COMPUTERS:
THE USER PERSPECTIVE

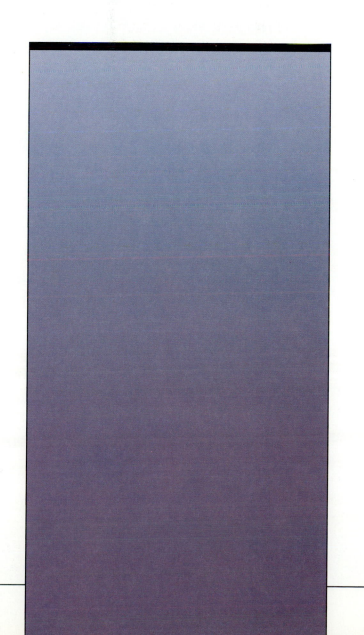

THE TIMES MIRROR/MOSBY
DATA PROCESSING AND INFORMATION SYSTEM SERIES

COMPUTERS: THE USER PERSPECTIVE

WARREN D. STALLINGS

SARAH E. HUTCHINSON

STACEY C. SAWYER

TIMES MIRROR/MOSBY COLLEGE PUBLISHING
ST. LOUIS   TORONTO   SANTA CLARA
1988

FIRST EDITION   Copyright © 1988 by Times Mirror/Mosby College Publishing
A division of the C. V. Mosby Company
11830 Westline Industrial Drive, St. Louis, MO 63146

Printed in the United States of America

Editor: Susan A. Solomon
Developmental Editor: Rebecca A. Reece
Production Coordinator: Stacey C. Sawyer
Art Director and Production Designer: Nancy Benedict
Preproduction Designer: Diane Beasley
Copyeditor: Leland Moss
Cover Illustrator: Kristen Throop
Illustrators: Bob Haydock, Irene Imfeld, Mary Burkhardt, Bob Mascolo, Gary Crounse, and Paula McKenzie
Photo Researcher: Judy Mason
Proofreaders: Patricia Cain, Elizabeth Judd, Ph.D.
Compositor: Typothetae (Anita Wagner, Joan Sorensen, Beth Brann, Leticia Bejarano, John Nelson, Cletus Coble, Carl Yoshihara, Ron Guzman, and Vicki Martinez)
Color Separator: Colorific Litho, Inc. (Emma Dankoski)

LIBRARY OF CONGRESS CATALOGING-IN-PUBLICATION DATA

Stallings, Warren D.
  Computers: the user perspective.

  Includes index.
  1. Microcomputers.   I. Hutchinson, Sarah E.
II. Sawyer, Stacey C.   III. Title.
QA76.5.S696 1988   004.16   87-26684
ISBN 0-8016-4752-5

TY/VH/VH   9 8 7 6 5 4 3 2   03/B/372

SUPPLEMENTS

Our collection of software and supplements was thoroughly developed to meet your teaching needs. All supplements have been reviewed to ensure their quality.

■

SOFTWARE SUPPLEMENTS
Educational versions of:

WordPerfect (5026)

SuperCalc4 (5026)

dBase III Plus (5026)

■

FOR THE STUDENT

Laboratory Manual (5118)

Study Guide (4791)

■

FOR THE INSTRUCTOR
Instructor's Manual with
Transparency Masters (14752)
Overhead Transparencies (5025)
Test Bank (5004)
MicroTest (IBM 4999; Apple 5024)

■

CONTENTS IN BRIEF

CONTENTS IN BRIEF

CONTENTS IN DETAIL

PART ONE

THE BEGINNING: BECOMING A COMPUTER USER   1

CONTENTS IN DETAIL

SPORTINGLIFE

EPISODE 1
Do You Really Need a Computer?   66

CONTENTS IN DETAIL

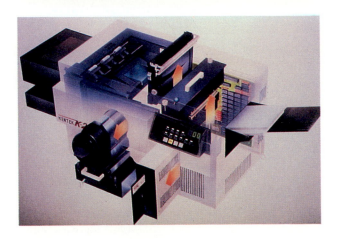

PART TWO

HARDWARE 71

CONTENTS IN DETAIL

Contents in Detail

SPORTINGLIFE

Contents in Detail

Part Three

Software   217

CONTENTS IN DETAIL

CONTENTS IN DETAIL

PART FOUR
SYSTEMS CONCEPTS AND APPLICATIONS   303

CONTENTS IN DETAIL

CONTENTS IN DETAIL

CONTENTS IN DETAIL

PART FIVE

TRENDS 443

CONTENTS IN DETAIL

PART SIX

MICROCOMPUTER SOFTWARE   473

CONTENTS IN DETAIL

CONTENTS IN DETAIL

Contents in Detail

CONTENTS IN DETAIL

Preface

Why We Wrote This Book: The Needs of the Users

This book is oriented toward future computer *users*, not future computer specialists. Users—also called *end users*—treat the computer as a tool for helping them with reports, spreadsheets, databases, and the like. They are not the specialists who will write programs for computers or who will design computer systems.

Too many introductory texts, we believe, try to please both users and specialists, and as a result fail both: They don't provide enough technical detail for the specialist, but they offer too much detail and not enough practical, business-related information for the user.

Why We Believe You Should Consider This Book

We believe that our book offers many of the features desired by today's instructors of the introductory course. We wrote our book to provide instructors and students with:

A USER ORIENTATION   Our book is directly relevant to the user. It prepares students to use microcomputers in business and to communicate effectively with computer specialists such as programmers. Everything in this book—every topic, illustration, case, and so on—is geared to the user, providing what he or she needs to know to prepare for a business career. If the user doesn't need to know it, it's not in this book. For example, in Chapter 10, "Systems Development Life Cycle," we explain the phases of the cycle so that students can see where they'll be involved in the process as users and thus better communicate with the analysts and programmers to get their needs met.

A Straightforward Look and Approach We conducted market research to learn what instructors really want from an introductory book. We learned that many instructors are becoming increasingly disgruntled with the overdone, confusing look and style of the books. They are concerned about the numerous boxed features, margin notes, cartoons, and crossword puzzles. They've made comments such as, "There are so many things on a page. Where do students look first?" and "Now where does the continuing boxed feature end so that we can get back to the chapter content?" We've taken your concerns to heart and provided solid, meaningful, and practical coverage that is not obscured by endless margin notes and boxed features that compete for students' attention.

Also, we use full color *meaningfully* to enhance content, not overpower it. We use four specific colors to indicate input, storage, processing, and output. As Figure 1.4 shows, *red* is used for input, *blue/green* for storage, *rust* for processing, and *gold* for output. Furthermore, in Modules C and E we use blue and maroon to help students differentiate between Lotus 1-2-3 and SuperCalc4 commands.

FIGURE 1.4

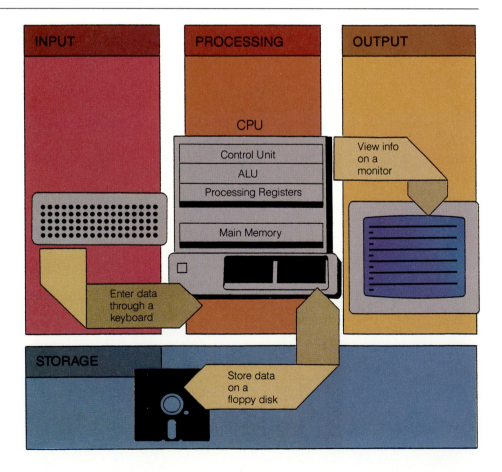

FLEXIBILITY   Our market research has shown that some instructors teach only concepts in this course; others offer exposure to software packages; still others want students to learn packages plus some BASIC programming. In an attempt to keep up to date and meet employers' needs, instructors end up frequently changing books.

Thus, we've designed our book to allow you to teach the course the way you want. The first five parts of our book cover fundamentals: introduction, hardware, software, systems concepts, and trends. Part 6, "Microcomputer Software," consists of five modules that cover microcomputer operating systems, word processing, spreadsheets, database, and graphics. Each module concludes with a tutorial, **In the Lab,** which introduces the student to a popular commercial business package—DOS, WordPerfect, Lotus 1-2-3, SuperCalc4, and dBase III Plus. Because each module is self-contained, you can choose the application(s) you want to cover and teach them in the order you like. Our appendix on BASIC is also self-contained. It was written by two programming specialists, Eli Cohen and Betty Boyd, who are authors of another successful Times Mirror textbook on BASIC programming, *Business BASIC for the IBM PC with Cases.* This appendix was included within the book to allow users to take that extra step—try some programming—and thus learn to better communicate with programmers.

A MICROCOMPUTER ORIENTATION   This book covers all types of computers—supercomputers, mainframes, minicomputers, and microcomputers. When the topic lends itself, particular focus is given to microcomputers. For examples, see the following sections:

- Chapter 4   "Direct Access Storage for Microcomputers," pp. 127–139
- Chapter 5   "RAM for Microcomputers," pp. 166–169
- Chapter 7   "Systems Software for Microcomputers," pp. 240–243
- Chapter 14   "Desktop Publishing," pp. 457–463

And, too, microcomputer use is the theme of Part 6, "Microcomputer Software."

A CONTINUING BUSINESS CASE—"SPORTING LIFE"   "Sporting Life" is the name of the sporting goods store featured in our on-going case. The four episodes are thought-provoking rather than hands-on. Students at this stage need real-life examples to put the concepts they've learned into perspective, but they don't yet have the background to, for example, actually choose the hardware and software for a company. By putting themselves in the shoes of Sporting Life's owner, they gain insight into the trials and tribulations of computerizing a business.

AN INTERESTING WRITING STYLE   Reviewers of drafts of this book consistently praised our writing style. Our primary goal is to reach students—to make all the explanations as clear, relevant, and interesting as possible.

PEDAGOGY   We've carefully developed our learning aids to maximize student comprehension:

- *The User Perspective* opens each chapter, explaining why the user needs to know the material in that chapter.

- *History* is covered as it naturally arises in the discussion of each topic, making it more immediately relevant than if it were isolated within a separate chapter.

- *Onward* is a section at the end of each chapter that indicates how the user might apply that chapter's information to his or her future job and relates that chapter's content to the next chapter's.

- *Summary* sections that students can use for review conclude each chapter.

- *Key Terms* sections list all the important terms covered in the chapter.

- *Exercises*—matching, multiple choice, short answer, and outside projects—test students' comprehension and encourage them to learn more about computers on their own.

SUPPLEMENTS

Our market research showed that it's not important how *many* supplements a book has. What's important is what they are, how useful they are, and whether they're of high quality. We offer a number of supplements that we believe you'll find especially beneficial. You'll also find them to be of high quality; to ensure that they're truly useful and accurate, we've had them reviewed by instructors teaching this course.

APPLICATIONS SOFTWARE MASTER DISKS

The software that accompanies this text includes:

WordPerfect Version 4.2
dBase III Plus
SuperCalc4 Version 1.0

SOFTWARE LICENSING   Five master diskettes (one for WordPerfect and two each for dBase III Plus and SuperCalc4) are provided free to you if you adopt our text. As long as you require students to purchase this text, you may make one copy of each master diskette for each student in your course. After the course, students are free to take their copies with them.

DESCRIPTION OF THE SOFTWARE   The software—WordPerfect, dBase III Plus, and SuperCalc4—is provided by Times Mirror/Mosby through contractual arrangements with WordPerfect Corporation, Ashton-Tate, and Computer Associates International, Inc., respectively. The three applications packages are educational versions, which contain all the features of the commercial versions. The only differences are as follows:

- For WordPerfect Version 4.2—The educational version saves files up to 4 K (files can be linked), supports one parallel printer port, prints *WPC randomly at the ends of paragraphs, prints the standard ASCII character set (rather than the extended ASCII set), provides a reproduction of the template in lieu of help menus, and includes a demonstration of the thesaurus and speller.
- For dBase III Plus—The educational version can accommodate as many as 31 records.
- For SuperCalc4—This educational version provides a 26 × 40 spreadsheet, supports one font, and prints across the width of the page rather than sideways.

In all other respects, these three packages are the same as the commercial versions.

ORDERING THE SOFTWARE   Copies of the diskettes are available for review by qualified potential adopters. Merely contact your local Times Mirror/Mosby Publishing Representative or call toll-free (800) 325-4177 to request your diskettes from a Sales Service Representative.

WORDPERFECT DISCOUNT FORM   Times Mirror/Mosby in cooperation with WordPerfect Corporation is pleased to offer faculty members and students an additional value with this book. At the back of this text, you'll find the WordPerfect Corporation School Direct Order Form, a value worth several hundred dollars in savings. Send the form with your order to WordPerfect; photocopies of the form are acceptable.

INSTRUCTOR'S MANUAL WITH TRANSPARENCY MASTERS

This supplement, written by Sarah E. Hutchinson, contains:

Course Planning Guidelines

A Guide to the Educational Software Master Disks

Chapter/Module Outlines

Teaching Tips

Suggestions for Using the Transparency Masters and Full-Color Overhead Transparencies

Suggestions for Using the Lab Manual and Study Guide

Answers to the BASIC Appendix Questions/Exercises

100 Transparency Masters

OVERHEAD TRANSPARENCIES

Seventy-five full-color transparencies of key illustrations and tables are available to qualified adoptors.

TEST BANK

For each chapter/module, this supplement contains:

True/False, Multiple Choice, and Fill-in-the-Blank questions, graded in difficulty

Two forms of a Reading Quiz to test students' comprehension of the material

A sample Final Exam for the entire text

All Answers

MICROTEST

This computerized test bank is available to qualified adoptors.

LABORATORY MANUAL

This manual is by Jeffrey Mock of Diablo Valley. It includes additional software lessons that amplify the In the Lab sections in the text. These lessons center on the Sporting Life sporting goods store presented in the running case episodes of the text. Also, this manual contains command reference guides for the applications software provided with the text.

STUDY GUIDE

Written by Sarah E. Hutchinson, this supplement contains for each chapter and module:

An Outline

A Summary on why coverage is important to the user

Study Tips

Self-Test Questions (fill-in-the-blank, true/false, matching, multiple choice) with answers

QUALITY

We are pleased to publish this book with Times Mirror/Mosby College Publishing. Their developmental model helped ensure that we have published a quality project. Unlike many other introductory textbooks available, our book can boast the following quality control steps:

ACQUISITION AND DEVELOPMENTAL EDITORS

Our acquisition and developmental editors served in an invaluable on-line, quality control capacity to guarantee that the Stallings-Hutchinson-Sawyer text approaches, as closely as possible, the ideal textbook of potential adoptors. These editors worked on a weekly, and often daily, basis with us. Few, if any, publishers offer this high degree of editorial assistance and attention to detail.

DEVELOPMENTAL EDIT

A word-by-word developmental edit of each draft of the entire manuscript ensured an accurate, clear, and consistent presentation of content and pedagogical flexibility throughout.

MARKET RESEARCH

Throughout the evolution of this project, constant market research was conducted to ensure that the book would meet instructors' preferences in terms of coverage, organization, pedagogical approach, type, and quantity of examples and applications. Within this process, instructors at more than 400 schools were asked how their present text met their needs and what they *really* needed.

FIRST DRAFT REVIEW

As the first draft of the manuscript was completed, 28 different instructors reviewed it. From this feedback, we initiated the detailed process of tailoring the text to meet instructors' needs. Each instructor was carefully chosen on the basis of course objectives, teaching experience, and book in use. Throughout development of the manuscript, all reviewers read and commented on the *entire* manuscript.

SECOND DRAFT REVIEW

Twenty-one instructors carefully critiqued this revised draft and, in doing so, provided us with extensive commentary for additional manuscript refinement.

THIRD DRAFT REVIEW

Nine instructors critically and thoroughly appraised the third draft of the manuscript for accuracy, organization, level of detail, user orientation, microcomputer coverage, writing style, and pedagogical effectiveness to provide the highest-quality, most market-driven introduction to computers text available today.

SPECIALISTS REVIEW

The nature and breadth of the introduction to computers course make specialized knowledge in each major subject difficult. Therefore, 13 specialists were enlisted to thoroughly examine the modules, as well as the chapters on hardware (Chapters 3, 4, 5, and 6), software (Chapters 7, 8, and 9), systems analysis and design (Chapter 10), information systems (Chapter 11), database (Chapter 12), and data communications (Chapter 13). These authoritative reviews ensured the accuracy and clarity of these key chapters.

CLASS TESTING

Various drafts of the manuscript were class tested. Students commented on the strengths and weaknesses of the manuscript from their perspectives and made substantial contributions to its refinement.

FINAL DRAFT

Using the input gained from the three reviewed drafts, specialist's reviews, further analysis of the market's needs, and class testing, we completed a final draft. No other new introduction to computers text can claim such rigorous development.

PHOTO AND ILLUSTRATION RESEARCH

Throughout development of the text, a professional photo researcher worked closely with us and our editors to select illustrations that would most effectively reinforce and complement the textual narrative. Consequently, each photograph and illustration that appears in the text is *directly* related to our examples and applications.

DEVELOPMENT OF THE SUPPLEMENTS PACKAGE

As with the text itself, producing supplements of extraordinary quality and utility was a primary objective for both us and the publisher. Too often, emphasis and investment in these items are based on quantity, not utility. All supplements that accompany our text, from the Test Bank to the Study Guide, have been thoroughly reviewed. Additionally, much attention has been given throughout the developmental process to provide supplements with features that have been requested by both experienced and inexperienced instructors alike. We know that in this market, the supplements package can be almost as important as the text—our package successfully addresses that concern.

ACKNOWLEDGMENTS

We wish to thank the reviewers, who contributed greatly to the content, organization and focus of this book and its supplements.

REVIEWERS

Joyce Abler
Central Michigan
University

Marvin Albin
Western Kentucky
University

Virginia Bender
William Rainey Harper
College

James Adair
Bentley College

Anthony Basilico
Community College of
Rhode Island

Jane Burcham
University of Missouri,
Columbia

Shirley J. Chann
Pima Community
College

Marvin Clark
Boise State University

Fred L. Collins
Chabot College

Louise Darcey
Texas A & M
University

Donald L. Davis
University of Mississippi

Ken Gorham
Los Angeles Mission
College

Carol C. Grimm
Palm Beach Junior
College

P.J. Guinan
Boston University

Fran Gustavson
Pace University

Thomas M. Harris
Ball State University

Robin Hill
Metropolitan State
College

Seth Hock
Columbus Technical
Institute

C. Brian Honess
University of South
Carolina, Columbia

Peter L. Irwin
Richland College

David A. Kay
Moorpark Community
College

Gary Klotz
Milwaukee Area
Technical College

Riki Kucheck
Orange Coast
Community College

Rose M. Laird
Northern Virginia
Community College,
Annandale

James F. LaSalle
University of Arizona

Paul M. Leidig
James Madison
University

Robert Lind
University of Texas,
El Paso

Paul Loeber
Wayne County
Community College

C. Gardner Mallonee
Essex Community
College

Nick Mavros
Elgin Community
College

Duncan Meier
Moorhead State
University

Richard M. Meyer
Hartnell College

Marilyn Meyers
Fresno City College

Lewis D. Miller
Canada College

Mary Amundson-Miller
University of
Wisconsin, Eau Claire

Margaret Miller
Skyline College

Jeffrey Mock
Diablo Valley College

Leonard A. Nicholas
Weber State College

Robert Norton
Mesa Community
College

William O'Hare
Prince George's
Community College

Ernest F. Phillip
Northern Virginia
Community College,
Arlington

Ernst Rilki
Harper College

Thomas J. Seymour
State University of
North Dakota, Minot

Peter Simis
California State
University, Fresno

Martin W. Sivula
Johnson & Wales
College

Gregory L. Smith
Colorado State
University

Glenn Smith
James Madison
University

Robert Smith
Kent State University

Richard G. Stearns
Parkland College

Margaret C. Thomas
Ohio University, Athens

Terry M. Walker
University of
Southwestern Louisiana

SPECIALISTS

To ensure quality and accuracy, we enlisted the help of specialists in the field to review specific chapters. We are grateful to these specialists for their insightful comments and recommendations.

Lonnie D. Bentley
Purdue University

Marilyn Bohl
Digital Research

Eli B. Cohen
Bradley University

James F. Courtney, Jr.
Texas A & M
University

John K. Gotwals
Purdue University

Peter L. Irwin
Richland College

John Maniotes
Purdue University,
Calumet

Fred R. McFadden
University of Colorado,
Colorado Springs

Kathryn P. Rea
The Consulting Edge,
Inc.

John Shepherd
Duquesne University

Jerry F. Sitek
Southern Illinois
University, Edwardsville

Mary Sumner
Southern Illinois
University, Edwardsville

OTHER CONTRIBUTORS

We also wish to thank Karen M. Gardner of Golden Gate University for her contribution on artificial intelligence and expert systems in Chapter 11, "Management Information Systems," and Chapter 14, "Computer Trends: The User Perspective."

The complexities and difficulties of preparing and producing a textbook like this one can be overwhelming at times—and insurmountable without the help of good people and organizations, such as those whose names are listed on the copyright page. These people—highly talented professionals—have all helped establish this book's high level of quality, and we are very grateful for their help. Special appreciation goes to Susan Solomon and Rebecca Reece for assistance above and beyond the call of duty!

Finally, we need to know: was this book truly *useful* to users? We'd like to hear from you about any misstatements we might correct or improvements we might make. Write to us in care of our publisher, Times Mirror/Mosby College Publishing.

Warren D. Stallings
Sarah E. Hutchinson
Stacey C. Sawyer

1

THE BEGINNING: BECOMING A COMPUTER USER

The user—this is a term often heard in computer and data processing circles. Actually, the user is *you*—the person at the end of the chain who receives the computer's services.

In this first part of the book, we describe what computer systems are and their critical role in business—and where you, as the user, fit in.

■

CHAPTER ONE

COMPUTERS: THE NEW TOOL FOR AN INFORMATION AGE

The job interview can be a stressful experience for many. But would you believe that some people actually *enjoy* interviewing for jobs? The secret, perhaps, lies in being prepared—knowing the job and company for which you are applying, being certain of your accomplishments, and knowing which questions to ask (and which to answer).

Two questions apt to be asked nowadays are, "What do you know about computers? What kind of software are you familiar with?" The more you know about how to use the computer as a resource, the more prepared you will be to handle such questions.

PREVIEW

When you have completed this chapter, you will be able to:

■

Describe who the user is and explain what a computer system is by focusing on computer hardware, software, and people

■

Describe the three main types of computer systems and how each might be used in business

■

Describe the impact computers have had on the processing of data into information and on business and society

■

THE USER PERSPECTIVE

The automatic teller machine. The supermarket price scanner. The magic "wand" used in department stores to "read" clothing price tags. A voice on the phone that told you to "Please hang up and dial your call again."

Did you come in contact with one of these special-purpose computer devices today? If not, then you probably encountered something similar, for the average person interacts with a computer several times a day (Figure 1.1). You, then, are already a *user* of computer-produced information.

But you want to become more than that. You want to go beyond push buttons and digitized voices and become a true user, someone who can join a business and use the computer as a problem-solving tool.

WHO IS THE USER?

To help you better understand who the computer user is, consider the following distinction:

- A **computer professional** is a person in the field of computers who has had formal education in the technical aspects of using computers—a programmer or systems analyst or computer operator who is concerned only with supporting the computer's physical functions in producing information for the user.

- The **user** is a person perhaps like yourself—someone without much technical knowledge of computers but who makes decisions based on reports and other results that computers produce.

This distinction seems clear enough, except for one thing: The computer user of the early 1980s used reports produced by the computer but did not necessarily deal

FIGURE 1.1
Computers in daily life. As these commonplace examples show, today it is almost impossible to avoid using a computer; (left) automated teller machine; (right) computerized checkout.

directly with the computer. However, today the user is becoming more directly involved in the production of reports through the hands-on use of *microcomputers, a type of computer that is often referred to as a personal, or desktop, computer.* Later in this chapter we describe a microcomputer in more detail.

As a user, you should realize that computers aren't just a passing fad. Business depends on computers; your job will depend on knowing how to use them. In other words, you must become computer literate.

"COMPUTER LITERACY": MIGHTY MICROS AND OTHER COMPUTERS

Computer literacy has been a rapidly changing term. In the early 1980s, most computer professionals thought of it simply as "technical knowledge"; to users it usually meant only "computer awareness." Today, however, you are probably considered computer literate if you have a basic understanding of what a computer is and how it can be used as a resource. You are certainly considered computer literate if you can use a computer, probably a microcomputer, as a business tool to assist in producing the information necessary to make intelligent decisions. This change of definition is a direct result of the increased use of microcomputers in business in the past decade, as shown in Figure 1.2. Because many management professionals already know how to use microcomputers, success in the business world—*your* success—depends on mastering this skill, too.

Being computer literate means not only acknowledging the importance of computers and determining to overcome any fears about them, but also actively involving yourself with them. As a computer literate person you should:

FIGURE 1.2
Micro millions. The number of microcomputers used in business has soared astronomically in the 1980s.

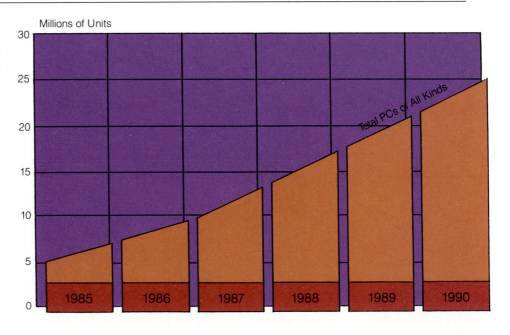

- Master the terminology used when talking about what a computer is and how to use one
- Learn to identify and describe the functions of the various components of a computer
- Learn to use a computer to produce the information you need

The objective of this book is to describe what a computer system is and how to use it—to help you achieve a level of computer literacy that will give you valuable skills in business.

WHAT IS A COMPUTER SYSTEM? THE SUM OF THREE PARTS

The term computer is used to describe a device made up of a combination of electronic and electromechanical (part electronic and part mechanical) components. By itself, a computer has no intelligence and is referred to as hardware. A computer, or computer hardware, doesn't come to life until it is connected to other parts of a system. A computer system is a combination of three elements: hardware, software, and people. Software is a term used to describe the instructions that direct hardware on how to perform a task; without software instructions, the hardware doesn't know what to do. People, however, constitute the most critical component of the computer system. People design, build, and operate computer hardware; people create computer software instructions and respond to the procedures that those instructions present. Figure 1.3 shows a computer system in operation.

The purpose of a computer system is to convert data into information. Data is all the raw, unevaluated facts, concepts, or instructions that form the basic materials for transforming, or processing, the facts into useful information. People "capture" data in a variety of ways, including verbalization and observation, and then record it on a document. For example, Roger Shu records his name on an employee timecard by first entering the letter R. Each letter of his name is an element of data, as is the number 5, used to indicate the number of overtime hours worked.

Information is the product of data processing. This processing includes refining, summarizing, categorizing, and otherwise manipulating the data into a useful form for decision making. Information adds context to data; for example, the number 5 becomes information when viewed in the context of *5 hours of overtime* worked by employee Roger Shu. We shall now describe the hardware devices that convert data into information in a typical computer system.

COMPUTER HARDWARE

If, at a job interview, you are asked about what kind of hardware you've used before or what you know about hardware, and you don't have an answer, your interviewer will probably perceive you as a person who doesn't take an active role in what's going on around you—a perception that could dramatically hurt your chances of getting the job you want. In today's business world, not knowing what computer hardware is and what typical hardware components do is similar to being a taxi driver and not knowing what a car is and that it has components such as an engine, doors, windows, and so on.

In Chapters 3 through 6 we talk in detail about the different categories of computer hardware. In this section, however, we provide a brief description of the components found in each category of hardware so that you can see how they relate to one another and how they fit into the larger picture of computers in business.

Computer hardware can be divided into four categories: (1) input hardware, (2) storage hardware, (3) processing hardware, and (4) output hardware. Figure 1.4 shows the typical configuration of computer hardware.

INPUT HARDWARE   The purpose of input hardware is to collect data and convert it into a form suitable for computer processing. The most common input device is a keyboard. It looks very much like a typewriter keyboard with four or five rows of keys arranged in the typical typewriter layout, as well as a number of additional keys used to enter special computer-related codes. Although it isn't the only type of input device available, the computer keyboard is the one most generally used by the business community. We will describe other types of input devices in Chapter 3.

STORAGE HARDWARE   The purpose of storage hardware is to provide a means of storing computer instructions and data in a form that is relatively permanent, or nonvolatile—that is, the data is not lost when the power is turned off—and easy to retrieve when needed for processing. Storage hardware serves the same basic functions as do office filing systems except that it stores data magnetically, commonly on disk or tape, rather than on paper. Storage devices are discussed in Chapter 4.

FIGURE 1.3
Three to go. Hardware, software, and people make a computer run.

PROCESSING HARDWARE   The purpose of processing hardware is to retrieve, interpret, and direct the execution of software instructions provided to the computer. The most common components of processing hardware are the central processing unit and internal memory.

The **central processing unit (CPU),** which is like the brain of the computer, is made up of a control unit, an arithmetic/logic unit, and processing registers. The **control unit** reads and interprets software instructions and coordinates the processing activities that must take place. The **arithmetic/logic unit (ALU)** performs mathematical calculations and any data comparisons that may be requested (for example, "How does this year's total overtime hours for all employees compare to last year's?"). The **processing registers,** which are located in the CPU, hold the data or the instructions being acted on. If you think of the inside of a computer as resembling the surface of your desk, with data being the various stacks of paper on the desktop, the processing registers are like the space right in front of you, where data is instantaneously acted on (by the CPU), after which it is returned to other places on the desk (places inside the computer) for final disposition later.

FIGURE 1.4
Typical hardware components. The four categories of computer hardware are input, storage, processing, and output.

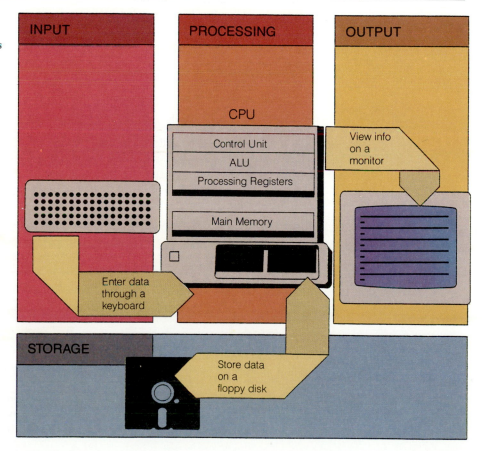

The design of the CPU affects the processing power and the speed of the computer, as well as the amount of internal memory it can use effectively: The bigger the CPU's registers, for example, the faster the processing. With a well-designed CPU in your computer, you can perform highly sophisticated tasks in a very short time.

Internal memory (also called *main memory*) can, as we mentioned, be thought of as an electronic desktop. The more desk surface you have in front of you, the more you can place on it. Similarly, if your computer has a lot of internal memory, you can place more software instructions in it. The amount of internal memory available determines whether you can run simple or sophisticated software: A larger memory is more capable of holding the thousands of instructions that are contained in the more sophisticated software programs. Having a large amount of internal memory in your computer also allows you to work with and manipulate great amounts of data and information at one time. Quite simply, the more internal memory you have in your computer, the more you can accomplish.

In Chapter 5, we describe in much more detail exactly how a computer processes data into information.

OUTPUT HARDWARE   The purpose of output hardware is to provide the user with the means to view information produced by the computer system. Information is output in either **hardcopy** or **softcopy** form. Hardcopy output can be held in your hand, such as paper with copy (words or numbers, for example) printed on it. Softcopy output is displayed on a **monitor,** a television-like screen on which you can read copy. We describe other types of output devices in Chapter 6.

COMPUTER SOFTWARE

As we have said, a computer is an inanimate device that has no intelligence of its own and must be supplied with instructions so that it knows what to do and how and when to do it. These instructions are called software. The importance of software can't be overestimated. You might have what most people consider the "best" computer sitting on your desk in front of you; however, without software to "feed" it, the computer will do nothing more than take up space.

Software is made up of a group of related **programs,** each of which is a group of related instructions that perform very specific processing tasks. Software acquired to perform a general business function is often referred to as a **software package.** Software packages, which are usually created by professional software writers, are accompanied by **documentation**—users' manuals—that explains how to use the software.

Software can generally be divided into three categories: (1) systems software; (2) applications software; and (3) software development tools. Chapters 7 and 8 explore each of these categories in detail. For now, some basic information will suffice.

SYSTEMS SOFTWARE   Programs designed to function as the principal interface between all the hardware components, the user, and, for example, a business software package are called **systems software.** In many ways, systems software functions in the same way as a business manager: It tells the hardware what to do and how and when to do it, as well as coordinating other, more complex tasks.

APPLICATIONS SOFTWARE Any instructions or collection of related programs designed to be carried out by a computer to satisfy a user's specific needs are **applications software**. A group of programs written to perform payroll processing is one type of applications software, as are programs written to maintain personnel records, update an inventory system, or help you calculate a budget.

Applications software can be purchased "off the shelf"—that is, already programmed, or written—or it can be written to order by qualified programmers. If, for example, its payroll processing requirements are fairly routine, a company can probably purchase one or more payroll applications software programs off the shelf to handle the job. However, if a company has unique payroll requirements, such as a need to handle the records of hourly employees, salaried employees, and commissioned employees, then off-the-shelf software may not be satisfactory. It may be more cost-effective to have the payroll programs written to exact specifications than to try to modify off-the-shelf programs to do something they were never intended to do.

Figure 1.5 shows a variety of packaged applications software available at computer stores.

SOFTWARE DEVELOPMENT TOOLS Applications software is created by **software development tools**. The most traditional tools are the "languages" used to write programs, such as BASIC, COBOL, and FORTRAN. Even though programming languages have been improved and refined over the years, writing applications software still takes a lot of time and effort. As a result, other tools have been created to help speed up the process (essentially, these are software packages with programming capabilities). It is not uncommon today for an employer to require employees to use one or more of the newer software development tools. These tools, as well as programming languages, are described in detail in Chapter 8.

WE THE PEOPLE

People, whether computer professionals or users, are the most important component in the computer system. Although our role may seem rather obvious, it is often underestimated. Here are some of the many ways people can affect computer operations:

1. Computer professionals design computer hardware and related equipment.
2. Computer professionals design, create, and develop computer software.
3. Professional computer operators run the computer systems and monitor their activities during processing.
4. Professional data entry clerks key in vast amounts of data every day in computer-usable form for storage and processing at a later time.
5. Users input data to be processed right away, depending on the design of the computer system.

6. Users create specialized applications software using one or more of the newer software development tools.

7. Users review information produced by the computer for use in making effective business decisions.

TYPES OF COMPUTER SYSTEMS: WHAT'S THE DIFFERENCE?   The difference is important for you to know about if you want to show a potential employer that you have a fundamental knowledge of computers. Computers come in a variety of sizes and shapes and with a variety of processing capabilities. The earliest computers were quite large because of the crude technologies used; as technological improvements

FIGURE 1.5
Software supermarket. Need help with your budget? Want to design and print some greeting cards? Thinking of printing your own newsletter? Buying software is becoming more and more like buying albums and tapes. Most computer stores offer a wide variety of applications software packages.

were made in computer components, the overall size of computers began to shrink. Today, the complete CPU of a computer can be as small as a postage stamp.

To provide a basis for comparing their capabilities, computers are generally grouped into three basic categories: (1) mainframe computers, which are the most powerful type of computer; (2) minicomputers, which are the next most powerful; and (3) microcomputers, which are the least powerful—but which you most likely will be required to use in business.

MAINFRAMES, MINICOMPUTERS, AND MICROCOMPUTERS

It's hard to assign a worthwhile definition to each type of computer because definitions can get bogged down in potentially confusing technical jargon. Nevertheless, the following definitions can suffice:

- A **mainframe computer** is a large computer, usually housed in a controlled environment, that can support the processing requirements of hundreds and often thousands of users and computer professionals.

- A **minicomputer** is similar to but less powerful than a mainframe computer; it can support from 2 to 50 users and computer professionals. Minicomputers and mainframe computers can work up to 100 times faster than microcomputers and have up to 16 times more storage positions in internal memory.

- A **microcomputer** is a relatively small, general-purpose computer system that uses a microprocessor chip as its CPU. Made of silicon, a material refined from sand, a **chip** can be as small as a quarter-inch square, as shown in Figure 1.6. This chip holds the circuits that run the computer. A microcomputer, as we think of it today, can usually be used by only one person at one time.

FIGURE 1.6
A chip off what kind of block? This gives you an idea of how small a chip is.

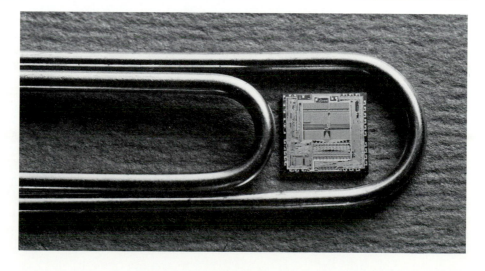

Of course, as technology advances, the definitions change. Microcomputers that have become as powerful as minicomputers are often referred to as *supermicros*, and some minicomputers with capabilities of mainframe computers are called *superminis*. Some mainframe computers have grown so vastly powerful that they are called *supercomputers*. For simplicity's sake, we will focus on the three broad categories.

Figure 1.7 shows examples of the three major types of computers. How to categorize a computer depends on the following parameters:

FIGURE 1.7
Small, medium, and large. The microcomputer is top left. On the right is a minicomputer, and underneath is a mainframe.

1. *The type of CPU and size of processing registers* —As noted, microcomputers use microprocessors. The larger computers tend to use CPUs made up of separate, high-speed, sophisticated components. The size of the processing registers determines how much data can be dealt with in a single processing cycle—the more data the registers can carry at once, the more work that can be done in a cycle. The size of the registers is usually measured in bits. A bit, short for binary digit, is the basic element of the coding scheme used in computers to represent data. It takes 8 bits to represent one character, or byte, such as the letter A, in a computer. (This is discussed in more detail in Chapter 4.)

2. *The amount of internal memory the CPU can use*—A computer equipped with a large amount of internal memory can support more sophisticated programs and can even hold several different programs in memory at the same time. The amount of internal memory a computer can support is usually measured in **K** (kilobyte; 1 K = 1024 characters of 8 bits each, or 8192 bits) or **MB** (megabyte; 1 MB = 1000 K, approximately 1 million characters).

3. *The capacity of the storage devices*—The larger computer systems tend to be equipped with higher capacity storage devices. Like internal memory, the capacity of storage devices is usually measured in K or MB.

4. *The speed of the output devices*—The speed of microcomputer output devices tends to be rated in terms of the number of **characters per second (CPS)** that can be printed—usually in tens and hundreds of CPS. Larger computers' output devices are faster and are usually rated at speeds of hundreds or thousands of *lines* that can be printed per minute.

5. *The processing speed in millions of instructions per second (**MIPS**)*—The term *instruction* is used here to describe a basic task the software asks the computer to perform while also identifying the data to be affected. The processing speed of the smaller computers tends to be less than 12 MIPS. The speed of larger computers can range up to 50 MIPS. In other words, a mainframe computer can process your data a great deal faster than a microcomputer.

6. *The number of users that can access the computer at a time*—Most smaller computers can support only a single user; some can support as many as two or three at a time. Larger computers can support hundreds of users simultaneously.

7. *The cost of the computer system*—Business systems can cost as little as $1500 (for a microcomputer) to $5 million (for a mainframe).

Table 1.1 compares the three categories of computers.

The microcomputer is often the only type of computer that many people use on the job. Larger computer systems tend to be operated by computer specialists and are usually located in specially equipped areas. If your company has one of the larger computer systems, your only contact with it may be through a terminal that has a keyboard and a video display screen connected to the computer by some type of cable. Figure 1.8 shows a computer terminal in use that is connected to a larger computer system.

THE ANATOMY OF A MICROCOMPUTER

Chances are that, when you enter the business environment, you will be required to know how to use a microcomputer to perform many of your job-related functions. It is estimated that by 1990 at least one out of every three office workers will be using a microcomputer. It is therefore critical that you understand the typical components of a microcomputer system—to use it effectively and talk about it intelligently. The more you know about it, the more valuable you will be to a current or potential employer. To understand the tremendous role microcomputers now play in business, it's helpful to look at how the role has developed.

With the introduction of the Apple II and the Radio Shack Model I and II systems in the late 1970s, the business community began to adopt microcomputers. Then a number of additional vendors, including Atari, Commodore, Osborne, and Kaypro, entered the marketplace with computers designed to be used in the office or in the home. The interest in microcomputers grew rather slowly at first for several reasons: (1) The initial cost for some microcomputer systems was quite high, ranging up to $6000; (2) the average person did not have sufficient background in computer-related subjects to use the computer without difficulty; and (3) there were no industry-wide standards to ensure the **compatibility**—that is, the usability—of data and software on different types of microcomputer systems.

However, when IBM introduced the IBM PC in 1981, so many businesses adopted the product that an industry standard was set. Most vendors now design their products to be compatible with this standard. The only other relatively successful

TABLE 1.1   The Three Kinds of Computers

Component	Microcomputer	Minicomputer	Mainframe
Registers	8, 16, or 32 bit	16 or 32 bit	64 bit
Memory	64 K–7 MB	1–16 MB	8–128 MB
Storage Capacity	10–130 MB	100–1000 MB	600–10,000 MB
Processing Speed	.65–12 MIPS	2–10 MIPS	5–50 MIPS
Number of Users	1–3	3–100	50–500
Cost	$1500–$11,000	$10,000–$200,000	$200,000–$5,000,000

FIGURE 1.8
The mainframe's connected to the keyboard . . . If you use a large computer, you will probably need a terminal (top) that has a keyboard, a video display screen (monitor), and a cable that is connected to the computer (bottom) (which is usually in a different room). You will input data through the keyboard and review the output on your screen. All of the processing, however, is done remotely by the large computer (a mainframe or a minicomputer).

microcomputer product lines today that have maintained their own unique standards are the Apple II and the Macintosh. The Apple II retains a fiercely loyal group of users who have supported it since its introduction in the late 1970s. Although the Apple II has been overshadowed in the business world by IBM PC-compatible products, Apple introduced a much more powerful version of its system—the Apple II GS—in June 1986.

The large number of different types of microcomputer systems in the marketplace makes it difficult to select one "best system." As a result, our discussion of the microcomputer will center on the three basic hardware devices found in most desktop microcomputer systems used in business today: the keyboard, the monitor, and the system unit (the main computer system cabinet). Figure 1.9 shows these components as featured on an ITT XTRA XL 286 system.

KEYBOARD   The microcomputer input device that you will use the most, the keyboard, is made up of a circuit board and related electronic components that generate a unique electronic code when each key is pressed. This code is passed along the keyboard cord to the computer system unit where it is translated into a usable form for processing. The number of keys and their positions on the keyboard vary among machines. You should select a keyboard that is comfortable for you to use.

MONITOR   The term *monitor* is used interchangeably with *screen*, *video display screen*, and *cathode-ray tube (CRT)*. This output device provides your principal visual contact with the microcomputer system. When you enter commands or data from the keyboard, you see the results on the monitor. A **monochrome monitor** displays text and, in some cases, graphics in a single color—commonly green or amber—usually on a dark background. A **color monitor**, often referred to as an **RGB monitor** (for red, green, blue), can display text and graphics in various colors. Most of the capabilities of the monitor, including image clarity and the ability to do graphics, are determined by the sophistication of the video display board, if any, contained within the system unit.

SYSTEM UNIT   The main computer system cabinet, called the **system unit,** usually houses the power supply, the motherboard, and the storage devices (although some storage devices—disk drives, for example—are often housed in cabinets outside the system unit). These elements can be defined as follows:

1. The **power supply** provides electrical power to all components housed in the system unit. In some microcomputers—such as the Macintosh, the ITT XTRA, and the Compaq—it also provides power to the monitor.
2. The **motherboard** is the main circuit board of the microcomputer system. It normally includes (1) the microprocessor chip (or CPU), (2) internal memory chips, (3) all related support circuitry, and (4) the expansion slots where additional components can be plugged in.
3. The **storage devices** are one or more floppy disk drives and a high-capacity hard disk drive or hard card. A **floppy disk** is a thin plastic disk enclosed in a paper or plastic covering that can be magnetically encoded with data. **Hard**

FIGURE 1.9
Basic anatomy of a micro-
computer. The top part
of this illustration shows
a high-performance ITT
XTRA XL with monitor,
keyboard, and cabinet with
disk drives; on the bottom
is a cutaway drawing of a
standard microcomputer
setup. The different parts
will be discussed in detail
in the following chapters.

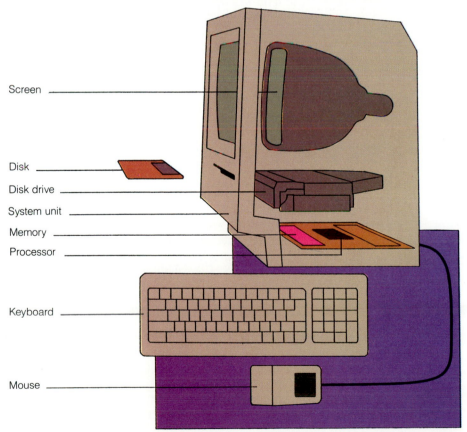

Screen

Disk

Disk drive

System unit

Memory

Processor

Keyboard

Mouse

disks are rigid disks capable of storing from about 8 to 112 times as much data as a floppy disk. **Hard cards** are similar to hard disks except they are located on a board that is connected to an expansion slot on the mother-board. Hard disks and cards are quite a bit more expensive than floppy disks. Whereas a typical floppy disk costs between $1 and $6, depending on size and storage capacity, hard disks and cards range in price from $375 to $1200. Since most hard cards and most hard disks are permanently installed in the system unit, floppy disks, which can be carried around, are often used to move data from one computer to another. Floppy disks, hard disks, and hard cards are all controlled by a *disk controller board*.

4. **Additional components:** The expansion slots on the motherboard allow us to add new components to our computer system. The most popular add-on components include: (1) a memory card containing internal memory chips that give you additional internal memory; (2) an internal modem to facilitate data communications between computers over phone lines and similar cables; (3) a battery-powered clock and calendar mechanism; (4) additional printer ports ("hook-ups") that allow you to communicate with several types of output devices; (5) video display boards; (6) a disk controller board; and others.

All these components will be explained in detail later in the book. Figure 1.10 gives you a general idea of what the parts of the system unit look like.

Microcomputers are likely to become a very important part of your career. Pay attention to them and focus on what they can do for you! Turn their power on—to your advantage.

The History of Computer Processing

In the last section, we gave you some historical information about the use of microcomputers in business since the early 1980s so that you could put into perspective their role in business today. In this section, we go back a little farther—almost 5000 years—to impress on you the tremendous effect that computers have had on data processing in general, which in turn has profoundly affected the society of which you are a part. To help you to appreciate where our society is today in terms of the amount of information it is capable of producing, we describe in this section how data was processed into information before and after computers.

Data Processing Before Computers

To record and communicate data and information, prehistoric cave dwellers painted pictures on the walls of their caves, and the ancient Egyptians wrote on a crude form of paper called *papyrus*. Around 3000 B.C., the Sumerians created a device for representing numbers that consisted of a box containing stones. About 2000 years later, in 1000 B.C., the Chinese took that idea one step further when they strung stones on threads in a wooden frame. The Chinese device was named after their name for box, *baccus*. The *abacus*, as we know it, remains in wide use even today and is still considered a powerful tool for performing mathematical computations.

Over the centuries, people have developed an amazing variety of data processing tools and techniques. The most notable tools in use between the mid-1600s and the early 1900s are described in Figure 1.11.

FIGURE 1.10
The system unit. Here you see the system unit with its cover removed.

THE EVOLUTION OF COMPUTERS

The first large-scale electronic computer, the Electronic Numerical Integrator and Computer (ENIAC), became operational in 1946 (Figure 1.12). It contained approximately 18,000 electronic vacuum tubes—tubes the size of light bulbs that

FIGURE 1.11
Which came first—computers or data processing? Many people think that we have been turning data into information only since computers came into use. The truth is that we have been processing data since prehistoric times. This illustration shows a few of the data processing methods used between the mid-1600s and the early 1900s. (a) Pascaline calculator (mid-1600s), the first automatic adding and subtracting machine; (b) Leibniz Wheel (early 1700s), the first general-purpose calculating machine; (c) Jacquard loom (1801), run by punched cards; (d) Thomas's arithmometer (1860), the first commercially successful adding and subtracting machine; (e) Hollerith's tabulating machine, used in the 1890 U.S. census; and (f) early IBM calculating machine (c. 1930).

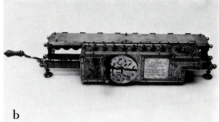

control the flow of electric current. The ENIAC, which weighed 30 tons and occupied about 1500 square feet of floor space—a huge machine compared to today's standards—was able to perform a scientific calculation involving the multiplication of four numbers in approximately 9 milliseconds (9/1000ths of a second). Since that time, the technology used in the design and production of computers has accelerated at a remarkable pace.

The term *generation* was applied to different types of computers to help delineate the major technological developments in hardware and software. To date, computer technology has evolved through four distinct generations and is currently developing into a fifth generation. As you read about each generation, you should be thinking about how each has affected data processing, because each development has had (and in the case of the later generations, will continue to have) an effect on you—on the job and in society in general. The major characteristics of each generation are outlined below:

FIRST GENERATION (1951–1958)   During this time, computers were first used in business. Most input and output media were punched cards and magnetic tape, and internal memory was almost exclusively made up of vacuum tubes—although one computer used a magnetic drum for internal memory. These computers were slow and large and produced a tremendous amount of heat.

FIGURE 1.12
ENIAC. The first large-scale electronic computer.

Second Generation (1959–1963)   In the early 1960s, transistors and some other solid-state devices that were much smaller than vacuum tubes were used for much of the circuitry. Magnetic cores, which looked like very small metal washers strung together by wires that carried electricity, became the most widely used type of internal memory, and removable magnetic disk packs, a stack of disks tied together by a common spindle (like a stack of records), were introduced for direct access storage. Second-generation machines tended to be smaller, more reliable, and significantly faster than first-generation computers.

Third Generation (1964–1970)   During this period, the integrated circuit—a complete electronic circuit on a silicon chip—replaced transistorized circuitry. The use of magnetic disks became widespread, and computers began to support such capabilities as multiprogramming (processing several programs simultaneously) and timesharing (people using the same computer simultaneously). Minicomputers were being widely used by the early 1970s. The production of operating systems—a type of systems software—and applications software packages increased rapidly.

Fourth Generation (1971–1987)   In 1971, the first electronic computers were introduced that used Large-Scale Integration (LSI) circuits—thousands of integrated circuits on a chip—for internal memory and logic circuitry (the circuitry that performs the logical operations of the CPU; different types of chips had different functions). These computers had a much larger capacity to support internal memory (as much as 16 million characters). This period also saw increased use of input and output devices that allowed data and instructions to be entered directly through the keyboard. The microprocessor, introduced in 1971, combined all of the circuitry for the central processing unit on a single chip.

Fifth Generation (Now–?)   Definitions of what constitutes fifth-generation computers do not always agree. Some people think that the new microcomputers with faster operating speeds, greater processing capacity, and virtually unlimited memory should be included. Other people believe that fifth-generation computers will have circuitry based on gallium arsenide instead of silicon. This substance offers a fivefold speed increase and uses only one-tenth of the power that silicon uses. Many fifth-generation computers will also incorporate hundreds or thousands of processors that operate in parallel—that is, simultaneously. Traditional computers act on only one problem at a time; *parallel processing* means that many processors will work on the problem at the same time. As you will see later on, this concept promises to provide tremendously more efficient processing than the traditional kind.

The processing speeds of fifth-generation computers will approach 10,000 Mflops (millions of floating point operations per second; *floating point* refers to a scientific form of notation used to handle very large numbers in which the decimal point is allowed to move around, or "float"). The most powerful supercomputer in operation today is the Cray 2 with a speed of 200 Mflops. To prevent overheating, fifth-generation computers may need to have their components bathed in super-cooled liquids.

What Does All This Mean?

Don't worry if you don't understand all the terms used to describe the sequence of computer generations. As you work through the book, the differences between them will become clear. In the meantime, to continue putting the progress of computing technology in its proper perspective, we will now compare the performance of the first electronic computer with the performances of today's typical micro- and supercomputers.

ENIAC, the first-generation computer, could perform about 333 operations per second. The IBM Personal Computer, introduced in 1981, can perform approximately 4.75 million operations per second. The Cray 2 has a theoretical ability to process data at the incredible rate of more than 200 million operations per second. Figure 1.13 will give you an idea of what can be done in one second.

The net effect of the tremendous increase in processing power provided by the computer is that more data can be processed faster than ever before. This means that all the information you need in your job to make decisions will be quickly available—a necessity in today's rapidly changing business environment.

The catch to all this, however, is that the power of the computer has grown so much that it can often generate more information than we can effectively deal with at one time. As a result, we must be selective about the type of information produced. It must be concise and relevant so that we avoid getting buried under an avalanche of unnecessary information.

The Impact of Computers on Processing Data and Information

New generations of computer technology will continue to affect the processing of data and information. Data collection continues to become easier and easier, data processing is getting faster and faster, mathematical calculations continue to be performed with increased precision, and information is being provided to users in more useful forms. And one of the best improvements that new technology brings us is that computers continue to become easier to use.

FIGURE 1.13
Nanosecond to none. For a computer to carry out millions of operations per second, it must be able to carry out individual operations in a few billionths of a second—that is, in a few *nanoseconds.*

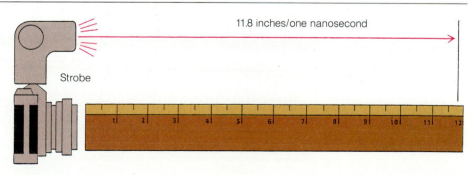

DATA COLLECTION: HARD LABOR TO EASY TIME

Before computers were invented, data was collected and processed by hand in a variety of tedious ways. And the data often had to be copied and recopied more than once before it could be processed into information. Data collection for early computers was often done by transcribing hardcopy data into computer-usable forms such as punched cards or paper tape (Figure 1.14). The data was recorded by punching a series of holes according to a standardized coding scheme. Technological advancements in data collection have made this cumbersome collection method obsolete. Chapter 3 discusses modern data collection devices in detail.

THE PRODUCTION OF INFORMATION: FASTER, EASIER, BETTER

It's no wonder that so many businesses have adopted computers so readily. Quick and easy production of accurate information has become a reality to businesspeople who used to dream about it. The U.S. government was one of the first institutions to benefit from increased data processing speed. In the last century, census taking was one of the most arduous processing tasks ever undertaken in this country. Almost 50,000 people collected data by hand, completing forms for approximately 13 million households. Processing this data by hand usually took more than eight years; no sooner would the population be tallied than the new census would begin. As a result, in 1890, the U.S. Congress authorized the Census Office to hold a competition to select the most efficient new method for recording and tabulating the census. Herman Hollerith won the contest with his system for electric tabulating using data input on punched cards. Although at the time the speed of this data processing method was a major breakthrough—it took Hollerith six weeks to compute an unofficial census—a modern personal computer can process the same amount of data in about half the time, after capturing it in a computer-usable form.

Thanks to the science of *ergonomics* (also called *human engineering*), which designs things to be easily used by people, the convenience of computer use has also

FIGURE 1.14
Taking a collection. An early method of collecting data for the computer involved the transcribing of hardcopy data into a computer-usable form on punched cards and paper tape. Fortunately, the technology for data collection has advanced to the point where such methods have become extremely rare.

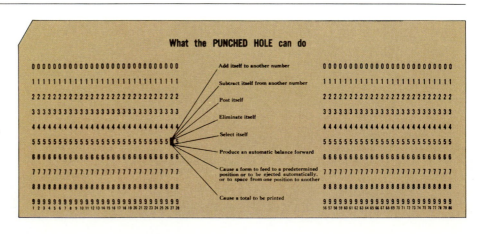

improved over the years. Many people have been afraid of computers, but great strides have been made in transforming the computer into a friendlier, less mysterious tool. Input devices have become easier to use (see Figure 1.15), and software is easier to understand than ever before (Figure 1.16).

In addition to being fast and easy to use, the computer also brings us a math facility that many of us thought was eternally beyond our reach. Have you ever had

FIGURE 1.15
An ergonomic input device. A relatively new input device is the *mouse* (a), a hand-held device that is moved around the desktop (b). It controls the position indicator (cursor) on the video screen, and it can also be used to make selections of options offered by the software shown on the screen and to create graphics. The keyboard is still used to type characters.

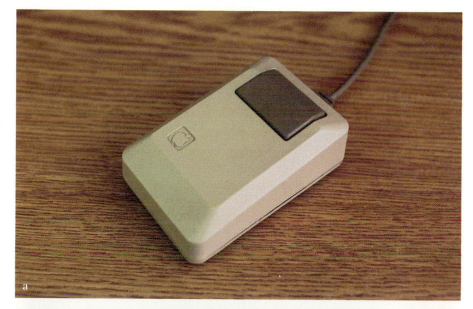

difficulty balancing your checkbook or creating a budget? Many of us find it difficult to consistently perform mathematical calculations accurately by hand. Sooner or later we make a mistake. One of the major advantages of a computer is that, once it is properly programmed to do computations, it will continue from then on to perform the calculations quickly and accurately. Many calculations are performed with much greater precision and speed than would be possible manually.

Information in Usable Forms:
For the Computer and for the User

The need for business-related data to be retrieved, manipulated, and analyzed is constant. In the past, data was collected by hand and analyzed manually to produce a report. Then you had to go through the same procedure again if you wanted to use the same data to produce a different report. The computer allows us to capture data in computer-usable form. Once the data is available in this form, the computer can repeatedly retrieve and manipulate it to produce information tailored—in people-usable form—to meet specific needs.

HARDCOPY OUTPUT   Information presented in a printed report, a type of hardcopy output, has probably been the most widely used form of computer output. In recent years, many improvements have been made in producing printed output. First, the speed of standard printing devices has been increased to the point where 2000 lines (about 30 pages) per minute is not uncommon; 100 pages per minute can be achieved with one of today's more advanced printing devices, such as a laser printer.

FIGURE 1.16
What will you have? Some computers and software use *menus* (a series of choices presented on the screen; see top left area of the screen shown here) and *icons* (pictures representing options; see the right side of the screen) to make it easier for people to run the system.

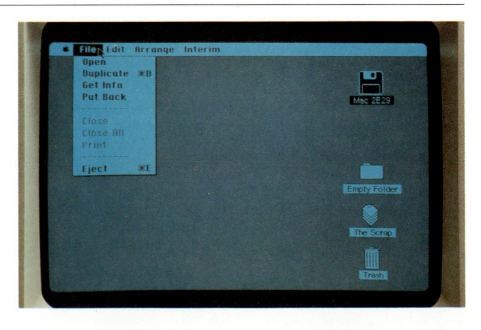

Second, the number of type styles available has put computer typesetting, or "desktop publishing," within reach of us all. A modern microcomputer-level laser printer can handle 60 type fonts (different typeface designs and sizes) and full-page graphics with a resolution, or image clarity, of 300 or more dots per square inch. Figure 1.17 shows a text sample that was printed using a laser printer.

SOFTCOPY OUTPUT   Improvements have also been made in softcopy output. You are now able to see more text on the screen, and the images are clearer, thus preventing eyestrain. As a result, more information is being displayed in softcopy form now than ever before. People used to print out mounds of paper because video display screens did not contain enough space (characters per line) to provide the same coverage as wide computer paper (132 columns per line). However, a number of new computer terminals and microcomputer systems can now easily display up to 150 characters per line on the video display screen.

Voice output is another form of softcopy output that is being used more frequently. In many parts of the country, when you request a phone number from the information operator, a computer takes over and searches the file, locates the listing, and provides it to you using a computerized voice output device.

THE IMPACT OF COMPUTERS ON SOCIETY

We have seen that computers have essentially revolutionized data processing. Computers have also changed some industries and actually created others. The design and manufacture of computer hardware has become an enormous industry, and the need for software by all sorts of businesses—from apple growers to zoo managers—has led to the development of the applications software industry. Major retail sales and wholesale distribution operations have developed to sell these hardware and software products.

FIGURE 1.17
Good copy. This is a sample of hardcopy output produced using a microcomputer and a laser printer. Before laser technology was widely available for use with microcomputers, users did not have many type styles to choose from, and it was difficult for them to produce high-quality graphics.

"I think there is a world market for about five computers."
— Thomas J. Watson, founder of IBM

All these industries have one thing in common: They need workers. In fact, the growth of the computer information industry has created a vast and varied number of jobs. As you will see in the next section, no matter what type of business you go into, you will probably be using computers. Figure 1.18 shows a few examples of current job opportunities.

OPPORTUNITIES FOR EMPLOYMENT

The employment picture for computer professionals looks good and is getting better. It is estimated that approximately 2.5 million people are employed as computer programmers, computer operators, systems analysts, data entry clerks, and other more technical workers. The growth of the microcomputer hardware and software industries in recent years has created a large number of new jobs in the retail sales and marketing of computers as well. Many jobs have also been created by companies that manufacture the various computer components and by companies that specialize in computer repair—most recently, microcomputer system repair.

The employment picture for users (you) is good if you have had some experience using computers. Many employers now require some degree of computer

FIGURE 1.18
Write when you find work. These assorted newspaper ads give only a small sampling of the types of jobs available for people who know how to use computers.

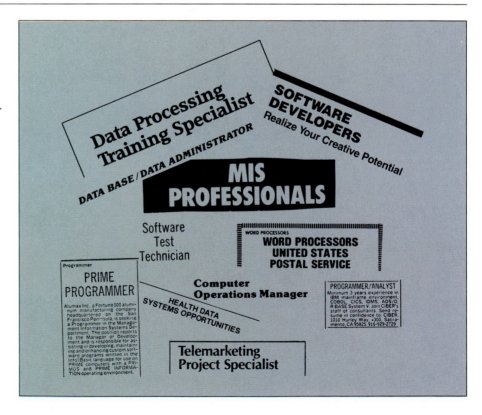

literacy as a prerequisite for employment. Computers are becoming standard business tools for all employees, from the president of the company to the clerks in the typing pool. For example, accounting departments and public accounting firms now seek college graduates who have substantial hands-on microcomputer experience. Many administrative and managerial employees are also using microcomputers or computer terminals in their offices. To meet the demand for computer literacy, many schools offer extension courses or seminars in computer skills.

The most popular courses cover word processing programs (designed to output professional documents in a short amount of time), database management system programs (designed to easily store, update, and manipulate large amounts of data), and electronic spreadsheet programs (designed to handle calculations and update complex financial forms). Attendance in these courses by working professionals has increased dramatically in the past few years. An informal survey of several universities has shown that people enroll for training for three reasons:

- *To satisfy job requirements*—Some of those surveyed stated that they were strongly encouraged or required by their employers to learn more computer skills.

- *To increase job skill and marketability*—Others surveyed said that because microcomputers and related software tools were becoming so popular, they felt they needed some additional skills to keep their jobs or to be considered for advancement.

- *To learn to use a computer as a personal resource*—The remaining people indicated that they wanted to learn to use the computer as a personal resource on the job and at home. These people were not required to use computers on the job but felt computers could help them perform their jobs more efficiently.

COMPUTERS IN BUSINESS

The computer has been used by businesses to assist with such day-to-day operating activities as:

- *Sales Order Entry*—The procedures for handling customer orders, including receipt of the order and verification of availability of ordered stock

- *Inventory Management and Control*—The procedures for tracking, counting, and reordering stock items

- *Personnel Management*—The procedures for maintaining employee information (such as hire date, salary, performance rating, and date of last review) for both development and reporting purposes

- *Payroll*—The procedures for producing paychecks and reports on employee compensation

- *Accounting*—The procedures for maintaining the company's financial records

Computers are also being used to collect and analyze data, to produce concise information for management in a clear format suitable for making decisions, and to help managers avoid being overloaded with unnecessary information.

COMPUTERS IN GOVERNMENT

Government is by far one of the biggest computer users in the world today. It would almost be impossible to collect, tabulate, and categorize the colossal amount of data the U.S. government must deal with daily without the aid of a huge network of computers. For example, the Internal Revenue Service has ten huge data centers throughout the country solely dedicated to processing income tax returns. Even so, it takes most of the year to process the prior year's tax returns. Figure 1.19 shows the large collection of computer hardware at one of the regional processing centers for the IRS.

To a large extent, the defense of this country is based on computer technology. Vast networks of computers work together to coordinate and disseminate strategic information relating to the management and deployment of our armed forces. Satellites are used to collect and communicate data and information, and all our weapons systems have computerized components. Many of our weapons are now considered "smart" weapons because they can collect data, process it into information, and use it in military strategies.

COMPUTERS IN THE LEGAL PROFESSION

Law enforcement agencies use computers to collect and analyze evidence. Many agencies are now equipped with data processing facilities that enable them to connect with large, country-wide law enforcement computer systems from which they can obtain and with which they can share information on criminal activities.

FIGURE 1.19
A taxing situation. The Internal Revenue Service uses computers to process the massive amounts of data included in our tax returns.

As shown in Figure 1.20, police cars are now equipped with computer terminals so that an officer can access immediate information about a suspect or a vehicle.

The criminal justice system uses computers to help manage large amounts of information. The documentation created when a suspect is arrested and tried can easily take up several hundred pages. Without computerized information processing, it would be next to impossible today to collect the data, process it, and keep track of the status of cases.

COMPUTERS IN MEDICINE

The use of computers in the health-care industry has grown tremendously in the past ten years. The computer has become a valuable resource in the management of records for physicians, hospitals, and medical insurance companies, as well as in patient diagnosis and physiological monitoring. Computers are used to process mountains of medical administrative paperwork, including millions of patient insurance claims; patient billing forms; inventory control accounts to track the availability and use of beds; and extensive patient records and histories of test results, treatments, and medicines.

The most recent computer-related developments in the medical profession involve the use of computer systems to assist in patient diagnosis. CAT and PET scanners (not named after animals, but acronyms from long technical names) can take computerized "pictures" of the interior of the brain and other parts of the body. Many of the devices found in intensive care units are also computerized—such as the electrocardiograph system used to record the pulses that cause a patient's heartbeat.

FIGURE 1.20
Sherlock Holmes takes on a new look. Computers are used to collect and analyze evidence. This police car is equipped with a Motorola mobile computer terminal that can access information from the main police station about suspects' vehicles.

COMPUTERS IN EDUCATION

In recent years educators have been involved with computers in three ways: (1) They teach students about computers; (2) they teach students about a variety of subjects, such as math, language skills, reading, grammar using computers (computer-assisted instruction); and (3) they use computers as classroom management tools (computer-managed instruction). Computer classes have been offered at the college level since the mid-1950s. Today many schools at all levels offer students some exposure to computers. Many colleges and universities now have their own micro-computer training labs, as shown in Figure 1.21.

COMPUTERS IN THE HOME

Computers are such versatile tools that people are bringing them into their homes in increasing numbers (see Figure 1.22). A wide variety of software is available for home use, including (1) educational software for young children, (2) personal financial management software, and (3) entertainment software. Many professionals also use their home computers to do some work-related tasks at home.

ONWARD: MAKING USE OF INFORMATION

Chapter 2 focuses on the activities that normally take place in computer-based information systems (when data is processed into information using a computer).

FIGURE 1.21
Computer labs. Micro-computer training labs such as this one, which uses several different Macintosh models, are common at the university level, and more and more labs are being constructed and used at the high school and grammar school levels.

You need to understand where you will fit into this system before you can learn to use a computer efficiently. Chapter 2 also describes the different ways companies may use computers, as well as the different kinds of computer facilities you may come into contact with when working in a business that uses computers.

SUMMARY

Why are you studying this book? Because computers have become the backbone of modern business and you want to become a success in the job of your choice. The need to know how to input, process, store, and output data and information has become increasingly relevant to anyone who plans to enter the business environment. Your survival in the business world of today and tomorrow depends more and more on how well you understand what a computer is, how it works, and what it can be used for.

A computer system is composed of computer hardware, software, and people. People have always been extremely important to the functioning of a computer system. In the past, however, when computers weren't so commonplace in business, many people were able to ignore them. Today it is much more difficult to avoid being a part of a computer system, because most business professionals must use a computer to get their jobs done. Knowledge of a microcomputer is especially relevant for people in business today. If you're familiar with the basic microcomputer hardware components—the keyboard, the monitor, and the system unit—you're already on the way to improving your usefulness in business. And if

FIGURE 1.22
You *can* take it with you. Computers are being used more and more in the home for entertainment, educational and financial management purposes, and to catch up on work taken home from the office.

you have had experience using some of the popular "off-the-shelf" software programs, you are already a more valuable employee.

Business has seen many improvements in the area of data processing since the introduction of computers:

- Data can be collected more easily.
- Data can be processed with much greater speed.
- Data can be manipulated over and over again with ease.
- Calculations are performed not only faster but with greater accuracy.
- Output can be produced in more usable forms.

Significant progress has been made in making the computer easier to use by, for example, introducing the mouse, using menus and icons, and improving the clarity of the images displayed on the monitor.

The impact of the computer on society can be felt everywhere: in business, government, the legal profession, the medical profession, and in the home.

KEY TERMS

applications software
arithmetic/logic unit
   (ALU)
binary digit
bit
byte
central processing unit
   (CPU)
chip
compatibility
computer
computer literacy
computer professional
computer system
control unit
CPS (characters per
   second)

data
data processing
documentation
floppy disk
hard card
hardcopy
hard disk
hardware
information
internal memory
K (kilobyte)
keyboard
mainframe computer
MB (megabyte)
microcomputer
minicomputer
MIPS (millions of in-
   structions per second)

monitor
monochrome monitor
motherboard
nonvolatile
power supply
processing registers
program
RGB (color) monitor
softcopy
software
software development
   tool
software package
storage devices
   (hardware)
systems software
system unit
user

EXERCISES

MATCHING

Match each of the following terms to the phrase that is the most closely related:

1. _____ computer literacy
2. _____ computer
3. _____ data
4. _____ software package
5. _____ chip
6. _____ bit
7. _____ data processing
8. _____ information
9. _____ computer system
10. _____ central processing unit
11. _____ microcomputer
12. _____ K
13. _____ floppy disk
14. _____ monitor
15. _____ user
16. _____ computer professional

a. This hardware component made of silicon holds the circuits that run a computer.
b. This hardware component is made up of a control unit, arithmetic/logic unit, processing registers, and internal memory.
c. This device provides your principal visual contact with a computer system.
d. The combination of hardware, software, and people.
e. This flexible storage device is commonly used with microcomputers and is capable of magnetically storing data on its surface.
f. A collection of raw, unevaluated facts, concepts, or instructions.
g. The processing of data into information.
h. The product of the computerized processing of data.
i. Software that has been created by professional software writers and that is accompanied by a users' manual.
j. This hardware component provides the electrical power to all components housed in the system unit.
k. A relatively small, general-purpose computer system that uses a microprocessor chip as a central processing unit.
l. This term is used to describe the equivalent of 1024 characters stored either in internal memory or on a storage hardware device.
m. A basic understanding of what a computer is and how it can be used as a resource.
n. The smallest element of data; eight of these form a character.
o. A person without much technical knowledge about computers but who uses computers to produce information used in decision making.
p. The main circuit board of the computer.
q. This device is a combination of electronic and electromechanical components that can perform computations.
r. A person in the field of computers who has had formal education in the technical aspects of using computers.

MULTIPLE CHOICE

1. Data can be differentiated from information because:
   a. There is no difference between data and information.
   b. Data always has a context; information doesn't.
   c. Information always contains data.
   d. Information always has a context and data doesn't.

2. Which of the following represents a step toward achieving computer literacy?
   a. learn how to talk about computers
   b. learn how to use a computer to produce the information you need
   c. learn to describe the various components of a computer
   d. acknowledge the importance of computers in our society
   e. all of the above

3. Which of the following terms is unrelated to the others?
   a. arithmetic/logic unit
   b. processing registers
   c. monitor
   d. control unit
   e. central processing unit

4. Which of the following isn't a factor when deciding whether a computer is a mainframe, a mini, or a micro?
   a. amount of internal memory the CPU can use
   b. processing speed in millions of instructions per second
   c. capacity of the storage devices
   d. amount of electricity required to process
   e. number of users that can use the computer at any given time

5. Which of the following is an important component of a microcomputer system?
   a. K
   b. microprocessor
   c. MB
   d. byte
   e. none of the above

6. Which of the following statements relates to the effect computers have had on society?
   a. Computers shorten the time it takes to process data into information.
   b. Computers can perform calculations accurately.
   c. Computers manipulate data with ease.
   d. Computers can collect data in more usable forms.
   e. all of the above

7. Which of the following statements isn't true?
   a. A modern computer can perform around 1 billion operations per second.
   b. Herman Hollerith invented the punched card.
   c. There was no data processing before computers.
   d. Computers normally allow us to process data with greater accuracy.

8. Which of these characteristics does not apply to first-generation computers?
   a. Most of the input and output mediums were punched cards and magnetic tape.
   b. Internal memory was made up almost exclusively of transistors.
   c. The computers produced a tremendous amount of heat.
   d. The computers were slow and large.

e. Computer training at the high school level is becoming more and more popular.

9. Which of these characteristics applies to fourth-generation computers?
   a. have a very large capacity for internal memory
   b. use a wide variety of input and output devices
   c. include the development of the microcomputer
   d. use large-scale integration circuits for main memory and logic
   e. all of the above

10. Which of the following is a category of computer hardware?
   a. input
   b. storage
   c. output
   d. processing
   e. all of the above

SHORT ANSWER

1. Why are people so important to a computer system?
2. In what ways have computers affected the processing of data into information?
3. What are some of the ways in which computers have affected society?
4. What are the three main categories of software?
5. What do you need to know to be considered "computer literate"?
6. What is the difference between a computer professional and a user? How has the definition of *user* changed over the years?
7. What are the typical hardware components found in a computer system?
8. What are the most notable characteristics of computers in each of the five generations?
9. What is meant by the terms *mainframe, minicomputer,* and *microcomputer*? Why is it difficult to define these terms?
10. What is the difference between data and information?

PROJECTS

1. Write a report about how computers are being used at your school or where you work. You can describe the use of computers in all departments or focus on the use of computers in one department. If possible, determine how the computers affect data processing.
2. Your task is to convince some friends that they will be more marketable to potential employers if they become computer literate. Incorporate one or more of the following techniques into your argument:

    a. Interview personnel in the job placement department at your school to determine what employers require of job applicants.

    b. Interview personnel in charge of hiring at a company to see if they view a job applicant with computer skills more favorably than one without any computer skills.

    c. Survey the employment section of various publications to see what percentage of jobs require some type of computer skills.

3. Go to a local computer store and ask the salesperson the following questions:

    a. What types of questions do customers ask when they come to buy a computer?

    b. What do you think the customer should know before buying a computer? Do you make sure the customer knows all of these things before you sell them a computer?

CHAPTER TWO

THE COMPUTER-BASED INFORMATION SYSTEM

The past is prologue—the beginning of the present. Now that we have discussed the past and learned some basic concepts, let us move on to the present and explore how you can use the computer to turn data into useful information.

The goal of this book is to provide you with tools that you can take with you into your career right away. With that goal in mind, we have devised a series of episodes that shows you how to use a computer in your own business. The first such episode immediately follows this chapter.

PREVIEW

When you have completed this chapter, you will be able to:

■

State what your role might be in a computer-based information system

■

Name the five components of a basic computer-based information system, and describe its four phases of activity

■

Describe the role of computer software and hardware in a computer-based information system

■

Discuss four different approaches a company can take to organize computerized data processing

■

The User Perspective

Can data be turned into information *without* the use of a computer? Of course—and it has been, for all the centuries of human history. Whether fingers or pebbles or coins are used to represent quantities, they may be manipulated in all sorts of ways. The difference between then and now is speed: The computer enormously enhances the rapidity of converting data into information. The invention of computers and their speed, however, has created another important difference: what people have to do to data and to the computer in order to get information.

Not all your business information problems will be best solved using a computer. Right now you're not in the position to judge when to use the computer, but you will be when you understand what is known as a *computer-based information system*—the collection and processing of data, and the storage and output of information. In the following pages, we will describe exactly what this system is, how it fits into a typical business organization, and what you need to know. But first let's determine where you fit in the overall picture.

Where Do You Fit in?

Perhaps a secret anxiety of many users like you is the knowledge that computers don't run by themselves—a human presence, *your* presence, is required to make things happen. Indeed, you *are* a critical part of a computer-based information system, but we will lead you through it step by step so that it won't look quite so fearsome by the time you reach the end of the chapter.

As Figure 2.1 shows, during normal business activities users interact with the system at two points—at the beginning and at the end. At the beginning, data must be converted into a form suitable for input to the computer. At the end, information is produced for review and is then used as a basis for making decisions.

The user may also interact with the computer-based information system at a third point: the development of business software. This doesn't mean that you, the user, have to *write* the software; it means that you may have to help define the business-related requirements in enough detail so that the computer professionals assigned to develop the software understand what is to happen, when it is to happen, and how. For example, if you want the computer to prepare reports on budgeted versus actual sales of bridge paint, your requirements for how the report is to be produced must be carefully thought out. What level of detail do you require? Should reports cover information only on orange bridge paint, or should purple be included? How often do you want reports? when? in what form? and so on.

Some type of computer hardware is required at every stage of processing. The larger the computer system is, the more removed the users are from the computer hardware. If your company uses a mainframe or minicomputer system, you may work only with a terminal connected to the system and never even see the computer. In this case, you will need to learn how to establish communication with the central computer system and to follow the established procedures for requesting that certain programs be run in your behalf. However, if your company has only microcomputers for staff use, you will need to know a great deal more about the hardware.

WHAT IS A COMPUTER-BASED INFORMATION SYSTEM?

In a **computer-based information system,** the user is concerned with collecting data (input), processing it into information (in a form usable for decision making), and

FIGURE 2.1
The user's part in a computer-based information system. At the system's starting point, the user inputs data to the computer (a). After processing, at the system's end point, the user reviews output information (b).

storing information for future reference. The system has five components and four phases of activity.

SYSTEM COMPONENTS

You'll recall from Chapter 1 that any computer system has three basic parts: people, hardware, and software. In the business-related system, we must be concerned with two additional components: data and information (Figure 2.2). The people (users and computer professionals) interface with the system at points where **data** must be

FIGURE 2.2
The five components of a computer-based information system. People (1), data (2), hardware (3), processing procedures and software (4), and information (5).

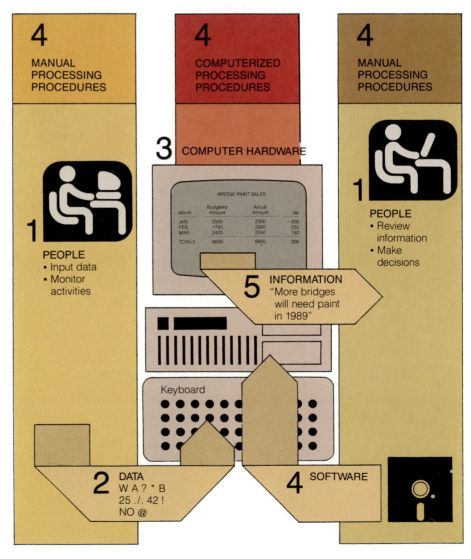

input and **information** must be output, reviewed, and analyzed in order to make decisions.

The computer hardware performs tasks as directed by the processing procedures, which fall into two categories: manual procedures (activities performed by people when they interact with the information system) and computerized procedures (specifically written software programs stored in computer-usable form to be retrieved and used by the hardware to perform the desired processing activities) (Figure 2.2).

PHASES OF ACTIVITY

A computer-based information system includes four major phases of activity: input, processing, output, and storage (see Figure 2.3). Each phase has a major objective, and each requires specific software and people to direct the activities and one or more computer hardware components to perform tasks.

FIGURE 2.3
The four phases of a computer-based information system. Input (1), processing (2), output (3), and storage (4).

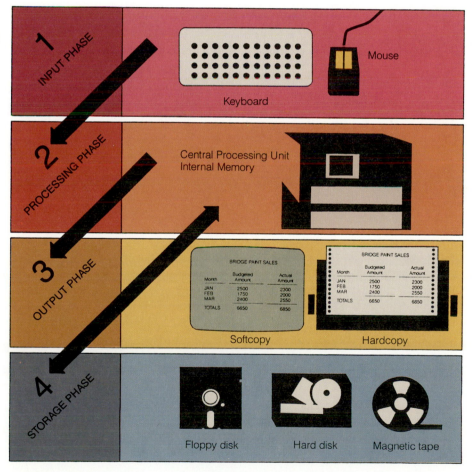

INPUT PHASE   During the input phase of a computer-based information system, business-related data is "captured" and converted to a form that can be processed by a computer. In this phase people will:

- Collect the data, either in document form or verbally
- Instruct the computer to begin data input activities
- Input data (using a keyboard or a mouse, for example) into a device (such as a computer terminal) that captures the data in a computer-usable form
- Supervise the data collection and input process

Manual procedures—which sometimes are used together with computerized procedures—direct and control each activity in terms of who is supposed to do what, when, and how. For example, when data from sales receipts is being entered, someone must check to see that the sales records from which the data is being taken have been properly filled out; all the documents must be accounted for, and—after the data is input—someone must make sure that all the data has been entered. And, of course, the collection of documents and inputting of data must be scheduled. Computerized procedures are required for:

- Coordinating the keying and processing of the data
- Checking the validity of the data (Was the product number you entered a valid one? Was the data keyed in without typos?)
- Storing the data in computer-usable form for processing
- Producing a control report that both summarizes the amount of data keyed in and provides totals on selected data elements (such as gallons of purple bridge paint sold yesterday) to ensure accurate entry

The computer hardware devices used most often during the input phase are the keyboard, video display screen, disk storage unit, and printer (to produce a control report).

PROCESSING PHASE   In the processing phase of a computer-based information system, all the number and character manipulation activities are done that are necessary to convert the data into an appropriate form. As shown in Figure 2.4, this includes performing calculations, classifying the input data, sorting the data, summarizing the data, and performing logical processing activities (such as updating files, which are collections of related records, each containing data relating to one topic; more on this later).

In a well-designed computer-based information system, people rarely need to do more than issue instructions that tell the computer what procedures to perform. The manual procedures focus on how to begin, then how to monitor the computer processing procedures. The hardware components used most during this phase of activity are the central processing unit (CPU) and internal memory.

OUTPUT PHASE   The output phase of the system provides the user with all the necessary information to perform and manage day-to-day business activities, as well as tactical planning (monitoring current company operations) and strategic planning (planning long-range goals for the company). The computer hardware used most often in this phase of activity includes (1) hardcopy output devices, such as printers and plotters (used to prepare hardcopy graphics), and (2) video display screens, or monitors.

FIGURE 2.4
Examples of processing activities. Computer processing is useful for organizing different forms of output. Information may be listed, summarized, categorized, sorted, or classified.

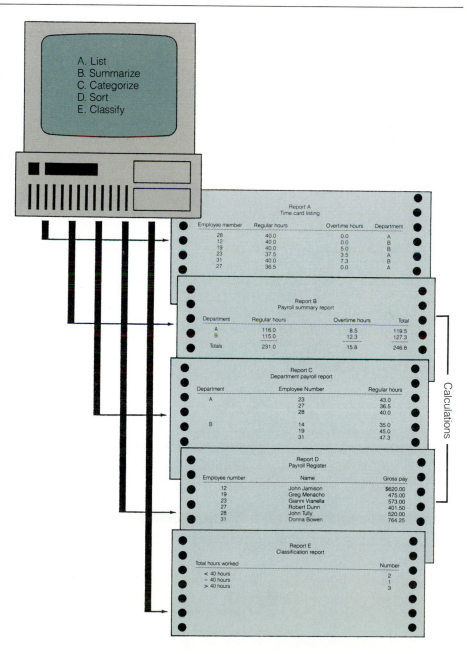

The form in which information is produced as output will vary according to needs. For example, some information can be output in printed form on regular paper or on special forms (hardcopy), whereas other information may be more useful if displayed immediately on a video display terminal in the form of text and images (softcopy). Hardcopy reports are commonly used; softcopy output is best for information that needs to be viewed only occasionally or only for a few moments.

Technological improvements have made it much more practical to produce both hardcopy and softcopy output that incorporates graphics with text. Sometimes information is also produced in an audio form, such as a telephone number given over the phone by directory assistance.

In the output phase people usually:

- Prepare the output for distribution
- Distribute the output to the intended recipients
- Review the output by analyzing the information, then write reports and make decisions based on the results of the analysis

The preparation and distribution of the output (manual procedures) would normally be controlled by a company's established standards and procedures. However, procedures for output review, analysis, and decision-making activities are rarely documented formally.

STORAGE PHASE　The storage phase of a computer-based information system involves storing data, information, and processing instructions in computer-usable form for retrieval, as well as processing and updating as required. There is little need for human involvement in the computerized storage of data. The computer program directs the computer to store the data in computer-usable form. People do get involved, however, in the maintenance of computer-based files. Someone has to monitor how long data should be retained, decide whether backup copies are required, and determine when data should be removed from the system. These activities are normally directed by formal policies and procedures relating to file retention. Indeed, much of the information stored on computers—medical records, for example—must be maintained by law for specified periods of time.

THE FOUR PHASES OF ACTIVITY AT INTOUCH OFFICE SUPPLIES, INC.

In almost every business it's easy to identify the four phases of activity in the computer-based information system. The user procedures may differ slightly, as may the hardware components; however, the general flow of activities—from the input of data into computer-usable form and the processing of data into information to the output or storage of information—remains the same.

In this section we use sales order entry—necessary to many businesses—to illustrate each phase of activity. Refer to Figure 2.5, which shows the entire process, throughout this section.

INTOUCH SALES ORDER ENTRY: INPUT PHASE　Suppose you were running an office supply store named Intouch Office Supplies, Inc. One of the first things you need to do in the input phase of the sales order entry process is to identify the different *types* of input required for processing. Obviously, you have to input data that has to do with the price and amount of goods ordered by and sold to customers on a daily basis. In addition, the stock within the store must be replenished. So data about the receipt of goods into stock must also be entered into the computer.

Data related to customer orders can be received in at least three ways: (1) A customer may call and place an order; (2) a customer may send an order in the mail; (3) a customer may stop by the store, pick out the needed items from the shelves, and bring them to the cash register. The input procedures might differ slightly for each circumstance.

When a customer calls on the phone, you might record the order data on an order form (**source document**) for later entry into computer-usable form. As an alternative, if your store is equipped with modern computer processing facilities, you might enter the data immediately into the computer through a video display terminal. This approach has some distinct advantages. For example, if the data is entered into computer-usable form immediately, the computer could automatically check the inventory file to ensure that a sufficient quantity is on hand to fill the order.

The orders received in the mail would probably be collected, grouped into small batches (a **batch** is a group of documents intended for input to the computer in a controlled fashion), and entered all at once into the system through a video display terminal.

Customer orders placed at the store could be handled in several ways. If all the items in the store have the bar-coded tags we often see at the supermarket, you could use a bar-code reading device to automatically scan the product data into computer-usable form. You could also simply use the keyboard on a video display terminal at the counter to enter the data on the items ordered. Some stores still use cash registers to key in the price and amounts of each item; managers of such operations can determine the number of items sold only by periodically counting the number left on the shelf.

To keep track of the number of items in stock, the data relating to goods received must also be entered into the computer. The product numbers and number of items received can be taken from the vendor's bill of lading (a document identifying the contents of a shipment) and entered directly into the computer.

INTOUCH SALES ORDER ENTRY: PROCESSING PHASE   During the processing phase, the data (now in computer-usable form) is transformed into information. Processing includes performing calculations, classifying the input data, sorting the data, summarizing the data, and performing logical processing activities such as updating files.

At Intouch, Inc., you probably process the customer order data in the following fashion. First, you process the data relating to the items ordered. The product number for each item is verified by comparing it with the number contained in the inventory master file. Each item's price is retrieved, as well as the detailed item description. The inventory master file is updated to reflect the number of items ordered and removed from stock. Then all the order data is processed to produce the information necessary to produce an invoice—the bill for the customer. In the invoice, the quantity of each item ordered is multiplied by its unit price (the price of one item) to produce a line total. All the line totals are added to produce an invoice subtotal. The subtotal, as well as the customer's status, is analyzed to determine what type of discount, if any, should be allowed. (For example, customers who owe no money and who order more than 20 gold paper clips at one time

FIGURE 2.5 (a)
Sales order entry. At Intouch Office Supplies, customer order data is taken by mail, phone, and in the store. The data (product numbers plus prices and amount of items sold) is input to the computer and processed. Processed data is used to update stored inventory, customer files, and sales order files and to output information in the form of invoices and reports.

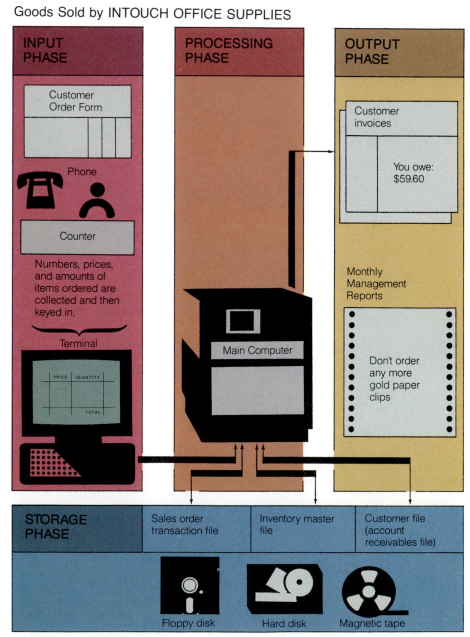

get a 5% reduction in price.) The discount amount is computed, as well as any state and local taxes that apply. Finally the invoice total is computed. The last step in processing customer order data involves updating the file of unpaid customer invoices (accounts receivable) with a summary of the invoice-related data.

Figure 2.5 (b)
To fill orders effectively, Intouch, Inc., also needs to process data relating to receipt of product shipments to replenish inventory. Data (numbers and amounts of items delivered) taken from the bills of lading is input to the computer and used to update stored inventory files and to output information in the form of inventory status reports and reorder requests.

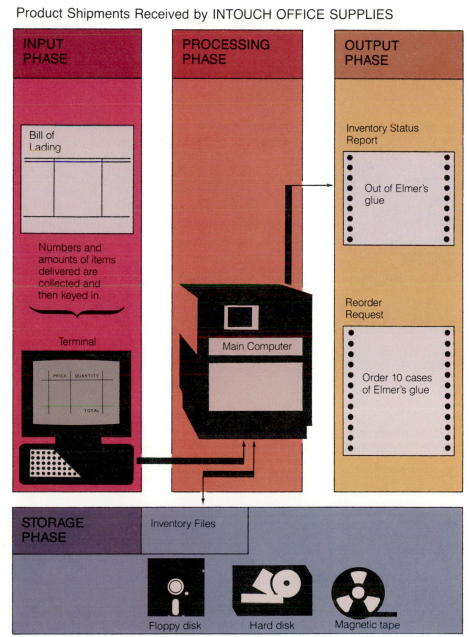

Product Shipments Received by INTOUCH OFFICE SUPPLIES

INPUT PHASE

Bill of Lading

Numbers and amounts of items delivered are collected and then keyed in.

Terminal

PRICE   QUANTITY

TOTAL

PROCESSING PHASE

Main Computer

OUTPUT PHASE

Inventory Status Report

Out of Elmer's glue

Reorder Request

Order 10 cases of Elmer's glue

STORAGE PHASE

Inventory Files

Floppy disk   Hard disk   Magnetic tape

The processing of the bill of lading data involves updating the master inventory file to reflect the number of additional items placed in stock and updating the accounts payable file—that is, the file that shows amounts owed to suppliers for what shipments.

INTOUCH SALES ORDER ENTRY: OUTPUT PHASE   Intouch Office Supplies probably produces two main types of output regularly in its sales order entry system: (1) customer invoices, printed out and sent to customers for payment, and (2) management reports, produced monthly to summarize and categorize the products sold.

In addition, status reports of all goods in stock are produced periodically; in other words, the number of items actually on the shelves is compared with the number indicated by the computerized records. "Exception" reports are produced whenever the quantity of an item on hand falls below the minimum stocking level (sometimes referred to as the *reorder point*).

INTOUCH SALES ORDER ENTRY: STORAGE PHASE   Your office supply company is involved with computerized storage in three ways. First, the order data and the data on goods received (to restock inventory) is entered into a temporary storage file (called a **transaction file**) and stored until needed for processing. Second, during processing, information stored in a permanent customer file and an inventory master file is retrieved for use in performing calculations and other processing activities. Third, information stored in the inventory master file and the accounts receivable file is updated.

In addition, all processing instructions are stored in a permanent form for easy retrieval.

METHODS OF INPUT AND PROCESSING

We used the sales order entry process of Intouch Office Supplies to illustrate the activities that might take place in each phase of a computer-based information system; but the activities we described were specific to that example. Any organization that uses computers to process data into information has a computer-based information system. However, the activities of each phase will be different depending on what overall input and processing approach, or combination of approaches, is used.

In this section, we describe four different approaches an organization might use to computerize its information system: (1) batch; (2) on-line; (3) on-line real-time; and (4) off-line. Deciding which approach is best depends on how the organization inputs data, when data needs to be processed (immediately or later), and when output (information) is needed. We will use Intouch Office Supplies to illustrate the activities that might take place using each of the four approaches.

BATCH APPROACH: DELAYED INPUT

An organization that uses the batch approach collects data in the form of source documents (for example, customer sales orders) and places them into groups (*batches*). Once all of the data has been collected and batched, it is forwarded to a data entry person or group responsible for keying it into computer-usable form. As the data is keyed in, it is stored in a transaction file. In some cases the data may be stored for only a few hours, but in other cases it may be stored for a week or a month

FIGURE 2.6
Batching it. Source documents are collected over a period of time. Then their data is entered into the computer in batches. After being temporarily stored in the transaction files, the data is processed for output and updating of permanent files.

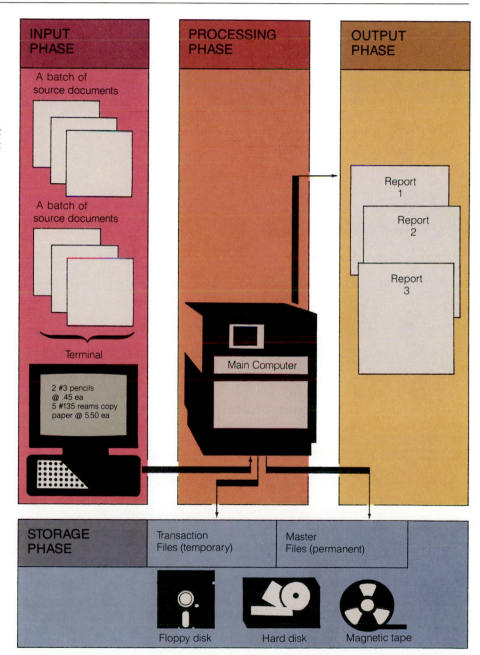

INPUT PHASE

A batch of source documents

A batch of source documents

Terminal

2 #3 pencils
@ .45 ea
5 #135 reams copy
paper @ 5.50 ea

PROCESSING PHASE

Main Computer

OUTPUT PHASE

Report 1

Report 2

Report 3

STORAGE PHASE

Transaction Files (temporary)

Master Files (permanent)

Floppy disk   Hard disk   Magnetic tape

before the regular processing activities are scheduled. At this time each transaction in the batch is processed, one after another, until all related output has been produced and appropriate files have been updated. Figure 2.6 (on the previous page) shows the typical activities that take place in the batch approach to a computer-based information system.

Intouch Office Supplies would probably use the batch approach to handle pertinent transaction data from mailed customer orders and bills of lading from suppliers. After collecting the data into batches, a clerk would be assigned the task of entering the data into the computer for temporary storage. (Sometimes the data is transcribed onto some other type of form or source document before it is input to the computer.) The processing activities would probably take place at the end of the workday or in the evening so as not to tie up the computer during the day.

ON-LINE APPROACH: IMMEDIATE INPUT

An organization that uses the **on-line** approach doesn't record data for input on a source document. Instead, as shown in Figure 2.7, the relevant data from each transaction is immediately translated into computer-usable form. However, the data is not necessarily processed immediately. It may be held in temporary storage until needed for regularly scheduled processing activities.

Intouch Office Supplies would probably use the on-line approach to take sales orders over the phone and over the counter. As the order data is received from the customer, it is input to the computer via a video display terminal and immediately recorded directly into a transaction file; the data is not manually recorded on an order form first. (However, if desired, the company could use a modern video display that can create a picture of an order form on the screen. The clerk would then key in the appropriate data elements as if completing a hardcopy order form.) The data is held in a transaction file until the end of the day, when the computer sorts it into the same order as the master file to be updated; then the data is processed all at once.

ON-LINE REAL-TIME APPROACH: IMMEDIATE INPUT AND IMMEDIATE PROCESSING

Similarities exist between the on-line and the on-line real-time processing approaches. In both cases the transaction data is immediately translated into computer-usable form. However, in the case of **on-line real-time processing,** each transaction is fully processed when input into the system so that there is immediate feedback and action can be taken right away, based on the results of the processing (see Figure 2.8). There is no delay; all related computer files affected by the transaction are updated immediately. An airline reservation system is an example of a system that requires immediate processing of transactions; airlines need to use the on-line real-time approach to keep an accurate up-to-date record of reservations, cancellations, and scheduled flights and flight changes. Some automatic teller transactions are also handled on an on-line real-time basis: When you withdraw money, your balance is immediately updated and printed on your receipt.

Adding a few refinements to Intouch's sales order system could qualify it as an on-line real-time system. The primary change would be the manner in which each transaction is processed by the software.

FIGURE 2.7
On-line. This type of processing uses no source documents with manually recorded data. Instead, data is input immediately and stored temporarily in a transaction file for later processing, which produces output and updates permanent files.

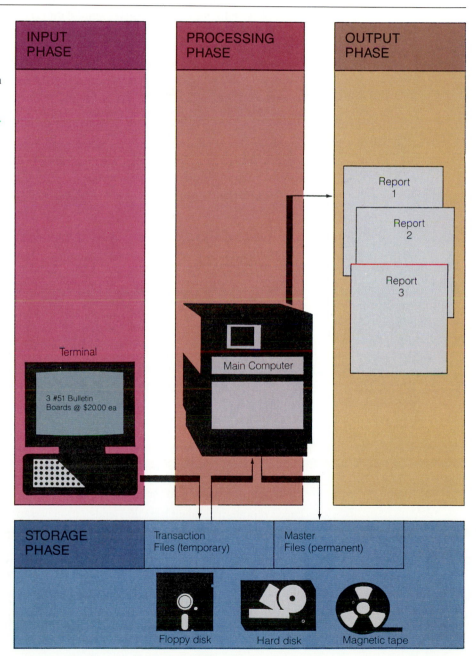

INPUT PHASE

PROCESSING PHASE

OUTPUT PHASE

Report 1

Report 2

Report 3

Terminal

3 #51 Bulletin Boards @ $20.00 ea

Main Computer

STORAGE PHASE

Transaction Files (temporary)

Master Files (permanent)

Floppy disk

Hard disk

Magnetic tape

First, you enter the customer identification code in the space provided on the order-form image on the video display screen. The system immediately verifies the code by checking against the customer master file. If the code is incorrect, a message will prompt you to try again. After you have entered a valid code, the system will respond by retrieving the related customer name, address, and credit information and displaying the information on the screen. Next, you enter the product code and the quantity of the item being sold.

The system then immediately verifies the code by checking it against the inventory master file. Again, if the code is incorrect, you will see an error message on your video display screen. If the code is correct, the product description is retrieved and the quantity ordered is deducted from the balance on hand in the inventory master file for that product. The system also verifies that the quantity on hand is sufficient to satisfy the order. If the quantity on hand is insufficient, you will see a message to that effect on the screen.

These procedures are repeated for each item ordered. When all the product information has been entered, the system then performs all the necessary computations to produce the customer invoice and to update the accounts receivable file to reflect the amount of money owed by the customer.

The key characteristics to note in the preceding example of on-line real-time processing are:

- Customer order data is acted on immediately.
- The inventory master file is updated immediately to reflect the number of items removed from inventory.
- The customer invoice is produced on the spot.
- The accounts receivable file (money owed to Intouch Office Supplies) is updated immediately to reflect the new invoice data.

The on-line real-time approach is used for the most time-sensitive applications, when processing must be immediate and the resulting information needs to be available for decision making as quickly as possible. Some organizations use a combination of batch, on-line, and on-line real-time processing at different points in their operations, depending on whether processing needs are routine or time sensitive.

OFF-LINE APPROACH: DELAYED, HEAVY-DUTY PROCESSING

An organization that uses **off-line processing** generally performs a great number of large-volume, redundant tasks that tend to unnecessarily tie up the processing power of a mainframe computer system. A specialized computer is used to handle these types of tasks. The task most often handled using off-line processing is printing large-volume output reports. For example, a typical large corporate data processing center produces 250,000 pages per month or more, and a public utility, with literally millions of customers, could easily produce 20 million pages per month of output reports and bills.

Off-line processing occurs after regular processing has been completed. During regular processing, regardless of whether it was done in batch or on-line processing mode, the output is recorded onto disk or tape. This is because the main computer system can record the data onto disk or tape much more quickly than the printers can produce it in hardcopy form. The stored output (now in computer-usable form

FIGURE 2.8
On-line real-time. This approach uses immediate input and processing to produce information without delay—including the customer's invoice.

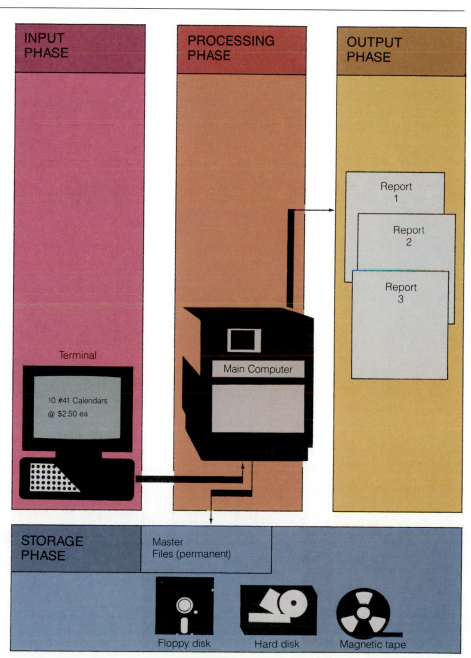

because it's already on disk or tape) is ready to be processed off-line, which involves one or more high-speed printers to get the hardcopy output produced as quickly as possible (see Figure 2.9).

MANAGEMENT PHILOSOPHY AND THE USE OF COMPUTERS

When a company acquires a minicomputer or mainframe computer system, it also usually sets up a special organizational unit, or department, to operate it. (Because microcomputers are still generally used by only one user at a time, a special department does not need to be set up to operate them.) The name of this unit may

FIGURE 2.9
Off-line. This approach frees up the main computer for regular processing. A special computer and one or more high-speed printers are used to generate large amounts of repetitive reports that were output in special report files.

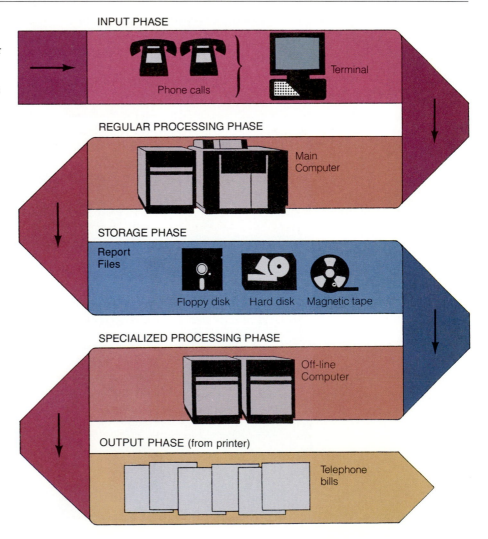

vary from the Data Processing Department to the Information Systems Department. The computer system and related equipment plus the area set aside for the employees who staff the department are often called the *computer facility*. How a computer facility functions and how it is used within an organization tends to reflect management's organizational philosophy. You, as a user, should know how your company's computer facility is organized so that you can efficiently perform your job-related activities. Figure 2.10 diagrams the characteristics of the three types of facilities: centralized, decentralized, and distributed.

CENTRALIZED COMPUTER FACILITY: ONE FOR ALL

When an organization has established a single computer department to provide data processing services, this department is often referred to as a **centralized computer facility.** It is called *centralized* because it alone supplies data processing support to all other departments in the company. The position of a centralized facility in the organizational structure varies. However, it often reports to one of the following: (1) the Controller, who is in charge of all accounting procedures, (2) the Vice President of Finance, or (3) directly to top management through a Vice President of Information Systems.

When computerized information processing was first introduced to business, it was most often used in the areas of accounting and finance. To have the computer facility staff report to the head of the department to which it provided services seemed only natural. Because many organizations computerized their accounting activities first, the data processing facility usually reported to the head of accounting.

As businesses gained experience in using computerized information processing, more departments began to recognize the value of the computer. This led to competition for the use of the computer resource, which in turn led to problems in establishing priorities. To resolve this problem, many organizations established the computer facility as a separate functional unit, or department, that reported to upper management. The management set up an independent management steering committee to objectively consider all requests for computer support and establish priorities, which were then followed by the staff of the computer facility.

The principal advantages of the centralized processing approach are:

- *Cost-effectiveness*—The cost effectiveness of computer hardware resources is increased because equipment is not duplicated at different locations.

- *Coordination and control*—Processing activities are easier to coordinate and control in a centralized facility.

- *Standards*—The ability to impose and enforce processing standards is easier in a centralized facility.

In some cases, the centralized approach proved unsatisfactory because of:

- *Lack of accountability*—It is difficult to track and fairly allocate the costs of the computer processing facility to the specific departments based on individual departmental use.

- *Unfamiliarity*—The computer specialists responsible for the design of computer applications software ended up being responsible for working in many areas of the company with which they were unfamiliar. As a result, the specialists often took a lot of time to understand the processing requirements of a new department. This problem often caused delays in a project and sometimes led to misunderstandings—in other words, some of the software developed failed to meet the needs of the department, or failed to meet them in time.

- *Delays*—In many cases the data processing staff in centralized computer facilities had so many demands placed on their time that users had to wait for months (or even years) for their projects to be completed.

Concerns with problems such as these led some organizations to organize their computer facility differently.

DECENTRALIZED COMPUTER FACILITIES: ALL FOR ONE

An organization that uses a separate computer facility to service the needs of each major organizational unit has **decentralized computer facilities.** The size of each facility is determined by the processing requirements of the department it services. Smaller departments may have a decentralized processing facility that is staffed with only one or two computer operators to initiate and control processing activities on a minicomputer. Other organizational units may have a large data processing facility with computer operators, data entry personnel, programmers, and systems analysts. (Systems analysts determine users' computer-related processing requirements and then design a computerized applications system to meet those requirements.)

Although this approach solves some problems created by centralized facilities, it also creates new ones. For one, the approach makes it difficult to obtain consolidated, company-wide management information, because each organizational unit has its own key data and information stored on its own computer system. Because the format and content of this data and information are not consistent between organizational units, it can't be easily accessed or subjected to a simple consolidation procedure. For example, suppose one company uses six different types of microcomputer: Accounting has an IBM PC-AT; the Vice President of Finance uses an Apple IIe; Personnel, a Compaq Deskpro; Marketing, a Macintosh; Production, a Tandy Model 3000 (with three terminals); and the Controller has an old Kaypro 10. Each computer is unable to exchange data or software easily with the others—the computers are not *compatible*. This eliminates the ability to share data in a form that can immediately be processed by a computer. As a result, the only way to share data is in printed form, and the only way to process combined data is to re-input it into a form compatible with the computer intended to process it.

Another drawback of decentralized facilities is that the duplication of hardware, software, and personnel to run them becomes an unmanageable expense.

DISTRIBUTED COMPUTER FACILITY: SOMETHING FOR EVERYONE

A combination of centralized and decentralized computer facilities has been used recently to try to capture the advantages of both while minimizing their weaknesses. In this system, called a **distributed computer facility,** users have their own computer equipment, and one or more computer terminals are connected to a bigger system—a few microcomputers, a minicomputer, or in some cases a mainframe computer—depending on processing requirements.

To illustrate, let's consider a company with four divisions located in different cities throughout the country with its corporate headquarters on the West Coast.

FIGURE 2.10
Three different computer facilities. Companies may organize computer facilities so that they are centralized, decentralized, or distributed. Management philosophy determines the choice of facility.

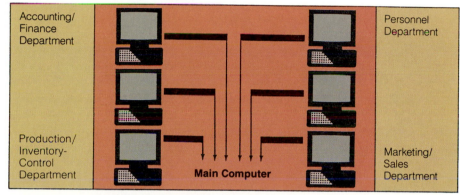

CENTRALIZED COMPUTER FACILITY

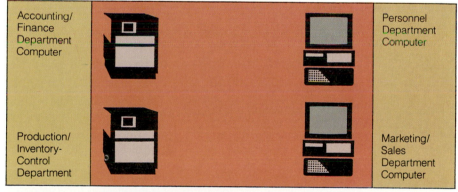

DECENTRALIZED COMPUTER FACILITY

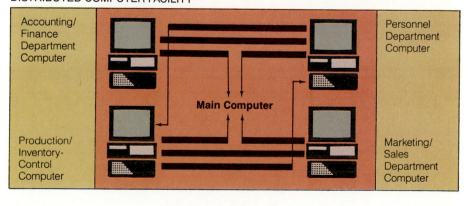

DISTRIBUTED COMPUTER FACILITY

Headquarters has a large mainframe computer system, and each division has a smaller minicomputer to handle its own local processing needs. Some individual users in various departments at the division level have microcomputers to increase their productivity. The mainframe computer performs all corporate-level processing and passes pertinent data and information to each division as needed through a communications facility built into the computer systems at all locations. The greatest processing needs at the division level are handled by the division's minicomputer system. In many cases, several departments have microcomputer terminals connected to the minicomputer system. These personal computers may be used for a variety of processing requirements. The more sophisticated personal computers are able to exchange data with the division-level computer system.

In a distributed computer environment, the corporate-level facility is ultimately responsible for the control and the coordination of processing activities at all company levels. This is usually accomplished through corporate-level policies and procedures, as well as by direct support from the corporate data processing department, which oversees equipment selection and systems design to maintain compatibility.

Without careful planning, the compatibility of data files can become a problem when users capture data on a microcomputer and then wish to transfer it to the central computer system. The reverse is also often true. Microcomputers use a different coding scheme for data than many larger computers do. Unless special steps are taken—adding special hardware components and using special software—data cannot be exchanged in either direction. However, when the proper steps are taken, the problem of data file compatibility is eliminated. Then the microcomputer can be a significant tool in distributing computer processing power to the users.

In some cases, the central facility also develops software and turns it over to the users to operate. (Users generally develop their own applications software for microcomputers—perhaps with some consultation with the central computer facility.)

The principal advantages of the distributed processing approach are:

- *User involvement*—The users are more directly involved in the processing activities than they would be in a centralized structure.

- *Cost allocation*—Computer processing costs are easier to allocate than they are in a centralized computer facility.

- *Familiarity*—The computer staff is more familiar with the activities and needs of the specific organizational unit they support than they are in a centralized setup.

- *Corporate processing needs*—The central computer facility can focus more on corporate processing needs than it can when the organization uses only a centralized facility to support all its departments.

- *Fewer personnel*—There is less duplication of personnel than with the decentralized approach.

- *Coordination*—There is more coordination between the corporate computer facility and the division-level computer facilities than with other approaches.

A company that has many widely dispersed units is likely to have a decentralized or a distributed computer facility. Of the two, the decentralized approach will work better when the different units are involved in unrelated activities that require little overall coordination and control. Distributed computer facilities are often found in companies where the organizational units are separate but still closely related and where corporate coordination is very important. Companies with one large headquarters are likely to have a centralized computer facility.

ONWARD:
APPLYING WHAT YOU'VE LEARNED

Part One has offered you an overview of many of the basic concepts that provide a foundation for understanding how computers are used in business. You should now have a general sense of what a computer system is, how it has affected the processing of data into information, and what basic steps are involved in a computer-based information system.

Now we proceed to Episode 1 of establishing your own business—a chance for you to start applying what you've learned.

SUMMARY

A computer-based information system involves collecting data (input), processing it into information, and storing the information for future reference and output. The system has five basic components—people, computer hardware, manual and computerized processing procedures (software), data, and information—and four major phases of activity—input, processing, output, and storage. People are most directly involved during the input and output phases.

Each organization has different processing requirements, depending on the nature of its business and activities and how quickly the data needs to be processed. To accommodate these differing needs the computer-based information system can be designed to use one or more of four basic types of processing approaches: the batch approach, the on-line approach, the on-line real-time approach, and the off-line approach. These approaches differ in terms of the methods for collecting the data for input, the amount of time that passes between data input and actual processing, and the speed with which the output is produced.

In many organizations, we can see a direct relationship between computer-related functions and management's organizational philosophy. As a result, organizations set up their computer facilities differently, using either a centralized, decentralized, or distributed computer facility.

KEY TERMS

batch
batch processing

centralized computer
   facility

computer-based
   information system

data
information
on-line real-time
decentralized computer
off-line processing
  processing
  facility
on-line processing
source document
distributed computer
transaction file
  facility

EXERCISES

MATCHING

Match each of the following terms to the phrase that is the most closely related:

1. _____ computer-based information system
2. _____ input phase
3. _____ processing phase
4. _____ output phase
5. _____ storage phase
6. _____ on-line processing
7. _____ on-line real-time processing
8. _____ off-line processing
9. _____ batch processing
10. _____ decentralized computer facility
11. _____ centralized computer facility
12. _____ distributed computer facility

a. Uses a separate computer to service the needs of each major department.
b. The overall activities involved with the input, processing, output, and storage of data and information by computer.
c. This approach to computerizing an information system involves fully processing each transaction's data when it is input so that the user can receive immediate feedback.
d. The phase in a computer-based information system when data is "captured" and converted to a form that can be processed by a computer.
e. An organization has this when it uses one computer to service the needs of the entire organization.
f. This approach to computerizing an information system tends to relieve the central computer from performing a large number of redundant tasks.
g. The phase in a computer-based information system when all the number and character manipulation activities are performed.
h. In this approach to computerizing an information system, the data needed for each transaction is immediately put into computer-usable form but might be held in storage for later processing.
i. Uses a combination of centralized and decentralized computer facilities.
j. The phase in a computer-based information system when the user receives information from a computer that can be used to help in decision making and to perform day-to-day business activities.

k. The phase in a computer-based information system when data and information are held in computer-usable form on something like magnetic tape or disk.

l. This approach to computerizing an information system involves collecting data in the form of source documents and placing them into groups for later input into the computer.

MULTIPLE CHOICE

1. In the input phase of a computer-based information system, which of the following activities isn't normally performed?
   a. collecting data
   b. supervising the data collection process
   c. using an input device to key data in
   d. performing mathematical calculations
   e. instructing the computer to begin data input activities

2. Which of the following statements is false? In the output phase of a computer-based information system:
   a. People are usually involved in analyzing information.
   b. Both hardcopy and softcopy output are usually produced.
   c. Printers, plotters, and video display screens are often used.
   d. Hardcopy output is best for reviewing information that needs to be viewed only occasionally or for a short period of time.

3. Which of the following processing approaches is used when data that will be used for input isn't recorded on a source document?
   a. off-line processing
   b. batch processing
   c. on-line processing
   d. none of the above

4. Which of the following processing approaches is generally used to increase the processing power of a mainframe computer that performs a great number of redundant tasks?
   a. off-line processing
   b. batch processing
   c. on-line processing
   d. on-line real-time processing
   e. none of the above

5. If your task is to design a computer facility in such a way that each organizational unit within your company is serviced by its own computer, you would be designing a(an):
   a. centralized computer facility
   b. decentralized computer facility
   c. distributed computer facility
   d. on-line real-time computer facility
   e. none of the above

6. A computer facility that maximizes the advantages of a centralized computer

facility and a decentralized computer facility is known as a(an):
   a. centralized computer facility
   b. decentralized computer facility
   c. distributed computer facility
   d. on-line real-time computer facility
   e. none of the above

7. Which of the following is not an advantage of the distributed approach to organizing a computer facility?
   a. The users are more directly involved with the processing activities than when using the decentralized approach.
   b. The computer staff is more familiar with the needs of each organizational unit.
   c. Computer processing costs are easier to allocate than in a centralized computer facility.
   d. The organization uses a central computer to service the needs of each organizational unit so that hardware resources aren't duplicated at different locations.
   e. none of the above

8. Which of the following activities doesn't normally occur in the processing phase of a computer-based information system?
   a. A copy of the processing instructions is placed into internal memory.
   b. A copy of the data to be processed is placed into internal memory.
   c. A copy of the information produced is temporarily placed into internal memory.
   d. The CPU carries out instructions in memory.
   e. none of the above

9. In which of the following two phases in a computer-based information system are people involved the most?
   a. output, storage
   b. input, storage
   c. processing, storage
   d. input, output
   e. processing, output

10. Which of the following activities does a user normally perform in the storage phase of a computer-based information system?
   a. maintain computer-based files
   b. monitor how long data should be maintained
   c. decide whether backup copies of data are required
   d. determine when data should be removed from the system
   e. all of the above

SHORT ANSWER

1. What do you think your role would be as a user of a microcomputer in a company?

2. What is the purpose of internal memory during the processing phase of a computer-based information system?

3. What activities typically take place in the storage phase of a computer-based information system, and what might your role be in this phase?

4. What are the advantages and disadvantages of using a centralized computer facility in an organization?

5. What are the advantages and disadvantages of using a decentralized computer facility in an organization?

6. How does a distributed computer facility minimize the weaknesses and maximize the strengths of centralized and decentralized facilities?

7. How does on-line processing differ from on-line real-time processing?

8. What is meant by the term *computer-based information system*, and why should you be familiar with it?

9. Why is there little need for human involvement in the storage phase of a computer-based information system?

10. When might a company want to use the batch approach to computerize its information system?

PROJECTS

1. You are in charge of generally defining a registration system for a school that is about the same size as the one you are currently attending. Using your school's registration system as a model, focus on defining the following:
   a. What will the probable inputs for the system be?
   b. What will the probable outputs for the system be?
   c. What will your storage and processing requirements be?
   d. Identify the five components of the registration information system.

2. Identify an organization (for example, your school; a fast food restaurant; a car repair business; a stock brokerage) that uses computers. Describe the organization's use of computers by focusing on its processing approach (batch, on-line, and so on) and on the approach it has taken to organizing its computer facility (centralized or another approach).

EPISODE 1

DO YOU REALLY NEED A COMPUTER?

THE BEGINNING

There is no point in having computer skills unless you are going to use them. Let us, therefore, help you to do that.

Suppose we encourage you to start your own business. "What? Not me," you say. "I wouldn't know the first thing about it." That's how we're going to help.

Obviously, you should go into a business that you are interested in—motivation is important. Because we have no idea what that might be, let us suggest one. Taking advantage of the national interest in health and fitness and your location near a college campus, let us suggest you open a store—perhaps the first of many—that carries a full line of health, sports, aerobic, exercise, and dance equipment and clothing. You can make up your own name for it, but we will suggest one: Sporting Life.

After borrowing the money to buy the initial stock of goods, you spend the first few years doing the day-to-day work of running the store yourself: identifying what goods are to be sold, keeping the shelves stocked, and doing the bookkeeping. By the end of three years, you're on a roll: Business is so good that you are able to expand the store and add to the stock. That means you also need to add to the staff. By the end of five years, you've built quite an organization, one that could be represented by the chart shown in Figure E1.1. The most important members of your staff are you; Roy, in charge of inventory control; and Mary, who is the company's controller and is in charge of accounting.

Mary, the company's controller, has a full-time staff of four to assist her, including two cashiers, one accountant, and a clerk to handle personnel and payroll activities. In addition, you employ six part-timers from the local high schools and the university.

In its first year of business, Sporting Life carried 115 items, occupied 2000 square feet of space, and had a gross income (before expenses) of $150,000. After five years, 600 items were carried in stock, and the store's size had more than doubled to 4500 square feet. Gross sales that year topped $1,400,000. In the latest year for which figures are available, Sporting Life carried just under 1000 items in stock and its gross income was $2,250,000.

HOW TO TRACK INVENTORY

Since Sporting Life was founded, you've kept your inventory records in a ledger book, one page for each item carried in inventory. When one page gets full, you take it out and replace it with a new blank page with the balance carried over. Inventory information includes a description of the item, its product number, the name of the supplier, an entry for weekly sales, and a running balance of the number of items on hand. Figure E1.2 shows a page from the inventory record ledger. Roy's job is to keep an accurate count of all items on hand, to advise you when items need to be reordered, and to restock the shelves with items from the storeroom when necessary.

The procedure for maintaining inventory records can be broken down into five separate steps, as shown in Figure E1.3. Let us explain each step:

1. The inventory ledger is reviewed for accuracy once each quarter when a physical inventory is conducted. Each item in inventory is counted. The balance on hand for each item is compared to the total in the inventory ledger. Discrepancies are researched and resolved, or adjustments are made in the ledger to account for the losses.

2. Copies of all sales receipts are collected in a stock folder.

EPISODE 1, CONTINUED

3. Once every two weeks, you take all the sales receipts from the stock folder and do the following:

—Sort them into order by type of purchase.
—Tally the amount of each item purchased (how many).
—Record on each item's ledger page the amount sold and the current balance of items in stock (the current balance is computed by subtracting the items sold from the balance on hand).

4. When the balance on hand for an item is relatively low, you prepare a purchase order and send it out to your supplier.

FIGURE E1.1
Your organization. After five years, the organizational chart for your store looks like this. Connecting lines between the boxes indicate who supervises whom.

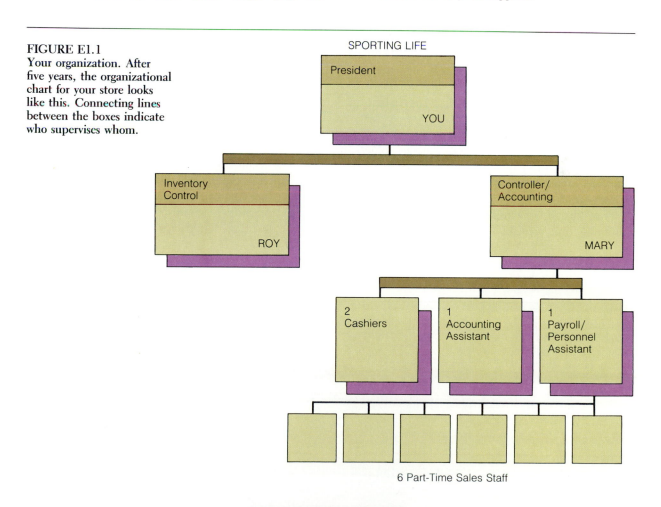

SPORTINGLIFE

EPISODE 1, CONTINUED

5. When the ordered goods are received, you take the bill of lading (the document identifying the contents of the shipment received) and record the information in the inventory ledger. The number of items received is added to the prior balance to give the updated balance on hand.

HOW MARY HANDLES FINANCES

Mary's methods for handling her record-keeping responsibilities at Sporting Life have remained basically the same since the business began. She has maintained financial records in a general ledger book where sales activities are posted in order by date. Figure E1.4 shows a sample of a few of the accounting entries recorded in Mary's general ledger. She keeps separate folders for records of accounts receivable (money owed to Sporting Life) and accounts payable (money Sporting Life owes to suppliers).

In addition, a payroll folder is maintained for each employee, and a single checking account for the com-

pany is maintained in a local bank. All payroll and tax forms are prepared manually. Employees are paid twice a month.

SIZING UP THE SITUATION: YOU CAN'T GO ON LIKE THIS!

Because nearly 1000 items are now carried in stock, compared to only 115 when the business began, you're having trouble keeping inventory records current. Your traditional ledger method worked fine five years ago, but with the ninefold increase in stock on hand, you've spotted some problems.

Far too many slow-selling items are being kept in stock, whereas some very popular items are always out of stock. Mary is having difficulties keeping her accounting records up to date, even with the help of her staff. She says she would like to review the records, prepare some financial reports, and even try to do some simple forecasting about Sporting Life's projected growth. But there simply isn't enough time. Besides,

FIGURE E1.2
Track record. This shows a page from the traditional inventory record ledger book that you and Roy use in your business.

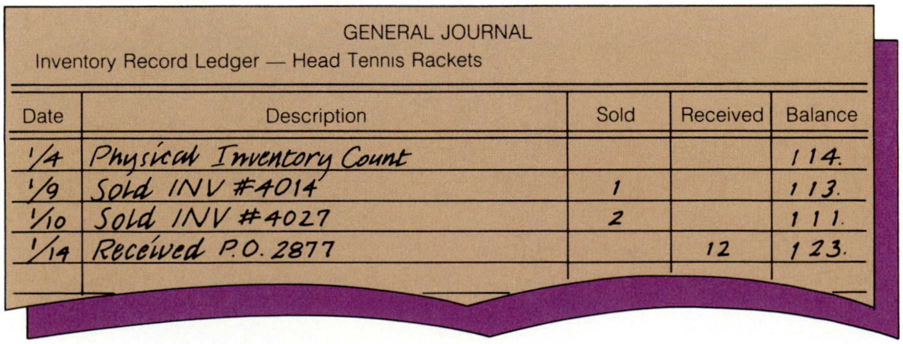

GENERAL JOURNAL				
Inventory Record Ledger — Head Tennis Rackets				
Date	Description	Sold	Received	Balance
1/4	Physical Inventory Count			114.
1/9	Sold INV #4014	1		113.
1/10	Sold INV #4027	2		111.
1/14	Received P.O. 2877		12	123.

68

EPISODE 1, CONTINUED

although she's excellent at basic math, Mary admits that she's not entirely comfortable with the idea of reports and financial projections because, even if she had the time to do them, she isn't sure what procedures she should follow.

WHAT DO YOU THINK?

You've considered buying a microcomputer to help track inventory and automate the accounting records. However, your employees are a bit anxious about com-

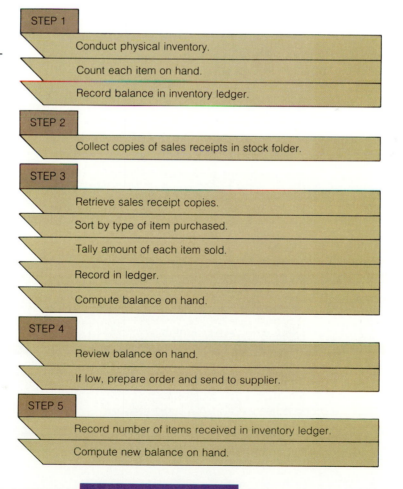

FIGURE E1.3
Keeping in step. These are the five steps you would take to keep track of the inventory (or movement of stock) in your store.

STEP 1
Conduct physical inventory.
Count each item on hand.
Record balance in inventory ledger.

STEP 2
Collect copies of sales receipts in stock folder.

STEP 3
Retrieve sales receipt copies.
Sort by type of item purchased.
Tally amount of each item sold.
Record in ledger.
Compute balance on hand.

STEP 4
Review balance on hand.
If low, prepare order and send to supplier.

STEP 5
Record number of items received in inventory ledger.
Compute new balance on hand.

EPISODE 1, CONTINUED

puterizing the business. On the basis of what you know about the subject, discuss their concerns:

1. Because buying a computer is a big investment, Mary wants to do some research before you make any decisions about hardware and software. Which processing approach should she investigate for cashier and inventory purposes? Batch? On-line? On-line real time? Off-line? Why? Would this approach also be advantageous for Mary to use for accounting and payroll records?

2. Roy knows the computer will help him track inventory more efficiently and effectively, but he knows nothing about how it will affect his current inventory procedures. Also, he is worried about having to unlearn the methods that have become ingrained after many years in the business. Based on your knowledge of computerized sales entry and the five steps for tracking inventory, describe for Roy a hypothetical computerized system for tracking inventory. What kinds of data do you want to track? Discuss the roles of input, processing, storage, and output.

3. The staff is worried that the computer will have a negative effect on the family atmosphere of the company. Do you agree?

FIGURE E1.4
The general ledger. These are some of the accounting entries Mary or you might make in a general ledger book. This activity is labor intensive, because anytime anyone wants the balance in any account, every debit and credit made to an account must be determined.

GENERAL LEDGER					
Date	Description	Post Ref.	Debit	Credit
1/14 87	PAID INVOICE #AQ 459			
	CASH (CHK 1049)	101		175.50
	OFFICE SUPPLIES	508	175.50	
1/14 87	DAILY SALES TICKETS			
	CASH	101	1419.23	
	INCOME	401		1419.23
1/14 87	PAID INVOICE #73914			
	CASH (CHK 1050)	101		1575.00
	RENT	5013	1575.00	
1/14 87	RECEIVED INVOICE #1183			
	A/P	201		107.75
	TELEPHONE	506	107.75	

PART TWO

2

HARDWARE

We can certainly make any computer user one promise: The hardware—the equipment— will probably change drastically in the next decade. The processing power contained in a refrigerator-size minicomputer is already available on a desktop machine (can we then any longer call it a "micro-computer"?), and the power of upcoming super-computers will be truly awesome, perhaps a thousand times more powerful than the machines used by research scientists today. Data will be input not only through the keyboard, that time-honored device, but also through more exotic equipment— for example, devices that understand human voices. Output will be on printers capable of extra-ordinary speeds and clarity. Still, the general principles behind new hardware will remain the same as those you are about to study in the next four chapters: input, storage, processing, and output.

■

CHAPTER THREE

3

INPUT HARDWARE

D o you know how to type?

Perhaps it may not be necessary to learn. No doubt during our lifetime many ways of inputting data and software instructions to a computer system will be invented that will no longer require a keyboard. We believe, however, that if you *do* know how to type, you are much better off. No matter what organization you join after reading this book, it will most likely want to hire people who can handle a computer keyboard—not just clerks and typists, but managers and executives as well.

PREVIEW

When you have completed this chapter, you will be able to:

■

Identify the most widely used input media and hardware

■

List six different types of terminals used for data input and describe three kinds of dedicated data input systems

■

Describe the importance of input controls in today's computerized society

■

List points to consider when choosing input hardware and methods

■

The User Perspective

If you find a typewriter or computer keyboard somewhat cumbersome, be glad you are entering the field now rather than back in the '60s. Then, the principal means of inputting data to a computer system was on punched cards—the so-called "IBM cards"—that a generation of college students were admonished never to "fold, spindle, or mutilate." Although these cards are still in use in some quarters, their numbers are very few compared to the 150,000 tons of them that were used every year in the 1960s—enough that, put end to end, would stretch 8 million miles.

As you already know, computers by their very nature can deal only with instructions and data that have been converted into a computer-usable form—that is, a form the central processing unit can directly access from internal memory or retrieve from a storage device and put into internal memory. For more than 20 years the physical activity required to convert an organization's data into computer-usable form was the largest single personnel expense in operating a computer facility. Fortunately, great technological progress has been made in terms of input hardware devices and input methods. Because sometime during your career you may well have to decide which devices and methods are best for your organization, in this chapter we will teach you the basic information you'll need to make such a decision.

Input Fundamentals

As we discussed in Chapters 1 and 2, the term *input* is used to describe the process of capturing or collecting raw data—at the beginning of a computer-based information system—into a form that is usable by the computer for processing. Sometimes the data is processed right away (on-line or on-line real-time processing), sometimes hours or days later, or even longer (batch or off-line processing). As a result, data is often stored in a computer-usable form, where it can be quickly retrieved at the time of processing with little or no human intervention.

Input Media: What Is Data Stored on?

The objective of the input phase of a computer-based information system is to capture raw data and convert it into computer-usable form as quickly and efficiently as possible. The approaches devised to accomplish this can be categorized to some extent according to the type of material on which the data is recorded. In data processing, these materials are called **media** (the singular is **medium**). Although in a few sophisticated systems data can be captured in audible form (sounds and spoken words) and even in the form of eye movement, two kinds of media are used most often: paper and magnetic, as shown in Figure 3.1. For many years, the most widely used media to record input data were paper-based products such as 80-column and 96-column punched cards and punched paper tape. Figure 3.2 shows an example of an 80-column card as well as the hardware components of a typical **keypunch machine.** The operator of a keypunch machine transcribes data from a source document by punching holes in the cards via a keyboard according to a special code. (The 96-column card, which was developed to store 20% more data in a small amount of space, never found widespread use.)

Today, punched cards are rarely used; however, they still play an occasional role as turnaround documents. A **turnaround document** is a computer-produced output document that is forwarded to a recipient who then records any necessary additional data on the document and returns it to the sender. This data serves as input to further computer processing. Examples of turnaround documents are many utility bills, phone bills and charge account statements (Figure 3.3).

FIGURE 3.1
Paper and magnetic storage media. Two basic kinds of media are used to record data and information. Today, magnetic media are by far the most popular.

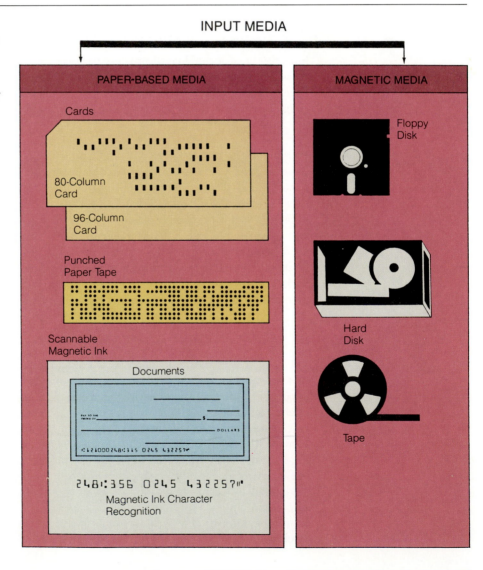

Paper-based media are also being used today in new ways because of technological improvements—such as scanners, connected to computers, that can "read" typed or handwritten data. The banking industry has long relied on paper-based

FIGURE 3.2
The keypunch machine and card reader and the 80-column card.

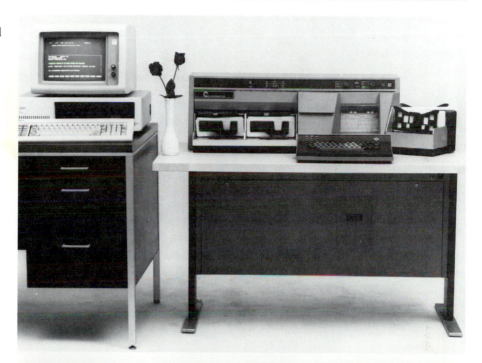

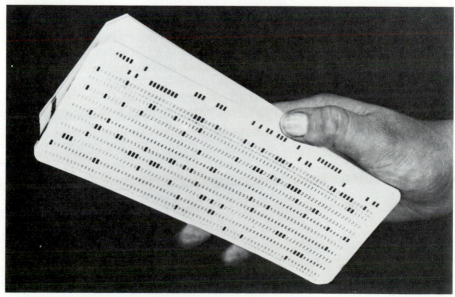

FIGURE 3.3
Utilitarian approach. Some retail stores and utility companies use turnaround documents to help process bills. The amount written in by the customer—$59.18 in the figure to the right— is input to the company's computer system after the statement is returned.

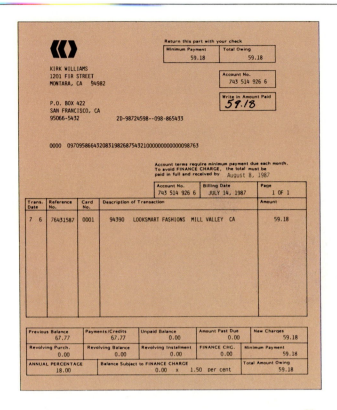

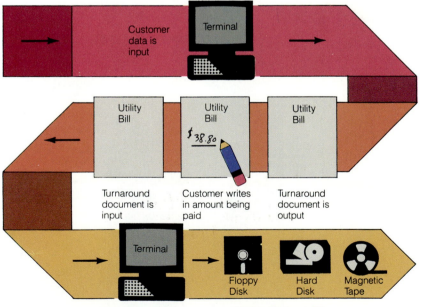

Update Customer File

input media: Our checks are printed using a special magnetic ink that can be scanned optically for magnetic retrieval of data for input to computers for processing. Optically oriented input devices are now available for use with microcomputer systems, too, which puts this type of input within the reach of small businesses. For example, even a small, independently owned grocery store may have a microcomputer at the checkstand and a hand-held optical scanning device to read the product numbers on purchased items. (The product numbers access stored computer files with the current prices, which then show on the register.)

The most widely used input media today are magnetic media in tape or disk form. The major advantages of magnetic media are their reusability, low cost, great flexibility for accessing the data during the input process, and high speed compared to punched cards and manual keyboard entry. We'll discuss magnetic media more fully in the next chapter.

CATEGORIZING INPUT HARDWARE

When you start work, chances are that your company will have already purchased input hardware. However, if input hardware has not yet been acquired, you may find yourself in the position of helping to decide which input hardware is best suited to your needs. In this section we describe the different types of input hardware devices that you will typically find in a business environment.

One of the easiest ways to categorize input hardware is according to whether or not it uses a keyboard to initially capture data (see Figure 3.4). Most commonly used input devices do rely on a keyboard, and these devices generally fall into two groups: (1) terminals connected to general-purpose computer systems (microcomputers fall into this group also), and (2) dedicated data entry systems, which are specialized, single-purpose systems used for nothing else but entering data.

The non-keyboard input devices, often called *specialized input devices*, include optical scanners, mice, light pens, touch screens, and voice recognition equipment (to be discussed shortly), among others.

DATA INPUT USING TERMINALS

You'll recall that a **terminal,** typically consisting of a video display screen, a keyboard, and usually a connecting cable, is used for inputting data to and sometimes also retrieving data and information from a remotely located general-purpose computer system. Terminals can be "dumb," "smart," or "intelligent," according to their capabilities. A **dumb terminal** is entirely dependent for all its capabilities on the computer system to which it is connected. It cannot do any processing of its own and provides only a keyboard for data entry and a monitor to display output. A **smart terminal** may have sufficient processing capabilities of its own to allow some editing and storage of data without interacting with the central computer system, but it cannot be used for programming (that is, for creating new instructions). An **intelligent terminal** can input and receive data, as well as allow users to edit and do programming.

A variety of computer terminals are used to enter data, including the following most popular types:

- Desktop terminals
- Point-of-sale terminals
- Financial transaction terminals
- Executive workstations
- Portable terminals
- Microcomputers used for input

But before we discuss the different types of terminals, you need to know something about the keyboard.

THE KEYBOARD

A computer **keyboard** is a rather sophisticated electromechanical component designed to create special standardized electronic codes when a key is pressed. The

FIGURE 3.4
To key or not to key . . . Input hardware can be categorized according to whether or not it uses a keyboard.

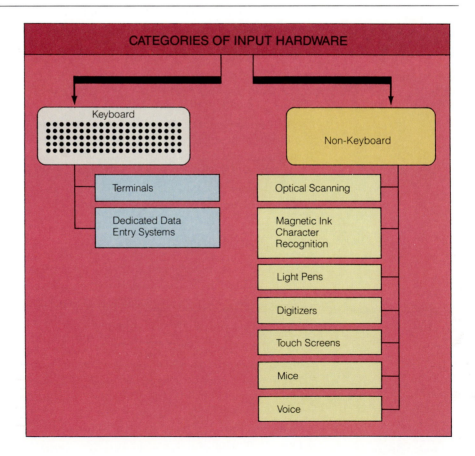

codes are transmitted along the cable that connects the keyboard to the computer system unit or terminal, where the incoming code is analyzed and converted into the appropriate computer-usable code.

Keyboards come in a variety of sizes and shapes, but most keyboards used with computer systems have a certain number of features in common (Figure 3.5): (1) standard typewriter keys, (2) special function keys, (3) cursor movement keys, and (4) numeric keys.

Computer keyboards almost always have a central group of keys similar in layout to a standard typewriter keyboard. However, several keys in the central group are used slightly differently: for example, the *Caps Lock* key, the alternate *(Alt)* key, and the control *(Ctrl)* key. The *Caps Lock* key is used to place all of the alphabetic keys into an uppercase position (that is, capital letters only). This key is similar to a shift-lock key on a typewriter, with one difference. The shift-lock key allows you to type the upper character on any typewriter key, whereas the *Caps Lock* key affects *only* the alphabetic keys on the computer keyboard. For example, the * is the upper character on the number 8 key on the keyboard shown in Figure 3.5. The shift-lock key on a typewriter would allow you to press the number 8 key to make * appear. However, if you use the *Caps Lock* key on the keyboard, an 8 appears unless you hold down the regular shift key. The control *(Ctrl)* and alternate *(Alt)* keys on most microcomputer keyboards are used in conjunction with other keys to issue commands—that is, to tell the computer what operation to perform. For example, in one software package (WordStar), the *Ctrl* and the G keys allow you to delete a character. In another package (WordPerfect), pressing the *Alt* and the *F4* keys allows you to begin marking a whole portion of text to be moved to another place in your document.

Many terminals and microcomputer keyboards have groups of special **function keys,** also called *programmable keys.* These keys are used to issue commands, among other things. Not all software programs use the special function keys the same way; for instance, on the IBM PC keyboard, which has ten function keys, underlining is done by the *F5* key in WordStar, but by the *F8* key in WordPerfect.

On the keyboards used with the early IBM PC-compatible microcomputers, which are still used in many businesses today, the keys for cursor movement were combined with the numeric keypad—the keys used to enter numbers (see Figure 3.5). (The **cursor** is the symbol, or indicator, on the video display screen that shows where the next character that is input will be positioned; in other words, the cursor shows you where you are on the screen.) On this keyboard, you have to remember to press the numeric lock *(Num Lock)* or a shift key before using the keys to enter numbers. Newer keyboards have cursor movement keys that are separate from numeric keypad keys.

If you have used a typewriter keyboard, you should find it easy to learn to work with a computer keyboard. However, since some of the keys are different, you—along with keyboard novices—may want to experiment with some of the keyboard familiarization software programs on the market today. These provide computer users with a dual opportunity—to become familiar with the layout of the keyboard and to develop typing proficiency.

FIGURE 3.5
90 words per minute? These are two kinds of micro-computer keyboards—an IBM PC keyboard on the left and an "enhanced" IBM PC keyboard on the right (the keyboard on the right has a numeric keypad separate from the cursor movement keys).

DESKTOP TERMINALS

Desktop terminals are commonly found in organizations whose computer systems support multiple-user activities—that is, more than one person uses the central computer at one time. A **desktop terminal**—which, as its name suggests, fits on top of the user's desk—usually has a video display screen 12–14 inches in diagonal width and produces a monochrome (single-color) image. The resolution (screen image clarity) of the terminal is normally good. The keyboards will differ slightly according to the manufacturer. Figure 3.6 shows a picture of Hewlett-Packard desktop terminals.

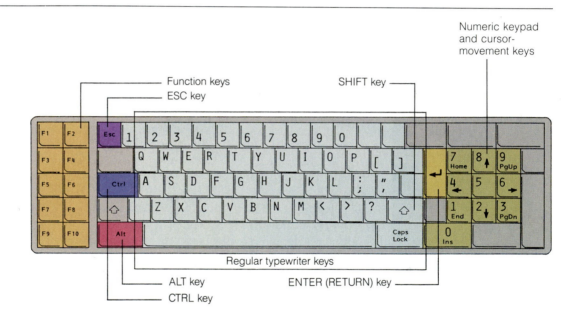

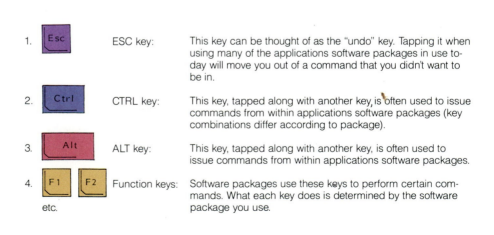

1. ESC key: This key can be thought of as the "undo" key. Tapping it when using many of the applications software packages in use today will move you out of a command that you didn't want to be in.

2. CTRL key: This key, tapped along with another key, is often used to issue commands from within applications software packages (key combinations differ according to package).

3. ALT key: This key, tapped along with another key, is often used to issue commands from within applications software packages.

4. Function keys: Software packages use these keys to perform certain com-
   etc.   mands. What each key does is determined by the software package you use.

Desktop terminals can be found in a number of places throughout an organization. For example, the computer specialists who develop software usually have desktop terminals handy to enter program instructions, run the programs, and make corrections as necessary. The warehouse or supply room often has a desktop terminal to enter data on new shipments received and orders filled. The personnel department in many companies has a desktop terminal to enter new employee data and change-of-status data on existing employees. Such desktop terminals are connected to the same central computer, usually by a cable, in which case they cannot be more than about 4000 feet apart. Other methods of connecting terminals to the central computer include telephone lines or other types of communications technology.

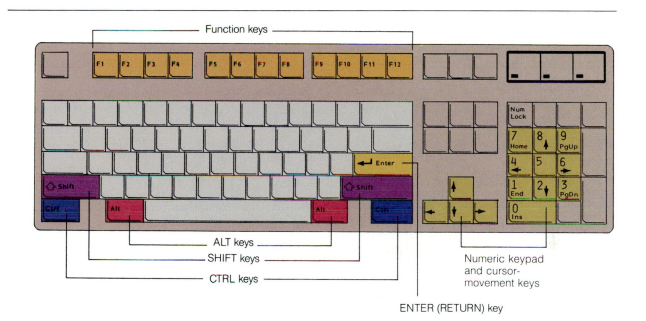

5. 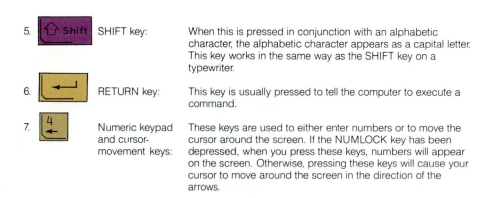 SHIFT key: When this is pressed in conjunction with an alphabetic character, the alphabetic character appears as a capital letter. This key works in the same way as the SHIFT key on a typewriter.

6. RETURN key: This key is usually pressed to tell the computer to execute a command.

7. Numeric keypad and cursor-movement keys: These keys are used to either enter numbers or to move the cursor around the screen. If the NUMLOCK key has been depressed, when you press these keys, numbers will appear on the screen. Otherwise, pressing these keys will cause your cursor to move around the screen in the direction of the arrows.

POINT-OF-SALE TERMINALS

A **point-of-sale terminal** is used very much like a cash register (Figure 3.7), but it also captures sales and inventory data at the point of sale and sends it to the central computer for processing. Point-of-sale terminals are used in a growing number of retail businesses. As mentioned earlier, many supermarkets have cash registers that are connected directly to a central computer so that the sales dollars and product-sold data can be immediately recorded. This type of terminal usually displays the price, the product number, and possibly the product description. In addition, this type of terminal is equipped with a cash-register-type keyboard, a cash drawer, and a printer to print the receipt.

FINANCIAL TRANSACTION TERMINALS

A **financial transaction terminal** is used to store data and to retrieve data from a central computer to perform banking-related activities. The two types of financial transaction terminals we see most often are the automated teller machines (ATMs) located outside of most banks (Figure 3.8) and the specialized terminals used by bank tellers to verify the account balance when a customer withdraws or deposits money in person. The teller terminals (Figure 3.9) are usually quite small and specialized. The keyboard has special keys that allow the teller to identify which type of account is being used (savings or checking) and to enter the account number. The video display is usually quite small and monochrome.

FIGURE 3.6
Terminal work. These Hewlett-Packard desktop terminals are being used for data entry.

EXECUTIVE WORKSTATIONS

Executive workstations, or **integrated workstations,** are terminals used by management professionals to assist them in their daily activities (Figure 3.10). These work-

FIGURE 3.7
A smart sale. This point-of-sale terminal is being used to record goods sold at a variety store.

FIGURE 3.8
Midnight money. The automated teller machine has become more than just a convenience for those who can't get to the bank during regular banking hours—and for those who need cash for late-night snack attacks or unexpected emergencies.

stations can be operated by themselves or in connection with a main computer, and they usually have voice and data communications capabilities, meaning that the terminal includes a phone for regular communication and components for special computerized communication. However, the design and features of this type of terminal tend to vary widely. Most executive terminals have built-in software (often referred to as *desk management software*) to handle desk calendar, phone book, and desk calculator functions. Executive workstations are not used for high-volume data input. In most cases, the user enters a request for data or information to be retrieved and displayed. These terminals usually include a full-sized keyboard and a number of special function keys. Most also have some graphics capabilities (monochrome or color).

PORTABLE TERMINALS

A **portable terminal** is a terminal that users can carry with them to hook up to a central computer from remote locations, often via telecommunications facilities. (The term *telecommunications* refers to communication at a distance by telephone, tele-

FIGURE 3.9
Taking it into account. The teller terminals used in banks enable tellers to quickly identify your account and its balance.

vision, or some other means.) Most portable terminals are connected to the central computer by means of telephone lines. These terminals have components called *modems* built into them that convert the data being transmitted into a form suitable for sending and receiving over the phone. If the terminal is dumb, it can do little more than send data to and receive data from the main computer. (Some of the smallest portable terminals can only send data.) If the portable terminal is smart, some data may be entered and edited before the connection to the main computer is made.

Portable terminals are available in a wide variety of sizes and shapes. Most portable terminals include a full typewriter-like keyboard. Some specialized portable terminals are so small they are called *hand-held* terminals. The hand-held terminal weighs up to about 3 pounds and can be used for a variety of purposes, including checking the stock market and identifying cars with many unpaid parking tickets (Figure 3.11).

Many older-model portable terminals use only printers to display the data that has been input and the computer's response because standard video display screens are a bit cumbersome and easily damaged. However, newer portable terminals use the latest technologies to provide smaller, flat screen displays that show as much text as a desktop terminal. Like executive workstations, portable terminals are rarely used for high-volume data input.

FIGURE 3.10
High-tech management tool. The executive work-station helps managers take care of daily business through the use of desk management software and communications and data processing capabilities.

MICROCOMPUTERS USED FOR INPUT

The market for general-purpose portable terminals has been overshadowed by many of the new portable microcomputers in the marketplace today. Although, as you know, microcomputers can be used on their own for processing, they can also be used as smart or intelligent terminals or workstations; the type of software used determines what kind of terminal the microcomputer "becomes." This flexibility is very attractive to many businesses. Data entry programs can be created for the microcomputer so that data can be input and stored locally—where the user is. When data entry is complete, the microcomputer can then be used as a terminal, and the data can be uploaded (transmitted from the microcomputer to the main computer) very quickly. For example, a small editorial production office in San Francisco with a microcomputer equipped with a modem and certain software can arrange with the local telephone company to have telex capabilities activated and a telex number assigned. Then the office can input data—page proof corrections, for example—that is telexed to a typesetter in Singapore, who transfers the data into the computerized typesetting system after reading it on a microcomputer screen. In turn, the typesetter can telex data back to the editorial office in San Francisco.

Some microcomputers on the market today have been designed *specifically* to be used both as stand-alone processors (that is, they operate on their own without being hooked up to a main computer) *and* as terminals. The NCR supermicro shown in Figure 3.12 is a good example. For microcomputers that were not specifically designed to fulfill both functions, manufacturers have produced special hardware that can be purchased and placed into the microcomputer to enable it to communicate with a larger computer.

FIGURE 3.11
Will you lose your car? Hand-held terminals are used for many purposes today. For example, the parking control officer—after checking the number of unpaid parking tickets on your car—may decide to have it towed while printing out your latest parking ticket.

DEDICATED SYSTEMS

When an organization has high-volume data input requirements, such as the Internal Revenue Service at tax time, it often uses a secondary computer—usually a minicomputer—that temporarily stores previously keyed-in data for later processing by the main computer. This processing usually takes place at night, when the main computer's time is not taken by user requests. The group of terminals connected to the minicomputer that handle data entry and storage are called a **dedicated data entry system**—they do nothing but input and store data. Today, data in such systems is usually stored on high-capacity magnetic disks, which we discuss in more detail in the next chapter. However, data is still occasionally stored on tape.

KEY-TO-TAPE SYSTEMS

Key-to-tape input devices were first introduced in the mid-1960s as a replacement for punched cards. A **key-to-tape data recorder** (Figure 3.13) functions similarly to a keypunch machine except that data is no longer represented by holes punched in a card; instead, data is represented by magnetized spots on magnetic tape. This new dedicated input system provided several advantages:

1. Magnetic media are much less expensive than punched cards, are easier to handle, and take up less space.

FIGURE 3.12
Double duty. Microcomputers can be used on a stand-alone basis or as terminals connected to a main computer—in this case, a minicomputer. Some new micros have been specially designed to do both; others must have special hardware components installed to act as a terminal.

2. Data entry onto tape is faster than punching holes in cards.
3. Unlike punched cards—which still had to be read by a card reader into a computer and stored until needed for processing—data keyed directly onto tape was immediately ready for processing.
4. Magnetic tape is reusable.

Early key-to-tape units had a keyboard and tape for each operator. In 1968, more sophisticated key-to-tape systems were introduced that consolidated all data onto a single tape. However, even these newer systems had two major disadvantages: First, the data recorded on magnetic tape cannot be altered without creating an entire new tape. Second, key-to-tape systems do not allow editing, nor do they allow you to validate the data being entered under software control—meaning that they do not allow you to check to see that you have entered, for example, a valid product number. Advances in data input technology have solved these problems, so key-to-tape systems are no longer used extensively. However, these systems represented a major step because they used magnetic media to input data directly into a computer-usable form.

KEY-TO-DISK SYSTEMS

In the late 1960s, key-to-disk technology was introduced for high-volume, dedicated data entry. A **key-to-disk system** consists of several terminals connected to a dedicated computer—usually a minicomputer—that stores data on magnetic disks that resemble long-playing records until all the data has been input, when it is either

FIGURE 3.13
Magnetic personality. Key-to-tape data input systems departed from punched paper cards and used magnetic tape as an input medium.

transmitted directly to the central computer or transferred to magnetic tape and then transferred to the main computer system.

The ability to enter data directly to disk provided new capabilities. First, more than one user can enter data at the same time to a shared disk, and this data can then be immediately accessed by the computer controlling the activities. Second, the computer can run specialized data entry programs, which display specific input screens on the user's video display screen. An **input screen** is a combination of displayed text and graphics, or pictorial, data (graphics are not always used) that identifies the elements of data to be entered and in which order they are to be entered. Input screens allow the operators to verify visually all data being entered. Third, each input record can be immediately edited and validated by the data entry program. In this way any errors can be corrected by the operator before he or she continues with the next document to be entered. Figure 3.14 shows a key-to-disk system.

FIGURE 3.14
Key-to-disk. Several terminals are connected to a dedicated computer that stores data for later transferral to the main computer system.

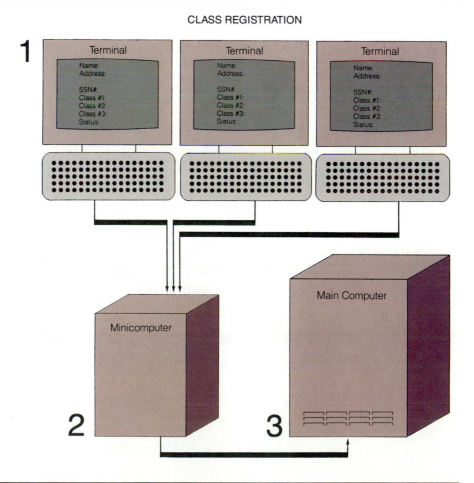

The editing and self-validation capabilities of the key-to-disk systems and their ability to manage data entry activities frees up the main computer. In other words, they can do things that the main computer used to have to do. Key-to-disk systems are still in wide use today in organizations with high-volume batch-oriented data entry requirements.

Key-to-Diskette Systems

In 1972, IBM introduced the 3741 Data Station, the first dedicated key-to-diskette data entry system. A **key-to-diskette system** is similar to a key-to-disk system except data is stored on floppy diskettes that are smaller than the disks used in key-to-disk systems. Companies with a large number of key-to-diskette devices use special equipment to handle data stored on many floppy diskettes. The disks are placed in a hopper where the data is automatically transferred to magnetic tape for the main computer system. Today, it is more likely you will encounter microcomputers used to key data to diskette rather than dedicated key-to-diskette systems.

Specialized Non-Keyboard Devices

Some of the most exciting kinds of input systems are those that use specialized, or non-keyboard, input devices. For example, did you know that you can touch a video display screen or use a "magic" wand to input data? Talk to the computer? Even use the movement of your eyes to tell the computer what to do? Non-keyboard data entry systems minimize the amount of human activity required to get data into a computer-usable form. The ones receiving the most attention today are: (1) card readers for microcomputer systems, (2) devices that read data optically, (3) devices that read magnetically encoded data, (4) voice input devices, and (5) so-called pointing devices.

Card Readers

The use of punched cards has dropped dramatically in the last ten years because of the speed and cost-effectiveness of the newer input devices. However, some organizations—such as the military, some government offices, and some schools— still use cards. A **card reader** is used to read the holes in punched cards and transfer the appropriate electrical signals as input to the computer. In the past two years, punched card readers have become available for use with microcomputers. These devices are used mostly by schools and small businesses whose data input is small. Figure 3.15 shows the Cardamation data card reader, which is often used in schools for scoring tests and tabulating daily attendance.

Optical Character Recognition (OCR) Devices

So much business-related data and information is recorded on paper that most of us would have difficulty imagining the amount. Before many of our modern input devices and systems were available, a lot of research was devoted to eliminating the expensive and time-consuming step of inputting all this hardcopy data manually by keying it in. As a result, in the 1950s a number of **optical character recognition (OCR)** input devices were developed to read hardcopy data from source documents into computer-usable form. These devices use light-sensitive equipment to read bar codes, optical marks, typewritten characters, and handwriting.

BAR-CODE READERS   By now you have probably become familiar with bar codes similar to the one shown in Figure 3.16. They're on the clothes you buy, the groceries you try to determine the prices of, the latest paperback novel, and so on. **Bar codes** are recorded on the products by the manufacturers and usually carry the inventory stock number (also called the *product number*). The coding scheme—called the *Universal Product Code*—for recording the data is based on the width of the bars and the space between them. Two types of input scanning devices are used to read the bar codes. The first is a hand-held wand (Figure 3.17a) that the clerk passes over the tag with the bar code. The wand has a scanning device that analyzes the light and dark bars for width and spacing, translating this data into electrical signals for the computer. The second is found most often in supermarkets and is built into the countertop (Figure 3.17b) along with a computerized cash register. The function of the countertop scanning device is similar to the hand-held wand; however, in many cases the light source of the former may be a laser.

Bar-code readers have proven to be very valuable as data entry devices for two reasons:

■ The price and product inventory numbers do not need to be keyed in, elimi-

FIGURE 3.15
Making the grade. The Cardamation data card reader can be used with a microcomputer to read punched cards, display the input on the screen, and store the data on diskette or hard disk for later processing. Such card readers are often used in schools for grading.

nating the potential for many keying errors. (Quantities of items, however, *are* keyed in.)

■ The sales data and inventory status stored on file are kept current.

However, when you're checking out at the supermarket, keep your eye on the computerized price and item description display on the register. As we mentioned earlier, the product numbers are recorded in the bar codes on the items you buy, but the corresponding price files must be updated at the supermarket. If someone forgets to enter today's special 50% reduction in cat food prices in the store's computer, you'll end up paying the old price.

OPTICAL-MARK READERS   When you took the College Board SAT (Scholastic Aptitude Test) or similar examination and marked the answers on a preprinted sheet using a No. 2 lead pencil, you worked with the simplest form of optical data recording—**optical marks** (Figure 3.18). Data recorded in this form is converted into computer-usable form by an **optical-mark reader (OMR).** The OMR device has a high-intensity light inside that is directed in the form of a beam at the sheets of paper being fed through it. The beam scans the marked forms and detects the number and the location of the pencil marks. The data is then converted into electrical signals for the computer. OMRs come in a variety of sizes and shapes that depend on the size of the forms to be read and the required loading and processing capacity of the reader.

The optical-mark technology is used widely for scoring examinations and inputting raw data recorded on questionnaires. For OMRs to read the data accurately, the forms must be carefully designed and manufactured, and the marks must be carefully recorded—which is why the College Board is so insistent on your using a No. 2 pencil. OMR technology has just recently been made available for micro-

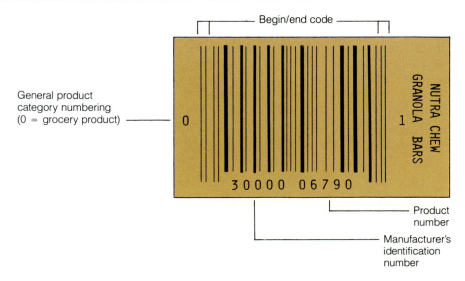

FIGURE 3.16
Bar gains. Bar codes such as this Universal Product Code found on many supermarket items contain product data that is read by an OCR device and sent to the computer.

FIGURE 3.17
Bar hopping. Bar-code reading devices can be hand-held, such as this Radio Shack wand reader (a), or built into the counter at the checkout stand, like this supermarket scanning equipment (b).

computers. Figure 3.19 shows an OMR device that will work with both Apple and IBM-compatible personal computers.

TYPEWRITTEN- AND TYPESET-CHARACTER READERS   For many years, typewritten data on source documents had to be rekeyed to be entered in a computer—in some cases, it still is today. As we mentioned before, optical character recognition tech-

FIGURE 3.18
On your mark . . . The College Board examination answer form requires you to mark answers—according to numbers in the test booklet—using a No. 2 lead pencil. The marks are later read and tabulated by an optical-mark reader.

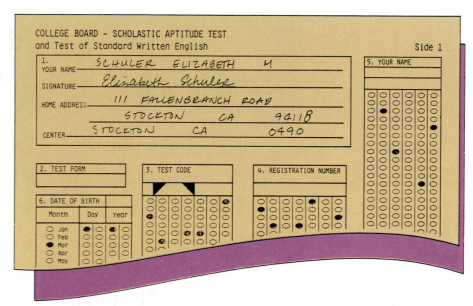

FIGURE 3.19
SCANTRON Model 1100 Optical Mark Reader. This optical-mark reader can be used with Apple and IBM-compatible computers.

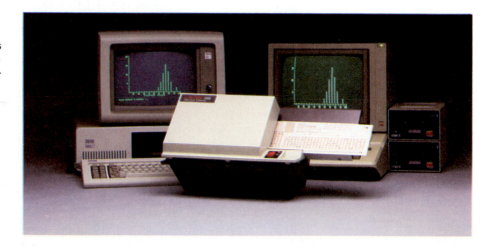

nology was developed to avoid this massive duplication of effort. To help speed up and reduce the cost of converting typewritten (and typeset) data to computer-usable form, certain manufacturers developed special type fonts (typeface styles) to be read by a scanning device. To assist this process the American National Standards Institute adopted a standard type font called OCR-A for use with optical character reading devices (Figure 3.20). OCR-A has become the most commonly used font used for OCR devices. However, the more expensive OCR devices can read a variety of type fonts.

In the early 1980s, small-capacity devices (called *scanners*) designed to read OCR-A, a variety of other type fonts, and illustrations began to appear on the market for use with microcomputers (Figure 3.21). One professor reports being rescued by one of these OCR-A readers for microcomputers. After preparing 65 pages of material for a seminar, he lost the disk they were stored on. Fortunately he had

FIGURE 3.20
OCR-A font. The OCR-A typeface style on top was designed to be read by a special scanning device, shown at bottom.

printed out hardcopy of the text, which he then took to a friend, whose system was able to scan all 65 pages onto an IBM PC-compatible diskette in about 30 minutes.

HANDWRITTEN-CHARACTER READERS   Although the percentage of data recorded by hand has dropped substantially over the last 50 years, quite a bit of data is still recorded this way. As OCR technology advanced, designers felt that it would be possible to also convert handwritten data into computer-usable form in much the same way that typewritten data is. Devices with this capability are the most sophisticated and versatile of the OCR devices. Because handwriting varies widely, specific guidelines must be followed so that the OCR reader will interpret the characters accurately (see Table 3.1).

MAGNETIC-INK CHARACTER RECOGNITION (MICR)

As many as 750 million personal checks are processed each month in the United States. This number does not even include the business checks written each month, which total more than triple the number of personal checks. How does the banking industry handle this mountain of data?

The American Bankers Association (ABA), anticipating this problem in the mid-1950s, adopted the **magnetic-ink character recognition (MICR)** technology as its primary means of data entry for processing checks. This technology involves the reading of numeric characters and a few special symbols printed on checks with

FIGURE 3.21
DEST's PC Scan Plus. This scanner, used here with a Macintosh Plus and IBM PC-AT microcomputer, can read a variety of type fonts and illustrations, producing them either as softcopy output on the screen or hardcopy output from the printer. In many cases, the images may also be stored.

TABLE 3.1   Handwriting Guidelines for OCR Readers

- Print using block letters and numbers.

- Make the size of each character fairly large.

- When writing a character or letter that has a loop (like 6, 9, or *g*), carefully close the loop.

- When writing a character or letter with connecting lines (like *T, I, 4,* or *5*), carefully connect the lines.

- Do not use script (it connects the letters), and do not connect series of zeros together in numbers.

- If necessary, use special forms that have an individual box for each handwritten character.

TABLE 3.2   The Standard MICR Character Set

- The numbers 0–9
- An amount symbol (⊞)
- A dash symbol (▮▮▮)
- A transit symbol (▮⋮)
- An "on-us" symbol (▮▮▪) (tells who is the payer and who is the payee)

magnetic ink. (Alphabetic characters are not used with this technology.) Figure 3.22 shows the layout of the MICR encoding on a personal check. The data is divided into five groups: (1) check routing symbol, (2) ABA transit number, (3) customer acccunt number, (4) check number, and (5) check amount. The check amount in the bottom right corner is keyed in manually at the branch where the check is received for processing.

Have you ever noticed a check, returned by your bank with your monthly statement, that had a piece of paper taped to the bottom? That piece of paper contains a duplicate of the MICR encoding on the check. What has happened is that the MICR symbols have been damaged, or your signature strayed too far below the line into the area where the MICR symbols for the check amount are entered. As a result, the MICR reader rejected your check. So one of the clerks at the bank rekeyed the MICR symbols onto a separate slip of paper and taped it to your check. In 1960, when it became apparent that some standardization was needed in the MICR type font, the ABA adopted a standard character set consisting of 14 symbols (Table 3.2).

The banking industry would not be as efficient as it is today if it had never adopted the MICR technology. Recently, the banking industry has begun to take steps to minimize the amount of paper handling necessary. That is why we are seeing more automated teller machines that use electronic "checks" instead of paper ones and why we are starting to hear about so-called "smart cards."

SMART CARDS   **Smart cards** (Figure 3.23), which were pioneered in France, are designed to be carried like credit cards but used like tiny transaction computers. To use it, the cardholder inserts the card into a special card-reading point-of-sale terminal and then enters a password on the keyboard. The cards have microchips that can keep permanent records, which are updated each time the card is used. The transaction data stored on the card can later be read into the computer for the user's bank—perhaps via an ATM—to update the user's bank records. In France and Britain smart cards are used to pay bills (while keeping current bank balances on file on the card), buy merchandise, make phone calls, buy postal money orders, get exam results from the university, store emergency medical information, and to perform other common activities.

FIGURE 3.22
Check it out. Your personal checks are encoded with magnetic ink that is read by MICR equipment. The data is then stored for processing. Note that the printed check amount in the bottom right corner is encoded by an MICR inscriber.

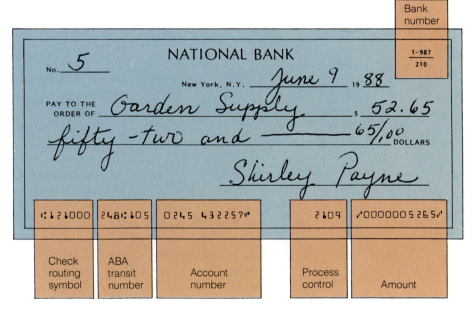

Processing Your Check

1. Checks are fed into large, high-capacity MICR reader/sorter devices.
2. MICR characters on checks are read electronically.
3. Check data is stored on tape or disk for processing.
4. Checks are sorted by bank number and returned to your bank.
5. If you wish, a bank may sort checks by account number and return them to you with the monthly statements.

The cards are being used to some extent in the United States—by the U.S. Navy, for example, for purchasing procedures—and will become increasingly common. Some manufacturers are already talking about a "supersmart card" that will incorporate a keypad and a display unit along with the memory and processing capabilities. Other manufacturers are developing smart cards to use as "keys" that users must employ to gain access to certain types of computer systems. For now you can use your bank card with its magnetically encoded strip to pay for gasoline and groceries at some gas stations and supermarkets; the purchase amount is automatically deducted from your bank balance, without any further action from you.

VOICE INPUT DEVICES

In an effort to increase worker productivity, a substantial amount of research is being done in voice recognition—programming the computer to recognize spoken commands. **Voice input devices** (Figure 3.24) convert spoken words into electrical signals by comparing the electrical patterns produced by the speaker's voice to a set of prerecorded patterns. If a matching pattern is found, the computer accepts this pattern as a part of its standard "vocabulary." This technology is also used by people whose jobs do not allow them to keep their hands free to input data and by handicapped people who are not able to use traditional input devices. NASA is currently developing experimental space suits that use microprocessors and storage devices to allow astronauts to view computerized display across their helmet visors. These displays would be activated and manipulated by spoken command—convenient when you've got both hands busy on an outer-space repair job!

FIGURE 3.23
Smart card. A French version.

To date, the biggest problems with this technology involve limitations on the size of the computer's vocabulary, pronunciation differences among individuals, and the computer's inability to accept continuous speech. However, research continues at a fast pace. Several voice input units are currently available for use with microcomputers.

LIGHT PENS, MICE, TOUCH SCREENS, AND DIGITIZERS

Data input also involves entering commands and selecting options. The light pen, the mouse, the touch screen, and the digitizer tablet were all developed to make this easy. Each of these devices allows the user to identify and select the necessary command or option by, in effect, moving the position indicator (cursor) to a certain location on the screen or tablet and sending a signal to the computer. For this reason they are sometimes called *pointing devices*, and they are used in **menu-driven** programs—that is, programs that offer varying levels of menus, or choices, to the user to lead him or her through the program functions.

LIGHT PEN   The **light pen** uses a light-sensitive photoelectric cell to signal screen position to the computer (Figure 3.25a). The pen is touched to the video display screen at the desired location and the switch on the pen is pushed to close the photoelectric circuit, thereby indicating the *x-y* screen coordinates to the computer. Light pens are frequently used by graphics designers, illustrators, and drafting engineers. (Of course, data may also be entered using keyboards.)

FIGURE 3.24
Voice input. Such devices convert spoken words into electrical signals.

MOUSE   The **mouse,** briefly discussed in Chapter 2, is a hand-held device connected to the computer by a small cable. As the mouse is rolled across the desktop (Figure 3.25b), the cursor moves across the screen. When the cursor reaches the desired location, the user usually pushes a button on the mouse once or twice to signal a menu selection or a command to the computer. Mouse technology is often used with graphics-oriented microcomputers like the Macintosh. With special software for graphics, the mouse can be used like a pen or a paintbrush to create figures and patterns directly on the video display screen. Foot mice are available for people who do not want to take up desktop space with a traditional mouse.

TOUCH SCREEN   Limited amounts of data can be entered via a terminal or a microcomputer that has a **touch screen.** The user simply touches the screen at the desired locations, marked by labeled boxes, to "point out" choices to the computer (Figure 3.25c).

DIGITIZER   An interesting method of input that is used in mapmaking is the **digitizer,** or **digitizing tablet** (Figure 3.25d). The tablets, which come in different sizes, are the working surface. Each is covered by a grid of many tiny wires that is connected to the computer. Drawings placed over this grid can be traced and entered into the computer by the use of a special pen or mouse-like device with crosshairs that opens and closes electrical circuits in the grid and thus identifies x-y coordinates. Original drawings may also be entered. As it progresses, the drawing is

FIGURE 3.25
Four common non-keyboard input devices. (a) Light pen; (b) mouse; (c) touch screen; (d) digitizer.

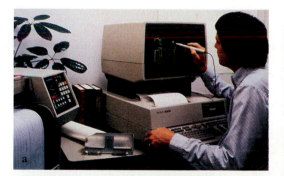

displayed on the screen. Digitizers are also used in design and engineering businesses—such as those that develop aircraft or computer chips.

Most specialized, non-keyboard input devices are used in conjunction with a keyboard, because the specialized devices can't be used to input all types of data and instructions. An exception may be the Eyescan Communicator that translates eye movements into signals for a computer. This innovation—still under development—allows people who cannot speak or use keyboards to communicate using a computer.

INPUT CONTROLS: PRESERVING DATA INTEGRITY

No matter how sophisticated your input hardware is and how well thought out your input methods are, you still run the risk of generating inaccurate or even useless information. The completeness and accuracy of information produced by a computer system depends to a great extent on how much care was taken in capturing the raw data that served as input to the processing procedures. An old computer-related saying summarizes this point: "Garbage In, Garbage Out." If you input incomplete and inaccurate data (Garbage In), then you can expect the information that is produced to be correspondingly incomplete and inaccurate (Garbage Out). How do you ensure that input data is accurate and complete?

Input controls include a combination of manual and computerized control procedures designed to ensure that all input data has been accurately put into computer-usable form. A variety of control techniques can be used, depending on the design of the computer system and the nature of the processing activities taking place.

When source documents (papers, forms, and so on) are used that contain data to be keyed into computer-usable form, the most commonly used control technique is the *batch control technique*, which involves the following steps:

- The source documents are collected into groups or stacks (batches).
- A batch control slip is attached to the batch, and someone in the user department where the batch was prepared records: (1) date and batch control number; (2) count of the number of documents in the batch; (3) a total of particular elements such as hours worked, number of customers, or the like for comparison purposes.
- The batch number and control slip information are recorded on a control log, providing the means to determine which batches have been forwarded for data entry.
- The batch of documents and control slip are forwarded to the personnel responsible for keying the data into the computer—someone in the same department, or, in most cases, the data entry group within what used to be called the *Data Processing Department* but is now called the *Information Center* or the *Information Systems Department*.
- The batches are logged in by the data entry group and assigned to individual clerks for input.

- The data entry clerk keys the data into the data entry device. The computer counts the number of documents entered and accumulates a matching control total to compare with the sample total of one area's data on the batch control slip.

- After a batch has been entered, the input device displays all the control information accumulated. The clerk can then compare this information to the batch control slip. If the control information matches, the batch is considered complete. If the control information does not match, the clerk will review the entries made (usually on a video display screen) and make the necessary adjustments.

- Once the data has been put into computer-usable form, it is processed by the computer to ensure no additional errors have been made. The computer will look for invalid customer numbers, invalid part numbers, invalid account numbers, and so on. The errors are listed in an *input control report*.

- The batches and the report are sent back to the original department for review and correction. The corrections are then forwarded to the data entry group for input.

The input control techniques differ for on-line and on-line real-time systems—that is, when source documents aren't used, and data has been keyed in through a terminal. In these cases, the user typically has a computer terminal on the desk or sales counter. As data is provided by the customer or other source, it is keyed into the computer immediately. The main computer is usually programmed to immediately verify the accuracy of the data (customer number, product number, account number, and so on) by matching it to the appropriate master computer files. In other words, the input controls in the form of editing and validation are written into the software and the user can see error messages on the screen. Corrections can generally be made immediately by the user.

How important are input controls? Consider the modest-living couple who got a phone bill or a local store's invoice for $450,000 and spent months trying to convince the company it was a mistake. The customer service personnel and the data processing staff were probably trying to identify the glitch in the input control procedures. The computer doesn't make mistakes; the people who input data and monitor input procedures do. Even software writers are not infallible. Without input controls mistakes might be impossible to detect or correct. Imagine the consequences this could have on the level of international trade, politics, and military activities.

Onward: Holding on to What You've Got

Now that you've learned something about the hardware and the methods used to input data, it's time to move on to where and how you store the data. "On magnetic tape or disk," you say—but there's more to it than that, as the next chapter will show.

SUMMARY

As a computer user, you will not be able to avoid entering data of some sort. The more you understand about the input hardware and methods, the better you will be able to do the job.

Input hardware can be broken down into three categories: computer terminals (with keyboards and monitors), dedicated data entry systems, and specialized, non-keyboard input devices. The keyboard, which comes in many shapes and sizes, is probably the most widely used mechanism for entering data into a computer-usable form. Many of its keys resemble typewriter keys; however, it also has special function keys to issue commands (among other things), cursor movement keys, and numeric keys (to enter numbers).

The types of computer terminals most often used for data input are (1) desktop terminals, (2) point-of-sale terminals, (3) financial transaction terminals, (4) executive workstations, (5) portable terminals, and (6) microcomputers used as input terminals.

There are three types of dedicated data entry systems: (1) key-to-tape systems, (2) key-to-disk systems, and (3) key-to-diskette systems. Key-to-tape systems are rarely used today. They have been largely supplanted by the disk- and diskette-based systems (or microcomputers).

Popular specialized data input devices today include: (1) card readers for microcomputer systems, (2) devices that read data optically, (3) devices that read magnetically encoded data, (4) voice input devices, and (5) light pens, mice, touch screens, and digitizers (sometimes called *pointing devices*).

Most data that is input to a computer-usable form is not processed immediately; instead it is held on storage media until needed for processing. These media include paper and magnetic tape and disk—magnetic media being the most widely used today. Punched cards and paper tape were the first paper-based input media, but they are not used much anymore. Today, specialized input devices are being used frequently to read data recorded by hand, typed, or typeset on paper documents.

The conversion of data into a computer-usable form is a vital part of a computer-based information system. Input control procedures are needed to safeguard the data's integrity and to ensure the production of complete and accurate information—in other words, to ensure no "garbage in" to avoid getting "garbage out."

KEY TERMS

bar-code reader	digitizer	input controls
card reader	dumb terminal	input screen
cursor	executive workstation	integrated workstation
dedicated data entry	financial transaction	intelligent terminal
system	terminal	keyboard
desktop terminal	function keys	keypunch machine

key-to-disk data entry
key-to-diskette data
  entry
key-to-tape data entry
light pen
magnetic ink character
  recognition
media

menu-driven
mouse
optical character
  recognition
optical mark
optical-mark reader
point-of-sale terminal

portable terminal
smart card
smart terminal
terminal
touch screen
turnaround document
voice input device

EXERCISES

MATCHING

Match each of the following terms to the phrase that is the most closely related:

1. _____ turnaround document
2. _____ key-to-tape system
3. _____ key-to-disk system
4. _____ voice input devices
5. _____ point-of-sale terminal
6. _____ portable terminal
7. _____ cursor
8. _____ function keys

9. _____ keyboard
10. _____ light pen
11. _____ touch screen
12. _____ input controls
13. _____ desktop terminal
14. _____ mouse
15. _____ optical character
    recognition

a. A combination of manual and computerized procedures designed to ensure that all input data has been accurately and completely put into computer-usable form.

b. A sophisticated electromechanical component designed to create special standardized electronic codes when a key is pressed.

c. A symbol on the video display screen that shows where the next character that is input will be positioned.

d. Programmable keys that are used for, among other things, issuing commands.

e. A terminal used to capture sales and inventory data on the spot; the data is later sent to a central computer for processing.

f. A terminal that can be used to access a central computer from remote locations; these terminals can be easily moved.

g. A system that functions similarly to a keypunch machine, except data is recorded in the form of magnetic spots on magnetic tape, instead of punched in a card.

h. A system that consists of a number of keying devices connected to a dedicated computer that stores data on disk.

i. These devices convert spoken words into electrical signals.

j. An input device with a photosensitive cell that signals the position on the screen to the computer.

k. An input device that the user can simply touch to tell the computer to perform certain activities.

l. A terminal that fits on top of the user's desk and usually has a video display screen 12 to 14 inches in diagonal width that produces a single-color image.

m. A computer-produced hardcopy output that is forwarded to a recipient who then records additional data on it and returns it to the sender for updated input.

n. Computerized reading of hardcopy data from source documents and subsequent conversion of the data into computer-usable form.

o. Specialized input device that the user rolls around on the desk surface.

MULTIPLE CHOICE

1. Which of the following would be the best purchase if your goal is to have portability, use applications software to help you with your daily activities, and communicate with a larger computer?
    a. desktop terminal
    b. portable terminal
    c. executive workstation
    d. point-of-sale terminal
    e. none of the above

2. Which of the following would probably be the best purchase if your job requires you to access the company's central computer frequently to obtain data even when you are in another state on business?
    a. desktop terminal
    b. portable terminal
    c. executive workstation
    d. point-of-sale terminal
    e. none of the above

3. Which of the following is part of the standard microcomputer keyboard?
    a. caps lock key
    b. alternate key
    c. cursor movement keys
    d. return key
    e. all of the above

4. Which of the following would you most likely use at home as well as in the office connected to a central computer?
    a. microcomputer
    b. executive workstation
    c. mainframe computer
    d. desktop terminal
    e. point-of-sale terminal

5. Which of the following do you think does not fall into the "specialized input device" category?
    a. keyboard
    b. light pen
    c. optical-mark reader
    d. mouse

     e. voice input device

6. Which of the following types of input devices was developed to reduce the amount of time that was necessary to transfer hardcopy data (such as a page of text) into computer-usable form?
   a. keyboard
   b. light pen
   c. optical character reader
   d. mouse
   e. voice input device

7. Which of the following input devices was developed to make it easier for the user to identify and select a command or menu option?
   a. light pen
   b. touch screen
   c. mouse
   d. digitizer
   e. all of the above

8. Which of the following is a major advantage of magnetic input media?
   a. reusability
   b. low cost
   c. flexibility in accessing data
   d. high speed
   e. all of the above

9. Which of the following is most often used to categorize input hardware?
   a. whether the device uses a keyboard
   b. whether the device can be held in your hand
   c. whether the device is heavy
   d. whether the device is expensive
   e. none of the above

10. Which of the following is not used to describe terminals?
   a. intelligent
   b. dumb
   c. quick
   d. smart
   e. all of the above

SHORT ANSWER

1. Why do you think that your grocery business would benefit from using point-of-sale terminals that are connected to a central computer?

2. What are input controls, and why is it important to establish them in an organization that uses computers?

3. What is a turnaround document?

4. What is meant by the term *computer-usable input*?

5. Describe the different types of keys on a standard microcomputer keyboard and what their functions are.

6. What type of terminal are you most likely to find on the top of an executive's desk? Why?

7. What is meant by the term *dedicated data entry system*? Briefly describe three types of data entry systems.

8. What are some of the non-keyboard input devices that are being used today? Describe where you would probably find each of these devices being used.

9. What is a smart card? How do you think it might be used in the future?

10. Describe what voice input devices are used for. What are the current limitations of voice technology?

PROJECTS

1. Go to a local computer store and see what types of input devices are displayed there. Ask for a demonstration of the different input devices used with microcomputers. Write a report on the devices you saw and the ones that were demonstrated.

2. Observe the use of input devices in a few stores, such as supermarkets. Some stores use tedious methods for data input and some use efficient methods. What are they?

3. Identify a turnaround document that you receive monthly, such as a utility bill. Trace what you think its path has been and will be within the sending organization. What input method(s) do you think the sender uses to process this document? What input controls do you think the sender uses?

CHAPTER FOUR

STORAGE HARDWARE

A great deal of business has to do with keeping score, with record keeping. Indeed, very few businesses can operate without keeping a running account of daily transactions: who owes what to whom, who collected what, when something is scheduled to happen, and so on. We have already described the fundamentals of the computer-based information system and how data can be converted into computer-usable form. Now let us consider how this computerized data is stored and retrieved.

PREVIEW

When you have completed this chapter, you will be able to:

■

Describe the difference between primary and secondary storage, and how data is represented in each

■

List three data storage and retrieval methods

■

List and describe the storage devices used most often with microcomputers

■

List and describe the storage devices used most often with minicomputers and mainframes

■

THE USER PERSPECTIVE

If a business cannot store data and information, it cannot work—computerized or not. In a noncomputerized office, data is stored temporarily in in-boxes and out-boxes, and semipermanently in file cabinets and on microfilm. In a computerized information processing environment, data is stored in a form that is directly usable by the computer for processing—that is, in computer-usable form (Figure 4.1).

FIGURE 4.1
Out with the old. The storage phase in the computer-based information system.

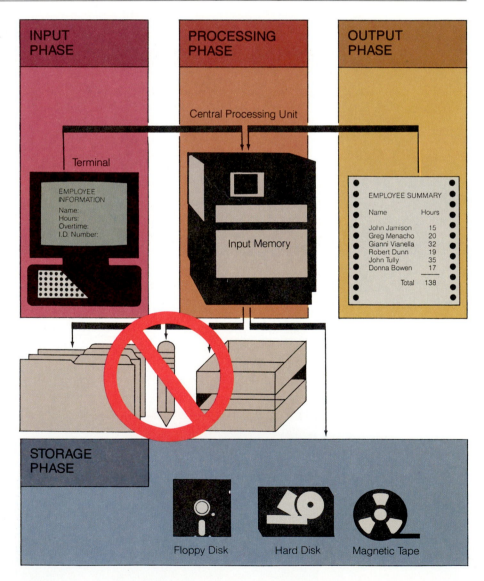

If until now the computer-based information system has seemed a vague abstraction, this chapter will demonstrate how useful it can be—and why your understanding of it is so important.

WHY IS STORAGE AN IMPORTANT CONCEPT?

Not understanding the concept of computer storage is like not understanding the concept of a car's gasoline tank. Without using a gasoline tank, you won't be able to get your car to go very far because, of course, without the tank, you can't use gasoline. Similarly, if you don't use a storage device with your computer you won't have the capability to store the data that will make your computer useful.

In general, data is stored in a computer system for three principal reasons. First, current input data needs to be held for processing. For instance, the sales order data for boogie boards sold today at Sporting Life must be input and stored until needed to produce invoices. Second, some types of data are stored on a relatively permanent basis and retrieved as required during processing. For example, to produce your invoices for boogie boards sold, you need data from the customer file: customer's name, address, billing instructions, and terms. Third, data is stored to be periodically updated. In our case, after the invoices have been produced, some of the files on accounts payable (the records reflecting what customers owe) need to be updated to reflect the latest boogie board purchases. In addition to all this data, the computer software instructions must be stored in a computer-usable form because a copy of the software must be read into internal memory from a storage device before data processing can begin.

WHAT DO YOU NEED TO KNOW ABOUT STORAGE?

As you rise in the organizational world, you will very likely be required to write reports for your supervisor or manager. Picture yourself sitting down in front of a microcomputer for the first time with the intent of creating a report for your boss. Before you can begin, you must determine where the software that you will use to write the report is stored. Once you have written your report, you will need to save a copy of it on a storage device (particularly if you don't finish it in a single sitting). To do these things, you have to know about storage. Also, if you are going to create a very large report, the capacity of your storage medium and device may be a consideration. For example, depending on your particular computer system and the storage devices connected to it, a 100-page document may not fit on one diskette. How, then, do you write your report? This chapter covers these issues and more.

STORAGE FUNDAMENTALS

By now you know that storage hardware provides the capability to store data and program instructions—either temporarily or permanently—for quick retrieval and use during computer processing. You also know that the term *media* means the materials on which data can be recorded (magnetic media are the most popular). But to fully appreciate the storage capabilities available in computer systems, you must understand a number of storage fundamentals.

PRIMARY AND SECONDARY STORAGE

The term **primary storage** refers to the internal memory of a computer, where both data and instructions are held for immediate access and use by the computer's central processing unit during processing. Although the technology is changing, most primary storage today is considered a **volatile** form of storage, meaning that the data and instructions are lost when the computer is turned off. **Secondary storage** (or **auxiliary storage**) is any storage device designed to retain data and instructions (programs) in a more permanent form. Secondary storage is **nonvolatile,** meaning that the data and instructions remain intact when the computer is turned off.

The easiest way to differentiate between primary and secondary storage is to consider the reason data is placed in them. Data is placed in primary storage (internal, or main, memory—sometimes just called *memory*) only when it is needed for immediate processing. Data in secondary storage, or auxiliary storage, remains there until overwritten with new data or deleted and is accessed when needed. In very general terms, a secondary storage device can be thought of as a file cabinet. We store data there until we need it. Then we open the drawer, grab the appropriate folder (file), and place it on the top of our desk (primary storage, or internal memory), where we work on it—perhaps writing a few things in it or throwing away a few papers. When we are done with the file, we take it off the desktop and return it to the cabinet.

DATA REPRESENTATION: BINARY CODE

When you begin to write your report, you have quite a collection of symbols to choose from: the letters A–Z, both upper- and lowercase; the numbers 0–9; and numerous punctuation and other special symbols, such as ?, $, and %. People understand what these characters mean; computers cannot. Computers deal with data converted into the simplest form that can be processed magnetically or electronically—that is, binary form. The term *binary* is used to refer to two distinct states—on or off, yes or no, present or absent, 1 or 0. For example, a light switch can be either on or off, so it can be viewed as a binary device. When data is stored on magnetic tape or disk, it appears as the presence or absence—"on" or "off"—of magnetic spots.

To store and process data in binary form, a way of representing characters, numbers, and other symbols had to be developed. In other words, *coding schemes* had to be devised as standardized methods of encoding data for use in computer storage and processing.

A scheme for encoding data using a series of binary digits is called a **binary code.** A **binary digit (bit)** is either the character 1 (on) or the character 0 (off). It represents one of two distinct states—magnetically, electrically, or optically. You can think of a bit as a light switch. One switch—one bit—can be either on or off. However, as shown in Figure 4.2, when you have two light switches operating together, you can now set them in four different combinations: on-on, on-off,

off-on, and off-off. As you can see, the number of elements of data that a series of light switches—bits—can represent is equal to the number 2 (the number of states, on or off) raised to the power of the number of light switches. In other words, if you have 2 states and 4 switches, you have 2^4, or 16, combinations (elements of data). It usually takes 8 bits—known as one **byte**—to form a character.

Two specific individuals contributed greatly to the coding scheme used to record and process data in computer-usable form: Herman Hollerith and Samuel F.B. Morse. Herman Hollerith, of U.S. Census fame, developed a binary coding scheme for representing data on paper cards through patterns of punched holes. Morse is responsible for the development of one of the earliest forms of electronic data communication—the telegraph. His dream was to break down the information to be communicated into a coding scheme based on electrical pulses. The code for each letter and number was formed by a combination of long and short electrical pulses. A short pulse was a "dot," and a long pulse was a "dash" (Figure 4.3).

The combined contributions of Morse and Hollerith (and others) laid the foundation for the storage and processing of data in magnetic and electrical form. Several coding schemes for the computer have been adopted that rely on the binary

FIGURE 4.2
Every little bit counts. The smallest unit of data that can be stored is a bit, short for binary digit. A bit can be 0 or 1—off or on, just like a light switch. Different combinations of 0s and 1s are electronically translated into computerized codes.

A bit is the smallest possible unit of data; it is 1 or 0 — that is, on or off:

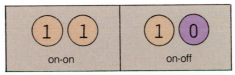

2 bits can have four possible combinations:

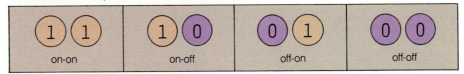

3 bits can have 8 possible combinations:

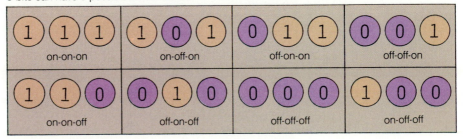

4 bits yield 16 possible combinations.

8 bits yield 256 possible combinations, enough to represent all the letters of the alphabet, numbers 0-9, and special symbols.

FIGURE 4.3
An early binary code. Samuel F.B. Morse, developer of the Morse Code, showed that data elements (characters) could be represented by using two "states"—long and short, otherwise known as dash and dot.

FIGURE 4.4
ASCII and EBCDIC. These are two commonly used coding schemes for data representation.

Character	ASCII	EBCDIC	Character	ASCII	EBCDIC
A	100 0001	1100 0001	N	100 1110	1101 0101
B	100 0010	1100 0010	O	100 1111	1101 0110
C	100 0011	1100 0011	P	101 0000	1101 0111
D	100 0100	1100 0100	Q	101 0001	1101 1000
E	100 0101	1100 0101	R	101 0010	1101 1001
F	100 0110	1100 0110	S	101 0011	1101 0010
G	100 0111	1100 0111	T	101 0100	1110 0011
H	100 1000	1100 1000	U	101 0101	1110 0100
I	100 1001	1100 1001	V	101 0110	1110 0101
J	100 1010	1101 0001	W	101 0111	1110 0110
K	100 1011	1101 0010	X	101 1000	1110 0111
L	100 1100	1101 0011	Y	101 1001	1110 1000
M	100 1101	1101 0100	Z	101 1010	1110 1001
0	011 0000	1110 0000	5	011 0101	1111 0101
1	011 0001	1110 0001	6	011 0111	1111 0110
2	011 0010	1111 0010	7	011 1000	1111 0111
3	011 0011	1111 0011	8	011 1001	1111 1000
4	011 0100	1111 0100	9	011 1010	1111 1001

representation. Two commonly used codes are ASCII (pronounced "as-key") and EBCDIC (pronounced "eb-see-dick").

ASCII   The acronym **ASCII** stands for the **American Standard Code for Information Interchange,** which is widely used to represent characters in microcomputers and many minicomputers. Because microcomputers operate on data in 8-bit groups, ASCII uses 8 bits to represent a character—only 7 bits are meaningful, but you don't need to worry about that. For example, the character A in ASCII is 01000001.

The number of characters that can be represented using ASCII depends on the number of different combinations that can be made using the 7 bits that represent data, which is 128. There are 128 valid codes (or characters) that can be formulated using ASCII; Figure 4.4 shows 36 of them.

EBCDIC   The acronym **EBCDIC** refers to **Extended Binary Coded Decimal Interchange Code,** which is the most popular code used for IBM and IBM-compatible mainframe computers. Unlike ASCII, this scheme uses all 8 bits to represent data. Using all 8 bits in the coding scheme makes 256 character codes, or bit combinations, available. In EBCDIC, A is 11000001. Figure 4.4 shows a list of EBCDIC characters.

As you can see in Figure 4.4, characters are coded differently in ASCII and EBCDIC. Because of these differences, transferring data between computers using different coding schemes requires special hardware and software.

FILES AND DATA HIERARCHY

No matter what size or shape computer you work with, you will be working with files. But before we can put data files in their proper perspective, we need to examine the levels of data, known as the **data storage hierarchy.** If you look at Figure 4.5, at the top of the data hierarchy you'll see the term *file*. A **file** is made up of a group of related records. A **record** is defined as a collection of related fields, and a **field** is defined as a collection of related characters, or bytes, of data. And finally, a byte of data, as you learned in the last section, is made up of 8 bits.

To illustrate this concept, let's examine an inventory file for basketballs from a manufacturer of sporting goods from whom Sporting Life often buys. This particular inventory *file* is made up of a group of *records*, one record for each item in inventory. Each record contains the same number of *fields* such as: (1) item or product number, (2) item or product description, (3) unit price, and (4) quantity on hand. Each field contains a number of *characters*. As an example, the product number field of one record contains the expression "3618A" (5 characters) and the quantity-on-hand field of that record contains the characters "24" (2 characters), indicating that there are 24 items with the product number 3618A in stock.

Up to this point, we've described various types of files in general terms, such as master files (used to permanently store data for access and updating) and transaction files (used to temporarily hold data for processing). Now that we've described how data is represented on a storage medium (with bits and bytes) and how the data hierarchy is structured, we can get a "bit" more detailed in our description of what a file is, what it does, and where it's kept.

Files generally fall into two categories: (1) files containing data (often referred to generically as *data files*) and (2) files containing software instructions (often referred to generically as *program files*). Data files, in turn, tend to be categorized according to how they are used—as a (1) transaction file, (2) master file, (3) report file, (4) output file, (5) history file, or (6) backup file (Figure 4.6). The amount of time that data needs to be stored and the purpose of storing the data vary substantially, depending on the processing objectives. These objectives determine what type of file you'll be storing data in.

You'll recall that some data is input into computer-usable form and then retained only until it is time to process. This type of data is referred to as *transaction data*, and it is stored in an input **transaction file.**

Some data is stored in computer-usable form for lengthy periods of time, after which it is used for retrieval and is updated during processing. A file containing this type of data is referred to as a **master file.**

In large computer systems, the volume of reports to be produced is so immense that a special, smaller computer system is set up just to control and coordinate the

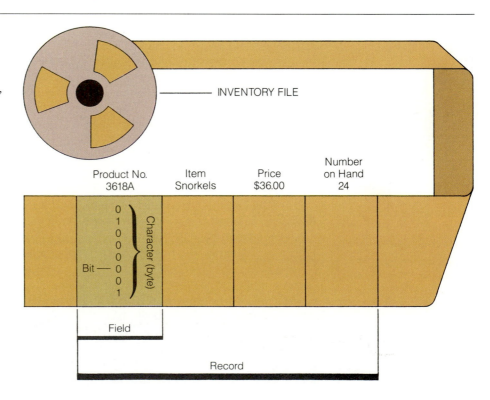

FIGURE 4.5
Data storage hierarchy. Computer files are made up of four subordinate parts: bit, character (byte), field, and record.

printing of reports. This is often true of major utility companies that produce millions of customer bills and statements each month. To make this process easier, the data necessary to produce the reports is captured in a **report file,** which is then transferred to the special computer system for printing after it has been processed in the main computer.

Many computer software applications are designed to produce data as output to be used by another program or application at a later time. (An application is usually a group of related programs, such as a payroll application consisting of 14 programs.) A file created for this purpose is referred to as an **output file** at the time it is produced. However, it becomes an *input transaction file* when it is read into another program for processing.

Many organizations find it useful to produce reports that require analysis of data on past company operations. A file created to collect data for long-term reporting purposes is referred to as a **history file.**

Backup files are copies of other types of files that are made to ensure that data and programs will not be lost if the original files are damaged or destroyed. Occasionally data is extracted from backup files to use like data in historical files.

Program files are simply programs stored on disk or tape. They are usually controlled by the computer operations group and maintained in libraries.

FIGURE 4.6
Types of files. The basic types of data files are determined by how the files are used.

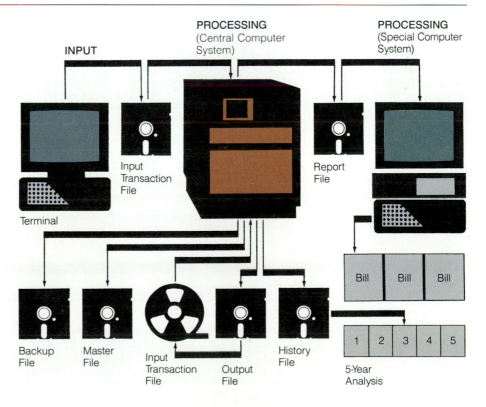

HOW IS DATA STORED?

To store data for later use you need two things: a storage *medium* and a storage *device*. The storage device records the data onto the medium, where the data is held until needed. The process of recording data onto media, which is coordinated by software, involves four basic steps (Figure 4.7):

1. After input, the data to be recorded by a storage device begins its journey from its temporary location in internal memory to the controller board for the storage device.

FIGURE 4.7
For the record. (1) After the computer has been given the appropriate command, data to be stored on a floppy disk enters and then leaves internal memory (a kind of transfer point). (2) Software instructions determine where the data is to be recorded on the disk. (3) The data goes to the disk controller board. (4) From here it flows to the read/write heads in the disk storage device and is recorded on the storage medium—the floppy disk.

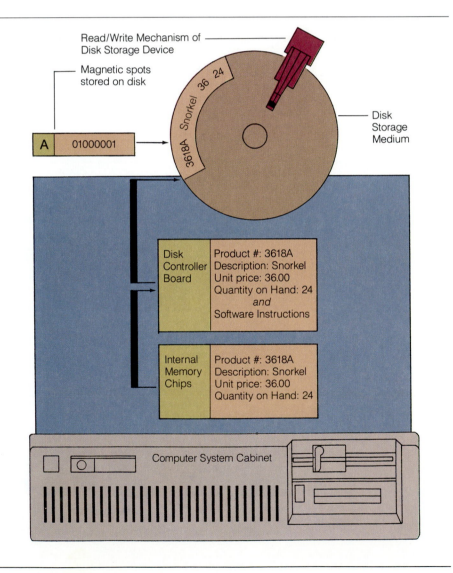

2. Software instructions then determine where the data is to be recorded on the storage medium.

3. The controller board for the storage device positions the recording mechanism over the appropriate location on the storage medium. [For storage on disk, this mechanism is referred to in most cases as a **read/write head** because it can both "read" (accept) magnetic spots and convert them to electrical impulses and "write" (enter) the spots on the disk; it can also erase the spots.]

4. The recording mechanism is activated and converts electrical impulses to magnetic spots placed on the surface of the medium as required to record the data according to the coding scheme being used (ASCII, for example).

DATA STORAGE AND RETRIEVAL METHODS

Most of us read a novel from the first page to the end of the book in sequence because we have an interest in following the story in the order that the author intended. However, in a catalog you may wish to locate the information for just a single item. It would take much more time to locate the page you desired if you started at the beginning and read all the pages instead of looking up the item in the index. The same kind of principle applies to the storage and retrieval of data in computer-usable form.

Your old filing system at Sporting Life can be used as a good example of the basic storage and retrieval concepts. In most cases, when a file cabinet is first organized, the file folders are placed in each drawer in a certain order. For a customer file, the folders are placed into drawers in sequential order by customer number or customer name. If new customers are added later, their folders are inserted into the correct location between the existing folders. When you need to retrieve data from the file cabinet, the way you get it depends on what needs to be done. For example, if you are going to prepare a report on customer status, you will probably review each folder in order. However, if a specific customer calls and asks about the status of one invoice, you will go to the file cabinet and locate and remove that one customer's folder.

In the computerized environment, a file cabinet is usually thought of as a database (a collection of interrelated files stored together), a file drawer is thought of as a file (master file, transaction file, history file, and so forth), and a folder is thought of as a record. The three principal methods of storing and retrieving the data are: (1) sequential, meaning that records are stored and retrieved in sequential order, (2) direct, meaning that records are not stored or retrieved in any special order, and (3) indexed sequential, a combination of the preceding two methods whereby records are stored in sequential order but with an index that allows both sequential and random retrieval.

Each of these three approaches to computerized data storage and retrieval is suited to different applications and processing requirements. For most users, the selection of a storage method has been left up to the technical professionals involved in developing the software. However, if you find yourself involved in a project where the requirements for new software are being specified, be sure that the information system specialists understand how you need to store and retrieve the data. Your processing requirements should be used as the basis for selecting the file storage and retrieval method.

SEQUENTIAL STORAGE AND RETRIEVAL

The **sequential storage and retrieval** method (Figure 4.8) is ideal for situations in which all records in a file need to be accessed for processing—such as producing payroll (because everyone gets a check) or preparing a comprehensive inventory report by part number. In this approach, data is retrieved in the sequence in which it was recorded on the storage media. It's relatively easy to write software instructions (procedures) to retrieve records from a file that is organized sequentially. However, it's more difficult to retrieve data when the sequential storage and retrieval method isn't used.

The evolution of the sequential storage and retrieval method was based, at least in part, on the characteristics and limitations of the early storage media and devices. As you know, punched cards were used as one of the earliest types of secondary storage media. The cards were always handled in sequential order as they were read by the card reader. If the forty-third card had the data you wanted, all of the preceding cards had to be read first before you could get it. To develop a mechanical device that could selectively read or extract a single card from the middle of the stack proved to be too cumbersome.

The use of new storage media such as magnetic tape, disks, and diskettes has improved the situation. However, although they can all support sequential storage

FIGURE 4.8
Sequential access. Records are accessed one at a time and in the order in which they were recorded.

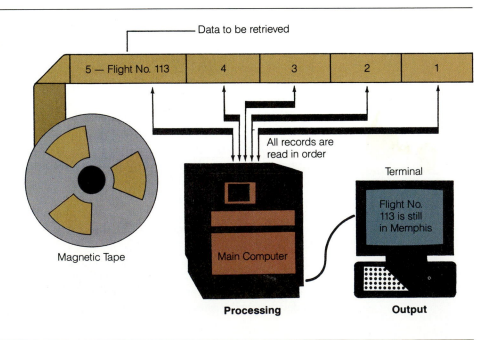

and retrieval of data, they can't all be used for direct and indexed sequential storage and retrieval of data.

DIRECT ACCESS STORAGE AND RETRIEVAL

The **direct access storage and retrieval** method—also called *random access*—is best suited to situations in which only a few records in a file need to be accessed in no particular sequence (Figure 4.9). Airline reservations systems rely heavily on this method. Because there is no predictable pattern in which customers call to inquire about the status of flights, the individual records containing the status of the flights need to be stored in a fashion whereby they can be directly retrieved in any order— meaning that all the records in front of the record containing status data on your flight No. 113 from Memphis to Cincinnati do not have to be read first.

There are a number of ways to access records directly in no particular order. The most common approach is to use a unique element of data—called a **key field** or **key**—contained in each record as a basis for identifying the record and for determining which storage location on the disk the record should be stored in or retrieved from. For example, in an airline reservations system, each flight has a different number that can be used as a key field. To determine where to store a record so it can be retrieved directly, the computer performs a mathematical calculation—called *hashing*—on the key field value. This eliminates the need for an index by translating the record's key field directly into an address. Obviously, no two key fields should be given the same address; hashing prevents this by using a mathematical formula that (almost always) produces a unique number. This can be done, for example, by dividing the key field number by the prime number closest to, but not greater than, the number of records to be stored. (A prime number can be divided only by itself or by 1.) The resulting number is then translated into a disk surface number, sector number, and track number.

The direct access storage and retrieval method is ideal for applications like an airline reservations system or the computerized telephone information service,

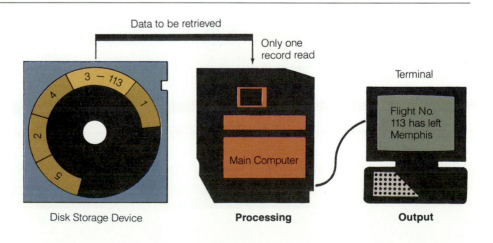

FIGURE 4.9
Direct access. Records are stored and retrieved in any order.

Data to be retrieved

Only one record read

Terminal

3 – 113

Main Computer

Flight No. 113 has left Memphis

Disk Storage Device

Processing

Output

where records need to be retrieved only one at a time and there is no fixed pattern or sequence to the requests for data and records. However, this method cannot be used with magnetic tape, and it is very inefficient in situations that require accessing all records in sequential order: Because the records are not stored in any particular order, following the key sequence in order to retrieve them may involve jumping back and forth around the storage medium, which takes too much time.

INDEXED SEQUENTIAL STORAGE AND RETRIEVAL

In a payroll system, all records are usually accessed in order of employee number—that is, sequentially—when payroll checks are produced. However, occasionally a clerk in the payroll department may need to check on the status of a particular employee. In this case, processing the records sequentially just to access data for a single employee is impractical. To be able to access stored data in either a sequential *or* a direct fashion, a third storage and retrieval methodology was developed—the **indexed sequential access method (ISAM)** (Figure 4.10). This method is used almost exclusively with random access microcomputer storage devices to provide

FIGURE 4.10
Indexed sequential access. Records are stored sequentially but with an index that allows both sequential and direct, random access.

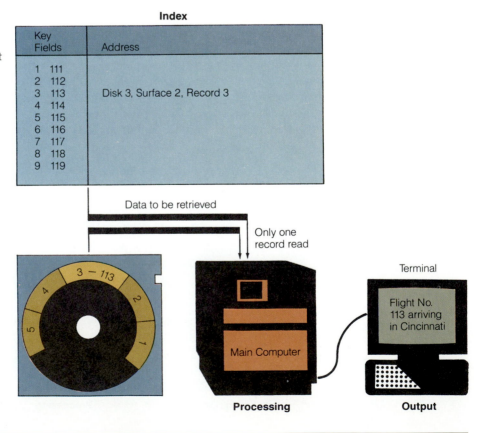

maximum flexibility for processing and has proven to be the most flexible for business applications.

The easiest way to grasp the concept of indexed sequential access is to consider how you locate a specific product in a catalog. You can either search from the first page until you find what you need or you can look up the product in the index and go directly to the page that describes it.

To use the indexed sequential access approach, you first must create an ISAM file by recording the records in sequential order by key field. One or more indexes are created at the same time. Each index consists of two columns of entries: the key field and the address of each record. Then, to access the data in the ISAM file, you can direct the computer to (1) read the records in sequential order starting from the beginning of the file, (2) read them in sequential order starting from any specified record (by key field) in the file, or (3) read individually specified (by key field) records directly. The index needs to be accessed only once to determine where to find the first record. After that, all records can be retrieved in exactly the same fashion as a standard sequential file. It's also possible to create more than one index for a file, which allows the file to be accessed using different key fields. For example, at least two indexes may be created for a personnel master file: an index by the primary key field (employee number) and a second index by, say, social security number. The first index could be used to provide sequential or direct access by employee number. The second index could be used to process the file to inquire about a specific employee by social security number.

TAPE STORAGE DEVICES

The development of magnetic tape was stimulated by the search for a faster, more convenient, and more cost-effective means than punched cards of recording and processing data sequentially. Magnetic tape is made of a thin plastic-like material called *Mylar* that can be easily magnetized to store data. The tape is 1/2 inch wide and is produced in a variety of lengths ranging from 200 to 3600 feet—the latter weighs about 4 pounds and has a reel about 10 1/2 inches in diameter. A modern tape storage unit can store the equivalent of more than 2.25 million punched cards—which would weigh over 10,000 pounds and could cost over $50,000. A reel of tape typically costs less than $25. (Tape cartridges, discussed a bit later in this chapter, cost about $20.)

RECORDING DATA ON MAGNETIC TAPE

Data is recorded across the width of a magnetic tape in columns of magnetic spots (Figure 4.11). Among the coding schemes used on magnetic tape are ASCII and EBCDIC. EBCDIC for standard magnetic tapes involves nine rows, also called *tracks* or *channels*, that run the full length of the tape. The number of columns of data that can be recorded per inch varies from 800 to 6250 depending on the capabilities of the tape drive mechanism. The capacity, or storage density, of a magnetic tape is measured in bits per inch (bpi), or columns per inch. Eight of the bits in each column are used to record the code for each character of data to be stored. (The ninth bit is for an error detection scheme, which will be described later.) The codes are recorded by writing magnetic spots in the rows of a column where a binary 1 is needed. The rows in the column where a binary 0 is needed are left blank (that is, no magnetic spot is recorded).

Records can be recorded onto the tape one at a time or in groups referred to as **blocks.** Blocks, also known as **physical records,** are made up of **logical records,** which are defined by the user according to the logic of the program being used. Each record, or block, is separated by a fixed length of blank tape. This section of tape is needed to compensate for the acceleration and deceleration of the tape as the individual records or blocks are positioned over or under the read/write head assembly. The blank sections are called **interrecord gaps (IRGs)** or **interblock gaps (IBGs)** (Figure 4.12). When records are blocked, space on the tape is not wasted because fewer gaps are needed. Also, records recorded in blocks can be retrieved much faster than the same number of records can be retrieved individually.

THE TAPE DRIVE MECHANISM

Figure 4.13 shows the components of a magnetic tape storage device. The reel of tape is placed on the left spindle and locked in place so that it does not come loose as it spins at high speed. The tape is fed through a **drive capstan,** a small cylindrical pulley used to regulate the speed of the tape. Several feet of tape are used as slack and then the tape is run through another capstan called a **stop capstan.** Then the

FIGURE 4.11
A. This figure shows the character *A* **recorded in EBCDIC across the width of a section of magnetic tape.**

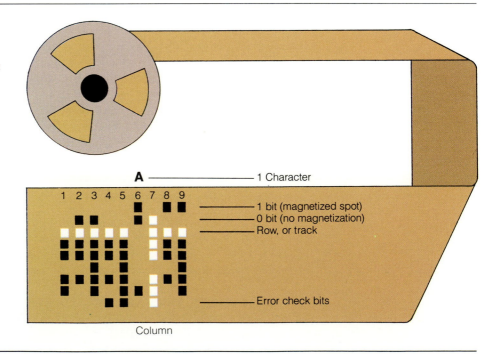

tape is run through the read/write head assembly and the right half of the tape mechanism, which is a mirror image of the left side. The stop capstans work together to hold the tape still long enough for data to be written or read. An empty tape reel is used to temporarily hold the tape after it has been read or written on. The tape moves at speeds approaching 200 inches per second. This translates into an ability to record or read data at an average speed of from 100,000 to 1,250,000 characters per second.

MAGNETIC TAPE PROCESSING CHARACTERISTICS

Magnetic tape is ideal for applications that require only sequential access to data. Many public utilities still use magnetic tape for storing their enormous customer master files. A file with millions of customer records could easily take up close to 100 reels of magnetic tape. Because of the number of tapes to be handled, many companies hire a librarian to manage them. A special room, called a *library*, is often set aside to store the tapes, and procedures are established to control their use (Figure 4.14).

To ensure that the correct version of a tape is used for processing, an **external label** (Figure 4.15a) is placed on the tape reel and an **internal label** is recorded on the tape magnetically. The internal label is often referred to as a *header label* and is examined by a program before processing begins to ensure it is the correct tape.

Tapes are protected from being accidentally overwritten by the use of a **file protection ring,** a plastic ring inserted into the back of a tape reel (Figure 4.15b). A tape can only be written on when the ring is in place, so it's the *absence* of the ring that protects the file from changes. When a new master file is created, the ring is immediately removed to prevent the accidental reuse of the tape.

FIGURE 4.12
Communication gaps. Inter-record and interblock gaps are used on tape to compensate for varying tape speeds.

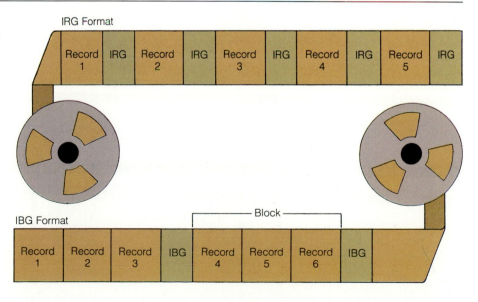

FIGURE 4.13
Play it again, Sam. This magnetic tape storage device (a) is an IBM 3420; (b) shows the components of the magnetic tape device.

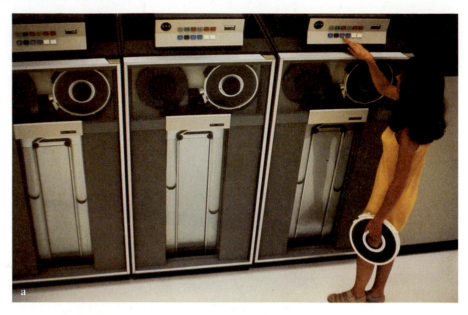

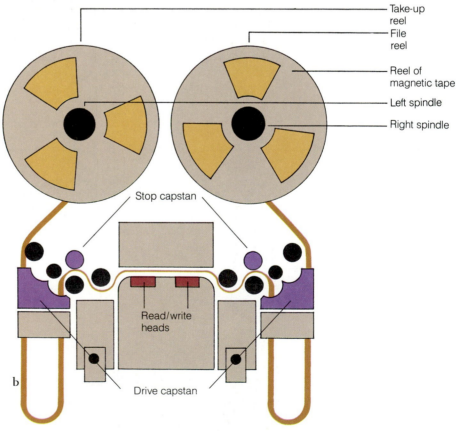

LIMITATIONS OF MAGNETIC TAPE

Although magnetic tape has provided a major improvement in the secondary storage capabilities of computer systems, it has two major drawbacks. First, the data recorded on tape cannot be practically altered—that is, it cannot be updated or changed in place. When records need to be changed, added in sequence, or deleted, a completely new tape must be created. Second, the data is recorded on the tape sequentially and can be accessed only sequentially. These limitations make magnetic tape less attractive for applications that require an update-in-place capability and access other than sequential. As the cost of direct access storage devices dropped, magnetic tape began to lose its popularity. However, despite its limitations, magnetic tape is still used widely today in minicomputer and mainframe computer systems. It remains an ideal medium for making backup copies of data stored on disk to enable businesses to recover from a data center disaster.

DIRECT ACCESS STORAGE FOR MICROCOMPUTERS

The Apple II and Tandy-Radio Shack (TRS-80) Model I personal computer systems were among the first to be made available to the public (1977). These two systems—as well as many of the others that entered the marketplace shortly thereafter—initially offered only cassette-tape storage devices. These devices, much like a per-

FIGURE 4.14
In the stacks. Large organizations often have extensive tape libraries.

sonal tape recorder, proved to be remarkably slow and awkward to use. As the microcomputer began to move from the home into the business environment, the need for fast direct access storage and retrieval became a significant issue.

This problem was solved when IBM introduced the diskette as a direct access storage medium. As a result, the microcomputer has dramatically expanded its role in information processing—and continues to do so.

DISKETTES: EASY ACCESS

The storage medium most commonly used by people in business is the **diskette,** also known as a **floppy disk.** Like magnetic tape, diskettes are made of Mylar that has

FIGURE 4.15
No ring, no write. (a) An external label. (b) Tapes are protected from accidental changes by the use of a file protection ring that must be inserted in the center of the tape reel before the tape can be recorded on or erased.

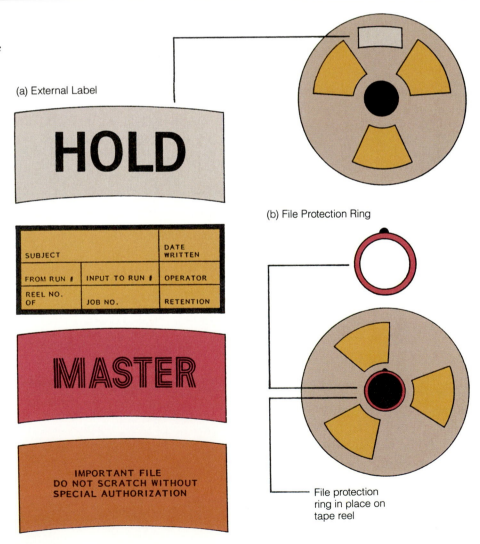

(a) External Label

HOLD

SUBJECT		DATE WRITTEN
FROM RUN #	INPUT TO RUN #	OPERATOR
REEL NO. OF	JOB NO.	RETENTION

MASTER

IMPORTANT FILE
DO NOT SCRATCH WITHOUT
SPECIAL AUTHORIZATION

(b) File Protection Ring

File protection
ring in place on
tape reel

been coated with a film of material that can easily be magnetized. Diskettes—more commonly called just *disks*—are often referred to as "floppy" because they are made of flexible material. As Figure 4.16 shows, the disk is enclosed in a protective jacket lined with a soft material specially treated to reduce friction and static. The disk jacket has four openings: (1) hub, (2) data access area, (3) write/protect notch, and

FIGURE 4.16
Floppy disk. Diskettes, or floppy disks, were developed to replace cassette tape as data storage media for use with microcomputers and to provide fast direct-access capabilities. (a) 5¼″ disk; (b) 3½″ disk.

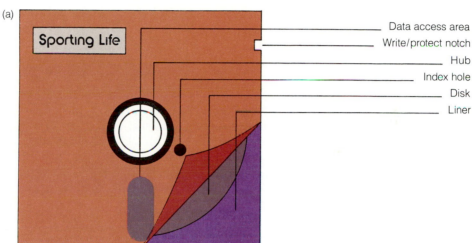

(a)

Sporting Life

Data access area
Write/protect notch
Hub
Index hole
Disk
Liner

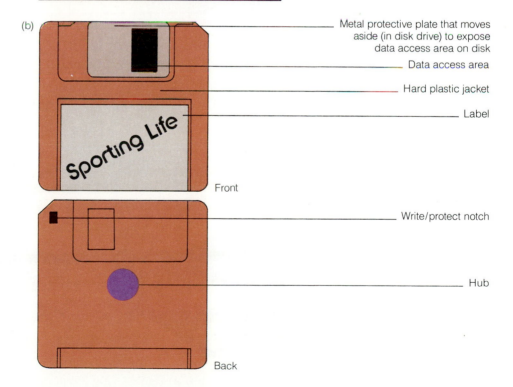

(b)

Sporting Life

Front

Back

Metal protective plate that moves aside (in disk drive) to expose data access area on disk
Data access area
Hard plastic jacket
Label

Write/protect notch

Hub

(4) index hole. To store and retrieve data from a disk, you must place it into a **disk drive** (Figure 4.17), which contains special mechanical components for storing and retrieving data.

The **hub** of the floppy disk is the round opening in the center. When the disk is placed into the disk drive, the hub fits over a mount, or spindle, in the drive. If you are using an IBM PC, before you can access any data on the diskette, you must close the **disk drive gate,** or door. (Some personal computers, like the Macintosh, do not have drive doors.) The act of closing the disk drive gate moves a lever over the drive and clamps the disk over the spindle of the drive mechanism (Figure 4.17).

When data is stored or retrieved, the disk spins inside its jacket, and the read/write heads are clamped on the surface in the **data access area** of the disk (the exposed part of the disk). Most disk drives are equipped with two read/write heads so that the top and bottom surfaces of the disk can be accessed simultaneously. The read/write heads are moved back and forth over the data access area in small increments to retrieve or record data as needed. Just inside the disk drive unit, a small mechanism checks to determine if the disk's **write/protect notch** is covered. If the notch is covered with tape, a switch is activated that prevents the read/write head from being able to touch the surface of the disk, which means no data can be recorded. Covering the write/protect notch prevents accidental erasure or over-writing of data. The **index hole** in the jacket is positioned over a photoelectric sensing mechanism. As the disk spins in the jacket (when data is being recorded or

FIGURE 4.17
Take it for a drive. This cutaway illustration shows the main parts of a disk drive.

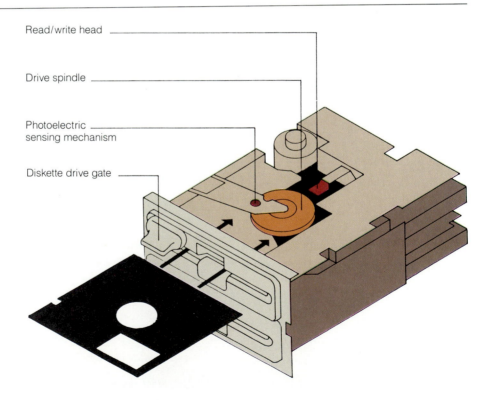

Read/write head

Drive spindle

Photoelectric
sensing mechanism

Diskette drive gate

retrieved), the hole (or holes—some disks have more than one) in the disk passes under the index hole in the jacket and a switch is activated. The activation of the switch each time the disk revolves is used as the basis for timing. The timing activity is critical because this is how the mechanism determines which portion of the disk is over or under the read/write heads. The disk spins at a fixed speed of about 300 revolutions per minute (RPM).

FLOPPY DISK SIZES AND SHAPES   The initial floppy disk introduced by IBM was 8 inches in diameter. Although no longer frequently used, this size and the format in which the data was recorded was the standard for many years. A few of the larger microcomputer systems and dedicated systems still use the 8-inch-diameter disks; in most cases the 8-inch size is selected because the format in which data is stored is relatively standard and can be used for data transfer to a larger computer system.

The use of 5 1/4-inch floppy disks by IBM in their personal computer system in 1981 led to the de facto adoption of this size as the microcomputer industry standard. However, since the Apple Macintosh introduced the 3 1/2-inch disk and disk drive in 1984 and IBM switched to this size in 1987 in its new PS/2 microcomputer systems, the standard has been changing. Although they are smaller in size, the 3 1/2-inch disks are capable of storing more data than 5 1/4-inch diskettes, and they are also less susceptible to damage because they are covered by a hard plastic jacket rather than a paper jacket. (The care of floppy disks is discussed later in the chapter.)

FLOPPY DISK STORAGE CAPACITY   The byte is the unit of measure used most often to determine the capacity of a storage device used with any type of computer. Storage capacities are usually measured in thousands of bytes (Table 4.1). In computer terminology, 1000 bytes is referred to as 1 **kilobyte (K).** (Technically, 1 K equals 1024 bytes.) 1000 K, or a million bytes, is referred to as 1 **megabyte (MB).** One billion bytes is called a **gigabyte (GB),** and a **terabyte (TB)** is one trillion bytes. The capacity of disks varies dramatically. Some disks hold as little as 90 K characters, and others as much as 1.44 MB, which is the equivalent of about a 500-page textbook.

The capacity of a disk does not necessarily depend only on its size. A number of factors affect how much data can be stored on a disk, including (1) whether the

TABLE 4.1   Take a Byte

bit	a binary digit; 0 or 1
byte	8 bits, or 1 character
kilobyte (K)	1000 bytes
megabyte (MB)	1,000,000 bytes
gigabyte (GB)	1,000,000,000 bytes
terabyte (TB)	1,000,000,000,000 bytes

disk stores data on only one side (single-sided disk) or both sides (double-sided disk), (2) whether the disk drive is equipped with read/write heads for both the top and the bottom surfaces of the disk, (3) what the data recording density is (the number of bits that can be stored per inch), and (4) what the track density is (the number of tracks per inch—tracks being circular bands on the disk similar to grooves on a phonograph record—in which data is recorded).

The first floppy disks introduced were **single-sided.** But as the need to store more data became a significant concern in the business community, technology produced the **double-sided** disk, which is capable of storing twice the amount of data as a comparable single-sided disk. To take advantage of a double-sided disk, however, you must have a computer with a **double-sided disk drive.** Double-sided disk drives are equipped with read/write heads for both the top and bottom surfaces of a disk. This allows data to be read from or written to both surfaces simultaneously. (The heads move together on the same mechanism so that they are positioned over corresponding locations on the surfaces of the disk.)

Disk capacity also depends on the recording density capabilities of the disk drive. **Recording density** refers to the number of bits per inch (bpi) of data that can be written onto the surface of the disk. Disks and drives are typically rated as having one of three recording densities: (1) **single-density,** (2) **double-density,** or (3) **quad-density.** The specifications for the exact number of bits per inch for each recording density vary from one manufacturer to another. The disk manufacturers use the

FIGURE 4.18
Staying on track. Tracks are concentric circles on disks on which data is recorded. The tracks are separated by small gaps.

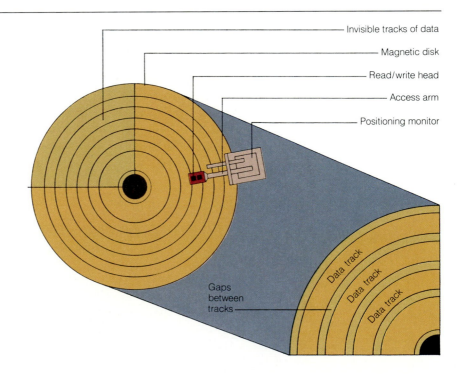

Invisible tracks of data

Magnetic disk

Read/write head

Access arm

Positioning monitor

Gaps between tracks

Data track
Data track
Data track

recording density designation as a measure of the maximum bpi their disks can reliably be expected to store.

A double-sided, double-density 5 1/4-inch disk has a storage capacity of about 362 K; a double-sided, quad-density disk has a capacity of approximately 1250 K. In 1986 Kodak introduced a new floppy disk drive unit with a storage capacity of about 5000 K. The floppy disks in the new IBM PS/2 series of microcomputers hold from 720 K to 1.44 MB. As technology advances, even more data will be stored in a smaller amount of space.

The final factor affecting disk capacity is the track density. As pictured in Figure 4.18, data is recorded on disks in circular bands referred to as **tracks.** The read/write heads are designed to move in small increments across the data access area of the disk to find the appropriate track. The number of tracks that can be used depends on how small an increment the heads can be moved mechanically and the precision with which the heads have been manufactured. The more mechanically precise the read/write head mechanism is, the thinner the track that data can be stored on and retrieved from. The two most common **track densities** in use today are 48 tracks per inch (tpi) and 96 tpi. The recording surface of a 5 1/4-inch disk is slightly less than 1 inch; therefore, the usable tracks per inch are 40 or 80 in most cases.

SECTORS   Typically a disk is divided up into eight or nine **sectors,** or pie-shaped "wedges" used for storage reference purposes (Figure 4.19). The point at which a sector intersects a track is used to reference the data location; the track number indicates where to position the read/write head, and the sector number indicates when to activate the read/write head as the disk spins. When data is read from or written onto a diskette, a minimum of one entire sector is involved—partial sectors cannot be used. Disks and drives are identified as being either hard-sectored or soft-

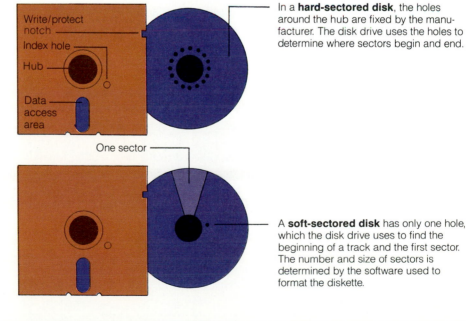

FIGURE 4.19
Hard and soft sectors. In hard-sectored diskettes, the number of sectors is predetermined by the manufacturer. The sectors on a soft-sectored disk are fixed by the user's software.

Write/protect notch
Index hole
Hub
Data access area

One sector

In a **hard-sectored disk**, the holes around the hub are fixed by the manufacturer. The disk drive uses the holes to determine where sectors begin and end.

A **soft-sectored disk** has only one hole, which the disk drive uses to find the beginning of a track and the first sector. The number and size of sectors is determined by the software used to format the diskette.

sectored (Figure 4.19, on the previous page). **Hard-sectored disks** always have the same number and size of sectors, which are fixed by the manufacturer. Today most microcomputer systems use soft-sectored disks. **Soft-sectored disks** are marked magnetically by the user's computer system during a process called *formatting*, which determines the size and number of sectors on the disk. These characteristics vary, depending on the software you are using.

The advantage of the soft-sectored disk is that it can be used in a variety of computers and formatted to assume the recording density of the computer system being used. For example, a double-sided, double-density disk can be formatted on an Apple II to hold about 150 K of data, on a Kaypro II to hold approximately 192 K, or on an ITT XTRA to hold about 362 K. However, the soft-sectored disk should not be formatted to hold more than its maximum recording density will allow.

A hard-sectored disk can be used only on the computer system for which it was created. The presence of the hard-sector marks allows data to be retrieved from the disk with less effort than from a double-sided, double-density soft-sectored disk. Hard-sectored disks have been used most often with dedicated computer systems that handle the manipulation and production of text (called *word processing*).

ACCESS TIME   The responsiveness of your computer depends to a great extent on the time it takes to locate the instructions or data being sought and then load a copy into internal memory. The term **access time** refers to the average speed with which this is done. The access time of your computer's disk drive is determined by measuring the time it takes to perform each of the following activities: (1) positioning the read/write heads over the proper track (the time it takes to do this is called the **seek time**); (2) waiting for the disk to revolve until the correct sector is under or over the read/write heads (this is called **rotational delay** or **latency**); (3) placing the read/write head(s) in contact with the disks, called **setting time;** (4) transferring the data from the disk into the computer's internal memory (at a speed called the *data transfer rate*).

The average access time for floppy disks ranges from 150 milliseconds (150 thousandths of a second) to 300 milliseconds, depending on the operating characteristics of the disk drive mechanism. This may not seem like very long, but access time can be a major performance factor for the following reasons: (1) Large application software packages keep only a portion of the instructions in memory at one time and must retrieve additional instructions periodically to perform a specific task. (2) The processing of large files is done only a few records at a time, so a substantial amount of time can be spent going back and forth to the disk to get the next few records.

Before you proceed to the next section to study hard disks, you need to know how to care for your floppies—abuse means lost data. The accompanying chart refers to 5 1/4-inch disks; however, just because the 3 1/2-inch disks have hard plastic jackets does not mean that they cannot be damaged too!

HARD DISKS: TAKING GIANT BYTES

The introduction of high-capacity **hard disks** for microcomputer systems solved two serious problems related to the limited storage capacity of floppy disks. First, as a

Handle with care! This illustration shows how to avoid disk damage.

1. Do not touch the disk surface. It is easily contaminated, which causes errors.

2. Do not use alcohol, thinners, or freon to clean the disk.

3. Do not use near magnetic field, including that of a telephone. Data can be lost if exposed.

4. Do not bend or fold the disk.

5. Do not place heavy objects on the disk.

6. Do not use rubber bands or paper clips on the disk.

7. Do not use erasers on the disk.

8. Do not expose the disk to excessive heat or sunlight.

Manufacturer's Label

9. Apply the index label to the right of the manufacturer's label. Do not use labels in layers.

10. Write on the index label with felt tip pen only, not pencil or ball-point pen.

Disk drive

11. Insert carefully, by grasping upper edge of disk and placing it into the disk drive.

12. Keep disk in its protective envelope when not in use.

business begins to use microcomputers extensively, the amount of software acquired and data collected tends to grow substantially. As a result, the number of floppy disks to be handled increases dramatically. It is not uncommon for one person to have a library of 100 floppies or more. Second, the largest file that can be worked with is limited to the capacity of the storage medium. So, if the capacity of a floppy disk is 360 K, no files larger than that can be stored. Hard disks can store much larger files; for example, it is no longer impractical to set up an inventory system on a microcomputer that calls for working with a 45,000-item inventory master file.

In some hard disk systems, data is stored in the same way as it is on floppy disks. A series of tracks are divided into sectors when the disk is formatted. As their name suggests, hard disks are made out of a rigid substance that is capable of storing a greater amount of data than the soft material used for floppy disks. Hard disk drives for microcomputers (Figure 4.20) can be *internal* (built into the computer cabinet and nonremovable) or *external* (outside the computer cabinet and connected to it by a short cable).

The capacity of floppy disks in wide use today ranges from 362 K to 1.44 MB each. Microcomputer hard disk capacity ranges from 10 MB to 130 MB or higher. Hard disks' larger capacity allows the user to store larger files and larger programs than can be used with floppy disks. Also, the access time of floppy disks is greater than that of hard disks, which means that hard disks can store and retrieve data much faster than a floppy disk unit.

Hard disks have the following characteristics: (1) They are rigid metal platters connected to a central spindle; (2) the entire disk unit (disks and read/write heads) is placed in a permanently sealed container; (3) air that flows through the container is filtered to prevent contamination; and (4) the disks are rotated at very high speed (usually around 3600 RPM; floppy disks rotate at about 300 RPM). These disk drives can have four or more disk platters in a sealed unit. In most of these disk units (which are often called *Winchester disk drives*), the read/write heads never touch the surfaces of the disks. Instead, they are designed to float from .5 to 1.25 millionths of an inch from the disk surface; because of this characteristic, the design is often referred to as a *flying head* design.

Hard disk technology was first introduced by IBM in the early 1970s. Hard disks for microcomputer systems began to appear in the marketplace in 1980. Since then, hard disk units have become increasingly smaller. The first units introduced for microcomputers used 8-inch-diameter disk platters. The most popular units today use 5 1/4-inch disks; the newest disk units are 3 1/2 inches in diameter. The initial 5 1/4-inch disk drives were approximately 3 1/2 inches high, whereas the newer disk drives are just over 1 1/2 inches high; this means that you can put at least twice as much disk capacity in the same space you used before. Two floppy disks and their drives now fit where only one used to fit, and two hard disk units can occupy the space that one did. This type of configuration provides a powerful system in a small work space.

Hard Disk Storage Capacity   The capacity of microcomputer hard disk units varies from 10 MB to 130 MB, depending on the design of the unit. The principal factors affecting capacity are: (1) the number of platters, (2) the recording density, and (3) the track density. As mentioned earlier, the number of platters in a hard disk unit varies from one to four. In most units, data can be recorded on both surfaces. Thus a disk unit with four platters would have eight recording surfaces. The recording density of these disks varies from 6000 to 9500 bits per inch, as compared to between 2700 and 6000 bpi with a floppy disk. The wide variation in recording densities is a result of the different approaches used by vendors to record data on the disk. The track density varies for the same reason. Typical hard disk track densities range from 300 tpi to 1000 tpi, as compared to from 48 to 96 tpi with a floppy disk. The bottom line is that hard disks are much more efficient than floppy disks.

HARD DISK ACCESS TIME   Hard disks typically have much shorter access times and faster data transfer rates than floppy disks. This is because hard disks spin more than ten times faster and access at least twice as much data per track. The read/write heads are positioned in corresponding locations on the disk surfaces. In a hard disk unit with eight disks, the heads can read data from all eight surfaces at the same time. The typical access time for hard disks ranges from 9.5 to 90 milliseconds—much faster than floppy disks. The hard disk data transfer rate is also much faster—as fast as 5 million bits of data per second. The typical data transfer rate for floppy disks is around 250 thousand bits per second. The improvement in performance offered by hard disk units is dramatic and well worth the investment. Hard disks are used widely in business microcomputers today. Chances are good that you'll be using them in your job.

DISK CARTRIDGES

Removable **disk cartridges** are an alternative to hard disk units as a form of secondary storage. The cartridges usually contain one or two platters and are enclosed in a hard

FIGURE 4.20
Hard disk unit. This illustration shows the main components of a hard disk unit. Note that the sealed unit has been opened to enable you to see inside. The read/write head is clearly visible over the surface of the hard disk.

plastic case that is inserted into the disk drive much like a music tape cassette. The capacity of the most widely used cartridges ranges from 5 to 10 MB, somewhat lower than hard disk units but still substantially superior to floppy disks. Disk cartridges are typically used (1) as a means of backing up large-capacity hard disk units, perhaps about once a week, and (2) as secondary storage devices on their own, with separate cartridges for each major application like payroll and inventory. Cartridges come in 5 1/4- and 3 1/2-inch sizes. Figure 4.21 shows a cartridge disk unit that can be used in a personal computer system.

CARTRIDGE-TAPE DRIVES

As high-capacity hard disk units increased in popularity, the problem of making backup copies of disk contents became a significant concern. (Backup copies of *all* stored data files should be made to ensure that you don't lose your data if the original storage medium is damaged or destroyed.) It takes approximately 30 floppy disks to back up the contents of one 10-MB hard disk. Imagine how many floppy disks would have to be used to back up a 144-MB hard disk!

This concern prompted the development and refinement of **cartridge-tape drive** technology to back up high-capacity hard disks. The most popular tape cartridges use 1/4-inch tape in reels up to 1000 feet long to record data using the **streaming tape method.** In this method, the data is written onto the tape in one

FIGURE 4.21
Disk cartridge unit. This Tandon PAC 286, which is compatible with the IBM PC AT, has two receptacles for Personal Data Pac 30-MB removable hard disk drives.

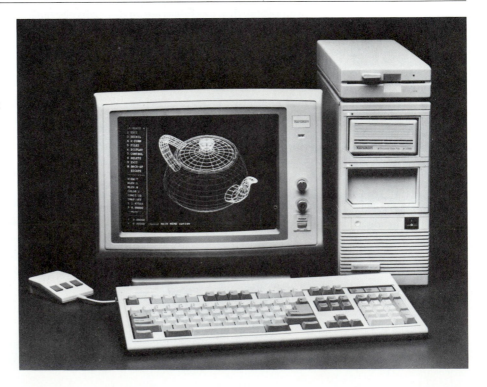

continuous stream. There is no starting or stopping, no gaps between blocks (or records) of data being recorded. Tape cartridges have a capacity (per cartridge) ranging from 10 MB to 60 MB. Their recording density ranges from 1600 to 10,000 bpi, and their data transfer rate ranges from 11 K to 720 K per second.

Cartridge-tape drive units (Figure 4.22) are available in two basic configurations: stand-alone units and integrated units. The stand-alone units are designed to be connected to a system that already has a hard disk. These units have their own power supplies and can "stand" on their own. Integrated units come with a hard disk and a cartridge-tape unit. These units are ideal for users who originally purchased a microcomputer with two floppy disk drives and no hard disk drives. There would be no room for a hard disk or a cartridge unless you took something out—but you can solve the problem by hooking up an integrated cartridge-tape unit.

FIGURE 4.22
Cartridge-tape units. The Irwin 400 series of external tape subsystems can be used to back up many types of microcomputers.

DIRECT ACCESS STORAGE DEVICES FOR MINIS AND MAINFRAMES

The data storage requirements for large computer systems are enormous compared to the needs of microcomputer-based applications. The access time and the data transfer rate have to be much faster, and the capacity of the disk storage devices must be considerably larger. Early storage devices used with minicomputers and mainframes were limited in storage capacity and were costly. However, modern technology has overcome these problems. Today, three distinct types of direct access storage devices are used with large computers: (1) removable disks, (2) fixed disks, and (3) disk cartridges.

REMOVABLE DISKS

In large computer systems, hard disks are sometimes contained in packs that are removable (Figure 4.23), meaning that they can be removed from the computer and replaced at will. **Disk packs** typically hold 6 to 12 platters that are usually 14 inches in diameter.

The capacity of removable disk packs varies by manufacturer and ranges from 150 to 250 MB. A minicomputer system with four disk drives can have 1 billion characters of data on line—that is, available—at one time for direct access. The total storage capacity could be dramatically increased by having a dozen or so extra disk packs to be interchanged with the packs in the disk drives.

Individual disk packs are often used for specific purposes. The computer operator simply mounts on the computer the disk pack containing the files for a particular application when they are needed for processing. Despite their ease of use and great storage capacity, removable disk packs have a few limitations. The fact that disk packs are removable and are therefore frequently handled can lead to accidental damage to disk surfaces and possible contamination by dust and other foreign matter. In addition, the mechanics of a removable disk drive mechanism have proven limiting in terms of reliability and their adverse effects on storage capacity. Because they are not used extensively today, you may not have to handle removable disk packs.

FIXED DISKS

The limitations of removable disk technology led to substantial research to improve **fixed disks**—disks that cannot be removed from the disk drive. For technical reasons, the storage capacity of disk packs (in terms of recording density and track density) could not be significantly improved; also needed to improve capacity was a contamination-free environment like that of hard disks.

The first of the fixed disk units used widely had a storage capacity of 70 MB, an average access time of about 35 milliseconds, and a data transfer rate of just under 1 million bytes per second. The capacity of fixed disk units has been improved using thin-film technology to the point where the IBM 3380 direct access storage unit (with two spindles) has a capacity of 1260 MB per spindle, an average access time of less than 24 milliseconds, and a data transfer rate of 3 million bytes per second. A large computer system with 20 IBM 3380s would have an on-line direct access storage capacity of approximately 45 billion bytes (45 gigabytes). This would be the equivalent of 4500 10-MB microcomputer systems!

DISK CARTRIDGES

The first disk cartridges for minicomputers were introduced to meet the growing demand for direct access storage capacity in small businesses. The cartridges usually have one or two 14-inch disk platters sealed in a hard plastic case and typically have a capacity of 2 to 20 MB. The cases have a handle for easy removal and handling. These disk cartridges (large in comparison to those used with microcomputers) are not used extensively today; instead, newer disk-cartridge technology is used, both with large computer systems and with microcomputer systems.

FIGURE 4.23
Pack it in. Hard disks are sometimes contained in removable packs.

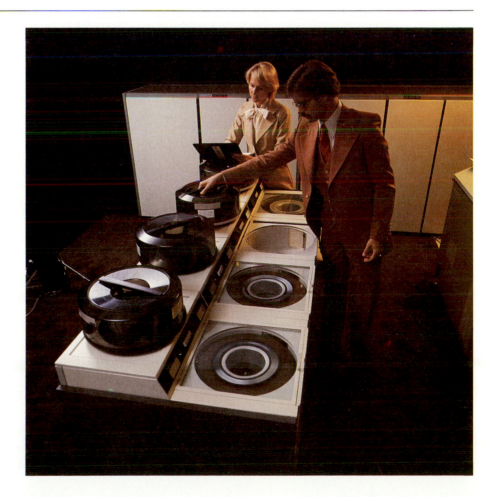

MASS STORAGE SYSTEMS

In spite of all the improvements that have been made in magnetic disk storage technology, there still never seems to be enough capacity. Major banks, for example, each do about 600 terabytes worth of check-related processing a year. One terabyte is equivalent to the storage capacity of 1250 reels of high-density magnetic tape. Can you imagine trying to manage 750,000 reels of tape in your tape library?

The ability to use multiple reels of tape and removable disk packs does extend an organization's ability to store a large amount of data. However, as you learned earlier, magnetic tape does not support direct access storage. And removable disk packs provide some flexibility, but the time required to remove a disk pack, retrieve the replacement, mount the replacement, and return the pack to the library just takes up too much time.

Mass storage systems (Figure 4.24) were developed to remedy this situation: These systems are composed of banks of as many as 2000 data cartridges. Each cartridge contains a strip of magnetic tape about 3 inches wide and from 150 to 770 inches long. Each bank of cartridges is serviced by a mechanical unit that retrieves the cartridges individually and positions them under a special read/write head for data transfer. IBM and Control Data Corporation both offer mass storage systems similar in capacity and capabilities. The IBM system is designed so that the data is transferred from the cartridge to a high-speed fixed disk. The Control Data System is designed (with a cartridge capacity of 8 MB) so that the contents of the entire cartridge can be loaded directly into internal memory, which provides much faster access to the data.

FIGURE 4.24
UNISYS Corporation
system for mass storage.

NEW STORAGE TECHNOLOGIES

The appetite for secondary storage capacity has proven almost impossible to satisfy. The days of the personal computer with only two 360-K floppy disks are gone. By the end of 1987, a typical personal computer system was equipped with a minimum of 40 MB of disk storage capacity. Current mass storage technologies have helped assuage the hunger to some extent; however, the general feeling is that there will never be enough storage capacity. To keep pace with the need, research and development have concentrated on two areas: (1) improving magnetic disk storage technology, including hard cards, and (2) refining optical disk storage technology.

CAN MAGNETIC DISK STORAGE TECHNOLOGY BE IMPROVED?

Magnetic disk storage technology has advanced very far during the past 25 years. The latest advancements include: (1) thin-film read/write heads, (2) thin-film disks, (3) vertical recording, and (4) hard cards.

THIN-FILM READ/WRITE HEADS AND DISKS   Improvements in the manufacturing of read/write heads have made them not only much smaller, but also capable of producing much higher data recording and track densities. To further improve the technology, experiments in coating the disk surfaces with a substance other than ferric oxide were conducted. It was found that, if the surface of the disk was plated with a thin film of a special metallic substance, very small magnetic spots could be reliably recorded. This technology holds great promise and is expected to be widely available by 1990.

VERTICAL RECORDING   Another promising technology involves changing the way the data is magnetically recorded on the disk. Consider a magnetic spot recorded on a disk as a small bar magnet. One end of the bar acts as a north pole, and the other end acts as a south pole. In the past, magnetic spots have been recorded in a manner equivalent to laying the bar magnet down on the disk surface horizontally. In **vertical recording** the spot is standing on end, with the north pole on top. It has been predicted that this technology, which saves space on the recording surface, could produce recording densities of 100 MB per square inch by the end of the decade.

HARD CARD   Until recently, adding a hard disk to your microcomputer system meant either losing one of your internal floppy disk drives or taking up desk space with an external hard disk drive. The **hard card,** a new type of storage device that is plugged into one of the microcomputer's expansion slots, can solve this problem for most users (Figure 4.25). (Some computers, like the original Macintosh, do not have expansion slots.) To insert a hard card into an expansion slot, one takes the cover off the computer cabinet (using a screwdriver) and pushes the card, which contains a hard disk, into an empty slot—almost like a plug. Hard cards can store approximately 20 MB of data.

OPTICAL STORAGE   The most promising new secondary storage technology, **optical storage,** involves the use of a high-power laser beam to burn microscopic spots in a disk's surface coating (Figure 4.26). Data is represented by the presence (binary 1) and the absence (binary 0) of holes in the storage locations. A much lower power laser beam is used to retrieve the data. The patterns of spots detected by the laser (during a read operation) are converted into electrical signals.

The capacity of optical disk systems is enormous. The recording density is over 15,000 bits per inch, and the track density is 15,000 tracks per inch. The track density is phenomenal when compared with the 400-track-per-inch density of most magnetic disk storage devices. This technology promises a storage capacity in excess of 100 gigabytes for a single 12-inch disk. This large storage capacity is especially useful in situations where images must be stored; images take up much more storage space than alphanumeric or numeric data.

A number of microcomputer storage devices have already been introduced that use a 5 1/2-inch optical disk—the same size as a compact disk for a stereo system. The cost of optical media has proven to be about 1/10 that of magnetic tape and 1/100 that of magnetic disk. Their average access time and data transfer rates are equally faster—or better. In addition, unlike on magnetic storage media, the data

FIGURE 4.25
Hard card. Hardcard™ hard disk expansion cards provide personal computer users with an easy way to upgrade the storage capacity and performance of their equipment.

recorded on optical media is not damaged by stray magnetic fields and surface problems like fingerprints, dust, scratches, and so on.

However, optical disks present one big problem: Once the data has been recorded, it cannot be erased (once a hole has been burned into the surface coating, it cannot be removed). This limits the current use of the disks to applications where large amounts of nonchanging data are written once and read as often as needed—such as archives, medical records, historical data. And prerecorded optical disks can be purchased that function as input devices; for example, a research firm can buy optical disks that contain whole encyclopedias stored on them for input when necessary.

Massive efforts are underway to improve this technology to the point where data can be recorded without making a permanent hole in the surface of the disk. When these efforts prove successful, we will see a whole new generation of direct access storage devices, including optical storage cards and tape. These devices will make almost limitless storage capacity available to us.

FIGURE 4.26
What you see is what you get. This optical disk can store much more data than traditional storage media. It is also faster and cheaper; however, for now you cannot erase or change the data you write on optical storage media.

ONWARD:
PROCESSING THE INGREDIENTS

Now that you know several ways to hold on to your data after you've input it, you need to find out what to do to it—what you *can* do to it. The third part of the computer-based information system is the processing phase, the topic of the next chapter.

SUMMARY

Storage and storage needs must be properly evaluated if a business is to run smoothly. The requirements for storage capacity, speed of data retrieval, size, cost, complexity of equipment, and so on vary from business to business.

Basically there are two types of storage: primary storage, also called *internal memory* or *memory*, where data is volatile, and secondary storage (also called *auxiliary storage*), where data is nonvolatile. If data is volatile, it is lost when the power to the computer is turned off; nonvolatile data remains intact.

In storage, data is represented using a binary code, a system of combinations of binary digits (bits)—0, meaning "off" (no magnetic spot present), and 1, meaning "on" (magnetic spot present). Two common binary coding schemes are the American Standard Code for Information Interchange (ASCII) and the Extended Binary Coded Decimal Interchange Code (EBCDIC). ASCII is typically used to represent data on microcomputers, and EBCDIC is used on larger computers.

Data is stored in files, which can be understood by means of the data storage hierarchy. A file is a collection of records; a record is a collection of fields, which comprise a collection of bytes. A byte, or a character, is a collection of eight bits. Files can be categorized as follows: (1) transaction file, (2) master file, (3) report file, (4) output file, (5) history file, and (6) backup file.

The three methods used to store and retrieve data in files are (1) sequential, (2) direct, and (3) indexed sequential. In the sequential method, data can be retrieved only in the order in which it is stored. All records must be read to get to the data you want. Direct access avoids that problem by allowing you to go straight to the data you want. Key fields are used by the computer as identifiers to locate the data. The indexed sequential method allows both sequential and direct access through the use of an index set up by the computer according to key fields and locations on the storage media. Your business needs should determine the type of storage and retrieval method you use.

Introduced in the early 1950s, magnetic tape quickly overcame the limitations of punched cards as a storage medium. On magnetic tape, data is stored only in sequential fashion using either the ASCII or EBCDIC coding schemes. Unfortunately, data put on tape can't be reorganized or altered without creating a new tape. Because of this limitation, direct access storage media were developed for microcomputers, including floppy disk(ette)s and hard disks. The direct access storage media used with the larger computers include removable disk packs, fixed disks, and disk cartridges.

Data is stored on disk surfaces in sectors and tracks. The higher the track density (tracks per inch) and the recording density (bits per inch), the more data that can be placed on the disk. Storage capacity is measured in thousands of bytes (kilobyte—K), millions of bytes (megabyte—MB), billions of bytes (gigabyte—GB), and trillions of bytes (terabyte—TB). The disk devices used on larger computers are typically capable of storing a greater amount of data in a smaller amount of space than those used for microcomputers. Microcomputer storage technology is rapidly advancing, however, so the difference in storage capacity may not last.

There never seems to be enough storage room. Out of this persistent reality have come two new storage technologies. The first has to do with improving magnetic storage capacities. The second focuses on storing data optically. The storage capacity and speed of optical disks are tremendous; however, because data is burned on them with a laser beam, it cannot be erased or changed thereafter. Once this difficulty is resolved, this technology will be widely used.

KEY TERMS

access time
American Standard
    Code for Information
    Interchange (ASCII)
backup file
binary code
binary digit (bit)
block
byte
cartridge-tape drive
data access area
data storage hierarchy
direct access storage
    and retrieval
disk cartridge
disk drive
disk drive gate (door)
diskette
disk pack
double-density
double-sided disk drive
drive capstan
Extended Binary Coded
    Decimal Interchange

Code (EBCDIC)
external label
field
file
file protection ring
fixed disk
floppy disk
gigabyte (GB)
hard card
hard disk
hard-sectored disk
history file
hub
indexed sequential ac-
    cess method (ISAM)
index hole
interblock gap (IBG)
internal label
interrecord gap (IRG)
key
key field
kilobyte (K)
logical record
mass storage system

master file
megabyte (MB)
nonvolatile
optical storage
output file
physical record
primary storage
quad-density
read/write head
record
recording density
report file
rotational delay
    (latency)
secondary (auxiliary)
    storage
sector
seek time
sequential storage and
    retrieval
setting time
single-density
single-sided
soft-sectored disk
stop capstan

streaming tape method   track density   volatile
terabyte (TB)   transaction file   write/protect notch
track   vertical recording

EXERCISES

MATCHING

Match each of the following terms to the phrase that is the most closely related:

1. _____ primary storage   9. _____ binary code
2. _____ secondary storage   10. _____ transaction file
3. _____ file   11. _____ master file
4. _____ read/write head   12. _____ optical storage
5. _____ tracks   13. _____ logical record
6. _____ file protection ring   14. _____ access time
7. _____ recording density   15. _____ track density
8. _____ volatile

   a. This term describes primary storage, because when the computer is turned off, all the data and instructions are lost.
   b. Number of tracks per inch on a disk.
   c. Many people think this type of storage is similar in concept to a filing cabinet.
   d. A group of related records.
   e. Another name for internal memory.
   f. This type of file contains software instructions.
   g. This type of file contains data that is waiting to be processed.
   h. A mechanism that reads magnetic spots on a storage medium and converts them into electrical pulses and that also records magnetic spots on the storage medium.
   i. A scheme for encoding data using a series of binary digits.
   j. This storage technology involves the use of a laser beam to burn microscopic spots into a disk's surface coating.
   k. The amount of time it takes to locate the instructions or data being sought and then load a copy into internal memory.
   l. The use of this device prevents tapes from being accidentally overwritten.
   m. Many people think of these as similar in concept to the circular grooves on a phonograph record in which data is stored.
   n. This type of record is defined by the user according to the logic of the program being used.
   o. Number of bits that can be stored per inch.
   p. Pie-shaped "wedges" used for magnetic storage reference purposes.
   q. This type of file contains data stored in computer-usable form for lengthy periods of time that is used for retrieval and updating.

MULTIPLE CHOICE

1. Which of the following statements about primary and secondary storage is true?
   a. Most primary storage is volatile.
   b. Secondary storage is designed to retain data, information, and software instructions.
   c. Primary storage contains data for immediate processing.
   d. Secondary storage is nonvolatile.
   e. all of the above

2. Which of the following accurately describes how data is represented when using microcomputers and minicomputers?
   a. The ASCII coding scheme, which uses 7 bits to represent data, is used to represent up to 256 different characters.
   b. The EBCDIC coding scheme, which uses 8 bits to represent data, is used to represent up to 256 different characters.
   c. The ASCII coding scheme, which uses 7 bits to represent data, is used to represent up to 128 different characters.
   d. The EBCDIC coding scheme, which uses 7 bits to represent data, is used to represent up to 128 different characters.
   e. none of the above

3. With the data storage hierarchy in mind, which of the following is the least true?
   a. Fields are composed of a number of characters.
   b. Records are composed of a number of fields.
   c. Files are composed of a number of records.
   d. Fields are composed of a number of bytes.
   e. none of the above

4. Which of the following data file types would you have to use if your computer applications have been designed to produce data to be used by another program or application?
   a. history file
   b. report file
   c. master file
   d. output file
   e. none of the above

5. Which of the following storage and retrieval methods would be well suited to your processing requirements if you only need to retrieve records one at a time and there is no fixed pattern to the requests for data and records?
   a. sequential
   b. direct
   c. indexed sequential
   d. indexed direct
   e. none of the above

6. Which of the following factors should you ignore when determining the storage capacity of a hard disk?
   a. number of platters

    b. recording density

    c. track density

    d. height of the hard disk drive

    e. none of the above

7. Which of the following isn't a characteristic of a Winchester hard disk?

    a. The disk is removable.

    b. The unit consists of one or more rigid metal platters connected to a central spindle.

    c. The entire disk unit is placed in a permanently sealed container.

    d. Air is filtered through the container to prevent contamination.

    e. The disks are rotated at very high speed.

8. Which of the following is the best way of measuring the storage capacity of a floppy disk?

    a. disk drive mechanism

    b. internal memory capacity

    c. number of floppy disks in the computer

    d. recording and track density

    e. all of the above

9. Which of the following storage technologies is the least likely to be used with mini and mainframe computers?

    a. fixed disks

    b. floppy disks

    c. removable disks

    d. disk cartridges

    e. none of the above

10. Which of the following is characteristic of a floppy disk?

    a. hub

    b. data access area

    c. write/protect notch

    d. index hole

    e. all of the above

SHORT ANSWER

1. Why does transferring data between a microcomputer and a mainframe computer require special hardware and software?

2. You currently use a filing cabinet containing folders to store customer-related data. When a customer calls to ask about the status of his or her account, the process of locating the correct file and information is cumbersome. If you were to computerize your filing cabinet, which storage and retrieval method(s) would work the best for you? Why?

3. You own a microcomputer. If given the choice, why would you want to store your data on a hard disk rather than a floppy disk?

4. What new technologies are in development that will dramatically increase storage capacity?

5. How is data stored and retrieved from a floppy disk?

6. Describe what a file is by describing the data storage hierarchy.

7. Respond to the following: "Access time has no relationship to your computer's responsiveness." Why?

8. What are the advantages and disadvantages of the optical storage technology?

9. Why do you think the storage requirements of large computer systems (minis, mainframes) are so much greater than those of smaller computer systems (microcomputers)?

10. Why is it important for you to understand the concept of storage as it relates to computers?

PROJECTS

1. What storage hardware is currently being used in your school? What are the advantages and disadvantages of this technology? Would you recommend an alternate storage technology? Why? Why not? Is the storage technology being used similar to that being used by other schools in the area?

2. Research one of the newer storage technologies. How is this technology being applied now? How do you think it will be applied in the future?

3. Visit a local computer store to see some of the storage media and devices described in this chapter. What kinds of devices are being sold most often? What kinds of devices don't you see that were described in this chapter? Why don't you see them in this store?

PROCESSING HARDWARE

5

When you look at a computer, you can see and even touch most of the input, output, and storage equipment—the keyboard or the mouse, the video display screen, the printer, the disk drive doors or the tape cartridge. But you cannot actually *see* the equipment that does the processing—the electronic circuitry inside the cabinet of the computer itself. Although you have no need to puzzle out wiring diagrams and the like, you should have some understanding of processing hardware, because the processing hardware used will affect how much the computer can do for you and how quickly it can do it.

PREVIEW

When you have completed this chapter, you will be able to:

■

Describe why it is important for a user to know about a computer's processing hardware and power

■

Describe the importance of and distinguish between random access memory and the different types of read-only memory

■

Describe the factors that should be considered when evaluating the processing power of a computer

■

The User Perspective

You may never have to look inside a computer—although if a computer technician comes to your office to fix your microcomputer, we recommend that you look over his or her shoulder and ask the technician to identify some of the internal components, just so you can get a general idea of what's going on inside. But why, essentially, do you need to know anything about the processing hardware and activities—any more than you need to know how the engine of a car works? We think there are two reasons:

- Just as some people like to work on their own cars, you may decide it's economical for you to do some work on your microcomputer. For instance, you may find that some new software programs are too sophisticated for your computer—that your computer cannot hold enough data or instructions or process them fast enough—and that you need to add some more internal memory. This may well be something you can do yourself.
- More likely, you will some day need to make a buying decision about a microcomputer, either for yourself or for an organization. You may have to judge whether it's worth buying a machine that takes five hours to accomplish what another machine—perhaps not a microcomputer but a minicomputer or a mainframe—can accomplish in seconds.

Before we look at processing activities, let's start our discussion of hardware components by going to the heart of the matter—the CPU.

The Central Processing Unit

The **central processing unit (CPU)** is the heart of the computer system. Among other things, its configuration determines whether a computer is very fast or—while still being fast, of course—is relatively slow. The CPU is the most complex computer system component, responsible for directing most of the computer system activities based on the instructions provided. As one computer generation has evolved to the next, the size of the CPU has become smaller and smaller, while its speed and capacity have increased tremendously. Indeed, these changes resulted in the microcomputer that is small enough to fit on your desk or your lap. As we mentioned earlier, the CPU circuitry of a microcomputer—called a **microprocessor**—fits on a chip about the size of your thumbnail, or smaller.

The CPU is composed of three distinct parts: (1) the control unit, (2) the arithmetic/logic unit, and (3) the processing registers (locations in the CPU where data and instructions are accepted, temporarily stored, and transferred very quickly). These three parts of the CPU are usually connected by an electronic component referred to as a **bus,** which acts as an electronic highway between them (Figure 5.1). Different kinds of buses will be discussed later.

CONTROL UNIT

The **control unit,** a maze of complex electronic circuitry, is responsible for directing and coordinating most of the computer system activities. It does not execute instructions itself; it tells other parts of the computer system what to do.

Just as a car is useless without gas, a computer is not much good without software instructions. When we use a software program, we are working with high-level (English-language-like) instructions that are to be carried out by the control unit. These instructions are converted by a language processor into a low-level form of instructions the computer can work with—**machine language,** the only language that the CPU can understand (Figure 5.2). In machine language, data and instructions are represented in binary form, and each type of computer—microcomputer, minicomputer, mainframe—responds to a unique version. Once the instructions have been converted into this form, they can be retrieved from internal memory and interpreted by the control unit (sometimes referred to as *decoding*). According to each specific instruction, the control unit issues the necessary signals to other computer system components as needed to satisfy the processing requirements. This could involve, for example, directing that data be retrieved from a disk storage device, "telling" the printer to print the letter you just wrote, or simply directing the arithmetic/logic unit to add two numbers.

ARITHMETIC/LOGIC UNIT (ALU)

Without the **arithmetic/logic unit,** Mary would not be able to do those financial forecasts for Sporting Life on the computer, and you would not be able to use

FIGURE 5.1
Travel by bus. Buses, a kind of electronic transportation system, connect the main components of the central processing unit.

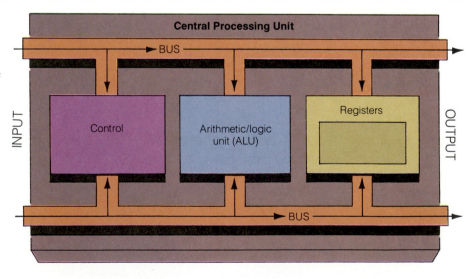

Ticketron to find out if you and your friends can get five seats at the Lemon Bowl. In fact, without the ALU, computers would not be able to do most of the tasks that we find useful. The ALU performs all the arithmetic and logical (comparison) functions—that is, it adds, subtracts, multiplies, divides, and does comparisons. These comparisons, which are basically "less than," "greater than," or "equal to," can be combined into several common expressions, such as "greater than or equal to." The objective of most instructions that use comparisons is to determine which instructions should be executed next.

A computer that performs arithmetic operations at a very high speed has usually been designed to perform the basic addition and subtraction operations in **parallel;** that is, each calculation is processed simultaneously in a single operation, rather than on one digit at a time, which is called **serial addition.** The computer handles serial addition much like we do: The number of times addition is performed directly relates to the number of digits to be added. In parallel addition, the time needed to perform an addition operation does not depend on the number of digits being added.

The ALUs in some microprocessors are not very sophisticated; they process mathematics serially. As a result, a personal computer system can get bogged down doing a substantial amount of arithmetic data manipulation. This could happen, for example, when you try to process Sporting Life's very large annual financial report. To help ease this computational burden, some major microprocessor manufacturers have designed special mathematical **coprocessor chips** to help speed up processing. When such a chip (Figure 5.3) is put on a board in the microcomputer, it allows the microcomputer to do parallel addition. Numeric coprocessors are said to improve the speed with which some mathematical operations can be performed by a factor of between 10 and 100—a significant improvement and a worthwhile addition to any microcomputer system that will be used to perform a large number of mathematical operations.

FIGURE 5.2
Machine language. This illustration shows the Apple and the IBM machine language instructions for adding two numbers. IBM computers are incompatible with Apple computers because they use different versions of machine language instructions. For a software program used on one computer to be used on another, both computers must use the same version.

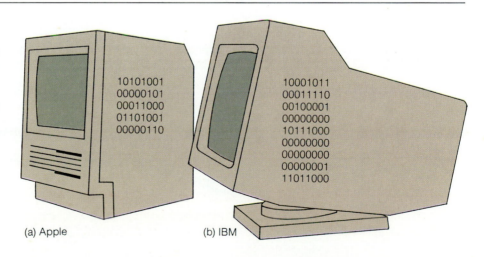

10101001
00000101
00011000
01101001
00000110

10001011
00011110
00100001
00000000
10111000
00000000
00000000
00000001
11011000

(a) Apple

(b) IBM

REGISTERS

A **register** is a special temporary storage location within the CPU. Registers very quickly accept, store, and transfer data and instructions that are being used immediately (internal memory holds data that will be used shortly; secondary storage holds data that will be used later). The number and types of registers in a CPU vary according to the CPU's design. An instruction that is to be executed must be retrieved from internal memory and placed into a register. The control unit interprets the instruction and then fetches the necessary data required to perform the requested operation. The data is then placed into special registers that can be accessed by the ALU.

The size (capacity) and number of registers can dramatically affect the processing power of a computer system. In general, the "larger" the register (the more bits it can carry at once), the greater the processing power. Some personal computers have general-purpose registers that hold only 8 bits; others hold 16 bits; newer microcomputers have 32-bit registers. The difference in processing power due to difference in register size can be illustrated by the difference between trying to put out a fire with a small drinking glass and with a 5-gallon bucket.

BUS

The term **bus** refers to an electrical pathway through which bits are transmitted between the various computer components in a computer system. Depending on the design of a system, as many as three different types of buses may be present: data bus, address bus, and control bus.

FIGURE 5.3
Numeric coprocessor. This type of chip—shown here as part of a Quadram accelerator board—can be added to your personal computer to increase its ability to manage large-scale arithmetic operations efficiently.

The **data bus,** which carries data between the components of the computer system, is the most important of the three types of buses. The wider the data bus, the more data it can carry at one time, and thus the greater the processing speed of the computer. The data bus in the Intel 8088 processor is 8 bits wide, meaning that it can carry 8 bits—or one character—at a time. In contrast, the data buses in the Motorola 68020 processor (in the new Macintosh II microcomputer) and the Intel 80386 processor (in the new IBM PS/2 Model 80 microcomputer) are 32 bits wide—they can move four times more data through their data buses than the Intel bus can. Table 5.1 shows the data bus capacity (called *dataword length*) of several microprocessor chips.

The **address bus,** if present in the design of the system, is used to access internal memory storage locations that contain data needed by instructions. When data and instructions reside in the same portion of internal memory, they generally share the data bus for movement into the CPU.

The **control bus** carries the control signals generated by the control unit to the appropriate computer system components.

TABLE 5.1 Dataword Length Comparison of Several Microprocessors Used Today

Company	Micro-processor	Word Size (bits)	Address Bus (bits)	Data Bus (bits)	Max RAM	Clock Speed (MHz)	Micros Using This Chip
Zilog	Z-80A	8	8	8	64 K	4	Radio Shack Personal Desktop Sanyo Business Systems MBC/250 Epson QX-10
Mostek	6502	8	8	8	64 K	4	Apple IIe Atari 800 Commodore 64
Intel	8088	16	20	8	1 MB	8	IBM PC and XT Compaq Portable HP 150 touch screen
Intel	8086	16	20	16	1 MB	8	Some IBM compatibles
Motorola	68000	32	24	16	16 MB	12.5	Radio Shack TRS-80 Model 16B Corvus Concept Apple Macintosh
Intel	80286	16	24	16	16 MB	8–12	IBM AT ITT XTRA 286
Motorola	68020	32	32	32	4 GB	12.5–32	Macintosh II
Intel	80386	32	32	32	4 GB	16–32	Compaq 380 IBM PS/2 Model 80

FIGURE 5.4
Chip off the new block. Chips with minute circuitry (a)(b) are manufactured in groups on wafers (c), which are sliced from blocks of silicon. This photo (d) shows the Advanced Micro Devices laboratory, where chips are manufactured.

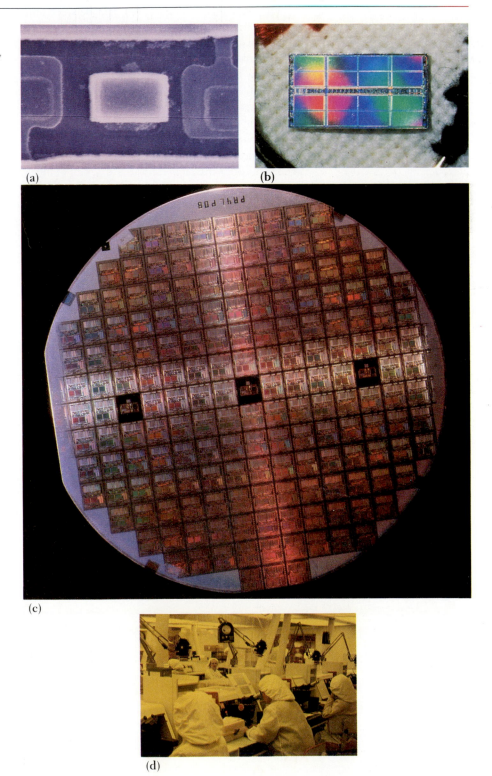

(a)

(b)

(c)

(d)

THE MICROPROCESSOR: HOW IS IT MADE?

Having the CPU available on a tiny chip revolutionized the computer industry and created the business market for microcomputers—basically providing the reason why you are reading this book now. How is this chip—the microprocessor—made?

The microprocessor contains at least a control unit and an ALU. Some of the more sophisticated microprocessor chips also include different types of memory (to be discussed shortly) and circuitry necessary to support specialized hardware devices. The microprocessor chips in early microcomputer systems weren't nearly as powerful as the CPUs in large computers, but with each technological advance—which seems to occur almost every day—microprocessors are becoming more and more powerful. Some of today's microcomputers, equipped with powerful microprocessor chips, rival the processing power found in many of today's minicomputers.

As we mentioned earlier, a large dataword length—that is, the number of bits a data bus can carry at once—translates directly into high processing speed. An 8-bit computer can do anything a 32-bit computer can, just slower. And an 8-bit microprocessor costs a lot less than a 32-bit microprocessor, because its circuitry is much less sophisticated.

A microprocessor's circuitry may be as small as a 1/4″ square. To develop such complicated circuitry in such a small package requires a combination of technologies. Hundreds of microprocessors can be produced on a single disk—called a *wafer*—sliced from an ingot of silicon, a nonmetallic element that, after oxygen, is the most common in the earth's crust. A wafer is about 4/1000 of an inch thick; an ingot is about 2 feet long and 6 inches in diameter (Figure 5.4). Chips are made to do different things in addition to being a CPU—for example, to expand a computer's ability to handle numeric computation (the numeric coprocessors mentioned previously) and to expand a computer's memory.

INSTRUCTION EXECUTION CYCLE

To execute an instruction, the control unit of the CPU retrieves it from internal memory and places it into a register. The typical operations that take place in the processing of instructions are part of either the instruction cycle or the execution cycle.

The **instruction cycle,** or I-cycle, refers to the retrieval of an instruction from internal memory and its subsequent decoding (the process of alerting the circuits in the CPU to perform the specified operation). The time it takes to go through the instruction cycle is referred to as **I-time.**

The **execution cycle,** or E-cycle, refers to the execution of the instruction and the subsequent storing of the result in a register. The time it takes to go through the execution cycle is referred to as **E-time.** The instruction cycle and the execution cycle together, as they apply to one instruction, are referred to as a **machine cycle** (Figure 5.5). The CPU has an internal **clock** that synchronizes all operations in the cycle.

INTERNAL MEMORY

CPUs, ALUs, registers, buses, instructions, input, output, storage . . . what good are they if you have no material to work with? You wouldn't have any if it weren't for **internal memory** (also called *primary storage* and *memory*), the part of the processing hardware that temporarily holds data and instructions needed by the CPU.

HISTORY OF INTERNAL MEMORY

For many years internal memory was one of the most expensive computer components to manufacture. However, technology has revolutionized internal memory components over the past forty or so years: Their size has been drastically reduced, and they have become less expensive as the manufacturing materials have changed from vacuum tubes to magnetic cores to transistors and finally to the chips we know today (Figure 5.6).

The earliest form of internal memory was based on vacuum tubes. Today's technology can put 64 K bytes on a single internal memory chip; the equivalent internal memory capacity would have required a shelf of vacuum tubes more than a mile long. And tubes were not reliable: Their power requirements were high, they generated heat, they failed frequently, and they were slow. The transistor, invented in 1947, was a much smaller and more reliable provider of internal memory. It also

FIGURE 5.5
The machine cycle—the instruction cycle and the execution cycle as they apply to one instruction.

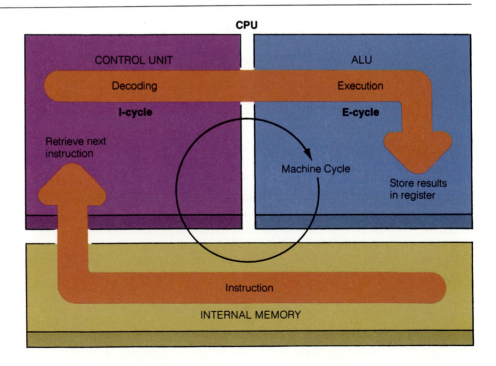

had smaller power requirements and failed less frequently than vacuum tubes. Magnetic cores were smaller still.

However, by the mid-1970s, work had begun on a new type of internal memory technology—semiconductor memory. (A **semiconductor** is a material that conducts electricity poorly but that, when "impurities" are added to it, can be used to form electrical circuits.) The internal memory of almost all computers today is based on this technology, which involves coating a silicon chip with a material that can take on two different states once the circuits have been etched onto the surface: The material either will or will not conduct electricity (binary "on" and "off"). Chips are very small and relatively inexpensive to manufacture, and they do not consume as much power as older forms of internal memory. The use of chips has greatly increased the memory capacity of computers. In 1979 a microcomputer with 64 K of internal memory was considered to be a satisfactory system. Today a microcomputer system with less than 640 K of internal memory may be considered underpowered.

THE FUNCTION OF INTERNAL MEMORY

The main function of internal memory is to act as a buffer between the central processing unit (CPU) and the rest of the computer system components. It functions as a sort of desktop on which you place the things with which you are about to begin to work. There are two basic types of internal memory chips—read-only memory

FIGURE 5.6
From tubes to chips. The materials used to manufacture internal memory and the size of the components have changed dramatically over the past forty years.

(ROM) and random access memory (RAM). The main difference between them is that the data and programs in ROM are permanent—usually placed there by the manufacturer—and can only be "read" and not changed, whereas the data and programs in RAM can be both read *and* changed by the user.

Read-Only Memory (ROM)

How does your computer know what to do when you turn it on? How does it know to check out your hardware components (such as the keyboard or the monitor) to see that they have been connected correctly? How does it know what to do with your business software? Instructions to perform such operations, which are critical to the operation of a computer, are stored permanently on **read-only memory (ROM)** chips (Figure 5.7) in a permanently accessible, nonvolatile form. When the power in the computer is turned off, the instructions stored in ROM—permanently recorded there by the chip manufacturer—are not lost.

It is necessary, and also convenient, to have instructions stored in ROM. For example, if you are using a microcomputer with floppy disk drives, the more instructions in ROM, the fewer floppy disks you may have to handle. If you could have *all* the program instructions you'll ever need to use in ROM, you would have everything you need for processing data and information at your fingertips—always.

Unfortunately, until recently, the process of manufacturing ROM chips and recording data on them was more expensive than the process of producing random access memory chips (to be discussed in the next section). As a result, manufacturers tended to record in ROM only those instructions that were crucial to the operation

FIGURE 5.7
Thanks for the memory: ROM chips.

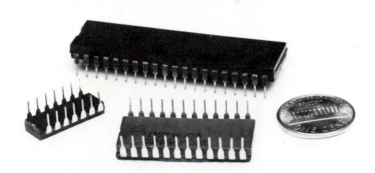

of the computer. In recent years improvements in the manufacturing process of ROM chips have lowered their cost to the point where manufacturers are beginning to include additional software instructions.

PROM, EPROM, EEPROM   In addition to ROM, three additional categories of nonvolatile memory are used in some computer systems—namely PROMs, EPROMs, and EEPROMS. **PROM** stands for **programmable read-only memory.** This type of memory functions in the same way a regular ROM component does with one major exception: The data or program instructions are not prerecorded on the PROM chip when it is manufactured. Instead, users can record their own data or instructions (frequently, the most-used data and instructions), which provides added convenience for the user. The only problem with PROM chips is that, like ROM chips, once data is recorded on them, it can't be changed.

   Erasable programmable read-only memory (EPROM) (Figure 5.8) chips were developed as an improvement over PROM chips. EPROM functions exactly the same as PROM; however, with the help of a special device that uses ultraviolet light, the data or instructions on an EPROM chip can be erased, and new data can be recorded in its place. To change instructions on an EPROM chip, the chip must be taken out of the machine and then put back when changes have been made.

   Electrically erasable programmable read-only memory (EEPROM) (Figure 5.8), the latest addition to the ROM family of chips, avoids the inconvenience of having to take chips out of the computer to change data and instructions. Instead, changes can be made electrically byte by byte under software control. These chips are being used in point-of-sale terminals to record price-related data for products.

FIGURE 5.8
EPROM (left), and
EEPROM (right): Nothing
to wear a corsage for.

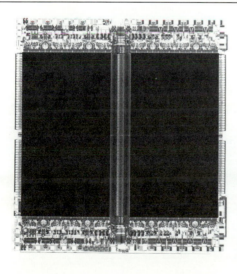
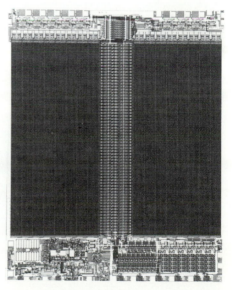

The prices recorded on them can be easily updated as needed. The only disadvantage of EEPROM chips is that they currently cost substantially more than regular ROM chips.

RANDOM ACCESS MEMORY (RAM)

The volatile part of internal memory is called **random access memory,** or **RAM.** The name derives from the fact that data can be stored in and retrieved at random—from anywhere—in the electronic internal memory chips in approximately the same amount of time, no matter where the data is. RAM is reusable in the sense that, when a program has completed processing, the space the instructions took in RAM is freed so that it can be used again by the next program loaded into RAM.

Internal memory is nonmechanical in nature. Copies of data and programs from input devices and secondary storage media are stored and retrieved in the form of electronic signals traveling at the speed of light. With no moving parts involved, the data can be retrieved in about the same amount of time from different locations, no matter where it is in internal memory. By contrast, disk and tape storage devices—because they are mechanical—require time to retrieve data, depending on where it is located on the surface of the storage media.

In general, RAM is used for the following purposes:

■ Storage of a copy of the main software program that controls the general operation of the computer. This copy is loaded into internal memory when the

FIGURE 5.9
Going to the bank. This photo shows banks of RAM chips (left) on the motherboard of a microcomputer.

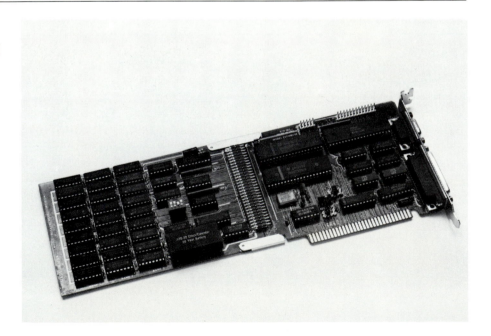

computer is turned on (you'll find out how later), and it stays there as long as the computer is on.

- Temporary storage of a copy of application program instructions (the specific software you are using in your business) to be retrieved by the central processing unit (CPU) for interpretation and execution.

- Temporary storage of data that has been input from the keyboard or other input device until instructions call for the data to be transferred into the CPU for processing.

- Temporary storage of data that has been produced as a result of processing until instructions call for the data to be used again in subsequent processing or to be transferred to an output device such as the screen, a printer, or a disk storage device.

Figure 5.9 shows the banks (a group of usually nine chips arranged in a row) of RAM chips found on the motherboard of a personal computer. Many people erroneously assume that a memory chip with a capacity of 64 K can hold a substantial number of characters of data; however, in internal memory it takes nine chips to store one character. Each chip can be thought of as representing a column of 64 K electronic light switches that can be read one row at a time. The code for a character, such as the letter X, is stored in the same row across the entire bank of memory chips (Figure 5.10). The first 8 bits build the character; the ninth chip, called the **parity chip**, holds the *parity bit*, or *check bit*, that is used for error detection.

FIGURE 5.10
Chipping away at words. Many people think that a character of data can be stored in a chip, but it takes eight chips to store one character. The ninth chip, called the *parity chip*, is used for error detection.

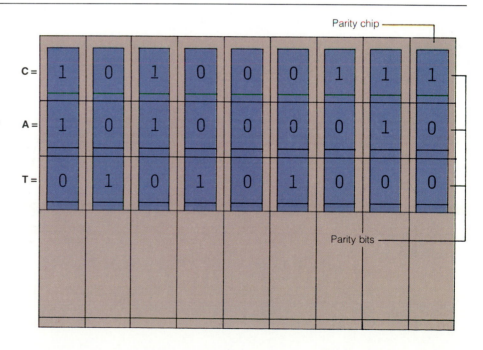

When data is written across a bank of memory chips, the number of binary 1's in the code are counted to determine what bit should be placed in the corresponding parity chip. If the manufacturer has adopted an *even-parity scheme*, then the total number of binary 1's in all nine chips must be an even number. So if the code for the letter X is to be stored and the parity scheme is even, the parity chip would have a binary 1 placed in it because there are an odd number of binary 1's in the character code itself. The *odd-parity scheme* works in the reverse fashion. The parity bit used assures that there will always be an odd number of binary 1's in each character stored in the memory bank. (Figure 5.10 shows an odd-parity scheme.)

Parity schemes were adopted because the data in internal memory is stored in a volatile electrical form. The slightest electrical power surge or static charge can reverse the charge in one of the rows in a chip or even cause the entire chip to fail. The electrical charges placed in each electrical junction tend to fade with time, so the contents of the memory locations must be constantly refreshed to keep the data from being lost. As a part of this process, each bank of memory is scanned by the system software to determine if any parity errors are present—that is, if a character has an odd number of 1's in an even-parity scheme, for example. If a parity error is detected, an error message is usually generated to advise the operator of the problem. Depending on the location of the memory bank with the parity error, the processing may be halted when the condition occurs. This usually results in the failure of your keyboard or other input device to function.

RAM FOR MICROCOMPUTERS

The amount of random access memory you have in your microcomputer directly affects the level of sophistication of the software you can use. Sophisticated, or powerful, programs take up a lot of space in RAM. Many of today's software programs require a minimum of 320 K to run.

Early microcomputer systems were not equipped with very much random access memory by today's standards for two basic reasons. First, the architecture of microprocessors did not allow very much RAM to be directly controlled—the early microprocessors were able to directly access and control up to only 64 K RAM. Microprocessors currently allow users to access up to 7 MB RAM.

Second, the price of RAM chips was much higher than it is now. To upgrade the random access memory of a computer from 16 K to 48 K in 1979 could easily have cost several hundred dollars. Today 64 K of internal memory can be purchased for less than $10. The price drop of internal memory chips occurred because of increases in manufacturing efficiency and technological improvements that provided more capacity per chip. Early microcomputers were equipped with banks of memory chips with an individual capacity per chip of 16 K. In 1982, microcomputers with 64 K memory chips began to appear. By 1985, computers with 256 K memory chips were on the market; these chips are currently being used in many microcomputers, such as IBM's PS/2 models.

The software available for microcomputers did not require much internal memory until certain new products began to appear on the market around 1984.

With the introduction of special software to handle large financial reports, the need for increased internal memory grew rapidly. Now, for a microcomputer to effectively use many of the newer software products, it should probably have 640 K of internal memory available.

But what if your microcomputer is not brand new and has an internal memory capacity of only 256 K? This capacity would include four banks of 64 K memory chips. Unfortunately, you cannot simply pull out two of the 64 K chips and replace them with 256 K chips to increase the amount of internal memory available to 640 K because of the component referred to as the **dynamic memory access (DMA)** controller (Figure 5.11). In most older microcomputer systems, the DMA chip was designed to work with only one size of memory chip. However, in newer systems the DMA controller is designed to allow a mix of banks of 64 K and 256 K memory chips. The DMA chip or module is responsible for managing the use of all internal memory. It keeps track of which memory locations are in use (and by what) and which are available for use.

ADD-ON MEMORY BOARDS   As we just described, users of early microcomputer systems couldn't increase the amount of internal memory located on the motherboard. This situation led to the development of a wide variety of new products allowing the memory to be increased through the use of an **add-on memory board,** or *card,* sometimes referred to as an *external memory board.* This board is simply pressed into an expansion slot on the motherboard. (An expansion slot is a "plug-in"

FIGURE 5.11
Dynamic memory access controller. This AST DMA controller module manages the use of all internal memory in all Q-bus and MicroVAX II systems.

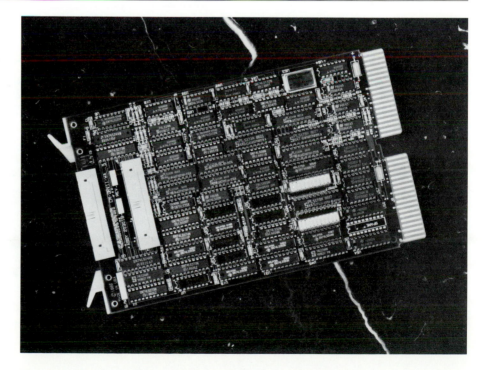

spot on the motherboard specifically meant to support add-on components.) This connects the add-on board with the power supply for the computer and links the board with the buses for moving data and instructions. Then some switch settings in the computer may need to be adjusted to account for the increased amount of memory, because the computer won't know how much internal memory it has unless you tell it. The entire process takes only a screwdriver and about ten minutes. Figure 5.12 shows an external memory board that provides an extra 384 K of internal memory in the form of one bank of 256 K memory chips and two banks of 64 K memory chips.

Some microcomputer users need even more memory. New software programs are getting more demanding, and many of them already require more than the maximum memory capacity of 640 K (such as the IBM PS/2 models, which support the 80286 and the 80386 microprocessors). The internal memory capacity of all but the newest microcomputers is limited to 640 K for two basic reasons: microprocessor architecture and the IBM PC. The Intel 8088 microprocessor used in the IBM PC and almost all PC-compatibles can access and control 1 MB of internal memory. The design of the IBM PC allocates 360 K of this capacity to ROM and 640 K to RAM. To help overcome the 640 K internal memory barrier, a new product called **expanded memory** was introduced in 1985. This product can provide additional internal memory over and above the 640 K maximum (up to 8 MB) through the use of an add-on memory board and the addition of special driver software to your systems software disk.

The first major expanded memory product, introduced in 1985 under the joint sponsorship of Lotus, Intel Corporation, and Microsoft, is referred to as the Lotus/Intel/Microsoft Expanded Memory Specification, or LIM EMS. Later in the year

FIGURE 5.12
How to improve your memory. Banks of 256 K and 64 K chips can be attached as an add-on board like the one shown here to the motherboard in your microcomputer to substantially increase its internal memory capacity.

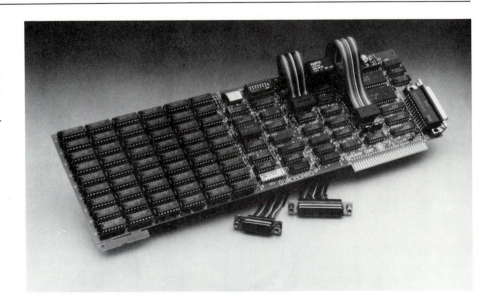

two other major vendors, AST Research and Quadram Corporation, introduced a competing product (see Figure 5.3).

To take advantage of expanded memory, you must use a software product that is designed to work with it (as most new software packages are designed to do). If you are using older software that is not designed to work with expanded memory technology, you can still increase your memory capacity in some ways; however, these techniques are a bit technical to go into here. Just remember that increased memory capacity means better performance. If you don't know how to improve the memory of your microcomputer, ask a computer professional in your company or a computer store.

MEASURING THE PROCESSING POWER OF A COMPUTER

The proliferation of microcomputers in our society means that more and more people are becoming familiar with the processing power of computers in general. Many individuals are considering the purchase of a microcomputer, or personal computer, on their own, with the result that more and more people are asking, "How do you determine how powerful a computer is?"

This question is fairly easy to answer. However, understanding the answer requires knowledge of a few more computer fundamentals.

ADDRESSING SCHEME

The **addressing scheme** is a computer design feature that directly determines the amount of internal memory that can be controlled by the central processing unit at any one time. The addressing scheme is based on the size (in bits) of a special register that is used only for addressing. The early microcomputer CPUs were limited in memory addressing capability to 64 K. The popular IBM PC-compatible computers have a memory addressing capability of 1024 K. The most recent model, IBM PS/2 model 80, uses a processor that allows access to approximately 16,000 K, or 16 MB, of internal memory, which is equal to the addressing capability of current mini-computers. Some "super" minicomputer systems can access even more than that. Mainframes usually have an addressing scheme that allows access to between 32 and 128 MB or more of RAM.

REGISTER SIZE

In addition to the register used for addressing, computers have a number of registers (often referred to as **general-purpose registers**) that are used for a variety of purposes including arithmetic operations. The more of these registers you have and the larger they are, the more processing power you have. The registers in early microcomputers could hold only 8 bits each. The Intel 8088-type microprocessor was equipped with eight general-purpose registers, each capable of holding 16 bits. The Motorola 68000 processor, used in the Macintosh, has sixteen general-purpose registers that can hold 32 bits each. Each 32-bit general-purpose register can process twice as much data in each machine cycle per register as a 16-bit register can. If you compare the size and number of registers of the Intel 8088 processor and the Motorola 68000, you can see that the 8088 has a total general-purpose register capacity of 128 bits, whereas the 68000 has a capacity of 512 bits. This means that the Motorola 68000 provides substantially more work space for data during processing.

The registers in minicomputers today are usually 32 bits. Mainframes generally have registers at least 64 bits in size.

DATA BUS CAPACITY

As you learned earlier, the data bus is like a pipeline used to move data and instructions between internal memory, the central processing unit, and other computer system components. The size of the data bus controls the amount of data that can travel down the pipeline at one time and thus can significantly affect a computer's performance. The early computers had data buses large enough to allow 8 bits of data to pass at one time; the latest model IBM AT has a data bus that is 16 bits wide. As you can imagine, the larger data bus allows data to be moved around the system much faster. The Intel 80386 microprocessor is expected to be one of the most widely used of the new generation 32-bit microprocessors.

CLOCK SPEED

The clock, mentioned in the section on the instruction execution cycle, is the part of the CPU that synchronizes and sets the speed of all the operations in the machine cycle. The speed at which computers perform operations is measured in millions of cycles per second (megaHertz, or MHz). The early microcomputers operated at speeds of around 1 MHz. This means that those computers had approximately 1,000,000 processing cycles available per second to perform useful work. The newest model personal computers are operating at speeds of 10–12 or even 16 MHz. Modern mini- and mainframe computers operate at clock speeds greater than 20 MHz.

INSTRUCTION SET

The early 8-bit microprocessors were extremely slow when performing mathematical operations. They were designed to handle only addition and subtraction; a more sophisticated operation (such as division or multiplication) had to be performed by a series of special program instructions, often called *subroutines*. For example, to multiply 6 times 2, a subroutine would add the number 2 together 6 times. The more powerful 16-bit microcomputers use additional instructions that handle mathematical operations in a single processing cycle. The 16-bit microprocessors also use single *blocks* of instructions (called *instruction sets*) that can cause whole blocks of data to be moved from one place to another. On the 8-bit microcomputers, this type of operation would also have to be handled by a subroutine (lots of "small," individual instructions).

CHECKLIST

In general, keep these points in mind when trying to determine the processing power of a computer:

- *Addressing scheme:* The larger the addressing capability, the more internal memory the computer can control.
- *Register size:* The larger the general-purpose registers, the more data the CPU can operate on in one machine cycle.
- *Data bus:* The larger the data buses, the more efficiently and quickly data and instructions can be moved between the processing components of the computer.
- *Clock speed:* The faster the clock speed, the more machine cycles are completed per second and the faster the computer can perform processing operations.
- *Instruction set:* The more powerful the instruction set, the fewer instructions and processing cycles it takes to perform certain tasks.

ONWARD: OUT WITH IT!

Now that you have learned more hardware-related terms than you ever cared to know about, we're going to give you one more hardware group to study—output hardware. The output phase of a computer-based information system is most important to the user. After all, the whole object of inputting and storing data and instructions for processing is to produce *information* that you can use to make decisions in your office or profession.

SUMMARY

If you are "tuned in" to the amount of processing power in your computer, you won't fall into the trap that many people do—namely, of buying a software program that won't run on your computer or expecting the computer to do something it isn't capable of doing.

The most important processing hardware component is the central processing unit (CPU), which comprises the control unit, the arithmetic/logic unit (ALU), and processing registers. CPUs used to be made of vacuum tubes, magnetic cores, and transistors, which were all relatively expensive, slow, and unreliable by today's standards. Today CPUs are manufactured from silicon; one wafer from a silicon ingot can hold hundreds of chips, also called *microprocessors*. The electric circuitry that forms the CPU is etched onto the surface of the chip.

The control unit of the CPU is responsible for directing and coordinating most of the computer system activities. It uses machine language to run the show. Unfortunately, the binary codes that make up machine language differ among machines, which creates a problem of incompatibility.

The arithmetic/logic unit (ALU) performs all arithmetic and logical (comparison) functions. Some computers do arithmetic operations in parallel, meaning that they perform all calculations simultaneously in a single operation. Parallel addition is faster than serial addition. Computers that add and subtract serially perform calculations one at a time, in order, like most people do. To help ease the computational burden placed on some microcomputers, manufacturers have developed numeric coprocessor chips to be added to computers to speed up processing.

Registers are special temporary storage locations within the CPU that very quickly accept, store, and transfer data and instructions that are being used immediately. The number and types of registers in a computer vary according to the computer's design.

To get data and instructions moving between the various components of the system, the computer needs buses. The wider the bus, the more data it can carry at one time. Computers may have three types of buses: (1) data bus, (2) address bus, and (3) control bus.

The cycle that the computer goes through to execute one instruction is called the *machine cycle*. In the instruction cycle part of the machine cycle, an instruction is retrieved from internal memory and is decoded in the CPU. The time it takes to do this is called *I-time*. In the execution cycle, the instruction is executed and the result is stored. The time this takes is *E-time*. An internal clock in the CPU sets the speed of the machine cycle, which is measured in MHz—megaHertz, or millions of cycles per second.

A computer system could not operate without internal memory, also called *main memory*, *primary memory*, and simply *memory*, of which there are two basic types: read-only memory (ROM) and random access memory (RAM). The main difference between ROM and RAM is that the data and programs in ROM are permanent—they are placed there by the manufacturer and cannot be changed by the user—whereas the data and programs in RAM can be both read and changed by the user.

In general, ROM is nonvolatile—the data and programs are not lost when the power to the computer is turned off. RAM, however, is volatile in most cases. The data vanishes when the power goes.

Certain types of ROM chips give users added flexibility. Programmable read-only memory (PROM) chips allow you to put your own data and programs on them—you don't have to rely on manufacturers to do it. Erasable programmable read-only memory chips can be changed by using a special ultraviolet light device; however, you have to take EPROM chips out of the computer to change the data and programs on them. Electrically erasable programmable read-only memory chips (EEPROM) can be changed without taking them out of the computer.

In general, RAM is used (1) to store a copy of the main software program that controls the general operation of the computer; (2) to store a copy of the business application software you are using; (3) to temporarily store data that has been input from the keyboard or other storage device until it is transferred for processing; and (4) to temporarily store data that has been produced as a result of processing until it is transferred to output or secondary storage.

In a microcomputer, RAM chips are usually found in banks of nine on the motherboard. A character's 8 bits are stored in a row of chips; the ninth chip holds the parity bit, which is a 1 or a 0 based on whether the parity scheme is odd or even. The parity scheme is used to check for errors produced by interferences with the electrical current.

The greater your machine's memory capacity, the better because:

- It can create and use much larger programs.
- It can hold copies of more than one program in internal memory to support the sharing of the computer by more than one user at a time.
- It can operate faster and more efficiently.
- It will be able to use new, sophisticated software.

If you have a microcomputer that needs to have its memory expanded beyond 640 K RAM to handle new types of software, you can purchase an add-on board, also called an *expanded memory board*, to "plug in" to the motherboard.

The processing power of a computer can be determined using the following factors: (1) addressing scheme, (2) register size, (3) data bus, (4) clock speed, and (5) the instruction set.

KEY TERMS

add-on memory board
address bus
addressing scheme
arithmetic/logic unit
    (ALU)
bus
central processing unit
    (CPU)
clock
control bus
control unit
coprocessor chip
data bus
dynamic memory
    access (DMA)

electrically erasable pro-
    grammable read-only
    memory (EEPROM)
erasable programmable
    read-only memory
    (EPROM)
E-time
execution cycle
expanded memory
general-purpose register
instruction cycle
internal memory
I-time
machine cycle

machine language
microprocessor
parallel addition
parity chip
programmable read-
    only memory
    (PROM)
random access memory
    (RAM)
read-only memory
    (ROM)
register
semiconductor
serial addition

EXERCISES

MATCHING

Match each of the following terms to the phrase that is the most closely related.

1. _____ machine language
2. _____ microprocessor
3. _____ register
4. _____ bus
5. _____ machine cycle
6. _____ parity chip
7. _____ addressing scheme
8. _____ clock
9. _____ I-time
10. _____ E-time
11. _____ ROM
12. _____ parallel addition
13. _____ serial addition
14. _____ RAM
15. _____ address bus

   a. The CPU circuitry of a microcomputer.
   b. The only language that can be understood by the CPU.
   c. It takes a single operation to process all calculations.
   d. All calculations are processed one digit at a time.
   e. A temporary storage location within the CPU.
   f. Without this, no bits can be transmitted between various components in a computer system.
   g. The time it takes to retrieve an instruction from internal memory and decode it.
   h. The instruction cycle and the execution cycle together.
   i. The time it takes to execute an instruction and store the result in a register.
   j. Data and instructions stored here are in a nonvolatile state.
   k. Used for error detection in a bank of chips.
   l. Determines the amount of internal memory that can be controlled.
   m. The type of memory that is volatile.
   n. Synchronizes and sets the speed of all the operations in the machine cycle.
   o. Used to access internal memory storage locations that contain data needed by instructions.

MULTIPLE CHOICE

1. Which of the following affects processing power?
   a. addressing scheme
   b. register size
   c. data bus capacity
   d. clock speed
   e. all of the above

2. Which of the following hardware components is the most volatile?
   a. ROM
   b. RAM
   c. PROM
   d. EPROM
   e. EEPROM

3. Which of the following isn't a function of RAM?
   a. to store a copy of the main software program that controls the general operation of the computer
   b. to store instructions permanently until they are transferred to an output device
   c. to store a copy of application program instructions
   d. to store data that has been input from the keyboard
   e. to store data as a result of processing that is waiting to be output to a storage device

4. Which of the following can't be found in a CPU?
   a. ALU
   b. control unit
   c. RAM
   d. processing registers
   e. none of the above

5. Which of the following isn't related to the instruction execution cycle?
   a. instruction cycle
   b. decoding
   c. machine cycle
   d. E-time
   e. M-time

6. Which of the following registers is used to determine where data and instructions are located in internal memory?
   a. instruction register
   b. address register
   c. accumulator register
   d. general-purpose register
   e. none of the above

7. Why is the width of a data bus so important to the processing speed of a computer?
   a. The narrower it is, the greater the computer's processing speed.
   b. The wider it is, the more data that can fit into internal memory.
   c. The wider it is, the greater the computer's processing speed.
   d. The wider it is, the slower the computer's processing speed.
   e. The data bus isn't important to the processing speed of a computer.

8. Which of the following is the most characteristic of ROM?
   a. It performs mathematical calculations.
   b. It is volatile.
   c. It is nonvolatile.
   d. It is wide.
   e. none of the above

9. What is a major characteristic of EEPROM?
   a. Users can record their own data and instructions.
   b. Recorded data and instructions can be changed if necessary.
   c. Changes to data and instructions are done electrically byte by byte.

    d. a type of ROM
    e. all of the above

10. Which of the following is used to detect errors in how data is stored in internal memory?
    a. ROM
    b. arithmetic/logic unit
    c. control unit
    d. parity chip
    e. none of the above

SHORT ANSWER

1. What are the main factors affecting the processing power of a computer?

2. Why is internal memory in a computer important?

3. What happens in a typical machine cycle? Does it take long?

4. How might a PROM, EPROM, or EEPROM chip help to eliminate your use of floppy disks? What are the advantages of an EEPROM chip over a PROM or an EPROM chip?

5. What is the difference between serial addition and parallel addition, and why is this difference relevant to you?

6. What are parity schemes and why are they important?

7. Why might it be important for you to know about the activities performed by the processing hardware in your computer?

8. What would a good indication be that two computers are incompatible? Why is knowing this important to you?

9. Why is it much faster to retrieve data from RAM than from a disk storage device?

10. What led to the development of expanded memory?

PROJECTS

1. Advances are made almost every day in microprocessor chip technology. Specifically, what are some of these advances? In what computers are these chips being used? How might these advances affect the way we currently use microcomputers? Research the latest advances by reviewing the most current computer magazines and periodicals.

2. Research the current uses of and the latest advances in ROM technology. How do you think ROM technology will affect the way we currently use microcomputers? Will we see a lessened need for storage media?

CHAPTER SIX

6

OUTPUT HARDWARE

In business, presentation is important—how you present yourself, your product, your information. Although computers may not be able to help you with your wardrobe or your public speaking skills, they *can* help you create clear and attractive informational presentations quickly. But because computers can produce beautiful, professional, seemingly error-free printouts or exciting colorful graphics on a screen, we are apt to believe that the information is more truthful than the same results scribbled on a yellow pad. In fact, the information that is output—the basis on which you and others will be making decisions—is no better than the quality of the data that was input.

PREVIEW

When you have completed this chapter, you will be able to:

■

Describe the basic forms of output and categories of output media and hardware

■

Describe the advantages and disadvantages of the major types of hardcopy and softcopy output devices

■

Explain why it is important to implement output controls

■

The User Perspective

The success of a business today can depend to a large extent on how relevant and timely the information is that the computer can produce—that is, the **output**. Having the right information, in the right hands, in the best form, at the right time—these are the keys to effective decision making (Figure 6.1).

Output can take many forms. For instance, when you use an automated teller machine you are dealing with the following types of output: (1) the messages displayed on the video display, (2) the paper transaction receipt that is printed out, and (3) the funds dispensed. And just as forms of output vary, so do types of output devices that you can use to view computer-produced information. Different types of hardware suit different informational needs, and very few businesses use all types. Determining what type of hardware is best suited to a business takes careful consideration. If you are in charge of acquiring an output device for your office, you must first analyze your output needs—determine what *forms* of output you need. Then you can determine what kind of output hardware will best serve those needs.

Output Fundamentals

To be effective, information must be produced in a usable form. To achieve this goal, you may need to use more than one output device and output medium, such as a display on a video screen as well as paper and a printer (as in our automated teller example). Each type of output device has advantages and disadvantages. Is the hardware going to make a lot of noise? What is the quality of the output produced? Is the hardware slow? Is the hardware expensive? Is it compatible with the equipment you already have? Not all types of computers work with all types of output hardware devices; neither do all software programs. How do you know which to use? To choose wisely, you must be familiar with the categories of computer output.

How Do We Categorize Output?

There are four basic categories of computer-produced output: (1) *text*, (2) *graphics*, (3) *voice*, and (4) *computer-usable*. Text, which is the most often used type of output, can appear in a variety of forms: a memo summarizing the sales activities for the first quarter, a budget report, a list of items in inventory that are nearing the reorder point, a utility bill, a bank statement, a form letter. Over 85% of all computer-produced output presents information in text form.

In the past six years, interest in the presentation of information in the form of graphic images has grown substantially, partially because of improvements in the quality of graphics hardware and advancements in the capabilities and flexibility of graphics software. Examples of graphic output are bar charts, graphs, and pie charts.

Voice output has recently begun to be used more often. For example, these days the telephone is used more frequently for voice output: The last time you dialed telephone information (directory assistance), the number you were given was probably provided in the form of computer-generated voice output. Some specialized computer devices are also being used to disseminate messages and marketing information automatically over the phone. The computer begins dialing a long list of telephone numbers. When the phone is answered, a message is automatically transmitted—perhaps to the annoyance of the person being called. When there is no answer or the line is busy, the computer takes note and automatically tries again later. More and more applications are being found each year that use voice as a form of computer output.

As you know, information produced as output by one program or system as the result of processing is often needed as input by another program or system. For example, when payroll processing is performed, some information is usually stored in computer-usable form on magnetic tape or disk so that it can be passed along to other parts of the accounting system. This is computer-usable output. Prerecorded optical disks—such as those that hold an entire encyclopedia—can also be thought of as computer-usable output.

MEDIA

There are two basic types of output media: hardcopy and softcopy. The term *hardcopy*, as defined in Chapter 1, refers to information that has been recorded on a tangible medium (meaning you can touch it) such as paper, special forms, or microfiche (sheets of microfilm that hold computer-produced "photos" of information at

FIGURE 6.1
What form of output is best? As a computer user in the business environment, your output needs will be determined by the kind of decisions you need to make to perform your regular job duties, the type of information that will facilitate making those decisions, and the frequency with which you must make decisions.

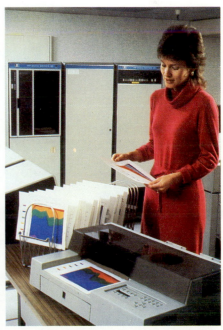

a greatly reduced size). The term *softcopy* refers to information that has been produced in a seemingly intangible form (meaning you can't touch it). Many people think of information recorded in computer-usable form as softcopy output, because they cannot see the magnetic spots recorded on the tape or disk. However, since the medium is indeed tangible, this form of output could be classified as hardcopy;

FIGURE 6.2
Feed the printer. Continuous-form paper is used to avoid having to hand-feed individual sheets of paper to the printer (called *friction feed*) when you are printing reports. The holes on both sides of the paper fit onto a *tractor feed* mechanism attached to the printer that guides the paper and pushes it forward, as directed by the software. Continuous-form paper is used more often in business than are single sheets.

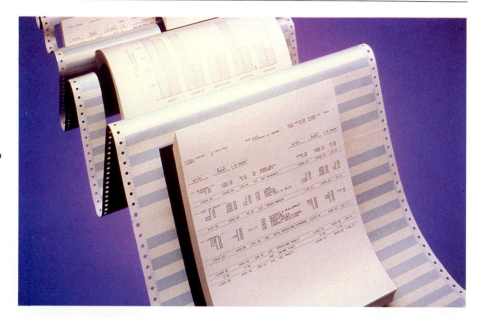

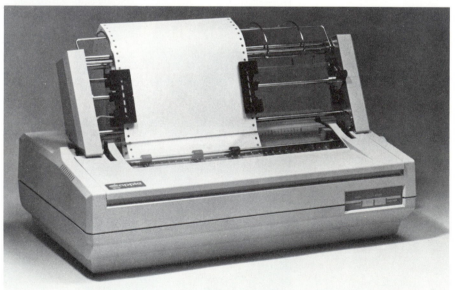

nonetheless, we usually refer to information displayed on a video display screen or provided in voice form as softcopy.

Paper is one of the most widely used output media. Paper products come in a variety of forms including:

- Lined computer paper (11 × 14 5/8 inches)
- Plain computer paper (8 1/2 × 11 inches)
- Special preprinted forms
- Labels

Individually placing these paper products in an output device (such as a printer) takes a lot of time, so they are all available in *continuous form* (Figure 6.2).

The second most widely used output medium is the video display image. You look at a video display screen to get instructions while completing an automated teller machine transaction. Many shopping malls now provide computer terminals that allow visitors to locate businesses quickly in a computerized directory. The two types of display screen used most often are a computer terminal connected to a large computer system and a monitor attached to a microcomputer system.

The advantages and disadvantages of each output medium must be considered carefully to ensure that outputs are produced in the most usable form. When computer display devices are not readily available and information has some value over time, it is best produced as hardcopy. When computer display devices are readily available and information must be quickly accessible, it is best produced as softcopy.

Hardware

Output hardware is categorized according to whether it produces hardcopy or softcopy (Figure 6.3). The principal hardcopy output devices are printers and plotters. The principal softcopy output devices are cathode-ray tube video screens (CRTs), flat screens, camera output microfilm and microfiche systems, and voice output systems.

As you read the next two sections, consider which types of output hardware would best satisfy the information needs that exist in your chosen field or profession. By doing so, you'll be moving even closer to computer literacy.

Hardcopy Output Devices

Among the wide variety of hardcopy output devices, printers and plotters are used the most. A **printer** is capable of printing characters, symbols, and sometimes graphics on paper. Printers are categorized according to whether or not the image produced is formed by physical contact of the print mechanism with the paper. *Impact printers* do have contact; *nonimpact printers* do not. A **plotter** is used most often for creating graphics because it can produce specialized and free-form drawings on paper. Plotters are categorized according to whether or not they use pens, how the paper is placed in them, and which of their parts move. To suit the needs of many different users, different types of printers and plotters are available with slightly different characteristics and capabilities—cost, quality, and speed will determine which are best for you.

IMPACT PRINTERS

An **impact printer** makes contact with the paper. It usually forms the print image by pressing an inked ribbon against the paper with a hammer-like mechanism. In one type of impact printer, called a *letter-quality printer*, the hammer presses images of fully formed characters against the ribbon, just like a typewriter. The print

FIGURE 6.3
Hard job, soft job? Output devices are categorized according to whether they produce hardcopy or softcopy.

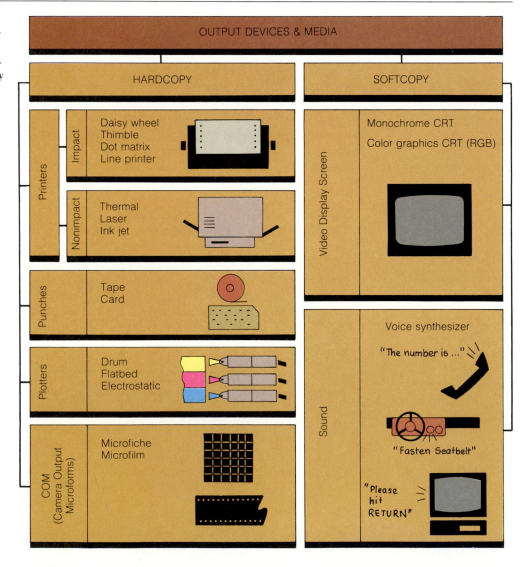

mechanism in another type of impact printer, called a *dot-matrix printer*, is made of separate pin-like hammers that strike the ribbon against the paper in computer-determined patterns of dots. Letter-quality printers and dot-matrix printers are used with microcomputer systems. Larger computer systems, which often must produce a high volume of output, use high-speed printers that fall into a separate category.

LETTER-QUALITY PRINTERS **Letter-quality printers**—also called *character printers*—produce a very high-quality print image (one that is very clear and precise) because the entire character is formed with a single impact. Letter-quality output is generally used for important business letters, memos, and reports. The two most widely used letter-quality printers are (1) the daisy wheel printer and (2) the thimble printer. The **daisy wheel printer** (Figure 6.4) has a print "wheel" with a set of print characters on the outside tips of the flat spokes. To print a specific character, the wheel is spun until the appropriate spoke is lined up with the print hammer. The print hammer is then fired, and the print character is forced against the ribbon and paper with sufficient force to make a clear, crisp impression. The **thimble printer** works similarly, except that the spokes curve upward, instead of lying flat.

Some early letter-quality printers had print mechanisms similar to the IBM Selectric typewriter ball. However, the daisy wheel and thimble printer technologies have proven superior in terms of speed. The range of speeds for letter-quality printers varies from about 20 characters per second (cps) to a maximum of about 95 cps. This speed translates into approximately 240 to 1140 words per minute (based on an average of five characters per word)! The principal advantage of letter-quality printers is the excellent image produced. However, they do have some disadvantages:

- They are still too slow for many large-volume output situations.
- They are very noisy.
- To change the typeface style, the operator must halt the machine and change the print wheel.
- They cannot produce graphics.

DOT-MATRIX PRINTERS **Dot-matrix printers** were developed with two objectives in mind: greater speed and more flexibility. The images are formed by a print head that is composed of a series of little print hammers that look like the heads of pins. These print hammers strike the ribbon individually as the print mechanism moves across the entire print line in both directions—that is, from left to right, then right to left, and so on. They can produce a variety of type styles and graphics without requiring an operator to stop the printer or change the print wheel.

Figure 6.5 shows how a dot-matrix print head is constructed. The print head of a dot-matrix printer usually has nine pins. However, new high-quality dot-matrix printers have print heads with as many as 24 pins, which allows a much more precise image to be produced. Figure 6.6 gives an example of graphics produced by a dot-matrix printer.

The speed of dot-matrix printers ranges from 20 cps to 400 cps—about 240 to 4800 words per minute. They generate less noise than letter-quality printers, and many of the dot-matrix printers can achieve a near-letter-quality mode when the print head makes more than one pass for each print line, creating a darker, thicker character (Figure 6.7). Table 6.1 compares letter-quality and dot-matrix printers.

FIGURE 6.4
Daisy wheel (top) and daisy wheel printer (bottom).

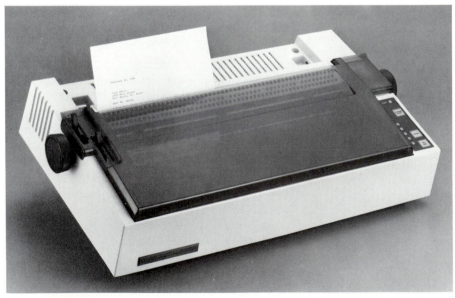

FIGURE 6.5
Dot-matrix print head. Part
(a) is an enlarged view of a
group of pins, or print hammers, striking the printer
ribbon; part (b) shows the
print head. The same group
of pins can be used to create a variety of characters.

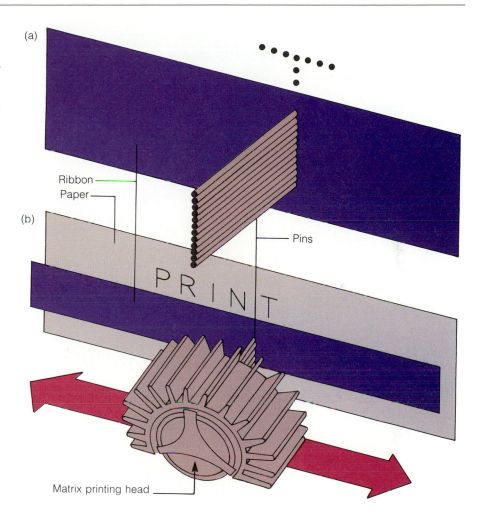

FIGURE 6.6
Dot-matrix sample. Graph-
ics produced by a nine-pin
dot-matrix printer.

FIGURE 6.7
The second time around. To produce a near-letter-quality image with a dot-matrix printer, the character is printed twice (a); the second time the print head is positioned slightly to the right of the original image. (b) shows a "real" (daisy wheel) letter-quality character for comparison.

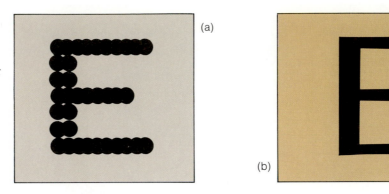

(a)

(b)

TABLE 6.1   Comparison of Letter-Quality and Dot-Matrix Printers

	Letter-Quality	Dot-Matrix
Draft-Quality Speed	n/a	80–400 cps
Letter-Quality Speed	20–95 cps	20–100 cps (near-letter-quality)
Image Quality	Excellent	Good to very good
Graphics Capabilities	None	Extensive
Cost	$350–3000	$250–1500
Print Mechanism	Daisy wheel or thimble	9- 18-, or 24-pin print head

HIGH-SPEED PRINTERS   Several types of high-speed printers have been developed to satisfy the high-volume output requirements of most large computer installations, which cannot be satisfied by dot-matrix or letter-quality printers. These **line printers,** so called because they print a whole line of characters practically at once, come in several varieties, including **band printers** (Figure 6.8), **belt printers,** and **print-chain printers.** Each of these printers has several copies of each printable character on a band, a belt, or a print chain, with a separate print hammer for each print position across the width of the paper guide. As the band, belt, or print chain revolves around the print line, the hammers are activated as the appropriate characters pass in front of them.

Whereas speed in letter-quality and dot-matrix printers is measured in characters per second, the speed of these faster printers is measured in lines per minute. The speed achieved by this type of printer ranges from 200 to 3000 lines per minute (lpm), which translates into about 5280 to approximately 79,000 words per minute. Some high-speed printers can print more than 20,000 lines per minute—an astounding 528,000 words per minute! (A highly trained typist can do about 90–120 words per minute on a typewriter.) Line printers with speeds in the 200–1000 lpm range are used with minicomputers. The faster ones are used with mainframes. (Some mainframe computer systems produce so much hardcopy output that they have a whole room full of high-speed and very-high-speed printers.)

Speed is the obvious advantage of this type of printer. Unless your business produces an extremely large volume of hardcopy output, though, you probably will not need to use one. The major disadvantages are noise and relatively poor image quality. However, these limitations are being overcome by new printer technologies (such as laser printers, which we'll describe in the next section).

Nonimpact Printers

Printers that do not strike characters against ribbon or paper when they print are **nonimpact printers.** The main categories of nonimpact printers are ink-jet printers, thermal printers, and laser printers. These printers generate much less noise than impact printers. However, if you're using a nonimpact printer, don't try to print on multiple-part carbon forms: Because no impact is being made on the paper, you'll end up with no copies! Believe it or not, quite a few people have purchased a nonimpact printer, put carbon forms into it, and been gravely disappointed when the carbon copies didn't materialize.

INK-JET PRINTERS **Ink-jet printers** (Figures 6.9, 6.10) work in much the same fashion as dot-matrix printers in that they form images or characters with little dots. However, the dots are formed, not by hammer-like pins, but by tiny droplets of ink.

FIGURE 6.8
Steel print band. Some high-speed printers use bands to print a whole line of characters almost at once.

These printers can almost match the speed of dot-matrix printers—up to about 270 cps—and they produce less noise.

Because several manufacturers now produce color ink-jet printers, this type of printer is being used more often as a color graphics output device. The right side of

FIGURE 6.9
Ink-jet printer.

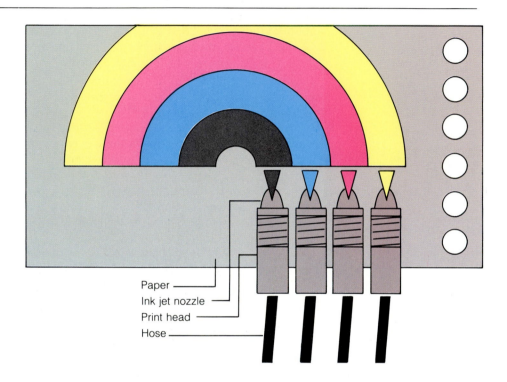

Paper
Ink jet nozzle
Print head
Hose

FIGURE 6.10
Jet set graphics. Free-form images can be printed in color using a color ink-jet printer.

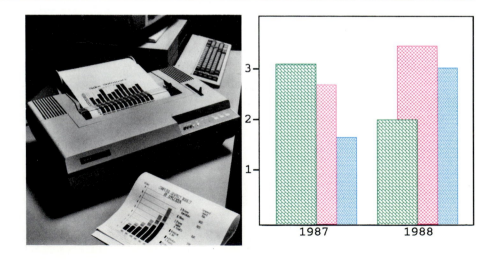

Figure 6.10 was produced using an ink-jet printer. Problems experienced with this type of printer include clogged ink jets (from which the ink is fired) and relatively poor image quality of color graphics compared to those produced by a plotter (shown in Figure 6.15). However, many users find the quality to be quite acceptable.

THERMAL PRINTERS   **Thermal printers** use heat to produce an image on special paper (Figure 6.11). The print mechanism is designed to heat the surface of chemically treated paper so that a dot is produced based on the reaction of the chemical to the heat. No ribbon or ink is involved. The primary advantage of this type of printer is its low noise level; however, it is relatively slow, the paper is usually costly and degrades with storage, and it can print only in a single color.

Recent developments have made **thermal transfer printers** capable of providing high-quality output. This type of thermal printer has a print head that is heated and applied to an inked ribbon, which has been coated with wax. The heat of the print head melts the wax, which in turn sticks to the surface of regular paper. This process

FIGURE 6.11
Hot topic. Thermal printers produce images by heating chemically treated paper until dots appear.

FIGURE 6.12
Laser printing process and print sample. A microprocessor controls a small laser beam that is bounced off a mirror (a) millions of times per second onto a positively charged drum. The spots where the laser beam hits become neutralized (b), enabling a special toner to stick to them and then print out on paper, through the use of heat and pressure. The drum is then recharged for its next cycle.

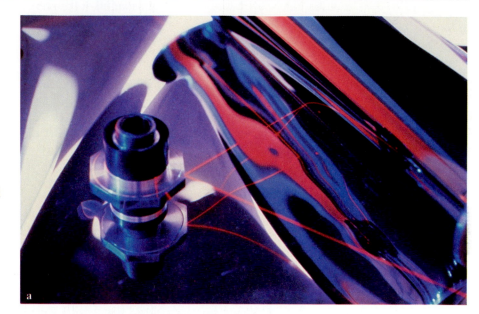

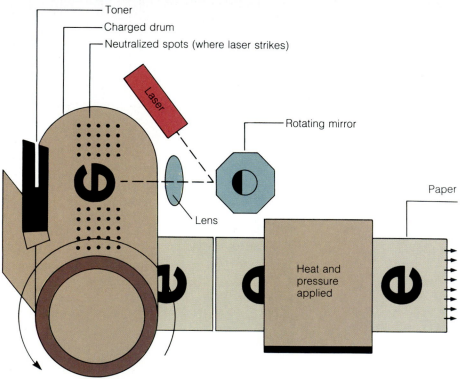

costs less and produces a higher image quality than regular (untreated) thermal printers.

LASER PRINTERS **Laser printer** technology is much less mechanical than impact printing (that is, no print heads move, no print hammers fire), resulting in much higher speeds and quieter operation. The process resembles the operation of a photocopy machine (Figure 6.12): A laser beam is directed across the surface of a light-sensitive drum and fired as needed to record an image in the form of a pattern of tiny dots. The image is then transferred to the paper—a page at a time—in the same fashion as a copy machine, using a special toner.

The major advantages of laser printers are:

- Very high speed
- Low noise level
- Low maintenance requirements
- Very high image quality
- Excellent graphics capabilities
- A variety of type sizes and styles
- On large, high-speed laser printers, forms can be printed at the same time data is recorded in them.

When high-speed laser printers (also called *page printers*) were introduced, they were very expensive. Their cost could only be justified in large data processing organizations where a print speed capability of between 10,000 and 20,000 lines (about 300 pages) per minute was required. Figure 6.13 shows a large high-speed laser printer system. However, recent laser printer technology has made desktop versions available at very reasonable prices. For less than $3000, a small, desktop laser printer can be obtained that can produce up to ten pages of printed material per minute—more than ten times the speed of a letter-quality printer. Laser printers that handle about 20 pages per minute are also available for minicomputer systems.

The desktop laser printer has become a very popular output device for microcomputer-based systems. Many practitioners of "desktop publishing," which is publishing you do yourself, prefer desktop laser printers because of the high-quality images they produce. Figure 6.14 shows a popular desktop laser printer.

The primary limitation of laser printers at this time is restriction to single-color output. And desktop laser printers need a minimum of 1200–2000 K internal memory (RAM) to build a high-resolution full-page image (300 × 300 dots per square inch). However, they are very popular in the business community. To help you understand why, Table 6.2 compares the various types of nonimpact printers.

PLOTTERS

A plotter is a specialized output device designed to produce high-quality graphics in a variety of colors. There are two basic types of plotters: those that use pens and those that don't. Drum plotters and flatbed plotters both use pens. Electrostatic plotters do not.

In a **drum plotter,** the paper is mounted on the surface of a drum. The drum revolves and the plotter pens (which are similar to felt-tip pens) are horizontally positioned over the target area. When the paper has rotated to the correct point, the pens are dropped to the surface and moved left and right under program control across the paper as the drum revolves. When the image is complete, the pens are

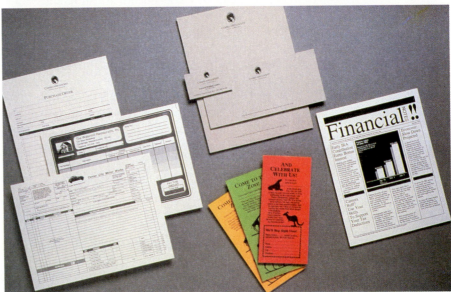

FIGURE 6.13
High-speed laser printer system from Hewlett-Packard with sample output.

TABLE 6.2 Comparison of Nonimpact Printers

Type	Major Use	Technology	Advantages	Disadvantages	Typical Speed	Approximate Cost
Thermal	Low-speed	Temperature-sensitive; paper changes color when treated; characters are formed by selectively heating print head	Quiet; relatively inexpensive	Special paper required; paper fades (poor print quality)	Several dozen to several hundred characters per second	Under $10,000
Ink-Jet	High-speed	Electrostatically charged drops hit paper	High-quality printing	Relatively slow; clogged jets	Several hundred characters per second	Usually under $30,000
Laser	High-speed	Laser beam directed onto a drum, "etching" spots that attract toner, which is then transferred to paper	Very high speed; excellent quality	High cost	Several hundred pages per minute (desktop lasers print 6–10 pages per minute)	Several hundred thousand dollars ($1600–$7000 for desktop laser printers)

FIGURE 6.14
Desktop laser printer. This model is made by Hewlett-Packard.

raised from the surface. **Flatbed plotters** are designed so that the paper is placed flat and one or more pens move horizontally and vertically across the paper. **Electrostatic plotters** use electrostatic charges to create images out of very small dots on specially treated paper. The paper is run through a developer to allow the image to appear. Electrostatic plotters are faster than pen plotters and can produce images of very high resolution.

Figure 6.15 shows a drum plotter, a flatbed plotter, and an electrostatic plotter. Figure 6.16 shows a plotted graph that was generated on a flatbed plotter. The cost of a plotter can range from about $1000 to more than $100,000, depending on the machine's speed and ability to generate high-resolution images. Several 2- to 8-pen flatbed plotters are available for microcomputer systems, as are some small drum plotters; large plotters, used with large computer systems, can produce drawings up to 8 feet by 8 feet, or sometimes even larger.

FIGURE 6.15
Not a plodder. Two commonly used pen plotters are (top) the flatbed plotter and (below left) the drum plotter. The electrostatic plotter (below right) uses electrostatic charges to produce images. All produce high-quality graphic output for presentations.

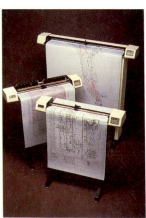

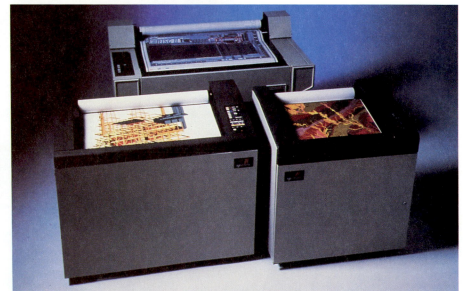

SOFTCOPY OUTPUT DEVICES

Eyestrain. Headaches. Neck cramps. What is a frequent cause of these complaints? The video display screen, the output device that many business users deal with the most. Actually, complaints have diminished as video display technology and ergonomics, the science of human comfort, have advanced. The two main types of video screens are the cathode-ray tube (CRT) and the flat panel.

CATHODE-RAY TUBE

The **cathode-ray tube (CRT),** probably the most popular softcopy output device, is used with terminals connected to large computer systems and as a monitor for microcomputer systems. This type of video display screen is used to allow the operator to view data entered into the computer and information produced by the computer as a result of processing.

The principal components of a CRT are (1) an electron gun, (2) a yoke, (3) a shadow mask, and (4) a phosphor-coated screen (Figure 6.17). To create an image on the screen, the **electron gun** fires a beam of electrons at the inside of the screen, which causes the phosphors to glow. The light from the phosphors creates the display you see on the screen. The electron beam is directed across the screen horizontally and vertically by the magnetic field produced by the yoke under the control of the computer software. The **yoke** is a cylinder placed in front of the electron gun that can generate a controlled magnetic field (like a directional magnet). The **shadow mask** is a shield with holes drilled in it that is used to prevent the dispersion of the beam (because the beam naturally tends to get wider as it travels toward the screen), so that only a small, precise portion of the beam reaches the screen.

The distance between any two adjacent holes in the shadow mask is referred to as **dot pitch.** The smaller the dot pitch, the smaller the impact point will be on the screen and the more precise the resulting image will be. The glowing phosphors,

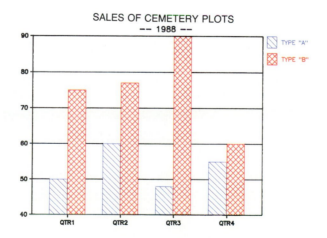

FIGURE 6.16
Cemetery plot. This graph was produced in about 5 minutes using a flatbed plotter.

which are the picture elements, are called **pixels** for short. The smaller the pixels (the more points that can be illuminated on the screen), the better the image clarity, or **resolution.**

It takes more than one illuminated pixel to form a whole character, such as the letter *e* in the word *Help* (Figure 6.18). And a finite number of characters can be displayed on a screen at once. The screen can be thought of as divided into a series of **character boxes**—fixed locations on the screen where a standard character can be placed. Most screens are capable of displaying 80 characters of data horizontally and 25 lines vertically. By multiplying the two numbers we can determine the number of character boxes that the electron gun can target—namely, 2000. The more pixels that fit into a character box, the higher the resolution of the resulting image.

As mentioned earlier, the term *resolution* refers to the crispness of the image displayed on the screen. Three factors are used to measure resolution: lines of resolution (vertical and horizontal), raster scan rate, and bandwidth. To determine the number of lines of resolution that a video display can display vertically, simply multiply the number of pixels in each character box vertically times the number of lines of text that can be displayed on the screen at one time—say, 25. If a character

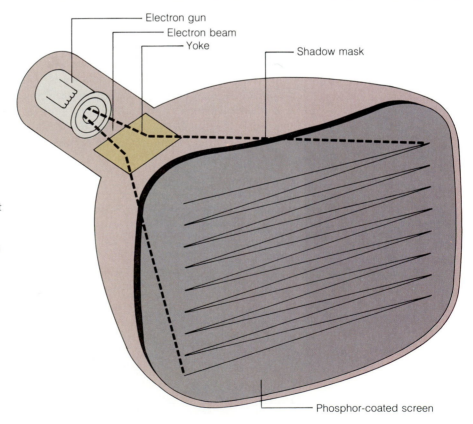

FIGURE 6.17
CRT does not stand for Computer-Run Television. But, in a way, it could, because the screen resembles a TV screen, and the production of images is run by computer software. This illustration shows how. The electron gun emits a beam of electrons that moves across the phosphor-coated screen under the control of the yoke's magnetic field. The glowing phosphors emit light, which makes up the image on the screen. The distance between the points of light is fixed by the shadow mask.

Electron gun
Electron beam
Yoke
Shadow mask
Phosphor-coated screen

box has 14 pixels vertically, the display would have a vertical resolution of 14 × 25, which equals 350. To determine the number of lines of resolution horizontally, we simply multiply the number of pixels in each character box horizontally times the number of characters that can be displayed per line—say, 80. Thus, if a character box has 9 pixels horizontally, the horizontal resolution would be 9 × 80, or 720. For this monitor, the lines of resolution would be stated as 720 × 350. When you select a monitor, choose one with the highest possible number of lines of resolution.

The term **raster scan rate** refers to how many times per second the image on the screen can be *refreshed*—that is, "lit up" again. Because the phosphors hit by the electron beam do not glow very long, the electron beam must continuously sweep across the screen from left to right. If the raster scan rate is too low, the image will begin to fade and the screen will seem to flicker, which can be very hard on the eyes. The higher the raster scan rate, the better the image quality—and the less eyestrain.

The final factor that affects image resolution is the **bandwidth.** This term refers to the rate at which data can be sent to the electron gun to control its movement, positioning, and firing. The higher the bandwidth, the faster the electron gun can be directed to do its job.

FIGURE 6.18
Building character. Each character on the screen is made up of a number of pixels, or picture elements.

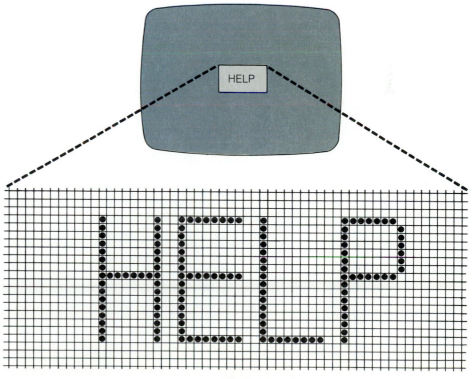

Pixels

CRTs have some disadvantages that recent technology has been trying to overcome, most notably: (1) size, (2) power consumption, and (3) fragility. The CRT is rather large and bulky because of the need to separate the electron gun from the screen by a particular distance, so it is unsuitable as a display screen for portable computers. The CRT also tends to draw a substantial amount of electric power, again making it unsuitable to be used with portable computers, which occasionally need to run on batteries. Finally, as with a television, the CRT's glass tube and screen can be damaged if not handled carefully.

MONOCHROME AND COLOR MONITORS   A **monochrome monitor** (a monitor capable of displaying only a single-color image) and an **RGB color monitor** (RGB stands for red, green, blue) differ in two principal ways. First, they have different numbers of electron guns. A monochrome monitor has only one electron gun (Figure 6.17); however, as shown in Figure 6.19, an RGB color monitor has three electron guns. Second, the screen in an RGB color monitor is coated with three types of phosphors: red, green, and blue.

FIGURE 6.19
RGB monitor. The workings of an RGB color monitor are similar to those of a monochrome CRT, except that three types of phosphors—red, green, and blue—are hit by three electron beams. Each pixel has three color dots that are activated to different degrees to produce a wide range of colors.

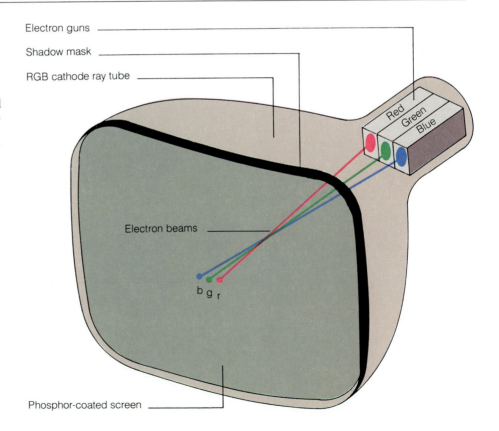

The operation principles of both monitors are almost exactly the same. However, each pixel in an RGB monitor is made up of three dots of phosphors, one of each color. The three electron guns direct their beams together. Each gun is aimed precisely so that it can hit a specific color dot in each pixel. A wide variety of colors can be created by controlling which guns fire and how long a burst they project at each dot. For example, if all three guns are fired at full intensity, a specific color is created for that pixel. If only two guns are fired at full intensity and the third gun is fired at half intensity, an entirely different color results. By varying the intensity with which the guns fire, RGB monitors are capable of displaying a large number of different colors. As you might expect, the control circuitry and software to direct the operation of an RGB monitor are somewhat more sophisticated than the corresponding components for a monochrome monitor.

Recent developments in color "cards" and circuit boards are providing microcomputers with improved color capabilities. With appropriate software, sufficient internal memory, and compatible monitors, Color Graphics Adapters (CGA), Enhanced Color Adapters (ECA), and Hercules graphics cards—plugged into the motherboard of a personal computer—provide painting and drawing functions. These cards also support laser printers, such as the Hewlett-Packard Laserjet.

CHARACTER-MAPPED DISPLAY   The patterns of pixels used to represent the standard characters displayed on a monitor (the alphabetic characters, numbers, and special symbols) in **character-mapped display** are drawn from prerecorded templates (guides) stored in a video display ROM chip. When the user's software sends a request to display, for example, the letter A at a specific location, the template for that pixel pattern is looked up in the video display ROM chip. The electron gun then uses this pattern when it fires at the phosphors in the appropriate character box. In a personal computer the screen has 25 lines with 80 characters per line; this means that there are 2000 positions on the screen where a predefined character can be placed.

BIT-MAPPED DISPLAY   Character-mapped display cannot be used for extensive graphics because of the limited number of templates available. To create the variety of images necessary to produce graphics, the computer needs to be able to direct each electron beam individually at each pixel on the screen, not just superimpose a template over a character box. This approach requires more sophisticated control circuitry, software, and internal memory than character-mapped display requires.

In a video display with **bit-mapped,** also called *dot-addressable* or *all-points-addressable*, graphics capability, the entire screen is a single character box. A screen that can display 25 lines of text with 80 characters per line contains about 252,000 pixels; as a result, bit-mapped graphics-capable monitors require an ample supply of internal memory to store all the image specifications before electron gun firing can begin. A minimum of 64 K of RAM should be dedicated to creating the image specification. The more memory available, the more sophisticated the graphic image that can be created on the screen—subject to the hardware limitations of the CRT, of course.

FLAT SCREEN TECHNOLOGIES

The disadvantages of the CRT—large size, high power consumption, and fragility—plus occasional flickering images and low (very low!) levels of emitted radiation have led to the development of **flat screen** technologies.

Flat screen technology is particularly useful for lap-top computers, which can be used in the office and then taken home or on trips. Producing a truly lap-size, or lap-top, computer—that is, fully functional and weighing 10 pounds or less—has not been easy, and designing the video display unit has been the most difficult problem.

Interest in lap-top computers encouraged researchers to explore different approaches to developing high-resolution, low-power-consumption flat screens with the same graphics capabilities of the traditional CRT. The most effective results to date have been achieved in three areas: liquid crystal display, electroluminescent display, and gas plasma display.

LIQUID CRYSTAL DISPLAY   The **liquid crystal display (LCD)** has been the most popular choice of many manufacturers of lap-top computers. (You can also find LCDs on the faces of clocks, watches, calculators, and the like.) LCDs use a clear liquid chemical trapped in tiny pockets between two pieces of glass. Each pocket of liquid is covered both front and back by very thin wires. When a small amount of current is applied to both wires, a chemical reaction turns the chemical a dark color—thereby blocking light. The point of blocked light is the pixel.

The principal advantages of LCDs are:

- Low power consumption
- Low cost
- Small size

The biggest disadvantages are:

- LCDs do not emit light; as a result, the image has very little contrast.
- The screen is very susceptible to glare, so the optimum viewing angle is very narrow.
- LCDs as yet have no color capability.
- The resolution is not as good as that of a CRT.

Significant research is being conducted to overcome the limitations of LCD screens. The recent development of the back-lit "twisted" screen, for example, decreases glare and improves contrast, thereby making the screen easier to look at. The Zenith 181 was the first to use this technology; other vendors, such as IBM, Toshiba, and Grid Systems, are following suit. Several companies are also actively working on the development of LCDs with full color capability. It is anticipated that LCD will continue to be a popular technology for some time. Figure 6.20 shows three of the currently popular lap-top computers that use LCDs.

ELECTROLUMINESCENT DISPLAY   The first flat panel display used in a powerful lap-top computer was **electroluminescent (EL) display;** however, it uses too much power to be suitable for battery-powered lap-top computers. As you can see in Figure 6.21, the circuitry of an electroluminescent display takes up much less space than that of a CRT. EL display has two main components: a light-emitting layer of phosphor and two sets of electrodes. The electrodes surround the phosphor layer much like the slices of bread surround the ham in a sandwich. On one side, the electrodes form vertical columns (usually 512), and on the other side, they form horizontal rows (usually 256). To form a pixel on the screen, current is sent to the intersection of the appropriate row and column; the combined voltages from the row and the column cause the phosphor to glow at that point.

FIGURE 6.20
LCDs on display. Three of the most popular lap-top computers that use liquid crystal display are (top) the Hewlett-Packard Portable Plus, (bottom left) the Zenith 181, and (bottom right) the Grid Lite.

EL display provides very high image resolution and excellent graphics capability; it also generates its own light (called an *active display*), unlike LCD, which only reflects light. Several manufacturers are currently working on the development of

FIGURE 6.21
CRTs are fatter than electroluminescent display screens.

FIGURE 6.22
Gas plasma display. This modern portable personal computer by Grid Systems uses a gas plasma display.

electroluminescent displays with full color capability. Most experts have predicted that this technology will come closest to matching or even surpassing all of the capabilities of the traditional CRT. The major limitation of this technology has been cost.

GAS PLASMA DISPLAY   The oldest flat screen technology is the **gas plasma display** (Figure 6.22). The first flat screen display produced by a major vendor was produced by IBM. This unit, which was quite large, could display up to four pages of text at one time. This technology involves the use of three pieces of glass sandwiched together. The inner layer has a large number of small holes drilled in it. As the outer two layers are placed on either side of the middle one, the holes are filled with a gas mixture—usually a mixture of argon and neon. Both outer layers of glass contain a thin grid of vertical and horizontal wires. A pixel is turned on by charging the appropriate horizontal and vertical wires. Depending on the mixture of gases, the color displayed ranges from orange to red.

The principal advantages of gas plasma display are:

- The images are much brighter than on a standard CRT.
- The resolution is excellent.
- Glare is not a significant problem.
- The screen does not flicker like some CRTs.

The main disadvantages are:

- Only a single color is available (reddish orange).
- The technology is expensive.
- It uses a lot of power.

Several new lap-top computers use gas plasma display, including a new model of the Grid Compass, the Ericsson Portable PC, the Sharp Executive PC, and the Toshiba 3100. Table 6.3 compares the different flat screen technologies.

TABLE 6.3   Comparison of Flat Screen Technologies

	LCD	Back-Lit, "Twisted" LCD	Gas Plasma	Electroluminescent
Power consumption	low	low	high	high
Battery operation?	yes	yes	no	no
Contrast	low	medium-high	high	high
Image color	black	blue-black	red orange	yellow
Screen background	dull	light (varies)	dark	dark
Cost	low	medium	high	high
Graphics capability	low	low-medium	high	high

ALTERNATIVES TO TRADITIONAL HARDCOPY AND SOFTCOPY OUTPUT

The volume of information produced by computers is staggering. If we were limited to regular hardcopy output, it is likely that most Americans would be knee-deep in paper by now. However, what do you use when you don't want to take up space with regular hardcopy output, but softcopy output on display screens is inappropriate?

CAMERA OUTPUT MICROFILM/MICROFICHE (COM) SYSTEMS

Camera output systems have been in use for more than ten years. The two most popular systems capture computer output on microfilm or microfiche. The principal advantages of this technology are:

- *Speed*—COM systems can easily handle output at a rate in excess of 30,000 lines per minute. This is about 50% faster than most large laser printers.
- *Size*—The output is condensed in size (compared to hardcopy output) by a factor ranging from 20 to 100.
- *Cost*—The cost per page of printed material is less than that of regular hardcopy output methods.

The major disadvantage of COM systems is that, because of the reduced visual size of the output, special equipment must be used to read the output that has been stored. Figure 6.23 shows a microfiche panel and one of the reader devices used to display the information. Because of the high cost of camera output systems (they can exceed $100,000), companies may not buy very many readers, so users may have to share them or go to another department to find one, which may be inconvenient. Microfilm and microfiche are most widely used by libraries for records and reference materials.

VOICE OUTPUT SYSTEMS

"Please close the door." "Please fasten your seatbelt." "You are now exceeding 65 miles per hour." Does your car talk to you? Many new cars have voice output devices, as do the telephone systems we've already mentioned. **Voice output systems** are relatively new and can be used in some situations where traditional display-screen softcopy output is inappropriate: It is certainly more helpful to hear a warning that you are speeding than to take your eyes off the road to check a display.

Voice output technology has had to overcome many hurdles. The most difficult has been that every individual perceives speech differently; that is, the voice patterns, pitches, and inflections we can hear and understand are different for all of us. It is not always easy to understand an unfamiliar voice pattern. At this point, two different approaches to voice output have evolved: speech coding and speech synthesis. **Speech coding** relies on human speech as a reservoir of sounds to draw from in building the words and phrases to be output. Sounds are codified and stored on disk to be retrieved and translated back as sounds. Speech coding has been used in applications such as automobiles, toys, and games. **Speech synthesis** relies on the

FIGURE 6.23
COM: Camera Output Microfilm/Microfiche. (Top) Microfiche; (bottom) this equipment enlarges microfilm and can print output on paper.

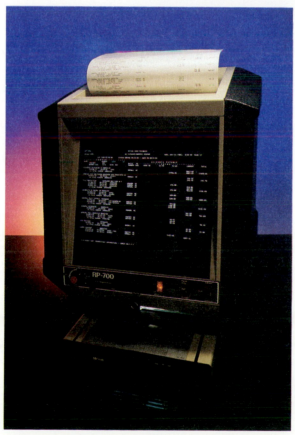

use of a set of basic speech sounds that are created electronically without the use of a human voice.

Researchers are continuing to develop and improve voice output technologies. Many new products using voice output are expected to appear in the marketplace during the next decade. The largest application to date for the speech synthesis approach to voice output—converting text into "spoken" words—has many potential uses, including providing reading machines for the blind.

OUTPUT CONTROLS   We have emphasized that the quality of information the user produces must be very high, because decisions are made on the basis of this information, and much of the business runs according to it. You have learned that data you enter must be accurate and complete and that input control methods have been designed to ensure just that. You also learned that different input and processing methods can produce information more quickly than others, thus affecting the timeliness of the information you are dealing with.

In addition, measures need to be taken to protect stored data so that not just anyone can get to it; this precaution should also be taken with sensitive output. Information should be accessible only to authorized personnel, and output that contains sensitive information should be destroyed when it is no longer needed.

Some examples of typical output controls are:

- A distribution list for all reports, so that only those people on the list receive the information
- Requiring signatures on a predetermined form from those people who receive reports
- A delivery schedule for reports so that people expecting them can follow up if the reports do not arrive on time
- Requiring users to enter passwords when attempting to obtain softcopy output on the video display screen
- Guidelines on how, when, and where to destroy reports after they are no longer needed
- Securing sensitive data and information in an inaccessible location when it is not being actively reviewed

The degree to which output control measures are taken must be determined by the needs of the business and both the people who run it and those who work there. Obviously, the extent of the controls is directly related to the value and the sensitivity of the information.

ONWARD:
SOFTWARE—TAKING CARE OF BUSINESS

This chapter completes the section on hardware. Now that you know the basics about the hardware associated with the four parts of a computer-based information system—input, storage, processing, and output—you may wonder how you can possibly stay current with new developments after you have finished your courses or your degree and joined the work force. One of the best ways is to check reviews and articles in popular weekly and monthly computer newspapers and magazines—*PC World, Info World, PC Week, Macworld,* and *Computerworld,* to cite a few. Such publications are also good sources for staying current with the topic of our next chapter—software—as you shall see, after briefly revisiting your booming business, Sporting Life.

SUMMARY

Before deciding which output hardware and media to use, business users must determine what *kinds* of output they need based on the kind of information they need in order to perform regular job duties and to make decisions (and on how often they need to do both). Users should also consider how much noise the equipment makes, how fast it works, how expensive it is, and, above all, whether it is compatible with the equipment they already have.

The four basic categories of computer-produced output are (1) text, (2) graphics, (3) voice, and (4) computer-usable. Text is the type of output used most often. Within these categories there are two types of output media: hardcopy, which is generally thought of as being tangible, or "touchable," and softcopy, which is thought of as intangible. Paper, the most-used hardcopy output medium, comes in a variety of forms. Continuous-form paper, which uses a tractor feed, was developed for use in computer printers so that users would not have to feed individual sheets into the computer one at a time. (When this is done, it is called *friction feed.*)

The second most commonly used output medium is a softcopy one—the video display image. The two types of display screen used most often are a computer terminal connected to a large computer system and a monitor attached to a microcomputer system. When computer display devices are not readily available and information has some value over time, it is most often produced in hardcopy form. When computer display devices are readily available and information must be accessed quickly, it is often produced in softcopy form.

Output hardware is categorized according to whether the hardware produces hardcopy or softcopy. The main hardcopy output devices are printers and plotters.

A printer can print characters, symbols, and sometimes graphics on paper. Printers are categorized according to whether or not the image produced is formed by physical contact of the print mechanism with the paper. Impact printers make contact; nonimpact printers do not.

Impact printers usually form images by pressing an inked ribbon against the paper with a hammer-like mechanism. A letter-quality printer, like a typewriter, presses fully formed characters against the ribbon. A dot-matrix printer uses separate pin-like hammers to form characters out of dot patterns. Letter-quality printers produce higher quality images than dot-matrix printers do and are generally used for business letters, important memos, and reports. However, letter-quality printers are slower and noisier than dot-matrix printers, and they cannot produce graphics. The common types of letter-quality printers are the daisy wheel printer and the thimble printer. Dot-matrix printers, because they do not print fully formed characters, are more flexible and can be used to print graphics.

The high-volume output requirements of most large computer installations cannot be satisfied by dot-matrix or letter-quality printers. Large computer systems often use special high-speed printers, called *line printers*, because they print a whole line at a time. Three common types of line printers are band printers, belt printers, and print-chain printers.

The main categories of nonimpact printers are ink-jet printers, thermal printers, and laser printers. These printers make much less noise than impact printers, but they cannot be used to generate carbon copies.

Ink-jet printers, which are about as fast as dot-matrix printers, form images with tiny droplets of ink fired through a plate with holes drilled in it. Color ink-jet printers are used to produce graphics; however, ink jets can get clogged, and the image quality is not considered to be as good as that produced by plotters.

Thermal printers use heat to produce an image on specially treated paper. They are very quiet; however, they are slow, the special paper is expensive, and they can print only in a single color. The new thermal transfer printer uses a heated print head and an inked ribbon coated with wax to press images onto paper. This process costs less and produces a higher quality image than regular thermal printers do.

Laser printers are nonmechanical, nonimpact printers. Because the process uses no print heads to move or print hammers to fire, the result is high speed and quiet operation. Laser printers work somewhat like photocopying machines. They use laser beams to transfer images to sensitive paper that is then coated with toner—the toner sticks to the spots sensitized by the laser. Laser printers print a page at a time and can produce very high-quality images, so they are often used for graphics. They also have low maintenance requirements. Laser printers used to be very expensive; however, because their prices have fallen, small laser printers are now within reach of users wanting a high-quality desktop printer. They are frequently used in desktop publishing, which uses microcomputers, special software packages, and laser printers to produce material ready to be published.

A plotter is most often used for producing graphics because it can output free-form drawings on paper in color. Plotters are categorized according to whether or not they use pens, how the paper is placed into them, and which of their parts move. Drum plotters and flatbed plotters use pens; electrostatic printers do not. In a drum plotter, paper is mounted on a rotating drum onto which pens are dropped and moved left and right to create images. In flatbed plotters, the paper is flat and the pens move horizontally and vertically across the paper. Electrostatic plotters use electrostatic charges to create images out of very small dots on specially treated paper, which is then run through a developer to allow the image to appear. Electrostatic plotters are faster than pen plotters and can produce images of very high resolution.

The main softcopy output devices are cathode-ray tube (CRT) video screens and flat video screens. Camera output microfilm/microfiche systems and voice output systems are sometimes considered to be softcopy output systems, but we have categorized them separately.

The CRT, which is used with terminals connected to large computer systems and as a monitor for microcomputer systems, has an electron gun that fires at phosphors on the inside of the screen, causing them to glow. The yoke and the shadow mask keep the electrons that are fired by the gun under control. The glowing phosphors become the picture elements—pixels, for short. It takes a group of pixels to form one character, and there is a finite number of characters that can be displayed on the screen at once. Most screens display 80 characters horizontally and 25 lines vertically, which yields 2000 character boxes. The more pixels that fit into a character box to form a character, the higher the resolution—or crispness—of the resulting image.

The three factors used to measure resolution are the lines of resolution (vertical and horizontal), the raster scan rate, and the bandwidth. Vertical resolution is found by multiplying the number of vertical pixels in the character box by the number of lines displayed on the screen; horizontal resolution is found by multiplying the number of horizontal pixels in the character box by the number of characters displayed on the line. Raster scan rate refers to how many times per second the image on the screen is refreshed—how many times the fading phosphors are "relit." The higher the raster scan rate, the better the quality of the screen image and the less strain on the eyes. The bandwidth refers to the rate at which data is sent to the electron gun—the higher the bandwidth, the faster the electron gun can be directed to do its job.

CRTs can display images in one color (monochrome) or several colors. The RGB (red, green, blue) monitor uses three electron guns to illuminate red, green, and blue phosphors.

The most notable disadvantages of CRTs are their large size (to accommodate the electron gun setup), their high rate of power consumption, and their fragility.

Graphics are best shown in bit-mapped display, rather than character-mapped display. In the latter, characters are imposed by templates—kinds of preformed guides—controlled by the software; this approach does not lend itself to free-form drawing. In bit-mapped displays, the individual pixels on the screen can be controlled. Bit-mapped graphics-capable monitors require a large supply of internal memory to store all the image specifications before electron gun firing. The more memory available, the more sophisticated the image that can be created on the screen.

The disadvantages of the CRT and rising interest in portable and lap-top computers led to the development of flat screen technology, which is becoming a favored alternative to the CRT. The three most common types of flat panel displays are liquid crystal display (LCD), electroluminescent (EL) display, and gas plasma display.

Liquid crystal display involves trapping tiny pockets of a liquid chemical between two pieces of glass. Each pocket is covered with wires that can pass electric current to it, thereby causing a chemical reaction—the liquid turns dark and blocks light, becoming a "pixel." LCDs have a low rate of power consumption, are inexpensive, and are conveniently small. However, many use reflected light and do not emit their own light, so contrast is low and eyestrain can result. Also, they have no color capability at this time, and the resolution is not as good as that of a CRT.

The electroluminescent display uses a layer of phosphors and two sets of electrodes to create points of light (pixels). An EL display is conveniently small and its resolution and graphics capability are excellent; however, it uses too much power to be used in battery powered lap-top computers, and it is relatively expensive.

Gas plasma display uses a mixture of gases and a thin grid of wires held between pieces of glass to create a display of pixels illuminated by electrical charges. The color of the display ranges from orange to red. The images in a gas plasma display are brighter than on a CRT, the resolution is excellent, and glare is not a problem as it can be with LCDs.

Camera output systems are often used by companies that don't want to take up space with a lot of regular hardcopy output, like paper, but have needs not met by softcopy output. These systems capture computer output on microfilm or microfiche—both approaches can be referred to as COM. COM systems are fast, produce output condensed in size, and are not particularly expensive. However, special equipment is needed to read the output that has been stored.

Voice output systems are relatively new; they can be used in situations where hardcopy is inappropriate and commonly used softcopy output devices are inconvenient.

As with input and storage, care must be taken to ensure that output is responsibly generated, shared, and disposed of. Control methods should be established to ensure that only authorized users see sensitive output and that output is properly secured.

KEY TERMS

band printer
bandwidth
belt printer
bit-mapped display
camera output
   microfilm/microfiche
   systems (COM)
cathode-ray tube (CRT)
character box
character-mapped
   display
daisy wheel printer
dot-matrix printer
dot pitch
drum plotter
electroluminescent (EL)
   display

electron gun
electrostatic plotter
flatbed plotter
flat screen
gas plasma display
impact printer
ink-jet printer
laser printer
letter-quality printer
line printer
liquid crystal display
   (LCD)
monochrome monitor
nonimpact printer
output
pixel
plotter

print-chain printer
printer
raster scan rate
resolution
RGB color monitor
shadow mask
speech coding
speech synthesis
thermal printer
thermal transfer printer
thimble printer
voice output system
yoke

EXERCISES

MATCHING

Match each of the following terms to the phrase that is the most closely related:

1. _____ output
2. _____ thermal printer
3. _____ shadow mask
4. _____ dot pitch
5. _____ nonimpact printer
6. _____ raster scan rate
7. _____ flatbed plotter
8. _____ pixel

9. _____ resolution
10. _____ impact printer
11. _____ dot-matrix printer
12. _____ speech coding
13. _____ RGB monitor
14. _____ character box
15. _____ laser printer
16. _____ monochrome monitor

a. A softcopy output device capable of displaying only one color.
b. A hardcopy output device that uses pens to produce high-quality graphics in a variety of colors.
c. An approach used in voice output technology.
d. Information produced by a computer.
e. This component of a CRT fires a beam of electrons at the inside of a screen and causes the phosphors to glow.
f. The crispness of the image displayed on a screen.
g. A softcopy output device capable of displaying a variety of colors.
h. This type of hardcopy output device uses heat to produce an image.
i. A CRT component that serves to prevent the dispersion of an electron beam.
j. This hardcopy output device operates with a technology that resembles that of a photocopy machine.
k. The distance between any two holes in a shadow mask, which helps determine the quality of the image on the screen.
l. A hardcopy output device that makes contact with the paper.
m. A printer that doesn't form an image by striking characters against a ribbon.
n. The print mechanism in this type of impact printer is made up of separate pin-like hammers that create an image with dots.
o. The number of times a CRT screen must be scanned by the electron gun to maintain an image on the screen.
p. Fixed locations on the screen where a standard character can be placed.
q. Picture elements that make up a softcopy image.

MULTIPLE CHOICE

1. Which of the following printer types will you not use if your intent is to print on multipart carbon forms?
   a. laser
   b. dot-matrix
   c. daisy wheel

  d. thimble
  e. none of the above

2. Which of the following factors does not affect resolution?
  a. screen size
  b. raster scan rate
  c. vertical and horizontal lines of resolution
  d. bandwidth
  e. none of the above

3. Which of the following is a type of impact printer?
  a. laser
  b. thermal
  c. dot-matrix
  d. ink-jet
  e. thermal transfer

4. Which of the following is a disadvantage of using a camera output system?
  a. speed
  b. size
  c. specialized equipment needed to read output
  d. cost
  e. none of the above

5. Which of the following is not a component of a CRT?
  a. electron gun
  b. gas plasma
  c. shadow mask
  d. phosphor screen
  e. none of the above

6. If your intent is to produce high-quality graphics and you have the following output hardware devices to choose from, which would you choose?
  a. dot-matrix printer
  b. laser printer
  c. thimble printer
  d. plotter
  e. electroluminescent display

7. Which of the following is a principal difference between a monochrome monitor and an RGB monitor?
  a. number of electron guns
  b. resolution
  c. size
  d. cost
  e. gas plasma

8. Which of the following is not considered to be a type of flat screen technology?
  a. gas plasma
  b. liquid crystal display
  c. electroluminescent display
  d. RGB monitor

e. none of the above

9. What is the principal hurdle to be overcome before voice output technology will be more widely used?
   a. size of the specialized equipment
   b. high cost
   c. differences in how individuals perceive speech
   d. need for specialized equipment

10. Which of the following is considered to be the major limitation to CRT technology?
   a. size
   b. power consumption
   c. fragility
   d. all of the above

SHORT ANSWER

1. When might you want output to be in a computer-usable form.
2. What are the differences between hardcopy output and softcopy output, and when would you consider using each?
3. Why has there been such interest in developing flat screen technologies?
4. What advantages does the laser printer have over other printers? What is its principal limitation?
5. If you, a member of an organization, are in charge of purchasing output hardware, what questions will you want to ask before you buy anything?
6. What are the limitations of CRT technology?
7. Describe a situation in which an alternative to the traditional forms of hardcopy and softcopy output might be necessary.
8. What is meant by the term *output controls*? Why are output controls important?
9. When do you think you might find a need to use a plotter to output information? Why?
10. What are the principal differences between how an image is formed on a monochrome monitor and on an RGB monitor?

PROJECTS

1. Review the current computer publications for articles relating to uses of the flat screen technology. Where and for what purposes are flat screens being used?
2. Research the answer to the following question by reviewing the current computer publications: "What is the state of the art in printer technology, and how is it currently being used?"
3. Visit a local computer store to see what output devices are being displayed. What types of output devices that we've described in this chapter are not displayed? Why do you think this is? Ask the salesperson to verify your opinion.

WHAT DO YOU WANT THE COMPUTER TO DO FOR YOU?

THE STORY CONTINUES . . .

When we left you at Sporting Life, you were thinking about buying a computer to help you with inventory and general ledger record keeping. However, a lot has gone on since then, and like many people, you have put off acquiring a computer until the work load and related problems have become too serious to ignore.

For example, when the company next door moved out, you acquired the space to accommodate your increasing level of business. And, to support your expanded business, you have extended your hours to seven days a week: 9:00 A.M. to 9:00 P.M. Monday through Friday and 10:00 A.M. to 6:00 P.M. on Saturday and Sunday. You have also increased your product lines to include more than 1300 different items. As a result, your sales have increased from just over $2 million to more than $4.2 million!

HELP!

Roy is losing control of inventory; an increasing number of popular items are out of stock. Inventory records can't be kept up to date. In addition, the overall dollar investment in inventory has gone up substantially, and Roy feels that the money is not being properly managed. Meanwhile, Mary has run into difficulties handling the accounting work load; it's hard for her to keep up with the manual recording of all the daily sales entries to the sales journal.

All your employees now agree that your business definitely needs a computer: But what exactly do you want it to do for you? Before making *any* purchases, you must decide what you want to achieve in the areas of input, processing, storage, and output. The preceding four chapters (Part Two) have taught you the basic concepts in these areas as they relate to hardware. This information is enough for you to begin to think practically about how computers are useful in business.

After you have read the section on software, you will be able to get more specific about choosing software and compatible hardware for your business. In the meantime, to resolve the question posed above, you call a meeting to determine what the data and information needs of your staff are.

SIZING UP THE SITUATION

Mary says she expects the computer to produce a substantial amount of useful accounting information and to take over the major burden of accounting-related processing activities. She thinks that:

- She and the staff will need to retrieve information—for example, the status of customers' accounts—from the files and review it on the computer's display screen.
- A large volume of hardcopy reports will have to be produced, including:
  —Accounting ledgers: single copies, 80 columns wide, about 300 pages per week
  —Customer invoices: 3 copies of each, 80 columns wide, about 75 per day
  —Special reports: single copies, 132 columns wide, about 50 pages per day

Mary also thinks that it would be a good idea to analyze in graphic form the trend in accounts receivable and accounts payable. She is looking forward to being able to review graphs on the screen, as well as print them out occasionally.

Roy says that he needs the computer to provide assistance in tracking the status of inventory as a whole and in restocking inventory. He thinks that:

- The computer will have to allow him to quickly check on a terminal the status of any item in inventory.

EPISODE 2, CONTINUED

- He will have to track inventory turnover.
- The following reports will have to be produced:
  —Detailed inventory listings: 2 copies of each, 132 columns wide, about 30 pages daily
  —Inventory reorder report: single copies, 132 columns wide, about 2 pages a day
  —Purchase orders: three copies, 80 columns wide, about 75 per week

In addition, you, Roy, and Mary agree that you need to store the following kinds of computer files:

- Invoice files: both paid and unpaid invoices (about 5000 invoices)
- Purchase orders: both filled and unfilled (about 500)
- Customer information: about 2500 customers
- Employee files: folders are kept for each employee (average 25, including part-time employees)
- Accounting files: these records currently fill six filing cabinets
- Inventory files: all the data on items you order, store, and sell (item number, description, unit price)

SPECIFIC POINTS FOR DISCUSSION: WHAT'S YOUR OPINION?

Now that you know what your basic data and information needs are at Sporting Life, discuss the following points:

1. Which input hardware and methods would be best suited to your business?
   - Will the volume of input activity be high enough to warrant dedicated data entry systems? Or will you be better served by a less expensive general-purpose system?
   - Do you anticipate planning for on-line input or will batch input be satisfactory? Could you use both methods?
   - Do you think a bar code scanner might be useful? If so, how?
   - How about an optical scanner?
   - You'll probably need several types of printers. Based on your output needs, for which kinds will you research cost and limitations?

2. What factors would you consider to determine the types of computerized storage you need?
   - Do you think there will be a place for the use of floppy disks? If so, how will they be used?
   - Will you need a high-capacity hard disk? Why or why not?
   - Have you considered how important making backup copies of files will be? How could this be done?

3. Will you need both hardcopy and softcopy output? Give examples.
   - Are hardcopy or softcopy graphics going to be used? Give examples.

4. How powerful a computer system do you really need?
   - What factors would you consider in determining whether you need a microcomputer system, minicomputer system, or mainframe computer system?

Discussing the preceding questions should have helped you clarify what a computer could do for a business. But don't rush out and buy anything yet. First you must learn about software—how it is developed, what forms it comes in, and what it can do. After that, in the next episode, you will learn how to choose software that will fulfill Sporting Life's needs and be compatible with the types of hardware you are interested in.

PART THREE

3

SOFTWARE

Once upon a time the term *hardware* described iron fittings, tools, and other things created by the village blacksmith; military jargon then expanded the definition to include machines and, still later, computer equipment. In 1962, someone used this precedent to coin a new term to describe the programs, procedures, and related documentation associated with computers—*software*. No doubt the definition of software will change as much as hardware in the coming years, but in both cases many underlying concepts will probably remain the same. In the next three chapters, we will describe systems software, which has more to do with the computer than the user, and off-the-shelf applications software such as word processing or database managers that you will find useful in your career and that you may eventually use to develop your own particular kinds of applications.

■

CHAPTER SEVEN

7

APPLICATIONS SOFTWARE AND SYSTEMS SOFTWARE

Why can't you simply buy a floppy disk with the software program you need, put it into your microcomputer's disk drive, start it up, and have it run? Unfortunately, it's not often that easy; buying software is not like buying an audio cassette of your favorite music and slapping it into a tape deck, or renting a movie to play on your VCR. Computer software comes in two forms: applications software and systems software. Because different systems software is made for different purposes, and some applications software is not compatible with some systems software, it is important for business users to understand the fundamental concepts and features of these two types of software.

PREVIEW

When you have completed this chapter, you will be able to:

■

Explain why you should try to evaluate your applications software requirements before your other hardware and software requirements

■

Describe what applications software is and categorize the types of applications software

■

List and describe four types of systems software

■

The User Perspective

Can you use a daisy wheel letter-quality printer to print out a portrait of Abraham Lincoln? Can you use an RGB monitor to show the colors of the rainbow? With your knowledge of hardware, you know the answers to these questions. Different equipment has different uses. Likewise with software: A software program designed to handle text may not necessarily be used to draw charts and graphs or manipulate rows and columns of numbers.

To help you begin to understand the differences among types of software, let us repeat the definitions we gave back in Chapter 1 for applications and systems software. **Applications software** is a collection of related programs designed to perform a specific task—to solve a particular problem for the user. The task or problem may require, for example, computations for payroll processing or for maintaining different types of data in different types of files. A **systems software** program starts up the computer and functions as the principal coordinator of all hardware components and applications software programs. Without systems software loaded into the internal memory of your computer, your hardware and applications software will be useless.

How Does Software Affect You?

No such thing as software existed in the earliest computers. Instead, to change computer instructions, technicians would actually have to *rewire* the equipment (Figure 7.1). Then, in the 1950s, computer researchers—following the approach of Herman Hollerith and his census-tabulating machine—began to use punched cards to store program instructions. In the mid-1950s, high-speed storage devices that were developed for ready retrieval eliminated the need for hand-wired control panels. Since that time, the sophistication of computer hardware and software has increased exponentially.

Until the late 1970s, only trained computer operators and other computer specialists interacted directly with computer hardware. The appearance of the microcomputer in the late 1970s made computer hardware and software accessible to many more people because it was more affordable, easier to use, and flexible enough to handle very specific job-related tasks. Because of this accessibility, a large pool of applications software has been created to satisfy almost any business requirement. In other words, you do not have to be a specialist to use computer software to solve complicated and tedious problems in your work. However, you will be entering the job race without your running shoes if you do not understand the uses of—and the differences among—types of software.

What Software Is Available and How Good Is It?

Many people will buy an applications software program just because it was recommended by a friend. They do not bother to evaluate whether the program offers all

FIGURE 7.1
Software evolution. (a) At first only the most highly skilled specialists could use or "run" computer software. They would have to rewire the computer for each new task they wanted the computer to perform. (b) Today, because of the sophistication of modern software, people as diverse as schoolchildren and accountants are able to use computers for common tasks.

the features and processing capabilities necessary to meet their needs. It's much easier in the short run to simply take the friend's recommendation, but, in the long run, a lot of extra time and money will be spent. Knowing what software is available—and how to evaluate it—is vital to satisfy processing requirements.

For large computer systems, the choice of systems software tends to be made by computer specialists. Fewer systems software choices are available for microcomputers; the user makes the final selection on the basis of which systems software is compatible with the most applications software available to suit his or her needs and, of course, which computer hardware the systems software is compatible with.

If you are starting from scratch, you should choose your applications software *first*, after you identify your processing needs. Then choose compatible hardware models and systems software that will allow you to use your applications software efficiently and to expand your system if necessary. (Sometimes the systems software is automatically included with the computer.) By choosing your applications software first, you will ensure that all your processing requirements will be satisfied: You won't be forced to buy a software package that is your second choice simply because your first choice wasn't compatible with the hardware or systems software already purchased.

When you go to work in an office, chances are that the computer hardware and systems software will already be in operation, so if you have to choose anything, it will most likely be applications software to help you do your job. If you do find yourself in a position to choose applications software, make sure not only that it will satisfy the processing requirements of your job, but also that it is compatible with your company's hardware and software.

There is much more applications software to choose from than systems software. Applications software can be purchased off the shelf of a computer store to satisfy almost any business requirement; this software is often referred to as **off-the-shelf software.** The decision on what applications program to use therefore requires very careful analysis.

So much software is available today that even in the microcomputer software industry people need a directory or catalog of software to keep track of it. In the course of a year, *Software Reviews on File* (Figure 7.2) publishes hundred-word excerpts from some 3000 reviews of more than 500 new programs for microcomputers. Figure 7.3 shows a page from *PC World*, the "business magazine of PC products and solutions." Data Pro Publications also provides a valuable guide to computer hardware, software, services, and related topics of interest; however, the annual cost of subscribing to Data Pro Publications is more than $500. Figure 7.4 shows a typical software review found in *InfoWorld* magazine. Figure 7.5 shows some software reviews from the *Whole Earth Software Catalog*.

FIGURE 7.2
Software Reviews on File.
Each 64-page issue covers
approximately 40
programs—name, author,
producer, date, price, physical contents, and system
hardware requirements.

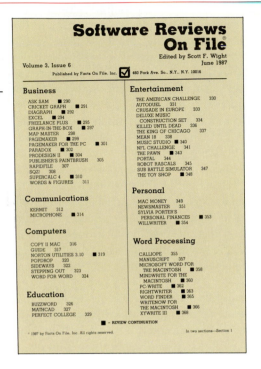

FIGURE 7.3
PC World review. This
"Executive Summary" is
typical of software reviews
published by PCW Com-
munications, Inc., in *PC
World* magazine, available
on newsstands.

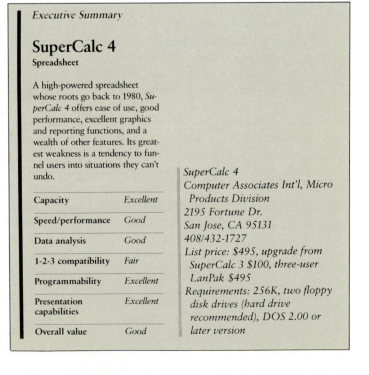

FIGURE 7.4
InfoWorld software review. *InfoWorld* magazine publishes reviews like this in every issue.

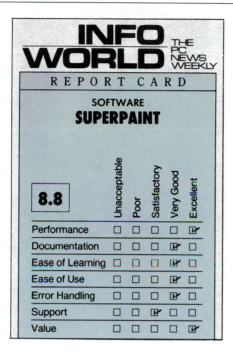

FIGURE 7.5
Whole Earth Software Catalog. The table of contents.

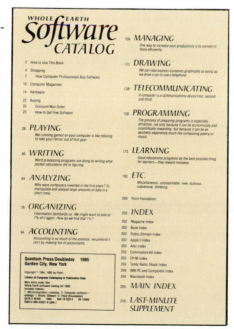

APPLICATIONS SOFTWARE

After the days of rewiring computers had passed, only two sources existed for basic applications software: (1) Software could be purchased from a computer hardware vendor, or (2) if you were a programmer, you could develop your own. Today, computer software has become a multibillion-dollar industry. More than a thousand companies have entered the applications software industry, and they have developed a wide variety of products. As a result, the number of sources of applications software has grown. Applications software can be acquired directly from a software manufacturer or from the growing number of businesses that specialize in the sale and support of microcomputer hardware and software. Most independent and computer chain stores devote a substantial amount of shelf space to applications software programs; some businesses specialize in selling only software.

If you can't find off-the-shelf software to meet your needs, you can develop—or have someone else develop—your own. If you don't know how to do it yourself, you can have the data processing professionals within your own organization develop the software, or you can hire outside consultants to do it. Unfortunately, hiring a professional to write software for you can become much more costly than the price of off-the-shelf software.

TYPES OF POPULAR APPLICATIONS SOFTWARE

Just as the subject matter of a book determines what literary category it falls into (such as history, gardening, cooking, or fiction), the capabilities of an applications software program determine how it is categorized. Applications software categories that are used most often include:

- General business management
- Industry-specific
- Special disciplines
- Education
- Personal/home management
- General-purpose software for the user

General business management software, the largest group of applications software, includes products that cover the vast majority of business software needs, including accounting, inventory control, finance and planning, personnel, office administration, project management, and many others. However, some industries have very specialized applications software requirements; special industry-specific software is designed to meet these needs. Typical industries requiring specific products include specialized accounting services, advertising, agriculture and farm management, architecture, banking, construction, dentistry, engineering, legal services, leasing and rental companies, personnel agencies, property management, publishing, and others.

Special-disciplines software is a category set aside for such hobbies and special-interest areas as amateur radio, astrology, geography, mathematics, music, sports and leisure, visual arts, and others. Education applications software products focus on educational administration, computer-aided instruction (CAI), and special education. Personal/home management software tends to group products according to whether they relate to education, entertainment, finance, or home management.

The following list highlights the types of general-purpose applications software programs you are likely to use in the business environment. Each type is covered in greater detail in the modules that follow Chapter 14.

WORD PROCESSING SOFTWARE   This software offers capabilities that greatly enhance the user's ability to create and edit documents (Figure 7.6). It enables the user to easily insert, delete, and move words, sentences, and paragraphs without ever using an eraser. **Word processing** programs also offer a number of features for "dressing up" documents with variable margins and type sizes and styles. For a more thorough and practical understanding of word processing software, refer to Module B.

FIGURE 7.6
My word! With word processing software you can get (b) without having to go through (a).

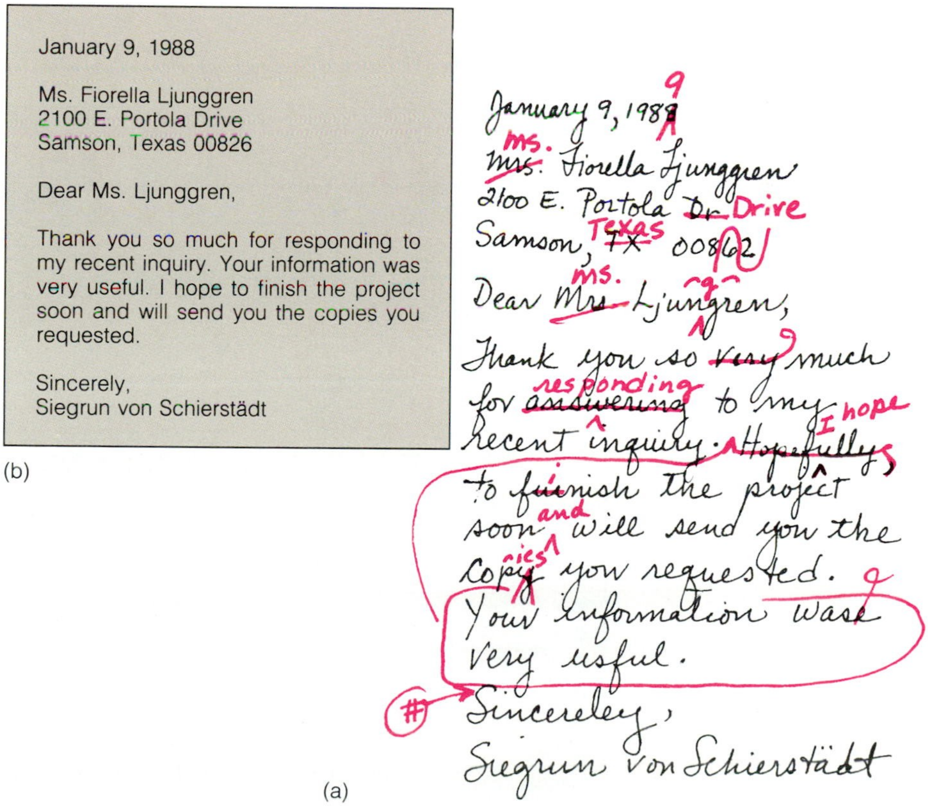

January 9, 1988

Ms. Fiorella Ljunggren
2100 E. Portola Drive
Samson, Texas 00826

Dear Ms. Ljunggren,

Thank you so much for responding to my recent inquiry. Your information was very useful. I hope to finish the project soon and will send you the copies you requested.

Sincerely,
Siegrun von Schierstädt

(b)

(a)

ELECTRONIC SPREADSHEET SOFTWARE   With this software the user can develop personalized reports involving the use of extensive mathematical, financial, statistical, and logical processing. Its automatic calculation abilities can save the user almost a lifetime of tedious arithmetic. The flexibility of this tool is as great as the user's imagination. The **spreadsheet** shown in Figure 7.7 was created by a beginner in less than an hour. This spreadsheet is designed to calculate expense totals and percentages. Module C covers electronic spreadsheets in detail.

DATABASE MANAGEMENT SYSTEMS (DBMS) SOFTWARE   This software allows the user to store large amounts of data that can be easily retrieved and manipulated with great flexibility to produce meaningful management reports. With **database management** software, you can compile huge lists of data and manipulate, store, and retrieve it without having to touch a single filing cabinet or folder. What would you rather have sitting in the corner of your office—two huge filing cabinets or that nice floor-to-ceiling poster you always wanted? Module D gives a practical presentation of database management systems software.

FIGURE 7.7
The calculating type. Electronic spreadsheets (b) look much like spreadsheets created manually (a). However, when a number is changed in an electronic spreadsheet, the totals are automatically updated—certainly not the case when you fill out a spreadsheet by hand!

(a)

EXPENSE	JAN.	FEB.	MAR.	TOTAL
TEL	48.50	51.00	37.90	137.40
UTIL	21.70	30.00	25.00	76.70
RENT	465.00	465.00	465.00	1,395.00
AUTO	35.00	211.00	42.00	228.00
MISC	120.00	93.00	41.43	254.43
TOTAL	$690.20	$850.00	$611.33	$2,091.53

(b)

EXPENSE TYPE	JAN	FEB	MAR	TOTAL	PERCENT
TELEPHONE	$48.50	$51.00	$37.90	$137.40	6.57%
UTILITIES	$21.70	$30.00	$25.00	$76.70	3.67%
RENT	$465.00	$465.00	$465.00	$1,395.00	66.69%
AUTOMOBILE	$35.00	$211.00	$42.00	$228.00	10.90%
MISCELLANEOUS	$120.00	$93.00	$41.43	$254.43	12.16%
TOTAL	$690.20	$850.00	$611.33	$2,091.53	100.00%

GRAPHICS SOFTWARE   One picture is often worth a thousand words. Thus, reports and presentations that include graphics can be much more effective than those that don't. **Graphics** software (Figure 7.8) enables users to produce many types of graphic creations. Module E explores the capabilities of a microcomputer graphics program. Specialized graphics software also exists for other systems.

INTEGRATED SOFTWARE   This software represents the industry's effort to combine all the software capabilities that the typical user may need into a single "package" with a common set of commands and rules for its use. The objective is to allow the user to perform a variety of tasks without having to switch software programs and learn different commands and procedures to run each one. Integrated software combines the capabilities of word processing, electronic spreadsheets, database management systems, graphics, data communications (using telephone lines, satellites, and other communications technology to transmit data and information), and other types of software into one program. In Figure 7.9 the user is creating a graph in one section of the screen, called a *window*, while referring to data in another section of the screen. Symphony, by Lotus Development Corporation, is a popular integrated software package used in business today.

RAM-RESIDENT SOFTWARE   As the name suggests, this type of software is designed to be available at any time to the user by residing in internal memory at all times, even when not in use. In other words, once a **RAM-resident** program is loaded into your computer (for example, from a floppy disk), it stays in RAM, "underneath" any other software you may be using from other disks, until you turn the power off. As long as the power is on, you do not have to put the RAM-resident software disk back in the drive to use the program—you simply access it from RAM with certain keystrokes. Different types of RAM-resident software allow the user to computerize many routine activities, including using a calculator, organizing an appointment calendar, taking notes, looking up words in a dictionary to make sure they are spelled correctly, and many more. The bottom line is that RAM-resident software can save the user time. Pop-Up Windows and Sidekick are two popular RAM-resident software packages.

DESKTOP PUBLISHING SOFTWARE   This software allows the user to use a microcomputer and a desktop-size laser printer to produce near-typeset-quality text and other images for newsletters, documentation manuals, forms, and even certain types of books without going to the expense of using a typesetting service. Figure 7.10 was produced using a laser printer and desktop publishing software. We will describe **desktop publishing** software in more detail in Chapter 14.

COMMUNICATIONS SOFTWARE   This software allows users to access software and data from a computer in a remote location and to transmit data to a computer in a remote location. For example, communications software is required for the traveling business professional in Seattle, Washington, who needs to access client information daily from the company's main computer in San Diego, California. Chapter 13 describes communications software in more detail.

FIGURE 7.8
Graphic description. As
more and more business
users understood the value
of using graphics to convey
information, the need for
graphics software increased
dramatically. This illustration shows (top) several
popular graphics software
packages and (bottom) a
common type of graphic
display, the bar graph.

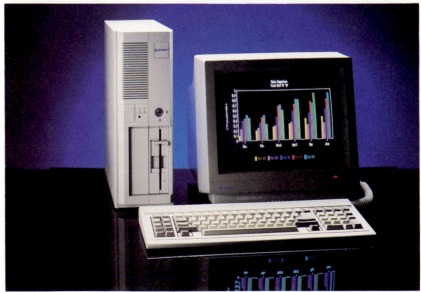

FIGURE 7.9
Using integrated software. Because integrated software combines the capabilities of several types of software programs, this user is able to create a graphic presentation in one section of the screen while referring to data in a second section— and perhaps send the information at the same time to someone in another part of the country or the world.

FIGURE 7.10
Do it yourself! This ad for Sporting Life was done in less than one hour on a Macintosh SE and a Laser-Writer Plus using Adobe Illustrator and PageMaker software.

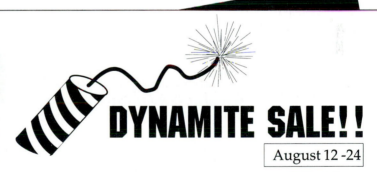

SYSTEMS SOFTWARE

Without systems software you won't be able to use any of the sophisticated software described in the last section. Systems software tells the computer how to interpret data and instructions, how to run peripheral equipment like printers, keyboards, and disk drives, and how to use the hardware in general; and it allows you, the user, to interact with the computer. Systems software comprises (1) internal command instructions, (2) external command instructions, (3) language processors, and (4) operating environments. Because systems software is critical to your interaction with the computer (no matter what kind), you must be familiar with it.

INTERNAL COMMAND INSTRUCTIONS

Internal command instructions can be thought of as the innermost layer of software (Figure 7.11). They combine programs permanently "wired" in the computer's circuitry (in the chips) and programs on disk to direct and coordinate other types of software and the computer hardware. These instructions are loaded into internal memory as part of turning on the computer—called **booting**—and reside in inter-

FIGURE 7.11
Who's the boss? Without the operating system, the most important type of systems software, you won't be able to use your applications software or your hardware, because the operating system runs the show.

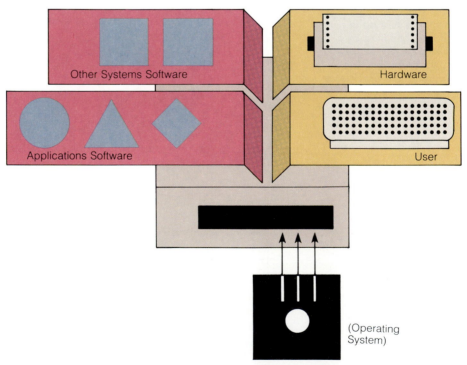

Other Systems Software

Applications Software

Hardware

User

(Operating System)

Internal Command Instructions

nal memory until the computer is turned off. (That is why they are referred to as *internal* command instructions.) Without these instructions in internal memory, a computer can be likened to a race car without fuel for the engine and without a driver to decide where to go and how fast. That is why the primary purpose of the procedures followed in starting up a computer is to load a copy of these instructions into internal memory so they can be accessed by the CPU. The level of sophistication of internal instructions depends on the size of the computer they operate and the tasks the computer is intended to perform.

Internal command instructions are sometimes referred to generally as the **operating system,** abbreviated **OS.** For microcomputers, the operating system is called a **disk operating system,** or **DOS.**

The "captain" of the operating system is often referred to as the **supervisor,** or the **control program.** The supervisor remains in internal memory and calls in other parts of the operating system as needed from secondary storage (Figure 7.12). The supervisor controls all other programs in the computer.

The first operating systems for computers, which were relatively simple by today's standards, could support the use of only one program by one user at a time. As the power of computer hardware grew over the years, operating systems were improved substantially to allow the user to take advantage of the increased power. And, as the power of the microcomputer hardware continues to increase, new versions of microcomputer operating systems appear that offer many capabilities once found only on large computer systems.

The operating systems used on minicomputers and mainframes are more sophisticated and much larger in terms of the number of programs and routines they comprise and the amount of internal memory space taken up by the supervisor. Microcomputer operating systems can sometimes allow the execution of more than one program at a time. Minicomputers can execute dozens of programs at a time, and mainframes can execute hundreds of programs at a time.

Fortunately, you probably will not have to become familiar with the technical intricacies of communicating with the operating systems of large computer systems. As mentioned earlier, one of the major considerations in deciding which microcomputer operating system to use is finding out what compatible applications software programs are available. Some operating systems are compatible with more applications software than others.

EXTERNAL COMMAND INSTRUCTIONS

External command instructions, often referred to as **utility programs,** are general-purpose instructions that take care of what many people call "housekeeping tasks." External command instructions are not needed to run applications software; for this reason, they reside in secondary storage, instead of internal memory, until needed. They are called in by the supervisor to handle such jobs as, for example, sorting files and formatting, or initializing, disks so they are ready to receive and store data. Some systems software has only a few utility programs, whereas other systems software may have hundreds.

Utility programs are generally provided by the computer manufacturer when you purchase a computer. However, some software firms specialize in developing high-performance utility software that can be acquired when needed. Utility programs are available to assist in a wide variety of areas, including:

- Sorting and merging large files with great speed and flexibility
- Keeping track of computer system activity—identifying who is using the computer system, what the computer is being used for, and what users should be charged
- Monitoring the operating characteristics of computer hardware and software to ensure they are being used effectively and efficiently
- Backing up and restoring data from disk storage devices
- Encrypting (or coding) and decrypting (or decoding) files to prevent unauthorized disclosure of sensitive data

FIGURE 7.12
Loading the supervisor. The part of the operating system called the *supervisor* stays in internal memory and runs the systems; it calls in other parts of the operating system from secondary storage as needed.

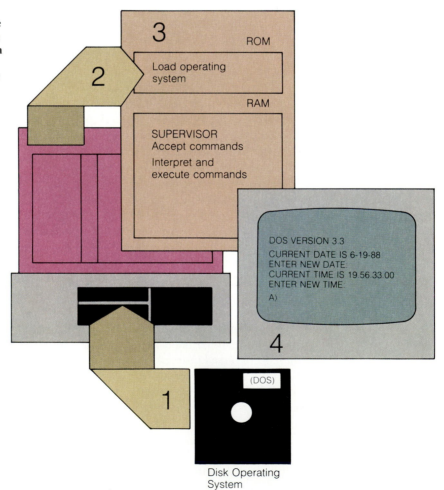

ROM

3

Load operating system

RAM

SUPERVISOR
Accept commands

Interpret and execute commands

2

DOS VERSION 3.3
CURRENT DATE IS 6-19-88
ENTER NEW DATE:
CURRENT TIME IS 19.56.33.00
ENTER NEW TIME:
A)

4

(DOS)

1

Disk Operating System

■ Converting files from one storage medium to another (for example, tape to disk or 5-1/4 inch disk to 3-1/2 inch disk)

LANGUAGE PROCESSORS

You will recall that computers understand only one language—machine language, "written" using the digits 1 and 0. Most people, however, use more convenient languages when they work with computers. Writing instructions in machine language is very tedious and time-consuming and, like most detailed tasks, invites a high rate of error. How, then, does the computer "understand" the user? **Language processors,** or **translators,** translate the user's software into language that the CPU can understand. Without them, programmers would be forced to write instructions in machine language so that the computer could execute their instructions.

The first step in the development of language processors was the creation of programming languages that used symbolic abbreviations to represent machine-language instructions. These languages, which somewhat simplified the programmer's job, are called **assembly languages,** or **low-level programming languages,** and they are machine-specific, or machine-dependent, meaning they are written to be understood by specific makes and models of computers. This, of course, means that an assembly language is compatible only with machines it is written for. Because of this problem, applications software programs are not normally written in assembly language. Also, as you may imagine, writing instructions in assembly language, although an improvement over writing in machine language, is still time-consuming.

To overcome the problem of incompatibility of programs written in assembly language, a group of newer programming languages, called **high-level programming languages,** was developed whose structure was less machine-dependent. These languages are easier to learn and use than assembly language, are less time-consuming, and can be used on more than one type of machine. Since 1950, many different programming languages have been developed for use in business, industry, science, and education.

Like the low-level languages, high-level language programs must still be converted into machine-language instructions before they can be carried out by the computer. This conversion process is handled in one of two ways: by specialized language processors called *interpreters* or by *compilers*.

The **interpreter** is a language processor that converts high-level program instructions into machine language one instruction statement at a time (Figure 7.13). To accomplish this, the interpreter first examines the statement, checks its structure, and then interprets and executes that statement. This process of interpretation is then repeated with the next high-level language statement. An interpreted program is easier to write and test because it interacts directly with the computer as each statement is executed, thus enabling the programmer to immediately identify which instruction is in error (perhaps because of a typographical error) and to correct it. The interpreter program is usually stored on the operating system disk or permanently wired into the computer.

The **compiler** is a language processor that examines an *entire* high-level language program, referred to as the **source program,** and, if the source program contains no language errors, creates a new version of the program, called the **object program,** consisting entirely of machine-language instructions (Figure 7.14). Because a compiler does not check instructions a line at a time, it does not provide the operator with the same convenience of fixing errors.

Most business users who write high-level language programs use language processors that function as interpreters. The development of compiled software requires a slightly more complex procedure and is usually performed by trained software development specialists. However, if you are working with microcomputers at home or in the office, you won't have to worry about compiling or interpreting—the software packages have already been compiled and you will not even be able to look at the machine-level language the computer uses.

FIGURE 7.13
The interpreter. When an interpreter is used to convert high-level program instructions into machine language, each instruction is interpreted and executed one at a time. The programmer using an interpreter gets immediate feedback about the accuracy of the program statements.

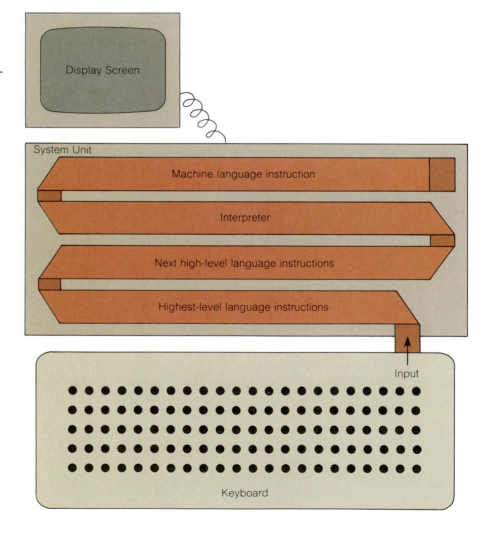

Operating Environments

In the mid-1980s a new category of systems software products was introduced to help improve and simplify the users' procedures for communicating with and using the capabilities of systems software and applications software. These new products, often referred to as **operating environments,** were first released in early 1985.

Operating environments reside in internal memory, along with the supervisor, at all times after the computer has been turned on. Because the software is RAM-resident, it can be activated at any time and allows the user to interrupt whatever is being done to perform another task—the current program is interrupted and control is temporarily turned over to the operating environment. The commands available in the operating environment program are displayed in a menu in a window that has

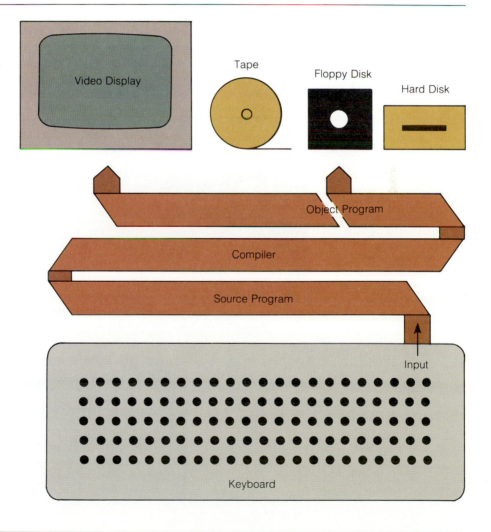

FIGURE 7.14
Compiling a program. In this example, the computer is compiling the *source program,* written in a high-level language, as it was input through an intelligent terminal. The machine-language version of the program is the *object program.*

been opened up somewhere on the screen, as shown in Figure 7.15. Commands are given simply by tapping a key. All activity that takes place during the new operation is displayed in the window area of the screen. Once the operation is complete, it's an easy matter to return to the original operation. Because they make computers easier for users to work with, operating environments are expected to grow in popularity and importance in the next few years.

As the sophistication of microcomputer operating systems increases, the number and complexity of the commands will also increase. Many users find long lists of commands and programming languages so difficult that they are discouraged from using computers. However, operating environments can help. You don't have to memorize a long list of commands or memorize a language if you can simply look at a menu and say "I want to do that" by tapping a key or two. Substantial effort has also gone into improving user interface with minicomputer and mainframe computer systems.

OTHER SYSTEMS SOFTWARE CAPABILITIES

Since the appearance of the first business computer, advances in hardware technology have increased the power of computers a hundred-thousandfold or more. To make that power available to users, systems software has been steadily improved to include new capabilities. You are likely to be using systems software that supports

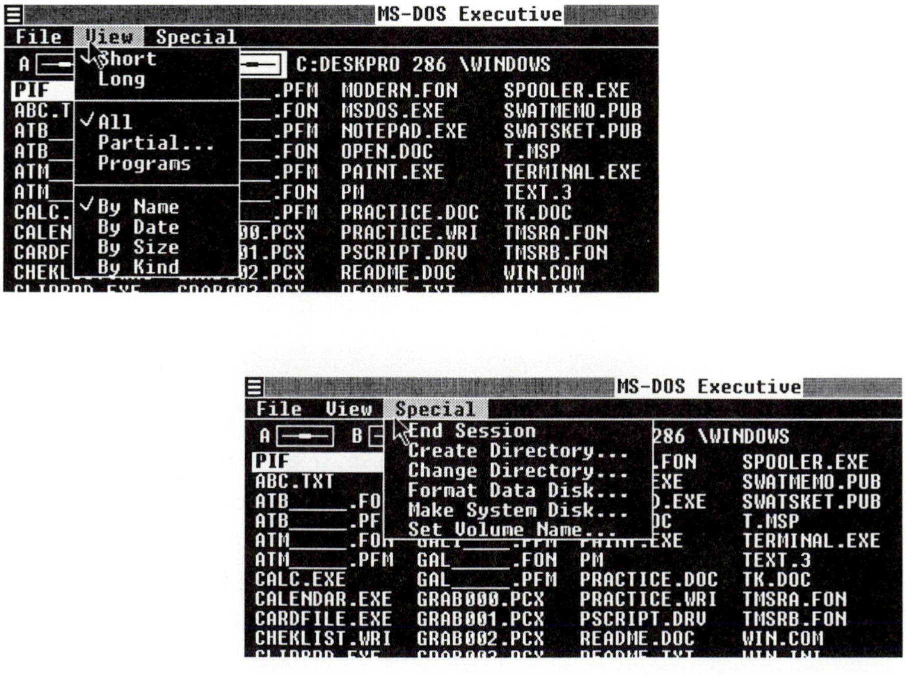

FIGURE 7.15
Operating environment. This illustration shows two pull-down menus of Microsoft Windows, a popular operating environment for use on microcomputers; it makes programming operating systems commands easier for the user.

one or more of these capabilities in the business environment. Therefore, understanding these capabilities will be useful to you.

MULTITASKING   As we have mentioned, the first operating systems were designed for computers with limited processing speed and limited internal memory and storage capacity. These early operating systems were referred to as *single-user operating systems* because they could accept commands from only a single terminal or other input source and could manage only a single program in internal memory at one time. Modern large computer systems are designed to be shared by many users, so very few, if any, have single-user operating systems. Although most operating systems for microcomputers are considered single-user/single-program operating systems, some new microcomputer operating systems are single-user but can do **multitasking,** or **multiprogramming;** that is, they can execute more than one task or program at a time.

In multitasking, a copy of each program to be executed is placed in a reserved portion of internal memory, usually called a *partition* (Figure 7.16). The supervisor is more sophisticated in an operating system with multitasking capabilities because it coordinates the execution of each program. It directs the central processing unit to spend a predetermined amount of time executing the instructions for each

FIGURE 7.16
Multitasking. An operating system that can handle more than one program at a time is capable of multitasking, or multiprogramming.

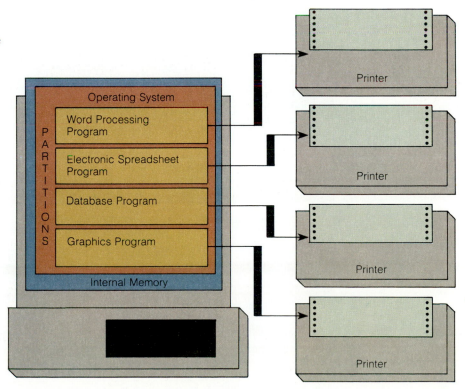

program, one at a time. In essence, a small amount of each program is processed, and then the CPU moves to the remaining programs, one at a time, processing small parts of each. This cycle is repeated until processing is complete. The processing speed of the CPU is usually so fast that it seems as if all the programs are being executed at the same time. However, the CPU is still executing only one instruction at a time, no matter how it may appear to users.

MULTIPROCESSING   A multitasking operating system works with only one CPU. However, the computer is so fast that, if it spends a little bit of time working on each of several programs in turn, it can allow a number of users to make progress at the same time. The key is that the operating system can keep track of the status of each program so that it knows where it left off and where to continue processing. The **multiprocessing** operating system is much more sophisticated; it manages the *simultaneous* execution of programs with two or more CPUs (Figure 7.17). This can entail processing instructions from different programs or different instructions from

FIGURE 7.17
Multiprocessing. Some large computer operating systems use two or more CPUs to process programs simultaneously.

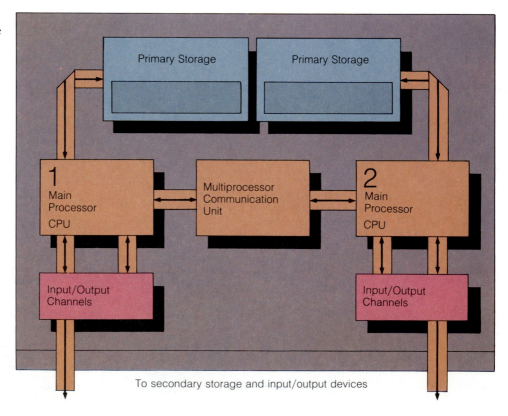

the same program. Multiprocessing configurations are becoming very popular in large computing systems.

TIMESHARING   A **timesharing** computer system supports many user stations or terminals simultaneously; in other words, the users share time on the computer. The processing requirements of an operating system with timesharing capabilities are great. As a result, in some cases a computer called a **front-end processor,** which is smaller than the main computer, is used to schedule and control all the user requests entering the system from the terminals. The use of a front-end processor allows the main computer to concentrate solely on processing applications as quickly as possible (Figure 7.18).

Timesharing systems are most often used for three purposes: (1) As general-purpose systems, they enable users to create and run their own applications software

FIGURE 7.18
Do you have the time? In a timesharing environment, the front-end processor schedules and controls users' processing requests. The main computer is thus freed up for processing.

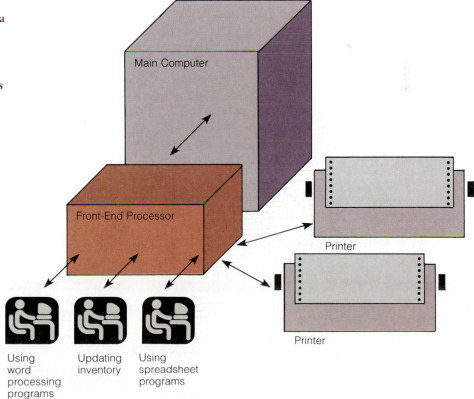

using a variety of programming languages. (2) As a commercial service to other companies, they access the system with terminals to run a wide variety of existing programs that the companies would otherwise have to buy or write themselves. (3) As a service bureau, they offer companies without their own computer access to the software and hardware required to do all of their processing. The service bureau has the computer, the computer operators, and all of the support staff. The users enter only the data required by the programs and submit requests for the reports that need to be produced. One typical use of such a service is payroll processing. The obvious advantage of using a service bureau is that users do not have to purchase the computer or the software.

VIRTUAL MEMORY   **Virtual memory,** or **virtual storage,** is an operating system element that enables the computer to process as if it contained an almost unlimited supply of internal memory. One of the major tasks of all operating systems is to manage the use of internal memory carefully. Virtual storage enables a program to be broken into modules, or small sections, that can be loaded into internal memory when needed. Modules not currently in use are stored on a very high-speed disk and retrieved one at a time when the operating system determines that the current module has completed executing. In the past, all computer operating systems were designed so that an entire program had to be loaded into internal memory before it could begin execution. As a result, the size and sophistication of a program was limited by the amount of internal memory available. As you may guess, the use of virtual memory facilitates multitasking.

SYSTEMS SOFTWARE FOR MICROCOMPUTERS

Because more of you will be using microcomputers than minicomputers and mainframe computers, we have chosen to give you a few more details about the operating systems available for microcomputers. Although problems of compatibility between operating systems and applications software packages are becoming less significant as computer technology advances, they still deserve your attention.

In the late 1970s and early 1980s, a number of microcomputer hardware vendors introduced products that included their own individual, machine-specific operating systems. This created a software compatibility problem because each software package was written for specific operating systems and machines—if it worked with one type, it couldn't be used with another. This problem was lessened when software vendors decided to concentrate on developing software for the most popular operating systems in use—that is, Apple DOS, TRS-DOS, CP/M, PC-DOS, and UNIX.

APPLE DOS AND TRS-DOS

The Apple Computer Corporation and Tandy/Radio Shack both introduced popular types of personal computer systems in the late 1970s. Because the machines were based on entirely different microprocessors, their operating systems were incompatible. The net effect of this incompatibility was an inability to share data and instructions. The Apple disk operating system is called **Apple DOS** (pronounced "doss"), and the Tandy/Radio Shack disk operating system is named **TRS-DOS.** Over the years, a substantial amount of applications software was developed for both operating systems. But even though adequate software was available, the lack of compatibility was of great concern to software developers, users, and hardware vendors.

CP/M

CP/M, Control Program for Microcomputers, is a disk operating system designed to operate on microcomputer systems using the Intel 8080 or Zilog Z80 microprocessor families. Developed in the mid-1970s by Dr. Gary Kildall and marketed by Digital Research Corporation (the company he formed), the CP/M operating system filled a major consumer need. As more vendors moved toward entering the growing microcomputer marketplace, they balked at the projected research and development costs required to produce their own exclusive operating systems. The vendors were impressed with CP/M because it could run on just about any Intel 8080- or Zilog Z80-based microcomputer system. In addition, CP/M was very "device friendly" in that it permitted a wide variety of disk drives (5-1/4" or 8") to be hooked up to the computer and used without difficulty. For these reasons, many vendors decided to adopt CP/M as their standard operating system.

In 1981, a number of major vendors, including IBM, Hewlett-Packard, and Xerox, introduced microcomputer systems that offered CP/M as the standard operating system or as an option. The version of CP/M designed to work with the new 16-bit microprocessors was dubbed CP/M-86. It is estimated that versions of the CP/M operating system were used on more than 300 different microcomputer system products. Even the Apple Computer Corporation introduced an add-on processor board that included a Z80 microprocessor and permitted users to run CP/M and the related applications software.

DOS

Another major microcomputer operating system is simply called **DOS.** Its development began in 1978 when Intel Corporation announced the development of a newer and much more powerful microprocessor, the Intel 8086. The new processor could use much more internal memory and was substantially faster than the older 8080 series of processors.

Because of some differences between the old and the new processors, it became apparent that a new operating system would have to be developed to take advantage of the power of the 8086. In 1979 Tim Paterson of Seattle Computer Products began developing a new operating system called 86-DOS. The system was patterned after CP/M to some extent but included many enhancements that the new processor could support. The rights to distribute 86-DOS were acquired by Microsoft Corporation; Microsoft then entered into an agreement with IBM to make 86-DOS the operating system for the new personal computer IBM had under development. IBM added additional program enhancements to 86-DOS and released the product in

1981 as IBM **PC-DOS** (IBM Personal Computer Disk Operating System). The impact of IBM's entry into the microcomputer marketplace was so strong that users and vendors began to indicate a preference for PC-DOS and its generic equivalent, **MS-DOS** (Microsoft Disk Operating System). By 1985 it was clear that DOS had become the industry standard for microcomputers. In fact, PC-DOS/MS-DOS has become so common that in 1987 Apple released new versions of its popular Macintosh computer (using Apple DOS) that can run PC-DOS/MS-DOS-compatible software by means of an add-on board. The latest version of PC-DOS, DOS 3.30, was introduced in April of 1987.

The CP/M and PC-DOS operating systems were designed principally to perform a single task for a single user. However, as the power of microcomputer hardware continued to grow, so did the need for more powerful operating systems. Digital Research Corporation introduced several new versions of its operating systems to help satisfy the demand: MP/M, Concurrent CP/M, and Concurrent DOS. These new operating systems can support more than one task on the same microcomputer at one time.

As the demand for products with these capabilities began to increase, users became concerned about the compatibility of microcomputer software and files with larger computer systems. As a result, a growing number of products have been developed that facilitate the exchange of data and instructions between microcomputers and larger computer systems.

In 1988, IBM introduced Operating System/2 (**OS/2**), which is designed to take advantage of the 80286 and 80386 microprocessors. OS/2 (sometimes also referred to as DOS5, NewDOS, AdvancedDOS, ADOS, and 286DOS) supports

TABLE 7.1   Microcomputer Operating Systems

Processor	Apple DOS	TRS-DOS	CP/M	MS/PC-DOS	OS/2	Concurrent DOS	UNIX
Intel 8080			x				
Zilog Z80			x				
M6502	x						
Intel 8088			x	x		x	
8086			x	x		x	x
80286			x	x	x	x	x
80386				x	x	x	x
Single-user	x	x	x	x		x	
Multitask					x		x
Multiuser							x

multitasking and will allow new software applications to directly address up to 16 MB of internal memory. Because of the many instructions that comprise OS/2 (over 1.5 million), the minimum system requirements to use it are 1.5 MB of internal memory and a hard disk.

UNIX

The **UNIX** operating system was developed at Bell Laboratories, where the earliest version was released in 1971. This operating system was initially created for mini-computers and provides a wide range of capabilities, including virtual storage, multiprogramming, and timesharing. In 1973, the system was rewritten in a high-level language, which allowed it to be used on a wider variety of computers, ranging from the largest mainframe computers to some of the more powerful micro-computers. One of the biggest advantages of this operating system, in addition to its adaptability to a wide variety of computers, was its extensive library of tools created for the computer software specialist to develop programs.

Before finalizing its agreement with IBM regarding the DOS operating system for microcomputers, Microsoft acquired the rights to create a version of UNIX to run on the new Intel 8086 family of microprocessors. The resulting product, called XENIX, is licensed as a multiuser, multitasking operating system.

MAKING YOUR CHOICE

If you ever have to choose a microcomputer, consider carefully the systems software choices available in light of your specific processing needs. The choice you make should be determined by:

- The quantity of compatible applications software
- The ease of use by both users and programmers
- The speed of operation
- The capability to support multitasking and multiuser needs
- The types of compatible hardware you will need
- The availability of trained technical support personnel available to help you solve problems using your equipment and software

Table 7.1 reviews the main operating systems used with microcomputers.

ONWARD: DO IT YOURSELF?

Chapter 7 described what is available for you in the way of software—systems software and applications software—or what you may find in place when you start your job. But what if you want to update your software yourself? This is not necessarily a job only for someone with a brain like a computer. The next chapter will describe the tools available for creating software and give you a few ideas about how you could use them.

SUMMARY

Software plays a critical role in computer-based information systems, because our hardware would be useless without it. Software comprises the instructions that tell the hardware what to do. If possible, you should first select the software that meets your information needs, then choose compatible hardware.

Software can be divided into two major categories—systems software and applications software. Applications software is a collection of related programs designed to perform a specific task—to solve a particular problem for the user. Systems software starts up (boots) the computer and functions as the principal coordinator of all the hardware components and applications software programs.

Many off-the-shelf applications software packages are available to the user, and reviews of these packages can be found in several types of publications, including popular computer magazines. The six major categories of applications software are general business management, industry-specific, special disciplines, education, personal/home management, and general-purpose for the user. In the category of general-purpose software, the main types of software you will encounter in an average business are:

1. Word processing software, which enables the user to easily insert, delete, and move words, sentences, and paragraphs automatically and also to change the appearance of the written material

2. Electronic spreadsheet software, with which the user can conveniently develop reports involving the use of extensive mathematical, financial, statistical, and logical processing

3. Database management systems (DBMS) software, which allows the user to store large amounts of data that can then be easily retrieved and manipulated with great flexibility to produce reports

4. Graphics software, which gives the user the ability to make reports and presentations even more effective through the use of graphs and other types of drawings

5. Integrated software, which combines the software capabilities of several types of software programs to enable the user to perform different types of tasks without having to change software and to transmit data and information to other computers through the use of telephone lines, satellites, and other communications technology

6. RAM-resident software, which is loaded into internal memory and which stays there, "underneath" other software, until the power is turned off; it allows the user to interrupt one task, switch over to the RAM-resident software, perform another task, and switch back to the original package

7. Desktop publishing software, which allows the user to take advantage of particular text and graphics software and use laser printers to produce material of publishable quality

The four types of systems software are (1) internal instructions (operating system), (2) external instructions (utilities), (3) language processors, and (4) operating environments. A computer's internal instructions are most important; without them, the computer cannot operate. They must be loaded from storage when the computer is first turned on, or booted; otherwise none of the hardware components will function. Internal instructions remain in internal memory.

External instructions, or utilities, perform so-called housekeeping tasks, which frequently have to do with "desktop" management and file management. External instructions reside in secondary storage.

Language processors, or translators, convert the high-level language of the user's software into the only language the computer can understand—machine language. Some low-level languages, called assembly languages, were created using abbreviations to help programmers avoid the tedious and time-consuming task of writing programs in machine language (0's and 1's). High-level languages were developed to make the job even easier. However, both high-level and low-level languages must be translated into machine language for the CPU to use them. The translation can be done by interpreters, which convert software instructions a line at a time and thus allow for on-the-spot error correction, or compilers, which take the whole source program and create a program that the computer can understand (called an *object program*). The average business user will be using software that includes a translator and so will not have to get personally involved in the translation process.

Operating environments, the last type of systems software, make it easier for the user to communicate with the applications software. This RAM-resident software stays available to the user as long as the power to the computer is on. The commands available in the operating environment are shown in menus within windows on the screen.

The level of sophistication of systems software depends on the size of the computer it operates and the tasks it is intended to perform. When operating systems were first developed they could support only single users; some operating systems can now support multitasking (performing several tasks so fast that it appears they are being done at once), multiprocessing (using two or more CPUs to process two or more programs simultaneously), timesharing (allowing several users to work at the computer at the same time), and virtual storage (employing a piecemeal procedure for using secondary storage that increases the efficiency of internal memory use).

The most popular disk operating systems (DOS) for microcomputers are Apple DOS, TRS-DOS, CP/M, and PC/MS-DOS. These operating systems were originally developed to support single users and single tasks. However, as microcomputer hardware became more powerful, it was capable of supporting more sophisticated operating systems. One such operating system that can be used on a microcomputer is UNIX. Among its capabilities are the ability to support more than one user and to perform more than one task at a time. The new IBM OS/2 can also support multitasking.

Systems software is written to work with a particular type of microprocessor and is incompatible with machines that do not use that type of processor. Applications software is written to be used with particular systems software and is incompatible with others. Thus, the user who is in the position of acquiring a microcomputer should consider the availability of applications software needed and then pick systems software and hardware that are mutually compatible and compatible with the applications software. The user who picks hardware first may find himself or herself unable to use the software best qualified to do the job at hand.

KEY TERMS

Apple DOS
applications software
assembly language
booting
compiler
control program
CP/M
database management
    system (DBMS)
desktop publishing
disk operating system
    (DOS)
external command
    instructions
front-end processor
graphics

high-level programming
    language
integrated software
internal command
    instructions
interpreter
language processor
low-level programming
    language
MS-DOS
multiprocessing
multiprogramming
multitasking
object program
off-the-shelf software
operating environment

operating system (OS)
OS/2
PC-DOS
RAM-resident software
source program
spreadsheet
supervisor
systems software
timesharing
translator
TRS-DOS
UNIX
utility program
virtual memory
    (storage)
word processing

EXERCISES

MATCHING

Match each of the following terms to the phrase that is the most closely related:

1. _____ supervisor
2. _____ assembly language
3. _____ RAM-resident software
4. _____ electronic spreadsheet
       software
5. _____ interpreter
6. _____ virtual memory
7. _____ timesharing
8. _____ booting

9. _____ high-level programming
       languages
10. _____ word processing software
11. _____ compiler
12. _____ operating environment
13. _____ multitasking
14. _____ multiprocessing
15. _____ external command
       instructions

a. This software allows the user to easily insert and delete text and perform many other editing functions easily and quickly.

b. This software allows the user to produce reports involving the use of complex numeric processing that can be updated automatically.

c. This software is intended to be available for the user to use all the time because it always resides in internal memory.

d. Turning on the computer and loading the operating system into internal memory.

e. The portion of the operating system that always resides in internal memory and that calls in other parts of the operating system as needed from secondary storage.

f. A low-level programming language that is the symbolic representation of machine language.

g. Programming languages that fall into this category were developed to overcome the problem of incompatibility of programs written in assembly language with different types of computers.

h. A language processor that creates a machine-language version of high-level language statements all at once.

i. This type of software was designed to improve and simplify users' procedures for communicating with the systems software and applications software.

j. A language processor that converts high-level program instructions into machine-language instructions one instruction statement at a time.

k. A computer that has one CPU whose operating system can execute more than one program at a time.

l. A computer that has two or more CPUs whose operating system can execute more than one program at a time.

m. This element of an operating system enables the computer to process as if it contained an almost unlimited supply of internal memory.

n. A computer system that has been set up to support many terminals simultaneously.

o. This component of systems software contains instructions that are often referred to as utility programs.

MULTIPLE CHOICE

1. Which of the following types of software is the most different from the rest?
   a. operating system
   b. applications
   c. utilities
   d. language processors
   e. operating environments

2. Which of the following is a major consideration in choosing an operating system to use on your computer?
   a. Is it expensive?
   b. Is it compatible with your hardware?

    c. Is the applications software you want to use compatible with it?

    d. a and c

    e. b and c

3. Which of the following do programmers use to avoid writing software programs in machine language?

    a. front-end processor

    b. interpreter

    c. multiprocessing

    d. UNIX

    e. high-level programming languages

4. Identify the type of operating system used on a computer with two CPUs that can manage the execution of more than one program at a time.

    a. single-user

    b. multiprogramming

    c. multiprocessing

    d. timesharing

    e. none of the above

5. An operating system that is capable of multiprogramming does *not* use which of the following?

    a. CPU

    b. internal memory

    c. partitions

    d. supervisor

    e. none of the above

6. Which of the following is not a reason for acquiring an operating system that has the ability to support timesharing?

    a. You want users to be able to run their own applications at the same time.

    b. You want to operate as a service bureau that offers companies computer access to hardware and software.

    c. You want to be the only one who can use the computer.

    d. You want to operate as a commercial service to companies who want your software.

    e. all of the above

7. Which of the following microcomputer operating systems is both multiuser and multitasking?

    a. CP/M

    b. PC-DOS

    c. TRS-DOS

    d. UNIX

    e. Apple DOS

8. Which of the following should be the least likely to affect your decision about what type of operating system to acquire?

    a. quantity of compatible applications software

    b. speed of operation

    c. cost of the operating system

d. capability to support multitasking and multiuser needs

e. types of compatible hardware

9. Your computer will be totally useless to you without which of the following?

a. printer

b. systems software

c. applications software

d. programming languages

e. virtual memory

10. Which of the following is helpful in evaluating what applications software will best suit your needs?

a. objective software reviews

b. recommendations by friends

c. computer magazines

d. computer periodicals

e. all of the above

SHORT ANSWER

1. Why were high-level languages developed?

2. What are some types of general-purpose applications software programs that you are likely to use in the business environment?

3. What is the importance of internal command instructions to the process of booting your computer?

4. What are external command instructions? Why might you find it necessary to use them?

5. Why is it expected that the use of operating environment software will grow in the next few years?

6. What is the purpose of either compiling or interpreting a program? What are the advantages and disadvantages of each method?

7. What is the difference between multiprogramming and multiprocessing?

8. What is virtual memory and why is it significant?

9. If you are in a position to make a decision on what operating system software to acquire, what should you evaluate?

10. If you are in charge of acquiring microcomputer hardware and software, which should you select first? Why?

PROJECTS

1. Go to a local computer store and ask the salesperson to demonstrate some popular microcomputer system operating environment software such as Microsoft Windows, TopView, and the Macintosh operating system. Contrast this by attending a demonstration of the MS-DOS operating system. How do the operating environments differ in terms of what the user sees and what the operator

must do to initiate a command? Which of the operating environments did you enjoy working with the most? Why? What were its limitations?

2. Go to a local computer store and describe the different types of software you see for sale. Ask the salesperson what types of software sell the most. Why do you think this is so?

3. Research the answer to the following question: "What new capabilities will probably be added to the systems software currently used on microcomputers?" What capabilities does the systems software used on large computers have that you think might soon be supported by microcomputer systems software? Perform your research by reviewing current computer publications.

CHAPTER EIGHT

DEVELOPING APPLICATIONS SOFTWARE

At this point, just learning how to use computer hardware and software may seem challenging enough. Yet there often comes a day when users suddenly discover that the ready-made, off-the-shelf programs available to them won't do everything they want. People renovate their houses or modify their clothes for the same reasons that software users fiddle with their programs. Would you ever be able to create applications software yourself? Or be able to help someone else do so? In this chapter, we will describe two ways to develop or modify applications software—through the use of programming languages and existing software.

PREVIEW

When you have completed this chapter, you will be able to:

■

Describe what software development tools exist and which ones you are most likely to use

■

Describe some of the advantages and disadvantages of using each of the most popular high-level languages

■

Describe how a user could use existing microcomputer software to customize software

■

The User Perspective

One day, at work, you are tinkering with your database management program on your microcomputer when you suddenly realize you can't make it produce a sales report in just the right format. Or perhaps your spreadsheet won't automatically extract all the right data for a particularly useful analysis of an investment strategy. As new computer users gain more experience, they find it easier to identify areas where software can be modified or created to provide more useful and sophisticated processing capabilities above and beyond those of a purchased package. As we mentioned earlier, to obtain custom-made software the user can (1) hire an outside computer specialist to develop it, which can be costly and time-consuming; (2) ask the firm's computer specialists to do it, which may take a long time if they are backlogged with requests; or (3) go it alone. Regardless of the approach you take, you need to understand the process by which software is developed and be familiar with the tools available for you to use.

What Tools Are Available for Developing Software?

Just as many tools exist for building a house, many tools are available for creating, or writing, software. These tools comprise different types of programming languages, each of which consists of a number of different commands that are used to describe the type of processing to be done, such as multiplying two numbers together. Software development tools can best be categorized as falling into one of five generations of programming languages (Figure 8.1). The languages in each successive generation represent an improvement over those of the prior generation—just as the electric saw was an improvement over the manual one. Languages of later generations are easier to learn than earlier ones, and they can produce results (software) more quickly and more reliably. But just as a builder might need to use a manual saw occasionally to cut a tricky corner, professional programmers still need to use early generation languages (except machine language, which we'll explain shortly) to create software. Each of the five language generations will be described in detail in this chapter.

Compared with later generations, the early generation programming languages (first, second, and third) require the use of more complex vocabulary and syntax to write software; they are therefore used primarily by computer professionals. The term **syntax** refers to the precise rules and patterns required for the formation of the programming language sentences, or statements, that tell the computer what to do and how to do it. Programmers must use a language's syntax—just as you would use the rules of German, not French, grammar to communicate in German—to write a program in that language. Because more efficient software development tools are available, programmers don't create software using machine language anymore, and few use assembly language, except for programs with special processing requirements. However, third-generation languages are still in wide use today.

Fourth-generation languages still require the user to employ a specific syntax, but the syntax is easy to learn. In fact, fourth-generation programming languages are so much easier to use than those in prior generations that the non-computer professional can create software after about a day of training.

Many people believe that natural languages will constitute the fifth generation of languages. With this type of language, the user will be able to specify processing procedures using statements similar to idiomatic human speech—in our case, simple English statements. The use of natural language will not require the user to learn a specific syntax.

In addition to the five generations of programming languages, some microcomputer software packages (such as electronic spreadsheet and database management software) are widely used for creating software. Although these packages generally cannot be categorized into one of the five generations, many people consider some of the database management systems software used on microcomputers, such as dBase III Plus, to fall into the fourth-generation category.

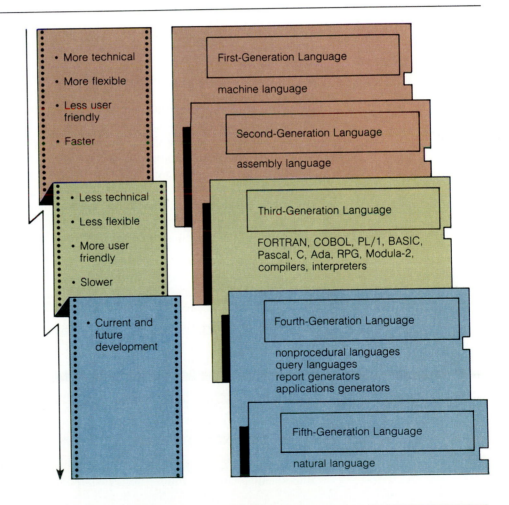

FIGURE 8.1
The five generations of programming languages.

WHICH TOOLS ARE YOU MOST LIKELY TO USE?

The decision about which software development tool to use depends on what processing procedures you need to perform. Developing software is like building a house: The work will go much faster if you have a plan and the right tools. However, the tools have little value if you don't know how to use them; consequently, one of the most important steps toward effective and efficient software development is the selection of the right development tool.

If you become a computer specialist, you will need to learn to use the most popular of the third-generation programming languages because much of the available applications software is based on them. In other words, the software that you buy off the shelf of a computer store has been created by a computer specialist using one of these languages. Also, computer specialists need to know how to use these languages in order to update, or maintain, this existing software to accommodate new processing and output requirements.

For the user who is not a computer specialist, the most popular tools for developing software will be the fourth-generation programming languages and existing off-the-shelf software packages such as electronic spreadsheets and database management systems software, because one does not have to be an experienced computer professional to use them. The user who is working with these tools can create specialized software applications, such as keeping track of a company's expenses by department (a good application for a spreadsheet package), or maintaining a comprehensive customer file used in a clothing store for billing, marketing, and checking customer credit status (a good application for a database package).

It's interesting to note that these software tools have served to decrease the number of professional computer programmers in the work force, because they allow users to create software without the expertise of a professional programmer. This has in turn helped to save companies thousands of dollars in programming fees. For a long time to come, however, the business environment will need professional programmers to create certain specialized and complex software programs and to maintain existing programs that were created using third-generation languages.

GENERATIONS OF SOFTWARE DEVELOPMENT TOOLS

Over the past 40 years, the programming languages used to develop software have been steadily improving in terms of ease of use, the time it takes to develop software, and the reliability of the finished product. In the following pages we describe the major characteristics of each generation of languages, or software development tools, and pay special attention to the tools you will likely be using in the business environment.

THE FIRST AND SECOND GENERATIONS

As you learned in Chapter 7, all higher-level language instructions are converted into machine-language form—**first-generation language**—before they can be carried out by the computer. As you learned in Chapter 4, machine-language instructions and data are represented by binary digits (a series of 1's and 0's corresponding to "on" and "off" electrical states). Because the specific format and content of the instructions vary according to the architecture of each type of computer, machine-language programs can be run only on the type of computer for which they were designed; that is, they are machine-dependent.

The first step in making software development easier and more efficient was the creation of assembly languages, also known as **second-generation languages.** (Some people consider them to be the first low-level languages and place machine language in a separate category.) You'll recall from the last chapter that assembly languages use symbols as abbreviations for major instructions instead of a long combination of binary digits. This means a programmer can use abbreviations instead of having to remember lengthy binary instruction codes. For example, it is much easier to remember L for Load, A for Add, B for Branch, and C for Compare than the binary equivalents—strings of different combinations of 0's and 1's.

Although assembly languages represented an improvement, they had obvious limitations. They can be used only by computer specialists familiar with the architecture of the computer being used. And because they are also machine-dependent, assembly languages are not easily converted to run on other types of computer. Assembly-language programs are still written today, but only when storage must be minimized or processing speed increased, results that can only be achieved by tailoring instructions to the architecture of the specific computer. For example, many small businesses have captured large amounts of data with a microcomputer using database management systems (DBMS) software. However, when a business attempts to sort stored data into a particular sequence for a certain job, the sorting activity may take as long as several hours. To drastically reduce this time, a "sort program" can be purchased that has been written in assembly language for the business's specific computer.

THE THIRD GENERATION

Third-generation languages, also known as *high-level languages*, are very much like everyday text and mathematical formulas in appearance. They are designed to run on a number of different computers with few or no changes. Unlike machine and assembly languages, then, many high-level languages are *machine-independent*. The most commonly used high-level programming languages are COBOL, FORTRAN, and BASIC. A large number of additional languages have been developed, each with its own strengths. The objectives of high-level languages are:

- To relieve the programmer of the detailed and tedious task of writing programs in machine language and assembly language
- To provide programs that can be used on more than one type of machine with very few changes
- To allow the programmer more time to focus on understanding the user's needs and designing the software required to meet those needs

Most high-level languages are considered to be procedure-oriented, or **procedural,** languages because the program instructions comprise lists of steps, or procedures, that tell the computer not only *what* to do but *how* to do it. High-level language statements generate, when translated, a comparatively greater number of assembly-language instructions and even more machine-language instructions (Figure 8.2). The programmer spends less time developing software with a high-level language than with assembly or machine language because fewer instructions have to be created.

A language processor is still required to convert a high-level language program into machine language. As described in Chapter 7, two types of language processors are used with high-level languages: compilers and interpreters, or translators. A compiled program normally runs in less time than an interpreted program because it doesn't need to convert program instructions from the high-level language form to machine-language form.

The importance of high-level languages was quickly recognized by the computer industry, and substantial human and financial resources were dedicated to their development. By the early 1960s, most computer manufacturers were working on a version of FORTRAN, the first widely used high-level language, for their computers. Various manufacturers' versions of FORTRAN were similar; however, their efforts to make one package better than the others resulted in a number of small differences. The problems associated with resolving these differences led to the realization that industry standards were needed to ensure complete compatibility of high-level language programs with different computers. The task of establishing such standards was turned over to the American Standards Association, and in 1966 the association released the first FORTRAN standards.

Since the late 1960s, the association—now known as the **American National Standards Institute (ANSI)**—worked with the **International Standards Organiza-**

FIGURE 8.2
Down through the generations. An example of a statement in COBOL, part of which is converted first to assembly language and then to machine language. As you can see, the high-level (third-generation) language requires few statements to create a large number of machine-language (first-generation) instructions. (*Computers and Information Processing,* O'Leary/Williams, © 1985, The Benjamin/Cummings Publishing Company.)

```
COBOL

MULTIPLY HOURS-WORKED BY PAY-RATE GIVING GROSS-PAY ROUNDED

Assembly

              PACK  210(8,13),02B(4,7)
              PACK  218(8,13),02F(4,7)
              MP    212(6,13),21D(3,13)
              SRP   213(5,13),03E(0),5
              UNPK  050(5,7),214(4,13)
              OI    054(7),X'F0'

Machine

     11110010  01110011  1101  001000010000  0111  000000101011
     11110010  01110011  1101  001000011000  0111  000000101111
     11111100  01010010  1101  001000010010  1101  001000011101
     11110000  01000101  1101  001000010011  0000  000000111110
     11110011  01000011  0111  000001010000  1101  001000010100
     10010110  11110000  0111  000001010100
```

tion (ISO) to develop standards for all high-level programming languages. All versions of programming languages that developers wish to have designated as meeting the standards must accommodate all the commands, syntax, and processing requirements formulated by the ANSI and the ISO. We'll now describe some popular standard high-level programming languages.

FORTRAN   The **FORTRAN**—short for FORmula TRANslator—programming language was first made available in 1957 by IBM. One of the very first high-level languages (Figure 8.3), FORTRAN was designed for technical and scientific applications. Its popularity grew rapidly, and, by the 1960s, a version of the language was available for almost all types of computers; however, it is used primarily on minicomputers and mainframes. Because the language was designed to handle research and analytical problems definable in terms of mathematical formulas and relationships, the majority of people using FORTRAN are mathematicians, scientists, and engineers.

As you would expect, the primary advantage of this language is the ease with which it can form complex mathematical and logical expressions. For that reason, FORTRAN is still widely used for technical programming today; however, although recent versions have been improved, the language has not found wide use in the business community because of its early disadvantages. FORTRAN was limited in both the flexibility and format with which it prepared printed reports, it did not handle input and output operations to storage devices very efficiently, and it had only a limited ability to express and process nonnumeric data.

COBOL   COmmon Business Oriented Language, or **COBOL** for short, was released in 1960. The U.S. Department of Defense, which is one of the world's largest buyers of data processing equipment, no longer wanted to commission the development of software in unalterable assembly language, so it funded the development of this programming language for business. The concern over the differences among versions of FORTRAN—all machine-dependent—led the developers of COBOL

**FIGURE 8.3
FORTRAN.** Here, a **FORTRAN** statement calculates a discount (7% of the invoice amount) if the invoice amount is greater than $500. Otherwise, no discount is given to the customer.

```
IF (XINVO .GT. 500.00) THEN

    DISCNT = 0.07 * XINVO

ELSE

    DISCNT = 0.0

ENDIF

XINVO = XINVO - DISCNT
```

to adopt machine independence as one of the primary objectives. The U.S. government then adopted a policy that required a computer to have the COBOL programming language available if the vendor wanted to sell or lease the equipment to the government. In 1968, COBOL was approved as the standard business programming language in the United States; the latest ANSI standards for COBOL were released in 1974.

The commands and syntax of COBOL's instruction statements are like English. As a result, it is much easier for a programmer to read and understand COBOL than FORTRAN. A COBOL program has four divisions: the *identification division*, which contains reference information such as program name and programmer's name; the *environment division*, which describes the type of computer to be used; the *data division*, which describes the data to be processed; and the *procedure division*, which contains the programming logic. Figure 8.4 shows an extract from the procedure division of a typical COBOL program.

The major strengths of COBOL, which is used primarily on minicomputers and mainframes and is the language most used for business applications, include its machine independence, its strong file-handling capabilities, the access it provides to database systems and data communications software, and its self-documenting English-language-like instructions. The major criticisms of COBOL have been directed toward the extensive length and wordiness of the programs it creates.

PL/1   The intended uses of FORTRAN and COBOL were always very clear. However, as the complexity and sophistication of the applications being developed for business increased, a language was needed that would be capable of dealing with computation *and* heavy-duty file handling. For this reason, IBM and two international organizations of computer users began to develop a general-purpose programming language, which was designated Programming Language 1, or **PL/1**. PL/1 was released in the mid-1960s for use on the IBM System 360 series of computers and has since been used primarily on mainframe computer systems. Figure 8.5 shows an extract from a PL/1 program.

FIGURE 8.4
COBOL. This COBOL statement shows the same discount calculation given in Figure 8.3.

```
OPEN-INVOICE-FILE.
    OPEN I-O INVOICE-FILE.

READ-INVOICE-PROCESS.
    PERFORM READ-NEXT-REC THROUGH READ-NEXT-REC-EXIT UNTIL END-OF-FILE.
    STOP RUN.

READ-NEXT-REC.
    READ INVOICE-REC
        INVALID KEY
            DISPLAY 'ERROR READING INVOICE FILE'
            MOVE 'Y' TO EOF-FLAG
            GOTO READ-NEXT-REC-EXIT.
    IF INVOICE-AMT > 500
        INVOICE-AMT = INVOICE-AMT - (INVOICE-AMT * .07)
        REWRITE INVOICE-REC.

READ-NEXT-REC-EXIT.
    EXIT.
```

The primary advantages of PL/1, which is used mostly on minicomputers and mainframes, are its power and flexibility and its combination of text- and arithmetic-processing capabilities. Using it, programmers can tap into virtually all available computer power without having to fall back on the use of assembly language to achieve a satisfactory degree of performance. The major drawbacks of PL/1 are that it requires a substantial amount of internal memory, has a very long list of options that are difficult to memorize, is sometimes more difficult to learn than COBOL, and is only available on a limited number of computer systems.

BASIC   Beginner's All-purpose Symbolic Instruction Code, or **BASIC**, was developed in the mid-1960s at Dartmouth College, where the large computer time-sharing system supported many student-terminals that allowed interactive testing of the new computer language. BASIC was intended to be a programming language that was easy to learn and flexible enough to solve a variety of simple problems. It was used primarily to teach people how to program.

By the late 1970s and early 1980s, BASIC had become so popular that it was selected as the primary language for implementation on microcomputers, although it can be used on all types of computers. Because of its popularity, a number of extensions have been added to the language to facilitate file creation and handling and the creation of graphics. Figure 8.6 shows an extract from a BASIC program.

The primary advantage of BASIC has been its ease of use. The primary limitation, aside from its slow processing speed, seems to be a lack of official standardization, although Microsoft's version of BASIC, called MS-BASIC, is accepted as a de facto standard. Each implementation of the language for a particular machine appears to have a few subtle differences that require specific attention when a program is to be run on a different machine. Although some ANSI standards were approved in 1978, they include only a small subset of the capabilities supported by most versions of the language. See the appendix for more detailed coverage of BASIC.

RPG   The Report Program Generator, or **RPG**, language was introduced by IBM in 1964 to help small businesses generate reports and update files easily. RPG is not

---

FIGURE 8.5
PL/1. The discount calculation of Figure 8.3 shown in PL/1.

```
/*CALCULATE DISCOUNT*/

GET LIST (INVOICE);

IF INVOICE > 500 THEN DISCOUNT = INVOICE * .07;

ELSE DISCOUNT = 0;

END;
```

as procedure-oriented as other third-generation languages. The programmer fills out a number of very detailed coding forms that are easy to learn to use; however, because RPG is designed to be used to solve clear-cut and relatively simple problems, it is much more limited than FORTRAN, COBOL, BASIC, and some other programming languages. RPG is used on a variety of IBM computers and has been *enhanced*, or improved, several times. The first revision, RPG II, was released in the early 1970s and provided enhanced capabilities for handling tape and disk files. The latest version of the language, RPG III (released in 1979), added the capabilities necessary to extract reports from data stored in a database system. Figure 8.7 shows some RPG forms with data entered.

The major advantages of RPG are the ease with which reports can be produced with minimal time and effort on the part of the programmer or user and the low number of formal rules for syntax and grammar compared to other high-level languages. However, the first version of RPG had limited computational capabilities

FIGURE 8.6
BASIC. Our discount calculation in BASIC.

```
10   REM    This Program Calculates a Discount Based on the Invoice Amount
20   REM         If Invoice Amount is Greater Than 500, Discount is 7%
30   REM         Otherwise Discount is 0
40   REM
50   INPUT "What is the Invoice Amount"; INV.AMT
60   IF INV.AMT > 500 THEN LET DISCOUNT = .07 ELSE LET DISCOUNT = 0
70   REM         Display results
80   PRINT "Original Amt", "Discount", "Amt after Discount"
90   PRINT INV.AMT, INV.AMT * DISCOUNT, INV.AMT - INV.AMT * DISCOUNT
100  END
```

FIGURE 8.7
RPG. The discount calculation.

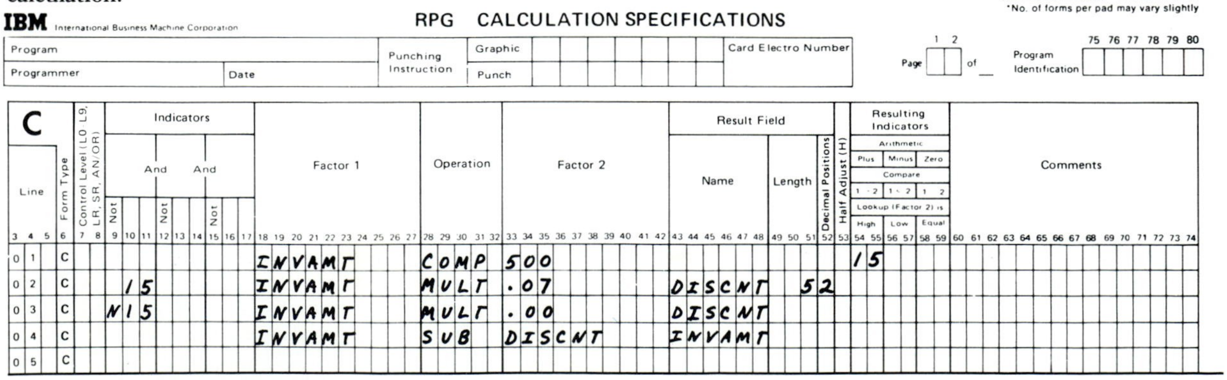

Line	Form Type	Control Level	Indicators	Factor 1	Operation	Factor 2	Result Field Name	Length	Decimal Positions	Resulting Indicators (High)
01	C			INVAMT	COMP	500				15
02	C		15	INVAMT	MULT	.07	DISCNT	5	2	
03	C		N15	INVAMT	MULT	.00	DISCNT			
04	C			INVAMT	SUB	DISCNT	INVAMT			
05	C									

and could not be used effectively in scientific or other applications requiring extensive mathematical processing. RPG II substantially corrected some of these limitations; RPG III, improved still further, is a powerful menu-driven, modern interactive language. However, no formal RPG standards have yet been introduced by the industry.

C This programming language, invented after the languages "A" and "B" had been developed, was introduced by Bell Laboratories in the early 1970s for use in writing systems software. C, which is quite sophisticated and difficult to learn, was used to create most of the UNIX operating system. The recent interest in UNIX as a powerful operating system for microcomputers has sparked interest in converting existing applications software to run with UNIX and in writing new software using C. Figure 8.8 shows an example of the C programming language.

PASCAL The **Pascal** language, named after the 17th-century French mathematician Blaise Pascal, was developed by the Swiss scientist Niklaus Wirth and introduced in the early 1970s. Available for both large and small computer systems, it was developed to teach programming as a systematic and structured activity; Pascal classes are offered at most universities and colleges because of its superior structured programming format. Structured programming, which we will cover in greater detail in the next chapter, is based on the principle that any desired programming procedures can be broken into three parts:

- Logic that allows a series of operations to be performed in sequence
- Logic that allows data elements to be compared and decisions to be made that determine the direction of subsequent processing
- Logic that allows procedures to be repeated a controlled number of times (looping)

Figure 8.9 is an extract from a Pascal program.

FIGURE 8.8
C. The C version of the 7% discount. C has many characteristics of both assembly and high-level programming languages, and, although it is a complex language to learn, it can be used on a variety of machines.

```
if (invoice_amount > 500.00)

    discount = 0.07 * invoice_amount;

else

    discount = 0.00;

invoice_amount = invoice_amount - discount;
```

The major advantages of Pascal are its strong capabilities for mathematical and scientific processing, its extensive graphics capabilities, and the ease with which it can be learned. The major drawback of Pascal is that, because its input and output operations are limited, it is a poor candidate for extensive use in business data processing.

MODULA-2   Developed by Niklaus Wirth as an improvement of Pascal and introduced in 1980, **Modula-2** is better suited for business use than Pascal, and it can be used as an applications software development tool. Because it is a relatively new language, it is not yet used extensively; however, many experts believe that it may become a popular business programming language.

ADA   In 1975, the U.S. Department of Defense began to encourage the creation of a language that would facilitate the development and maintenance of large programs that could be used for any type of application—from business to missile firing—and that could be used and modified over a long period of time. This decision was prompted by the results of a study that showed that lack of uniformity in the use of languages resulted in yearly software costs of billions of dollars. These costs were necessary to pay for the large staff of programmers required to support all the different languages used.

The programming language **Ada** was named after the daughter of the famous English poet Lord Byron, Augusta Ada, Countess of Lovelace, who worked with the mathematician Charles Babbage in the mid-1880s to develop mechanical computing devices. The Countess of Lovelace is considered to be the world's first programmer. This language is intended primarily for use in computer systems that are an integral part of another system for which they act as the control mechanism; that is, they are *embedded* systems. Many military weapons systems and equipment, for example, have embedded computer systems. However, the language can be used for commercial as well as military applications. Figure 8.10 is a sample extract of an Ada program.

FIGURE 8.9
Pascal. The customer discount calculation shown in Pascal.

```
if INVOICEAMOUNT > 500.00 then

    DISCOUNT := 0.07 * INVOICEAMOUNT

else

    DISCOUNT := 0.0;

INVOICEAMOUNT := INVOICEAMOUNT - DISCOUNT;
```

Ada's strong points are its extensive support of real-time procedures, automatic error recovery, fail-safe operation (that is, without error), and flexible input and output operations. Its disadvantages are that it is very complex and difficult to learn, its flexibility can lead to some inefficiency, and its language processor and resulting programs tend to demand extremely large storage requirements. Currently only a few Ada language processors are available; as a result, although Ada has great potential, it is not yet widely used.

How Does a Programmer Know Which Language to Use? We have discussed only a few of the most popular high-level programming languages—there are many more! However, if a programmer has a good understanding of what a program needs to accomplish, then deciding what language to use may not be difficult. The following factors are usually considered when a decision is made:

- Does the company already have a standard language that the programmers use?
- How easy is it to learn the language?
- What other languages are supported on the computer system?
- Do the processing requirements match the capabilities of the language? For example, FORTRAN is very effective for computations, whereas COBOL is very good at handling large volumes of business information.
- Will the program need to run on more than one type of computer system? If so, transportability becomes a consideration; that is, the degree of a language's machine dependence needs to be evaluated.
- Are the intended applications using the high-level language oriented toward a batch or an on-line environment?

No matter which language is selected to write a program, the principles of developing software are the same, even though the vocabulary and syntax may vary among languages. These principles will be covered in Chapter 9.

FIGURE 8.10
Ada. The 7% solution in Ada.

```
if INVOICE_AMOUNT > 500.00 then

    DISCOUNT := 0.07 * INVOICE_AMOUNT

else

    DISCOUNT := 0.00

endif;

INVOICE_AMOUNT := INVOICE_AMOUNT - DISCOUNT
```

THE FOURTH GENERATION

Also known as very-high-level languages, **fourth-generation languages (4GLs)** are as yet difficult to define, because they are defined differently by different vendors: Sometimes these languages are tied to a software package produced by the vendor, such as a database management system. Basically 4GLs are easier for programmers—and users—to handle than third-generation languages. Fourth-generation languages are **nonprocedural languages,** so named because they allow programmers and users to specify *what* the computer is supposed to do without having to specify *how* the computer is supposed to do it, which is done with third-generation, high-level (procedural) languages. Consequently, fourth-generation languages need approximately one-tenth the number of statements that a high-level language needs to achieve the same result. Because they are so much easier to use than third-generation languages, fourth-generation languages allow users, or non-computer professionals, to develop software. It is likely that, in the business environment, you will at some time use a fourth-generation language. Three basic types of language tools fall into the fourth-generation language category: query languages, report generators, and applications generators.

Query languages allow the user to ask questions about, or retrieve information from, database files by forming requests in normal English-language statements. Query languages do have a specific grammar, vocabulary, and syntax that must be mastered (like third-generation languages), but this is usually a simple task for both users and programmers. For example, a manager in charge of inventory may key in the following question of a database: How many items in inventory have a quantity-on-hand that is less than the reorder point? The query language will do the following to retrieve the information:

1. Copy the data for items with quantity-on-hand less than the reorder point into a temporary location in internal memory.
2. Sort the data into order by inventory number.
3. Present the information on the video display screen (or printer).

The manager now has the information necessary to proceed with reordering certain low-stock items. The important thing to note is that the manager didn't have to specify *how* to get the job done, only *what* needed to be done. In other words, in our example, the user needed only to specify the question, and the system automatically performed each of the three steps listed above.

Figure 8.11 provides an example of a query language, and Table 8.1 lists some of the popular query languages used today. Some query languages also allow the user to add data to and modify database files, which is identical to what database management systems software allows you to do. The difference between the definitions for query language and for database management systems software is so slight that most people consider the definitions to be the same.

Report generators are similar to query languages in that they allow users to ask questions of a database and retrieve information from it for a report (the output); however, in the case of a report generator, the user is unable to alter the contents of the database file. And with a report generator, the user has much greater control over what the output (or the result of a query) will look like. The user of a report generator can specify that the software automatically determine what the output should look like or can create his or her own customized output reports using special report-generator command instructions. In most reports, users require that a total or

---

FIGURE 8.11
Query language.

```
In order to produce a list of certain fields contained in an
organization's employee database (called Q.ORG), the SQL
instruction, or query, would be:


SELECT DEPTNUMB, DEPTNAME, MANAGER, DIVISION, LOCATION FROM Q.ORG


The result of the query might be:


DEPTNUMB  DEPTNAME       MANAGER   DIVISION     LOCATION
      10  HEAD OFFICE       160    CORPORATE    NEW YORK
      15  NEW ENGLAND        50    EASTERN      BOSTON
      20  MID ATLANTIC       10    EASTERN      WASHINGTON
      38  SOUTH ATLANTIC     30    EASTERN      ATLANTA
      42  GREAT LAKES       100    MIDWEST      CHICAGO
      51  PLAINS            140    MIDWEST      DALLAS
      66  PACIFIC           260    WESTERN      SAN FRANCISCO
      84  MOUNTAIN          290    WESTERN      DENVER
```

TABLE 8.1 Popular Query Languages

Category	Package/Language	Vendor
Query language	INTELLECT	Artificial Intelligence Corp.
	On-Line English	Culliname
	Query-By-Example	IBM
	Quick Query	Caci
	SQL	IBM
	Ingress/Star	Relational Technology
	Oracle	Oracle
Report generators	Easytrieve Plus	Pansophic
	GIS	IBM
	Mark IV	Informatics
	NOMAD	NCSS
Applications generators	ADS	Cullinet
	Application Factory	Cortex Corporation
	FOCUS	Information Builders
	MAPPER	Sperry
	MANTIS	CINCOM
	NATURAL	Software AG
	RAMIS	Mathematica, Inc.

totals of one or more groups of numbers appear at the bottom. And, if more than one category of information is to be included in the report, the user usually wants subtotals to appear for each category. In the case of a third-generation language, the number of instructions necessary to create totals is about ten times the number needed in a fourth-generation language, because the programmer needs to specify not only what to total, but how to total and where to place the total. Report generators have many built-in assumptions that relieve the user from having to make such tedious decisions. Table 8.1 lists the most widely used report generators.

Applications generators, as opposed to query languages and report generators, which allow the user to specify only output-related processing tasks (and some input-related tasks, in the case of query languages), allow the user to reduce the time it takes to *design* an entire software application that accepts input, ensures data has been input accurately, performs complex calculations and processing logic, and outputs information in the form of reports. The user must key into computer-usable form the specifications for "what" the program is supposed to do. The resulting specification file is input to the applications generator, which determines "how" to perform the tasks and which then produces the necessary instructions for the software program. Again, as with query languages and report generators, the user doesn't have to specify "how" to get the processing tasks performed. Table 8.1 lists some of the more popular applications generators used today.

THE FIFTH GENERATION

Some people consider **natural language** to represent the next step in the development of programming languages—the fifth generation. Natural language is similar to query language, with one difference: It eliminates the need for the user or programmer to learn a specific vocabulary, grammar, or syntax. The text of a natural-language statement very closely resembles human speech. In fact, one could word a statement in several ways—perhaps even misspelling some words or changing the order of the words—and get the same result. Natural language takes the user one step farther away from having to deal directly and in detail with computer hardware and software. Two natural languages already available are Clout (for microcomputers) and Intellect (for mainframes). However, because natural languages cannot yet handle complex logical operations, they are being used mainly in conjunction with database software.

The use of natural language touches on *expert systems*, computerized collections of the knowledge of many human experts in a given field, and *artificial intelligence*, independently smart computer systems—two topics that are now receiving much attention and development and will continue to do so in the future (see Chapters 12 and 14).

MICROCOMPUTER-BASED SOFTWARE DEVELOPMENT TOOLS

"And you can even buy it off the shelf of your computer store!" When electronic spreadsheet software and database management systems software were introduced to the business community in the early 1980s, the excitement was great, because this software placed programming power into the hands of the user, or non-computer professional. The sales of microcomputers soared as a result. These two types of software packages are considered to be software development tools because, with them, both programmer and user can create specialized applications to satisfy specific processing needs. As in the case of fourth-generation languages, electronic spreadsheet software and database management systems software require the user to specify only *what* processing is to be done, not *how* it should be done.

Spreadsheets

When spreadsheet software was introduced, businesses could immediately see that it could save them much time and money. For businesses that already had computers, money could be saved in professional programming fees. For the non-computerized business, electronic spreadsheets presented an economical way of computerizing routine and time-consuming activities. For example, in the business without computers, to "age" accounts receivables to penalize people with overdue account balances, someone has to manually calculate how many days have passed between the invoice date and the current date and then calculate an appropriate penalty based on the balance due. This can take hours of work. However, with an electronic spreadsheet package, in less than half an hour the user can create an application that will calculate accounts receivables automatically. And the application can be used over and over. Electronic spreadsheets provide users with the necessary analytical and processing tools to develop applications to satisfy many of the processing tasks encountered in the business environment. Module C describes electronic spreadsheet software in detail and teaches you how to use it.

Database Management Systems

Database management systems software has many of the features of fourth-generation languages. In fact, as mentioned earlier, many people believe that this type of software falls into the fourth-generation category. Database management systems software allows the user to store data in and maintain database files, to ask questions of, or query, the database files, and to generate stylized reports. Module D goes into these features in detail and discusses their use.

Onward:
Developing a Technique

Chapter 8 gave you a general picture of the kinds of tools available for developing computer software to perform useful business tasks. Chapter 9 will show you why you need to know about the basics of programming to communicate with programmers.

SUMMARY

Users need to know what software development tools, or programming languages, are used to create software. If you need additional processing capabilities that can't be satisfied by an off-the-shelf applications software program, you should know how to choose—or help a computer specialist to choose—the software development tool that can most efficiently and effectively satisfy your requirements.

Programming languages can be divided into five generations. Machine language, the only language the computer's processor can understand, is first-generation language—the digits 0 and 1. Assembly language, easier to work with than machine language because it allows the programmer to use abbreviations, is a second-generation language. (Both machine and assembly language are low-level languages.) High-level, or third-generation, languages were developed to make writing software programs even easier by using English-like statements. Of the hundreds of high-level languages used today, the following are some of the more popular:

- FORTRAN (FORmula TRANslator)—the first high-level language, which was formulated for scientific applications; this language does not handle the input and output of large volumes of data efficiently.

- COBOL (COmmon Business Oriented Language)—its development as a common programming language for business applications was funded by the U.S. government; this language is noted for its machine independence and its data processing and file-handling capabilities.

- PL/1 (Programming Language 1)—designed to combine the computational capabilities of FORTRAN and the data processing and file-handling capabilities of COBOL.

- BASIC (Beginners' All-purpose Symbolic Instruction Code)—developed at Dartmouth College for instructional purposes, but now used on microcomputers and certain business systems to solve a variety of relatively simple problems.

- RPG (Report Program Generator)—introduced by IBM as a program geared to deal with clear-cut problems and produce reports; users can produce reports by filling out special coding forms and then entering the recorded data.

- C—developed by Bell Laboratories as a tool for writing systems software, such as UNIX.

- Ada—named for Augusta Ada, Countess of Lovelace (the first programmer), and developed by the U.S. Department of Defense for use as an embedded system in computerized weapons systems.

- Pascal—named for 17th-century French mathematician Blaise Pascal; developed to teach structured programming; has strong mathematical and scientific processing capabilities and can be used on large and small computer systems; not used extensively in business.

- Modula-2—an improved version of Pascal, better suited for business.

Fourth-generation languages do not rely on a long list of detailed procedures that tell the computer *how* to do something. They just use English-like statements to tell the computer *what* to do. The three basic types of fourth-generation language tools are query languages, report generators, and applications generators.

Natural language, which some people refer to as fifth-generation language, allows users and programmers to interact with the computer by using human language patterns, including misspellings and mistakes. The fields of expert systems and artificial intelligence use natural languages.

The advantages and disadvantages of each programming language relative to the information and systems needs of a company should be analyzed before a programmer begins a programming project.

Most of the foregoing software development tools are commonly used by computer specialists—programmers—to write software programs. However, users have some relatively new microcomputer software packages—including electronic spreadsheets and database management systems—at their fingertips to help them create customized programs to solve unique needs. These packages are so much easier to use than typical programming languages and procedures that users who have used a computer for just a few hours can develop their own simple applications software.

KEY TERMS

Ada
American National
    Standards Institute
    (ANSI)
applications generator
BASIC
C
COBOL
database management
    systems software
first-generation language

FORTRAN
fourth-generation lan-
    guage (4GL)
International Standards
    Organization (ISO)
Modula-2
natural language
nonprocedural language
Pascal
PL/1

procedural language
query language
report generator
RPG
second-generation
    language
spreadsheet software
syntax
third-generation
    language

EXERCISES

MATCHING

Match each of the following terms with the phrase that is the most closely related:

1. _____ third-generation language
2. _____ second-generation language
3. _____ first-generation language
4. _____ syntax
5. _____ fourth-generation language
6. _____ query language
7. _____ C

8. _____ report generator
9. _____ natural language
10. _____ FORTRAN
11. _____ COBOL
12. _____ BASIC
13. _____ Ada

a. The precise rules and patterns required for the formation of programming language statements.
b. This high-level language is used to facilitate the development and maintenance of large programs that are used and modified over a long period of time.
c. This fourth-generation language was created to allow users to easily extract information from database files.
d. High-level languages fall into this generation of programming languages.
e. Languages that fall into this generation are considered to be nonprocedural languages.
f. This high-level language is often used for writing systems software.
g. This high-level programming language is often used for scientific and technical applications.
h. This type of language is similar to query language except that the user doesn't need to learn a specific vocabulary or syntax.
i. Machine language falls into this generation of programming languages.
j. This high-level programming language is easy to learn and can be used to solve a variety of simple problems.
k. This fourth-generation tool is used to speed up the process of producing reports.
l. Assembly language falls into this generation of programming languages.
m. This high-level programming language was developed to be machine-independent and is often used for business applications.
n. This high-level language was developed to combine the computational and file-handling capabilities of FORTRAN and COBOL.

MULTIPLE CHOICE

1. Which of the following is a specialized tool used to speed up the process of designing the initial version of an applications software program?
   a. compiler
   b. Ada

    c. applications generator

    d. interpreter

    e. all of the above

2. Which of the following is not a high-level programming language?

    a. assembly language

    b. COBOL

    c. BASIC

    d. FORTRAN

    e. PL/1

3. Which of the following high-level programming languages was approved as the standard business language in the United States?

    a. FORTRAN

    b. COBOL

    c. Pascal

    d. BASIC

    e. none of the above

4. Which of the following is not one of the four divisions of a COBOL program?

    a. identification division

    b. environment division

    c. data division

    d. logic division

    e. procedure division

5. Which of the following is an objective of high-level languages?

    a. to relieve the programmer of the tedious task of writing programs in either machine or assembly language

    b. to provide programs that can be used on more than one type of machine

    c. to meet specific needs of science and/or business

    d. to allow the programmer more time to focus on understanding the user's needs and designing software to meet those needs

    e. all of the above

6. If you were in charge of developing systems software, which of the following programming languages would you probably use?

    a. FORTRAN

    b. BASIC

    c. C

    d. PL/1

    e. Ada

7. Which of the following high-level languages would you probably use if you were commissioned to create a program that involved a large number of technical and scientific applications?

    a. FORTRAN

    b. BASIC

    c. C

    d. PL/1

    e. Ada

8. If you aren't a computer specialist but use a microcomputer in business, which type of software development tool will you most likely use?
   a. FORTRAN
   b. BASIC
   c. electronic spreadsheet
   d. PL/1
   e. Ada

9. What is the main characteristic of machine language?
   a. instructions and data are represented by binary digits
   b. machine-dependent
   c. first-generation language
   d. difficult to learn
   e. all of the above

SHORT ANSWER

1. Why is it important for you to know what tools are used to create software?

2. What were the reasons behind the development of high-level programming languages?

3. What is the advantage of using a fourth-generation language over a high-level language? Of using natural language?

4. Discuss the factors that should be considered in deciding which high-level language to use in developing software.

5. Why are programs still written in assembly language today even though more sophisticated software development tools are available?

6. What led to the development of high-level programming language standards by ANSI and ISO?

7. What is the purpose of a report generator?

8. What software development tools are you most likely to use? Why?

9. What is the main difference between procedural and nonprocedural languages?

10. What are the three main types of fourth-generation language tools?

PROJECTS

1. Visit the computer laboratory at your school.
    a. Identify which high-level languages are available.
    b. Determine if each language processor identified is a compiler or an interpreter.
    c. Determine if the language processors are available for microcomputers, larger computers, or both.
    d. Identify any microcomputer-based electronic spreadsheet software and data-base management systems software available.
2. Interview some professional programmers or students in advanced programming and find out why they think it's important for users to know the basics about developing software.

CHAPTER NINE

PROGRAMMING: WHAT THE USER NEEDS TO KNOW

Question: Why does a successful insurance salesperson study such seemingly remote subjects as tax law and inheritance law? *Answer*: To be an even better insurance salesperson. Knowing about these topics will improve the salesperson's ability to participate in clients' estate planning—and, of course, thereby sell insurance.

Similarly, learning about the fundamentals of programming will help you, the user, communicate with specialists and become an intelligent and effective contributor in your chosen field.

PREVIEW

When you have completed this chapter, you will be able to:

■

Identify the typical steps followed in developing a high-level language program and explain why they are important

■

Describe the importance of structured programming concepts and methods, including top-down design

■

Identify the basic operations common to most programs

■

Discuss the importance of program testing and documentation

■

The User Perspective

For a number of important reasons, the user should understand how a computer programmer develops software using a high-level language. The user may have to evaluate software vendors' claims about what their programs can do. More important, if the user fails to communicate clearly and precisely to the programmer the processing procedures and logic to be incorporated into a program, the programmer will have to make assumptions about what exactly should be done. If the assumptions are wrong, the user will probably end up with reports that contain erroneous information or reports that simply do not *have* the necessary information.

In addition, as we mentioned in the last chapter, some users today are using existing software packages such as electronic spreadsheets to customize their own software applications. If you are one of these people, you should be aware of a few facts. First, no matter how easy a software development tool is to use, you must understand the principal steps to take to "custom-tailor" an application. Second, the processing logic required for the procedures to be performed must be carefully mapped out. Third, you must understand the importance of testing and documenting the software to ensure it is doing exactly what is expected. Many users do not take this third step seriously, and, as a result, the software they develop often produces erroneous information.

Suppose your boss asks you to create an electronic spreadsheet that will produce information to be considered in making a multimillion-dollar bid for a new project. If you do not proceed carefully, you may end up with problems such as:

- A formula for computing costs does not include all the required values; as a result, the cost estimate will be too low.
- An estimate of the expected revenues from the project is incorrectly specified; as a result, the cash flow during the life of the project will be overestimated.

With millions of dollars at stake, you may quickly find yourself out of a job and your career ruined. An infinite number of problems can be created if you are not careful when using software. Many people assume that the numbers in a computer report are always correct. *They are correct only if the processing procedures have been carefully specified and thoroughly tested.*

Writing High-Level Language Programs

As you know, organizations that use computers to process data into information use applications software to perform specific business-related activities. This applications software comprises different applications software *programs*, each of which performs specific processing tasks, such as processing payroll or processing inventory. The orderly process that an organization goes through when identifying its applications software program requirements is referred to as the *Systems Development Life Cycle (SDLC)*, which is discussed in more detail in the next chapter. This chapter focuses on just a small part of the SDLC—namely, the steps involved in developing an applications software program once the requirements for the program have been identified. As mentioned earlier, you need to understand these steps so that you will be able to tell a programmer, in terms he or she can understand, exactly what your programming requirements are.

Writing a Program Step by Step

The primary steps in writing software programs are generally the same, no matter what kind of software is being written or what existing program is being modified. Once the general program requirements—the informational needs that it must fill—have been defined, the following steps are taken:

Step 1—Design the program

A. How will the intended program fit in with the other applications software programs in the organization? If the data or information produced by the program can't be used for further processing by any of the other programs, the program might not be of much value. For example, perhaps the information produced by a program in the payroll department needs to be passed along to a program in the human resources department. You should be aware of such needs so that you can communicate them to the programmers before they begin creating the program.

B. Identify the most efficient way of structuring the program to perform the intended tasks. This step is similar in concept to setting up a good outline for a lengthy term paper before starting to write it.

Step 2—Map out the program logic

After the program's design structure has been determined, deal with any areas where complex processing logic must be worked out. The programmer must work out **algorithms,** or diagrams of the solutions, before the program is written. The programmer may use a variety of tools to do this, including system flowcharts (covered in the next chapter), program flowcharts, and pseudocode (discussed later in this chapter). You probably won't ever need to use any of these tools, because they are used mostly by programmers mapping out complex logic or by those using third-generation languages. However, you should have a basic idea of how they are used in order to appreciate the detail that is necessary for a programmer to create a program. The more detail you can give the programmer about your processing requirements, the better the resulting program will be.

Step 3—Code the program

Translate the processing requirements of the program into the necessary programming language statements. The programmer usually drafts a program on scratch paper and then codes the instructions into the computer.

Step 4—Test the program

Review the program carefully to ensure that it is doing exactly what it is supposed to. Check computations and decision logic for accuracy, and review output reports to determine that they are in the correct format and contain all the required information. You can play an important role in identifying the "problem areas" in a program by testing it to see how it handles the types of tasks you want it to. The programmer can then fix the problems.

Step 5—Collate the documentation

Clearly document all the steps, procedures, logic tools, and testing results, as well as the goals of the program and other specific facts. Although listed as step 5, the activity of documenting the program actually goes on all the way through the design and coding process. This documentation, or manual, will tell future program operators, users, managers, and even programmers who may later have to modify the program exactly what the program does and how it does it, and what they need to do to use it. Documentation also helps programmers track down errors.

WRITING THE EGOLESS PROGRAM

The professional programmer is a highly skilled computer professional who puts a great deal of effort into writing a program. The time required to develop a program can stretch over many months. As a result, many programmers become so personally involved in their programs that they cannot take criticism resulting from program testing very well and become resistant to suggestions from peers and people who will be using the program—personality gets in the way of objectivity.

The result can be a poorly designed program that is not well documented. In 1971 Dr. Gerald Weinberg in his *The Psychology of Computer Programming* proposed a solution to the potentially protective attitude of the programmer. A program should be viewed as a product subject to the same quality assurance concerns as any other expensive technical mechanism. The purpose of quality assurance procedures is to ensure that the program does exactly what it is supposed to in the most efficient and effective manner possible. Thus, *egoless programming*—programming by a group of people who review one another's work—was born. In egoless programming, team members are equal; there is no chief. Assignments are determined democratically, and each member's work is the property of the team *and* the organization that has contracted the writing of the program. Peer review is an ongoing process.

TECHNIQUES FOR DOCUMENTING PROGRAM LOGIC

During the programming process, users must know how to express their processing requirements in the detailed terms necessary for the computer specialist to convert them into program logic. It may be easy to describe what you want accomplished to someone who is at least slightly familiar with the working of your department. However, you would be amazed at how much detail is required to communicate to a person unfamiliar with your work exactly what to do, when to do it, and how it is to be done. And exceptions must always be accounted for—a program has to be able to take care of the rare case as well as the routine ones.

A number of tools and techniques have been developed to assist in documenting the logic to be built into programs. We will discuss only program flowcharts and pseudocode, because it's unlikely that, as a general business user, you would come into direct contact with any other programming tools or techniques.

FIGURE 9.1
Standard flowchart symbols.
Programmers use plastic
templates (a) to trace standard ANSI flowchart sym-
bols when preparing plans
for program design (b).

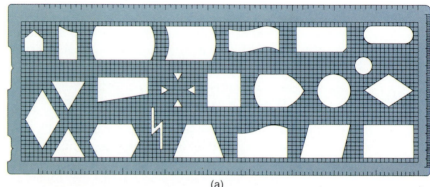

(a)

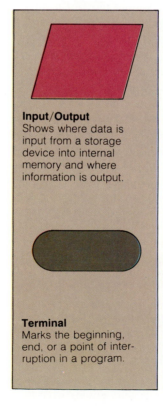

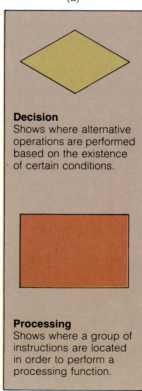

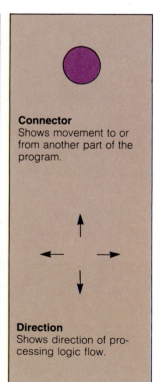

Input/Output
Shows where data is input from a storage device into internal memory and where information is output.

Decision
Shows where alternative operations are performed based on the existence of certain conditions.

Connector
Shows movement to or from another part of the program.

Terminal
Marks the beginning, end, or a point of interruption in a program.

Processing
Shows where a group of instructions are located in order to perform a processing function.

Direction
Shows direction of processing logic flow.

(b)

FLOWCHARTS

A **program flowchart** is a diagram that uses standard ANSI symbols to show the step-by-step processing activities and decision logic needed to solve a problem (Figure 9.1). (A *systems flowchart* maps the flow of data and information throughout an entire organization. This type of flowchart is drawn up as part of the systems development life cycle, which we will discuss in the next chapter.) How a program flowchart could show the processing logic used to calculate a salesclerk's bonus at Sporting Life is displayed in Figure 9.2. The flow of logic in a flowchart normally goes from top to bottom and left to right. Arrows are used to show a change from those directions.

Although program flowcharts have some disadvantages—their preparation may be time-consuming and they can be many pages long—they are considered to be a good tool for documenting the procedures to be used in the program, and they are often included in a program's documentation package.

PSEUDOCODE

The prefix *pseudo-* means *fake*; **pseudocode,** therefore, literally means *fake code*—that is, not the code that is actually entered into the computer. Pseudocode uses English-like statements instead of symbols (such as flowchart symbols) to represent

FIGURE 9.2
Logical Sporting Life bonus.
This shows the processing
logic necessary to calculate
a clerk's bonus depending
on whether actual sales
exceed goals by more than
20% (T = true; F = false).

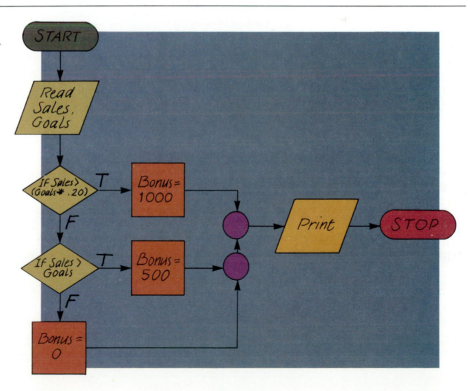

program logic. It is more precise in representing logic than regular, idiomatic English but does not follow a specific syntax. Using pseudocode to document program logic is much less time-consuming than flowcharting because the programmer doesn't have to spend time drawing symbols or boxes. Instead, the pseudocode statements can be composed and edited by hand or by using a typical off-the-shelf word processing program. Some people would argue further that pseudocode is much closer to actual code than are flowcharts, which makes pseudocode more productive than flowcharting. However, some programmers don't like to use pseudocode because it doesn't depict the program logic visually like a flowchart does.

Pseudocode uses four statement keywords to portray logic: IF, THEN, ELSE, and DO. Repetitive processing logic is portrayed using the statements DO WHILE (repeat an activity as long as a certain condition exists), DO UNTIL (repeat an activity until a certain condition is met), and END DO (stop repeating the activity). The processing logic is written out in narrative sentences. The logic statement

FIGURE 9.3
Pseudocode. Using pseudo-code to solve a crime.

START * murder of Grizzly Beans *

* Solve murder of Grizzly Beans *

DO WHILE there are suspects

    IF Roger's fingerprints are on the sword THEN

        Arrest Roger

    ELSE

        Question Matilda

        IF Matilda has an alibi THEN

            Grill Captain Murk

            Give Miss Turtle the third degree

            Identify fingerprints on sword

        ENDIF

    ENDIF

        Arrest murderer

END DO

END * murder of Grizzly Beans *

keywords are capitalized, and several levels of standard indentation are used to show decision processes and subprocesses. Figure 9.3 gives you an idea of how the keywords, statements, and indentation are used.

STRUCTURED PROGRAMMING CONCEPTS AND METHODS

Program flowcharts, pseudocode, and the rules and syntax of a high-level language enable a programmer to design and write software to solve a problem. However, for a long time many computer scientists felt that more structure and control were needed to standardize programming and make it more exact—to change it from an art to a science. Thus, in the mid-1960s, the concept of **structured programming** was developed. Structured programming uses top-down design, which you'll learn about shortly, and three basic control structures to "decompose" (break down) main functions into smaller ones (modules) for coding purposes. The **control structures**—sequence, selection (if-then-else), and iteration, or looping (do while)—can solve any problem in programming logic.

TOP-DOWN DESIGN

The objective of **top-down design** is to identify the main functions of the program and then to break those functions into smaller and smaller units, called **modules,** that are easy to work with. (In some programming languages, modules are often referred to as **subroutines.**) If possible, each module should have only a single function; indeed, many programmers think that each module should be limited to fifty or less lines of program instructions. This forces a limit to a module's size and complexity. **Structure charts,** also called *hierarchy charts* (Figure 9.4), are often used to picture the organization and breakdown of modules. [*Hierarchy Input Processing Output (HIPO)* charts, discussed in Chapter 10, diagram both the modular structure and the input/processing/ouput structure for each module.] A program that is considered modular in design usually has the following characteristics:

1. The functions of input and output are well defined and are usually in separate modules.

2. Each module has a single entry point (execution of the program statements always begins at the same instruction), and a single exit point (control always leaves the module on the same instruction) (Figure 9.5).

3. If one module refers to or transfers control to another module, the latter module returns control to the point from which it was "called" by the first module (Figure 9.6).

The principal advantage of modular program design for the user is that, if a program needs to be changed or updated, the work can be done in a short time, without affecting normal business activities; thus the use of this design method can often save the user money. More specifically, the advantages of a modular program are:

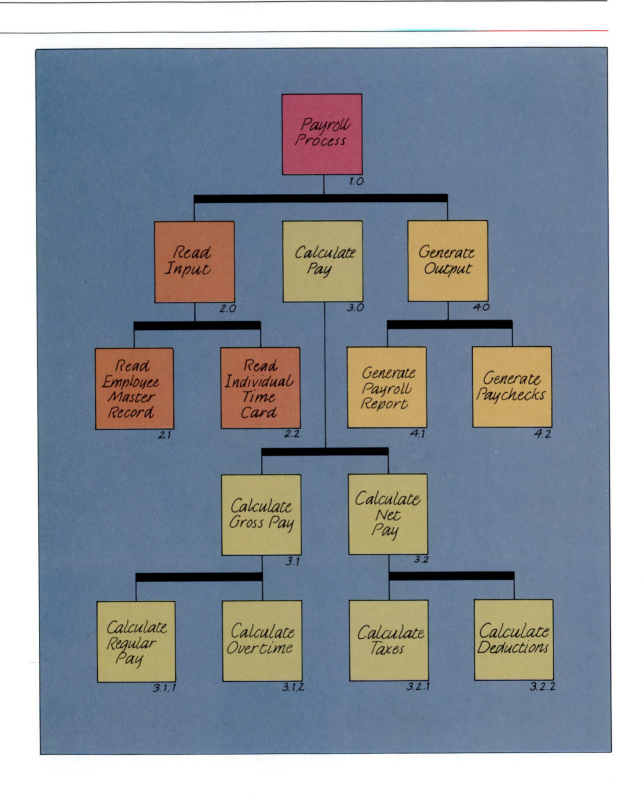

◄FIGURE 9.4
Structure chart for top-down design. In a structure chart, to perform the task given in the top of module (1.0), all substructured tasks must be performed first (for example, 2.1 and 2.2 to perform 2.0). Only one task is given each module.

- Complex programs can be organized into smaller and more manageable pieces in a relatively standard way.

- Programs can be modified with less effort than nonmodular programs because, when modular programming guidelines are followed carefully, each module is relatively independent and can be changed without affecting all the other parts of the program.

- A collection or library of standardized modules can be created that can be used in other programs (which saves the user money because similar processing tasks don't have to be programmed redundantly).

- Errors in logic can be quickly isolated and fixed. Figure 9.7(a) shows the logic flow in a nonmodular program. We can see that the different sections of code are interrelated and that each section is tied to several other sections. Because of these interrelationships, errors are not always easy to isolate. Figure 9.7(b) shows the flow of activity in a program that is modular in design.

SEQUENCE

According to the **sequence control structure** (Figure 9.8), when processing begins on any program, each instruction is executed in sequence. For example, consider the logic necessary to compute net pay (Figure 9.9). The first step is to input the number of hours worked, the pay rate, and the deduction percentage (taxes, insurance, and so on). The second step is to compute gross pay by multiplying the

FIGURE 9.5
One way in and one way out. Each module in a top-down program design has only one entry point and one exit point in the logical progression.

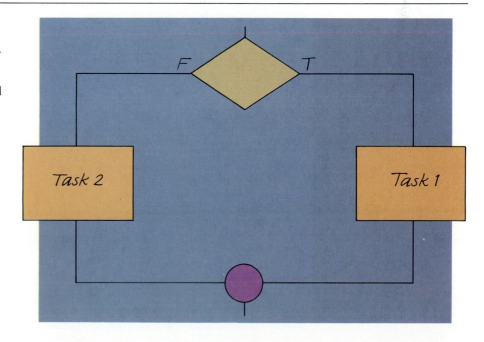

number of hours worked by the pay rate. The third step is to compute the deduction amount by multiplying the gross pay amount by the deduction percentage. The fourth and final step is to compute the net pay amount by subtracting the deduction amount from the gross pay amount. These events take place in sequence, one after the other, as specified.

SELECTION: IF-THEN-ELSE

The **if-then-else** control structure (Figure 9.10) allows a condition to be tested to determine which instruction(s) will be performed next; it allows the sequence con-

FIGURE 9.6
On call. When one module "calls" another module, meaning that it refers to or transfers control to another, the latter module returns control to the first one at the point where it was "called."

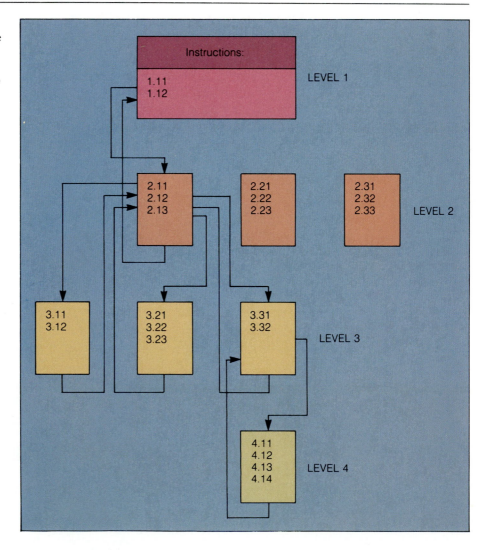

trol to be shifted depending on the outcome of the test. Thus the programmer can alter the basic sequence control structure when certain conditions apply. The intent of if-then-else is to determine which of two activities is to be performed—or *selected*—as the result of testing the condition. If the condition exists—that is, if it is true—one event takes place; if the condition does not exist—if it is false—a second, different event takes place. In other words, *if* a condition is true *then* do one thing, [or] *else* do another.

Figure 9.11 shows how the if-then-else control structure would look for figuring out whether or not an employee gets a bonus.

ITERATION: DO-WHILE

The **do-while** control structure allows an activity to be repeated (**iterated**) as long as a certain condition remains true (Figure 9.12). This is often referred to as a **loop**, because the program will keep repeating the activity until the condition becomes false. Loops simplify programming because they enable the programmer to specify certain instructions only once to have the computer execute them many times. The

FIGURE 9.7
Nonmodular and modular logic flow. Because the sections of code in a nonmodular program design (a) are interrelated, errors are harder to isolate and correct. In modular design (b), the instruction modules are relatively independent and can be changed without affecting all the other modules in the program.

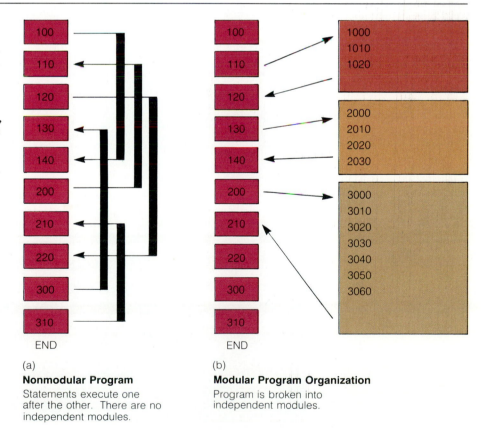

(a)
Nonmodular Program
Statements execute one after the other. There are no independent modules.

(b)
Modular Program Organization
Program is broken into independent modules.

do-while control structure is most often used in the processing logic for input/output operations.

Structured programming methods will continue to be used extensively in maintaining and modifying the large number of existing applications programs that have been written in a high-level procedural language such as COBOL. However, as you know, in recent years the newest tools and languages for developing software have become more flexible and "user friendly" (meaning that they are easier to use).

STRUCTURED WALKTHROUGH

When a group of programmers meets to review a program designed by another programmer, they perform what is called a **structured walkthrough**. Although the

FIGURE 9.8
Sequence control structure. One of the three principal control structures of structured programming specifies that all events take place in sequence, one after the other.

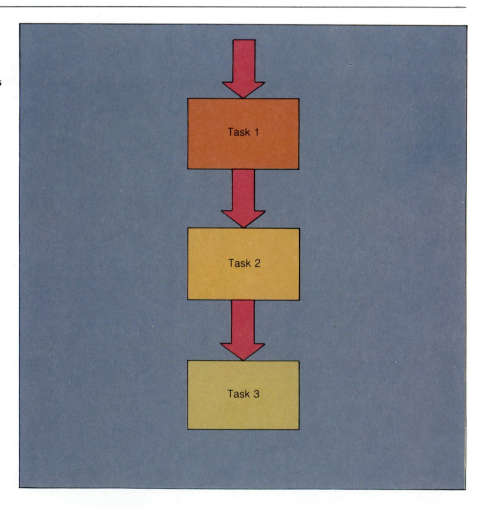

FIGURE 9.9
Sequencing to get net pay.
This example shows the
computation of net pay
using sequencing. The steps
are repeated until the end
of the file (EOF) is reached.

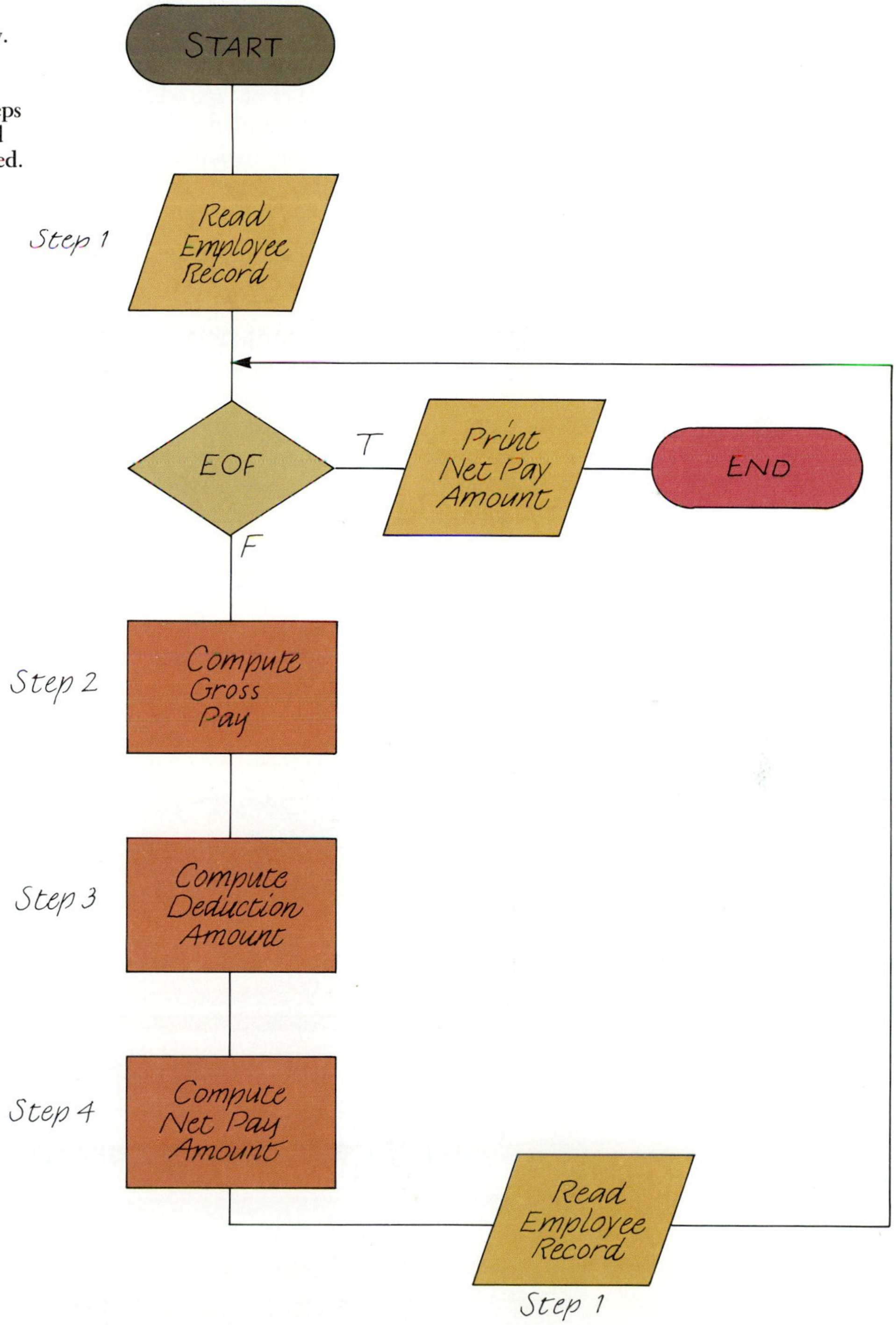

user isn't involved in the structured walkthrough, he or she should see a well-designed program as a result of the walkthrough. The group's manager does not attend, because the purpose of the meeting is not to evaluate the programmer's personal performance; rather, the purpose is to "walk through" the logic and identify what won't work, what is not clear, and what is inappropriate. As you can see, the structured walkthrough is related to the concept of egoless programming; indeed, it is organized by the programmer responsible for the work to be reviewed. A review may be called more than once, depending on the stage of work being done and the results of the previous review (if any).

FUNDAMENTAL PROGRAMMING CONCEPTS

The ways in which programs can vary are limited only by the programmer's level of skill and fund of imagination, the constraints of the programming language, and the user's needs. However, some common threads can be found in almost all programs, including (1) the types of data processed, (2) the operations performed on the data, (3) the need to perform input/output operations, (4) the need to count and accumulate totals for reporting purposes, and (5) the need to store data in and retrieve data from internal memory.

FIGURE 9.10
If-then-else control structure. If a condition is true, then one event takes place; if the event is false—that is, if it does not exist—then a second event takes place.

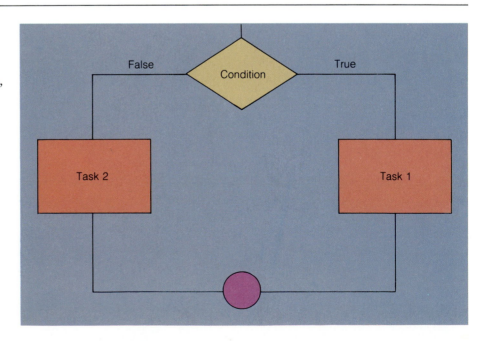

DATA TYPES

Programs set up instructions to process two basic types of data: numeric and alphanumeric. **Numeric data** describes an element of data that can be mathematically manipulated. An hourly pay rate of 10.50 is numeric data. Your age, the number of miles you travel to work, and your grade point average are all examples of numeric data. Numeric data is also categorized depending on whether or not it can include fractional values.

FIGURE 9.11
Selecting whether or not an employee gets a bonus. If the condition is true—that is, if actual sales exceed goals—the employee gets the bonus. If sales do not exceed goals, the employee is out of luck. A second true/false condition tested here is whether the sales goals are exceeded by more than or less than 20%.

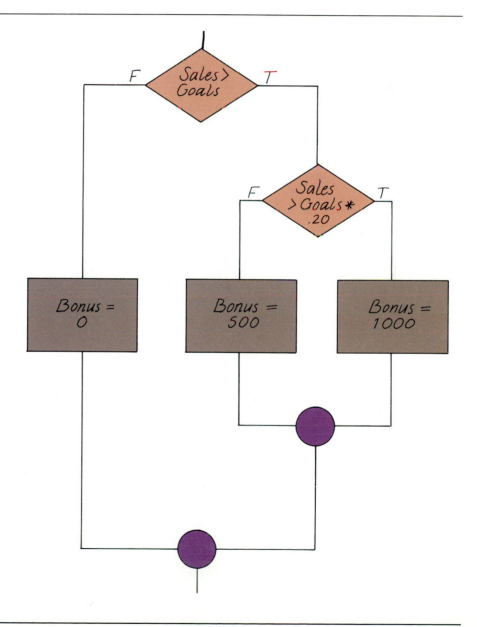

Alphanumeric data is data that is not intended to be mathematically manipulated; any attempt to do so would result in a meaningless response. Alphanumeric data can include any combination of alphabet characters, numeric digits, and special symbols (such as punctuation). A customer's name and address are examples of alphanumeric data, as is a car's license plate number.

OPERATIONS PERFORMED ON DATA

If you are going to be using a microcomputer to customize applications software, you should know about the different types of processing options available to you. The operations typically performed on data include arithmetic operations, relational operations, and logical operations.

Arithmetic operations include addition, subtraction, multiplication, division, and exponentiation.

Relational operations allow two elements of data to be compared to determine if a specific condition exists. One element of data can be greater than, less than, or equal to the other.

Logical operations allow comparisons to be combined into more complex tests of more than one part. The three basic logical operators are:

AND   Two separate conditions must be true before certain action is taken.

OR   At least one of two different conditions must be true before certain action is taken.

NOT   A certain action will be taken only when a particular condition is true.

These relational and logical operations form the building blocks for creating programming logic tailored to meet a user's needs. Additional logical operations exist, but they involve a higher level of detail than is appropriate for this text.

INPUT/OUTPUT (I/O)

Input and output are fundamental parts of most programs: The program must provide instructions for inputting data into internal memory and outputting information. These operations are often referred to as **input/output operations,** or **I/O.**

COUNTERS AND ACCUMULATORS

The most often used mathematical operations in a program involve counters, subtotals, and totals. The area set aside in internal memory to record the number of times an event, activity, or condition is encountered during processing is called a **counter.** The area set aside in internal memory to capture a total or a subtotal of certain numeric values is an **accumulator.** Most reports produced by the computer contain one or more totals or subtotals that have been accumulated during processing. Both counters and accumulators must be set to zero before processing begins; otherwise, values from prior processing runs will affect the final counts and make them inaccurate.

STORING DATA FOR PROCESSING: ARRAYS

Often it is valuable to create a program that can refer to and process data temporarily stored in internal memory and organized in rows and columns in tabular form, or an **array.** Most programming languages can set up programs with such capabilities. Arrays are valuable because they are a common way to represent data: Think of

FIGURE 9.12
Repeating the calculation of employee bonuses. As long as salespersons are listed for whom bonuses still need to be calculated, the program repeats the activity—the "loop" shown in the drawing.

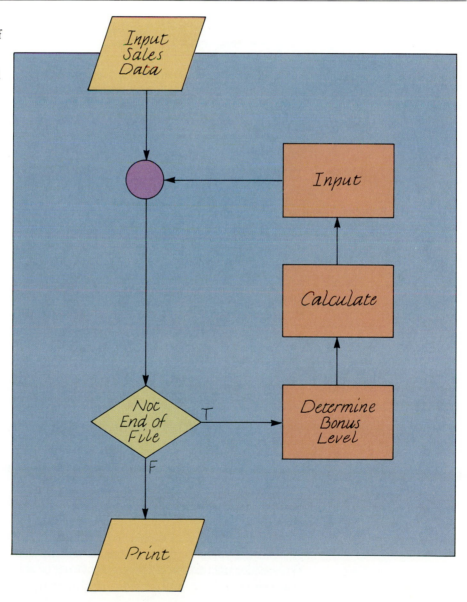

income tax tables, sales tax tables, life expectancy tables, calorie tables, and height and weight tables. The primary advantage of an array—also called a *matrix*—is that it allows data to be read by a search of a table rather than an extensive series of condition tests and computations. When array processing is used, the array can be maintained as a separate data file and simply loaded into memory during processing. That way, when values change, the entire program does not need to be changed, because the program consists of only the logic used to search for and process array values. A simple demonstration of the use of arrays in programming is given in the appendix.

PROGRAM TESTING: GETTING THE BUGS OUT

Even though a program is carefully designed and coded, it cannot be relied on to produce accurate information until it has been thoroughly tested. The object of testing is to "break" the program; if the program can be made not to work, that means it has "bugs" that must be eliminated. (The term *bug* originated in the early days of computers when a moth got inside the wiring and caused a computer to shut down.) When a program has passed all the necessary tests, the user can rely on the continued integrity of the results produced by the program.

Program testing—which is done at every level of program development—is done in three ways: (1) The program is examined to remove **syntax errors** (caused by typos and incorrect use of the programming language) and **logic errors** (caused by not using the correct control structures in the proper manner). (2) The program for several high-level modules is tested before the program is designed for the rest of the lower-level modules (subroutines). This process is sometimes called **stub testing** (the unprogrammed modules are the *stubs*). The objective is to test the individual components of a large and complex program as it is developed and thus eliminate as many errors as possible without having to write the whole program first. (3) The entire program is tested from beginning to end.

It is easy to create test data that is too narrow in scope, and a common mistake is to enter only valid test data. Although ensuring that the program will handle valid test data in the anticipated fashion is important, it is also necessary to ensure that the program will appropriately handle invalid test data— data that is incomprehensible to the program, incomplete, or in the wrong form (numeric instead of alphanumeric, for example). The point is to test the program's error functions—the functions that tell the user that data has been entered incorrectly.

DOCUMENTING THE PROGRAM

Program documentation should have been going on since the very beginning of program development. The importance of this step cannot be overemphasized: Without documentation, the program may not be able to be modified in the future; diagnosis of problems will be difficult; identifying and eliminating any remaining

bugs will be nightmarish; and users will have no instructions for using the program.
Program documentation should provide the following:

- A permanent record of what the program does.
- Instructions for program users on how to interact with the program.
- Instructions for computer operators on how to organize and control the processing of the program.
- Detailed documentation required to modify the program to meet new requirements.

As you can see, program documentation is required at several levels: user documentation, technical documentation, and operator's instructions.

User documentation is required for programs that have the user interacting directly with the computer during operation—such as entering data into the system, directing the processing, and requesting reports. User documentation usually consists of simple step-by-step procedures that describe what the user is to do and how to do it.

Technical documentation consists of a number of items prepared during the development of the program including:

- A narrative overview of what the program does.
- A series of flowcharts or paragraphs of pseudocode depicting processing logic. (Sometimes a combination of both are used.)
- Examples of all reports produced by the program.
- Examples of any display screen activity such as menus or softcopy reports.
- A listing of the program language statements.

Operator's instructions are required for programs that are run on large computer systems. These instructions identify exactly what is required for the computer operator to prepare the program to process, and they explain what steps are to be followed during processing.

As we have stated, the absence of good program documentation can create problems. Users can become frustrated when they try to work with the program. Programmers can have a very difficult time modifying programs they did not create if the documentation is inadequate. If a program is lost, it cannot be reconstructed without good documentation. And the need for good documentation doesn't apply just to custom-written programs: Be sure your microcomputer software comes with adequate documentation manuals!

Onward: SDLC

Now that you have an idea of how computer software programs are written, you need to learn how the program requirements are determined. How does an organization identify its information needs and data processing requirements? It goes through the systems development life cycle, or SDLC, to be discussed in Chapter 10. First, however, let's check back with Sporting Life to see how much you've learned about the world of computers.

SUMMARY

Regardless of whether a software program is being developed using a high-level programming language or an integrated microcomputer software package, the same steps should be taken once the program requirements have been established: (1) design the program, (2) map out the program logic—that is, work out the necessary algorithms, (3) code the program, (4) test the program, and (5) document the program.

Many tools and techniques are used to document program logic, including program flowcharts and pseudocode.

Program flowcharts use standard ANSI symbols to represent the step-by-step activities and decision logic needed to solve a processing problem. Logic flow normally goes from top to bottom and left to right.

Pseudocode is a "fake" code—that is, English-like statements that use the structure of the programming language statements to describe instructions but without being hard to understand. Pseudocode uses four keywords to portray logic: IF, THEN, ELSE, and DO. Repetitive processing logic is represented by DO WHILE, DO UNTIL, and END DO.

Structured programming is the method used by good programmers today. This method, used with one or more of the tools and techniques listed above, not only simplifies the task of writing a program but also makes it easier for the programmer to update, or make changes to, the program. Structured programming relies heavily on the concept of modularity (top-down design) and the use of structured walk-throughs. These programs all use the same three basic control structures to form the program code: (1) sequence, (2) selection (if-then-else), and (3) iteration, or looping (do while).

Top-down design identifies the main functions of the program and then breaks those functions down into smaller and smaller units, called *modules*, that are easy to work with. Each module should have only a single function and a single entry and exit point. Structure, or hierarchy, charts are often used to diagram the organization and breakdown of modules.

The sequence control structure determines that each program instruction is executed in sequence unless a particular instruction is intended to alter that sequence.

The selection control structure allows a condition to be tested (IF) to determine which instruction(s) will be performed next (THEN or ELSE). Using this structure, the programmer can alter the basic sequence structure.

The iteration control structure (looping) allows an activity to be repeated as long as a certain condition remains true. Loops simplify programming because they enable the programmer to specify instructions only once to have the computer execute them many times.

The structured walkthrough—conceptually related to egoless programming, or programming by a group of people—is a review of a programmer's work by his or her peers. No managers are present. During the review the programmer's work is evaluated and problems are identified. Structured walkthroughs should be scheduled at different stages of program development.

Although the ways in which programs can vary are virtually limitless, all programs (1) process one or more of the same types of data, (2) perform some of the same types of operations on data, (3) need to perform input/output (I/O) operations, (4) need to count and accumulate totals for reporting purposes, and (5) need to store data in and retrieve data from internal memory.

All programs deal with numeric and alphanumeric data. Numeric data is mathematically manipulated; alphanumeric data is not. Typical operations performed by most programs on data are arithmetic operations (addition, subtraction, multiplication, division, and exponentiation), relational operations (comparisons using less than, greater than, and/or equal to), and logical operations (AND, OR, NOT).

All programs must be repeatedly tested at all stages of development to identify and eliminate bugs (syntax and logic errors). Stub testing occurs when incomplete high-level program modules ("stubs") are tested before the rest of the program is written. Adequate test data must be designed to properly test the program.

Documentation, which should be done at each development stage, provides a permanent record of what the program does and how the program works. Documentation will be used by computer operators, programmers, managers, and users. Updating a program without good documentation is very difficult.

KEY TERMS

accumulator
algorithm
alphanumeric data
arithmetic operations
array
control structures
counter
input/output (I/O)
   operations
iteration (do-while)
   control structure

logical operations
logic error
loop
module
numeric data
program flowchart
pseudocode
relational operations
selection (if-then-else)
   control structure

sequence control
   structure
structure chart
structured programming
structured walkthrough
stub testing
subroutine
syntax error
top-down design

EXERCISES

MATCHING

Match each of the following terms with the phrase that is the most closely related:

1. _____ alphanumeric data
2. _____ pseudocode
3. _____ accumulator
4. _____ stub testing
5. _____ counter
6. _____ structured programming
7. _____ logical operations
8. _____ sequence control structure
9. _____ do-while (loop)
10. _____ array
11. _____ structure chart
12. _____ structured walkthrough
13. _____ if-then-else
14. _____ program flowchart
15. _____ modules

a. A tool used to assist in documenting the logic to be built into a program; it uses ANSI symbols to show the step-by-step processing activities and decision logic needed to solve a problem.

b. Used when programmers meet to review a program designed by another programmer.

c. English-like statements used to represent program logic.

d. Programming method that uses top-down design and three basic control structures to break main program functions into smaller ones.

e. The main functions of a program are broken into these smaller functions when the structured programming method is used.

f. Used to picture the organization and breakdown of programs, they are often referred to as hierarchy charts.

g. When this structure is followed while writing a program, each program instruction is executed in sequence unless a particular instruction is intended to alter that sequence.

h. When this structure is followed while writing a program, a condition can be tested to determine which instruction(s) will be performed next.

i. When this structure is followed while writing a program, an activity can be repeated as long as a certain condition remains true.

j. This type of data isn't intended to be mathematically manipulated.

k. These allow the relational operators to be combined into more complex tests of more than one part and form the building blocks for creating programming logic tailored to meet the user's needs.

l. An area set aside in internal memory to record the number of times an event, activity, or condition is encountered during processing.

m. An area set aside in internal memory to capture a total or a subtotal of certain numeric values.

n. Programs often refer to this arrangement in internal memory that stores data temporarily in rows and columns in tabular form.

o. This method is used to test the individual modules of a large and complex program.

MULTIPLE CHOICE

1. Which term is most unrelated to the structured programming method?
   a. modularity
   b. egoless programming
   c. structured walkthroughs
   d. alphanumeric data
   e. control structures

2. Which of the following is a program design technique used to depict program logic visually?
   a. flowchart
   b. egoless programming
   c. logical operations
   d. pseudocode
   e. none of the above

3. Which of the following is a program design technique that uses English-like statements to depict program logic?
   a. flowchart
   b. egoless programming
   c. logical operations
   d. pseudocode
   e. none of the above

4. Which of the following is used when creating a program using the structured programming method?
   a. if-then-else
   b. do-while
   c. sequence
   d. top-down design
   e. all of the above

5. Which of the following is common to all programs?
   a. need to store data in and retrieve data from internal memory
   b. operations performed on data
   c. need to perform input/output operations
   d. need to accumulate totals
   e. all of the above

6. Which of the following statements is false?
   a. Developing software involves preparing a documentation package.
   b. Computer-produced reports are always accurate.
   c. Programs should be tested with invalid and valid data.
   d. Stub testing is important when testing structured programs.
   e. all of the above

7. Which of the following is not an advantage of using the structured program design method?
   a. Complex programs can be organized into smaller pieces in a relatively standard way.

  b. A library of standardized modules can be collected to be used in other programs.

  c. Errors in logic can be quickly isolated and fixed.

  d. Programs can be modified with less effort.

  e. none of the above

8. Which of the following is not a characteristic of a structured program?
  a. Input/output functions are well defined.
  b. Each module has a single entry point and a single exit point.
  c. If one module gives control to another module, the other module will mark the end of processing.
  d. When the actual program instructions are written, they are indented in order to highlight the activities taking place.
  e. none of the above

9. Which of the following is part of the process of testing a program?
  a. The program is examined to remove syntax errors.
  b. The program is examined to remove logic errors.
  c. stub testing
  d. The entire program is tested from beginning to end.
  e. all of the above

10. Which of the following is an objective of documenting a program?
  a. Provide a permanent record of what the program does.
  b. Provide computer operators with instructions on how to organize and control the processing of the program.
  c. Provide programmers with the detailed documentation required to modify the program to meet new requirements.
  d. Provide program users with instructions on how to interact with the program.
  e. all of the above

SHORT ANSWER

1. Why should the user understand how a computer programmer develops software using a high-level language?

2. What steps does a programmer take to write a program once the general program requirements have been defined?

3. What is egoless programming and why is it important?

4. Why is documentation important?

5. What were the reasons behind the development of structured programming concepts and methods?

6. What common threads are found in almost all programs?

7. What is the importance of testing a program?

8. What is the importance of structured walkthroughs to program design?

9. What characteristics do modular programs usually have?

10. What are the advantages of a program design that is modular?

EPISODE 3

WHAT ARE THE GUIDELINES FOR BUYING A MICROCOMPUTER?

THE STORY CONTINUES . . .

By now things have become even wilder at Sporting Life. Two months ago your sales were $4.2 million, and climbing—good news, of course, but Roy is still struggling with his problem of trying to keep inventory records up to date and Mary is hard pressed to keep up with the accounting workload. Now that you have offered a discount to schools in your area (10% off all products bought by schools, and larger discounts for individual orders over $500), business is doing even better.

SIZING UP THE SITUATION

In the meeting described in Episode 2, Roy and Mary gave you their "wish lists"—a description of what they would like the computer to do. However, because most experts advise that you not buy hardware until you understand what software you will want to run, you have made no moves to install a computer system until you got some familiarity with software. Now you know something about both hardware *and* software, and you are in a position to buy.

What follows is a list of some important questions that you or *anyone*—student, businessperson, or hobbyist—can ask salespersons when shopping for computer hardware and software. The questions themselves are general; the examples we give, of course, are those that have grown out of the specific problems you're trying to solve at Sporting Life.

HOW MUCH MONEY DO YOU HAVE TO SPEND?

The salesperson may well ask this question (albeit more politely, perhaps wondering what is "in your price range"). You need not state your budget, but you should probably have your top figure in mind. The best strategy is to tell the salesperson the problems you are trying to solve, and then see if you can get the best hardware and software combination that will solve them for the least amount of money.

Note: The word to keep in mind is "upgrade." You can often start out with an inexpensive computer and then upgrade it by adding parts later. It is not necessary to buy an expensive system to take care of all your *future* needs—especially if you aren't sure what those needs will be. With Sporting Life, for instance, you might end up with 20 stores in five years, but you certainly don't want to buy a system for that now.

HOW SOPHISTICATED DO YOU WANT YOUR COMPUTER TO BE?

A microcomputer can be anything from a videogame machine to an "executive workstation." Sporting Life may be in the business of games, but you don't want a computer that just *plays* games. Here, then, are some matters to consider regarding sophistication:

1. Will the computer remain in your office (a desktop computer), or should it be portable (a laptop)—for example, so that you, Roy, and Mary can share it?

2. Should it be the same as, or compatible with, other computers—such as one at home or others linked by telephone?

3. Should it be able to use software you may already have?

4. Do you want it to show images in more than one color?

5. Should it be capable of holding a lot of information or large software programs?

6. Should it be upgradable and expandable? Will you be able to buy add-ons for it later that will make it faster, more powerful, more versatile, and so on?

EPISODE 3, CONTINUED

The answers to some of these questions depend on the kind of software you will need, as we shall discuss. At Sporting Life, right now it looks as though you don't need a portable computer or one that runs the same software you have at home. You may, however, want Roy to use a different one than Mary uses—but be sure their equipment is compatible!

WHAT KIND OF SOFTWARE WILL YOU WANT TO RUN?

The answer to this question lies in the answer to another question: What kind of tasks do you want the computer to do for you? You can get a computer and software that will enable you to play games, create art, compose electronic music, and track the stock market, but those are mainly home activities. Microcomputers used for work are another matter. Here are the most common questions to ask yourself—and the salesperson—about what you will use the computer for and, hence, what kind of software you will require:

1. *Word processing:* Will the computer be used for writing—such as letters, memos, reports, papers?

2. *Spreadsheets:* Will the computer be used to compute "what-if" types of financial possibilities—such as estimating costs, constructing bids, pricing products, calculating budgets, doing sales forecasts, and other forms of money management?

3. *File or database manager:* Will the computer be used to create mailing lists, address lists, lists of possessions or products, or other forms of record keeping?

4. *Telecommunications:* Will the computer need to exchange messages with other computer users and to access computer databanks?

5. *Graphics:* Will the computer be used to create charts and graphs?

6. *Integrated packages:* Will the computer have to mix any of the tasks listed above? For example, will sales figures be extracted from a file, manipulated on a spreadsheet, shown in graph form, put into a report, and/or transmitted by phone to another computer user?

7. *Special requirements:* Will the computer be used for desktop publishing (for, say, publishing a newsletter for Sporting Life Employees)? Will it be used to do accounting tasks? Plan business strategy? Do stock market analysis? Special-interest or industry-specific software is available for all kinds of tasks.

At Sporting Life, Roy needs a program to keep track of inventory; a database program, such as dBase III Plus or R:base 5000, would be helpful for him (see Module D for a description of dBase III Plus). Mary needs software for accounting—a specific accounting program, perhaps, but she might be able to use an integrated package that can retrieve information from a file, display it in spreadsheet or graph form, and print out reports and purchase orders. Symphony or Framework might be the best solution; however, such programs will run only on certain machines (such as the IBM Personal Computer) with a minimum required amount of memory (for instance, 640 K).

WHAT KIND OF HARDWARE SHOULD YOU BUY?

Because the software is available only for certain brands of computers, your choice automatically rules out some makes. Programs available for an Apple IIe, for example, will not run on an IBM PC. In addition, certain programs will run only on certain *models* of a particular make: Some software will run on the AT model of an IBM Personal Computer but not on the original PC model. Moreover, if the software requires certain kinds of disk drives, availability of color video display, or access to a printer, those factors will also determine the kind of computer you buy.

EPISODE 3, CONTINUED

The following are basic questions to ask:

1. *Processor:* Does the software require a machine with 8-, 16-, or 32-bit processor?

2. *Memory:* How much memory (in kilobytes) does the software need?

3. *Expandability:* Is the computer that you are considering expandable in memory capacity? That is, can you add plug-in circuit boards or otherwise increase the memory capacity? Are there limits?

4. *Secondary storage:* Does the software run on 3½-inch or 5¼-inch disks? Does it require a hard disk drive?

5. *Video display:* What kind of monitor or video display screen is standard with the computer being considered? Is it adequate to run the software? Will it display 80 columns (usually necessary with most software)? Is a monochrome (one-color) monitor sufficient and, if so, is it green or amber (colors that are less eye-fatiguing than white-on-black)? Is a color monitor warranted with the software you're considering? Is the screen resolution high enough for your purposes?

6. *Interfaces:* Will the computer interface (connect with) the devices such as printers and telecommunications devices that you need to run your software? Note that printers, for instance, may have either serial or parallel interfaces.

7. *Printer:* What kind of printer will you need to take advantage of the software? Do you need a letter-quality printer to prepare professional-looking letters or other documents being prepared for the public? Do you need a dot-matrix printer in order to print out graphics (pictures)? Do you need a laser printer (which will do both text and graphics and is quieter, but may be expensive)? Is the printer fast enough for your needs? Will it have the kind of paper-feed de-vice (friction feed, pin feed, or tractor feed) that will enable you to print with the kinds of paper or forms you want to use? Can you use just a printer for normal width (8½-inch-wide) paper, or do you need a wider printer for accounting or financial planning?

8. *Modem:* With one exception—telecommunications—most software can be run on the equipment we have discussed above. To communicate with another computer over a telephone line, however, you need a peripheral (add-on) device called a modem to connect your computer with a telephone. If you need one, you should ask: How fast is the baud rate—300 (which transmits 30 characters per second) or 1200 (120 cps)? The 1200 version, which may be more expensive, may be easier on the phone bills if you're sending a lot of information. Can the modem both originate and receive messages?

9. *Other peripheral devices:* Do you need a keyboard with a separate numeric keypad for entering lots of numbers? Does your software require a mouse to manipulate images on the screen? Do you need sound effects (for music or speech output), optical scanner, bar code scanner, voice-recognition device, or a chip-mounted real-time clock inside the computer?

An analysis of Mary's present needs at Sporting Life suggests that, to keep track of the accounting records (part of which involves analyzing accounts payable and accounts receivable in graphic form) and the personnel/payroll records, she needs the following hardware and software configuration:

1. Spreadsheet, database, and word processing software (or an integrated package)

2. A microcomputer of at least 16 bits, with at least 640 K and expandable memory

3. A 20-MB (or larger) hard disk drive

EPISODE 3, CONTINUED

4. A color monitor to display graphics
5. A laser printer capable of printing out wide accounting reports, with a tractor feed for forms such as invoices and purchase orders, and an envelope feeder

Mary, her accounting assistant, and her personnel/payroll assistant are the three people who will be using this microcomputer system; they will make up a schedule showing the times each will be using it.

As the controller of accounting, Mary is also in charge of Sporting Life's two cashiers. To track sales, each cashier requires the following microcomputer configuration:

1. A software program that prompts the cashier to enter the item number and number of items purchased and that then prints out a list of the items and their prices, including a total, for the customer
2. A microcomputer of at least 16 bits, with at least 640 K and expandable memory
3. A 20-MB (or larger) hard disk drive that stores an inventory file containing the item numbers and prices of every item in stock, as well as one or more transaction files (depending on the day's activities) that contain data about the number of items sold and returned each day. (*Note:* A transaction file can't be larger than the storage capacity of a floppy disk because the disks later need to be transferred to Roy, who will update the master inventory file.)
4. A monochrome monitor
5. A small printer that will print out sales receipts

At the end of each day, the cashiers make two copies of the transaction file(s) onto one or more floppy disks; one copy goes to Roy so that he can update the master transaction file and determine the status of inventory, and the other copy goes to Mary so that she can keep the accounting records current.

The main function of Roy's computer is to keep track of inventory. He requires a microcomputer system similar to Mary's, although he should have at least a 30-MB hard disk drive to accommodate all the data that relates to the more than 1300 different items that are carried in stock. Roy doesn't need a color monitor; a monochrome monitor would be fine. He should have a laser printer capable of printing out wide inventory reports, although it doesn't need a tractor feed or an envelope feeder. Roy will be the only one using this microcomputer system, unless he hires someone to update the master inventory file at the end of each day.

Of course, you—because you're the boss—get to use the computers almost any time you want!

WHAT KIND OF SUPPORT COMES WITH THE COMPUTER SYSTEM?

Before you move on to the next chapters and Episode 4, which deals with databases and communications, you need to consider your support system. The purpose of a computer is to save time. But if you have to figure everything out by yourself or fix it yourself, the time your computer saves may be minimal. Thus, questions about support should be as follows:

1. Is the computer and software retailer able to give you advice and assistance—either by virtue of being close by or, if a mail-order house, by technical support over the telephone?
2. Does the seller offer training classes?
3. Does the seller offer any help in financing your purchases?
4. Can a maintenance contract be purchased to cover parts and labor in case of breakdowns?
5. Is the documentation accompanying each piece of hardware and software clear?

PART FOUR

SYSTEMS CONCEPTS AND APPLICATIONS

If you choose a descriptive word at random—*nervous*, *planetary*, *educational*—and put it in front of the word *system*, you immediately suggest something powerful: a collection of items forming a whole or serving some purpose more important than the items themselves. Systems are an important concept of computers in business. In the following four chapters, we will see how you can use the concept as a way of solving problems, managing information, organizing databases, and communicating data.

10

SYSTEMS DEVELOPMENT LIFE CYCLE

No matter what your position in an organization, you will undoubtedly come in contact with a systems development life cycle (SDLC)—the process of setting up an *information system*. Regardless of the circumstances, the user has a definite role in a systems development life cycle. And if you, the user, understand its principles, you will be able to apply them to solving *any* type of problem, not just business- and/or computer-related ones.

PREVIEW

When you have completed this chapter, you will be able to:

■

Explain why some systems fail

■

Identify six phases of a systems development life cycle

■

List the techniques for gathering and analyzing data describing the current system

■

Describe the extent to which the requirements for a new information system must be defined before it is designed

■

Identify the major factors to consider in designing the input, output, and processing procedures and storage requirements of a new system

■

The User Perspective

How might you have to deal with systems development? You may be a manager whose staff is unable to handle the current work load and who has requested a study to see if a computer will improve the situation. Or you may be a staff member faced with the task of learning how to use and evaluate a new sales order entry system. Perhaps the division vice-president has decided that some departments need computers, and you are asked to submit a report on your department's need for one. And, as you will see, you may be involved with the SDLC process in even more ways.

The extent to which your job brings you in contact with your company's **systems development life cycle (SDLC)** will vary depending on a number of factors, including the size of the organization, your job description, your relevant experience, and your educational background in information-processing concepts, tools, and techniques. In large companies the SDLC is usually a formal process with clearly defined standards and procedures. Although the technical aspects of each phase of the cycle will undoubtedly be handled by computer specialists, you are often likely to interface with these specialists. For example:

- It may be necessary for you to explain how the current system works in your department: the manual procedures you use or what you do to support an existing computerized system.

- You could easily find yourself in a meeting discussing the nature of problems with the current system and how it can be improved.

- You may be required to provide the departmental objectives and requirements that the system must meet to systems analysts and designers. For instance, if you expect to have the new system produce useful reports, then you should plan to assist the computer specialists in designing them.

- As the development of a new system nears completion, you may help in testing it to ensure that it works as expected.

- You may attend briefings and training sessions to learn how the new system will affect your job and what its new operating procedures will be.

- And last, but certainly not least, you will end up using the new system. This may involve preparing data for input or using information produced by the system.

In addition:

- If your company doesn't have a data processing staff or department, you may have to develop a system yourself—using the same steps that systems analysts and designers use.

- With the ever-increasing use of fourth-generation languages and other microcomputer development tools, you will likely become more involved in developing systems themselves (through prototyping—the building of a small, simple model of the system—which we will discuss later).

- You may often be involved in the approval of projects and budgets as a member of a special steering committee (which we also discuss in more detail later).

In a sizable company the SDLC may seem like a large and complex process to which you are only peripherally related; however, your role in it is still important. Although in a small organization you are likely to be involved in more phases of the SDLC, and your role in each phase will tend to be more detailed, you shouldn't assume that the principles of an SDLC apply only to large computer systems and applications. Users often assume that they can purchase a microcomputer and a payroll software package on Monday and have a staff member produce paychecks on Friday. Unfortunately, it just isn't that simple. The basic principles of an SDLC should be followed even at the microcomputer level.

THE SYSTEMS DEVELOPMENT LIFE CYCLE:

Businesses are made up of many systems and subsystems, including many manual and mechanized procedures. Some systems are very simple: An order entry system could be just a set of procedures for taking down a telephone order from a customer and seeing that the appropriate catalog item is delivered. Other systems are very complicated: A large company's payroll system involves a number of subsystems for tracking employee turnover, pay rate changes, tax exemption status, types of insurance deductions, overtime rates and bonuses, and so on.

A system for which a computer is used to perform some of the procedures is called a **computer-based information system**. No computer-based system can stand on its own. As we discussed in Chapter 1, people must interact with the system and perform the manual procedures required to feed it raw data, review the information produced, and take appropriate actions.

The scope of an SDLC can vary. In some cases, the effort will be so large that dozens of personnel will be involved for a year or more. In other cases, the scope will be much smaller—for example, the owner of a two-person book design business would not take long to set up an invoice and payment system. In both extremes, however, it is equally important to follow a clearly defined process. The degree of complexity of an SDLC and the amount of effort that goes into each of its phases will vary according to the scope of the project.

WHY DO SYSTEMS DEVELOPMENT PROJECTS FAIL?

The chances are great that a systems development project will fail if a clearly defined SDLC isn't followed. Sometimes, however, even when companies go to the trouble to establish a formal and comprehensive SDLC, projects still fail to achieve their objectives. Why? Most failures can be traced to a breakdown in communications between the users and the data processing group or among the computer specialists. The reasons for failure often include:

- *Inadequate user involvement*— Users must assume responsibility for educating the analyst about business applications, requirements, and policies. (For example, a system may fail because major functions weren't anticipated in the design—because users didn't make their needs known.)

- *Continuation of a project that should have been canceled*—Often it's tempting to *not* cancel a project because of the investment already made. Analysts should reevaluate the project at various phases to determine if it remains feasible.
- *The failure of two or more portions of the new system to fit together properly* (called *systems integration*)—This often results when major portions of the systems are worked on by different groups of technical specialists who do not communicate well.

Responses to systems failure vary. Project leaders may be fired; usually the systems requirements are reassessed, and the highest-priority requirements are identified to be satisfied by a smaller system that can be more easily controlled.

WANTED: ORDERLY DEVELOPMENT PROCESS

In most sizable companies, a great deal of money is allocated for information processing functions (hardware, software, and staff support). In such companies, a systems development project that costs more than $1 million is not uncommon. Hundreds, even thousands, of individual tasks may need to be performed as part of the development effort. These tasks may involve many people within an organization, often in several different organizational units. This multiplicity of effort can lead to conflicting objectives and result in a project that is difficult to coordinate. If the process of developing a system bogs down, the final product can be delayed, and the final cost can be more than double the original estimate. To avoid such difficulties, the SDLC is used as a guideline to direct and administer the activities and to control the financial resources expended—in other words, to impose order on the development process. In a small company the amount of money spent on project development may not be much; however, following the steps of the SDLC is no less significant. Some—but by no means all—risks of ignoring these steps include the following:

- *The new system does not meet the user's needs*—Inaccurate or incomplete information given by users to systems analysts and designers may result in the development of software that does not do what the user needs.
- *The acquisition of unnecessary hardware or too much hardware*— If personal computers and printers are sitting idle most of the time, then probably far too much money has been invested without a clear definition of how much processing power is needed.
- *The acquisition of insufficient hardware*—The system may be inefficient.
- *Software may be inadequately tested and thus may not perform as expected.* Users tend to rely heavily on the accuracy and completeness of the information provided by the computer. However, if software is not adequately tested before it is given to users, undetected programming logic errors may produce inaccurate or incomplete information.

Different organizations may refer to the systems development life cycle by different names—such as Systems Development Cycle (SDC) or Systems Life Cycle

(SLC); however, the general objectives will always be the same. The number of steps necessary to complete the cycle may also vary from one company to another, depending on the level of detail necessary to effectively administer and control the development of systems. One way to look at systems development is to divide it into six phases:

Phase 1 —Analyze current system.

Phase 2 —Define new systems requirements.

Phase 3 —Design new system.

Phase 4 —Develop new system.

Phase 5 —Implement new system.

Phase 6 —Evaluate performance of new system.

Using ANSI systems flowchart symbols (Figure 10.1), Figure 10.2 diagrams the six phases of the SDLC, as well as the points where management must make decisions about whether to allow the project to continue. (Systems flowcharts, which we discuss in more detail later, are similar to program flowcharts; they diagram the flow of data and the processing activities within a system.)

FIGURE 10.1
ANSI systems flowchart symbols. Systems flowcharts use symbols standardized by the American National Standards Institute, just as program flowcharts do (however, the symbols are not all the same).

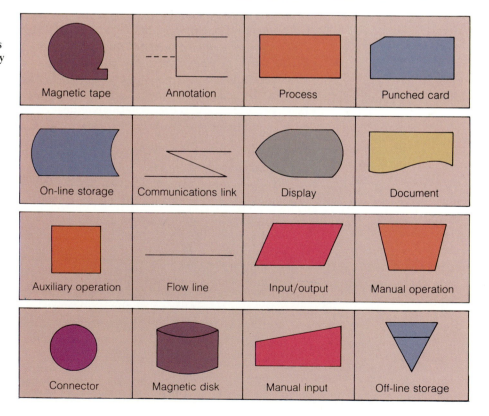

Magnetic tape	Annotation	Process	Punched card
On-line storage	Communications link	Display	Document
Auxiliary operation	Flow line	Input/output	Manual operation
Connector	Magnetic disk	Manual input	Off-line storage

WANTED: PARTICIPANTS

Three groups of personnel are usually involved in an SDLC project: the user group staff members (users), representatives of user management and data processing management (management), and a technical staff consisting of systems analysts and programmers (computer specialists). The users could come from a number of different departments, particularly in large systems. In smaller systems, the user may be a single individual or department.

Management participation in systems development is important because it lends support to the efforts underway. The cooperation of all staff members is much

FIGURE 10.2
The six phases of the SDLC. The diamond-shaped symbols indicate points at which management decides if the project is to continue. The activities of each phase are conducted by a professional systems analyst/designer; however, user input and review is a critical part of each phase.

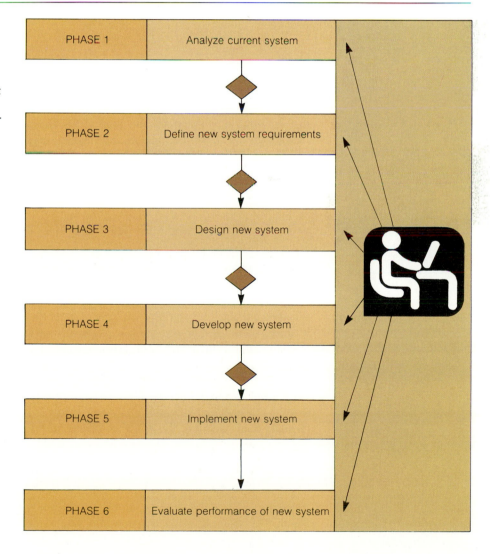

PHASE 1   Analyze current system

PHASE 2   Define new system requirements

PHASE 3   Design new system

PHASE 4   Develop new system

PHASE 5   Implement new system

PHASE 6   Evaluate performance of new system

easier to obtain when all levels of management have indicated their support for the project. Users must know that management will work with them to minimize any disruption caused by the project. In addition, management needs to review and approve progress as a project proceeds through each phase of the cycle. User management focuses on getting what is required; that is, it makes sure that the system fills all the stated requirements, and it evaluates the system's effect on staff and budget.

Occasionally *steering committees* are formed to help decide how to get started—that is, which systems development projects to work on first. A steering committee is a group of individuals from each department in an organization. It may hear reports from experts about the advantages, disadvantages, and costs of a particular project, after which it must decide whether it is in the organization's interest to implement the project. If it decides to go ahead, the systems development life cycle begins.

GETTING STARTED

The development of a system can be initiated in a number of ways. As we have indicated, a project request can come from a steering committee, which has already evaluated the project's potential benefits. In a large organization, a user department (for example, payroll department, personnel department, marketing department) may fill out a project request and submit it to management. Or top management may decide on its own to replace an archaic system—for instance, the manual accounting system—with a more modern and efficient one. Project requests may also originate from computer professionals or government. The requests are forwarded to the data processing department for review. Then the first phase of the SDLC begins.

PHASE 1: ANALYZE THE CURRENT SYSTEM

As we mentioned, the steering committee may request experts to report on a proposed project. This report, often called a *feasibility study*, is an optional step, but it can be considered part of the first phase of systems development. The goal of a feasibility study is to identify as quickly as possible whether the benefits of a proposed project appear to outweigh its expected cost and disruption. The analyst who conducts the study usually presents the findings to the steering committee along with a recommendation of how much priority should be assigned to the project. In many cases, it's a good idea to have the analyst conduct feasibility studies at various times throughout all phases of the SDLC to determine whether to continue the project.

PURPOSE OF PHASE 1

The objective of Phase 1 is to gain a clear understanding of the existing system and its shortcomings and to determine where improvements can be made; an analysis of the current system takes place regardless of whether it is manual or computer-based.

Figure 10.3 shows how you might have identified the problems in Sporting Life's manual accounting system, as well as areas in which a computer-based system could make improvements. The participants in this phase are usually the systems analyst, who must gain an understanding of the current system, and the users, who must educate the systems analyst about the current system.

Note: Users should keep in mind that, although systems analysts may be experts about computers and their applications, they are not necessarily knowledgeable about the business functions performed by the user. It is the user's responsibility to make sure the analyst is well informed about the current system.

FIGURE 10.3
Phase 1 analysis of Sporting Life's current accounting system. These are only a few of the general problems and objectives that may be identified.

```
Sporting Life Problem Definition--Accounting
System

The following problems have been detected in the
current accounting system:

1. Because files are spread among many filing
   cabinets in different locations, it takes too
   long to locate the required accounting files
   in order to update them. Often a file has been
   misplaced, or the file contains information
   that belongs somewhere else.

2. The procedures for updating all accounting
   files are not clearly defined. Mistakes are
   often made when entering accounting data.

3. The files that need to be updated daily
   include the General Ledger, Accounts Receiv-
   able, Accounts Payable, and the payroll files.
   Because it takes so much time to access the
   files, there is never enough time to get the
   job done; consequently, the job is often done
   haphazardly and updated only weekly.

4. Because data is filed in several places but
   under different labels, it is difficult to
   obtain information from the accounting files
   to generate the following types of reports:
      Summary reports about the financial status
      of the company (daily, weekly, monthly,
      yearly)
      Reports about the projected growth of the
      company.

Objectives

The new computer-based accounting system should:

1. Reduce by 50% the amount of time required to
   locate the files that have to be updated.

2. Include built-in procedures for the user to
   follow when updating the accounting files.

3. Establish built-in controls to reduce data
   input errors.

4. Make it easy to update the accounting files
   daily.

5. Make it easy to obtain information from the
   accounting files to generate reports.
```

Some aspects of the current system that are studied include:

- Inputs (transactions)
- Outputs
- Files
- Users' interaction
- Methods and procedures
- Data storage
- Controls
- Existing hardware and software

The systems analyst studies not only these components individually but also how they interact and how people *use* them. Users can assist the analyst by, first, expanding their thinking about the components being studied. For example, if you were helping a systems analyst study the existing filing system, you would have to describe *everything* used as a file, including not only files in file cabinets or on disk but also index card boxes, in/out boxes on your desk, the telephone book, notebook, log sheets, materials on your shelf—in other words, anything that is used as reference for obtaining data to help you make decisions. The analyst will also need to know *how* and *when* you use these references/files.

GATHERING DATA

As you can see, the principal activities in this phase involve gathering data about the current system and then analyzing the data. The analyst can use a number of techniques, including:

- Conducting interviews
- Reviewing policies and procedures
- Collecting sample forms, documents, memos, reports, and so on
- Observing operations
- Using questionnaires to conduct surveys

Needless to say, the systems analyst does not necessarily do these alone; users themselves can collect data on a current system using these techniques, perhaps in concert with the analyst.

INTERVIEWS   Interviews are probably the most widely used data-gathering technique. The analyst can learn a great deal about what is going on by interviewing the staff members who actually perform the work. Interviewing supervisory and management personnel allows the analyst to get comparative information on what is being done and how, so that he or she can identify any differences between how the supervisors and management believe the work is being done and how the staff is actually doing it. Eliciting feedback from more than one source is one way to avoid getting inaccurate information.

Interviews are usually conducted using an outline form that allows the person being interviewed to talk about what he or she feels comfortable with while still covering all the points the interviewer is interested in. (This is called a *structured interview*; if the questions deviate from the predetermined outline, it is called an *unstructured interview*.) Here are examples of questions and requests an analyst might ask of a user (in this case a payroll department supervisor):

- How many staff workers are currently in the department?
- Does your company have a formal organization chart? If so, may I obtain a copy?
- What are the responsibilities of each staff member? (The analyst would obtain copies of any formal job descriptions.)
- Please explain the company policies that affect the department. (The analyst would obtain any copies.)
- Please describe the daily processing activities in the department. (The analyst would obtain a copy of the procedures manual.)
- Please describe the current work load, including the times when it is heaviest and lightest.
- Please describe the operating procedure cycles—daily, weekly, monthly, and annual.
- Which activities are the most labor-intensive?
- Please discuss any problems, shortcomings, and inefficiencies.

REVIEWING POLICIES AND PROCEDURES   The extent to which the policies and procedures have been documented can give the analyst valuable insight into what is going on (see Chapter 9 for a review of the importance of documentation). A lack of formal documentation on current policies and procedures may indicate problems within the current system. The analyst should look over what documentation exists, thereby obtaining a picture of how current system activities were expected to operate. However, all documentation should be compared with the information obtained during interviews to determine if the documentation is up to date.

COLLECTING SAMPLE DOCUMENTS   Collecting samples of operating documents can also help the analyst to assemble an accurate picture of current systems activities. The term *document* refers to paper on which data has been recorded, including preprinted forms, handwritten forms, and computer-produced forms. The user must be sure to give the analyst copies of *all* documents used for data recording. A bill received in the mail or a customer purchase order are both examples of documents. Picture the system, or organizational unit, being studied as a box into which documents flow from outside the company or from other departments and from which documents flow outward to other departments or other companies. To help analyze the current system, the analyst should ask the user the following questions about both inward- and outward-bound documents:

- Why and from whom is each document received?
- What action is taken with each document received?

- Why is the document created?
- When is the document produced?
- For whom is each document intended and how is it used?

OBSERVING CURRENT OPERATIONS   The existing descriptions of procedures (if any) answer the question: What should be done and how? The information gathered during interviews, which represents the consensus of what people say they are doing, answers the question: What do users say is being done? Observing operations will confirm the analyst's understanding of what actually exists and answers the question: What are the users *actually* doing?

SURVEY QUESTIONNAIRES   Analysts find that using questionnaires to take a survey can be useful when information must be collected from a large group of individuals. Although questionnaires take less time than personal interviews, and many responses can be collected, they must be used with care. The questions must be precisely worded so that the user completing the questionnaire understands the instructions and does not need to interpret the questions. The principal drawbacks of using a questionnaire are that responses may be highly biased (intentionally or unintentionally), some users are reluctant to take the time to complete a questionnaire, and many people are cautious about expressing an opinion in writing.

ANALYZING DATA

After the analyst has gathered data on the current system, he or she must analyze the facts to identify problems—including their causes and effects—and opportunities for improvement. Some things that the analyst determines are:

- *Minimum, average, and maximum levels of activity*—for example, when do most sales orders come in?
- *Redundancy of procedures*—for example, are two users entering the same sales order data at different times?
- *Unusually labor-intensive and/or tedious activities*—manual activities that could be computerized, like filling out forms to record sales data.
- *Activities that require extensive (complex and/or repetitive) mathematical computation*—such as updating customer charge account balances and interest charges.
- *Procedures that have become obsolete*—perhaps your company's licensing requirements have changed, rendering the old procedures useless.

The analyst can use several tools to assist in the analysis, including **data flow diagrams** and special software packages, such as Excelerator. Data flow diagrams show the flow of data through a system—where it originates and where it goes. Like systems flowcharts, data flowcharts can be used for clarification in any phase of the systems development life cycle. Figure 10.4 shows the standard symbols used in data flow diagrams. The *process* symbol shows what is done to data in the current system—whether it is filed, printed out and forwarded, checked and discarded, and so on. The *source* symbol indicates where data has come from—that is, from which departments or individuals; a *sink* symbol indicates where data is going to—that is, it indicates the recipient. For example, a customer order record may be sent by Customer Services (*source*) to Inventory (*sink*). The *file* symbol indicates that data is deposited or stored—whether in an index card file or on magnetic tape, in a filing cabinet or on a desk notepad. *Vectors* show the direction of the data flow. To give you an example of how data flow symbols are used, Figure 10.5 diagrams how Sporting Life processes customer orders.

The first phase of the SDLC usually concludes with a report to management. The objectives of the Phase 1 report are to provide management personnel in affected departments and in the data processing department with a clear picture of what the system does, how it does it, and what the analysis identified as problems, causes and effects of problems, and areas where improvements can be made. After reading the report, management must be given an opportunity to ask for specific clarification of the points raised in the report and request a final recommendation from the analyst about whether or not to proceed.

FIGURE 10.4
Data flow diagram symbols. These are the standard symbols used to make data flow diagrams, which are prepared by systems analysts.

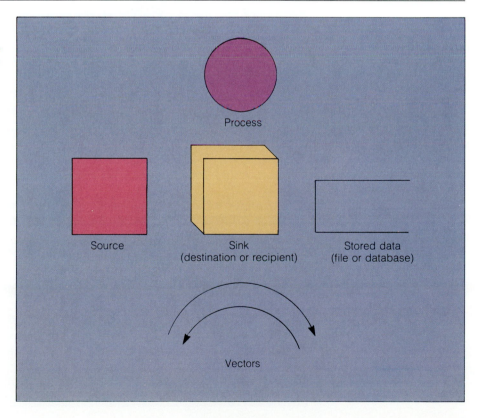

PHASE 2: DEFINE NEW SYSTEMS REQUIREMENTS

In Phase 2 the analyst focuses attention on what he or she—and the users—want the new system to do. But before the analyst can design it, he or she has to define the requirements that the new system must satisfy. And the requirements must be defined very carefully; otherwise the new system might not end up doing what the users hope it will do.

FIGURE 10.5
General data flow diagram of Sporting Life's system of processing customer orders. When an order is received, the inventory file is checked to make sure there are enough items in stock to satisfy the order (1). If there aren't, an out-of-stock notice (5) is given to the customer; otherwise, a credit check is performed (2). If the credit status is poor, the customer's order is not approved; otherwise, an invoice is prepared (3) and the goods and the invoice are given to the customer (4). (Some details are omitted from this diagram for the purpose of simplification.)

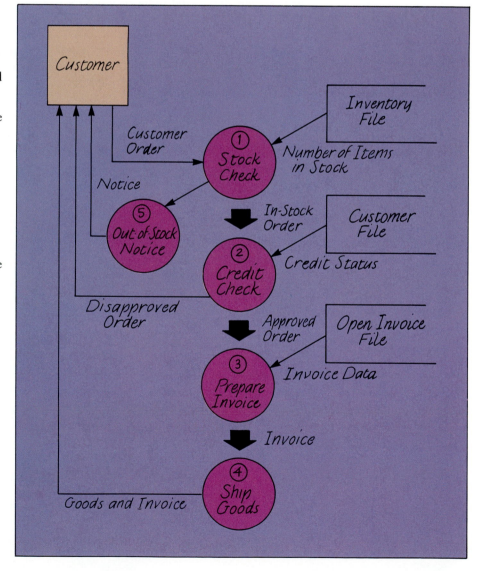

PURPOSE OF PHASE 2

In the second phase of the SDLC, the analyst defines the requirements for the new system in enough detail so that both computer professionals and users know exactly what the new system is going to do and how the system is going to do it. Needless to say, these requirements should solve the problems identified in the first phase.

The first requirements to be defined should be the *business* requirements—input, storage, processing, and output—that the system is able to accommodate. For example, do the personnel who fill customer orders find that certain inventory items are often out of stock and therefore want inventory reports to be issued more frequently? Has the number of files required by the current system grown so much that users spend too much time searching for customer account information? The requirement of the new system in this instance is to make the finding of file information quick and easy. Figure 10.6 shows some of the requirements identified for Sporting Life's payroll processing system. Computerization is not necessarily the answer to everything; manual as well as computerized procedures are often required. In some cases, a new manual system may fill a user's or a department's requirements.

Once the requirements of a system are known, then both manual and computer-based alternatives are evaluated for new and improved systems. Among the factors affecting what alternatives should be implemented are the availability of computer hardware that is technologically suited to the business's requirements and that fits within the budget of the proposed system. Cost becomes a major factor if software is necessary that must be created from scratch by a professional programmer, instead of being bought off the shelf.

REQUIREMENTS THAT AFFECT SOFTWARE   Once the business requirements have been defined, most systems analysts and designers focus on the *output* the system

FIGURE 10.6
Phase 2 requirements of Sporting Life's payroll portion of the new accounting system. These are only a few of the requirements that may be identified by the analyst.

```
Sporting Life: Requirements

The requirements for the Sporting Life payroll
processing system are as follows:

1.  Increase the number of time cards that can be
    processed once a week by 20% and decrease the
    time it takes to generate paychecks by 15%.

2.  Automatically update the personnel file with
    gross pay information when time cards are
    processed.

3.  Automatically calculate regular and overtime
    hourly amounts when time cards are processed.

4.  Automatically generate weekly-to-date and
    year-to-date personnel income figures when
    time cards are processed.
```

must produce. The output requirements fall into three general categories: hardcopy output (reports, special forms, and so on), softcopy output (displayed on video screen), and computer-usable output (a computer file created during processing for output in one system that is also used as input to another system—for example, a file produced by the payroll system that is later used in the general ledger system).

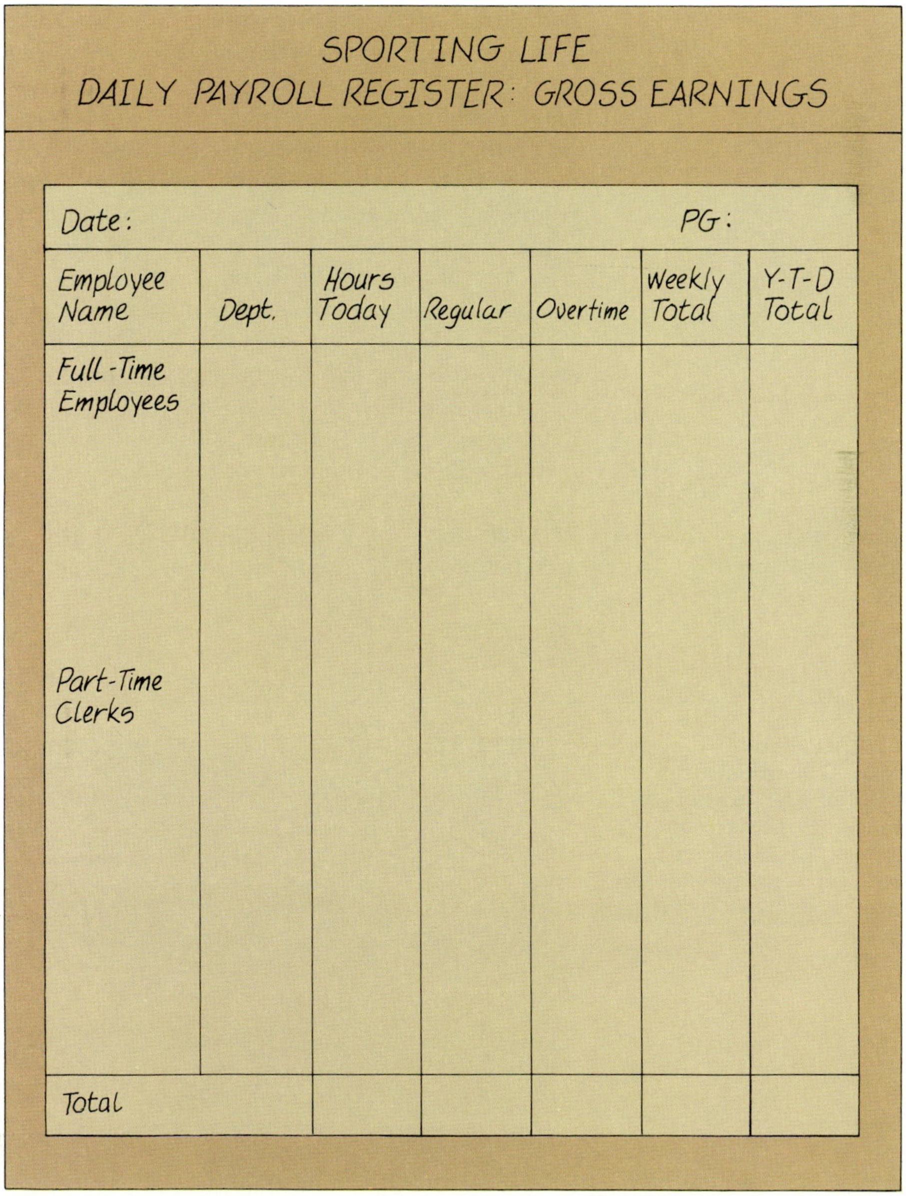

FIGURE 10.7
Specifying the requirements of one type of hardcopy output. In determining some requirements of Sporting Life's new accounting system, the analyst might sketch this output form for Mary to approve.

SPORTING LIFE
DAILY PAYROLL REGISTER: GROSS EARNINGS

Date:					PG:	
Employee Name	Dept.	Hours Today	Regular	Overtime	Weekly Total	Y-T-D Total
Full-Time Employees						
Part-Time Clerks						
Total						

To define the requirements for hardcopy and softcopy outputs, the analyst usually meets with each user who will be using each type of output and carefully identifies:

- The purpose of the output
- The elements of information it will contain
- How each element will be used
- How often and how fast the output will need to be produced

In some cases, the analyst will sketch forms for the user to approve (Figures 10.7 and 10.8).

The storage, processing, and input requirements are closely related to the output requirements. They are determined largely on the basis of where the information in an output is going to come from. Let's use the payroll register report sketched in Figure 10.7 as an example. The data on hours worked this week would probably come from an input transaction, such as a time card, so requirements would have to be determined for setting up time cards, collecting the data from them, and entering the data. The data on employee name and department would most likely be retrieved from storage—that is, the employee or payroll master file (entailing a need to set up requirements for establishing files, maintaining them, retrieving data from them, and so on). The year-to-date income figures would be calculated during processing. The data on hours worked this week (obtained from

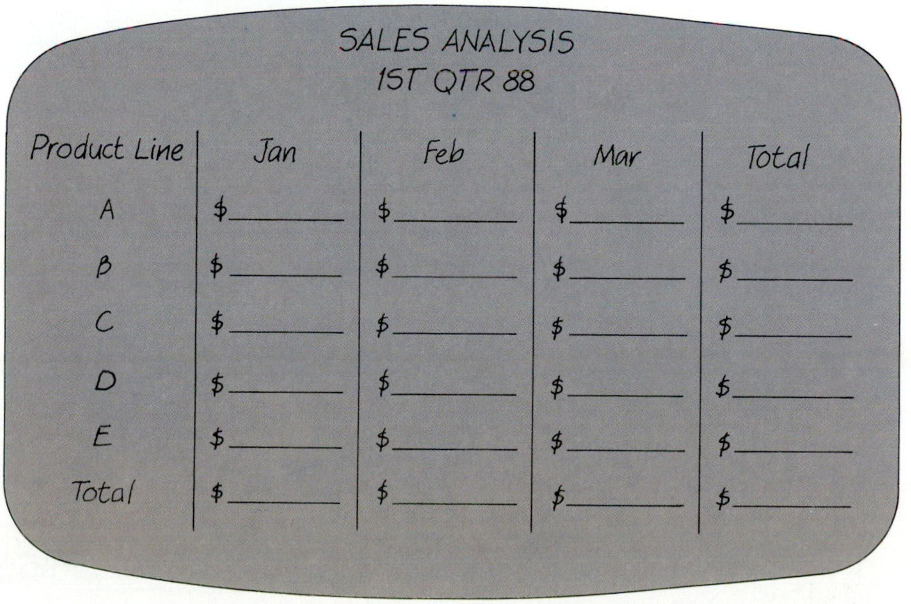

FIGURE 10.8
Specifying the contents of one type of softcopy output. This sketch shows what the analyst at Sporting Life thinks Mary needs to see on her screen when she has to do a sales analysis. The blank lines represent numbers. (In doing a sketch for softcopy output, the analyst must keep the space limitations of the screen in mind.)

SALES ANALYSIS
1ST QTR 88

Product Line	Jan	Feb	Mar	Total
A	$_____	$_____	$_____	$_____
B	$_____	$_____	$_____	$_____
C	$_____	$_____	$_____	$_____
D	$_____	$_____	$_____	$_____
E	$_____	$_____	$_____	$_____
Total	$_____	$_____	$_____	$_____

an input transaction) would be multiplied by the hourly pay rate data element (retrieved from storage in the employee master file). The resulting data would be added to the prior year-to-date income figure to form the new year-to-date figure to be reported. As you can see, the output requirements lead the systems designer to the identification of many of the input, storage, and processing requirements.

The input requirements are formulated in terms of:

- Who will be performing the input procedure
- The elements of data that will be entered
- The input screens (the information displayed on the screen that tells the user what data elements to enter)
- The control procedures to be exercised over the data entry process

Figure 10.9 shows a sketch of an input screen that the analyst might use for entering sales order information at Sporting Life. The control procedures for this type of input might include showing confirmation that the entered customer number and product numbers are valid and that data entered is complete. In addition,

FIGURE 10.9
Sketch of an input screen for Sporting Life.

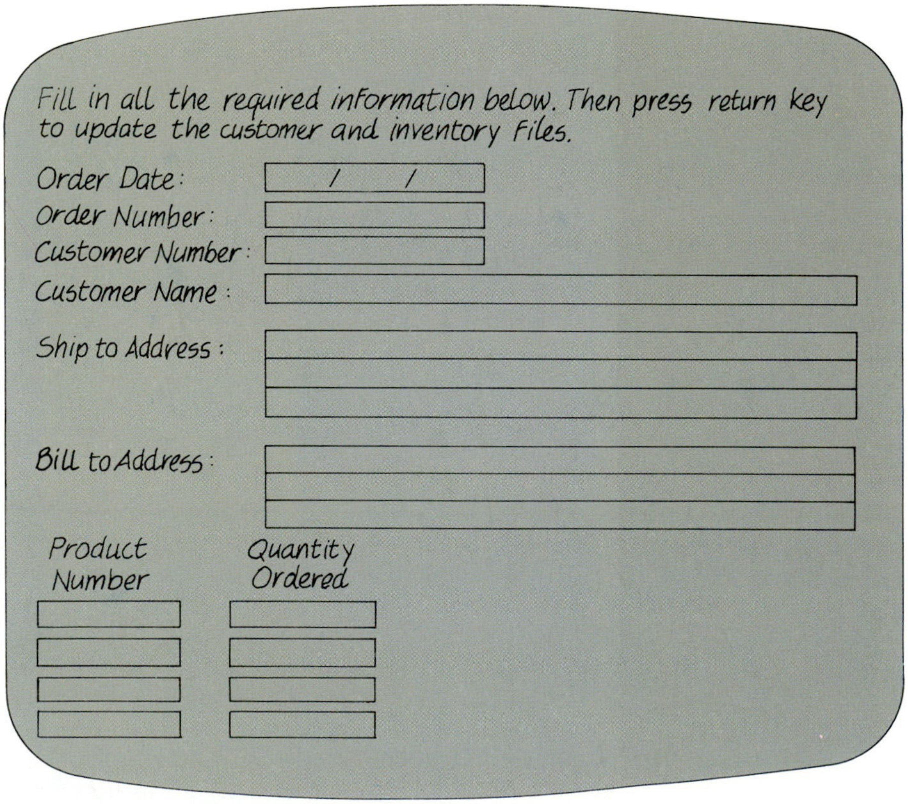

Fill in all the required information below. Then press return key to update the customer and inventory files.

Order Date:

Order Number:

Customer Number:

Customer Name:

Ship to Address:

Bill to Address:

Product Number   Quantity Ordered

the quantity ordered for each product could be checked against the quantity on hand (in the inventory master file) to ensure that enough units are available to fill the order. Of course, all desired control procedures would have to be identified as requirements for the new system to fill.

Storage requirements are defined in terms of the different files that will need to be created to satisfy the processing and output requirements. For instance, we already know that Sporting Life will be using (among other types of files) a master file, an inventory file, an accounts receivable file, an accounts payable file, input transaction and output/report files, and different backup files.

Processing requirements deal with processing schedules—that is, when data is to be input, when output is to be produced, and when files are to be updated—and the identification of logical and computational processing activities. For example, in Sporting Life's accounting system, payroll processing might include such activities as sorting lists of employee names alphabetically for certain reports (a logical activity of comparison, performed by the ALU; see Chapter 5); calculating deductions, sick pay, overtime pay, and final pay rates (computational activity, performed by the ALU); calculating withheld taxes for output on special tax forms (computational activity); and making sales projections for coming years (computational activity). The requirements for computational and logical processing procedures are usually documented in narrative or graphic form, or in a mathematical formula. If the processing logic is complex, pseudocode, data flow diagrams, flowcharts, and other tools may be used.

When all of the software-related requirements have been defined, they are usually summarized as a part of the New Systems Requirements Report (described later in this section). The detailed specifications are used as a basis for proceeding with the next phase of activity: design of the new system.

REQUIREMENTS THAT AFFECT HARDWARE   The new system's software requirements must be defined first to determine what type of computer hardware is needed. This may involve modifying equipment already owned or buying new equipment. Hardware requirements will be discussed in more detail in Phase 3.

EVALUATING ALTERNATIVES

Once the new system's requirements have been defined and ways to satisfy them have been suggested, the analyst should examine *alternative* approaches to satisfying the requirements. This step keeps people from jumping to conclusions. For example, perhaps an expensive conversion to a computer-based system from a manual one is not really necessary! The analyst carefully weighs the advantages and disadvantages of each alternative, including how each might affect the time required to get the new system in place and its estimated cost. As we discussed in Chapter 8, a company can modify existing software, hire computer specialists to develop it from scratch, or buy software packages off the shelf and perhaps modify them, if necessary. Hardware and software to support the new system should be selected, but it does not have to be purchased and in use before design begins.

SYSTEMS REQUIREMENTS REPORT

Phase 2 concludes with the analyst's preparation of a **systems requirements report** and a presentation to the steering committee, user department(s) management, and data processing management. The report provides the basis for the final determination of the completeness and accuracy of the new systems requirements, as well as the economic and practical feasibility of the new system. Data processing management reviews the report to determine if the alternatives have been adequately considered from a technical standpoint. After everyone has reviewed and discussed the report, a final decision is made about whether to proceed and, if so, which alternatives to adopt. Figure 10.10 shows what a systems requirements report might look like for the order entry portion of Sporting Life's new accounting system.

PHASE 3: DESIGN THE NEW SYSTEM

The third phase of the SDLC focuses on the design of the new system. To determine how the new system will be constructed, the analyst analyzes the requirements defined in Phase 2. The activities in this phase are carried out primarily by computer specialists—that is, programmers. Users may have little direct involvement in the design phase; however, their responses are critical when a programmer needs clarification of logical or computational processing requirements. Users should also be involved in the final approval of procedures that provide for user interface with the system—such as what type of dialog will show up on the terminal—and of proposed report forms, both hardcopy and softcopy. After all, the analysts can leave when their job is done; the users must live with the system!

FIGURE 10.10
Sporting Life's systems requirements report for order entry.

```
Statement of Systems Requirements
Pg. 5 of 20

3.1    Order Handling
       Information Required: customer name,
       product #, quantity ordered
       System Requirement: Produce information
       about quantity-on-hand for product ordered.
       Return order status of either "in-stock" or
       "out-of-stock."
       System Requirement: Produce information
       about customer credit status. Return status
       of either "approved" or disapproved"
       System Requirement: Produce necessary
       out-of-stock or disapproved order reports.
       Produce necessary invoice.
       System Requirement: Update open invoice file.
3.2    Accounts Receivable Status Reports
         .
         .
         .
```

PURPOSE OF PHASE 3

Phase 3 involves two main objectives: to design the new system and to establish a sound framework of controls within which the new system should operate. The tools and methods used to document the development of the design and the controls vary according to the preferences of the computer specialists and, if there is one, the standards and procedures of the data processing department. Three widely used tools and methods are systems flowcharts, hierarchy-input-processing-output (HIPO) design, and structured design.

SYSTEMS FLOWCHARTS

Chapter 9 described program flowcharts, which use ANSI symbols to diagram and document applications software programs. **Systems flowcharts,** which diagram and document the design of a new system, give designers and users an overview of the entire system, including the flow of data (points of input, output, and storage) and processing activities. Of course, all manual procedures must be included in the flowchart. Systems flowchart symbols were illustrated in Figure 10.1.

The systems flowchart for the accounts receivable portion of Sporting Life's accounting system is shown in Figure 10.11. The activity flows from top to bottom.

HIPO

The **hierarchy-input-processing-output (HIPO)** systems design method was developed in the early 1970s by IBM. The name was derived from the two basic types of diagrams used with this method: the *hierarchy (HD) diagram* and the *input-processing-output (IPO) diagram*. The HD, which resembles an organizational chart, presents a view of the new system broken down into its major functions and subfunctions (modules). This type of diagram is often referred to as a "visual table of contents" (VTOC) because each of the lower-level modules can be numbered and then referred to by number in the documentation.

IPO diagrams provide an overview of a module's input, processing, and output activities. They can be detailed enough to show all of the specific logic for the processing activities to be performed. A number of detailed IPO diagrams may be required to describe completely the processing activities taking place in a module.

Figure 10.12 shows a hierarchy diagram for Sporting Life's accounting system. The system is divided into three main modules: accounts payable module, accounts receivable module, and payroll/personnel module. Each main module is subdivided as necessary to depict clearly the logical groups of necessary processing activities. The accounts receivable module is divided into two submodules: order handling and accounts receivable status reports.

The detailed design for each module is documented using IPO diagrams that clearly show the flow of data into each module (input section), the processing activities that take place (process section), and the flow of information out of the module (output section). The processing activities are documented in a variety of ways depending on the complexity of the module. Usually they are described in detail in narrative form as a series of steps. The narrative is not as structured as pseudocode, which we discussed in Chapter 9. Instead, the narrative is an *in-depth* description. When a particular step involves a complex processing activity, it may refer to additional documentation, which may be in narrative, pseudocode, flow-chart, decision-tree, or decision-table form. In any case, all documentation is num-bered so that it can be tied directly to the numbered modules and submodules in the hierarchy diagram.

The IPO diagram for Sporting Life's order-handling module (module number 3.1) is shown in Figure 10.13. The inputs are three separate files—inventory file, customer and open invoice file, and customer order file. There are four outputs from this module: out-of-stock notice, disapproved order, invoice information to update the inventory file, and invoice.

STRUCTURED DESIGN

As with structured programming, which we discussed in the last chapter, **structured design** sets up a system from the top down to ensure that agreement is reached as

FIGURE 10.11
Systems flowchart for the accounts receivable portion of Sporting Life's new ac-counting system. Systems flowcharts give designers and users an overview of the entire system being designed.

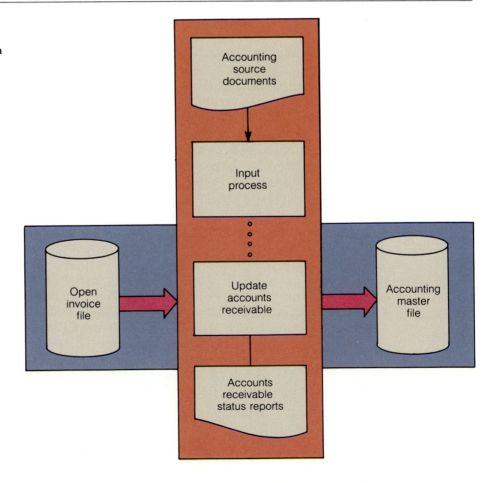

early as possible on the major design decisions. Structured design has three goals: simplicity, refinement by level, and modularity. Simplicity is necessary so that the design of a system can be clearly understood by all parties involved in the system's development and use. The system design will be easier to refine if it is broken down into levels on a step-by-step basis, one level at a time. Each new level of the design should provide more detail on exactly how the objectives of the level above will be met. A modular approach ensures that the design will consist of a series of well-designed single-purpose parts that can be integrated into a comprehensive system in which problems will be fairly easy to identify. Because each part can be easily understood, later modifications will be convenient to make.

The use of a structured approach to both analysis and design of new systems has gained great popularity in the last ten years. It fosters the kind of reasoning and logical analysis that must be followed to develop a sound design. Structured design involves the use of two basic types of diagrams to document the overall design of the new system: structure charts and data flow diagrams, both of which were discussed earlier.

OTHER SYSTEMS DESIGN TOOLS

Two of the additional tools and techniques that are used frequently during the systems design phase are data dictionaries and pseudocode. Although we described pseudocode in Chapter 9 in the context of developing a program (instead of in the more generalized context of the SDLC), it can also be used in designing a new system.

FIGURE 10.12
Hierarchy diagram for Sporting Life's accounting system. This type of diagram presents a view of the new system broken down into its major functions and subfunctions.

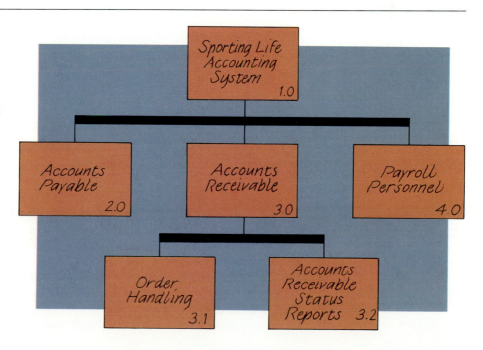

The **data dictionary** is a collection of the specifications for all elements of data to be used in the new system. This document identifies each element of data by name and describes:

- The type of data (numeric, alphabetic, a code)
- The length of the data elements (maximum number of characters to be allocated)
- Which program produces a computed (or derived) data element (for example, gross wages, deductions, and net pay are derived and computed from hours worked and hourly pay rate)
- The processing modules in the system that need access to the data element
- The output containing the data element

When the data dictionary has been completed by the designers and programmers after the systems design has been finalized, the data elements are analyzed to determine the best way to logically group them into files. Along with the anticipated level of activity, the type of access (direct or sequential) that will be needed to each file is considered to decide on the best file structure and organization scheme. (High activity means that a high percentage of the records are accessed during processing; low activity means that only a small percentage of records are accessed.)

DESIGNING NEW SYSTEMS CONTROLS

New systems must be designed to operate within a framework of controls, which must be defined and designed along with the new system. Controls involve both the manual procedures performed by users and data processing personnel and computerized procedures that provide information for review and follow-up. Systems generally fall into two distinct categories: general controls and applications controls.

General controls describe the organizational controls that need to be applied to the overall processing activities of all computer-based systems. General controls focus on five areas:

- The organization
- System and program documentation
- Software
- Physical security
- Management practices

Organizational controls ensure that there is an adequate segregation of duties for operating procedures both within the user department and within the data processing department. *Adequate segregation* means that users and computer operators have access only to those parts of the system and documentation that directly involve their particular routine activities.

The systems and program documentation controls ensure that documentation remains intact and available when needed as a resource during system maintenance. The documentation is usually stored in a documentation library and checked out only to personnel who have a current assignment calling for its use.

Software controls ensure that programs are run only by authorized personnel listed on an approved schedule and that programs can be accessed for modification only by programmers currently assigned to the program.

Physical security controls protect the security of computer hardware and software, whose loss or theft could cost the company money and time—not to mention valuable and possibly confidential information.

FIGURE 10.13
IPO diagram for Sporting Life's order-handling module. This type of diagram focuses on input/output functions.

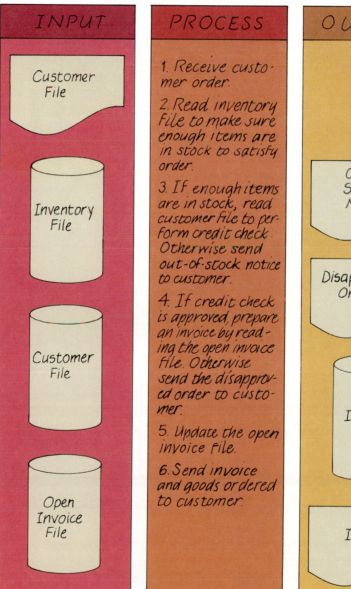

To have an effective framework of general controls, management practices must support well-defined policies, procedures, lines of authority, and supervision.

Applications controls focus on the flow of processing activities within the new system. They are designed to ensure that input and processing of data are accurate, complete, and properly authorized. These controls fall into four categories: input controls, processing controls, output controls, and authorization controls (Figure 10.14).

Input controls provide assurance that all transaction data has been input completely and accurately. This is most often done by the use of batch control totals and programmed checks. Batch control totals provide a way to ensure that all source documents containing data to be input to the computer are collected and converted into computer-usable form. This process can be as simple as manually counting the number of source documents in a batch being forwarded for data input and then comparing the number with the computer's total. Programmed checks establish the validity of the data being input to the computer for processing. Typical examples include verifying that a valid product number or customer number has been entered, determining if the quantity ordered exceeds the amount available in stock, and ensuring that all required fields of data have been keyed in.

Processing controls establish that all transactions collected during the input activity have been properly processed, all appropriate files were updated, and all expected outputs were produced and distributed to the intended recipients. Commonly used processing controls involve programmed procedures that collect and report critical control information for follow-up by users and computer operations personnel.

FIGURE 10.14
Applications controls ensure that input and processing of data are accurate, complete, and properly authorized.

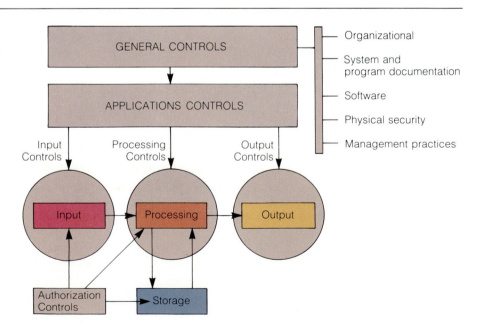

Output controls ensure that all expected outputs are produced on time, all reports are delivered to the intended recipients as quickly as possible, and reports are safeguarded so that only authorized persons have access to sensitive company information. Commonly used output techniques include using a schedule to track the data each report includes, keeping reports in a secured area until they are ready for delivery, asking users to initial a receipt on delivery of sensitive reports, and shredding reports with sensitive information rather than tossing them in the trash.

Authorization controls ensure that only approved transactions are entered into the computer for processing and that processing does not take place until all control reports have been reviewed and found to be in order.

CONCLUDING THE DESIGN PHASE

The completion of the design phase of the SDLC is marked by three events. First, the analyst/designer completes, organizes, and assembles the new systems design documentation, including records of the general and applications controls, by using a combination of the tools and techniques discussed earlier in the chapter. The documentation should include:

- A complete overview of the new system as a whole
- A description (narrative or graphic) of the major processing modules into which the system has been divided for design purposes
- Detailed documentation describing the input, processing, and output activities in each module and submodule
- Specifications of the storage requirements for the new system (data dictionary); a description of each file to be maintained in the system, including anticipated size and organization scheme/access method to be used
- A narrative description of the general and applications controls to be used with the new system

Second, the systems analyst(s) and data processing management meet to review the technical soundness of the design. Third, systems designer(s), user management, and data processing management meet to present and review the design. The outcome of the last meeting is either a decision to approve the design and proceed to the next phase of the SDLC—systems development—or to revise the design before continuing. Although most organizations would decide to discard a project entirely at an earlier phase, it is still possible that the project could be terminated at this time.

SELECTING HARDWARE

A company that is changing from a manual to a computer-based system (or modifying an existing computer-based system) cannot run out and buy hardware in Phase 1, analysis of the current system, because it doesn't yet know what the new system is supposed to do. The company shouldn't make the purchases during Phase 2 either because, although its requirements have been established, the new system has not yet been designed. Once Phase 3, systems design, is underway, hardware selection can begin.

Here are some points company representatives should keep in mind when buying (or leasing) hardware:

- If some computers have already been acquired, additional units need to be compatible.

- The minimum amount of internal memory to satisfy the processing requirements must be established. Some software products require a minimum of 320 K, whereas others require at least 512 K.

- If processing will involve extensive mathematical calculations, special math coprocessor chips may need to be installed in some computers.

- The video display units will need to be high resolution for certain applications, like graphics. If graphics are required, graphics adapter cards and RGB monitors may be required for certain computers.

- The storage requirements should be carefully analyzed to help determine what size system to purchase.

- The quality, volume, and type of printed output to be produced must be considered in determining the types of printers required.

- The delivery schedules for all equipment must be determined.

- Determine how many users the system will need to support now—and in a year or two.

- Determine the amount of multiusing and multitasking required.

- Determine the type of operating system that will ensure program compatibility and efficiency.

If using existing hardware, the new system design must be reviewed to determine if additional hardware (more personal computers, additional disk storage capacity, faster printers, more terminals, and so on) is required.

Once hardware needs have been identified, the company must determine which vendor to choose. Here are some considerations to keep in mind when deciding on the vendor:

- The financial stability of the vendor should be strong. You want the vendor to be in business when you call for assistance.

- The vendor should have a qualified technical support staff for ongoing maintenance and repair (toll-free lines are invaluable).

- The vendor should have staff available to assist in setting up the equipment and making sure it is ready to operate.

- The vendor should have staff available to provide training in the use of the equipment.

PHASE 4: DEVELOP THE NEW SYSTEM

Once the design of the new system has been completed, a very time-consuming part of the SDLC begins: the decisions about what—if any—software will be required by the new system. Because Chapter 9 described software development in detail, this section will review only the basics.

PURPOSE OF PHASE 4

The basic activities of this systems development phase include:

- Review the input, output, and processing requirements of the program
- Develop the logic for the program
- Review program designs with structured walkthroughs
- Code the programs
- Review (walk through) program code
- Test and debug the programs
- Document the programs (done at every step of development)

The number of programs needed within a system and the scope and processing requirements of the programs are determined by reviewing the systems design documentation. The programmers responsible for software development analyze this documentation to be sure they understand what the requirements are. They then develop the program logic.

Once the design of the programs has been formulated, it is reviewed at a meeting attended by experienced programmers and analysts: a design walkthrough. After problems are resolved, the process of writing the programs begins. Programming can be very time-consuming, depending on the language used and the complexity of the program being written. Most programmers compose the program at a desk, using the tools and techniques discussed in Chapter 9—for example, program flowcharts and pseudocode. Then they move to a keyboard—probably a terminal connected to a minicomputer or a mainframe—and enter the text of the program instructions.

Once a program has been written, it is thoroughly tested. After the problems identified during testing are solved, the final documentation from all the development stages is put together in a package that is kept in a special location—perhaps a library—under strict access controls.

PHASE 5: IMPLEMENT THE NEW SYSTEM

The process of developing a new system costs a great deal of time, energy, and money. However, even a beautifully designed and developed system can fail to meet its objectives if it is not carefully implemented. In this phase, users learn how to use the new system—they receive training in its use and, in turn, train other users.

PURPOSE OF PHASE 5

The implementation phase, which gets the new system up and running, involves five basic steps: (1) creating the operating documentation and procedures, (2) training the users to follow the new procedures and work with new equipment, (3) converting files, (4) performing the systems test, and (5) using the new system.

OPERATING DOCUMENTATION AND PROCEDURES

In the first step in getting ready to implement a new system, the analyst prepares the operating documentation and procedures that the users will need to perform regular processing activities. The procedures covered include entering data, making inquiries, directing processing activities, and distributing reports. In many cases, a "playscript" method is used, along with samples of video display screens, outputs, and other graphics, to enhance the clarity of procedural documentation. This documentation, used extensively to train users to operate the new system, can also help in training new employees. Playscripts (Figure 10.15) consist of a list of detailed processing procedures in columns with the position of the person responsible for performing the task located to the left of the procedure.

In a large system, the operating documentation and procedures must include the information needed by the data processing department for operating the system on a day-to-day basis and for future reference when the system must be modified. The computer operators must have operating documentation that identifies the processing schedule, files to be used, and programs to be run. The data entry group must have procedures on how the input data is to be entered. The control group must have procedures for monitoring system controls and coordinating the distribution of reports. Figure 10.16 shows some elements of a documentation package.

TRAINING THE USERS

In the next step—once the new system operating documentation and procedures have been prepared—the analyst trains the users to use the new system (trained users go on to train other users). Training usually includes familiarization with any new equipment (printers, terminals, and so on) and a complete review of the procedures. If the users are expected to interact directly with the system (for example, by using a computer terminal), hands-on training is provided to teach them how to use it. Hands-on training is equally important for the new user of a microcomputer.

FIGURE 10.15
Playscript procedure for order entry at Sporting Life.

```
1. Customer: Enter customer name, item number of item ordered,
   quantity ordered on customer order form.

2. Stock Clerk: Check inventory file to be sure enough items
   on hand to satisfy order. Clerk signs name and checks in-
   stock order box to see if order can be satisfied. Otherwise
   check out-of-stock order box and place in out-of-stock
   file. Inform customer of delay.

3. Credit Clerk: Mark with a check the received box on the in-
   stock order. Check customer file for customer credit status.
   If O.K., prepare invoice. Update invoice file by entering
   the amount of current invoice.

4. Stock Clerk: Review copy of invoice for number of items
   ordered. Fill customer order.
```

If your company does not provide in-house training in computer use, you might try one or more of the following suggestions:

- Read the manual and work through the practice lessons.
- Buy outside reference materials or books with better explanations and examples.
- Attend a community college course on computer hardware and software.
- Attend public training seminars using the software you have at the office.
- Purchase tutorial software and ask the company to reimburse you.

FIGURE 10.16
Sample documentation package.

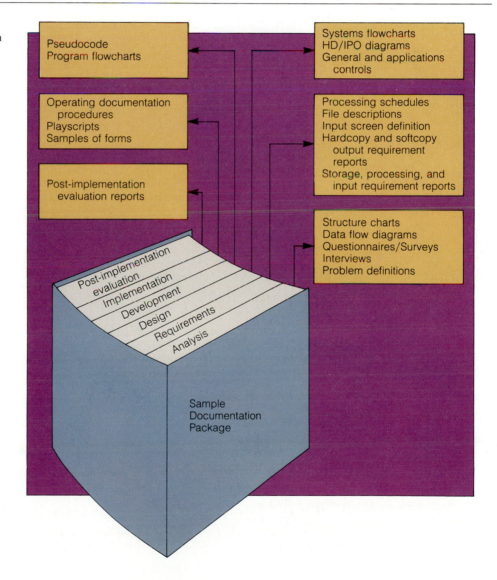

CONVERTING FILES

A new computer-based system cannot be used until all the data files are converted into computer-usable form. When a manual system is computerized, file conversion can become a monumental task. The time and effort required to sort through and key in the data—and the corresponding cost of doing it—are great. Outside assistance may be required for large file conversion tasks.

PERFORMING THE SYSTEMS TEST

The programs developed in Phase 4 were tested individually by computer specialists; now they need to be tested as a whole. The process of testing all the programs and all the related procedures for operating the new system is referred to as the **systems test.** The users of the new system participate heavily in the systems test; in most cases, they work closely with the project development team in creating comprehensive test data to test all the processing activities. Then, using this data, they perform the new systems operating procedures, including the entry of the test data, the direction of system processing, and the production and distribution of outputs. The outputs produced are reviewed carefully by both the users and the project team to ensure that data has been processed as expected.

USING THE NEW SYSTEM

Once it has been successfully tested, the system is ready for use. There are three basic approaches to implementing a new system: direct implementation, parallel implementation, and phased implementation. The concepts behind the three approaches are diagrammed in Figure 10.17.

In **direct implementation,** the change is made all at once. The old system is halted on a planned date and the new system is activated. This approach is most often used for small systems or larger systems for which a systems model was previously developed and thoroughly tested. Simply halting the old system and starting up the new system is a very simple approach; however, this method carries some risks. For example, in most large systems, there are far too many variables to be adequately tested. As a result, a few unexpected errors are almost always found during the initial implementation period. These errors are much more disruptive and difficult to correct when the old system has been halted, because normal processing cannot continue until they are fixed.

Parallel implementation involves running the old system and the new system at the same time for a specified period. The results of using the new system are compared to the old system. If the performance of the new system is satisfactory, use of the old system is discontinued. This approach is the safest because operations do not have to be shut down if the new system has problems; however, it is by far the most expensive and difficult approach to coordinate. Operating two systems instead of one takes much more time and effort. And, in addition to operating both systems, it is still necessary to compare the output from the new system to the old system and evaluate the results.

When the parallel implementation approach is used, a formal meeting of the project development team and the users is held at the end of the trial period. The performance of the new system is discussed and a decision is reached as to whether the findings are positive enough to warrant discontinuing the operation of the old system.

Some systems are just too broad in scope or are so large that they must be implemented in phases. **Phased implementation** can be handled in two different ways, depending on the system and the organization. First, if a system is very broad in scope, the effect of trying to implement all the components at once can be traumatic; implementation is more easily handled one phase at a time. For example, in an accounting system like Sporting Life's, the general ledger components could be implemented first. Once they are running, the accounts payable and accounts receivable components could be implemented. Second, if a system is to be implemented at many locations in a widely dispersed company, the task can be very difficult to manage all at once. To implement the system at one location at a time—and ensure that it is working correctly before moving on to other locations—is safer.

FIGURE 10.17
Three approaches to system implementation.

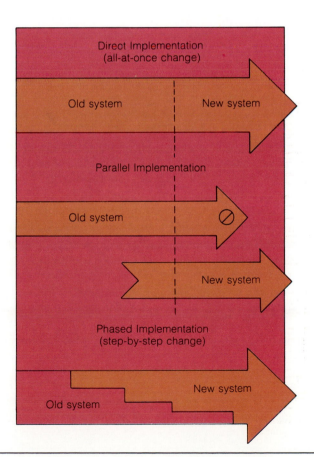

PHASE 6: POST-IMPLEMENTATION EVALUATION

Two very important activities take place after the new system has been implemented: systems maintenance and post-implementation evaluation. **Systems maintenance** is not actually part of the systems *development* life cycle; it refers to adjustments that need to be made to the system after it has been implemented. These adjustments may be needed because, as users gain experience in using the new system, they may discover minor processing errors. Or government reporting regulations may change, creating new requirements for a system to satisfy. Companies must remember to budget monies to pay for maintenance.

PURPOSE OF PHASE 6

After a new system has been in operation for several months and any necessary systems maintenance has been done, a formal evaluation—called a **post-implementation evaluation**—of the new system takes place. This evaluation determines either that the new system is meeting its objectives or that certain things need to be done so that it will meet its objectives.

The end of the final step in the SDLC is marked by the preparation of a new systems evaluation report. The report summarizes the extent to which the system meets the original objectives and includes a list of enhancements to be considered for future development and implementation.

PROTOTYPING

People are constantly searching for ways to refine and streamline the systems development process. **Prototyping,** a more recent approach to developing systems, is the process of building a small, simple model of the new system that can be prepared with a minimum of effort. The model is built during Phases 2 and 3. Several tools and techniques can be used, including report generators, applications generators, and database management systems software packages (discussed in detail in Chapter 12). In addition, analysts often use fourth-generation languages (Chapter 8) to rapidly develop prototypes. The objective of prototyping is to get feedback from the users as quickly as possible. The fact that a small-scale working model is available to try can help the user to define the new system requirements more carefully. Prototypes are also used to train users of the new system in Phase 5 of the SDLC.

In addition to improving the quality of requirements definition, prototyping can help reduce the time needed to develop a new system, as well as the time required for users to define their requirements. The experience of working with a model helps the users to think of needs that might otherwise have been overlooked. The main disadvantage of prototyping is that the initial model is often only an educated guess as to what the new system would do. Also, it addresses only user interface with the system, not all the components of complex processing that may be necessary.

In small systems involving simple applications, a prototype may be refined into a final system; in large, complex systems, the prototype is generally used for systems analysis and then discarded. The key to prototyping is knowing when the technique should be used and following up on user feedback.

WHAT SKILLS DOES THE USER NEED?

Now that you have learned a bit about systems analysis and design, you're probably wondering what *you* will have to know in a typical business situation. Whether or not you will need to use any of the tools and techniques for analyzing and documenting systems and their development depends on the type of organization you're with and the level of expertise you have gained. But, in most cases, you will need only a basic understanding of the life cycle used at your place of business and the objectives of each phase. You will need to develop your ability to communicate effectively with computer specialists to help your company operate efficiently and profitably. If you can't communicate your business needs clearly, your requirements may not be met by the new system.

ONWARD: WHO'S MINDING THE STORE?

By now you may be wondering how anyone can keep control of all the functions and parts of the computer-based information cycle—input, storage, processing, and output—and all the hardware and software that goes along with it, let alone the tasks of designing and writing programs and of developing systems. Who is put in charge of all this, and how do those in charge manage? How do they make sure what's produced is relevant to the needs of the business? How do they make decisions? The next chapter, on management information systems, will answer these questions.

SUMMARY

The systems development life cycle (SDLC) is the formal process by which organizations build computer-based information systems. Systems development life cycles may be known by different names and comprise varying numbers of phases, but their principles are basically the same. The participants in the SDLC are users, data processing staff, management of all departments, and computer specialists (programmers and analysts). Your role in the SDLC will depend on the size of the company you are involved with and your job description, educational background, and past experience. In any case, you will have to participate in the systems analysis and design process because you will have to explain to analysts and designers how you use the current system and what you think is wrong with it. In other words, you will have to help to define the new systems requirements. You will also have to be able to follow the charts, diagrams, and written procedures in the new systems documentation so that you will be able to use the new system effectively.

An SDLC is used as a guideline in directing and administering the activities involved in establishing business system requirements, developing the system, acquiring hardware and software, and controlling development costs. Without a reasoned approach to systems analysis and design, systems development can result in disruption of normal working procedures, acquisition of too much or too little computer hardware, development of inadequate software, misunderstood user needs and requirements, new system problems resulting from inadequate testing, and inadequate documentation for system maintenance and future modification.

An SDLC can be divided into six phases: Phase 1—analyze current system; Phase 2—define new systems requirements; Phase 3—design new system; Phase 4—develop new system; Phase 5—implement new system; and Phase 6—evaluate performance of new system. Table 10.1 summarizes the phases and their activities.

In Phase 1, the objective is to gain a clear understanding of the existing system, including its shortcomings, and determine where improvements can be made. Aspects of the system that are studied in Phase 1 include: inputs (transactions), outputs, files, users' interaction, methods and procedures, data storage, controls, and existing hardware and software.

To analyze the current system, analysts and users must gather data about the existing system using such techniques as interviews; reviewing written policies and procedures; collecting sample forms, reports, and other documents; observing operations, and using questionnaires to conduct surveys. After the data has been gathered, it must be analyzed. Problems and opportunities to improve the system are identified. Systems analysts use several tools and techniques to study the system and document the analysis, including data flow diagrams, systems flowcharts, and structure charts. Phase 1 concludes with a report and presentation to management that summarizes the current systems analysis and gives a recommendation about whether or not to proceed.

Phase 2 of the SDLC involves defining the business requirements for the new system—manual as well as computer-based procedures. Requirements should be defined in the areas of input, storage, processing, and output. Defining software requirements focuses first on the output that the users will need. Phase 2 concludes with a systems requirements report.

Phase 3 of the SDLC focuses on the technical design of the new system, using such techniques and methods as systems flowcharts, hierarchy-input-processing-output (HIPO) design, and structured design. HIPO design involves the use of hierarchy diagrams (HD) and input-processing-output (IPO) diagrams. Designing the new systems controls for both manual and computerized procedures is also an important part of Phase 3. The two major types of systems controls are general controls and applications controls.

Developing the new system, Phase 4 of the SDLC, involves designing programs, walkthroughs (review of technical design), writing programs, testing programs, and documenting programs. During this phase, programmers use tools such as program flowcharts and pseudocode to develop program logic; then they use a programming language to write the programs. Once the programs have been written, they are thoroughly tested, problems are solved, and all the documentation

TABLE 10.1 The SDLC's Six Phases

1. **ANALYSIS.** Gain a clear understanding of the current system. Summarize to management and recommend whether to proceed with the next phases in the SDLC.

Study the inputs, outputs, files, users' interaction, methods and procedures, data storage, controls, and existing hardware and software	*Gather data* conduct interviews review written policies and procedures collect sample forms observe distribute questionnaires	*Analyze data* data flow diagrams systems flowcharts structure charts *Identify problems*

2. **REQUIREMENTS.** Define the business requirements (software) for the new system. Hardware requirements will be finalized during and after the design phase. Prepare systems requirements report. Evaluate alternatives.

Output	*Input*	*Storage*	*Processing*
hardcopy softcopy computer-usable	input screens input controls	files	schedules *Start to build new system prototype*

3. **DESIGN.** Define the technical design of the new system using various methods and techniques. Establish a sound framework of controls within which the new system should operate. Assemble documentation about the design of the new system.

Systems flowcharts	*HIPO diagrams*	*IPO diagrams*	*Structured design*	*Controls*
Provide an overview of the entire system *Data dictionaries* *Pseudocode*	Provide an overview of the system in numbered modules (VTOC)	Provide a view of a module's input, processing, and output activities	Design from the top down to ensure simplicity, refinement, and modularity	general applications

4. **DEVELOPMENT.** Create or select the software required by the new system design.

Design programs	*Review designs*	*Write programs*	*Test programs*	*Assemble documentation*
flowcharts pseudocode	in a design walkthrough	using programming languages		from each of the development stages (and from prior stages)

5. **IMPLEMENTATION.** Get the new system running.

Create operating documentation and procedures	Train users	Convert files	Perform systems test	Use the system

6. **POST-IMPLEMENTATION EVALUATION.** Determine whether the new system is meeting its objectives.

Systems maintenance	Post-implementation evaluation

from every phase of development is put together for the benefit of operators, users, and programmers.

During the process of design and development, hardware must be selected that is compatible with any existing hardware that is to be retained. The need for internal memory, mathematical processing, graphics, storage, types and quantity of output, number of users, need for multitasking and multiusing, and the type of existing operating system (if any) must be considered before hardware is purchased or leased.

Phase 5 of the SDLC involves implementing the new system. This phase involves five steps: (1) creating operating documentation and procedures, (2) training users, (3) converting files, (4) performing the systems test, and (5) using the system. New systems can be implemented all at once (direct implementation), while the old system is still running (parallel implementation), or step by step (phased implementation).

Phase 6 of the SDLC involves post-implementation evaluation after any necessary systems maintenance has been done to adjust for problems. This evaluation determines whether or not the new system is meeting its objectives.

In some cases, to help define system requirements, small, simple models called *prototypes* are built for users to try out before the new system is designed and developed.

In general, a new system fails because of a lack of communication somewhere along the line. That is the main reason why you should understand the basics of the systems development life cycle—so that you can intelligently communicate to the computer specialists the problems with the current system as it affects your job and your requirements for the new system.

KEY TERMS

applications controls
computer-based
    information system
data dictionary
data flow diagram
direct implementation
general controls
hierarchy-input-

processing-output
    (HIPO) design
parallel implementation
phased implementation
post-implementation
    evaluation
prototyping
structured design

systems development
    life cycle (SDLC)
systems flowchart
systems maintenance
systems requirements
    report
systems test

EXERCISES

MATCHING

Match each of the following terms to the phrase that is the most closely related:

1. _____ applications controls
2. _____ computer-based information system
3. _____ data dictionary
4. _____ data flow diagram
5. _____ direct implementation
6. _____ general controls
7. _____ HIPO design
8. _____ parallel implementation
9. _____ phased implementation
10. _____ prototyping
11. _____ structured design
12. _____ systems flowcharts
13. _____ systems requirements report
14. _____ systems maintenance
15. _____ systems test
16. _____ post-implementation evaluation

  a. An information system in which a computer is used to perform some of the procedures.

  b. Used to diagram and document the design of a new system.

  c. A design method that sets up a system from the top down to ensure that agreement is reached as early as possible on the major design decisions.

  d. A design method that presents a view of a new system broken down into its major functions and subfunctions, which are numbered.

  e. This design tool is used by the systems analyst to show the flow of data through a system.

  f. A method for collecting data about the current system.

  g. A collection of the specifications for all of the elements of data to be used in the new system.

  h. The situation in which the old system and the new system are running at the same time for a specified period.

  i. The completion of the requirements phase of the SDLC, when the economic and practical feasibility of the new system is determined.

  j. The organizational controls that need to be applied to processing activities in all computer-based systems.

  k. This method for implementing a new system is used when the system is very broad in scope.

  l. The process of building a small, simple model of the new system that can be prepared with a minimum of effort.

  m. The controls that ensure the input and processing of data are accurate, complete, and properly authorized.

  n. The situation in which the old system is halted on a planned date and the new system is activated.

  o. The process of testing all the programs and related procedures for operating the new system.

  p. A formal evaluation of the new system.

  q. The adjustments that need to be made to the system after it has been implemented.

MULTIPLE CHOICE

1. In a business's SDLC, users often find themselves involved in:
   a. discussing the problems inherent in the current system
   b. providing some departmental objectives and requirements for the new system
   c. testing the new system
   d. using the new system
   e. all of the above

2. Which of the following techniques for gathering information about an existing system is probably the most widely used?
   a. observe operations
   b. collect samples
   c. conduct interviews
   d. review policies and procedures
   e. use a questionnaire

3. Which of the following is a major activity in the development phase of the SDLC?
   a. design the logic for the programs
   b. review the program code
   c. test programs
   d. document programs
   e. all of the above

4. Which of the following is studied in the analysis phase of the SDLC?
   a. users' interaction
   b. data storage
   c. controls
   d. inputs
   e. all of the above

5. Which of the following is used during the design phase of the SDLC?
   a. HIPO diagrams
   b. systems flowcharts
   c. structured design
   d. IPO diagrams
   e. all of the above

6. Which of the following is not a step in the implementation phase of the SDLC?
   a. training users
   b. converting files
   c. designing files
   d. using the new system
   e. performing the systems test

7. Which of the following situations indicates possible system failure?
   a. Major functions in the new system haven't been anticipated.
   b. A portion of the new system design isn't necessary.
   c. User involvement has been minimal.

d. Systems integration is lacking.

e. all of the above

8. Which of the following skills do you need to have in relation to the SDLC?

a. basic understanding of the SDLC

b. being able to communicate effectively with computer specialists

c. being able to follow simple data flow diagrams

d. being able to follow simple structure charts

e. all of the above

9. Which of the following would be explored during the analysis phase of the SDLC?

a. responsibilities of each staff member

b. activities that are the most labor-intensive

c. operating procedure cycles

d. the current organization chart

e. all of the above

10. Which of the following problems could occur if a company doesn't follow the steps in the SDLC?

a. New system doesn't meet the users' needs.

b. Too much hardware is acquired.

c. Too little hardware is acquired.

d. Software may not perform as expected.

e. all of the above

SHORT ANSWER

1. Why is it important for you to understand the principles of the SDLC and, in particular, your company's SDLC?

2. What determines the extent to which your job brings you in contact with your company's SDLC?

3. What are some risks that a company takes if it develops a project without following the steps in the SDLC?

4. Describe briefly the six phases in the SDLC.

5. What are some of the techniques used to gather data in the analysis phase of the SDLC?

6. What is the importance of first defining the output requirements of a proposed system?

7. What should company representatives keep in mind when buying (or leasing) hardware?

8. Describe the three basic approaches to implementing a new system.

9. What is the purpose of the post-implementation evaluation phase of the SDLC?

10. Describe the objectives of prototyping.

PROJECTS

1. *Conducting an interview.* You have been assigned the task of obtaining an understanding of the current activities in the payroll department of your company. The department is headed by a supervisor and three payroll clerks. The supervisor reports to the controller of the company.
   a. Develop a strategy for documenting the system.
   b. Make a list of objectives and questions you would ask the supervisor in a first interview.
   c. What steps would you take in analyzing the data collected?

2. *Designing system controls.* Your company is just beginning the process of computerizing the sales order entry activities. Currently, orders are received by mail, over the phone, and at the counter when customers stop by. The plan is to key the phone orders and counter orders into the computer immediately. The orders received in the mail will be entered into the computer in groups. A typical order contains customer information (such as number, name, and address) and product information (such as product number, description, quantity ordered, and unit price).
   a. Identify possible control techniques that could be designed into the system to ensure that all sales orders are completely input to the computer.
   b. Identify possible control techniques to help ensure all sales order data is accurately entered into the system.
   c. How would the control techniques for phone orders and counter orders differ from the orders received in the mail?

11

MANAGEMENT INFORMATION SYSTEMS

Now that you have a sense of how a systematic approach may be used as a problem-solving *tool*, let us look at the notion of systems as a *resource*, a way by which information may be organized to help different levels of managers—and you—make effective decisions. These kinds of systems are called *management information systems*.

PREVIEW

When you have completed this chapter, you will be able to:

■

Describe a management information system and explain its role in the organization

■

Describe the levels of management, the five basic functions of managers, and the types of decisions typically made at each level

■

Explain the difference between a transaction information system, a management information system, and a decision support system

■

Briefly explain the function of an information center and expert systems

■

The User Perspective

The best kinds of management information systems are invisible: When you call the telephone company for the number of a friend who has just moved, or when you call the service representative about a mysterious call for which you were billed but which you didn't make, you are probably not even aware that an information system exists. Only when someone answers "I can't find it in the computer" do you begin to realize that some system is supposed to help find information, but that it is not working correctly.

Today almost everyone is a consumer of computerized information. You need only try calling a large company about your bill to see that this is true. As a user or a manager who uses computer-based information to make decisions, you will find this chapter necessary to understand how organizations operate today and how you can use this knowledge to help further your career.

Information Systems: What They Are, How They Work

As you know, the heart of an organization, the **information system,** is a framework of standards and procedures for processing data into usable information; every business must have an information system to survive. A **procedure** is a specific sequence of steps performed to complete one or more information processing activities. In some organizations, these processing procedures are carried out only by the staff; in others they are carried out by a combination of the staff and the computer processing specialists. The information system can be manual or computer-based.

If you walk into a busy consumer products showroom, stand in a corner, and observe the activities taking place, you will probably see the following kinds of activities: Customers come in and browse around, looking at the display cases. Some customers decide to buy items and begin to fill out order forms. If they are completed properly, the order forms are taken at the counter by a clerk and placed into a *queue*—that is, in line to be processed. If an order form is not complete, the clerk asks the customer questions and completes it. Then a stock person takes the completed order forms into the warehouse and returns with the goods. A clerk takes each order form, marks it "filled," and rings up the sale on the cash register. All these activities form a procedure that is part of the *sales order entry system* (Figure 11.1).

A business is made up of many procedures, grouped logically into systems. The types of information systems found in companies vary according to the nature and structure of the business; however, the systems commonly found in many businesses include payroll, personnel, accounting, and inventory.

Businesses receive data from a variety of sources, including customers who purchase products or services, vendors from whom supplies are ordered, banks, government agencies, and insurance companies—just to name a few. Information systems help organizations process all this data into useful information. One of the

the most important purposes of a business's information system is to satisfy the information requirements of management.

WHAT IS MANAGEMENT?

You know what an information system is. After we consider what *management* consists of, we will see how the two concepts can be put together as a management information system.

Management often refers to those individuals in an organization who are responsible for providing leadership and direction in the areas of planning, organizing, staffing, supervising, and controlling business activities. These five functions, which are the primary tasks of management, may be defined as follows:

- *Planning* activities require the manager to formulate goals and objectives and develop short- and long-term plans to achieve these goals. For example, an office manager must work with top management to formulate a plan that satisfies the short- and long-term needs of the organization for office space; the vice-president of marketing must take many factors into account when planning short-term advertising campaigns and activities aimed at opening up new long-term markets.

FIGURE 11.1
Related procedures to complete information processing. This group of related procedures makes up a simple sales order entry system.

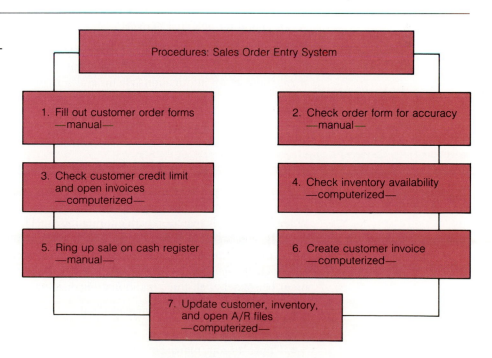

■ Management's responsibility for *organizing* includes the development of an organizational structure and a framework of standards, procedures, and policies designed to carry out ongoing business activities. For instance, top management must decide on the type and number of divisions and departments in the company and evaluate the effectiveness of the structure; it may decide to combine the personnel and the payroll departments to save money. Office managers establish working procedures, such as "Working overtime must be approved by the department supervisor in advance."

■ *Staffing* refers to management's responsibility for identifying the personnel needs of the organization and selecting the personnel, as well as training staff. Many companies have personnel managers to take charge of these activities.

■ *Supervising* refers to management's responsibility to provide employees with the supervision, guidance, and counseling necessary to keep them highly motivated and working efficiently toward the achievement of company objectives. This includes the recognition of good work, perhaps through certificates or bonuses, and concrete suggestions about how to improve performance. Company-wide educational seminars may also be held to upgrade employees' knowledge of the company in general or perhaps to help them deal with stress and improve their health.

■ *Controlling* refers to management's responsibility to monitor organizational performance and the business environment so that steps can be taken to improve performance and modify plans as necessary in response to the marketplace. This includes keeping alert to new opportunities in the marketplace and recognizing new business opportunities. Many new computer software products, for example, have been developed because software companies are ever watchful for potential markets.

Each primary management function involves making decisions, and information is required to make good decisions. Thus, to fulfill its responsibilities, management must set up information systems and subsystems.

WHAT IS A MANAGEMENT INFORMATION SYSTEM?

A **management information system (MIS)** comprises computer-based processing and/or manual procedures to provide useful and timely information to support management decision making in a rapidly changing business environment. The system must supply managers with information quickly, accurately, and completely.

The approaches that companies take to develop information systems for management differ to match the structure and management style of the organization. However, the scope of an MIS is generally company-wide, and it services management personnel at all three traditional organizational levels:

■ Low-level, or operating, management

■ Middle management

■ Upper, or top, management

The primary objective of the MIS is to satisfy the need that managers have for information that is *more summarized and relevant to the specific decisions that need to be made* than the information normally produced in an organization and that is *available soon enough to be of value in the decision-making process.* The information flows up and down through the three levels of management and is made available in various types of reports.

LEVELS OF MANAGEMENT: WHAT KINDS OF DECISIONS ARE MADE?

Each level of management (Figure 11.2) can be distinguished by the types of decisions made, the time frame considered in the decisions, and the types of report information needed to make decisions.

OPERATING MANAGEMENT   The lowest—and the largest—level of management, **operating management,** deals mostly with decisions that cover a relatively narrow time frame. Operating management, also called *supervisory management,* actualizes the plans of middle management and controls daily operations—the day-to-day

FIGURE 11.2
The three levels of management and kinds of decisions made. Different types of decisions are made, depending on the level of management. The higher the manager in an organization's hierarchy, the more decisions must be made from unstructured information. The four basic business functions or departments that top managers control are marketing, accounting and finance, production, and research and development.

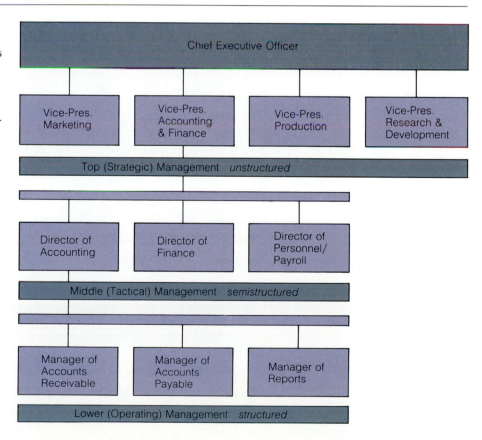

activities that keep the organization humming. Examples of operating managers are the warehouse manager in charge of inventory restocking and the materials manager, responsible for seeing that all necessary materials are on hand in a manufacturing firm to produce the product being manufactured. Most decisions at this level require easily defined information that relates to the current status and activities within the basic business functions—for example, the information needed to decide whether to restock inventory. This information is generally given to low-level man-

FIGURE 11.3
On report. (a) Low-level managers need information in the form of detail reports; (b) (c) (d) middle managers and top managers use summary reports and exception reports. These reports can be issued on demand, on a regularly scheduled basis (periodic), or on the occurrence of a specific event (event-initiated).

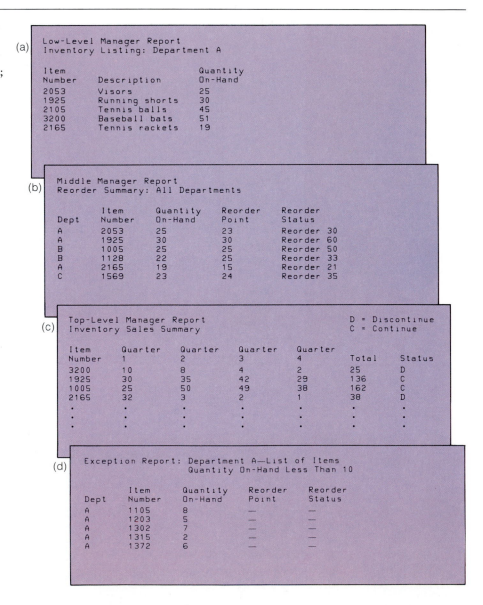

(a)
```
Low-Level Manager Report
Inventory Listing: Department A

Item                            Quantity
Number      Description         On-Hand
2053        Visors              25
1925        Running shorts      30
2105        Tennis balls        45
3200        Baseball bats       51
2165        Tennis rackets      19
```

(b)
```
Middle Manager Report
Reorder Summary: All Departments

          Item      Quantity    Reorder     Reorder
Dept      Number    On-Hand     Point       Status
A         2053      25          23          Reorder  30
A         1925      30          30          Reorder  60
B         1005      25          25          Reorder  50
B         1128      22          25          Reorder  33
A         2165      19          15          Reorder  21
C         1569      23          24          Reorder  35
```

(c)
```
Top-Level Manager Report                                            D = Discontinue
Inventory Sales Summary                                            C = Continue

Item      Quarter   Quarter   Quarter   Quarter
Number    1         2         3         4          Total    Status
3200      10        8         4         2          25       D
1925      30        35        42        29         136      C
1005      25        50        49        38         162      C
2165      32        3         2         1          38       D
 .         .         .         .         .          .        .
 .         .         .         .         .          .        .
 .         .         .         .         .          .        .
```

(d)
```
Exception Report: Department A—List of Items
              Quantity On-Hand Less Than 10

          Item      Quantity    Reorder     Reorder
Dept      Number    On-Hand     Point       Status
A         1105      8           —           —
A         1203      5           —           —
A         1302      7           —           —
A         1315      2           —           —
A         1372      6           —           —
```

agers in **detail reports** that contain specific information about routine activities (Figure 11.3a). Because these reports are structured—that is, their form is predetermined—and daily business operations data is readily available, their processing can be easily computerized.

Managers at this level, often referred to as **operational decision makers,** typically make structured decisions (Figure 11.4a). A **structured decision** is a predictable decision that can be made by following a well-defined set of routine procedures. For instance, a manager may not know exactly when inventory will need to be restocked, but knows that a decision to restock must be made soon. This type of decision can easily be programmed as a part of computerized data processing—for

FIGURE 11.4
(a) Structured decisions are typically made at the operating level of management by following clearly defined routine procedures. Operating managers need information that is detailed, focused on the present, and concerned with daily business activities. (b) Semistructured decisions, typically made at the middle management level, involve information that does not necessarily result from clearly defined, routine procedures. Middle managers need information that is less detailed and more summarized than information for operating managers and that compares the present with the recent past. (c) Unstructured decisions, typically made at the upper level of management, are supported by the management information system in the form of highly summarized reports. The information should cover large time periods and survey activities outside (as well as inside) the company.

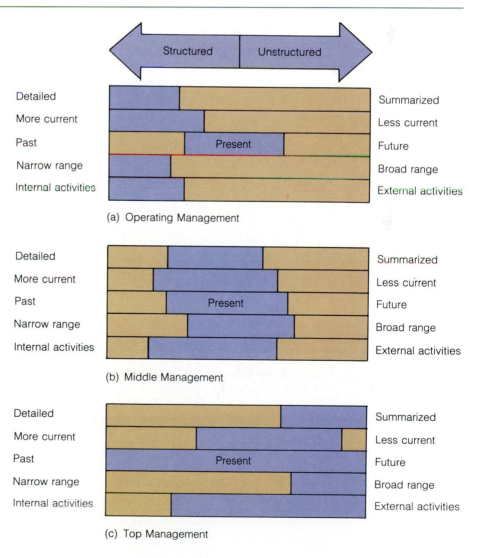

example, identifying the reorder point for a particular part or when to apply a discount to a customer's invoice. A clothing store floor manager's decision to accept your credit card to pay for some new clothes is a structured decision based on several well-defined criteria: (1) Does the customer have satisfactory identification? (2) Is the card current or expired? (3) Is the card number on the store's list of stolen or lost cards? (4) Is the amount of purchase under the cardholder's credit limit?

MIDDLE MANAGEMENT   The **middle** level of **management** deals with decisions that cover a somewhat broader range of time and involve more experience. Some common titles of middle managers are plant manager, division manager, sales manager, branch manager, and director of personnel. The information that middle managers need involves review, summarization, and analysis of historical data to help plan and control operations and implement policy that has been formulated by upper management. This information is usually given to middle managers in the form of **summary reports,** which show totals and trends—for example, total sales by office, by product, by salesperson, total overall sales—and **exception reports,** which show out-of-the-ordinary data—for example, inventory reports that list only those items that number fewer than ten in stock (see also Figure 11.3). These reports may be regularly scheduled (periodic reports), requested on a case-by-case basis (on-demand reports), or generated only when certain conditions exist (event-initiated reports).

Periodic reports are produced at predetermined times—daily, weekly, monthly, quarterly, or annually—and commonly include payroll reports, inventory status reports, sales reports, income statements, and balance sheets (we will discuss the last two in a bit more detail later). **On-demand reports** are usually requested by a manager when information is needed that focuses on a particular problem. For example, if a customer wants to establish a large charge account, a manager might request a special report on the customer's payment and order history. **Event-initiated reports** usually deal with a change in conditions that requires immediate attention, such as an out-of-stock report or a report on an equipment breakdown.

Managers at the middle level of management are often referred to as *tactical decision makers* who generally deal with semistructured decisions. A **semistructured decision** is a decision that, unlike structured decisions, must be made without a base of clearly defined informational procedures. In most cases, a semistructured decision (Figure 11.4b) is complex, requiring detailed analysis and extensive computations. Examples of semistructured decisions include deciding how many units of a specific product should be kept in inventory, whether or not to purchase a larger computer system, from what source to purchase personal computers, and whether to purchase a multiuser minicomputer system. At least some of the information requirements at this level can be met through computerized data processing.

UPPER MANAGEMENT   The **upper** level of **management** deals with decisions that are the broadest in scope and cover the widest time frame. Typical titles of managers at this level are president, chief executive officer, treasurer, controller, executive vice-president, and senior partner. Top managers include only a few powerful people who are in charge of the four basic functions of a business—marketing, accounting and finance, production, and research and development. Decisions made at this level are unpredictable, long-range, and related to the future—not just past and/or current activities; therefore, they demand the most experience and judgment.

A company's MIS must be able to supply information to upper management as needed in periodic reports, event-initiated reports, and on-demand reports. The information must show how all the company's operations and departments are related to and affected by one another. The major decisions made at this level tend to be directed toward (1) strategic planning—for example, how growth should be financed and which new markets should be tackled first; (2) allocation of resources, such as deciding whether to build or lease office space and whether to spend more money on advertising or the hiring of new staff members; and (3) policy formulation, such as determining the company's policy on hiring minorities and providing employee incentives. Managers at this level are often referred to as **strategic decision makers.**

Upper management typically makes unstructured decisions (Figure 11.4c). An **unstructured decision** is the most complex type of decision that managers are faced with. Because these decisions are rarely based on predetermined routine procedures, they involve the subjective judgment of the decision maker. As a result, this type of decision is the hardest to support from a computerized data processing standpoint. Examples of unstructured decisions include deciding five-year goals for the company, evaluating future financial resources, and deciding how to react to the actions of competitors.

THE ROLE OF MIS IN A BUSINESS

Now that you know what we mean by *managers* and understand their need for information, we can go on to describe in more detail the role of the management information system. First, as we have already pointed out, an MIS must provide managers with information (reports) to help them perform activities that directly relate to their specific areas of responsibility. For example, to effectively manage marketing responsibilities, the vice-president of marketing needs information about sales, competitors, and consumers. The head of the personnel department needs information about employee performance, work history, and job descriptions, among other things.

Second, a management information system must provide managers with information about other functional areas of the business—accounting and finance, marketing and sales, production, and research and development—so that they can coordinate their departmental activities with activities in these areas. For example, suppose that the accounting department (one functional area) has kept track of all customer invoices produced so far this year by maintaining an invoice history file. The file contains such information as (1) customer name, (2) customer address, (3) invoice date, (4) products sold, and (5) invoice amount. To better coordinate marketing activities, the vice-president of marketing (another functional area) can use this data to produce a variety of information, such as the year-to-date sales by month, a ranking of customers to whom the largest amounts of sales have been made, and an analysis of the months of highest sales. This same information could be passed along to the materials manager in production (another functional area),

FIGURE 11.5
Five steps of the decision-making process. At any step, feedback—a review of gathered information—may require the return to any of the previous steps.

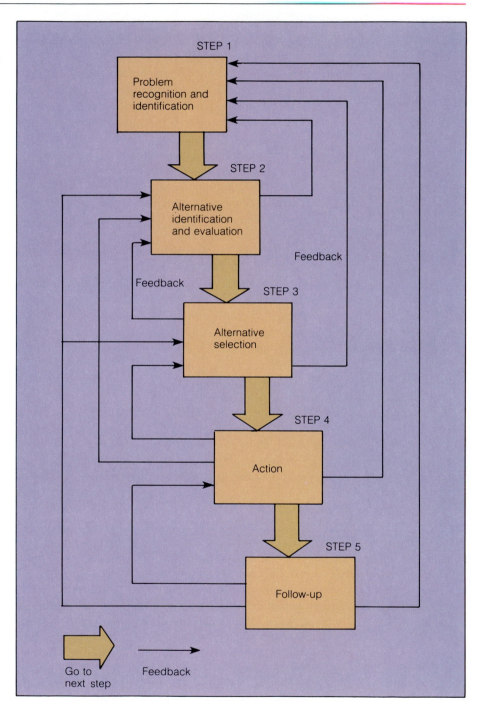

who can make informed decisions about when inventory levels should be raised or lowered to meet consumer demand.

But *how* do managers use information to make decisions? To understand how an MIS works, you must know something about the decision-making process.

HOW DOES MANAGEMENT MAKE DECISIONS?

Management styles vary. Some managers follow their instincts and deal with situations on a case-by-case basis. Other managers use a more systematic and structured approach to making decisions. If we approach decision making systematically, we can view it as a process involving five basic steps, as shown in Figure 11.5 and described below. Bear in mind that feedback, or review of the gathered information, is analyzed at each step, which may necessitate revisions or a return to a previous step. For example, suppose a company decides in Step 2 to purchase one of two software packages to help with in-house publishing; at Step 3 the company discovers that one of the two software manufacturers has gone out of business. The process must return to Step 2 to evaluate other software alternatives.

STEP 1: PROBLEM RECOGNITION AND IDENTIFICATION

In the first step of the decision-making process, the manager acknowledges a problem that affects the business. Take, for example, a small business like Bowman, Henderson, and Associates (B H & A), which provides training in the use of microcomputer hardware and software. The demand for training has grown so fast that the staff cannot handle it, and the facilities cannot support an increase in the number of students that can be taught per session. The fact that a problem exists becomes obvious when management notices that the staff is too busy to take a day off and everyone is always running around trying to take care of last-minute details. The seriousness of the problem becomes evident when staff morale begins to drop and potential customers are turned away.

STEP 2: IDENTIFICATION AND EVALUATION OF ALTERNATIVES

In the second step of the decision-making process, management considers various alternatives to solving the problem. In the case of B H & A, alternatives include (1) adding more staff and offering training in the existing facilities during expanded training hours (perhaps evenings and weekends) and (2) adding additional staff, purchasing additional equipment, and leasing additional training facilities. Once the alternative courses of action have been identified, they must be examined and compared in terms of anticipated costs and benefits.

STEP 3: ALTERNATIVE SELECTION

When each alternative has been carefully explored, the next step is to select the one that appears to best meet the manager's objectives. The logical choice would be the alternative that offers the most benefits for the least cost. However, the manager must ensure that the chosen action is not in conflict with other activities or organizational objectives.

STEP 4: ACTION

Once management has decided how to solve the problem, it must act on the decision. Suppose B H & A management selected the alternative that involved adding more staff and scheduling the use of existing facilities for additional hours. Implementing this decision would probably involve (1) defining specific staff requirements and skills, (2) advertising for additional staff, (3) interviewing prospective staff members, (4) selecting the best candidates, (5) notifying existing customers of the additional staff and expanded hours, and (6) scheduling the use of the facility during the new hours of operation.

STEP 5: FOLLOW-UP

In the final step of the decision-making process, management follows up on their choice of action to determine if it has been successful. Management assesses the degree to which original objectives and anticipated benefits are being achieved and takes corrective action when necessary. If the solution to the original problem has created a new problem, a new decision-making process begins to solve it.

WHAT KIND OF INFORMATION DOES MANAGEMENT USE TO MAKE DECISIONS?

Because decisions are made on the basis of information, the decision-making process is greatly affected by the scope and quality of the information provided by the MIS. This information is produced by processing data from three sources:

- Internally generated data (produced by normal data processing systems of the business)
- Data provided by higher or lower levels of management
- Externally generated data (produced by sources outside the company)

Information, as required by management, has four distinct properties that vary in significance depending on the organizational level and type of decision being made:

- Level of summarization
- Degree of accuracy
- Time frame

As you may have gathered from our discussion of the three management levels, the degree to which information needs to be *summarized* increases as the level of management goes up. Conversely, the lower the level of management, the more detailed the information needs to be. Top managers do not want to wade through mountains of details to make a decision. They want to be able to identify problems and trends at a glance in summary reports and exception reports; that is, they need only essential information, not nonessential details. Operational managers, however, need details on daily operations to make decisions regarding scheduling, inventory, payroll, and so on.

Of course, information must be *accurate* for wise decisions to be made. (Remember: garbage in, garbage out.) The higher the accuracy of the information, the higher the cost of the processing system, because more controls—both manual and computer-based—must be installed to increase the accuracy of output information. Some areas such as inventory may be able to live with an accuracy rate of 90–95%, but this rate is probably too low for the accounting department.

The *time frame* of management information involves how soon the information is needed and whether it needs to relate to the past, the present, or the future. When decisions are "time-sensitive" (they must be made quickly), the information system must accommodate this need. For example, whether a system is designed to use batch processing or on-line processing might be determined by how fast the information is needed by management. On the one hand, the kind of planning done by top management covers a broad time frame and requires reports that contain information covering past years as well as current performance. This type of decision making is not highly time-sensitive, so batch processing would probably be adequate. On the other hand, decisions related to banking activities may be highly time-sensitive and require on-line processing to provide up-to-date information.

TYPES OF MANAGEMENT INFORMATION SYSTEMS

The more structured the problem, the easier it is to develop computerized processing support to produce the information needed to solve it. As an organization matures in its use of the computer, the extent to which it uses computers to produce information for decision making grows.

TRANSACTION INFORMATION SYSTEM

The support of day-to-day business operating activities, or *transactions*, is usually the first and most important objective of an information system. These activities involve the processing of data received from external sources, as well as data generated internally. A computer-based **transaction information system,** also called an *operations information system (OIS)* or an *electronic data processing (EDP) system,* is focused at the operating level of a business (Figure 11.6). The management information produced by transaction information systems usually consists of detail reports of daily transactions (such as a list of items sold or all the accounting transactions that have been recorded in various ledgers and registers) or future transactions (such as lists of items that need to be ordered).

A transaction information system always includes two business transaction cycles—the income transaction cycle and the expenses transaction cycle. The *income transaction cycle* refers to the processing activities that relate to the sales of a product or service and the subsequent income, or money earned. The *expenses transaction cycle* refers to the processing activities that relate to the acquisition of assets, such as the buying of equipment and buildings, expendable resources (supplies that are used up, like office paper, pens, and so on), and the payment of bills.

The income transaction cycle usually includes such activities as the following:

■ Receiving a customer's order (and perhaps recording the order information on an order form)

■ Filling the customer's order and preparing an invoice

■ Performing the processing procedures necessary to record the sales information in the appropriate accounting records

■ Reporting the sales information in a variety of reports and statements

■ Receiving the customer's payment and recording the payment information in the appropriate accounting records

■ Reporting the payment data in appropriate reports

FIGURE 11.6
Three information systems for three levels of management.

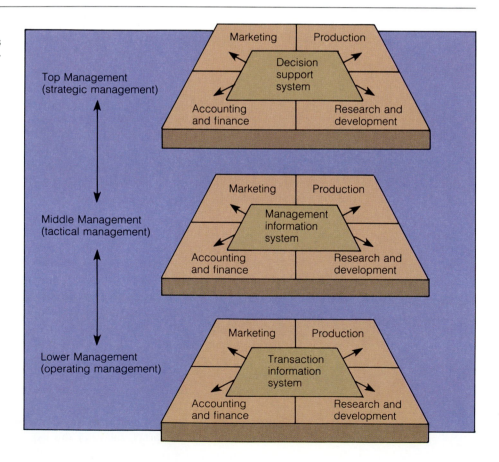

The expenses transaction cycle usually includes such processing activities as the following:

- Creating a purchase order for new supplies and forwarding it to the appropriate supplier
- Receiving a supplier's invoice and recording the data in the appropriate accounting records
- Creating a check for payment to the supplier and recording the payment data in the accounting records
- Reporting the payment data in appropriate reports

MANAGEMENT INFORMATION SYSTEM

Management information systems, also called *information reporting systems*, provide middle management with reports that summarize and categorize information derived from the company database (transaction processing data; Figure 11.3b). The purpose of the reports is to allow management to spot trends and to get an overview of current business activities.

The scope of the reports and the characteristics of their information vary according to their purpose. As you have seen, the reports can be periodic [such as income statements and balance sheets (Figure 11.7)], on-demand, or event-initiated, and they can summarize information or report on exceptional events or conditions.

DECISION SUPPORT SYSTEM

The most recent development in the evolution of computer use within an organization, the **decision support system (DSS),** makes very sophisticated use of the computer to produce information for decision making. There is no single DSS program to accomplish this; instead, DSS systems may use database management systems (covered in Chapter 12), query languages, financial modeling or spreadsheet programs, statistical analysis programs, report generators, and graphics programs to provide information.

To reach the DSS level of sophistication in information technology, an organization must have established a transaction information system and a management information system. But these two types of systems are not designed to handle unpredictable information and decisions well. Decision support systems *are* designed to handle the unstructured types of decisions—the "what if" types of decisions—that traditional management information systems were not designed to support (Figure 11.8). Moreover, decision support systems provide managers with tools to help them better analyze and make decisions about the information they have. Indeed, some people regard decision support systems as a separate type of information system altogether, not just a management information system for top management.

Although most DSSs are designed for large computer systems, electronic spreadsheet packages and database management packages are used by many businesspeople as tools for building a DSS for microcomputers. As microcomputers become more and more powerful, more and more microcomputer-based MISs will include a DSS using a database management system. The popularity of spreadsheet software among managers is due to the fact that it allows managers to examine a variety of business situations—that is, to "see what would happen" if business conditions changed—and to make projections, or guesses, about future developments based on sophisticated computer-based data analysis. Decision support systems designed for large computer systems collect large amounts of data and analyze it in more ways and with greater efficiency than a spreadsheet does.

Decision support systems generally fall into two distinct categories: general and institutional. A general DSS produces information that can be used in making a wide variety of management decisions. The electronic spreadsheet is an ideal tool for the development of general decision support systems for microcomputers. Large database management systems (see Chapter 12) and natural languages or query languages are used to develop decision support systems for large computer systems.

FIGURE 11.7
Common periodic business reports. The income statement describes the business's income and expenses, plus any profit or loss, for a given period. The balance sheet reports on the business's financial condition on a specific date.

```
Sporting Life
Income Statement for Year 1988
Sales Revenue                                          $5,109
Cost of Goods Sold                                      2,208
Gross Profit                                           $2,901
Operating Expenses                    $1525
Depreciation Expense                    119             1,644
Operating Earnings                                     $1,257
Interest Expense                                          105
Earnings Before Tax                                    $1,152
Income Tax Expense                                        550
Net Income                                            $   602
```

```
Balance Sheet at End of Year 1988
Cash                                                  $   190
Accounts Receivable                                       557
Inventory                                                806
Prepaid Expenses                                         111
Machinery, Equipment,
Furniture, and Fixtures               $ 435
Accumulated Depreciation              (105)
Undepreciated Cost                                        330
Total Assets                                          $1,994

Accounts Payable:
   Inventory                          $ 313
   Operating Expenses                    52           $   365
Accrued Expenses:
   Operations                         $ 109
   Interest                              17               126
Income Tax Payable                                        45
Short-Term Notes Payable                                 235
Long-Term  Notes Payable                                 300
Paid-in Capital                                          750
Retained Earnings                                        173
Total Liabilities and Stockholders' Equity           $1,994
```

An institutional DSS is much more industry- and function-specific. Examples include a DSS for the medical profession (including hospitals), which supports decision making in the areas of administration, patient diagnosis, determination and monitoring of drug dosages, medical records, and so on; a DSS for the advertising profession, which supports strategy in presenting products; and a DSS for the transportation industry, which supports traffic pattern analysis.

You will recall from Chapter 1 that the three major components of any computer-based information system are (1) the computer hardware and related equipment, (2) the people (the users and the technical computer specialists responsible for developing the software), and (3) the applications software and related manual procedures designed to process the data and produce the information required. Each component takes on specific characteristics when it is part of a decision support system.

DSS HARDWARE   In most cases, the computer hardware in a DSS is used mainly by management personnel. It is not uncommon to find a high-level manager sitting in front of a computer terminal or a personal computer to take advantage of the company's DSS. The terminal would be connected to a large multiuser computer system; the personal computer would have some processing capabilities of its own, but it would also need to be able to connect with the larger computer system for data exchange. In addition, personal printers and hardcopy graphics output devices (such as a plotter or a color ink-jet printer) are often available to the manager. The manager's collection of computer hardware is often called an *executive workstation* (see Chapter 3).

PEOPLE   The users of a DSS system must be reasonably comfortable working with the hardware and DSS software to be effective. Many managers develop substantial skills in using some of the microcomputer-based packages, such as electronic spreadsheets, that provide decision support processing capabilities. The software used for

FIGURE 11.8
Decision support system. These are some types of processing questions that the manager who has access to a decision support system can ask. (These questions are not keyed in word by word exactly as you see them here, but using a query language, such as SQL.)

1. If we discontinue selling baseball bats, will fewer people come into our stores?

2. If we add a new clothing line, will more people come into our stores?

3. How will offering the customer a 10% discount for all purchases totaling over $35 affect next year's net income?

4. What effect will hiring 50 additional sales employees have on the company's overall performance (i.e., profit)?

5. What effect will modernizing our stores have on sales?

DSSs on large computer systems is generally too complex for a noncomputer specialist to handle; the manager would use it only on a simple level—to ask questions and obtain reports.

Because a DSS is tailored to meet specific management information requirements, the non-management user would not likely be directly involved with it. However, this type of user might be involved in gathering data to be processed by the DSS and then used as information for management.

DSS SOFTWARE   DSS applications software is usually very complex in terms of the instructions of which it is composed. As mentioned earlier, many different types of programs can make up a DSS. In most cases, it can be divided into three levels: database management systems software, query language, and specialized software or languages.

Database management software provides managers with the ability to collect, maintain, manipulate, and retrieve huge amounts of data.

Query language, as you learned in Chapter 8, allows people to use software easily without having to learn countless lists of codes and procedures. This "layer" of DSS software helps managers use the database easily and perform a variety of activities, such as basic mathematical operations on fields of data contained in the database; calculation of ratios and various statistical measures; search of the database for records of a certain type; and extraction of records for the preparation of hardcopy reports and graphic representation of data.

Specialized software or languages are used to develop decision-making models. Some organizations purchase industry-specific modeling software for such common activities as financial risk analysis and forecasting (predicting future performance and conditions). However, the most sophisticated DSS users develop their own custom-made business activity and decision-making models.

DEVELOPING AND IMPLEMENTING A MANAGEMENT INFORMATION SYSTEM

The task of developing and implementing a management information system is a formidable one, requiring a great deal of planning. Business environments change rapidly, so unless management has great foresight (and the support of good specialists), an information system may be obsolete by the time it is implemented.

The successful development of a management information system requires:

- A long- and a short-range plan for the company; a company must have plans for the future to be able to decide what to do tomorrow, next week, and next month.

- A commitment from management to allocate the personnel and resources necessary to get the job done.

- A staff of technical specialists with the skills necessary to develop the computer-based parts of the system.

The most important step in undertaking the development of an MIS is the formation of a project development team (which, of course, would follow the steps of systems analysis, design, and development discussed in the preceding chapter). The team should be made up of managers, information system users, and technical computer specialists. All the team members should be familiar with the company's business objectives, current activities, and problems. And all the members must come to a general understanding of how the business operates. This task is not easy because many managers understand only how their department works but little, if anything, about other departments; many managers have difficulty explaining how their department works; and many managers, users, and computer specialists use jargon—special vocabulary and expressions—to explain what they do. Jargon is not generally understood by everyone. Modeling, or prototyping (discussed in the preceding chapter), is often useful in a situation like this.

The development of a comprehensive MIS is a massive undertaking that may take years to carefully plan and coordinate. However, the organizations that plan to survive the 1990s will have efficient management information systems—including decision support systems—to feed management the information it needs to be competitive.

EXPERT SYSTEMS: HUMAN EXPERTISE IN A COMPUTER

In the mid-1980s, a new type of system, called an *expert system*, was developed to support management in the decision-making process. This new type of system, which represents one of the first practical applications of artificial intelligence, is an exciting addition to the kinds of computer systems available to businesses. (**Artificial intelligence,** or **AI,** is the branch of computer science that intends to produce a new generation of computers that can perform tasks that previously only people could do; that is, it uses computers to simulate human thought processes. We will discuss artificial intelligence in more detail in the last chapter.)

An **expert system** solves problems that require substantial expertise to understand. The system's performance depends on the *body of facts* (knowledge) and the *heuristics* (rules of thumb) that are fed into the computer. The knowledge and the heuristics are gathered—largely through interviews—from human experts in the field for which the computer-based system is being designed to support decisions—fields such as medicine, engineering, or geology. (For example, in the field of medicine, one question that might be asked of an expert system is whether one treatment is better for a patient than another one.) An expert system has the capacity to store the collection of knowledge and manipulate it in response to user inquiries; in some cases, it can even explain responses to the user.

An expert system has four major program components (Figure 11.9): a natural language interface for the user, a knowledge base (like a database, where the facts are stored), an inference machine (which solves problems and makes logical inferences), and an explanation module (which explains its conclusions to the user).

One of the most famous expert systems—an older system now being replaced by updated ones—is MYCIN, a system that diagnoses infectious diseases and recommends appropriate drugs. For example, bacteremia can be a fatal disease if it is not treated quickly. Unfortunately, traditional tests for it require 24 to 48 hours to verify a diagnosis. However, MYCIN provides physicians with a diagnosis and recommended therapy within minutes. To use MYCIN, the physician enters data on a patient; as the data is being entered, MYCIN asks questions (for example, "Is patient a burn patient?"). As the questions are answered, MYCIN's inference machine "reasons" out a diagnosis: "IF the infection is primary bacteria, AND the site of the culture is the gastrointestinal tract, THEN there is evidence (0.7) that the identity of the organism causing the disease is *Bacteroides*." The "0.7" means that MYCIN "thinks" there is a 7 out of 10 chance that this diagnosis is correct. This pattern closely follows that of human thought: Much of our knowledge is inexact and incomplete, and we often reason using odds (such as "I think there's a 40%

FIGURE 11.9
Structure of an expert system.

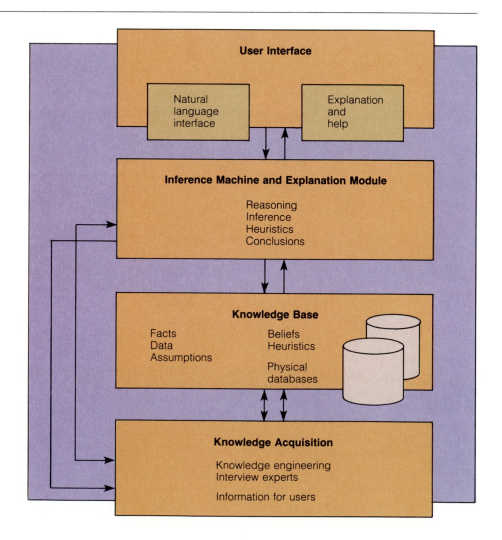

chance it's going to rain") when we don't have access to complete and accurate information.

Examples of other expert systems are XCON (a system that puts together the best arrangement of Digital Equipment Corporation (DEC) minicomputer system components for a given company), DENDRAL (a system that identifies chemical compounds), PROSPECTOR (a system that evaluates potential geological sites of oil, natural gas, and so on), and DRILLING ADVISOR (a system that assists in diagnosing and resolving oil rig problems).

Capturing human expertise for the computer is a difficult and time-consuming task. "Knowledge engineers" are trained to elicit knowledge (for example, by interview) from experts and build the expert system. The knowledge engineer may program the system in an artificial intelligence programming language, such as LISP or PROLOG, or may use system-building tools that provide a structure. Tools allow faster design but are less flexible than languages. An example of such a tool is EMYCIN, which is MYCIN without any of MYCIN's knowledge. A knowledge engineer can theoretically enter any knowledge (as long as it is describable in rules) into this empty shell and create a new system. The completed new system will solve problems as MYCIN does, but the subject matter in the knowledge base may be completely different (for example, car repair).

Expert systems are usually run on large computers—often dedicated artificial intelligence computers—because of the system's gigantic appetite for memory; however, some scaled-down expert systems run on microcomputers. Scaled-down systems do not have all the capabilities of large expert systems, and they have limited reasoning abilities. LISP and PROLOG compilers are available for microcomputers, as are some system-building tools such as EXPERT-EASE and INSIGHT.

IMPLICATIONS FOR BUSINESS

Expert systems will become increasingly important to business and manufacturing firms. However, it is difficult to define what constitutes "expertise" in business. Defining expertise in business (unlike in some other areas, notably math, medicine, and chemistry) is a formidable task because of its general and "soft" nature; that is, "business" is not made up of a specific set of inflexible facts and rules. Some business activities, however, do lend themselves to expert system development. DEC is developing several in-house expert systems, including ILPRS (which assists in long-range planning) and IPPMS (assists in project management). Other examples are TAXMAN, which evaluates the tax consequences of various proposed business reorganization schemes; AUDITOR, which helps auditors assess a company's allowance for bad debts; and TAXADVISOR, which makes tax planning recommendations.

Another issue that inhibits the use of expert systems in business is that businesses want systems that can be integrated into their existing computer systems. Many existing expert systems are designed to run on dedicated, specialized AI computers in a stand-alone mode. Furthermore, who will use the expert system? Who will be responsible for its maintenance? Who will have authority to add and/or delete knowledge in the expert system? What are the legal ramifications of decisions made by an expert system? These and other questions will have to be answered before expert systems are fully accepted in the business environment.

Cost is also a factor. Expert systems are still too expensive to build on a scale large enough to satisfy the needs of management across a wide spectrum of business and industry. However, a high priority has been set by the U.S. Department of Defense, the National Institutes of Health, and other government agencies for the development of expert systems. In Japan, the major focus of much development of new fifth-generation computers is on supercomputers that can provide high-power inference machines, or engines, for expert systems.

INFORMATION CENTERS

In an effort to further support management decision making, many large organizations have established **information centers** as part of their MIS. The people who staff an information center are technical experts on the hardware, software, and procedures that the company is using. The staff acts as "trouble shooters"—consultants and problem solvers.

The user is the person the information center was created for; the user is the only customer. If the user wants to request a computer, the information center staff will assist in identifying what kind of computer is appropriate. A user with an operating problem with hardware or software would call the information center for help, or for service requests and replacement parts. Information center staff also show users how to use available software to create their own customized applications and provide general training sessions for hardware and software use. In large systems with a mainframe computer, the information center will also assist users in accessing and storing data.

In systems without a mainframe, the information center is often called a *personal computer support center*. (Large information centers may also have a section specifically for the support of microcomputer users.) The services it provides are generally the same; however, it may have to access a remote mainframe computer (Chapter 13, Data Communications) for downloading of data.

ONWARD: DATABASICS

Neatly designed information systems would be useless if there were no organized way of handling all the data that makes up the information. A database management system helps you find the data you need, sort it, and manage it. We'll cover this topic in the next chapter.

SUMMARY

Every business needs accurate, complete, and timely information to make decisions and survive in today's competitive business environment. Management information systems—organized standards and procedures, both computer-based and manual, for processing data into useful information—help fulfill this need. They are used by three levels of management—operating management, middle management, and upper management—in the areas of planning, organizing, staffing, supervising, and controlling business activities in the departments of marketing, accounting and finance, production, and research and development.

The types of decisions made will differ according to the level of management. Operating management typically makes structured, short-term decisions. Middle management, or tactical management, generally makes semistructured decisions based on information that is less detailed (summarized to some degree). These types of decisions have some nonquantifiable aspects to them and require some subjective judgment on the part of the decision maker. Upper management, or strategic management, typically makes unstructured decisions, which are the most difficult to computerize because they are made with the most subjective judgment. Unstructured decisions are broad in scope, long range, and often unpredictable and future-oriented.

Information must be made available to management in the form of reports. Operating management generally uses detail reports that are issued on a regular, or periodic, basis. Middle and top management use summary and exception reports that are issued periodically or on demand or that are initiated by an event.

Managers generally follow five steps when making decisions: (1) problem recognition and identification, (2) identification and evaluation of alternatives, (3) selection of alternative, (4) action, and (5) follow-up. The data they use is generated internally (by normal data processing systems), externally (by sources outside the company), or by other levels of management. The information generated by processing the data into reports differs in level of summarization, degree of accuracy, and degree of time sensitivity, according to the management level.

A business can use three general types of management information systems to satisfy management's need for information. A transaction information system supports the day-to-day operating activities and is used mostly by operating management. A middle management information system (or simply a management information system) supports the decision making of middle management with reports that summarize and categorize information derived from data generated on the transaction level. A decision support system (DSS) supports the decision making of top management through a sophisticated software setup designed to answer "what if" questions and aid in making projections. Most DSSs are designed for large computer systems, although electronic spreadsheets and database management systems software can be used to build a type of DSS for microcomputers. General decision support systems produce information that can be used to make a wide variety of management decisions. Institutional decision support systems are much more industry- and function-specific. Managers using a DSS are usually provided with hardware at an executive workstation. DSS software generally uses a query language to make its use easy and specialized software languages to develop decision-making models; it also provides the manager with the ability to retrieve and manipulate huge amounts of data.

Expert systems, an application of artificial intelligence, are starting to appear in the business world to aid in the support of decision making. An expert system is a collection of knowledge (and rules for using it) gathered from human experts and fed into a computer system. Information centers and personal computer support centers, staffed by experts on a company's hardware, software, and business procedures, are also being used now to help managers and users in general to satisfy their ever-growing need for training and information.

KEY TERMS

artificial intelligence (AI)
decision support system (DSS)
detail report
event-initiated report
exception report
expert system
information center
information system

management
management information system (MIS)
middle management
on-demand report
operating management
operational decision maker
periodic report

procedure
semistructured decision
strategic decision maker
structured decision
summary report
transaction information system
unstructured decision
upper management

EXERCISES

MATCHING

Match each of the following terms with the phrase that is the most closely related:

1. _____ decision support system
2. _____ artificial intelligence
3. _____ information center
4. _____ transaction information system
5. _____ unstructured decision
6. _____ operating management
7. _____ middle management
8. _____ detail report
9. _____ expert system
10. _____ management
11. _____ procedure
12. _____ structured decision
13. _____ information system
14. _____ management information system
15. _____ exception report

a. A framework of standards and procedures for processing data into usable information.
b. A specific sequence of steps performed to complete one or more information processing activities.
c. Individuals in an organization who are responsible for providing leadership and direction in the areas of planning, organizing, staffing, supervising, and controlling business activities.
d. Combines computer-based processing and manual procedures to provide useful and timely information to support management's information requirements.

    e. This manager controls daily operations.

    f. This report contains specific information about routine activities.

    g. A predictable decision that can be made by following a defined set of routine procedures.

    h. Information is given to this type of manager in the form of summary reports and exception reports.

    i. This type of decision is unpredictable and requires subjective judgment on the part of the decision maker.

    j. An information system that supports day-to-day processing activities.

    k. This system allows a manager to obtain the answers to "what-if" types of questions.

    l. This system represents one of the first practical applications of artificial intelligence.

    m. A branch of computer science that attempts to do what human intelligence can do.

    n. Staff of technical experts who know all about a company's hardware, software, and procedures. They often act as trouble-shooters for users.

    o. The topmost level of management.

    p. This report shows out-of-the-ordinary data.

MULTIPLE CHOICE

1. Distinguishing between the different levels of management can be accomplished by analyzing:
   a. time frame considered in making decisions
   b. types of report information needed to make decisions
   c. frequency with which decisions are made
   d. types of decisions made
   e. all of the above

2. Which of the following is generally true about management reports?
   a. Middle managers use summary reports and exception reports.
   b. Top managers use summary reports and exception reports.
   c. Low-level managers need information in the form of detail reports.
   d. Reports can be issued on demand, periodically, or on the occurrence of a specific event.
   e. all of the above

3. Which of the following is not characteristic of upper management decisions?
   a. Decisions are unpredictable.
   b. Decisions are long range.
   c. Decisions are structured.
   d. Decisions require experience.
   e. Decisions require judgment.

4. Which of the following is part of the decision-making process?
   a. problem recognition
   b. problem identification
   c. alternative selection

   d. action
   e. all of the above

5. Information is produced by processing data from which of the following sources?
   a. internally generated data
   b. externally generated data
   c. data provided by lower levels of management
   d. data provided by higher levels of management
   e. all of the above

6. Which of the following statements is the most accurate?
   a. Middle managers make unstructured decisions.
   b. Low-level managers make unstructured decisions.
   c. The degree to which information needs to be summarized increases as one moves up through the management levels.
   d. Upper managers make structured decisions.
   e. Low-level managers need general information about operating activities.

7. Which of the following is characteristic of a transaction information system?
   a. used by upper management
   b. difficult to computerize
   c. fairly easy to computerize
   d. provides summary information
   e. none of the above

8. Which of the following is a requirement to develop a successful management information system?
   a. the development of a long-range goal for the system
   b. the development of a short-range goal for the system
   c. a commitment from management to allocate the personnel and resources necessary to get the job done
   d. a staff of technical specialists with the skills necessary to develop the computer-based parts of the system
   e. all of the above

9. Which of the following is a component of an expert system?
   a. natural language interface for the user
   b. knowledge base
   c. inference machine
   d. explanation module
   e. all of the above

10. Which of the following is not true about expert systems?
   a. Expert systems are expensive to design.
   b. Expert systems are usually designed to run on small general-purpose computers.
   c. Maintenance support may be difficult to obtain for an expert system.
   d. Expert systems are collections of human knowledge.
   e. all of the above

SHORT ANSWER

1. What is a management information system, and what is its role in an organization?

2. What are the five basic functions of managers, and how do these relate to management information systems?

3. What are the steps that management follows to make a decision?

4. Describe the relationship between the different levels of management and different types of decisions.

5. What are transaction information systems used for? What are the typical components of a transaction information system?

6. What is a decision support system?

7. What is the function of an information center?

8. Describe the current limitations of expert systems.

9. What are the differences between a transaction information system, a management information system, and a decision support system?

10. What does the development of a successful management information system require?

CHAPTER TWELVE

12

DATABASE MANAGEMENT SYSTEMS

Where does the power come from in a computer-based information system? Although your first answer may be "hardware and the speed with which it can process data," if you think about it a bit longer you will probably realize that the *real* power comes from the data. From data comes information, and access to information offers power. But the amounts of data being handled by companies in computer-based systems have grown so large in recent years that managing data properly has become a sophisticated operation.

PREVIEW

When you have completed this chapter, you will be able to:

■

Describe the difference between file management systems and database management systems

■

Describe how database management systems software relates to hardware and the user

■

Identify the advantages and disadvantages of the three database models and of database management systems in general

■

Explain the importance of administrating a database within an organization

■

THE USER PERSPECTIVE

As you have learned, managers need information to make effective decisions. The more accurate, relevant, and timely the information, the better informed management will be when making decisions. Now we turn our attention to the *organization* of the data that makes up the information. In many companies data was (and certainly still is) collected on a grand scale, even redundantly; that is, the same element of data was entered more than once and appeared in more than one file. Nevertheless, data needed for a report was often unavailable or at least not available in a form appropriate to the situation. And to extract data from uncoordinated files was difficult.

By the early 1970s it was apparent that traditional file-handling concepts were often no longer adequate to handle the large amounts of data and the sophisticated and complex informational needs of a business's information system. To improve the quality of management information—and information for users in general—as well as the ease with which it could be produced, a new tool was developed: the database management system.

In general, database management concepts are the same for large computer systems and for microcomputers. However, as a general business user, you will most likely be using a microcomputer, and you will almost certainly need to use data stored in a **database**—a large group of stored, integrated (cross-referenced) data elements that can be retrieved and manipulated with great flexibility to produce information. It is therefore important for you to understand not only what a database is but also what a database management system is, so that you can put them to effective use in your job.

WHAT IS A DATABASE MANAGEMENT SYSTEM?

A **database management system (DBMS)** is a comprehensive software tool that allows users to create, maintain, and manipulate an integrated base of business data to produce relevant management information. By *integrated* we mean that records are logically related to one another so that *all* data on a topic can be retrieved by simple requests. The database management systems software represents the interface between the user and the computer's operating system and database (Figure 12.1).

Picture a typical corporate office with a desk, chair, telephone, and a row of file cabinets along the wall. A wide variety of business data is stored in these cabinets. If the files have been carefully organized and maintained, then any piece of data that needs to be retrieved can quickly be located and removed. However, if the data has not been properly filed, some time and effort will be expended to find it. And, regardless of how carefully the files have been organized and maintained, you will always need to retrieve related pieces of data. For example, suppose you need to review the customer files for all invoices for payments due in excess of $2500 and prepare a simple report. How would you accomplish this task? First you would probably go through the customer files in alphabetical order, folder by folder. You would examine each invoice in the folders to determine if the amount is in excess of $2500 and remove and copy each invoice that meets the criterion. When you had examined all the customer folders and copied all the appropriate invoices, you would then review the copies and put together your report. Imagine how much time this could take. If there are a lot of customers, you would need to spend hours, if not days!

Now let's look at the situation in a different way. The environment is the same, except that, instead of file cabinets, you have a microcomputer and DBMS software that has access to a customer database file (Figure 12.2). In this file a row of customer data is referred to as a *record*, and an individual piece of data within a record, such as a name, is referred to as a *field*. (See Table 12.1 and Figure 12.3 for a review of filing and database terminology introduced in Chapter 4.) To get the invoice data you need, you would do something like this:

- Turn on the computer and the printer.
- Start up the DBMS software.
- Give the command to "open up" the customer database file stored on your disk, which is similar in concept to manually opening up the customer drawer in a filing cabinet.
- Give the command to search all the records in the database file and display copies of the records that meet your criterion (that is, the names of people with unpaid invoices greater than $2500). If you were using dBase III Plus, a popular microcomputer DBMS, the command would look something like:

```
LIST FOR INV_AMOUNT > 2500
```

If you were using SQL (Structured Query Language), the command would look like this:

```
SELECT NAME FROM CUSTOMER
     WHERE INV_AMOUNT > 2500
     ORDER BY NAME
```

In response to this command, all the records in the file that have an invoice amount greater than $2500 will be listed on the screen. (The SQL command would also function to sort the listing into order by name.) This whole procedure would take approximately five minutes or less!

The DBMS is a software tool designed to manage a large number of integrated, shared electronic "file cabinets." You describe the type of data you wish to store, and the DBMS is responsible for creating the database file(s) and providing an easy-to-use mechanism for storing, retrieving, and manipulating the data. (We discuss one DBMS software package, dBase III Plus, in Module D.)

WHY SHOULD YOU CARE ABOUT DATABASES?

In small businesses, databases may be both created and operated by the user. In moderate- to large-size businesses with extensive computer systems, the corporate database is usually created by technical information specialists, such as the database administrator, but the database management system is acquired by the information systems department. Users generate and extract data stored by the database management system. As with systems analysis and design, which we discussed in Chapter 10, to design a database the organization must describe its informational needs to the designers and specify the type of data needed. Users participate heavily in this process of defining what information needs to be stored in the database.

FIGURE 12.1
DBMS software as interface.
The database management
system is the facilitator that
allows the user to access
and manipulate integrated
data elements in a database.

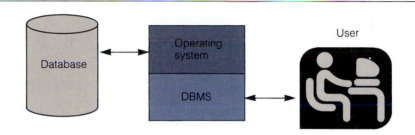

FIGURE 12.2
Customer database file.
This figure illustrates only a
small section of our hypothetical customer file. Data
stored electronically in a
DBMS can be more easily
retrieved than data stored in
filing cabinets.

Customer Name	Date	Item Ordered	Quantity Ordered	Invoice Amount
Arthene Ng	02/12/87	4065	5	2510.57
Pamela Robert	02/13/87	4128	7	1510.62
Jeff Arguello	02/13/87	4111	1	1905.00
Sylvia Arnold	02/14/87	4007	6	2950.93
Richard Mall	02/14/87	4019	1	63.55
Alan Steinberg	02/14/87	4021	3	1393.00
Harry Filbert	02/14/87	4106	2	940.56
Frances Chung	02/15/87	4008	5	2717.00
Bruce Chaney	02/15/87	4007	8	1720.00

Field   Record

Since the early 1980s, tremendous advances have been made in developing database management systems for microcomputers. They are now easy enough for users to learn to operate without assistance and powerful enough to produce valuable management information. Regardless of whether you're in a large or a small business, you cannot afford to do without the capabilities that a DBMS can provide. It is one of the most powerful tools available for use as an information resource.

DATA MANAGEMENT CONCEPTS

Chapter 4 discussed three methods for storing and retrieving data—sequential, direct, and indexed sequential. Each method stores records differently within a file, and each method is suited to particular applications and processing requirements.

TABLE 12.1   Short Glossary of Database Terminology

Data—the raw facts that make up information

Numeric data—data composed of numeric digits (numbers) used for mathematical calculations

Alphanumeric (character) data—data composed of a combination of letters, numbers, and other symbols (like punctuation marks) that are not used for mathematical calculations

Database—a large collection of stored, integrated (cross-referenced) records that can be maintained and manipulated with great flexibility; the top level in the data hierarchy

Bit—contraction of binary digit, which is either 1 ("on") or 0 ("off") in computerized data representation

Character—the lowest level in the data hierarchy; usually one letter or numerical digit; also called **byte** (8 bits)

Field, or **attribute**, or **data element**—a group of related characters (*attribute* is also a column of a relation in a relational database, discussed later); the second lowest level in the data hierarchy

Record—a group of related fields; the third level from the bottom in the data hierarchy (analogous to a *tuple*, or *row*, in a relational database)

Key—a unique field within a record that uniquely identifies the record

File—a group of related records; the fourth level from the bottom in the data hierarchy

Entity—any tangible or intangible object or concept on which an organization wishes to store data; entities have attributes, such as name, color, and price

Information—data that has value to or that has been interpreted by the user

In Chapter 4, we assumed that all data needed for processing is contained in a single file on a storage device. But what happens if needed data elements are spread among many files? For example, student records may be in one file, course and grade records in a second file, and billing records in a third file. The DBMS approach for storing and retrieving data in computer-usable form has evolved to allow users to easily retrieve and update data that is in more than one file. But before we describe why the DBMS approach is significant, and to facilitate your understanding of it, we will first describe in more detail the traditional system it evolved from—the file management system.

FILE MANAGEMENT SYSTEMS

Computers began to be widely used in the business community in the mid-1950s. At first, the processing performed was very straightforward. Applications software programs tended to be sequentially organized and stored in single file on magnetic tape that contained all the elements of data required for processing. The term **file**

FIGURE 12.3
Data hierarchy. This figure shows how most of the database terms in Table 12.1 fit into the data hierarchy.

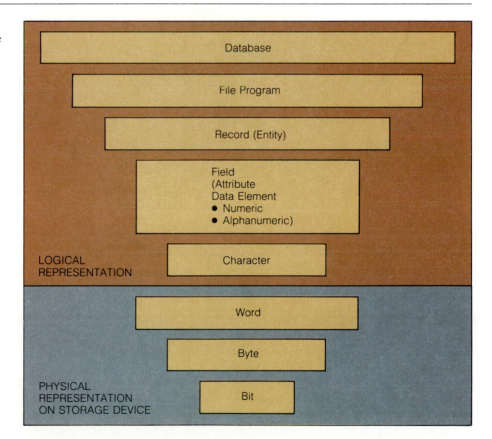

management system was coined to describe this traditional approach to managing business data and information (Figure 12.4). However, file management systems did not provide the user with an easy way to group records within a file or to establish relationships among the records in different files. As disk storage became more cost-effective and its capacity grew, new software applications were developed to access disk-based files. The need to access data stored in more than one file was quickly recognized and posed increasingly complex programming requirements.

The most serious problems of file management systems involve (1) data redundancy, (2) updating files and maintaining data integrity, and (3) lack of program and data independence. In the case of **data redundancy,** the same data elements appear in many different files and often in different formats, which makes updating files difficult, time-consuming, and prone to errors. For example, a payroll file and a personnel file may both contain an employee's ID number, name, address, and telephone number. Obviously, having many copies of the same data elements takes up unnecessary storage space.

In addition to wasted space, data redundancy creates a problem when it comes to **file updating.** When an element of data needs to be changed—for example, employee address—it must be updated in *all* the files, a tedious procedure. If some files are missed, data will be inconsistent—that is, **data integrity** is not maintained—and reports will be produced with erroneous information.

Another limitation of file management systems has to do with the lack of **program** and **data independence.** This lack of independence means that different files established in different arrangements, such as some with the date first and expense items second and others vice versa, cannot be used by the same program. Programs must be written by programmers to use a specific file format. This process takes a programmer a large amount of time and costs a company a great deal of money.

To deal with these problems and the ever-growing demands for a flexible, easy-to-use mechanism for managing data, the concept of a database was developed.

FIGURE 12.4
Single file: Traditional file management approach. In old file management systems, applications software programs accessed data from a single file stored on magnetic tape or disk.

Program A

Program B

Program C

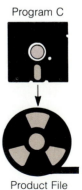

Payroll File

Personnel File

Product File

DATABASE MANAGEMENT SYSTEMS

As mentioned earlier, the term *database* describes a collection of related records that forms an integrated base of data, which can be accessed by a wide variety of applications programs and user requests. In a database management system, data needs to be entered into the system only once. When the user instructs the program to sort data or compile a list, the program searches quickly through the data in memory (or in storage), copying needed data into a new file for the purpose at hand. However, the original set of data is not changed in any way.

How is this done? Through software—which is what a database management system really is. However, the software must be considered together with the hardware and the database because the type and capacity of certain hardware components and the size of the database will affect both the sophistication and efficiency of the DBMS software.

HARDWARE: STORAGE COUNTS

Storage capacity is crucial to the operation of a database management system. Even the many megabytes of hard disk storage in an efficient, modern microcomputer can't handle the many gigabytes of data that move through large corporations. To manage these databases, large-scale database management systems need to use very high-capacity and high-speed disks for storage. It is not uncommon for database files in a comprehensive corporation information system to be so large that they use more than one disk storage device (plus additional backup devices).

Recent advances in the speed and capacity of hard disk drives for microcomputers have made them the main storage resource for microcomputer-based database management systems. Early microcomputer systems relied on floppy-disk-based storage devices with capacities ranging from 150 K to 1.2 MB. Although these capacities allowed small database files to be established, many business applications required files too large to be stored on floppy disk. The first hard disks introduced for microcomputers had 10 MB of storage capacity and an average access time of 90 milliseconds (ms). (Recall from Chapter 4 that *access time* refers to the average amount of time required to move the read/write mechanism to the appropriate disk-surface location and begin the process of retrieving data.) Recent hard disk units have cut this access time to less than 10 ms. The increase in speed improves both processing and response time for database applications.

Managers and other users in large organizations usually interact directly with the DBMS via a video display terminal connected to a large computer. The terminal allows users to communicate their requests for information to the system and view the results immediately. In the past, most information was displayed in the form of text. However, because many new terminals have color graphics capability, users can now view information in picture form, which may make it easier to understand (Figure 12.5).

Because database files represent a significant (in many organizations the most important) business resource, they must be protected from damage, loss, and unauthorized use. The most common way to protect the corporate database from loss or damage is to periodically make backup copies of it. In large database systems, backup copies are usually made on one or more reels of standard 1/2″ magnetic tape. The backup process for large corporate databases requires the involvement of computer operations specialists. The most popular form of backup for micro-computer hard disks is the streaming tape unit (Chapter 4). These devices are small, fast, and so easy to use that the user can perform the backup operation unassisted.

SOFTWARE: IN CONTROL

A database management system is an integrated set of software programs that pro-vides all the necessary capabilities for building and maintaining database files, extracting the information required for making decisions, and formatting the infor-mation into structured reports. It is intended to:

- *Make data independent of the applications programs being used, so that it is easy to access and change.* Say, for example, you have created a student database with many student records. After some time, you decide to change the structure of the student database to include phone numbers. With a DBMS you can do this and still use the applications program you were using before you changed the database structure, because the data's organization is independent of the program being used.

- *Establish relationships among records in different files.* The user can obtain *all* data related to important data elements.

FIGURE 12.5
Color graphic display of information being retrieved and manipulated by a DBMS. Users often find graphic displays to be more helpful than textual displays (like that on the monitor to the right).

- *Eliminate data redundancy.* Because data is independent of the applications program being used, it can be stored a single time in a file that can be accessed, for example, by the student billing applications program or the grade averaging program.

- *Define the characteristics of the data.* The user can create a database that has data stored in it based on particular informational needs.

- *Manage file access.* For example, the DBMS can "examine" user requests and clear them for access to retrieve data, thus maintaining data safe from unauthorized access.

- *Maintain data integrity.* Because data is not stored redundantly, it needs to be updated only in one place.

Using DBMS software, personnel can request that a program be run to produce information in a predefined format or extract information in a specific way. For example, if you are the manager of a school's registration department, you may want to review a report of the classes that currently have space available; however, the manager of the school's finance division may want to use the same data to generate a report on courses that had low enrollment over the past two years to determine whether to continue offering these courses.

The easiest way to view a DBMS is to think of it as a layer of software that surrounds the database files (Figure 12.6). The DBMS software usually includes a query language, report writers (microcomputers only), utilities, and an applications program language interface [usually called the *data manipulation language (DML)*]. Each of these will be described in the following sections.

QUERY LANGUAGE   Most managers and other users will find query language (see Chapter 8) to be the most valuable aspect of DBMS software. Traditionally, many managers rely on the information provided by periodic reports. However, this creates a problem when a decision must be made now and the information required to make it will not be produced until the end of the week. The objective of a query language is to allow managers to use simple English to produce information on demand that is also in simple English. To be effective, a query language must allow the user to phrase requests for information in a very flexible fashion. For example, take a request for inventory information. Here are some examples of questions that the user could ask using a query language when a single file is involved:

- List all items in the inventory database for which the quantity on hand equals zero. (Immediate orders would have to be placed to restock these items.)

- List all items in the database for which the quantity on hand is less than or equal to the reorder point. (This information would be used to process regular orders for restocking inventory.)

- List all items in the database for which the unit cost times the quantity on hand exceeds $10,000. (This would show the highest dollar volume items in inventory.)

Here are examples of questions that the user could ask using a query language when more than one file is involved:

- List the names and addresses of all customers who ordered items that were out of stock and that are now in stock. (This would involve using both the customer file and the inventory file and would show a listing of all customers who should be notified by mail that the items they ordered are now available for pick-up.)

- List the phone numbers of customers who ordered items that were out of stock and that aren't going to be restocked. (This would also involve using both the customer file and the inventory file and would show a listing of all customers who should be notified by phone that the item they ordered will no longer be carried in inventory.)

You, the user, can learn to use a typical query language effectively with about eight hours of instruction and practice. Once armed with this skill, you can prepare a special report in a few minutes instead of several days or weeks. Several powerful query languages, including SQL (IBM), dBase III Plus (Ashton-Tate), Oracle (Oracle), and INFORMIX, exist for use with microcomputers. About twenty different query languages are available for use with larger computer systems; four of the most widely used are NOMAD2, EASYTRIEVE PLUS, INTELLECT, and SQL.

FIGURE 12.6
DBMS software. The software that comprises the functions of a database management system can be thought of as a layer that surrounds the database files. Among other things, this software provides the user interface, which allows the user to interact easily with the system.

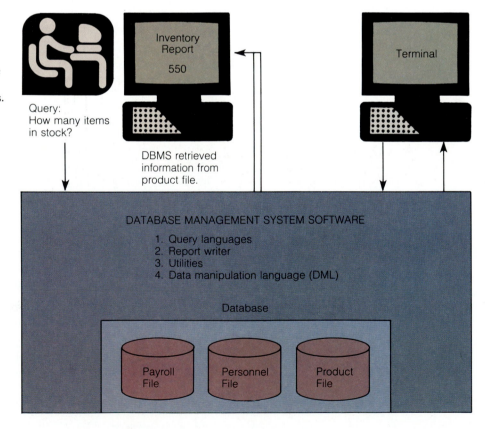

To further illustrate how you might use a query language, let's use an inventory database as an example again. The structure of the database is illustrated below.

Field Description	Name	Data Type	Size	Decimals
Part number	PNUM	Numeric	5	
Group code	GROUP	Character	1	
Description	DESCRIPT	Character	20	
Quantity on hand	QTYOH	Numeric	3	
Reorder point	ORDERPT	Numeric	3	
Unit cost	COST	Numeric	9	2
Supplier	SUPPLIER	Character	1	

Defining the size of a field tells the applications program how wide the field must be to store the numbers or characters in it; defining the decimals of a field applies only to numeric fields and refers to how many decimal places you want a number to be rounded to.

Let's suppose you are the inventory manager for a small company and will be attending a management meeting this afternoon to discuss the current budget. To prepare for the meeting you need to be able to discuss the status of inventory. You formulate some questions about inventory that you would like answered, including:

1. Which items in inventory are out of stock?
2. Which items in inventory are below the reorder point?
3. Which items to be ordered have a unit cost in excess of $25?
4. From which supplier will the company be ordering the most items?

If we assume that the database has been implemented on a microcomputer using a popular DBMS package such as dBase III Plus, you would use the following query language statements:

1. LIST FOR QTYOH = 0
2. LIST FOR QTYOH < ORDERPT
3. LIST FOR COST > 25 .AND. QTYOH < ORDERPT
4. LIST FOR QTYOH < ORDERPT .AND. SUPPLIER = "A"
   LIST FOR QTYOH < ORDERPT .AND. SUPPLIER = "B"
   LIST FOR QTYOH < ORDERPT .AND. SUPPLIER = "C"

The contents of the database and the results of the queries shown above are displayed in Figure 12.7.

```
Inventory Database Listing
Record#   PNUM GROUP DESCRIPT              QTYOH ORDERPT   COST SUPPLIER
     1    202  2     HAMMERS                 23     30    5.75 A
     2    207  2     NAILS                   14     25    2.75 B
     3    211  2     PLIERS                  30     25    8.65 A
     4    213  2     WRENCHES                 0     10   18.00 C
     5    202  2     SCREW DRIVERS           13     15    4.80 B
     6    218  2     SAW                      8      5   15.60 A
     7    309  1     BROOM                    0     10    9.99 C
     8    310  1     MOPS                     4     10   11.00 A
     9    308  1     SPONGES                 19     15    0.80 A
    10    308  3     LIGHT BULBS             10      8    7.80 B
    11    315  3     POWER CABLES            12     20   15.60 C
    12    300  3     EXTENSION CORDS          0     15    8.99 A
```

Quantity-on-hand is equal to zero.

```
Record#   PNUM GROUP DESCRIPT              QTYOH ORDERPT   COST SUPPLIER
     4    213  2     WRENCHES                 0     10   18.00 C
     7    309  1     BROOM                    0     10    9.99 C
    12    300  3     EXTENSION CORDS          0     15    8.99 A
```

Quantity-on-hand is less than the reorder point.

```
Record#   PNUM GROUP DESCRIPT              QTYOH ORDERPT   COST SUPPLIER
     1    202  2     HAMMERS                 23     30    5.75 A
     2    207  2     NAILS                   14     25    2.75 B
     4    213  2     WRENCHES                 0     10   18.00 C
     5    202  2     SCREW DRIVERS           13     15    4.80 B
     7    309  1     BROOM                    0     10    9.99 C
     8    310  1     MOPS                     4     10   11.00 A
    11    315  3     POWER CABLES            12     20   15.60 C
    12    300  3     EXTENSION CORDS          0     15    8.99 A
```

Cost is greater than 25 and quantity-on-hand is less than reorder point.

```
                        No records found.
```

Quantity-on-hand is less than the reorder point and supplier is equal to "A."

```
Record#   PNUM GROUP DESCRIPT              QTYOH ORDERPT   COST SUPPLIER
     1    202  2     HAMMERS                 23     30    5.75 A
     8    310  1     MOPS                     4     10   11.00 A
    12    300  3     EXTENSION CORDS          0     15    8.99 A
```

Quantity-on-hand is less than the reorder point and supplier is equal to "B."

```
Record#   PNUM GROUP DESCRIPT              QTYOH ORDERPT   COST SUPPLIER
     2    207  2     NAILS                   14     25    2.75 B
     5    202  2     SCREW DRIVERS           13     15    4.80 B
```

Quantity-on-hand is less than the reorder point and supplier is equal to "O."

```
Record#   PNUM GROUP DESCRIPT              QTYOH ORDERPT   COST SUPPLIER
     4    213  2     WRENCHES                 0     10   18.00 C
     7    309  1     BROOM                    0     10    9.99 C
    11    315  3     POWER CABLES            12     20   15.60 C
```

FIGURE 12.7 (opposite)
Results of database queries.
Here are the types of re-
sponses a DBMS would give
you based on the queries
listed in the text.

REPORT WRITER   The report writer aspect of DBMS software for microcomputers simplifies the process of generating reports. If we use our inventory file as an example, we might want to generate a report to be handed out at the afternoon meeting that shows the results of the queries given in Figure 12.7 in a polished format (Figure 12.8). The procedure is usually fairly easy and involves specifying column headings for the items to be included in the report, as well as any totals, subtotals, or other calculations.

UTILITIES   The utilities part of the DBMS software is used to maintain the database on an ongoing basis. This includes such tasks as:

- Creating and maintaining the data dictionary (described in more detail later in the chapter)

- Removing records flagged for deletion. (Most DBMSs have built-in protection schemes to prevent users from accidentally deleting records. To delete unwanted records from the database, the user must first mark, or "flag," them for deletion and then give the command to actually remove the flagged records.)

- Establishing control of access to portions of the database (protecting the database against unauthorized use)

- Providing an easy way to back up the database and recover data if the database is damaged

- Monitoring performance

DATA MANIPULATION LANGUAGE (DML)   The user needs the **data manipulation language** software in the DBMS to effect input to and output from the database files; in other words, all programs, including the query language, must go through the

FIGURE 12.8
DBMS-generated report.
Here is a more polished
report based on Query 2
of Figure 12.7.

```
Page No.        1
01/01/88
                    INVENTORY ITEMS
              QUANTITY-ON-HAND < REORDER POINT
PRODUCT NUMBER DESCRIPTION           SUPPLIER
          202 HAMMERS                A
          207 NAILS                  B
          211 PLIERS                 A
          213 WRENCHES               C
          202 SCREW DRIVERS          B
          218 SAW                    A
          309 BROOM                  C
          310 MOPS                   A
          308 SPONGES                A
          308 LIGHT BULBS            B
          315 POWER CABLES           C
          300 EXTENSION CORDS        A
```

DML, which comprises the technical instructions that make up the input/output routines in the DBMS. Each applications program that is written needs certain data elements to process to produce particular types of information. A list of the required elements of data is contained within each applications program. The DML uses these lists, identifies the elements of data required, and provides the link necessary to the database to supply the data to the program.

DATA DICTIONARIES AND TRANSACTION LOGS

Once a DBMS has been implemented, two types of files are constantly in use besides the database files—the data dictionary and a transaction log.

The **data dictionary** (which we discussed briefly in Chapter 10) is a file that contains the technical descriptions of each element of data to be stored within the database, including data element names, data element descriptions, type of data, maximum size allocated, and logical relationships to other data elements and applications programs (Figure 12.9). The dictionary is used constantly by the DBMS as a reference tool. When an applications program requests elements of data as part of a query, the DBMS refers to the data dictionary for guidance in retrieving them.

FIGURE 12.9
Data dictionary and transaction log.

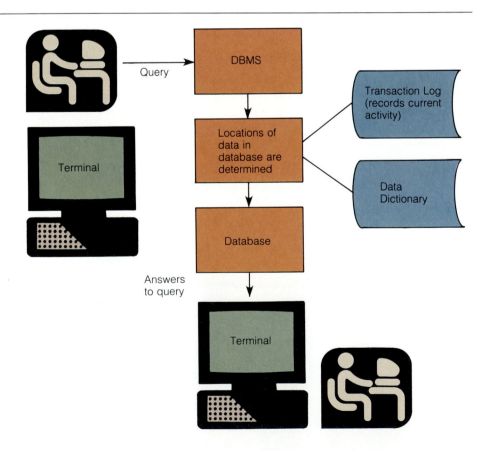

The information in the data dictionary varies from one DBMS package to another. However, in more complex systems, the data dictionary can contain several levels of information about each data element, including:

LEVEL	INFORMATION CONTAINED
1	Name of data element
	Type of data (numeric, alphanumeric)
	Maximum allowable size of data element
	Description of data element
2	Location where data element is stored
	Relationships to other data elements
	Programs that can access data element

The **transaction log** contains a complete record of all activity that affected the contents of a database during the course of a transaction period (Figure 12.9). This log aids in backup and in rebuilding database files (recovery) if they are accidentally destroyed or damaged. If a backup copy is made each time a database file is updated and a transaction log is created to document the current transaction period's activity, then recovery from the loss of the current copy of the database file(s) is simple. In this case, the previous day's copy of the database is considered to be the current copy, which is then updated by using the most current transaction log. Database management systems for microcomputers do not automatically create a transaction log file. Special provisions must be made in the program design to accommodate this requirement. Database management systems for minicomputers and mainframes usually build the transaction log automatically.

DATABASE MODELS

Three popular models are used to organize a database—hierarchical, network, and relational. These three models have evolved gradually as users and computer specialists gained experience in using database management systems. They differ in terms of the cost of implementation, speed, degree of data redundancy, ease with which they can satisfy information requirements, and ease with which they can be updated.

In use since the late 1960s, the hierarchical and network database models were first developed and used principally on mainframe computers. The concepts behind the relational database model were pioneered in the early 1970s by E. F. Codd and developed throughout the 1970s. This database model has been used extensively on microcomputers and is also being used more and more on larger computers for large-scale applications.

HIERARCHICAL MODEL

In the **hierarchical database model,** data is organized into related groups much like a family tree (Figure 12.10). The model comprises two types of records—parent

FIGURE 12.10
Hierarchical database
model for the Moser
Corporation. In this
database model, which
looks like a family tree, a
parent record can have
many child records, but
each child record can have
only one parent record.
The root record is the top-
most record.

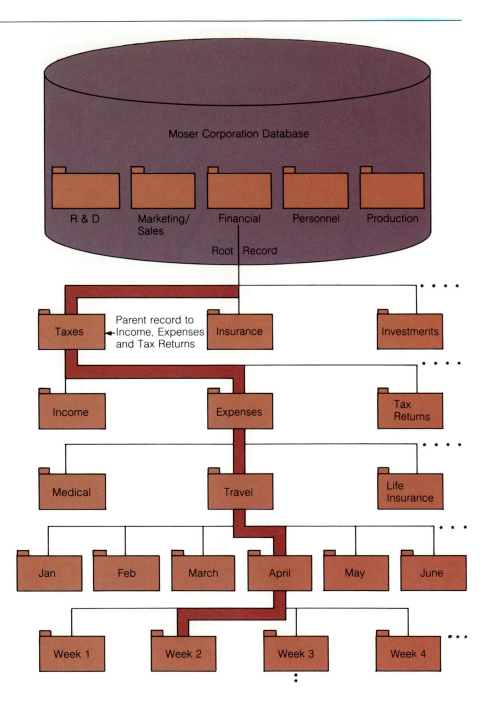

records and child records. **Parent records** are higher in the structure of the model than **child records.** Each "child" can have only one "parent"; that is, each record may have many records below it but only one record above it. The record at the highest level, or top of the "tree," is called the root record. The **root record,** which is the key to the model, connects the various branches.

The parent-child relationship between two record types in a hierarchical database model is also called a **one-to-many relationship,** which means that one parent record has many child records. To store or retrieve a record in a hierarchical model, the DBMS begins at the root occurrence and moves downward through each of the occurrences until the correct record is located. There is no connection between separate branches in this type of model. See, for example, the route that is followed in Figure 12.10 to locate the record of travel expenses for the second week in April.

The primary advantage of the hierarchical database model is the ease with which data can be stored and retrieved, as well as the ease with which data can be extracted for reporting purposes. A few DBMS packages using this model have been available for some time and thus have been refined for continued use.

The main disadvantage of this type of database model is that records in separate groups—in Figure 12.10, for example, medical, travel, and life insurance are separate groups—cannot be directly related without a great deal of effort. For example, the Moser Corporation might want to compare by month and by year the different expense amounts of each category to answer such questions as: "What percentage is each yearly expense amount of the total of all expenses for the year?" or "What is the average expense amount for each month and for the year?" But the user is confined to retrieving data that can be obtained from the established hierarchical links among records. Also, if you delete a parent from the model, you automatically delete all the child records. In addition, updating a hierarchical model is complex and requires a trained and experienced programmer who knows all the physical connections that exist between records. Another restriction is the inability to implement network models without a great deal of redundancy.

NETWORK MODEL

The **network database model** (Figure 12.11) is somewhat similar to the hierarchical model, but each record can have more than one parent. This model overcomes the principal limitation of the hierarchical model because it establishes relationships between records in different groups. Any record can be related to any other data element.

Figure 12.11 shows the expense types and expense periods for the first quarter of a year for Moser Corporation as part of a network database model. With this type of model, it would be easy to compare weekly or monthly expense amounts or to determine what percentage travel expenses are of all expenses for the first quarter.

The primary advantage of the network database model is its ability to provide sophisticated logical relationships among the records. However, as in the hierarchical model, the user is limited to retrieving data that can be accessed using the established links between records.

RELATIONAL DATABASE MODEL

The **relational database model** (Figure 12.12) is made up of many tables, called *relations*, in which related data elements are stored. The relations—similar in concept to files—are made up of rows and columns, and they provide data to the user about an *entity* class. A row (similar to a record) is called a *tuple*, and a column (similar to a field)—is called an *attribute*. For example, in Figure 12.12, Division Number, Department Number, and Department Name are attributes of the Department Table; the row that contains the values 1, 1, and accounting is one tuple.

The data content of a relation is determined by the relationship that the parts have to the whole. The main objective of the relational database model is to allow complex logical relationships between records to be expressed in a simple fashion.

Relational databases are useful because they can cross-reference data and retrieve data automatically. Users do not have to be aware of any "structure" to use a relational database, and they can use it with little effort or training. (The installation and use of hierarchical and network database models require the knowledge of a programming language such as Pascal or a particular query language.) Also, data can be easily added, deleted, or modified, and it can be accessed by content, instead of by address (as is the case with hierarchical and network models).

The main disadvantage of the relational model is that searching the database can be time-consuming, so it has primarily been used with smaller databases on microcomputers. Indeed, the relational model has become the most popular database model for microcomputer-based database management systems (dBase III Plus, for example, which is discussed at length in Module D). However, the relational model is finding more and more applications on mini- and mainframe computers.

FIGURE 12.11
Network database model for the Moser Corporation.

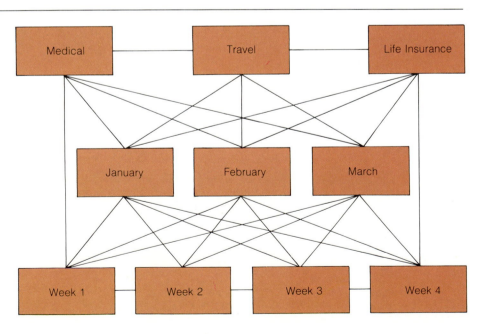

FIGURE 12.12
Relational database model.

Division Table

Division Number	Division Name
1	East Coast
2	West Coast
3	Europe

Department Table

Division Number	Dept. Number	Dept. Name
1	1	Accounting
1	2	Sales
3	1	Accounting
2	2	Sales
2	3	Personnel
	etc.	

Employee Personnel Table

Employee Number	Name	Address	Phone	Hire Date	Position Description	Date Eval.	Pref. Rating
501	Mary Adams						
502	Frank Sonter						
503	John Jones						
504	Susie Fischer						
505	Juan Valdez						

Employee Salary Table

Employee Number	Salary	YTD Pay	YTD Deductions	Number of Dependents
501	21000	3500	1225	2
502	31000	5166.66	2066.66	0
503	20000	3333	1166.55	2
504	28000	4666.66	1866.66	1
505	35000	5833.33	2624.99	0

Also, the relational model is the new ANSI standard (SQL) and will be included in OS/2 (extended) on IBM PS/2 microcomputers.

DESIGNING A DATABASE

Many users in the microcomputer environment will design a database and will actually build and implement it; however, users are less involved in database design and development when the database management system is intended to be used in minicomputer and mainframe computer environments. (Users are very involved in defining what data needs to be stored in the database, though.) In these situations, design and development is carried out by trained and experienced information system specialists.

MATCHING THE DESIGN TO THE ORGANIZATION

Most users working with microcomputer-based DBMS software focus on a very specific set of objectives and information processing needs—that is, their own. For many small applications this is a satisfactory approach. However, the objectives must be broader when working with a large corporation, a large computer system, and more complex and sophisticated DBMS software. And the plans for the use of the database management system must be integrated with the long-range plans for the company's total information system. The information processing needs of the entire corporation must be considered and viewed in terms of a corporate database that facilitates the collection, maintenance, and sharing of data among all the company's organizational units.

The design of a corporate-wide database is an enormous task. Tackling this task is often made easier by taking a modular approach—that is, proceeding department by department and identifying the information needs of each, then defining general information needs as they relate to the establishment of a database. Once the general information needs have been established, the design process can proceed. This process usually comprises two distinct phases of activity, the logical design phase and the physical design phase.

LOGICAL DESIGN

Logical design refers to *what* the database is as opposed to *how* it operates; in other words, the logical design is a detailed description of the database model from the business perspective rather than the technical perspective. The logical design of a database involves defining user information needs, analyzing data element requirements and logical groupings, finalizing the design, and creating the data dictionary. The major focus is on identifying every element of data necessary to produce the required management information systems reports and on the relationship among the records. This process involves defining two distinct views of the database—the schema and the subschema.

Schema refers to the organization of the database in its entirety, including the names of all the data elements and how the records are linked in useful ways. A

subschema is part of the schema; it refers to the manner in which certain records are linked in ways useful to a particular user—perhaps to produce a report or satisfy certain queries (often called *user-views*). (The data in a database should not be accessible to all the employees of a company.)

DEFINING DATABASE USER INFORMATION NEEDS   The objective of the first step in logical design is *information requirements analysis*—to identify specific user information needs and to group them logically. For example, let's assume that the personnel and payroll departments of a company have indicated that the following elements of data must be collected about each employee:

PERSONNEL DEPARTMENT	PAYROLL DEPARTMENT
Employee Name	Employee Name
Home Address	Home Address
Phone	Pay Rate
Hire Date	Number of Dependents
Department	Deductions
Job Title	Year-to-Date (YTD) Pay
Salary Level	
Date of Last Review	
Date of Next Review	
Performance Rating	
Number of Dependents	
Office Location	
Extension	

During this step in database design, the data elements required for each user department would be similarly identified and logically grouped by the database designer.

ANALYZING DATA ELEMENTS AND LOGICAL GROUPS   This step in logical design involves composing subschemas. First, the list of data elements that users have identified as necessary is analyzed to:

- Identify redundant data elements
- Identify the natural groups into which data elements can be organized
- Identify groups of data elements needed for specific applications programs

You'll note that there are three redundant elements of data in the items listed above for the personnel and payroll departments: employee name, home address, and number of dependents. And the items can be organized into at least four natural groups: employee data, position data, performance data, and salary data. The elements of data could be grouped as follows:

Employee Data
```
EMPLOYEE NUMBER
NAME
HOME ADDRESS
HOME PHONE
```

Position Data
```
EMPLOYEE NUMBER (needed as identifier)
DEPARTMENT
JOB TITLE
OFFICE LOCATION
EXTENSION
```

Performance Data
```
EMPLOYEE NUMBER
HIRE DATE
DATE OF LAST REVIEW
PERFORMANCE RATING
DATE OF NEXT REVIEW
```

Salary Data
```
EMPLOYEE NUMBER
PAY RATE
YTD PAY
DEDUCTIONS
NUMBER OF DEPENDENTS
```

Second, the major output reports to be produced from the database are identified along with the elements of data that will be required for each report. For example, if we know that we will need reports on the dates when a manager's employees are due for their next performance evaluations, we would include the following data elements: employee number, name, hire date, date of last review, performance rating, date of next review, and pay rate. This grouping of data elements would be considered a subschema.

FINALIZING THE DESIGN   The final step in the logical design of a database is to combine and refine the logical subsets of data—the subschemas—into an overall logical view of the relationships among all elements to be stored in the database—the schema. The schema includes a description of all the data elements to be stored, the logical records into which the data elements will be grouped, and the number of individual database files or relations to be maintained within the framework of the DBMS. In addition, the schema describes the relationships among the data elements and the structure of the database (that is, hierarchical, network, or relational model).

PHYSICAL DESIGN

Once the logical design of the database has been defined, the next step is to proceed with the physical design. The **physical design** of a database involves the specification of exactly *how* the data will be arranged and stored on the direct-access storage devices allocated for use by the DBMS. The objective of the physical design is to store data so that it can be updated and retrieved in the quickest and most efficient way possible.

One of the main considerations in the development of the physical design is the users' data-access patterns. In other words, how often will certain data elements need to be retrieved by the users? Knowing the patterns can improve speed and efficiency. Information about them is gathered during the logical design stage, often by counting the number of times users will access data elements by manual methods (such as opening a file drawer for a specific folder). Users' access patterns often change, so whatever physical design is developed must be continually reviewed and updated when necessary to conform to actual access patterns.

DATABASE ADMINISTRATION

The effective use of a database within an organization requires a great deal of cooperation and coordination. User requirements and needs throughout an organization need to be frequently reviewed, and the overall security and integrity of the database must be ensured. Organizations working with DBMSs quickly recognized the need for an individual or a group of individuals to coordinate all related activities and needs and to control the database. A **database administrator (DBA)** undertakes this function.

WHY ADMINISTER?

As we mentioned earlier, the development and implementation of a corporate-wide database is a major task that requires the complete support of management, a substantial amount of human resources, and often the expenditure of large sums of money. This task needs to be coordinated. In addition, the data in the database often represents the company's most precious asset, which must be managed well, so that it is not misused or damaged.

THE JOB OF THE DATABASE ADMINISTRATOR

The responsibilities for administering the database activities within an organization are usually assigned to an individual or a small group of individuals, depending on the size of the organization and the scope and complexity of the databases. The database administrator has six major responsibilities:

- *Database implementation.* The DBA plays a key role in the design and implementation of the database and participates in both the logical and the physical design phases. The DBA uses the data description language provided by the DBMS to create the data dictionary.
- *Coordination with user.* The DBA receives and reviews all user requests for additional DBMS support. The administrator establishes feasibility, resolves redundant or conflicting requests, and assists in the process of establishing priorities for the requests. In addition, the DBA is responsible for establishing and enforcing organization-wide DBMS standards for such things as techniques for accessing data, formats in which data elements will be stored, and data element names.

- *Backup and recovery.* The DBA is responsible for preparing a plan for periodically backing up the database(s) and for establishing procedures for recovering from the failure of the DBMS software or related hardware components.

- *Performance monitoring.* The DBA constantly monitors the performance of the DBMS using specialized software to calculate and record operating statistics. If a problem occurs, such as a slowdown in responsiveness, the DBA must identify the problem and take steps to improve the performance.

- *System security.* The DBA is responsible for designing and implementing a system of DBMS security that controls who has access to the database files, which DBMS operations can be performed, and which applications programs can be accessed. This system often involves the assignment of user identification codes and passwords.

Experience has shown that organizations that have a well-organized and well-staffed database administration department achieve a much higher degree of success in the use of the database management system to manage business information resources.

ADVANTAGES AND LIMITATIONS OF DBMS

The principal advantages of the DBMS approach include:

- *Elimination of data redundancy.* More storage becomes available when maintenance of redundant data elements among traditionally separate application files is rendered unnecessary.

- *Easy file updating.* Because there is only one copy of each data element, all applications have access to the most current data. In traditional systems in which the same element of data was kept on several different files, ensuring that all copies of the data element were updated when changes were made was a problem.

- *Data independence and simplification of program maintenance.* In a DBMS the programs are much more independent of the data than in traditional file processing systems. Previously, programs had to include a substantial amount of information about the format and structure of the fields and records in each file accessed. In a DBMS, this information is contained in the data dictionary; the programs do not need to contain these details. In traditional systems, when a change in format of one or more data elements was necessary, each program that used the data element had to be modified. In a DBMS only the data dictionary needs to be updated.

- *Increased user productivity.* The ability of a DBMS to respond quickly to user requests for additional information without involving the user in technical language manipulation encourages faster and more efficient work. The report generators and query languages associated with database management systems make them easy to use.

- *Increased security.* Centralized control of access to and use of the database is easily established. With traditional file processing systems, the data was too fragmented for effective security to be exercised.

- *Standardization of data definitions.* Before database management systems, each applications program could define similar elements of data with different names. However, the use of data dictionaries standardizes the names and descriptions of data elements.

Some disadvantages to using a database management system include:

- Database management systems are complex; extensive planning and a substantial amount of technical expertise are needed to implement and maintain a system.

- The costs associated with the development and operation of a corporate-wide DBMS can be substantial in terms of software and hardware acquisition, technical support personnel, and operations personnel.

- The consolidation of an entire business's information resources into a DBMS can create a high level of vulnerability. A natural disaster, a fire, or even a hardware- or software-related problem can cause the loss of the current version of the database files. This could be fatal for a business unless proper precautions are taken. A very thorough framework of policies and procedures must be established to ensure that backup copies of the database files are made on a regular basis, that a transaction log is maintained, and that documentation exists for recovery procedures.

ONWARD: SPREADING THE WORD

Having large amounts of integrated data available that can be efficiently and effectively retrieved and manipulated by a DBMS to help produce information gives power to the decision maker. But accessibility to data *beyond* the confines of one office system is often critical to successful decision making. This accessibility is provided by data communications and networking, the topics of the next chapter.

SUMMARY

Database management systems (DBMS)—comprehensive software tools that allow users to create, maintain, and manipulate an integrated base of business data—have become very popular in the business community as a means to support management information systems. In an integrated database, the records are logically keyed to one another so that all data on a topic can be retrieved by simple requests. Users will probably not get involved in designing databases (except for supplying job information needs to designers), but they will likely be involved in using a DBMS, especially on a microcomputer system.

File management systems used to be the only way of managing data and files. In these systems, data was stored in a series of unrelated files on tape or disk. The major problems associated with file management systems are (1) data redundancy—the same data appears in more than one file; (2) tedious updating procedures—because the same data appeared in many places, updating files was time-consuming; (3) poor data integrity—if some redundant data elements were missed during file updating, they were no longer current and could cause inaccurate information to be produced; and (4) lack of data and program independence—programmers could not use the data file to develop new programs because the data and the programs were restricted by existing formats. To update either the applications program or the data file became a major task.

Database management systems were developed to (1) make data independent of the programs, so that it is easy to access and change; (2) eliminate data redundancy; (3) establish relationships among records in different files; (4) define data character-istics; (5) manage file directories; (6) maintain data integrity; and (7) provide a means of securing access to the database.

DBMS software often uses a query language as an interface between the user and the system. This interface allows users to easily ask questions of the DBMS and obtain information to answer the questions and produce reports. DBMS software also includes capabilities to simplify report writing and maintain the database (util-ities) as well as to allow different applications programs to use the database (DML). During the design of the database, a data dictionary is constructed that contains all the data descriptions used by the DBMS to locate and retrieve data. The DBMS also can include a transaction log of current activity. This log can be used to update necessary backup copies of the database in case of failure of or damage to the operating database system.

A DBMS is usually modeled after one of three structures: hierarchical, network, or relational. These models differ in terms of the cost of implementation, speed, degree of data redundancy, ease with which they can satisfy information require-ments, and ease with which they can be updated.

The hierarchical database model resembles a family tree; the records are or-ganized in a one-to-many relationship, meaning that one parent record can have many child records. Records are retrieved from a hierarchical model by starting at the root record at the top and moving down through the structure. There is no connection between separate branches.

The network database model is similar to the hierarchical model, but it allows multiple one-to-many relationships (each child can have more than one parent) and relationships between records in different groups. Also, access to the database can be made from a number of points—not just from the top.

The relational database model is made up of many tables, called *relations*, in which related data elements are stored. The data elements are in rows, called *tuples*, and columns, called *attributes*. The main objective of the relational database model is to allow complex logical relationships between records to be expressed in a simple fashion.

In general, the hierarchical and network models are less expensive to imple-ment and allow faster access to data. However, they are more difficult to update and aren't as effective at satisfying information requirements as the relational model can be. Because the hierarchical and network models are older than the relational model, they are used most often on large computers. The newer relational model is used extensively on microcomputers; however, because relational models are so flexible in satisfying information requests, and because they aren't difficult to update, relational models are being used more and more on large computers.

The process of database design is usually carried out exclusively by specialists; however, users may have occasion to set up small databases for microcomputers. First, the logical design is set up; then the physical design. The logical design, which has to do with *what* the database is, from the business users' perspective, involves defining user information needs; analyzing data element requirements and logical groupings; finalizing the design; and creating the data dictionary. During the logical design the schema (the organization of the entire database, including the structure type) and the subschema (the way certain data elements are linked) are defined.

The physical design involves *how* the data will be physically arranged and stored on the storage devices used by the DBMS. During this design phase the database is actually set up, and the data is stored.

Databases are important business resources, and DBMS software is sophisticated; both of them must be carefully operated and controlled. For this purpose, the job of database administrator (DBA) has been created. The main responsibilities of a database administrator are (1) database implementation; (2) user coordination; (3) backup and recovery; (4) performance monitoring; and (5) system security.

In general, the main advantages of database management systems are (1) elimination of data redundancy; (2) increased ease of file updating; (3) increased data independence and simplification of program maintenance; (4) increased user productivity and efficiency; (5) increased security; and (6) standardization of data definitions.

The main disadvantages are (1) complexity; (2) high cost of implementation; and (3) vulnerability of consolidated business data in a central database.

KEY TERMS

child record
database
database administrator
  (DBA)
database management
  system (DBMS)
data dictionary
data independence
data integrity
data manipulation
  language (DML)

data redundancy
file management system
file updating
hierarchical database
  model
logical database design
network database
  model
one-to-many
  relationship

parent record
physical database design
program independence
relational database
  model
root record
schema
subschema
transaction log

EXERCISES

MATCHING

Match each of the following phrases with the statement that is the most closely related:

1. _____ database management system
2. _____ database
3. _____ data redundancy
4. _____ physical database design
5. _____ file management system
6. _____ data dictionary
7. _____ one-to-many relationship
8. _____ hierarchical database model
9. _____ transaction log
10. _____ network database model
11. _____ relational database model
12. _____ schema
13. _____ data independence
14. _____ database administrator
15. _____ record

a. A software tool that facilitates the creation and maintenance of databases.
b. Using this approach means that applications software programs can access data from only a single file.
c. A major limitation of file management systems.
d. A major advantage to using a database management system.
e. A collection of related files.
f. All the elements of data stored in a database.
g. A record of all activity that has affected a database during a period of time.
h. This model is composed of parent and child records (one parent to more than one child).
i. Hierarchical database model.
j. In this database model, each record can have more than one parent.
k. The most popular type of database model used on microcomputers.
l. The organization of a database in its entirety.
m. This involves specifying exactly how data will be arranged and stored on a storage device for use by the DBMS.
n. This person or group coordinates all related activities to control a database in an organization.
o. A group of related fields.

MULTIPLE CHOICE

1. Which of the following is characteristic of file management systems?
   a. data redundancy
   b. program dependence
   c. lack of data independence
   d. difficult to update
   e. all of the above

2. Which of the following is a type of DBMS software?
   a. query language
   b. report writer
   c. utilities
   d. data manipulation language
   e. all of the above

3. Which two files are constantly being used during DBMS use?
   a. data dictionary and query language
   b. data dictionary and transaction log
   c. query language and utilities
   d. data manipulation language and query language
   e. all of the above

4. Which of the following is characteristic of the network model?
   a. one-to-many
   b. many parents for each child
   c. program and data independence
   d. easy to update
   e. data redundancy

5. Which of the following is not characteristic of a relational database model?
   a. tables
   b. complex logical relationships
   c. fields
   d. records
   e. tree-like structure

6. Which of the following is a major step in designing a database?
   a. creating the physical database design
   b. creating the logical database design
   c. defining user information requirements
   d. development of an organization-wide model
   e. all of the above

7. Which of the following is not related to defining the logical design of a database?
   a. defining user information needs
   b. defining how data will be arranged on storage devices
   c. schema
   d. data dictionary
   e. none of the above

8. Which of the following is related to defining the physical design of a database?
   a. defining user information needs
   b. defining how data will be arranged on storage devices
   c. subschema
   d. data dictionary
   e. none of the above

9. Which of the following is not a database administrator's function?
   a. development of logical and physical database designs
   b. user coordination

    c. performance monitoring

    d. backing up the database

    e. none of the above

10. Which of the following best describes what a database is composed of?

    a. fields

    b. records

    c. files

    d. software

    e. none of the above

SHORT ANSWER

1. What are the advantages and disadvantages of a DBMS?

2. What are the advantages of organizing a database according to a relational model as opposed to a network model?

3. Why are DBMSs superior to file management systems?

4. What are the most important hardware components of a DBMS?

5. What are the major software components of most database management systems?

6. What are the differences between the logical and the physical designs of a database structure?

7. Why do you think microcomputer users are more likely than mainframe users to be involved with the design of a database?

8. Why is it important to administrate a company database?

9. What are data dictionaries and transaction logs? What are they used for?

10. What is a query language used for?

13

DATA COMMUNICATIONS

Getting from here to there has always fascinated human beings, going farther and doing it faster. Aside from the obvious thrills associated with speed, going places quickly means being able to stay connected with other people, to spread news and information and receive them in return—in other words, to *communicate*. Obviously, technology reached the point some time ago of allowing communication to occur without having to transport people from one place to another. But what about more recent developments? And what do they have to do with computers in business and the management of data and information? This chapter will explain how electronic data communications affects the business user.

PREVIEW

When you have completed this chapter, you will be able to:

■

Identify the basic characteristics of data communications

■

Briefly describe basic communications hardware

■

Name a few popular microcomputer communications software packages and discuss some of their capabilities

■

Explain what a communications network is and describe the typical network configurations

■

The User Perspective

The wheel, which is thought to have been invented around 3500 B.C., was a tremendous technological advancement; without it information would still be transported by people on foot or horseback, by smoke signals or drum sounds, by carrier pigeon. By now, however, people have refined the technology of motion to the point where mobility has become a way of life.

The invention of the computer and its introduction into the business environment in the early 1950s marked similar technological achievement. By the early 1960s, some information needed for business was available in computer-usable form "somewhere"; however, it may have been impossible or impractical to get it if the information needed was only available in a computer 1000 miles away. Modern **telecommunications,** or **electronic communications**—the movement of voice and data over long distances through the use of computers—has solved this problem.

You will encounter innumerable situations in the business environment that require data to be sent to, retrieved from, or shared among different locations. Here is a typical data retrieval scenario:

- A number of individual sales offices have accumulated their daily sales activity on their own computers.
- The company headquarters needs to prepare a daily summary of sales activity for offices by region and for all offices.
- At the end of each day, a computer operator at the headquarters location calls each office (or the call is made automatically by the computer) and directs the communications software to retrieve the daily sales summary file.
- To take advantage of low telephone rates, this entire activity takes place after the sales offices have closed for the day and all staff members have gone home.

The sending of data, or data transmission, could involve the following activities:

- At the end of each week, the company headquarters creates a summary file showing total sales for each week for each sales office.
- To provide each office with status information about how its sales total for the week compares with those of other offices, at the beginning of each week the company headquarters directs the communications software to send the previous week's sales summary file to each sales office.
- The company headquarters also uses data communications periodically throughout each week to make announcements about upcoming meetings, changes in sales prices, and so on.

Data can be shared among locations that have the hardware and software to access a database at a central location. And software can be shared among several users in one office through the use of a network configuration, which we will discuss later in the chapter. This chapter will provide you with the basis for understanding the communications activities you will likely perform in the business environment.

WHAT DOES IT TAKE TO COMMUNICATE?

To transmit or receive data, you must have special hardware—that is, a transmission method, which we will discuss shortly—as well as access to a telephone line or other transmission medium and special communications software on-line at both the sending and receiving locations. Learning to use the hardware and software involved in data communications in normal business situations is not difficult; in this chapter we will explain what they do.

CHARACTERISTICS OF DATA TRANSMISSION

When you are talking on the phone with another person who is a few houses away, you can probably hear that person clearly and do not need to speak loudly. However, often the farther away you are from the person, the harder it is to hear clearly what is being said because of static and other noise. A lot of noise increases the chance that parts of your message will be garbled or misinterpreted. This same problem can exist when data is transmitted over phone lines from computer to computer. To overcome this problem, alternative types of computerized data transmission have been developed, including satellite and microwave—although they are not without their own limitations, as you will see later on. But before we discuss the various methods of data communications, we need to discuss their common characteristics.

ANALOG AND DIGITAL SIGNALS

When we speak, we transmit continuous sound waves, or **analog signals,** that form what we call our "voice" (Figure 13.1). Analog signals could be compared to a steady stream of water coming out of a garden hose. These signals repeat a certain number of times over a certain time period—their **frequency,** which is measured in cycles per second, or *hertz*. Sometimes our voices sound high (composed of high-frequency sound waves) and sometimes our voices sound low (composed of low-frequency sound waves). Analog signals can also differ in **amplitude,** or loudness; a soft voice is at low amplitude. Telephone lines are currently an analog communications medium.

    Digital signals, in contrast, can be compared to the short bursts of water that shoot out of a timed garden sprinkler. These signals are discontinuous (discrete) pulses over a transmission medium (Figure 13.1). Computers communicate with each other in streams of binary digits (bits) transmitted in patterns of digital signals—a series of on and off electrical pulses. For data to travel from one computer to another across the phone lines, the sending computer's digital data must be converted into analog form and then reconverted into digital form at the receiving end—modulation and demodulation.

    Modulation refers to the process of converting digital signals into analog form so that data can be sent over the phone lines. **Demodulation** is the process of converting the analog signals back into digital form so that they can be processed by the receiving computer. The hardware that performs modulation and demodulation is called a **modem** (*mo*dulate/*dem*odulate); we'll describe modems in more detail later in the chapter. The sending computer must be connected to a modem that modulates the transmitted data, while the receiving computer must be connected to a modem to demodulate the data (Figure 13.2). Both modems are also connected to the telephone line.

FIGURE 13.1
Analog and digital signals. Analog signals are continuous waves whose patterns vary to represent the message being transmitted; digital signals are discontinuous, or discrete, bursts that form a transmission pattern. In this figure, the horizontal axis represents time and the vertical axis represents amplitude.

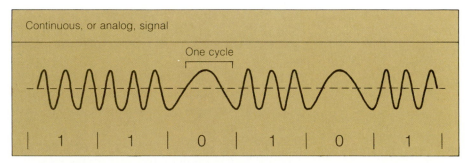

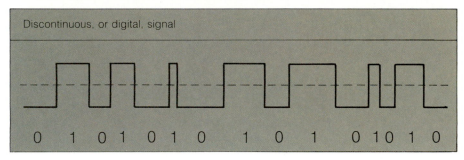

FIGURE 13.2
Helping computers wave to each other. Modems are hardware devices that translate digital signals into analog waves for transmission over phone lines and then back into digital signals again for processing.

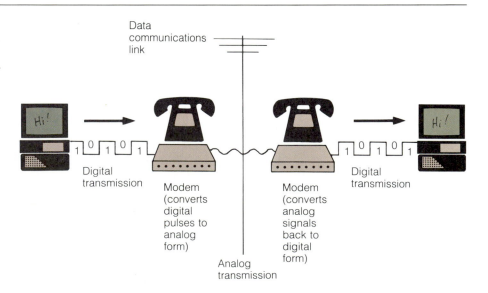

ASYNCHRONOUS AND SYNCHRONOUS TRANSMISSION

When signals are transmitted through modems from one computer to another, patterns of bits coded to represent data (Chapter 4) are sent one bit at a time. How does the receiving device know where one character ends and another starts? In **asynchronous transmission,** also called *start-stop transmission,* each string of bits that make up a character is bracketed by control bits (Figure 13.3). In effect, each group of digital or analog signals making up the code for one character is individually "wrapped" in an electronic "envelope" made of a start bit, one or two stop bits, and an error check bit (or parity bit). The error check bit is set according to a parity scheme that can be odd or even. (Recall from Chapter 5 that this means that the total number of bits representing a character must always be odd or always be even.)

For example, an ASCII "G" would be represented as 1000111, which has an even number of data bits in the "on" position (symbolized by a "1"). If an odd parity scheme is being used, then the start, stop, and error check bits would be set so that the overall total of bits in the "on" position would be odd—0100011101, per Figure 13.3.

FIGURE 13.3
Asynchronous and synchronous transmission. So that devices receiving data transmission can decode the beginnings and ends of data strings and check for transmission errors, the character strings are transmitted asynchronously or synchronously. Synchronous transmission takes less time because groups of characters are transmitted as blocks with no start and stop bits between characters.

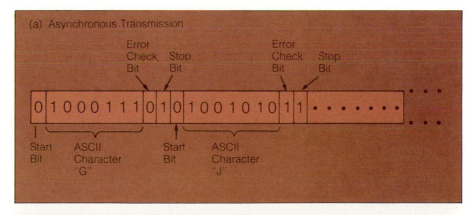

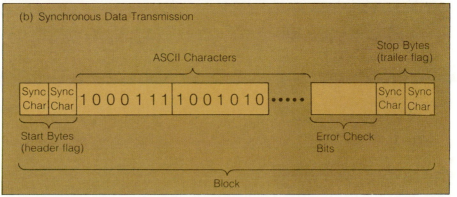

Users of both the sending and the receiving computers must agree on the parity scheme. The scheme chosen is set within a communications software program. For example, if computer A is transmitting to computer B, the users of both computers must first agree on a parity scheme (perhaps by having a telephone conversation), then load the communications software, and choose the agreed-on parity scheme. It doesn't matter which scheme is chosen as long as both computers are using the same one—odd or even.

Because asynchronous communication is inexpensive, it is widely used; however, it is also relatively slow, because of the number of parity and error check bits that must be transmitted with the data bits.

In **synchronous transmission,** characters can be sent much faster because they are sent as blocks. Header and trailer bytes, called *flags*, are inserted as identifiers at the beginnings and the ends of blocks. Synchronous transmission is used by large computers to transmit huge volumes of data at high speeds. Expensive and complex timing devices must be used to keep the transmission activities synchronized.

Most microcomputers are not equipped to handle synchronous data transmission. However, users recognize that synchronous transmission allows them to quickly download files from the company's main computer system into their microcomputers and to upload data that has been initially captured on these microcomputers to the company's main computer system, thus avoiding duplication of data entry on both systems. As a result, a number of vendors have produced "add-on" boards—for example, the IRMA board manufactured by Digital Communications Associates—that provide the microcomputer user with the hardware and software capabilities necessary for synchronous transmission (PC hookups to minis and mainframes).

SIMPLEX, HALF-DUPLEX, AND FULL-DUPLEX TRAFFIC

Besides signal type (analog or digital) and manner of data transmission (synchronous or asynchronous), data communications technology must also consider the *direction* of data traffic flow supported by communications links such as modems. In the **simplex** mode, data can travel in only one direction at all times (Figure 13.4). For example, environmental devices send information about temperature, humidity, and other conditions to a computer that monitors and adjusts office environmental settings automatically. However, the computer does not send information back to the devices. The simplex mode is also used occasionally in some local area networks, which we will discuss later.

A **half-duplex** communications link can support two-way traffic, but data can travel in only one direction at one time (Figure 13.4). This mode of transmission is similar to using a walkie-talkie. When you press the transmit button you can talk, but you cannot receive. After you release the transmit button, you can receive but you cannot transmit. Transmission of data in this mode over long distances can greatly increase the time it takes to communicate data. This delay is due to three factors: (1) the time needed for device A (at the receiving end) to change from receive to transmit mode, (2) the time required for device A to transmit a message to device B requesting confirmation that all is ready for transmission, and (3) the time required for device A to receive the confirmation that device B is ready to receive. The half-duplex transmission mode is most commonly used between a central computer system and the terminals connected to it.

Full-duplex transmission sends data in both directions simultaneously, similar to two trains passing each other in different directions on side-by-side tracks (Figure 13.4). This transmission mode eliminates the problem of transmission delay, but it is more expensive than the other two modes. However, when high-speed communication between computers and peripherals is necessary, the expense may be worthwhile.

FIGURE 13.4
Two-way, one-way, or the only way. Data traffic moves in simplex, half-duplex, or full-duplex modes.

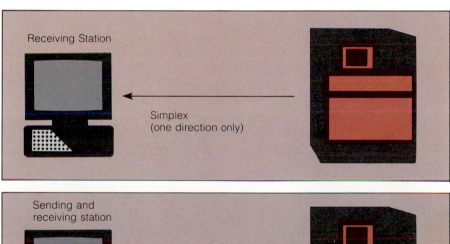

Receiving Station

Simplex
(one direction only)

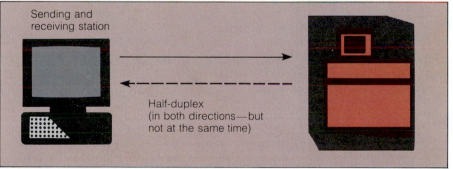

Sending and receiving station

Half-duplex
(in both directions—but not at the same time)

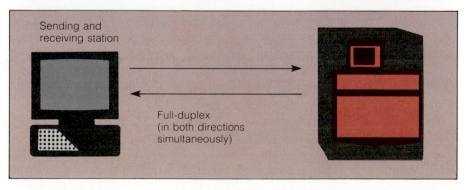

Sending and receiving station

Full-duplex
(in both directions simultaneously)

DATA TRANSMISSION MEDIA

To get from here to there, data must move *through* something. A telephone line, a cable, or the atmosphere are all transmission *media*, or *channels*. But before the data can be communicated, it must be converted into a form suitable for communication. The three basic forms into which data can be converted for communication are electrical pulses or charges (used to transmit voice and data over telephone lines), electromagnetic waves (similar to radio waves), or pulses of light.

The form or method of communications affects the maximum rate at which data can be moved through the channel and the level of noise that will exist—for example, light pulses travel faster than electromagnetic waves, and some types of satellite transmission systems are less noisy than transmission over telephone wires. Obviously, some situations require that data be moved as fast as possible; others don't. Channels that move data relatively slowly, like telegraph lines, are *narrowband* channels. Most telephone lines are *voiceband* channels, and they have a wider bandwidth than narrowband channels. *Broadband* channels (like coaxial cable, fiber optic cable, microwave circuits, and satellite systems) transmit large volumes of data at high speeds.

The transmission media used to support data transmission are telephone lines, coaxial cables, microwave systems, satellite systems, and fiber optic cables. Understanding how these media function will help you sort out the various rates and charges for them and determine which is the most appropriate in a given situation.

TELEPHONE LINES

The earliest type of telephone line was referred to as **open wire**—unsheathed copper wires strung on telephone poles and secured by glass insulators. Because it was uninsulated, this type of telephone line was highly susceptible to electromagnetic interference; the wires had to be spaced about 12 inches apart to minimize the problem. Although open wire can still be found in a few places, it has almost entirely been replaced with cable and other types of communications media. *Cable* is insulated wire. Insulated pairs of wires twisted around each other—called **twisted-pair cable**—can be packed into bundles of a thousand or more pairs. These wide-diameter cables are commonly used as telephone lines today and are often found in large buildings and under city streets. Even though this type of line is a major improvement over open wire, it still has many limitations. Twisted-pair cable is susceptible to a variety of types of electrical interference (noise), which limits the practical distance that data can be transmitted without being garbled. (To be received intact, digital signals must be "refreshed" every one to two miles through the use of an amplifier and related circuits, which together are referred to as a *repeater*. Although repeaters do increase the signal strength, which tends to weaken over long distances, they can be very expensive.)

COAXIAL CABLE

More expensive than twisted-pair wire, **coaxial cable** is a type of thickly insulated copper wire (Figure 13.5) that can carry a larger volume of data—about 100 million bits per second, or about 1800 to 3600 voice calls at once. The insulation is composed of a nonconductive material covered by a layer of woven wire mesh and heavy-duty rubber or plastic. Coaxial cable is similar to the cable used to connect your TV set to a cable TV service. Coaxial cables can also be bundled together into a much larger cable; this type of communications line has become very popular because of its capacity and reduced need for signals to be "refreshed," or strengthened (every two to four miles). Coaxial cables are most often used as the primary communications medium for locally connected networks in which all computer communication is within a limited geographic area.

MICROWAVE SYSTEMS

Instead of using wire or cable, **microwave** systems use the atmosphere as the medium through which to transmit signals. These systems are extensively used for high-volume as well as long-distance communication of both data and voice in the form of electromagnetic waves similar to radio waves but in a higher frequency range. Microwave signals are often referred to as "line-of-sight" signals because they cannot bend around the curvature of the earth; instead, they must be relayed from point to point by microwave towers, or relay stations, placed 20 to 30 miles apart (Figure 13.6). The distance between the towers depends on the curvature of the surface terrain in the vicinity. The surface of the earth typically curves about one foot every mile. The towers have either a dish- or a horn-shaped antenna. The size

FIGURE 13.5
Coaxial cable.

FIGURE 13.6
Microwave relay station.
Microwaves must be relayed
from point to point along
the earth's surface because
they cannot bend.

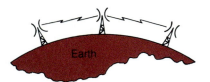

(a) Microwave line-of-sight links

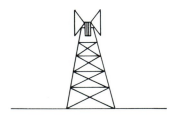

(b) Microwave tower

of the antenna varies according to the distance the signals must cover. A long-distance antenna could easily be 10 feet or larger in size; a dish of 2 to 4 feet in diameter, which you often see on city buildings, is large enough for small distances. Each tower facility receives incoming traffic, boosts the signal strength, and sends the signal to the next station.

The primary advantage of using microwave systems for voice and data communications is that direct cabling is not required. (Obviously, telephone lines and coaxial cable must physically connect all points in a communications system.) However, the saturation of the airwaves with microwave transmissions has reached the point where future needs will have to be satisfied by other communications methods, such as fiber optic cables or satellite systems.

SATELLITE SYSTEMS

Satellite communications systems transmit microwave signals (of a different frequency from those used on the earth's surface) from the earth to a satellite in stationary orbit around the earth (Figure 13.7). A **satellite** is a solar-powered electronic device that has up to 25 transponders (a small, specialized type of radio) that receive, amplify, and retransmit signals; the satellite acts as a relay station from microwave stations on the ground (called *earth stations*).

Although establishing satellite systems is costly (owing to the cost of a satellite and the problems associated with getting it into orbit above the earth's surface and compensating for failures), satellite communications systems have become the most popular and cost-effective method for moving large quantities of data over long distances. The primary advantage of satellite communications is the amount of area

FIGURE 13.7
**Satellite communications.
(a) The satellite orbiting the earth has solar-powered transponders that receive, amplify, and retransmit microwave signals to and from the earth's surface (b).**

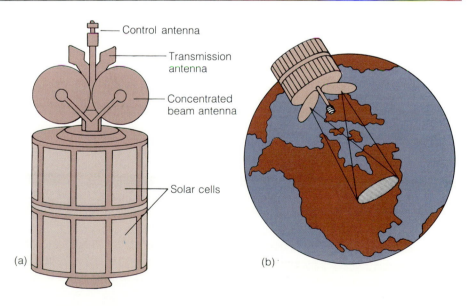

Control antenna

Transmission antenna

Concentrated beam antenna

Solar cells

(a)

(b)

that can be covered by a single satellite. Three satellites placed in particular orbits can cover the entire surface of the earth, with some overlap. However, satellite transmission does have some problems: (1) The signals can weaken over the long distances, and weather conditions and solar activity can cause noise interference. (2) A satellite is useful only for seven to ten years, after which it loses its orbit. (3) Anyone can listen in on satellite signals, so sensitive data must be sent in a secret, or encrypted, form. (4) Depending on the satellite's transmission frequency, microwave stations on earth can "jam," or prevent, transmission by operating at the same frequency.

Companies must lease satellite communications time from suppliers such as Westar (Western Union), Telstar (AT&T), Satellite Business Systems (partially owned by IBM), Galaxy (Hughes Aircraft), RCA, Comstar, and the American Satellite Company. Large companies with offices around the world benefit the most from satellite communications.

FIBER OPTICS

Although satellite systems are expected to be the dominant communications medium for long distances during the next decade, fiber optics technology is expected to revolutionize the communications industry because of its low cost, high transmission speed, low error rate, and message security. Fiber optic cables will probably replace copper wire as the major communications medium in buildings and cities; major communications companies are currently investing huge sums of money in fiber optics communications networks that can carry digital signals, thus eliminating the need for modems.

In **fiber optics** communications, signals are converted to light form and fired by laser in bursts through insulated, very thin (2000ths of an inch) glass or plastic fibers (Figure 13.8). The pulses of light represent the "on" state in electronic data representation and can occur nearly 1 billion times per second—nearly 1 billion bits can be communicated through a fiber optic cable per second. Equally important, fiber optic cables aren't cumbersome in size: A fiber optic cable (insulated fibers bound together) that is only 1/2 inch thick is capable of supporting nearly 250,000 voice conversations at the same time. However, since the data is communicated in the form of pulses of light, specialized communications equipment must be used.

Fiber optic cables are not susceptible to electronic noise and so have much lower error rates than normal telephone wire and cable. In addition, their potential speed for data communications is up to 10,000 times faster than that of microwave and satellite systems. Fiber optics communications is also very resistant to illegal data theft, because it is almost impossible to tap into it to listen to the data being transmitted—or to change it; in fact, it is currently being used by the CIA.

The communications needs of the 1984 Olympics in Los Angeles were supported by a fiber optics network that was set up by Pacific Bell. AT&T has already developed undersea optical fiber cables for transatlantic use in the belief that fiber optics will eventually replace satellite communications in terms of cost effectiveness and efficiency. And the Japanese have already laid an underwater fiber optic cable. Sprint is currently investing $2 million a day to complete a coast-to-coast, border-

FIGURE 13.8
Fiber optic cable. This figure shows a cross section of a fiber optic cable (top). Laser-fired light pulses (representing the "on" state in the binary system of data representation) are fired through a very thin glass or plastic fiber. (Bottom) Although dwarfed by a 1200-pair wire cable, typically used throughout the Bell system, the 144-fiber, half-inch diameter light-guide cable can carry nearly 50,000 simultaneous conversations—more than triple that of the larger cable.

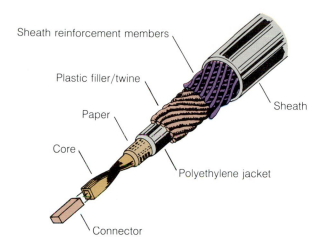

Sheath reinforcement members

Plastic filler/twine

Paper

Core

Sheath

Polyethylene jacket

Connector

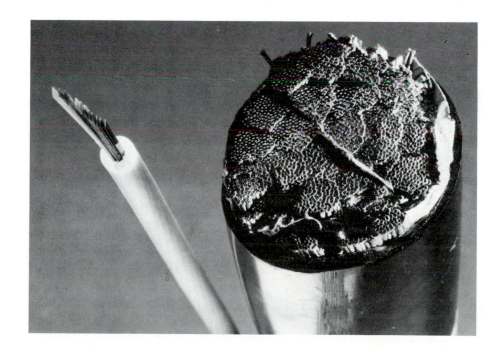

to-border fiber optics communications network laid along railroad rights-of-way in the United States that will be able to carry digital signals (analog voice signals will be converted to digital signals at company switching stations).

DATA COMMUNICATIONS HARDWARE

Much hardware used in data communications is operated by technical professionals and is rarely of immediate consequence to the user unless it stops working—when you're calling from New York and can't reach your division office in London, for example. However, you should become familiar with certain types of common business communications hardware: modems, which were described briefly at the beginning of this chapter, multiplexers, concentrators, controllers, front-end processors, and protocol converters.

MODEMS

Modems are probably the most widely used data communications hardware in business. They are certainly the most familiar to microcomputer users who communicate with one another or with a larger computer. As you learned earlier in this chapter, the word *modem* is actually a contraction of *mo*dulate and *dem*odulate; a modem's basic purpose is to convert digital computer signals to analog signals for transmission over phone lines, then to receive these signals and convert them back to digital signals for the receiving computer.

Most modems are categorized according to how they connect to the telephone line: acoustic or direct-connect. For many years, the **acoustic coupler** was the most widely used (Figure 13.9). This type of modem holds the telephone receiver in two rubber cups. The connection is then made acoustically (by sound). However, due to the nature of their connection to the phone line, they are very susceptible to noise, or interference. As a result, most acoustic modems are operated at speeds of only 300 bits per second or less, which is slow by today's standards.

In contrast, the **direct-connect modem** allows the user to directly connect the computer to the telephone line (Figure 13.10). The direct connection results in less interference and allows the modem to easily transmit and receive data at speeds from 300 to 2400 bits per second (bps, also called the *baud rate*). Some modems run at 9600 to almost 19,200 bps, but these modems, used with mini- and mainframe computers, are often more expensive than many microcomputers.

Direct-connect modems are either internal or external. An **internal modem** is located on a circuit board that is placed inside a microcomputer (actually plugged into an expansion slot). The internal modem draws its power directly from the computer's power supply. No special cable is required to connect the modem to the computer; instead, the phone line is plugged directly into the circuit board. The most recent internal modems have two phone plugs in the back. The second plug allows the user to plug in a telephone handset to carry on a voice conversation over the telephone line when necessary (you can't talk on a phone line that is being used to transmit data from computer to computer).

FIGURE 13.9
Acoustic coupler.
This type of modem holds
the telephone receiver in
two rubber cups to make
an acoustic connection between the computers using
the phone line.

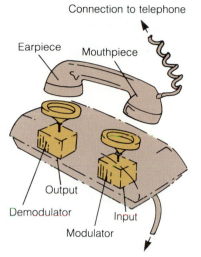

Connection to telephone

Earpiece   Mouthpiece

Output

Demodulator   Input

Modulator

Connection to computer

FIGURE 13.10
Direct-connect modems.
An internal direct-connect
modem (a) is placed inside
the computer; an external
direct-connect modem (b)
is outside the computer.

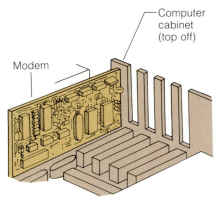

(a)

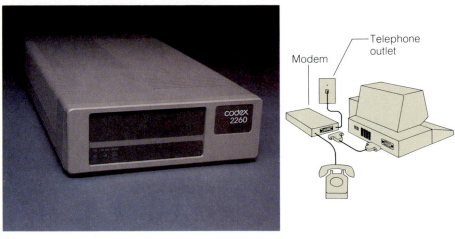

(b)

An **external** direct-connect **modem** is an independent hardware component—that is, it is outside the computer—and uses its own power supply (Figure 13.11). The modem is connected to the computer via a cable designed for the purpose. A simple external modem design to be used with a microcomputer costs less than $500; very fast, more complex modems can cost over several thousand dollars.

Business users who deal with modems and data communications must be sure they are communicating with compatible equipment; like other types of computer hardware and software, not all modems work with other modems, and not all modems work with the same type of software. In addition, microcomputer communications software packages—such as Smartcom II, CROSSTALK XVI, Red Ryder, InTalk, and MicroPhone—require users to set their systems at specific "parameters" so that their microcomputer can "talk" to another computer using the same parameters. (Parameters include speed of data transmission, parity scheme, direction of traffic, and so forth. The software package manual tells users how to set software parameters and how to use a small screwdriver to set certain switches in the external modem cabinet.) These software packages allow "smart" modems (with certain types of chips) to do more than simply transmit and receive; for example, you can arrange for automatic dialing and transmission, printing of incoming text, and storage of incoming data on disk.

MULTIPLEXERS, CONCENTRATORS, AND CONTROLLERS

When an organization's data communications needs grow, the number of lines available for that purpose often become overtaxed, even if the company has leased one or more private telephone lines—called *dedicated lines*—used only for data communications. *Multiplexing* optimizes the use of communications lines by allowing multiple users or devices to share one high-speed line (Figure 13.11), thereby reducing communications costs. Multiplexing can be done by multiplexers, concentrators, or controllers.

Briefly, a **multiplexer** is a data communications hardware device that allows up to eight, sixteen, or thirty-two or more (depending on the model) devices to share a single communications line. A **concentrator,** which also allows many devices to share a single communications line, is more "intelligent" than a multiplexer because it can store and forward transmissions. A **controller** also supports a group of devices (terminals and printers) connected to a computer. You won't need to get involved with many complex aspects of multiplexing unless you choose to take a high-level data communications course. If the computer in your office is connected to a multiplexer that is connected to a modem that is connected to a phone line that is connected to another modem connected to . . ., you won't have to learn more than the relatively simple steps involved to get data from one place to another.

FRONT-END PROCESSORS

In some computer systems, the main computer is conected directly into the multiplexer, controller, or concentrator. In other systems, it is first hooked to a **front-end processor,** a smaller computer that relieves the larger one of many data traffic management and communications functions (Figure 13.12). In effect, the front-end processor acts as a "mediator" between the network and the main computer, allow-

FIGURE 13.11
To multiplex or not to multiplex . . . This figure shows the basic difference between communicating with and without the use of a multiplexer.

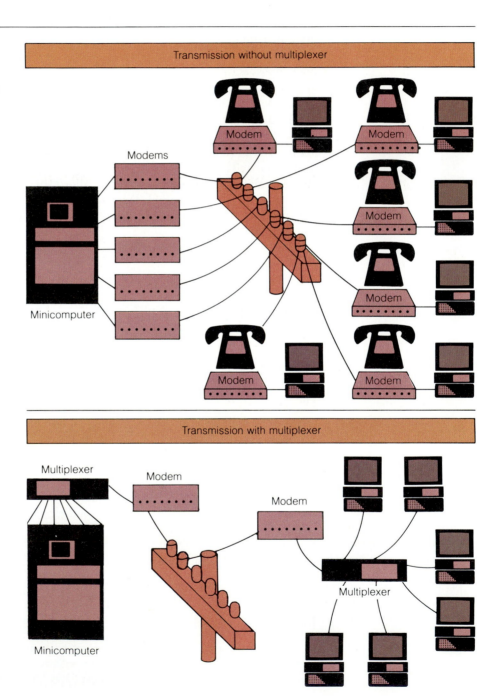

ing the main computer to concentrate on processing and improving the responsive-ness of the system to the user.

FIGURE 13.12
Help up front. A smaller computer, called a *front-end processor,* is often used to relieve the main computer of many communications functions.

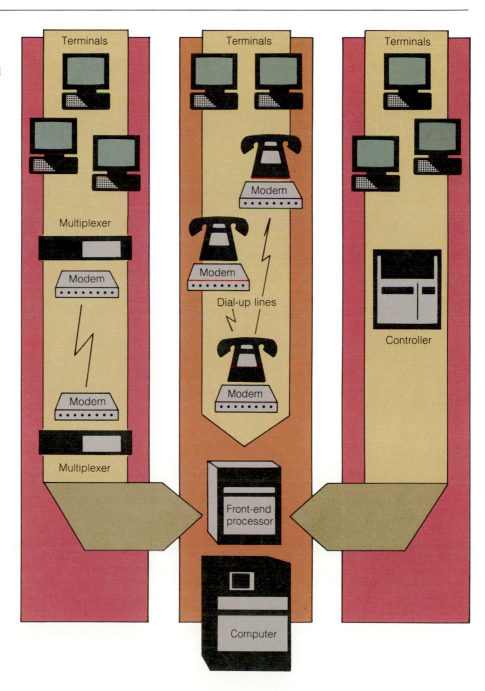

PROTOCOLS AND PROTOCOL CONVERTERS

One of the most frustrating aspects of data communications between different types of computers, especially between a microcomputer and a larger computer system, is that they often use different communications protocols. A **protocol** is the formal set of rules for communicating, including rules for timing of message exchanges, the type of electrical connections used by the communications devices, error detection techniques, means of gaining access to communications channels, and so on. To overcome this problem, a specialized type of intelligent multiplexer called a **protocol converter** can be used. Protocol converters are available that even allow a microcomputer operating in asynchronous mode to talk with a large IBM mainframe computer operating in synchronous mode. This type of device is being used by more and more companies that want to establish effective communications between personal computers and the main computer system.

COMMUNICATIONS NETWORKS

As we have talked about communications media and hardware, we have occasionally referred to communications *networks*. Networks are often used by business workers, and chances are that you will become acquainted with one or more types of communications networks in your job.

THE NETWORK: INTERCONNECTED COMMUNICATIONS

Information gains in value if it can be shared. A **network** is simply a collection of data communications hardware, computers, communications software, and communications media connected in a meaningful group to allow users to share information. The three most common types of networks are private, public, and international.

A **private network** is specifically designed to support the communications needs of a particular business organization. Many organizations with geographically separated facilities and a need for a large volume of data and voice communications implement or install their own private communications networks. The Southern Pacific Railroad was one of the first organizations to develop its own comprehensive microwave communications network to facilitate communication along all its rail lines. Its microwave towers can be seen along any of the major rail lines.

A **public network,** in contrast, is a comprehensive communications facility designed to provide subscribers (users who pay a fee) with voice and/or data communications over a large geographical area (in some cases coast-to-coast). Public networks are sometimes referred to as *common carriers* (for example, Bell Telephone and AT&T Communications) or *specialized common carriers* (public networks that provide more limited services, such as Western Union, the AT&T satellite system, Hughes Communications, and American Satellite Corporation, among others). Public networks provide a wide variety of services, including local telephone, long-distance telephone, satellite links, cellular radio (a type of mobile radio/telephone), telex (electronic transmission of text), and **teleconferencing** (the electronic linking of several people who participate in a conversation at the same time).

The term **international network** is used to describe a communications network specifically designed to provide users with intercontinental voice and data communications facilities. The majority of these networks use undersea cable or satellite communications.

NETWORK CONFIGURATIONS

A number of different network configurations, or shapes, are used to satisfy the needs of users in different situations. The basic types of configurations are star (and hierarchical) network, bus network, and ring (and token ring) network. Although each network configuration is actively used today by private, public, and international communications networks, you will most likely come into contact with one in the context of a local area network.

A **local area network (LAN)** is a communications network, connected by a length of wire, cable, or optical fiber, that serves a company or part of a company that is located on one floor, in a single building, or in offices within approximately two miles of one another; the LAN is generally owned by the company that is using it. Chances are that the microcomputer you will be using in your office will be part of a local area network. LANs allow office workers to share hardware—such as a laser printer or storage hardware—and to share software and data. The LAN also provides a communications link to outside communications systems, and it can be connected to other local area networks in different locations, either by public communications lines or by **dedicated lines**—lines leased by the company for its transmission purposes *only*. Note that modems are *not* needed within a local area network; special hardware and software are used instead.

In the 1970s, there were between 40 and 50 different plans available for LAN configurations. In an effort to standardize them, Xerox, Digital Equipment Corporation, and Intel Corporation joined to develop standard LAN guidelines that later became known as the Ethernet LAN. Among the requirements for the LAN are high data transmission rate, ability to cover a reasonable distance, low rate of data transmission error, ease of implementation, and low cost. Many companies today use the Ethernet standard for LANs.

STAR NETWORK   The **star network,** a popular network configuration, involves a central computer system that has a number of smaller computers and/or terminals tied into it (Figure 13.13). The small computers are often referred to as *nodes*. This type of network configuration is well suited to companies with one large data processing facility shared by a number of smaller departments. The central computer in the star network acts as the traffic controller between all the nodes and terminals in the system.

The primary limitation of a star network configuration is that the whole network is affected if the main computer "goes down" (fails to function). Since the nodes in the system are not designed to communicate directly with one another, all communication stops. Also, the cost of cabling the central system and the points of the star together can be very high.

When a number of star networks are configured into a single multilevel system, the resulting network is often referred to as a **hierarchical,** or **tree, network** (Figure 13.14). In this type of network a single large computer still controls all network activity. However, each (or some) of the computers connected into the main computer in the first level of the star has a star network of devices connected to it in turn.

Hierarchical network configuration is often used by large companies with a main communications center linked to regional processing centers. Each regional processing facility acts as a host computer to smaller offices or branch computer

FIGURE 13.13
Star network. In this network configuration, a central computer controls all the data traffic between smaller computers and terminals hooked up to it; it also controls communications to locations outside the LAN.

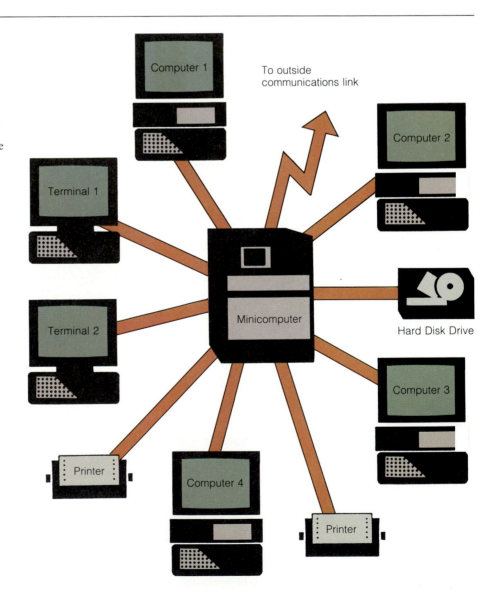

facilities within the region. The lowest-level computer facilities allow the users to do some stand-alone applications processing. The regional computer facilities are used to manage large business information resources (usually in the form of regional databases) and to provide processing support that the smaller computers cannot handle efficiently.

BUS NETWORK   In a **bus network,** a number of computers are connected by a single length of wire, cable, or optical fiber (Figure 13.15). The bus configuration is commonly used in local area networks in which office workers share hardware and software, as well as data. Because this configuration doesn't require a central computer

**FIGURE 13.14
Hierarchical network. This type of network configuration is basically a star network with smaller star networks attached to some of the nodes.**

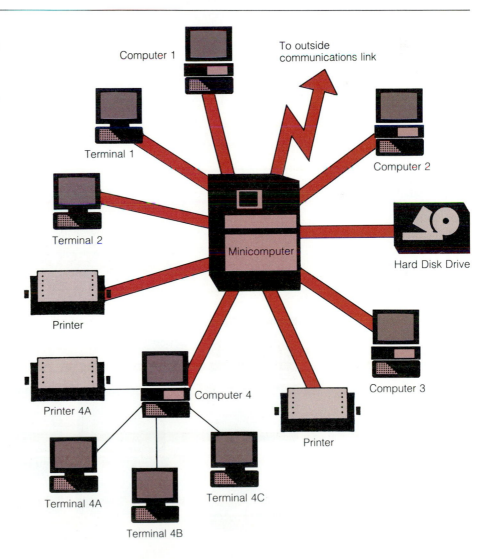

to control activity, none of the other computers is affected if one of the computers fails. Also, it is easy to connect additional computers to the network. Ethernet typically uses either the bus or the ring configuration (which we describe next).

RING NETWORK   A **ring network** is much like a bus network, except the length of wire, cable, or optical fiber connects to form a loop (Figure 13.16). This type of configuration does not require a central computer to control activity. Each computer connected to the network can communicate directly with the other computers in the network by using the common communications channel, and each computer does its own independent applications processing. When one computer needs data from another computer, the data is passed along the ring. The ring network is not as susceptible to breakdown as the star network, because when one computer in the ring fails, it does not necessarily affect the processing or communications capabilities of the other computers in the ring.

TOKEN RING NETWORK   In early 1986 IBM announced a new local area network for personal computers using the ring network configuration called the **token ring**

FIGURE 13.15
Bus network. All messages are transmitted to the entire network, traveling from the sender in both directions along the cable. Special access methods have been developed to allow computers to sense if the message is for them. The bus network does not need to be laid in a straight line; for example, it can also be U-shaped.

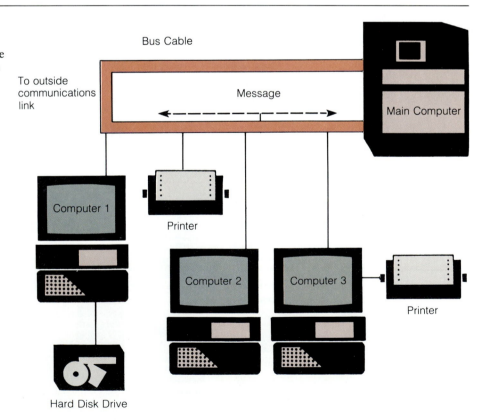

network (Figure 13.17). Before the token system was established, existing ring networks, such as Ethernet, used the following approach:

- A computer with a message to transmit monitored network activity, waited for a lull, and then transmitted the message.

FIGURE 13.16
Ring network. In this type of network configuration, messages flow in one direction from a source on the loop to a destination on the loop. Computers in between act as relay stations. If one computer fails, it can be bypassed, and the network can keep operating.

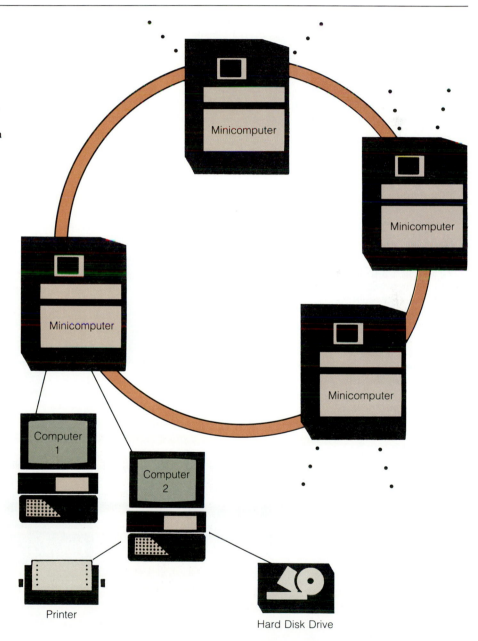

- This computer then checked to determine if other computers in the network tried to transmit a message at the same time, which might have garbled its message.
- If two or more computers did try to send messages at the same time, then both waited a different random period of time and tried to retransmit their messages.

Obviously, this procedure led to some message garbling and loss of time and productivity. In the token ring network, designed to eliminate these problems, a predefined pattern of bits, or *token*, is passed from computer to computer in the network. When a computer receives the token, it is allowed to transmit its message. Then the token is passed on. This method for transmitting messages (which can also be used in the bus network) prevents two computers from transmitting at the same time.

COMMUNICATIONS SERVICES, SYSTEMS, AND UTILITIES

If you have a microcomputer, a modem, a telephone, and data communications software, you can sell a printer, buy new software, play a game with one or more people, solve a complex problem by researching information in a database or having

FIGURE 13.17
Token ring network. In this type of ring network, each computer can get exclusive access to the communications channel by "grabbing" a "token" and altering it before attaching a message. The altered token acts as a message indicator for the receiving computer, which in turn generates a new token, freeing up the channel for another computer. Computers in between the sender and the receiver examine the token and regenerate the message if the token isn't theirs. Thus, only one computer can transmit a message at one time.

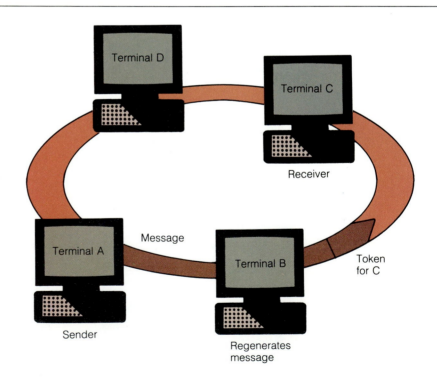

a conference with several experts, buy stock, book a plane reservation, send flowers, receive mail—all from your desk, using public communications networks. The introduction of the personal computer dramatically broadened the appeal of these networks to the business user and the general user. These networks provide users with the vast resources of (among other things) databases, teleconferencing services, information services, electronic bulletin boards, electronic mail, electronic stock trading, shopping, and banking.

Public Databanks/Information Services

Many industries and professions require access to large volumes of specialized information to conduct business. For example, a law firm must have access to a law library and other specialized legal information. Medical professionals must have access to a tremendous volume of patient histories and research-related information. To serve such needs, **public databanks,** or **information services,** were created by a number of organizations to provide users with access, for a fee, to large databases. (In addition to the fee, the user pays regular phone rates for hook-up time.) The user accesses the databank with a terminal or personal computer through one of the major common carrier networks (telephone lines). The databases contain information in text form and cover a wide range of topics such as health, education, law, humanities, science, government, and many others.

Some of the largest organizations providing public databases are Mead Data Central, Lockheed Information Systems, Systems Development Corporation, Data Resources, Inc., Interactive Data Corporation, Dow-Jones Information Service, The Source, and CompuServe.

Mead Data Central provides two very extensive public database services: LEXIS and NEXIS. The LEXIS database provides users with access to a tremendous pool of legal information for use in research. It incorporates data from a variety of sources including federal, state, and municipal court opinions, federal regulations, and a broad collection of recent publications in legal periodicals. The NEXIS database provides users with access to a huge amount of bibliographic data that has been collected from hundreds of magazines, newspapers, specialized newsletters, and other sources. In addition, NEXIS offers access to the complete text of the *Encyclopaedia Britannica*.

Lockheed Information Systems provides a public database service through its Dialog Information Service subsidiary. The DIALOG system provides users with access to close to 100 separate databanks covering a variety of areas, including science, business, agriculture, economics, energy, and engineering. DIALOG is regarded as the largest supplier of bibliographic data to computer users. To promote the use of the system after normal business hours, a special personal-computer-oriented service (called KNOWLEDGE INDEX) is made available at reduced rates.

Systems Development Corporation offers an information service called ORBIT SEARCH SERVICE. This service allows users access to over 70 specialized databases. Many of the databases available can also be accessed through the DIALOG system.

Data Resources, Inc., and Interactive Data Corporation both offer users access to a variety of statistical databanks covering such industries as banking, economics, insurance, transportation, and agriculture. The sources for their data include Chase Econometric Associates, Value Line, Standard & Poor's, and their own staff of economists.

The Dow-Jones Information Service provides users with access to one of the largest statistical databanks and a news retrieval service. The statistical databanks cover stock market activity from the New York and American stock exchanges. In addition, a substantial amount of financial data covering all of the corporations listed on both exchanges, as well as nearly a thousand others, is maintained. The Dow-Jones News/Retrieval system allows users to search bibliographic data on individual business and broad financial news compiled from a variety of sources including *Barron's* and *The Wall Street Journal*.

Since the early 1980s, several new information services have been created to provide personal computer users at home with easy access to the statistical and bibliographic databanks and other services. The most popular of these are The Source and CompuServe.

ELECTRONIC SHOPPING

One type of public network service provided to users is **electronic shopping** (Figure 13.18). To use this service, you dial into a network such as The Source or CompuServe and select the electronic shopping mode desired. A menu of major categories of items available is presented and you select one. You can then browse through the catalog—shown on the screen—looking for the desired item. When the item is found, you indicate that an order is to be placed and enter a previously

FIGURE 13.18
Spend money faster. Modems and communications software allow the computer user who subscribes to certain public network services to shop at home. In this example, if you want to buy a car stereo, you would tap the 5 key to see a list of brand names and types. You would then choose one of these to see a full item description, including price.

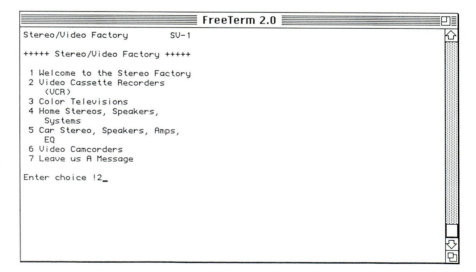

```
≡≡≡≡≡≡≡≡≡≡≡≡≡≡≡≡≡ FreeTerm 2.0 ≡≡≡≡≡≡≡≡≡≡

Stereo/Video Factory        SU-1

+++++ Stereo/Video Factory +++++

 1 Welcome to the Stereo Factory
 2 Video Cassette Recorders
   (VCR)
 3 Color Televisions
 4 Home Stereos, Speakers,
   Systems
 5 Car Stereo, Speakers, Amps,
   EQ
 6 Video Camcorders
 7 Leave us A Message

Enter choice !2_
```

assigned identification number and perhaps a credit card number (sometimes the credit card number is included in the user I.D. information).

The variety of goods available through electronic shopping has grown rapidly over the past four years and now includes a wide variety of name-brand goods at discount prices from nationally known stores and businesses. In fact, users now not only buy products but also make travel reservations.

ELECTRONIC BULLETIN BOARDS

The **electronic bulletin board** (Figure 13.19) is a popular information service that allows users to either place a message or advertisement into the system or scan the messages in the system. For example, suppose you have an item you would like to sell or trade—an automobile, bicycle, motorcycle, sports equipment, or even a personal computer or some software. After setting up your computer and modem with your communications software, you would dial the information service and select the electronic bulletin board mode. Next you would compose an electronic 3-by-5-inch card describing the item(s) for sale and include an electronic mailbox number to which inquiries can be directed. You can check back for responses over a period of days, or whatever is appropriate.

The procedure for scanning the bulletin board is very straightforward. Once you have entered the electronic bulletin board mode, you simply identify the type of item you would like to search for and let the computer do the work for you. You can also scan *all* the messages.

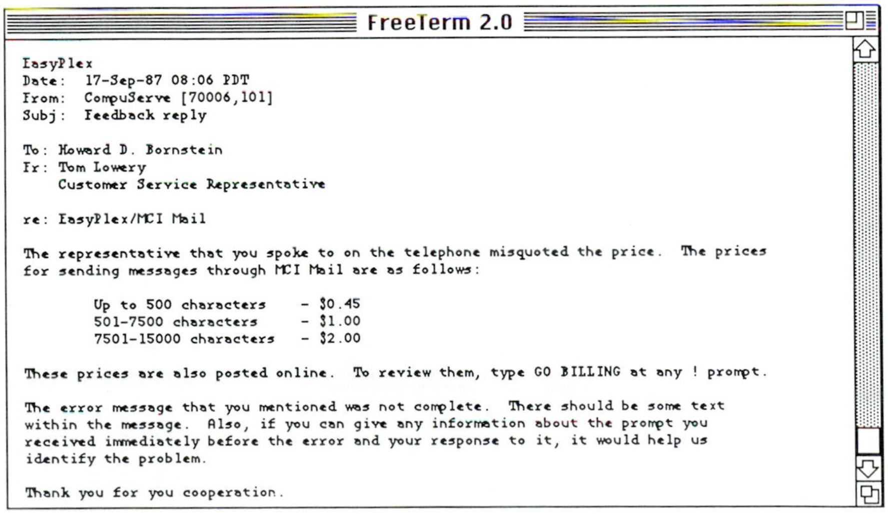

FIGURE 13.19
Have something to say? Electronic bulletin boards allow users to "post" messages on particular topics, read messages from other people, and reply to messages.

```
================= FreeTerm 2.0 =================

EasyPlex
Date:  17-Sep-87 08:06 PDT
From:  CompuServe [70006,101]
Subj:  Feedback reply

To: Howard D. Bornstein
Fr: Tom Lowery
    Customer Service Representative

re: EasyPlex/MCI Mail

The representative that you spoke to on the telephone misquoted the price.  The prices
for sending messages through MCI Mail are as follows:

        Up to 500 characters    - $0.45
        501-7500 characters     - $1.00
        7501-15000 characters   - $2.00

These prices are also posted online.  To review them, type GO BILLING at any ! prompt.

The error message that you mentioned was not complete.  There should be some text
within the message.  Also, if you can give any information about the prompt you
received immediately before the error and your response to it, it would help us
identify the problem.

Thank you for you cooperation.
```

ELECTRONIC MAIL

Many public information services provide an **electronic mail** service (Figure 13.20) for fast and inexpensive business and personal communications. Electronic mail is also used internally, within companies, to send and receive messages. Each user in the system is assigned a unique electronic mail address code. (This code is not tied to a specific location, as a ZIP code is.) When a message has been sent to a specific electronic mailbox, the user is automatically notified when he or she next logs onto the system. The user can then retrieve the message, print it, and send a response, as necessary. Once a message has been placed into the electronic system, it can be retrieved by the recipient from any location where the information service has established communications. Business users on the road often use their lap-top computers to check their electronic mailboxes for messages (the computer can be hooked up to the hotel telephone).

ELECTRONIC BANKING

In the past four years, many major financial institutions have begun to offer customers a new service referred to as **electronic banking.** This service allows customers to

FIGURE 13.20
No stamps necessary. Computer users can send and receive mail electronically, person-to-person. This Macintosh screen shows that Fred has no new mail to "open," 15 messages have been sent, and 3 messages remain to be sent. Fred's software also maintains an address book and a file for storing messages.

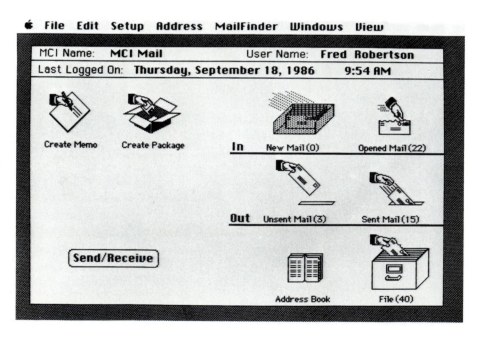

access banking services via a terminal or personal computer from the comfort of their offices or homes. The user just dials into the electronic banking service using the local-access telephone number. When the communications link has been established, the user is prompted to enter an identification code. If the code is accepted, the user can request a number of electronic banking services including:

- Retrieving the balance in checking and savings accounts
- Transferring funds between checking and savings accounts
- Directing that certain utility bills be paid directly by the bank
- Verifying the latest rates available on certificates of deposit, passbook savings accounts, and other investment options

ONWARD: WHAT'S NEW, WHAT'S NEXT?

You have spent a great deal of time learning about the computer-based information system: its components, what it does, how it's set up, and how it serves users and decision makers. However, one of the major problems involved with writing an introductory computer textbook is that many hardware components—and some software components—change so rapidly that it's hard to publish a book that is not out of date in some areas by the time it reaches the student. Therefore, in the next chapter we present trends and developments that are new right now and discuss the direction that information technology will probably take in the future—and how you, the user, may be affected.

SUMMARY

With the development of modern telecommunications, or electronic communications, business users and decision makers have been able to retrieve and send data quickly to and from widely scattered sources through the use of computers and communications hardware, software, and media.

To understand the basics of electronic data communications, one must know something about the characteristics of data transmission. When people speak, the sound travels as analog signals—continuous signals that repeat a certain number of times over a certain period (frequency) at certain amplitudes (degrees of loudness). Telephone lines carry analog signals. Computers, in contrast, use digital signals— discontinuous (discrete) pulses of electricity ("on") separated by pauses ("off").

When they communicate, the sending and receiving computers must use modems (*mo*dulate/*dem*odulate) to convert the digital signals into analog signals for transmission and then back again into digital signals for reception. Modems can be acoustic couplers (into which the telephone headset is placed), internal direct-connect (built into the computer or inserted on an add-on card or board), or external direct-connect (connected to the computer and the telephone by cable). Acoustic couplers are no longer commonly used.

When signals are transmitted from computer to computer, patterns of bits coded to represent data are sent one bit at a time. For the receiving computer to be able to determine where one character of data ends and another starts, data is sent either asynchronously or synchronously. In asynchronous transmission, each string of bits that make up a character is bracketed by control bits—a start bit, one or two stop bits, and an error check bit, or parity bit. Most microcomputers use asynchronous transmission.

In synchronous transmission, characters are sent as blocks with flags inserted as identifiers at the beginning and end of the blocks. This type of transmission is used by large computers to transmit huge volumes of data at high speeds.

Data communications technology must also consider the direction of data traffic: simplex (one way only), half-duplex (two-way traffic but only one direction at a time), or full-duplex (two-way traffic passing at the same time).

The media most commonly used for communication are telephone wires (open and twisted-wire), coaxial cables, atmosphere (microwave and satellite systems), and fiber optic cables. Each of these media differs in terms of the form of the transmitted data (electrical pulses, electromagnetic waves, or light pulses), the rate at which data moves through it, and its susceptibility to noise and "eavesdropping."

The hardware typically used to communicate between computers includes modems, multiplexers, concentrators, front-end processors, and microcomputer protocol converters. Multiplexers, concentrators, and front-end processors all allow multiplexing—the sharing of one high-speed communications line by multiple users or devices. A concentrator, which is like a multiplexer, is more "intelligent" because it can store and forward transmissions. A front-end processor, a smaller computer connected to the main computer, not only allows multiplexing but also relieves the main computer of many routine data traffic management and communications functions.

To communicate, the sending and receiving computers must follow the same rules, or protocols. In the case of microcomputer communications, the software parameters can be set on both ends to agree. In other cases, protocol converters must be used. For example, a protocol converter could be used to allow a microcomputer in asynchronous mode to communicate with a mainframe operating in synchronous mode.

Companies often set up communications networks, which are collections of data communications hardware, computers, communications software, and communications media connected in a meaningful group to allow users to share data and information. Three basic types of networks are private, public, and international. Private networks support the communications needs of particular business organizations. Public networks provide paying subscribers with voice or data communications over a large geographical area. International networks provide users with intercontinental voice and data communications facilities. Networks can be set up in different "shapes": star (and hierarchical) network, bus network, and ring (and token ring) network. The normal business user will encounter one of these network shapes in the context of a local area network (LAN), which is a network that serves a company or a part of a company that is located on one floor, in a single building, or in offices within approximately two miles of one another.

The star network uses a central computer connected to a number of smaller computers and/or terminals, called nodes. The nodes are not designed to communicate directly with one another, so if the main computer fails, the whole network "goes down."

In a more complicated star network called a hierarchical, or tree, network, some nodes have devices connected to them, in turn, in smaller star networks.

In a bus network, a number of computers are connected to a single communications line. In this network, if one computer fails, the others can continue to operate.

A ring network is much like a bus network, except that the communications line forms a loop. This network has no central computer, and each computer connected to the network can communicate directly with the others.

In the token ring network, predefined patterns of bits, or tokens, are passed from computer to computer. The computer with the token can transmit; the others cannot. This setup prevents the garbling of messages that occurs when more than one computer tries to transmit at the same time.

The business user can benefit from computer-to-computer communications using a number of public services and utilities to access data and information. Public databanks provide information about such topics as health, education, law, the humanities, science, and government. To use these databanks, the user pays a fee plus the regular phone charges. Public information services also provide the user with such conveniences as electronic shopping and banking, electronic bulletin boards, and electronic mail.

KEY TERMS

acoustic coupler
amplitude
analog signal
asynchronous
   transmission
bus network
coaxial cable
concentrator
controller
dedicated line
demodulation
digital signal
direct-connect modem
electronic banking
electronic bulletin
   board
electronic
   communications

electronic mail
electronic shopping
external modem
fiber optics
frequency
front-end processor
full-duplex
half-duplex
hierarchical network
information service
internal modem
international network
local area network
   (LAN)
microwave
modem
modulation
multiplexer

network
open wire
private network
protocol
protocol converter
public databank
public network
ring network
satellite
simplex
star network
synchronous
   transmission
telecommunications
teleconferencing
token ring network
tree network
twisted-pair cable

EXERCISES

MATCHING

Match each of the following terms with the phrase that is the most closely related:

1. _____ simplex
2. _____ modem
3. _____ modulation
4. _____ analog signals
5. _____ fiber optic cable
6. _____ full-duplex
7. _____ synchronous mode
8. _____ ring network

9. _____ multiplexer
10. _____ half-duplex
11. _____ direct-connect modem
12. _____ front-end processor
13. _____ asynchronous mode
14. _____ digital signals
15. _____ telecommunications

a. A type of modem—internal or external—that connects directly to the phone line and the computer.

b. The process of converting a digital signal into analog form so that data can be sent over the phone lines.

c. A communications medium that transmits data as pulses of light through strands of glass that are approximately two-thousandths of an inch thick.

d. Each character is transmitted one at a time—bracketed by start, stop, and parity bits—to the receiving computer.

e. A communications mode in which data is transmitted in two directions simultaneously.

f. A network configuration that operates with a number of computers connected in a closed loop.

g. Signals that are composed of continuous waves.

h. A data communications hardware component designed to allow two or more data transmissions to share a single communications line.

i. Signals that are composed of discontinuous electrical pulses.

j. The time it takes for a signal sent from one earth station to get to a satellite and the additional time it takes for the data to be rebroadcast from the satellite back to the receiving earth station.

k. The hardware component that performs modulation and demodulation.

l. A computer that relieves a larger computer of data traffic management and communications functions.

m. The number of frequencies that a channel can support.

n. A communications mode in which the data travels only in a single direction.

o. A communications mode in which data can move in two directions, but in only one direction at one time.

p. Characters are communicated in blocks with identifying flags to the receiving computer.

q. The movement of voice and data over long distances through the use of computers.

MULTIPLE CHOICE

1. The purpose of a modem is to:
   a. modulate
   b. change analog signals to digital signals
   c. demodulate
   d. change digital signals to analog signals
   e. all of the above

2. The modes that refer to how data is "packaged" to be sent from one computer to another are:
   a. digital and analog
   b. asynchronous and synchronous
   c. simplex, half-duplex, and full-duplex
   d. modulation and demodulation
   e. none of the above

3. Which of the following communications hardware devices converts analog signals to digital signals and vice versa?
   a. protocol converter
   b. front-end processor
   c. modem
   d. multiplexer
   e. none of the above

4. Which of the following communications hardware devices is the most important for a microcomputer to communicate with a mainframe?
   a. protocol converter
   b. front-end processor
   c. concentrator
   d. multiplexer
   e. none of the above

5. Which of the following is an advantage to using fiber optics data transmission?
   a. low noise level
   b. fast data transmission rate
   c. few transmission errors
   d. resistance to data theft
   e. all of the above

6. Which of the following communications services would be most useful if you want to get messages from your home company while you are on the road?
   a. electronic mail
   b. electronic shopping
   c. electronic bulletin board
   d. databanks
   e. electronic banking

7. Which of the following is required to communicate between two computers?
   a. protocol
   b. communications hardware

    c. access to transmission medium

    d. communications software

    e. all of the above

8. Which of the following might be used by a company to satisfy its growing communications needs?

    a. multiplexer

    b. concentrator

    c. controller

    d. front-end processor

    e. all of the above

9. Which of the following is considered a problem with satellite communications?

    a. Signals can weaken over long distances.

    b. A satellite is useful for only 7–10 years.

    c. Anyone can listen in on satellite signals.

    d. Satellite transmission can be "jammed."

    e. all of the above

10. Which of the following is composed of star networks?

    a. ring network

    b. hierarchical network

    c. local area network

    d. bus network

    e. none of the above

SHORT ANSWER

1. Describe a situation in which a computer user might want to communicate with another computer.

2. Describe the difference between synchronous and asynchronous transmission modes and how they affect the speed with which data can be communicated.

3. Describe the advantages and disadvantages of using the telephone line as a transmission medium.

4. Explain why a modem is necessary for computers to communicate over the phone lines.

5. Explain why some people think the biggest disadvantage of microwave systems is their popularity.

6. Describe the typical network configurations, or shapes, found in the business environment.

7. Describe the three modes of data traffic flow, and give an example of the use of each.

8. Describe four different types of transmission media, and give an example of how each is currently being used.

9. What are some of the advantages and disadvantages of satellite communications systems?

10. What is the function of a multiplexer?

BUILDING A DATABASE AND COMMUNICATING

THE STORY CONTINUES . . .

Two months have passed since we last checked on the progress of Sporting Life. In that period of time, you have opened a branch half the size of the original store on the north side of the city. The new store is also named Sporting Life; however, to keep the two stores straight, you refer to the second store as Sporting Life II. You have also purchased a complement of hardware and software that will help Roy with inventory, Mary with accounting, and the cashiers in both stores with sales transactions. A total of five computers were purchased, one of which will be used by the cashier in the new store. You had been wanting to open the new store for some time but waited until the plan for computerizing the two stores had been finalized. Episode 3 described the microcomputer systems purchased and the basic plan for using them. The cashier in the new store follows the same procedures as do the cashiers in the main store; he or she makes two copies of the day's transaction files on one or more floppy disks and hand-delivers one copy to Roy and one copy to Mary at the end of each day.

Although the plan, or logistics, for how the new microcomputer systems will be used was determined in the last episode, the physical implementation of the new system has yet to take place. In other words, Roy and Mary are still performing their inventory and accounting activities manually, and the cashiers are still tracking sales on multipart forms. Sporting Life has hired a consultant from Micro Mentor to help set up the new system. The consultant has noted that the following tasks need to be performed (these represent the types of tasks and training sessions that you may encounter in many jobs):

I. Tracking inventory on Roy's computer
   A. Using dBase III Plus (database management

systems software; Module D), design the structure for a database to be stored on Roy's computer that will keep track of inventory. Roy would like to be able to find answers to the following questions:

   - Which items in each store have fallen below the reorder point and need to be purchased?
   - Are any items in either store completely out of stock?
   - How many of each item have been sold so far this year?
   - What is the dollar investment in inventory, both overall and for specific product lines?

   B. Train Roy how to use dBase III Plus to add records to (update) the database, manipulate the database, and generate reports from the database about the status of inventory.

II. Tracking accounting on Mary's computer
   A. Design an electronic spreadsheet using Lotus 1-2-3 (Module C) to maintain the accounting ledgers and to process payroll.

   B. Train Mary and her two assistants to use Lotus 1-2-3 (Modules C and E) to perform the activities listed above and to produce business graphs, such as pie charts and bar charts, that will show the status of accounts receivable and accounts payable.

   C. Design the structure for a database using dBase III Plus to maintain customer records. Mary would like to be able to find answers to the following questions:

Episode 4, CONTINUED

- How many customers have shopped here more than once?
- Do most of our customers live in town?
- How many customers have been late on their payments more than once?

D. Train Mary and her two assistants to use dBase III Plus.

E. Train Mary how to use WordPerfect (word processing software; Module B) to generate reports.

III. Tracking sales on the cashiers' computers.

A. Using dBase III Plus, design the structure for a database that contains item number and price information that the cashiers can retrieve when processing a sale.

B. Using dBase III Plus, design the structure for a database that will allow the cashiers to track customer number if the customer has already established an account, customer name and address if the customer is a new customer, item purchased, quantity purchased, and method of payment (cash, check, or credit).

C. Train cashiers to use dBase III Plus to enter sales data into the database and to retrieve information from it.

IV. In addition, sometime soon you are going to purchase the necessary hardware and software (Cross-Talk IV) to allow the cashiers in both stores to communicate directly with both Roy and Mary's computers so that the cashiers don't have to hand-deliver daily transaction files to them on diskettes. Roy, Mary, and the cashiers will have to be trained to use the communications software to perform this activity.

Given the information available about what Roy, Mary, and the cashiers currently do when performing their respective activities—and what they would each *like* to do—the consultant is going to prepare the structures for the databases and spreadsheets and will conclude services by training each of them in how to use the databases and spreadsheets. Included in the consultant's services will be an evaluation of the feasibility of establishing communications between the cashiers' computers in both stores and Roy and Mary's computers in the main store.

TOPICS FOR DISCUSSION

The consultant used dBase III Plus to design the following data dictionaries.

A data dictionary to be used on Roy's computer for storing inventory data:

FIELD DESCRIPTION	FIELD NAME	FIELD TYPE	FIELD WIDTH	DECIMALS
Item Number	Itemno	Numeric	4	
Description	Desc	Character	15	
# in Stock	Instock	Numeric	3	
Reorder Point	Reorder	Numeric	3	
Vendor I.D.	Vendor	Character	10	

Episode 4, CONTINUED

A data dictionary to be used on Mary's computer for storing customer credit data:

FIELD DESCRIPTION	FIELD NAME	FIELD TYPE	FIELD WIDTH	DECIMALS
Customer #	Custno	Numeric	4	
Customer Name	Name	Character	20	
Address	Address	Character	20	
City	City	Character	20	
State	State	Character	2	
Zip	Zip	Numeric	10	
New Customer?	Type	Numeric	2	
Credit Status	Credit	Numeric	2	

1. If you had to create a data dictionary to be used on the cashiers' computers for tracking sales data, what fields would you include? (Keep in mind that the sales data is also used to update Roy's files and Mary's files. In addition, provision must be made for the different means of payment—cash, check, credit.)

2. What do you think the advantages would be if the cashiers' computers in both stores could act like terminals connected to Roy's computer? Could the inventory database on Roy's computer be automatically updated? Would time be saved? Are there any disadvantages? What type of network might be the most efficient?

3. What basic types of hardware and software would be required to set up the network in Question 2?

PART FIVE

5

TRENDS

How fast is fast, how small is small, how powerful is powerful? In the world of computers, yesterday's answer is not the same as today's answer, and neither answer is tomorrow's answer. But the major trend is clear: The speeds for processing, retrieving, and printing out information will increase, and, at the same time, further miniaturization will pack more hardware and software into smaller areas. Part Five examines this and other trends and discusses major developments in some specialized—and some new—areas of computer applications such as robotics, desktop publishing, artificial intelligence, and office design.

■

14

COMPUTER TRENDS:
THE USER PERSPECTIVE

Because it has radically changed the way information is produced and communicated, the computer will undoubtedly be labeled as one of the most significant inventions of the 20th century. But information technology is moving and changing so fast that it sometimes seems that we get the answers before we know the questions. Just where *is* computer technology going? And how will the new direction affect you, the user?

PREVIEW

When you have completed this chapter, you will be able to:

■

Describe some new hardware developments and some improvements in microcomputer processing that will affect the business user

■

Explain new developments in operating systems software and applications software

■

Describe how office setups are changing and how desktop publishing is becoming an increasingly important business tool

■

Name some uses of robotics, computer-aided design, computer-aided manufacturing, and computer-aided engineering

■

Discuss some social implications of the far-reaching role of computers in daily life

■

The User Perspective

In general, the life of the business user should get easier—at least as far as it relates to computers. Processing will get faster, equipment will take up less space, eyes will be subject to less strain, output quality will improve, electronic communications will become simpler, quicker, and less expensive. But will the new office become "paperless," as has been predicted for several years? Will you be able to avoid paper shuffling in your new job? Probably not. To help you understand why, we'll first examine trends in hardware and software, and we'll then describe developments in other areas of information technology that will affect the user. We'll conclude with a discussion of the role of the computer in society in general and leave you with a few things to think about.

Hardware

Computer hardware is rapidly becoming indispensable to the business user as it packs increasingly higher speeds and greater power into smaller units—thus bringing what used to be mainframe capabilities to the office desktop—and as it becomes more comfortable to use.

Display Technology: Thinner and Clearer

Although the CRT screen with improved resolution will continue to be the most-used desktop monitor, flat screens—in particular, liquid crystal display (LCD) and gas plasma display—will fulfill the need for PC compactness and portability, as proven by the success of the new lap-top computers. The LCD manufacturing process is complex, and quality control is difficult to maintain, but because of its low power consumption, which allows it to run for a reasonably long time on batteries, this type of flat panel display may be favored over gas plasma and electroluminescent display. Readability is being improved in LCD screens by backlighting (meaning that the screen has lighted panels *behind* the characters so that the user can read them without finding just the right angle of reflected light from a window or lamp), and experts expect the resolution to improve so that graphics will be of high quality. Color LCDs may also appear in the not-too-distant future.

In any case, as a new business user whose job involves some travel, you may expect to carry a lap-top computer with an LCD screen with you to update files, prepare reports, send information to your home company, check your company's database for product availability, and pick up messages from your electronic mailbox.

Printers: Eloquent Silence

As a new business user in an office, you can probably expect to be jangled by the loud noise of daisy wheel and dot-matrix printers—at least for a while yet. But as the cost of nonimpact laser printers decreases and their capabilities improve, more and more offices will turn to these quiet printers, especially in conjunction with desktop publishing (which we will discuss later). Laser printers already output hardcopy that looks almost like traditional typeset copy; soon you won't be able to tell the difference, and you will eventually be able to print out business charts and other graphics in color on laser printers. Laser printers will also get faster and smarter; that is, they will have more type fonts available and more memory, which will increase their flexibility (Figure 14.1). All these improvements mean that computerized businesses will be generating more paper than ever!

Something a bit farther down the road of laser printer developments is three-dimensional hardcopy—holograms. Some experts say that the technological pieces already exist; they just have to be put together to provide this innovative type of hardcopy. If you go to work, for example, for the health industry, for an architecture firm, or for an interior design firm, perhaps you will soon be helping to prepare three-dimensional reports. For instance, surgeons could view holographic output to study organs before operating on them; architects and interior designers could show clients more accurately how a building or an office will look.

In an effort to further increase printer speed, research is being done on other types of nonimpact printers, such as the light emitting diode (LED) printer (Figure 14.2), liquid crystal shutters, and ion-disposition printers. However, these printers are still in the research and development phase, and present trends indicate that you will not be dealing with them for quite a while.

DISKETTES: REDUCING THE STANDARD

Since IBM introduced its first microcomputer—the IBM PC—in 1981, the 5¼-inch diskette has been the industry standard, in spite of the fact that the popular Apple Macintosh computer (introduced in 1984) uses a 3½-inch diskette covered with sturdy plastic. Other computer manufacturers have also used the 3½-inch disk, including Hewlett-Packard, Grid Systems, and Toshiba in several popular lap-tops, but not until the introduction in early 1987 of the new IBM PS/2 series of micro-computers did the standard really change: IBM switched to the 3½-inch disk.

Because so much data has been recorded on 5¼-inch disks and because so many microcomputers that use this size disk are sitting in offices right now, the change to the 3½-inch size will not take place overnight. In other words, you will probably still be seeing and using the old familiar 5¼-inch floppy in your new job. Changing over will not be inexpensive, and it will take time. But it is already happening.

The 3½-inch disk has several advantages over the 5¼-inch floppy: First, it is more durable because it is covered by an inflexible plastic jacket that protects the disk from contamination and bending. Second, it can contain more data than the conventional 5¼-inch diskette—and in less space. The 3½-incher can fit in your shirt pocket. Third, the floppy disk drives that use these diskettes are smaller and lighter. Therefore, they require much less power to operate and they generate a lot less heat. And last, the 3½-inch drives are faster than the 5¼-inch drives because the read/write heads don't have to move as far to retrieve data; because data is stored more densely, the data transfer rate is greater.

FIGURE 14.1
LaserJet printer with font
cartridge (bottom). By
changing cartridges, the
user can change typestyles.

FIGURE 14.2
LED printer.

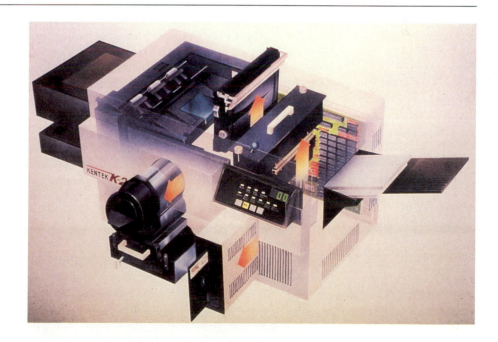

HARD DISKS: MORE BYTE

New hard disks are decreasing access time significantly, and their storage capacity is increasing. For example, a new 5¼-inch Winchester hard disk unit is available that stores 760 megabytes! And the new 3½-inch disk size standard is beginning to affect the hard disk market, too; one new 3½-inch hard disk unit that is sturdy enough to be dropped on the floor or even sent through the mail (a great improvement over current supersensitive hard disks) can store 30 MB.

What does this mean to you? As a personal computer user, it means that you will be able to manipulate more data faster, including graphics, which take up a lot of storage space. You'll even be able to build fair-sized databases on your own PC—much larger than current microcomputer users can build.

However, we are still talking about traditional *magnetic* hard disks. At the end of the century the typical business PC, which will manipulate *gigabytes* of data, will be using optical disks. Although at this point data is recorded by laser on optical disks either by the manufacturer (leaving the user with just read-only capabilities) or by the purchaser (WORM disks—for write once, read many), affordable read/write 5¼- and 3½-inch optical disks for microcomputers that can store 100 to 300 MB are expected to become available within the next few years. (Optical disk storage with a capacity of 1 trillion bytes is currently available for mainframes.) Optical storage will also be available in card form. Although optical disk access times are currently slower than magnetic hard disks, their speed is expected to improve dramatically. In the meantime, the new business user can expect to continue dealing with magnetic hard disks and floppy disks, with occasional magnetic tape backup.

MICROPROCESSORS

What in the 1940s weighed 5 tons, took up six rooms, processed about 10,000 instructions per second, and cost about $5 million now is 5 millimeters square, about ½-inch thick, can process about 4 million instructions per second, and costs less than $5. This revolution in computer processing was caused, as you know, by the development of the microprocessor. IBM's top-of-the-line PC, Model 80, priced at about $10,000, has essentially the same power as an IBM mainframe of more than ten years ago—but that machine cost $3.4 million at the time. If the automobile industry had advanced this fast since 1982, said Edward Lucente, the head of IBM's Information Systems Group, "Today we'd have cars that go zero to 60 in three seconds, circle the globe on a tank of gas, and cost half as much as they did six years ago. Of course, they would be difficult to get into, because they would be only half the size."

In general, current developments in the microcomputer industry indicate that the next generation of personal computers will change not so much in the way the hardware looks but in the way the computers work. That is, internal memory capacity will increase, operating systems will change, secondary storage will increase, and software will become more sophisticated and easier to use. In fact, PCs will have so much power that they will be able to devote 75% of their time to running software that improves interaction with the user and still calculate faster than current PCs.

Of course, many of these improvements relate to microprocessor developments. The processors that will enable you, the user, to enjoy these improvements have already been introduced—the Intel 80386, used in the Model 80 of the new IBM PS/2 series of microcomputers, and the Motorola 68020, used in the new Macintosh SE and Macintosh II. These 32-bit processors, which can process 32 bits, or 4 bytes, of data at a time, are much faster and more powerful than previous 8-bit or 16-bit microprocessors, and they allow microcomputers to support multitasking and increasingly sophisticated types of artificial intelligence programs, such as expert systems. The speed and power of microprocessors will continue to grow until the PC is no longer a uniprocessor system; that is, the PC will have specific processors for such functions as communications, graphics, and AI. Also, serial, or linear, processing—whereby instructions are executed one at a time—may become a thing of the past; true parallel processing—whereby many processors attack separate components of a problem simultaneously, which is already used to some degree in supercomputers—will eventually be available on microcomputers. (Some experts regard the 80386 processor as a miniature parallel processor because it can execute one instruction while simultaneously decoding a second and fetching a third.) Gallium arsinide (Figure 14.3), which works at least three times faster than silicon as a semiconductor, will probably be used to manufacture chips by the end of the

FIGURE 14.3
Gallium arsinide plant. A technician readies a carousel of gallium arsenide wafers for processing.

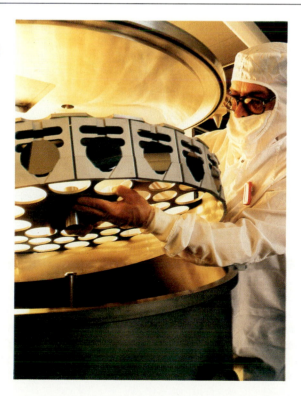

century (not that far away!)—that is, if other types of potentially cheaper and faster semiconductor material currently under research don't grab the spotlight.

How much the user gets out of the explosion in microprocessor power and speed will depend on what the software industry does with it. As we will discuss in more detail shortly, new operating systems are being developed to allow applications software manufacturers to take full advantage of the new microprocessors. In any case, when you start your new job, you will be able to "crunch" more data faster than current business users can.

INTERNAL MEMORY

One big limitation of early microprocessors and microcomputer systems was the amount of memory available. Chapter 5 told you that the amount of internal memory greatly affects the sophistication of the operating system and the applications software you can use. The best analogy for illustrating the importance of internal memory (RAM) is to liken the amount of RAM in your computer to the top of a desk. When you work at your desk, you like to have as much room as possible to spread things out. The early microcomputers had desktops large enough to hold only up to 64,000 characters (64 K) of data. Most later models usually supported 640,000 characters (640 K) of data (these models will continue to be used in business for several years yet). The new microprocessors can support even larger amounts of memory, but the 64 K and 256 K internal memory chips also had to be improved to take advantage of this support. (You'll recall that internal memory chips are combined in banks.) By making the chips more "dense"—that is, by making each chip capable of storing more data—new microcomputers can hold up to 2 MB RAM. This amount of internal memory will be necessary for you to take advantage of the new operating systems software and new, sophisticated applications software, especially the types that are highly memory-dependent, such as electronic spreadsheets, graphics, and AI-related programs.

MAINFRAMES, MINIS, AND SUPERCOMPUTERS

In Chapter 1, we said that some mainframe computers are so powerful that they are referred to as supercomputers. Indeed, supercomputers are "state-of-the-art" devices with such processing power and speed that ordinary computers pale by comparison. Early supercomputers were used in U.S. government agencies, such as the National Security Agency, or nuclear research facilities, such as the Lawrence Livermore and Los Alamos laboratories. Very few machines were available for either industrial or university research communities. However, in the early 1980s, universities and commercial users began to recognize that their processing needs had become so sophisticated that they needed supercomputers. As a result, the use of the supercomputers began to expand into research areas in government and industry such as chemistry, graphics, medical research, structural analysis, astronomy, geophysics, aerospace, weather forecasting, oil reservoir modeling, automobile engineering, particle physics, and defense.

Until 1983 these supercomputers were developed in the United States (indeed, the U.S. Department of Defense is still providing great opportunities for research in this area). However, as computer-related technologies have expanded into other countries, competition has begun to arise—notably from Japan. In 1985, there were reportedly fewer than 100 supercomputers in the world. This may not sound like much of a market; however, the value of these machines is enormous for two reasons. First, their development generates a great amount of pressure on technological research: When advances are made, they tend to filter down quickly into the mainframe, minicomputer, and microcomputer industry. Second, the supercomputer can tackle problems that other computers can't. These complex problems occur in areas such as aerodynamic design, weather prediction and analysis of planetary weather systems, development of nuclear weapons, compressing movies onto compact disks, animation, and holography. Some American universities use supercomputers on a timesharing basis at a cost of between $2000 and $3000 per hour. The NSF Supercomputer Network makes supercomputer cycles available to university researchers at a lower cost. (Universities in Japan can use such computers for less than $100 per hour, because of subsidies provided by the Japanese government to stimulate the development and use of supercomputers.) The Cray 2 (Figure 14.4), the Hitachi S810/20, and the Fujitsu VP200 are three commonly used

FIGURE 14.4
Cray 2 supercomputer.

supercomputers. These computers process at speeds of about 400 to 500 million operations per second (Mflops). Plans are already underway to develop supercomputers with performance capabilities of 10,000 to 30,000 Mflops.

The two basic approaches to developing a supercomputer differ in terms of the number of central processing units employed. In the first approach, a moderate number of very fast processors are linked together to perform linear processing. The second approach involves the use of a large number of processors to perform parallel processing; this is the supercomputer direction of the future. In supercomputer parallel processing, as many as 64,000 processors with a complexity of connectedness that begins to approach biological complexity will operate simultaneously to solve problems. The Connection Machine (Figure 14.5), invented by Danny Hillis of Thinking Machines in Cambridge, Massachusetts (who once put together a working computer made entirely from Tinkertoys), is a parallel processing supercomputer. The first one, sold to the Massachusetts Institute of Technology, stands 6 feet wide and 6 feet deep and costs about $1 million. It's currently being used to design its successor!

We know that developments in supercomputer-related technologies will lead to tremendous improvements in computer processing power. Many of these improvements will filter down and be used in the minicomputers and microcomputers that are used in business and industry to manage day-to-day activities. In addition, supercomputer vendors expect to sell more of these machines to universities in the United States and to the aerospace, automotive, and oil/gas exploration industries.

FIGURE 14.5
The Connection Machine. The 2500 Mflops/2500 Mips CM-2 is the newest member of the Connection Machine® family of parallel computers. The 5-foot cube houses the system's 64,000 processors. The Data Vault™ mass storage system uses dozens of small disk drives to provide very rapid access to 10 GB of data. Connection Machine systems are currently installed in major corporations, government laboratories, and universities.

SOFTWARE

As we mentioned, the degree to which you will be able to take advantage of computer hardware developments—especially new microprocessors—will be controlled by software developments. Some experts think that you will eventually be able to walk into your office and your PC will sense your presence, turn itself on, and automatically deliver your electronic mail before you even touch a key! Software will borrow techniques from artificial intelligence and allow PCs to "learn how" a particular user prefers to operate the system; different levels of complexity will be available to adjust to the user's skill level. But most experts agree that it will take several years for software companies to even bring their programs up to date with hardware introduced as early as 1987. In any case, software developments will make computer systems easier for you to use.

SYSTEMS SOFTWARE

Up to now, most users haven't been interested in operating systems—as long as they were compatible with the applications software the users wanted to run. This probably won't be true in the future. With the increased power of micros, operating systems software will offer many more useful capabilities to the user than basic file management programs such as copying files, renaming files, and so on. The operating systems of the future will offer the user standardized approaches to relatively routine operations like indexing files, networking, and windowing. They will also allow multitasking. IBM's new operating software, OS/2, which will support multitasking, will probably be available for its new PS/2 series of microcomputers by the time you are reading this book. So will an improved version of MS-DOS, version 3.3, by Microsoft. In the meantime, AT&T's UNIX operating system, which is compatible with a wide variety of microcomputers and minicomputers, will be used in increasing numbers of businesses to support multi-users and multitasking. New operating systems should allow users to work in simple English rather than jargon or seemingly cryptic statements.

Portability will also improve. This means that more operating systems will become standardized so that they can be used on different computers; thus, applications software will no longer have to be written in different versions for different operating systems. However, you, as a new user, will still have to deal with the current incompatibility of some operating systems with some hardware and the incompatibility of both of these with some software.

In addition, future operating systems will provide additional support for controlling and running local area networks so that businesses can share storage, peripherals, and software—not just data. They will also support transmitting and retrieving of information via modems from computers at other locations; in other words, they will take over some functions of current communications software.

Operating systems software may also be composed of different modules that perform different functions. In this way, the operating system can be tailored to specific pieces of hardware and specific users' needs.

Because the current trend is for operating systems to be easy to interface with, the use of graphics, icons, and mice will increase. As more and more capabilities are added to the operating system, it will be more difficult to distinguish where the operating system leaves off and the applications software begins.

APPLICATIONS SOFTWARE

Some experts think that, for microcomputer use to continue to grow, software must be more specialized. However, other experts believe that the next generation of software development tools will be so easy to use that specialized programs will be unnecessary. In fact, Apple recently released HyperCard for the Macintosh. This new type of software takes on some of the responsibilities of systems software while providing some ready-to-use applications—however, it allows ordinary users to write their own customized, specialized software easily, without writing in complex computer language. HyperCard can produce not only text and graphics, but also sound and video animation. Whatever the approach, applications software will become much more sophisticated. For example, given about 3 gigabytes of RAM, a 60-MHz 32-bit processor, and the right software, you will be able to set up a voice/video conference with your counterpart in Japan and have your PC program automatically transcribe—in both languages—the conversation, display a summary of past meetings, and telecommunicate all designated data to the locations you determine. For the time being, however, applications software developers are working on eliminating differing data formats. This means that the data created with one program will be accessible to all other programs—users can keep the applications software packages they're used to, such as dBase III Plus, Lotus 1-2-3, or Word-Perfect, but produce files that users with other packages can use.

COMMUNICATIONS

We have already mentioned the most important development that is changing the present and future of electronic communications—the fiber optics Integrated Services Digital Network, which will replace analog phone lines in most businesses. The use of fiber optics will improve the accuracy rate of data communications and protect data security. It will also enable the high-speed transmission of graphics, moving images, and voice and data messages. Until the change to fiber optic lines is complete, and modems are no longer needed, microcomputer modem speeds will increase from the currently common 1200 and 2400 baud (bits per second) to approximately 19,200 baud. Modems will also continue to become more intelligent and take over some of what now are microcomputer functions.

In addition, the use of local area networks (LANs) will increase to allow businesses to keep up with the increasing power of microcomputers. And most LANs will be connected to corporate communications networks. To guarantee the security of data available to users of a LAN, considerable security measures are currently incorporated into all levels of communications networks. In addition to measures commonly in use, companies can purchase retina-scanning devices called *Eye-dentify* to prevent unauthorized people from using the system. These devices can also identify people already on the network who are trying to get into a file they are not supposed to be using. The technology is based on the fact that no two people have the same pattern of blood vessels in their retinas. Retina-scanning devices are already used to guard large mainframe and minicomputer systems.

Research and development in communications is also working on a voice data terminal—a microcomputer with telephone and voice-mail messaging. This type of computer would use voice recognition to allow you to control the computer over the telephone (if you were on the road, for example).

ARTIFICIAL INTELLIGENCE

For years researchers have been exploring the way people think in the hope of creating a computer that thinks like a person. And little doubt exists that artificial intelligence (AI) has the complete attention of computer scientists; indeed, it is their main focus for the present and the future. However, no agreement exists about what artificial intelligence *is*. Existing definitions are contradictory: Some experts say that AI is the science of making machines do things that would require intelligence if done by a person. Others state that if we can imagine a computer that can collect, assemble, choose among, understand, perceive, and know, then we have *artificial intelligence*. Still others believe that there is no such thing as intelligence that is "artificial" and that, therefore, the term *knowledge-based system* should be used.

Why do the definitions differ? First of all, there is not—and never has been—a single agreed-on definition of *human* intelligence. Second, consensus on the point at which a machine exhibits intelligence is difficult to achieve. For example, years ago when a computer could play tic-tac-toe, some researchers considered it to be intelligent because it could choose the next best possible move and could beat its human opponents. Today most researchers no longer think that a machine's ability to play tic-tac-toe is enough to reflect intelligence. Other characteristics have been added to our definition of intelligent behavior—for example, the ability to reason logically and respond creatively to problems.

WHAT IS AI SUPPOSED TO DO?

The aim of AI is to produce a generation of machines that will be able to communicate with us by speech and hearing, use "vision" (scanning) that approximates the way people see, and be capable of intelligent problem solving. Some of the primary areas of research within AI of particular interest to business users are robotics, natural language processing, and expert systems. We have already discussed expert systems as part of decision support systems in a management information system. The next sections will briefly describe robotics and natural language processing.

ROBOTICS   According to *Webster's Ninth New Collegiate Dictionary*, a robot is an automatic device that performs functions ordinarily ascribed to human beings or that operates with what appears to be almost human intelligence. In the field of artificial intelligence, there are intelligent robots and unintelligent robots. Most robots are unintelligent; that is, they are programmed to do specific tasks, and they are incapable of showing initiative. An unintelligent robot cannot respond to a situation for which it has not been specifically programmed. Intelligence is provided either by a direct link to a computer or by on-board computers that reside in the robot. Robotic intelligence is primarily a question of extending the sensory (for example, vision) and mobility competence of robots in a working environment.

In the future, reasoning ability will be incorporated into robots, thus improving their ability to behave "intelligently." Robot vision has already been successfully implemented in many manufacturing systems. To "see," a computer measures varying intensities of light of a shape; each intensity has a numerical value that is compared to a template of intensity patterns stored in memory. One of the main reasons for the importance of vision is that production-line robots must be able to discriminate among parts. General Electric, for example, has Bin Vision Systems, which allow a robot to identify and pick up specific parts in an assembly-line format.

Another area of interest is the "personal" robot, familiar to us from science fiction. Existing personal robots exhibit relatively limited abilities, and whether a sophisticated home robot can be made cost-effective is debatable. B.O.B. (Brains On Board) is a device sold by Visual Machines that can speak (using prerecorded phrases), follow people around using infrared sensors, and avoid obstacles using ultrasonic sound. Software will allow the robot to bring its owner something to drink from the refrigerator. The performance limitations of personal robots reflect the difficulties in designing and building intelligent robots. In fact, we have just begun to appreciate how complicated such mundane tasks as recognizing a can of Pepsi in the refrigerator can be.

NATURAL LANGUAGE PROCESSING   The goal of natural language processing is to enable the computer to communicate with the user in the user's native language, such as English. The primary difficulty in implementing this kind of communication is the sheer complexity of everyday conversation. For example, we readily understand the sentence "The spirit is willing, but the flesh is weak." One natural language processing system, however, understood this sentence to mean "The wine is agreeable, but the meat has spoiled." It turns out that the system must have access to a much larger body of knowledge than just a dictionary of terms. People use their world knowledge to help them understand what another person is saying. For example, we know the question "Coffee?" means "Do you want a cup of coffee?" But a computer would have difficulty understanding this one-word question.

Most existing natural language systems run on large computers; however, scaled-down versions are now available for microcomputers. Intellect, for example, is the name of a commercial product that uses a limited English vocabulary to help users query databases on both mainframes and microcomputers. One of the most successful natural language systems is LUNAR, developed to help users analyze the rocks brought back from the moon. It has access to detailed world-extensive knowledge about geology in its knowledge database and answers users' questions.

The use of natural language on microcomputers isn't limited to database programs. In 1985 GNP Corporation introduced a product called HAL to the users of Lotus 1-2-3 (an electronic spreadsheet package). HAL interprets all the user's typed requests and then instructs the 1-2-3 program to execute the appropriate commands. HAL contains a limited amount of artificial intelligence that interprets sentences the user types in colloquial English. HAL understands more than just 1-2-3 terms; it knows quite a bit about microcomputer processing in general.

FUTURE DIRECTIONS

The field of artificial intelligence is still very much an emerging discipline, with contributions needed from a variety of other disciplines (for example, linguistics). These disciplines will shape the character of AI in the years ahead.

We can expect more AI products to be available in the commercial marketplace, particularly in business and manufacturing. Carnegie-Mellon and Westinghouse Corporation are developing the factory of the future, which will include the use of intelligent robots and expert systems. Personal computers will be parallel processing machines, each one with as many as 32 processors and 1 gigabyte of internal memory, working at a rate of 10 million instructions per second. With this kind of power available, we can expect large expert systems to migrate to microcomputers. At the moment, the general consensus is that *true* expert systems cannot run on microcomputers.

Expert systems will be available for most subject areas. Wherever human expertise exists, it may be possible to develop a computer model of this expertise. One consequence of this may be increased automation of specialist tasks (for example, credit scoring for loans) and concomitant unemployment among these specialists. Artificial intelligence is having, and will have, a social impact that will require our thoughtful attention.

DESKTOP PUBLISHING

"Corporate Publishing Takes Off," "Desktop Publishing Comes to the PC," "New Products Expected to Spur PC Publishing," "IBM, HP Gear Up to Assault Desktop Publishing Market." You'll find these and similar headlines if you pick up a computer magazine or periodical such as *InfoWorld*, *PC World*, or *Computerworld*. These articles, and hundreds more like them, are referring to what has come to be known as *desktop publishing*—a combination of microcomputer hardware and software that together provide the capability to produce near-typeset-quality output in a variety of sizes, styles, and type fonts (Figure 14.6). This technology can integrate, or combine, graphics and text on a professional-looking page.

Because it can lead to tremendous savings, desktop publishing should significantly affect anyone who currently sends text and/or graphics out to a professional typesetter. Instead of hiring a typesetter to format documents and graphics into reports, which can become extremely costly, with a desktop publishing system you can design the document yourself. This has the following advantages:

1. *You save money.* Sending a report out to a professional typesetter can easily cost a few hundred dollars.

2. *You save time.* Using a desktop publishing system can cut down the time spent on preparing documents by nearly 50%. Because you are preparing the report yourself electronically using a desktop publishing system, you can make any needed revisions immediately. The turnaround time necessary to make revisions when you are using a typesetter can easily add days onto a production deadline.

3. *You maintain control.* You are in charge of the final output and production schedule.

The disadvantages of desktop publishing center on the following issues:

1. The quality of an image that has been generated by a professional typesetter is still better. The clarity, or resolution, of an image is measured in terms of the number of dots per inch that make up the image. The resolution of an image that has been generated by a professional typesetter is around 1200 dots per inch; in comparison, the resolution of an image generated by a desktop publishing system is around 300 dots per inch. Most people, however, find it hard to tell the difference between the typeset image and the image that was desktop-published (Figure 14.7). Also, the dollars saved versus lower resolution is a fair trade-off for most people.

2. To produce a professional-looking report, the user not only needs the appropriate software but also some basic typesetting and design skills. You might

FIGURE 14.6
Integration of text and graphics. AST's desktop publishing system, the Premium Publisher, uses the IBM-AT-compatible CPU. This workstation is a powerful document-handling system that includes scanning, printing, computing, and integrated text and graphics display capabilities. Typical applications include layout and design of newsletters, brochures, ads, price lists, proposals, financial reports, manuals, and forms.

have the best hardware and software around, but if you don't follow some specific guidelines, your output will lose its effectiveness. Desktop publishing software provides the user with hundreds of different options for formatting text and graphics. What size type should you use in the headings? How many columns of text should you have on this page? Where should the bar chart be positioned on the page? How big should it be? Many people spend so much time dealing with questions such as these that time is wasted. Before attempting to generate a report using a desktop publishing system, the user should read at least a few of the many articles available in computer magazines that provide simple guidelines for generating effective reports.

Despite desktop publishing's disadvantages, it has been received very well in the business community. Understanding the highly manual and labor-intensive traditional methods for assembling business documents and graphics into reports will help you to understand why. When typesetting is required, most firms today still send the text to be included in a report to a professional typesetter. The document often needs to be re-keyed by the typesetter if it wasn't delivered in a computer-usable format (such as on a diskette), which can waste valuable time. The resin-coated paper onto which text is typeset can cost around 50 cents a sheet. For Sperry Corporation, which needs more than 120,000 typeset pages per year, the paper alone costs approximately $60,000 annually! In comparison to the cost of the manual cut-and-paste process that must be performed to put text and graphics together on report pages—for example, stylized headlines, business charts, and text in special formats such as multiple columns of text—the cost of paper is relatively

FIGURE 14.7
Typeset versus desktop-generated copy. As you can see, the typeset copy on the left does not look much different from the copy on the right, which was produced by a desktop laser printer. (From *The Art of Desktop Publishing* by T. Bove, C. Rhodes, and W. Thomas, Bantam Books, New York, 1987.)

Remember the last time you prepared some text to be typeset? Did you spend a lot of time on the preparation and proofreading, and also a lot of money on a vendor's service, without much control over the schedule? Would you prefer to do the typesetting in your office, see the results immediately, and make corrections at no extra charge? Wouldn't you rather use an inexpensive personal computer so that you only have to type the text once, and have the computer do all the proofreading?

Remember the last time you prepared some text to be typeset? Did you spend a lot of time on the preparation and proofreading, and also a lot of money on a vendor's service, without much control over the schedule? Would you prefer to do the typesetting in your office, see the results immediately, and make corrections at no extra charge? Wouldn't you rather use an inexpensive personal computer so that you only have to type the text once, and have the computer do all the proofreading?

insignificant. With revisions, an 8½-by-11-inch page can easily end up costing between $200 and $400. According to InterConsult of Cambridge, publishing is the second biggest expense for most companies (second to personnel) and typically consumes between 6 and 10 percent of a company's gross revenues.

Given the obvious cost savings that it can provide, why did it take so long for desktop publishing to catch on?

DESKTOP PUBLISHING'S HARDWARE REQUIREMENTS

Desktop publishing is the result of technological advancements in three areas: microprocessors, laser printers with memory, and sophisticated publishing software. First, because of improvements in the processing power of microcomputers, they are now capable of satisfying the processing requirements necessary to calculate character widths and to draw special fonts and images. Also, with the current high-capacity storage devices available for use with microcomputers, such as hard disks and hard cards, microcomputers can satisfy the tremendous storage requirements imposed by desktop publishing. The storage requirements for one page that combines text and graphics can be as much as 1 million bytes (one megabyte). Included in many desktop publishing systems is an external hard disk that is dedicated to storing the text and graphics outputs resulting from processing.

Second, desktop publishing requires that a laser printer be specially configured with a large amount of memory. For a laser printer to effectively combine text and graphics on a single page, a *page description language*, such as Adobe's Postscript, must be stored in the printer's memory. This special language can take up to half a megabyte of memory. Often this language is stored in the read-only memory (ROM) of the printer. Fortunately, laser printer technology has kept up with desktop publishing demands and can satisfy the memory requirements imposed by desktop publishing.

Third, sophisticated software, referred to as *page description software*, which takes advantage of both the increased processing power and storage capacities of a microcomputer and the flexibility in terms of output that a laser printer provides, allows the user to combine text and graphics in an organized format on a single page.

A typical desktop publishing system, including a microcomputer, laser printer, and page description software, costs between $6000 and $10,000. For the individual, this may sound like a lot of money, but when you consider that you might easily spend that much having just a few reports or projects professionally designed and typeset, the cost doesn't look so bad. For businesses that might easily spend over $100,000 per year, the $10,000 figure is something to celebrate. The cost of a desktop publishing system increases when certain other peripherals, such as an optical scanner for scanning drawings and photos into a report and a mouse and graphics tablet for drawing specialized images, are included in the overall system.

PAGE DESCRIPTION SOFTWARE   When a business user prepares a report, the text and graphics typically included in the report have been generated using a number of different software programs. Perhaps a word processing program was used to generate the text and an electronic spreadsheet program was used to generate the tables and business graphics for the report. Page description software allows the user to combine the elements from different files that have been generated using different software programs into one file, or output report. Page description software falls into two categories—code-oriented and "what-you-see-is-what-you-get" (WYSIWYG).

With a *code-oriented* page description language, formatting instructions are embedded (keyed) into a document in the form of codes. Code-oriented packages provide the user with more sophisticated desktop publishing options, compared to the WYSIWYG packages, and are based on traditional typesetting techniques, which also use formatting codes. There are two disadvantages to using this type of package. First, because of its high degree of sophistication, the user should have some typesetting experience before attempting to use the package. Second, the user can't see the final output until it's printed out. A user unfamiliar with how certain codes will affect the report may have to perform countless revisions. However, these programs usually require less internal memory, processing power, and storage requirements than the WYSIWYG programs. Among the code-oriented packages being used today are SC Laserplus, from Graham Software Corporation, and Deskset, from G.O. Graphics. With these programs, creating a report that combines text and graphics might involve the following:

1. The page description language is loaded into the memory of the computer.

2. A document that was created using a word processing program is retrieved from a storage device into internal memory.

3. Special codes (Figure 14.8) are embedded in the document that instruct the printer how to format the text in terms of type size, font style, and page layout. If a graph that was generated using a different program is also to be included in the report, the appropriate codes (which can be determined by looking in the documentation manual that accompanies the software) should be put into the document to instruct the printer what to do.

4. When the report is printed out, the user reviews the output to see if the codes used gave the intended results. If not, the user must modify the codes until the resulting report is in the desired format.

WYSIWYG programs (PageMaker from Aldus Corporation and Ventura Publisher Edition from Xerox Corporation) allow the user to see the report on the screen as it will appear when it is printed out (Figure 14.9). Many people prefer the WYSIWYG programs over the code-oriented programs for this very reason, because they don't have to wait until they print to see what a report will look like. With this type of program, the user chooses from menu options to format the text. This type of software is more power-, memory-, and storage-hungry than code-oriented software.

IS IT WORD PROCESSING OR DESKTOP PUBLISHING?

The distinction between the definitions of *word processing* and *desktop publishing* is already becoming blurred; by 1989 or 1990 the definitions may be one and the same. Traditional word processing packages provide the user with commands that allow for

FIGURE 14.8
Format codes.
The top two lines were
printed according to the
codes listed below. The
output was not displayed
before it was printed.

DR. SCIENCE

He's not a real comedian

```
%!
/paperheight 11 72 mul def
/paperwidth 8.5 72 mul def
/width paperheight def
/height paperwidth 2 div def
/margin .375 72 mul def
/xcenter paperwidth 2 div def
/ycenter paperheight 2 div def

%xcenter ycenter translate
%.25 .25 scale
%xcenter neg ycenter neg translate

90 rotate
0 0 moveto paperheight 0 rlineto 0 paperwidth neg rlineto
paperheight neg 0 rlineto closepath 0 setlinewidth stroke

/bumpersticker
{
    /AvantGarde-Demi findfont setfont
    (ASS, DR. SCIENCE) dup stringwidth pop
    width margin sub margin sub exch div /points exch def
    /AvantGarde-Demi findfont
    [points 0 0 points 1.5 mul 0 0 ] makefont setfont
    margin margin 135 add moveto show

    /AvantGarde-DemiOblique findfont setfont
    (He's not a real comedian) dup stringwidth pop
    width margin sub margin sub exch div /points exch def
    /AvantGarde-DemiOblique findfont
    [points 0 0 points 1.5 mul 0 0 ] makefont setfont
    margin margin 20 add moveto show
} def

0 height neg translate
0 0 moveto width 0 rlineto stroke
bumpersticker
0 height neg translate
bumpersticker

showpage
```

the easy entry, editing, and printing of text. More and more word processing programs, such as Microsoft Word, now include desktop publishing capabilities by providing the user with a set of format codes to embed in the document.

Microsoft Word is perfect for handling simple publications, such as newsletters and memos that don't require professional typesetting. It allows the user to perform complex formatting involving multiple columns of text and to design headlines. Microsoft Word also supports a number of different fonts and is compatible with such laser printers as the HP LaserJet and LaserJet Plus. Spellbinder Desktop Publisher, from Lexisoft, is a product that features a word processor and desktop publishing capabilities, including typesetting. This product allows for the integration of text and graphics into the same document.

FIGURE 14.9
WYSIWYG document. The menu below was displayed on the screen "as is" before it was printed out.

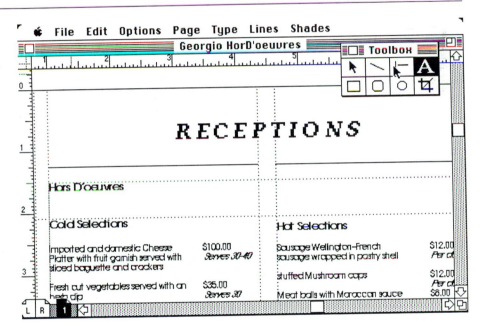

RECEPTIONS

Hors D'oeuvres

Cold Selections

Imported and domestic Cheese Platter with fruit garnish served with sliced baguette and crackers — $100.00 / Serves 30-40

Fresh cut vegetables served with an herb dip — $35.00 / Serves 30

Selection of duck, pork and chicken truffles pate — $40.00 / Serves 20

Hot Selections

Sausage Wellington–French sausage wrapped in pastry shell — $12.00 / Per dozen

stuffed Mushroom caps — $12.00 / Per dozen

Meat balls with Moroccan sauce — $8.00 / Per dozen

Onion Quiche — $12.00 / Serves 15

At this time, the desktop publishing capabilities provided by word processing packages aren't nearly as extensive as those provided by dedicated packages such as PageMaker, but many people believe that in the future desktop publishing and word processing may become one and the same.

COMPUTER-AIDED DESIGN, MANUFACTURING, AND ENGINEERING

Industry, especially manufacturing, has probably experienced the greatest economic impact of computer graphics. Mechanical drawings that used to take days or weeks to complete can now be done in less than a day. Among other things, the drawings can be three-dimensional, rotated, shown in detailed sections or as a whole, and automatically rendered on a different scale. But the use of computer graphics has evolved beyond the simple rendering of drawings; it is now used to help design, engineer, and manufacture products of all kinds, from nuts and bolts to computer chips to boats and airplanes. Computer-aided design (CAD) shortens the design cycle by allowing manufacturers to shape new products on the screen without having to first build expensive models (Figure 14.10). The final design data and images can be sent to a computer-aided engineering (CAE) system, which subjects the design to extensive analysis and testing that might be too expensive to do in the real world (Figure 14.11). From there, the data may be sent to a computer-aided manufacturing (CAM) system, which makes use of the stored computer images in automating the machines (unintelligent robots) that manufacture the finished products (Figure 14.12). Computer simulation in industry has increased productivity enormously and made previously expensive procedures affordable.

OFFICE TRENDS: UP-TO-DATE PLACES FOR KNOWLEDGE WORK

You will probably hear the term *knowledge worker* when you enter the business world. It was coined to describe users whose job responsibilities principally involve receiving or creating, processing, and transmitting information. Knowledge workers are the principal component in the information system and comprise the new majority in business. Knowledge workers' jobs depend on information instead of, for example, manufacturing goods or growing crops. Think of all the companies that manufacture, transport, or transmit information—overnight mail, computer information services, consulting firms, and so on. Because most knowledge work is done in the office, any improvements in how work is performed in the office will have an effect on productivity and on all of us who end up becoming knowledge workers. Better information equals better decisions, from the level of clerk through middle management to top management—all of whom may be knowledge workers.

In the mid-1970s, businesses began to be bothered by bottlenecks caused by the flood of information they had to deal with and its associated costs. To improve the

FIGURE 14.10
CAD. Computer-aided design allows new products to be shaped on the screen without first having to build expensive models.

FIGURE 14.11
CAE. This automation engineer is using a software package produced by Calma Company to put a robot through its paces on a computer screen—rather than through "trial and error" on the factory floor.

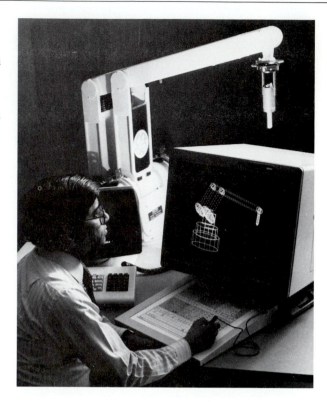

FIGURE 14.12
CAM. Automatic welding system at a Chrysler assembly plant uses computer-controlled robots for consistent welds of all components in the unitized body structure.

office situation, businesses started employing mechanization, then computerization, and now they are heading toward integration. *Mechanization* focused on individual tasks or activities. At this stage, sophisticated types of office equipment were acquired to speed up paper handling. *Computerization* focused on introducing some degree of computer-based data processing. In a large office, for example, a minicomputer or mainframe computer system may have been introduced to handle some of the more routine processing activities such as accounting, payroll, and personnel. In some cases, personal computers were introduced for use by staff members on an individual basis. In a small office, a personal computer may have been introduced as the only computerized processing component.

Very few offices, however, have reached the stage of *integration*—where the "office of today" is brought into the realm of the "office of tomorrow." Integration means using computers to relate all office and company activities to one another in an efficient and productive manner through the use of systems design and analysis, management information systems, and local area networks and electronic communications. Some of the activities and support services that will be integrated are document filing and retrieval, mail handling, word processing, personal productivity tools, report generation, decision support, and voice/video/data communications.

EFFECTS ON USERS

In general, users will be able to take care of more of their own needs—for example, through the use of fourth-generation languages, query languages, relational databases, and simple program writing. And the increased power, speed, and sophistication of hardware and software will allow users to generate more paper than ever! Perhaps the most notable change will be the complete computerization of all users' workstations.

THE ELECTRONIC WORKSTATION In many offices, the heart of the electronic workstation will be a personal computer system. The typical equipment configuration will include a keyboard, high-resolution screen with graphics capability, and perhaps a mouse. All workstations will have some individual storage capability (probably both floppy disk and hard disk) as well as the office-wide shared storage facility. The more advanced electronic workstations will also include voice and data communications capabilities—perhaps even video communications (Figure 14.13). Because users will be spending a great deal of time at their workstations, office designers are concentrating on comfort (ergonomics) as well as electronics.

ELECTRONIC FILING The substantial improvements in the software available for storage and retrieval of data have made electronic filing systems practical. These filing systems allow users to store, retrieve, and quickly manipulate more business information than ever before. The reduced cost of magnetic storage media and the introduction of high-capacity optical storage devices have increased the cost effectiveness of electronic filing. Improvements in digitizing and scanning technologies have even made it possible to convert hardcopy data (both text and graphics) into computer-usable form.

ELECTRONIC MAIL   Electronic "in-baskets" will become commonplace in the office. Memos will be distributed in electronic form throughout the office. If a staff member is not in the office at the time, as soon as his or her electronic workstation is activated, a "mail waiting" message will appear. Traveling staff members will take more frequent advantage of this function as lap-top computers become more popular. A simple call into the office system allows the user to check for mail. In addition, even if the office is closed, the staff member can leave mail for other staff members to retrieve the following day.

PRODUCTIVITY   To free users for more important activities, desktop software will take over mundane jobs such as maintaining calendars and scheduling appointments. This type of software began to appear in mid-1985 and continues to be improved. However, for it to be truly efficient, everyone in the office must use it. For example, to schedule a meeting in the office, everyone's calendar would be available in electronic form. First, the scheduling software would be activated. Then, the user scheduling the meeting would key in a request for a meeting of specified length with specified staff members by a certain date. The software would

FIGURE 14.13
Modern electronic workstation. Instead of using clumsy, space-eating cabinets, system units, and disk drives, this manager's workstation combines all computer-related elements in a single configuration. The keyboard has no cable (the back of the keyboard acts as a scanner) and the mouse is pen-shaped. The display screen's (center) position can be adjusted. The disk drives (left) can use regular disks, optical disks, and cards. Video camera, microphone, speaker, and video-conference screen enable the manager to participate in live conferences while displaying data and/or graphics at the same time (top right). The telephone and modem are built in.

then search all of the electronic calendars and identify the earliest date and time when all specified personnel could attend. All the appropriate calendars would be automatically updated and a brief notice would be printed out as a reminder of the meeting.

Many office staff members keep a Rolodex as a way of organizing the names, addresses, and phone numbers of key business contacts. Desktop software can handle this electronically. First a staff member is assigned the responsibility for building and maintaining the file. As business cards are acquired, this person keys in the data. Then, whenever anyone in the office needs a phone number, name, or address, he or she can obtain it quickly on the screen.

DECISION SUPPORT   The three business tools introduced in the early 1980s that have provided the office worker with tremendously powerful capabilities for manipulating data into business information will continue to be used—but used more efficiently. Electronic spreadsheets, microcomputer-based database management systems, and integrated software will be available to all personnel, thus extending the decision support system within the company. Both the software and the data will be shared among all authorized staff members.

TELECONFERENCING   The fully integrated office system will also have teleconferencing capabilities that will support meetings held by people in geographically separate locations. Teleconferencing saves time (eliminates travel) and money (eliminates travel costs). Users in each location will retrieve information electronically and use the decision support software to analyze it. In addition, messages can be sent back and forth among the locations—both in voice and digital form—and automatic summaries of the conferences will be transcribed by the computer.

SOCIAL IMPLICATIONS OF COMPUTERIZATION

Everything is connected to everything else. A change in one area will cause changes in other areas, even if they aren't readily apparent to us. This means that with opportunities also come problems. We are learning this lesson, for example, in the area of ecology. Are we also learning it in relation to the computer's growing role in business and society?

This question is becoming more important as information technology replaces energy as society's main resource. Many people are concerned that too much emphasis has been put on what the computer can do to streamline business and too little on how it may be affecting the quality of our lives. For example, is it distorting the meaning of thought? That is, is it absurd and dangerous to attribute the capabilities of thinking and creativity to a computer? People have experience, convictions, and cultural traditions. Are these qualities being devalued? If so, perhaps we are heading into an era in which machine-like qualities of speed and problem solving will be valued more highly than what used to be called *humane* qualities.

Many people believe that the computer's level of "thinking" can be compared simply to a muscle spasm and that too many computer enthusiasts are confusing data with ideas. After all, nothing is information until a *person* interprets it. And information is not the same as knowledge, which is gained by thinking. Further, knowledge can be gained without new information being received by the thinker. Can a machine do this? Do you want the equivalent of a muscle spasm in control of a weapons system? Society must guard against the creation of inhumane projects thought up only because a computer made them possible, and it must develop standard checking systems to ensure the integrity of data used to make strategic decisions in government as well as business.

In addition to the problems of computer-controlled nuclear weapons, the potential for abuse of power concerns many people. On the one hand, the computer could lead to equalization—that is, a democratic situation in which all people have access to the same information. On the other hand, this possibility could lead to the opposite situation: The existence of databases, electronic communications, and inexpensive portable computers has led some countries to outlaw personal possession of computers to avoid the free dissemination of information—clearly an abuse of power. Also, the existence of huge central databases that contain essentially all data related to everyone's public and private life can be frightening to consider.

Many people focus on the freedom from routine and boring work that computers give. This is certainly welcome in many situations, but we must remember that what is boring and routine work to one person may be life-saving employment to another. Traditionally, in the United States, many low-level jobs are held by young people and immigrants with language problems. Therefore, what at first seems like an advantage of computerization may really be a disadvantage. McDonalds restaurants came to this conclusion recently when they decided not to eliminate the order-cashier positions at the front counters staffed by people and replace them with machines that customers would use to key in their own orders. And maintaining human contact is still better for business.

One more problem to consider is the potential for computer-based systems in business to be used to monitor employees. What if terminals were programmed to check your speed, the pauses you make, the breaks you take, the rate of keying errors? Would it be fair for the company to do this to make sure it retains only the most efficient workers and thus increase the value of goods and services it has to sell? Or would this detract from your dignity as a human being—your right to do some things better than you do others? And would this type of company get high-quality decisions from its employees—or would the employees be too dissatisfied and afraid to work creatively?

These are only a few of the many computer-related issues that are being discussed today. These and other problems deserve attention—but don't let the problems obscure the opportunities that will be opened up to you if you know how to use computers in business!

ONWARD: HANDS ON

The next section of this text provides modules with hands-on tutorials to teach you the basics of working with operating systems software and some popular applications software including word processing, electronic spreadsheets, database management systems, and graphics. Chances are you have already started working through these modules!

DISCUSSION QUESTIONS

1. Do you think the "paperless office" will ever become a reality? Why or why not?

2. What is the issue surrounding the difficulty in defining "artificial intelligence"?

3. Do you think software for microcomputers will become more specialized? Why or why not?

4. Do you agree with using robots to perform low-level jobs? Explain your point of view.

5. How is desktop publishing used at your school? By your bank? At a local company? Interview at least three people who use desktop publishing and give a report on the advantages and disadvantages of the systems you observed.

6. Research the current use of natural language in business computer use. How is it likely to be used in the future? How do you think it will affect the input, storage, processing, and output requirements of computer systems?

7. Interview four or five people in management positions in business to determine their opinions on how students can best prepare themselves to enter the rapidly changing business world. Find out what computer skills *they* think are most important.

6

MICROCOMPUTER SOFTWARE

MODULE A

USING A MICROCOMPUTER'S OPERATING SYSTEM: DOS

This module focuses on the microcomputer operating system and its importance to the user. Before you proceed with this module, we recommend you read the following sections of the text: "The Anatomy of a Microcomputer" (Chapter 1); the discussion of hard and floppy disk drives and how they operate (Chapter 4); and "Applications Software" and "Categories of Systems Software" (Chapter 7).

■

PREVIEW

When you have completed this module, you will be able to:

- Describe the significance of disk-drive naming conventions, command hierarchy, command syntax, and file-naming conventions
- Boot a microcomputer
- Use DOS to:
  — Format a diskette
  — List, copy, rename, and erase files
  — Check the status of internal memory
  — Check the status of a diskette
- Create and use a directory
- Create and use a batch file
- Describe the MODE, BACKUP, SORT, FIND, and DISKCOPY commands

MICROCOMPUTER HARDWARE AND SOFTWARE REVIEW

We live in a computer age, and our main business tool is software. Software performs sophisticated tasks by providing the computer with instructions. Computers equipped with specialized software are being used in all types of businesses, including engineering, medicine, publishing, and education. Most computers used in these business environments are microcomputers. The modules that follow will introduce you to the most popular and practical microcomputer software currently available; this module provides the framework for understanding them.

Throughout this text we have emphasized the microcomputer when discussing hardware and software. In the section in Chapter 1 entitled "The Anatomy of a Microcomputer," we defined *microcomputer* as a relatively small general-purpose computer system that uses a microprocessor chip as its CPU. We described why microcomputers are being used in business today and why their use will surely continue to grow. We also described the different categories of microcomputers, including home computers, desktop computers, portable computers, and laptop computers. In addition, we described the main hardware components that make up the typical microcomputer system, including the keyboard, the monitor, and the system unit.

Among the components housed within the system unit are the disk drives (described in detail in Chapter 5). In recent years, more and more business professionals have begun using hard disks and hard cards for data storage, partially because the price for these components is steadily decreasing. But hard disks and hard cards are substantially superior to floppy disks for data storage for the following reasons:

- They can store much more data. A typical floppy disk can store between 100,000 and 1.4 million characters; a hard disk can store between 10 and roughly 70 million characters. Therefore, the maximum size of a file that can be stored on a hard disk is much larger than that stored on a floppy disk. Similar capacities are provided by hard cards.

- Accessing data doesn't take long. (For a description of how hard disks and floppy disks store and retrieve data, refer to Chapter 5.)
- They are virtually "wear-free." The device for storing and retrieving data from hard disks (the read/write head) is suspended a few millionths of a meter (microns) from the surface of the hard disk. However, a floppy disk's read/write head directly contacts the disk's surface when retrieving or recording data, wearing it out after 25 to 40 hours of use.

Hard disks and hard cards won't completely replace floppy disks, however. First, not all micros have a hard disk drive or a hard card, because these components are more expensive than floppy disks. Second, once installed, hard disks and cards aren't meant to be removed from the computer, whereas floppy disks are portable. For example, if you wanted to move a file stored on your hard disk to another computer, you would have to do the following:

1. Copy the file from your hard disk onto a floppy disk.
2. Take the floppy disk to the other computer.
3. Copy the file from the floppy disk onto the second computer's hard disk. (If the second computer didn't have a hard disk, the file would be copied onto another floppy disk.)

Third, and most significant, most hard disks are very sensitive to movement. For example, if you move a computer with a conventional hard disk and accidentally bump the computer against the side of a desk, all of the data stored on the hard disk will probably be lost: The read/write heads, suspended above the disk's surface, can crash down on the disk's surface with the slightest jolt. Special software programs are available that allow the user in effect to "lock" the read/write heads above the disk's surface. Even so, moving computers that contain conventional hard disks is a risky business. (Manufacturers of some 3½-inch hard disk drives claim that you can throw the drives downstairs without losing data!)

In Chapter 7 we described some "off-the-shelf" software programs typically used on microcomputers: word processing software, electronic spreadsheet software, database management software, graphics software, integrated software, RAM-resident software, and desktop publishing software. Modules B through E will cover many of these types of software in detail. We also described the components of systems software in Chapter 7: internal command instructions, external command instructions (utilities), language processors, and operating environments. Because this module focuses on internal and external command instructions (operating system), we recommend you review those sections of Chapter 7, as well as the section entitled "Systems Software for Microcomputers." These programs include Apple DOS, TRS-DOS (Tandy Radio Shack), CP/M, DOS (both IBM PC-DOS and its generic equivalent, MS-DOS from Microsoft), and UNIX. In the tutorial section of this module ("In the Lab"), you will be using the DOS operating system ("DOS" simply stands for Disk Operating System), which is the most widely used operating system in business today.

Operating System Software Fundamentals

Operating system software is the most important type of software for one simple reason: Your computer is useless without it. Before you can accomplish anything, you must first load the operating system software into your computer's memory. In this section, we will further define the role of operating system software in the microcomputer processing environment.

Disk-Drive Naming Conventions

As you know, the most common types of storage devices for the microcomputer are hard disks, hard cards, and floppy disks. Most microcomputers have one of the following disk-drive configurations: two floppy disk drives, one floppy disk drive and one hard disk drive or card, or two floppy disk drives and one hard disk or card. When you are working with applications software and want to save the work you've done, you need to tell the software onto which disk drive your work should be saved. (This concept is similar to telling someone in which drawer to put a folder.) To do this, you must follow certain disk-drive naming conventions.

Most of today's microcomputer operating systems refer to the first floppy disk drive as drive A (A:) and to a second floppy disk drive as drive B (B:). A hard disk is typically referred to as drive C (C:) (Figure A.1). The computers you use in your school will probably have either two floppy disk drives (drives A and B), one floppy disk drive (drive A) and one hard disk drive (drive C), or two floppy disk drives (drives A and B) and a hard disk (drive C). When the computer is first turned on, the instructions stored in read-only memory (ROM) will always check disk drive A for a diskette containing the operating system files necessary to **"boot"** the computer— that is, to get the computer up and running. If a disk is present in the drive (and the drive gate, or door is closed, which clamps the read/write heads on the disk), but the operating system files aren't on the disk, an error message such as "NON-SYSTEM DISK" will appear on the screen. If the gate is open, the loader program will automatically look onto the hard disk, or drive C, for a copy of the operating

FIGURE A.1
Disk drives. The floppy disk drives are drives A and B; if you have a hard disk drive, it is drive C.

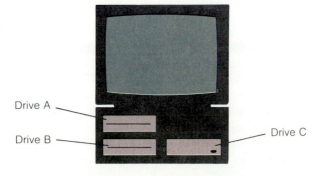

Drive A

Drive B

Drive C

system instructions necessary to boot the computer. With DOS, when the necessary instructions are found, you will be prompted for the current date and time, and then a SYSTEM PROMPT, which identifies the default disk drive, will appear on the screen.

The **default disk drive** is the disk drive automatically affected by commands unless the user specifies another disk drive (by a command). If the operating system files were retrieved from a disk in drive A, the default disk drive would be drive A. With DOS, if drive A is the default drive, the system prompt will appear as follows: A>. The letter represents the default disk drive, and the ">" sign, the **system prompt,** indicates that DOS is waiting for a command to be given. If drive C is the default drive (because a copy of the operating system files were retrieved from there), the system prompt will appear as follows: C>.

The default disk drive designation can be changed by entering the letter of the desired drive followed by a colon. For example, to change the default disk drive to B>, simply enter B: followed by pressing the RETURN key. The tutorial section of this module will cover disk-drive naming conventions in greater detail. The modules in the rest of the book will use these naming conventions frequently.

THE OPERATING SYSTEM COMMAND HIERARCHY

Once the system prompt appears on the screen, the operating system waits for you to issue one of two types of command: an operating system command or a command to start using an applications software program. **Operating system commands** are either internal commands or external commands (see Chapter 7) that allow you to manage disks and disk files (which is why DOS stands for Disk *Operating* System). The second type of command instructs the operating system to load a copy of the applications software program you want to use into internal memory. The instructions necessary to do so aren't on your operating system disk; they're present in a file on your applications software disk.

If the command you give doesn't fall into one of these two categories, an error message will appear on the screen. Figure A.2 diagrams the steps the operating system goes through when executing commands.

Because the typical user needs to be most familiar with **internal commands,** the instructions to perform these commands remain in internal memory the entire time the computer is on. There are three categories of internal commands: (1) standard user commands, (2) directory commands, which are used to create "directory structures" on a storage device (we'll discuss those later in this section), and (3) batch commands. **Batch commands** are used to create **batch command files,** which allow you to automate frequently used command sequences—thus certain tasks can be accomplished with fewer keystrokes. Although the commands used to create batch files are internal, batch files are considered external command files because the instructions in them aren't loaded into internal memory at the time the computer is booted (except in a special case that we'll describe later). We will describe how to use some of DOS's batch commands in the tutorial.

External commands are commands that the typical user doesn't use as much; therefore, the instructions to perform these commands remain on your operating system disk. Not all operating system commands can reside in internal memory; if they did, very little room would be left in internal memory for both a copy of the applications program you want to use and the results of your processing. For this reason, external command instructions are placed in internal memory only when you want to use them. When you want to issue an external command, the instructions necessary to carry out the command must be present on the default drive of your computer; otherwise you'll get an error message. Because internal commands reside in internal memory, you can execute them no matter what files are present on the default drive.

COMMAND SYNTAX

The operating system software interprets the commands issued through your input device (for example, the keyboard or a mouse) and communicates what you want accomplished to the computer. For the operating system software to understand

FIGURE A.2
The operating system goes through specific steps when executing commands. If the user tries to issue a command that doesn't fall into any of these categories, an error message will appear on the screen.

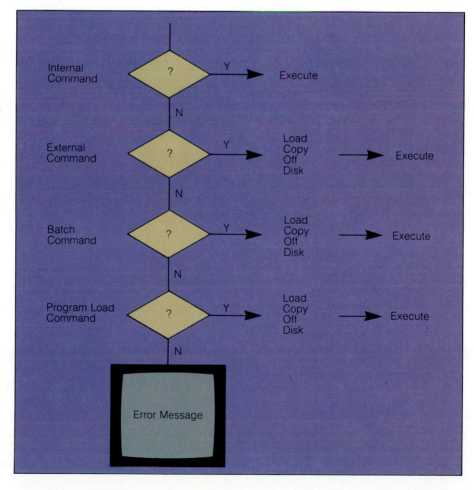

exactly what you want accomplished, your commands must use the correct **syntax**—just as you must use correct grammar when speaking or writing if you want to communicate clearly. However, unlike people, a computer won't pretend to understand you when you are unclear or imprecise; it will display an error message when your syntax is wrong. For example, if you misspell a command, you'll get an error message. However, the message rarely explains the reason for the error, so you must consult your operating system software manual to solve the problem. The tutorial section of this module will give you the correct syntax for each command discussed.

FILE-NAMING CONVENTIONS

When working with an applications program, you will need to name the data files you wish to save. Just as you must follow certain syntactical conventions, or rules, for issuing commands, you must name your files using the specific naming conventions of your operating system. If you don't know the conventions for naming your files, the operating system won't recognize them and thus won't know what to do with them.

Naming conventions vary among operating systems. DOS uses the following conventions:

1. The **file-name length** can be between 1 and 8 characters.
2. An **extension** (an "identifier" added to the file name) can be between 1 and 3 characters.
3. A file must have a name, but it doesn't have to have an extension.
4. The file name and the extension are separated by a period (.). (Both of the following are valid file names: BUDGET and BUDGET.MAR.)
5. If a file name has an extension, you must reference both parts of the name when telling DOS about the file.
6. The asterisk (*) and the question mark (?) are used as "global" characters that save you time if you need to carry out commands on more than one file. The asterisk is used to represent up to all eight characters in a file name or up to all three characters in the extension. The question mark is used to replace one character in a file name and/or an extension. In the tutorial section we will show you how to use these global characters when issuing a command.

Figure A.3 lists some valid and invalid file names.

File-name extensions allow users to distinguish between types of files. For example, you may want to end all of your report files with an extension of RPT and all of your budget files with an extension of BUD. User programs often assign an extension to files so that its files can be differentiated from files created by other programs. For example, Lotus 1-2-3 (Version 2.01) automatically assigns an extension of WK1 to all electronic spreadsheet files. Some extensions are reserved by DOS and have a special meaning, including EXE, COM, BAS, SYS, BAK, and BAT. Except for BAT, you should avoid using any of these extensions when giving names to files. (As you'll learn in the tutorial, the only time you should use BAT is when you are creating a batch file.)

THE ROOT DIRECTORY AND DIRECTORY STRUCTURES

Operating system software offers the user many useful capabilities, including the capability to create directory structures on a disk storage device, such as a floppy disk. Disk storage devices can become as full as office filing cabinets. What if two different departments are using the same filing cabinet to store business-related documents? Department A and Department B both store accounting, payroll, and inventory-related data in the cabinet. If each department's data is put into the drawer in no particular location or order, it would be difficult for either department to retrieve its data and easy to mix up the data. For this reason, filing cabinets usually contain dividers and subdividers (folders) that store documentation that relates to a common category, such as accounting or payroll.

When storing files on storage devices that are capable of holding large numbers of files, such as a hard disk, the user must be able to put files that are alike into the same folder, or subdirectory. A **subdirectory** is a file that contains other files and other subdirectories. A **directory structure** describes how a disk is organized into subdirectories. When you first boot your computer (turn it on) and see the operating system prompt, you are in the **root directory** of your storage device. The root directory is like a file cabinet: File cabinets are composed of drawers, which contain folders, which in turn contain other folders or files; similarly, the root directory can contain subdirectories (drawers) that can contain other subdirectories (**sub-subdirectories, or folders**) and other files. When you are working with subdirectories, you must be sure to tell the operating system which one you want to perform an action on; otherwise you may accidentally put a file into the wrong subdirectory (drawer or folder).

In the tutorial section of this module, you will use many commands necessary to create and maintain a directory structure. You will be surprised at how easy it is to maintain orderly disk storage.

FIGURE A.3
File-naming conventions. These are some of the valid and invalid files names that relate to the DOS operating system.

File Name and Extension	Status	Reason
1. QUARTER1	Valid	Contains 8 characters in file name
2. QUARTER1.BUD	Valid	Contains 8 characters in file name and 3 in extension
3. SAMPLEBUD	Invalid	Contains more than 8 characters in the file name
4. QUARTER1.BUD2	Invalid	Contains more than 3 characters in extension
5. A	Valid	Contains 1 character in file name

In the Lab:

Getting Started with DOS

A big problem that new users face when first using an operating system is how to decide which commands are the most important to master. This tutorial will help you solve this problem using DOS, which is the operating system most commonly used in business (your lab computer will use either PC-DOS from IBM or MS-DOS from Microsoft; the tutorial applies to both versions).

We assume you are using a computer that is configured with two floppy disk drives. You learned earlier that the first floppy drive is referred to as drive A and the second floppy drive is drive B. Floppy disk drives are positioned either one on top of the other or side by side in the computer cabinet. Depending on how your computer's disk drives are set up, drive A is either on the top or on the left, and drive B is either on the bottom or on the right. Drive A is the default drive, where your DOS files will be stored, and drive B will store your data.

A user who purchases DOS is supplied with a diskette containing most of the command files pictured in Figure A.4. Each command file is used by the user to

FIGURE A.4
Directory listing. A user purchasing DOS receives a documentation manual and a diskette with most of these files. The number of files may differ depending on the DOS version purchased.

```
COMMAND   COM    23210    3-07-85    1:43p
ANSI      SYS     1651    3-07-85    1:43p
ASSIGN    COM     1509    3-07-85    1:43p
ATTRIB    EXE    15091    3-07-85    1:43p
BACKUP    COM     5577    3-07-85    1:43p
BASIC     COM    17792    3-07-85    1:43p
BASICA    COM    27520    3-07-85    1:43p
CHKDSK    COM     9435    3-07-85    1:43p
COMP      COM     3664    3-07-85    1:43p
DISKCOMP  COM     4073    3-07-85    1:43p
DISKCOPY  COM     4329    3-07-85    1:43p
EDLIN     COM     7261    3-07-85    1:43p
FDISK     COM     8173    3-07-85    1:43p
FIND      EXE     6403    3-07-85    1:43p
FORMAT    COM     9398    3-07-85    1:43p
GRAFTABL  COM     1169    3-07-85    1:43p
GRAPHICS  COM     3111    3-07-85    1:43p
JOIN      EXE    15971    3-07-85    1:43p
KEYBFR    COM     2289    3-07-85    1:43p
KEYBGR    COM     2234    3-07-85    1:43p
KEYBIT    COM     2177    3-07-85    1:43p
KEYBSP    COM     2267    3-07-85    1:43p
KEYBUK    COM     2164    3-07-85    1:43p
LABEL     COM     1826    3-07-85    1:43p
MODE      COM     5295    3-07-85    1:43p
MORE      COM      282    3-07-85    1:43p
PRINT     COM     8291    3-07-85    1:43p
RECOVER   COM     4050    3-07-85    1:43p
RESTORE   COM     5410    3-07-85    1:43p
SELECT    COM     2084    3-07-85    1:43p
SHARE     EXE     8304    3-07-85    1:43p
SORT      EXE     1664    3-07-85    1:43p
SUBST     EXE    16611    3-07-85    1:43p
SYS       COM     3727    3-07-85    1:43p
TREE      COM     2831    3-07-85    1:43p
VDISK     SYS     3307    3-07-85    1:43p
LASER     BAT       42    6-14-85    1:41p
CONFIG    SYS      128    2-17-84    2:46a
```

perform specific functions. However, we do not have enough space in this module to illustrate the use of all of these command files. Instead, we will focus on the internal and external commands most relevant to the business user. (*Note:* You must have a new data disk to work through this tutorial. Make sure your data disk doesn't have any data on it, because we're going to be erasing it in the formatting section.)

LOADING DOS

Make sure your computer is off. Put your DOS disk in drive A. (*Note:* When you put a diskette into a disk drive, use the "rule of thumb." In other words, put your thumb on the label and then slide the diskette into the disk drive.) Close the disk drive gate. Turn your computer on. The computer will perform a few checks to make sure that your hardware is connected correctly and that the banks of internal memory chips in your computer are functioning properly. A message on the screen will identify any problem that is discovered. (*Note:* Before you call your instructor over to help you solve a problem, turn the computer off and make sure your disk has been correctly inserted into the disk drive and that the drive gate is completely closed. Then turn the computer on again.) Next you will be prompted for the current date (Figure A.5). You can either key in the current date according to the specified format and then press the RETURN key (on some keyboards, the RETURN key is labeled ENTER), or you can completely bypass the option by pressing the RETURN key. (For a review of the keys, check the keyboard section in Chapter 3.)

You will now be prompted to enter the current time (Figure A.6). Again, you

FIGURE A.5
Date prompt. When you boot DOS, if the computer finds the critical operating system files on the DOS diskette, you will be prompted for the date. "Current date" is the last date recorded; enter today's date.

```
Current date is Tue  1-01-1980
Enter new date (mm-dd-yy):
```

FIGURE A.6
Time prompt. After you have been prompted for the date, you will be prompted for the current time.

```
Current date is Tue  1-01-1980
Enter new date (mm-dd-yy):
Current time is  0:01:43.04
Enter new time:
```

can either enter the current time or bypass the option by pressing the RETURN key. Be sure to key in the current date and time when you know you will need to refer to them in your applications software program. Doing so is especially important with electronic spreadsheet programs, which are capable of performing calculations based on the current date and time.

You should now see the system prompt (A>) on the screen, which means DOS is waiting for you to issue a command. *Remember:* Regardless of what command you issue, you must always press the RETURN key next to let DOS know that the command should be executed.

THE FORMAT COMMAND

Because it prepares your new disks so that they can store data, the **FORMAT command** is probably the most important operating system command. The process of preparing your disks for storage is usually referred to as *formatting* or **initializing.** New disks are usually packaged unformatted.

The FORMAT command is an external command; the instructions necessary to carry out the formatting process are located on your DOS disk in a file called FORMAT.COM.

We are now going to format your data disk. When you key in the FORMAT command described below, DOS will look on the disk in the default drive for the instructions stored in the file FORMAT.COM and will place a copy of them into internal memory. If DOS doesn't find the file FORMAT.COM, an error message will appear on the screen. When the formatting process is complete, and the instructions are no longer needed, DOS automatically erases the instructions from internal memory.

Figure A.7 shows the syntax for the FORMAT command. To format your data disk, key in the following command:

```
A>format B:
```

Once you press the RETURN key, DOS will prompt you to insert your new data disk into drive B and to strike any key when ready (make sure that the disk-drive gate is closed). Once you've done this, you should see drive B's disk-drive light go on as the format program takes less than a minute to do the following:

FIGURE A.7
Syntax of the FORMAT command. Remember to tell the format program the location of the disk you want formatted.

FORMAT Command Syntax

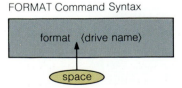

1. Writes a test pattern onto the disk

2. Reads the test pattern back to see if there are any problems with the data disk

3. Places an organization scheme onto the disk in which you can store data (this scheme prevents you from storing data in any "bad" (that is, non-functioning) areas on the disk)

4. Displays information about the total disk space available, the total bytes used by the system, the total bytes available on the disk, and a message that says "format complete"

The final message resulting from the FORMAT command asks you if you want to format another disk. Because you don't want to, type an N (for "no") and then press the RETURN key. You should now be back at the system prompt (A>). (If you had wanted to format an entire box of new disks, you would type a Y at this point. The FORMAT command would then prompt you to insert another new disk into drive B and would repeat the formatting process.)

With DOS, the user can specify a few special characteristics using the FORMAT command. The following are some examples:

1. `A>format B:/V`   The /V tells DOS you want to give the disk a name that is up to 11 characters long.

2. `A>format B:/4`   The /4 formats a disk (using DOS version 3.0 and higher) so tha. it can be both read from and written on in a 1.2-MB disk drive and a standard 362-K disk drive. (Note that a disk formatted in this way may not be reliable when used in a 362-K disk drive.)

3. `A>format B:/S`   This command puts the operating system files on disks of your choice to make them capable of booting a computer. With a floppy-disk-based microcomputer, this command is especially useful for preparing backup program disks, because you can use them to boot as well as to load your applications software. Thus you can reduce the number of times you have to put disks in and take disks out of your default disk drive.

If you use the formatting process on a disk that contains data, all the data will be erased. Some people format floppy disks over and over again if they want to erase all the data and, in effect, "clean them up." Users generally don't format their hard disks or cards often, but sometimes formatting them makes more efficient use of available storage space and speeds up the time it takes to access files.

THE DIR COMMAND

Probably the most widely used command, **DIR (DIRECTORY)** allows you to see what files you have on your disks and gives you descriptive information about the files (Figure A.8). Using this command is like looking in a file drawer to see what folders are there. Figure A.9 shows the syntax for the DIR command. Following is a list of some tasks you will be able to perform using the DIR command. (*Note:* When we tell you what to key in, we include the system prompt in the description. However, remember that the system prompt is supplied by DOS; you don't need to key it in.)

1. To display the names of files on the default drive, key in the following after the A prompt (don't forget to press the RETURN key after keying in a command):

   ```
   A>dir
   ```

   After the command has finished executing, you should again be at the system prompt.

2. The files will scroll across the screen too quickly for you to read all the names. Below are some options you can use to slow down the screen's scroll. The first option causes the list to PAUSE when the screen becomes full. Strike any key to continue the scroll. The second option allows you to display the list in a WIDE format.

   ```
   OPTION 1: A>dir /P
   OPTION 2: A>dir /W
   ```

3. To display the files on a drive other than the default drive, key in the letter corresponding to the drive where the files are located followed by a colon (:),

---

FIGURE A.8
Typical directory listing. The DIRECTORY command shows you what files you have on your disk, the size of each file, and the date and time that the file was created or last changed.

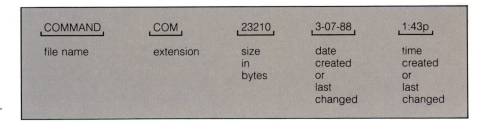

COMMAND	COM	23210	3-07-88	1:43p
file name	extension	size in bytes	date created or last changed	time created or last changed

---

FIGURE A.9
Syntax of the DIRECTORY command. You have the option of seeing the listing by page (/p) or in a wide display (/w).

DIR command syntax

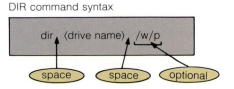

and then press the RETURN key:

```
A>dir B:
```

Because the disk in drive B is newly formatted, it has no files. You should see the message "File Not Found."

What if you want to see a list of a group of files on your DOS disk? As mentioned in the section entitled "File-Naming Conventions," to execute a command that involves more than one file, you can use DOS's global characters (* and ?):

4. `A>dir *.EXE`

This command will display those files on your DOS disk that have in their file names the extension EXE.

5. `A>dir ?O*.*`

This command will display those files on your DOS disk that have the letter O as the second letter in the file name.

GETTING READY TO PRACTICE MORE DOS COMMANDS

To practice some more DOS commands, we need to have files to work with. To make sure you have the correct files on your data disk, we are going to guide you through a procedure for creating a very short text file. Then you will make copies of it using DOS's COPY command so that we will have more than one file to work with.

You are now going to use an internal DOS command called the **COPY CON command.** (Although we aren't creating a batch file now, this command is quite frequently used for that purpose.)

The following command will instruct DOS to open up a new file on your data disk so that you can key something into it. Key in the following after the A prompt, pressing the RETURN key afer every line. (*Note:* the ⌃ means to hold the CTRL key down as you tap the letter Z.)

```
A>copy con B:TEXT1.DOC
   This is a sample text file for my DOS
   exercise.
   ^Z
```

After you press the RETURN key, you will then see the message:

```
1 File(s) copied
```

You should now have a file on your diskette called TEXT1.DOC. Just to check that this file *is* on your data disk, key in the following command:

```
A>dir B:
```

What you see on the screen should be the same as Figure A.10.

THE COPY COMMAND

Often you will want to make copies of files. The **COPY command**, an internal command, allows you to make copies of your files onto the same disk (but under different names) or onto another disk. Copying files is important because you need backup copies if files are accidentally erased. Figure A.11 shows the syntax for the COPY command.

Using the steps that follow, we are going to make five copies of the file called TEXT1.DOC onto your data disk. Because we are copying onto the same disk, we must give the copies different names. Key in the following commands (after each command press the RETURN key):

```
1. A>copy  B:TEXT1.DOC  B:TEXT2.DOC

2. A>copy  B:TEXT1.DOC  B:TEXT3.DOC

3. A>copy  B:TEXT1.DOC  B:REPORT.JAN

4. A>copy  B:TEXT1.DOC  B:REPORT.FEB

5. A>copy  B:TEXT1.DOC  B:REPORT.MAR

6. A>dir  B:
```

FIFURE A.10
New directory listing. Your data diskette should have only one file on it now called TEXT1.DOC.

```
    Volume in drive B has no label
    Directory of  B:\

TEXT1     DOC        49   1-10-88   12:41a
        1 File(s)       361472 bytes free
```

FIGURE A.11
Syntax of the COPY command.

COPY command syntax

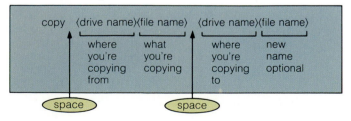

Your screen should now look like the one in Figure A.12. Assuming you have a DOS disk in drive A containing files similar to those pictured in Figure A.4, we are going to guide you through copying some files from the disk in drive A onto your data disk in drive B. Users often need to copy from one disk to another so that more than one user can have access to the same file. If for some reason you get the "file not found" message, you have either mistyped the command and/or name of the file you want to copy, or the file we want you to copy isn't on your DOS disk. (Check with your instructor in the latter case.)

Key in the following commands:

1. `A>copy A:COMMAND.COM B:`

   This command places a copy of the file COMMAND.COM onto your data disk.

2. `A>copy A:CHKDSK.COM B:`

3. `A>copy A:FIND.EXE B:LOST.EXE`

   This command copies the file called FIND.EXE from your DOS disk in drive A onto your data disk in drive B under a different name. The contents of FIND.EXE and LOST.EXE are identical.

What if you want to copy all the files from your DOS disk with the extension of EXE onto your data disk? If, for example, you have six files, do you have to issue the COPY command six times? What if there are 100 files? As mentioned in the section entitled "File-Naming Conventions," to execute a command that involves more than one file, we can use DOS's global characters.

Key in the following:

1. `A>copy A:*.EXE B:`

   DOS will copy all files with the extension EXE onto your data disk in drive B. The asterisk tells DOS "we don't care what the file *name* is; just copy all files with the *extension* EXE."

FIGURE A.12
New directory listing. Your data disk should now have six files on it. They should all contain the same number of bytes.

```
Volume in drive B has no label
 Directory of   B:\

TEXT1     DOC      49    1-10-88   12:41a
TEXT2     DOC      49    1-10-88   12:41a
TEXT3     DOC      49    1-10-88   12:41a
REPORT    JAN      49    1-10-88   12:41a
REPORT    FEB      49    1-10-88   12:41a
REPORT    MAR      49    1-10-88   12:41a
        6 File(s)    356352 bytes free
```

2. `A>copy A:A*.* B:`

DOS will copy all files that begin with the letter A from your DOS disk onto the disk in drive B.

3. `A>copy A:KE*.COM B:`

DOS will copy all files that begin with the letters *KE* and have the extension COM onto the disk in drive B.

4. `A>copy ?O*.* B:`

DOS will copy all files that have the letter O as the second character in the file name onto the disk in drive B.

5. `A>copy *.S* B:`

DOS will copy all files that have the letter *S* as the first character in the extension onto the disk in drive B.

6. `A>dir B:`

The directory listing of your data disk should look similar to the one in Figure A.13.

It's very important for you to know how to use the COPY command so that you can make backup copies of your files.

FIGURE A.13
Directory listing of the data disk after using the COPY command. Your directory listing should look like the one shown here. (The number of files may be slightly different.)

```
Volume in drive B has no label
Directory of  B:\

TEXT1     DOC       49    1-10-88   12:41a
TEXT2     DOC       49    1-10-88   12:41a
TEXT3     DOC       49    1-10-88   12:41a
REPORT    JAN       49    1-10-88   12:41a
REPORT    FEB       49    1-10-88   12:41a
REPORT    MAR       49    1-10-88   12:41a
COMMAND   COM    23210    3-07-85    1:43p
CHKDSK    COM     9435    3-07-85    1:43p
LOST      EXE     6403    3-07-85    1:43p
ATTRIB    EXE    15091    3-07-85    1:43p
FIND      EXE     6403    3-07-85    1:43p
JOIN      EXE    15971    3-07-85    1:43p
SHARE     EXE     8304    3-07-85    1:43p
SORT      EXE     1664    3-07-85    1:43p
SUBST     EXE    16611    3-07-85    1:43p
ANSI      SYS     1651    3-07-85    1:43p
ASSIGN    COM     1509    3-07-85    1:43p
KEYBFR    COM     2289    3-07-85    1:43p
KEYBGR    COM     2234    3-07-85    1:43p
KEYBIT    COM     2177    3-07-85    1:43p
KEYBSP    COM     2267    3-07-85    1:43p
KEYBUK    COM     2164    3-07-85    1:43p
COMP      COM     3664    3-07-85    1:43p
FORMAT    COM     9398    3-07-85    1:43p
MODE      COM     5295    3-07-85    1:43p
MORE      COM      282    3-07-85    1:43p
CONFIG    SYS      128    2-17-84    2:46a
VDISK     SYS     3307    3-07-85    1:43p
       28 File(s)     201728 bytes free
```

THE RENAME COMMAND

The **RENAME command,** an internal command, allows you to change the names of your files. Renaming files is essential when you have, for example, on two different disks two files that have the same name but different contents (Figure A.14). If you want to copy one of these files from one disk to the other, it will *replace* the second file (because both files have the same name). To avoid the loss of one file's contents, rename the file you are copying *before* you issue the command to copy. The syntax of the RENAME command is pictured in Figure A.15. Below are some examples of using the RENAME command:

```
1. A>rename B:TEXT1.DOC SAMPLE1.DOC
```

FIGURE A.14
Copying files. If you have two files with the same names on different disks and copy the file on one disk (A) to the second disk (B), the contents of the second file will be replaced with the contents of the first file. To avoid losing the contents of the second file, rename the file before copying from disk to disk.

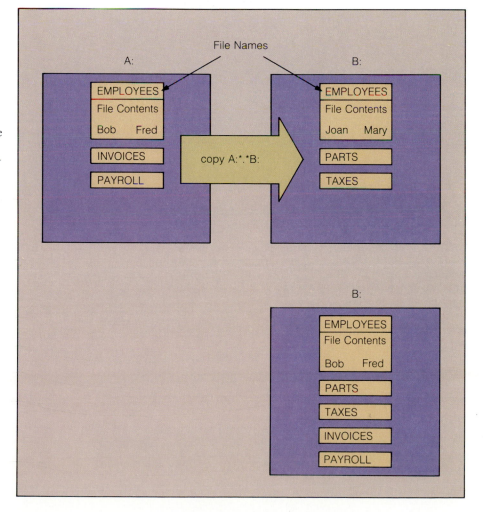

You should now have a file called SAMPLE1.DOC on your data disk. (To check the presence of this file, use the DIRECTORY command described earlier in this tutorial.) You shouldn't, however, have a file called TEXT1.DOC on your data disk.

2. `A>rename B:REPORT.JAN REPORT.APR`

You should now have a file called REPORT.APR on your data disk.

THE TYPE COMMAND

The **TYPE command,** an internal command, is especially helpful when you can't remember what is in a file, because it allows you to "take a peek" at the contents without having to open the file using an applications software program. When you issue the TYPE command, your file scrolls quickly down the screen. Text files (containing only alphanumeric data) appear in a legible format; however, other files may appear unreadable because of nonalphanumeric and nonnumeric characters. The syntax of the TYPE command is shown in Figure A.16.

Key in the following commands:

1. `A>type B:TEXT2.DOC`

You should see the contents of the file TEXT2.DOC on your screen.

2. `A>type B:REPORT.JAN`

The display should look similar to what you saw when you typed TEXT2.DOC, because the contents of the files are the same.

In the two steps listed above, we typed the names of files that contain text. What

FIGURE A.15
Syntax of the **RENAME** command. Specify the disk drive where the file you want to rename is located, the name of the file you want to rename, and the new file name.

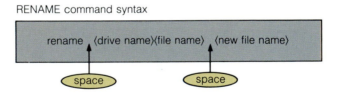

RENAME command syntax

rename ⟨drive name⟩⟨file name⟩ ⟨new file name⟩
        space   space

FIGURE A.16
Syntax of the **TYPE** command. Specify the disk drive where the file is located and the file name.

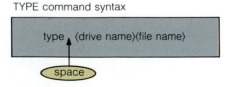

TYPE command syntax

type ⟨drive name⟩⟨file name⟩
     space

happens if we accidentally type the name of a file that contains special instructions that only the computer can understand? Key in the following:

```
A>type B:COMMAND.COM
```

You should see some very strange-looking characters on the screen. ALthough *we* can't make any sense of those characters, the computer knows exactly what they mean.

THE ERASE COMMAND

Just as it's sometimes necessary to "un-clutter" your desk and discard old notes and papers, it's occasionally necessary to discard old files stored on your data disks. The **ERASE command,** an internal command, is used for this purpose. The syntax for the ERASE command is shown in Figure A.17. Key in the following to learn the use of the ERASE command:

1. ```
   A>erase B:REPORT.MAR
   ```

   The file named REPORT.MAR should have been erased from your data disk. To make sure, use the DIR command to list the files on your data disk.

2. ```
   A>erase B:*.EXE
   ```

   DOS will erase all files from your data disk that have the extension EXE. It's valuable to know how to erase more than one file at a time because it can save you time.

THE CHKDSK COMMAND

The **CHKDSK command,** an external command, is used to analyze the directories on a disk to make sure all files have been recorded correctly. This command also gives the user information about the amount of memory available for use, as well as the amount of storage space available on disk. When you work with large files and software products that use a great deal of internal memory, periodically check the status of internal memory and disk storage space. The syntax for this command is shown in Figure A.18.

To use the CHKDSK command, key in the following:

```
A>chkdsk B:
```

The output from this command (seen on the screen) should look like Figure A.19.

FIGURE A.17
Syntax of the ERASE command. Specify which disk drive contains the file(s) you want to erase and the file name(s).

ERASE command syntax

FIGURE A.18
Syntax of the CHKDSK command. When using the CHKDSK command, if you want to check the status of a disk drive other than the default drive, you must specify it in the command.

CHKDSK command syntax

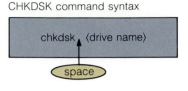

FIGURE A.19
Output from the CHKDSK command. The first three lines of the display describe the characteristics of your disk device, and the last two lines refer to internal memory.

```
362496 bytes total disk space
160768 bytes in 28 user files
201728 bytes available on disk

655360 bytes total memory
618304 bytes free
```

CREATING DIRECTORY STRUCTURES WITH DOS

Once you are working as a computer user in a business, you may find yourself creating so many files on a hard disk that the disk may become disorganized and cluttered. For example, if you are the manager of a sporting goods store like the one described in the episodes in this book, you may be dealing with the following file categories: invoice files, purchase order files, vendor files, employee files, and accounting files. Using so many files can lead to aggravating confusion; therefore, DOS has special commands that you can use to organize disk files into logical groups in a directory structure. The following sections will teach you how to use these commands. The directory structure you create will be the same as the hierarchical structure shown in Figure A.20.

Directory structures are usually created and used only on hard disks because they can store a great number of files. However, because we don't know if you have a hard disk in your computer, we will use the data disk you have in drive B. In the next two sections you will use the MKDIR, CHDIR, and RMDIR commands. Although the names are different, the syntax for these commands is identical (Figure A.21).

THE MKDIR (MD) COMMAND

The **MKDIR (MD) command** is used to make a directory. To create the structure shown in Figure A.20, key in the following commands:

1. `A>erase B:*.*`

   When you see the prompt "Are you sure Y/N," tap Y and then tap the RETURN key. This step isn't necessary to create a directory structure, but we want your disk to be empty so that it doesn't become cluttered as we proceed with this section.

2. `A>md B:\INVOICE`

   The backslash symbolizes the root directory, which is always at the top of the directory structure. (*Note:* There is no space between the colon and the backslash.) You have just created a subdirectory, right below the root directory, called *Invoice*, where you will store all invoice files. If you want to make sure that this subdirectory exists, use the DIR command to see what the directory listing of the root directory of your data disk looks like. You know you're in the root directory because the screen displays

FIGURE A.20
Hierarchical directory structure.

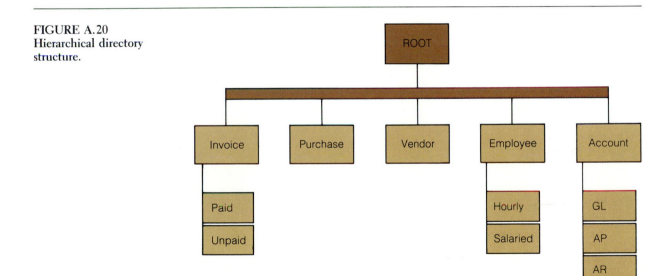

FIGURE A.21
Syntax of MKDIR, CHDIR, and RMDIR commands.

```
Directory of B:\
```

The extension for the Invoice directory should look like this:

```
<DIR>
```

3. `A>md B:\PURCHASE`

You have just created another subdirectory called *Purchase*, where you will store purchase order files.

Next you'll create the Vendor, Employee, and Accounting subdirectories on your data disk. The naming conventions for directories are identical to those for file names. We will abbreviate the name of the accounting directory so that it doesn't have more than eight characters.

4. `A>md B:\VENDOR`

5. `A>md B:\EMPLOYEE`

6. `A>md B:\ACCOUNT`

Key in the DIR command to see what the directory listing of your data disk looks like now. You should see that you've just created five subdirectories. Now we are going to create the lower-level subdirectories (sub-subdirectories). Key in the following:

7. `A>md B:\INVOICE\PAID`

You've just created a sub-subdirectory below the Invoice subdirectory.

8. `A>md B:\INVOICE\UNPAID`

You've just created a second sub-subdirectory below the Invoice sub-directory.

9. `A>md B:\EMPLOYEE\HOURLY`

10. `A>md B:\EMPLOYEE\SALARIED`

11. `A>md B:\ACCOUNT\GL`

This sub-subdirectory will contain all general ledger files.

12. `A>md B:\ACCOUNT\AP`

This sub-subdirectory will hold all accounts payable files.

13. `A>md B:\ACCOUNT\AR`

This sub-subdirectory will contain all accounts receivable files.

If you use the DIR command now, your listing won't show the lowest level of subdirectories (such as the Paid and Unpaid sub-subdirectories); because you are still in the root directory, you can see only the files and the first level of subdirectories that are in it. To see your sub-subdirectories, use the CHDIR command.

THE CHDIR (CD) COMMAND

The **CHDIR (CD) command** allows you to change the current directory. To practice moving around in the directory structure you've just created, and to make sure all the directories you wanted were actually made, key in the following:

1. `A>cd B:\INVOICE`

    You've now moved into the Invoice file drawer, or subdirectory, which is similar to pulling open a filing cabinet drawer so you can do something to the file folders inside. When you use the DIR command at this point, you'll see a listing of the Invoice drawer's contents, not the contents of the root directory (Figure A.22). DOS automatically places the designations . <DIR> and .. <DIR> in all of the subdirectories you create. In recent versions of DOS, . <DIR> provides the user with little or no functional purpose. However, .. <DIR>, when used in conjunction with the CHDIR command, allows the user to move up one level in a directory structure, which is similar to closing one filing cabinet drawer and opening the drawer above. To illustrate this, key in the following:

    `A>cd B:..`

    Now use the DIR command to list the files on your data disk; you should see the listing of the root directory.

2. `A>cd B:\INVOICE\PAID`

    You're now in the Paid file drawer. Use the DIR command to see what is present in the drawer. Note that, as in the case of the Invoice subdirectory, there are no folders, user files, or program files in this drawer.

3. `A>cd B:\ACCOUNT`

    You're now in the Accounting file drawer. If you use the DIR command, you will see that you have three folders (or sub-subdirectories) in it. Your directory listing should look like the one pictured in Figure A.23.

    Practice moving around in the directory structure a few more times until you feel comfortable with the procedure. After you're finished, move up to the root directory with the following command:

4. `A>cd B:\`

FIGURE A.22
Directory listing of the Invoice file drawer, or sub-directory.

```
    Volume in drive B has no label
    Directory of  B:\INVOICE

    .              <DIR>       1-10-88     1:32a
    ..             <DIR>       1-10-88     1:32a
    PAID           <DIR>       1-10-88     1:33a
    UNPAID         <DIR>       1-10-88     1:33a
            4 File(s)     350208 bytes free
```

FIGURE A.23
Directory listing of the
Account file subdirectory,
which contains three sub-
subdirectories.

```
     Volume in drive B has no label
     Directory of  B:\ACCOUNT

     .           <DIR>        1-10-88    1:32a
     ..          <DIR>        1-10-88    1:32a
     GL          <DIR>        1-10-88    1:33a
     AP          <DIR>        1-10-88    1:33a
     AR          <DIR>        1-10-88    1:33a
            5 File(s)      350208 bytes free
```

COPYING FILES INTO A DIRECTORY STRUCTURE

So far, no subdirectory contains any user or program files. In the next few steps, we will use the COPY command to copy some DOS files from your DOS disk in drive A into certain subdirectories on your data disk in drive B:

1. `A>copy A:KEY*.* B:\VENDOR`

   You have just copied all files on your DOS disk that begin with KEY into the Vendor file drawer on your data disk. To make sure the files were actually copied into the correct location, key in the following command:

   `A>dir B:\VENDOR`

   Note that you didn't have to actually change directories to see the files in the Vendor subdirectory; you just took a peek into it. You should still be in the root directory.

2. `A>copy A:*.EXE B:\INVOICE\UNPAID`

   You have just copied all files on your DOS disk that end with EXE into the Unpaid sub-subdirectory.

3. `A>copy A:COMMAND.COM B:\PURCHASE`

   You have just copied the file called COMMAND.COM into the Purchase subdirectory.

Copying files from one directory structure to another really isn't any different from copying files not in a directory structure. However, you must remember to specify the path—one or more directory names, each separated from the previous one by a backslash—from where you are copying *and* to where you are copying. What if you want to copy a file or files, from one subdirectory on your data disk to another subdirectory on the same disk? To practice this, key in the following:

4. `A>copy B:\INVOICE\UNPAID\*.EXE B:\ACCOUNT\GL`

   All files with the extension EXE will be copied from the Unpaid file drawer into the GL (general ledger) file drawer.

THE RMDIR (RD) COMMAND

Sometimes you'll create subdirectories and sub-subdirectories that you never use. The **RMDIR (RD) command** will allow you to remove them. But remember, when using DOS, only empty subdirectories can be removed. To illustrate this, key in the following:

1. `A>rd B:\INVOICE\UNPAID`

   You should have gotten an error message like the one in Figure A.24.

   To remove a subdirectory, you must first erase any files in it. Key in the following to erase the user-created files:

2. `A>erase B:\INVOICE\UNPAID\*.*`

You can now use the command in Step 1 to remove the Unpaid sub-subdirectory. To make sure it has been removed, key in the following:

`A>dir B:\INVOICE`

You should see only the Paid sub-subdirectory in the Invoice subdirectory.

THE TREE COMMAND

Business users often share computers. If the shared computer is configured with a hard disk, it probably also contains a directory structure that was created by the individual who uses the machine the most. What if you want to use the accounting files, but you don't know where to find them on the hard disk because they're hidden in a subdirectory? The **TREE command**, an external command, allows you to see subdirectories and sub-subdirectories and the files they contain. The syntax for the TREE command is given in Figure A.25.

FIGURE A.24
Error message. You can't remove a subdirectory that isn't empty.

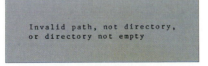

```
Invalid path, not directory,
or directory not empty
```

FIGURE A.25
Syntax of the TREE command. When using the TREE command to see a listing of all subdirectories on a disk, you must specify the disk drive where the directory is located.

TREE command syntax

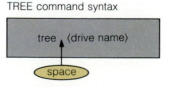

tree ˎ ⟨drive name⟩
space

Make sure your DOS disk is in drive A, because the TREE command is an external command, and key in the following:

1. `A>tree B:`

You should see a quick listing of the subdirectories located on your data disk. To slow down the screen display, and to see the display page by page, key in the following:

`A>tree B: | MORE`

Strike any key to continue the screen's scroll.

The last two commands showed you only subdirectories located on your data disk. What if you also want to see the files in the subdirectories? To do this you must use the /F option with the TREE command. Key in the following:

2. `A>tree B:/F | MORE`

You should see all subdirectories and the files they contain on your data disk. And, because we tacked on MORE to the end of the command, the screen displayed the listing page by page.

You should now feel relatively comfortable using DOS's directory commands. If you don't, work through the exercises at the end of this module.

Creating Batch Files with DOS

As manager of a sporting goods store, you will want to keep track of the files in your subdirectories—probably on a weekly basis. To do so, you can direct the output from the TREE command to the printer attached to your computer. (In the last section, when you issued the TREE command, the output from the command was directed to the screen.) But, because you will be performing this procedure week after week, and because someone who doesn't know as much about DOS as you do might occasionally need to perform this task, you'd be wise to automate this procedure by creating a batch file that contains the necessary commands. (As we mentioned earlier, a batch file is a collection of DOS commands that are automatically executed; this type of file is useful for executing frequently used series of commands. One of the most used batch files is the AUTOEXEC.BAT file, which DOS reads automatically whenever you boot your computer. Batch files can also include a set of special commands that allow you to write simple programs.) The following introduction to batch files should give you an understanding of how the batch file capability might be useful to you in the business environment.

Some Useful Batch Commands

The following commonly used batch commands can be found in most batch files:

1. ECHO OFF: This batch command causes the messages resulting from DOS commands not to be displayed on the screen.

2. ECHO: This batch command causes messages from commands to be displayed on the screen.

3. PAUSE: This batch command causes a batch file to interrupt processing and display the message "Strike a key when ready. . .". You can also add an optional remark (this will be covered in the next section).

4. CLS: This batch command, which clears the screen of all characters, is often used when directions or menus are to be displayed.

5. REM: When ECHO OFF is in effect, this batch command allows you to put remarks in your batch file that aren't displayed on the screen when the file is executed. This enables you to include descriptive text about the commands you're using in the file.

CREATING A SIMPLE BATCH FILE

The batch file you are going to create will function in the following way:

1. The ECHO OFF command turns off all messages so that only messages we've defined in the ECHO statements will be displayed on the screen.

2. The CLS command clears the screen so that messages can be displayed on an uncluttered background.

3. A message will be displayed on the screen describing the purpose of the batch file and asking you to make sure the printer is on; this is accomplished by ECHO statements.

4. The output from the TREE command will be directed not to the screen but to a file entitled DISKSTAT. This file will be placed in the root directory of your data disk.

5. A message will be displayed on the screen telling you to press the RETURN key when prompted to name your list device (what you're sending the output to).

6. When you press the RETURN key, the contents of the file DISKSTAT will be printed on the printer.

The batch file commands necessary to perform the activities listed above are given in Figure A.26. You are going to key them in using the COPY CON command (which you used in "Getting Ready to Practice More DOS Commands.") Key in the following:

1. A>copy con B:\TREEPRNT.BAT

   When you press the RETURN key, the cursor will move down one line and wait for you to enter keystrokes. Note that we used the extension BAT in the name of the batch file. All batch files must have this extension; otherwise DOS won't recognize them when you try to execute them. Key in the keystrokes shown in Figure A.26. Try not to make any mistakes, because the COPY CON command doesn't allow you to edit your files.

2. After you have entered the last line in the batch file, press the Return key; the cursor will then wait for you to enter something. To save the batch file,

hold the CONTROL (CTRL) key down while you tap the letter Z and then press the RETURN key. The message

```
1 File(s) copied
```

should appear on the screen.

To execute the batch file, which is located in the root directory of your data disk in drive B, you must make drive B your default drive, because DOS will look in the default directory for the file called TREEPRNT.BAT. Key in the following to execute the batch file:

3. `A>B:`

You have now made drive B the default disk drive.

4. `B>TREEPRNT`

The keystrokes in the file TREEPRNT.BAT should now be executing. If you follow the instructions in the batch file, the tree structure on your data disk should be printed out by the printer.

THE AUTOEXEC.BAT FILE

As mentioned earlier, an **AUTOEXEC.BAT file** is a special type of batch file placed in the root directory of your default disk (the disk that contains the files necessary to boot your computer) so that all its instructions will be executed when the computer boots. For example, someone who uses a computer principally for word processing might put instructions in an AUTOEXEC.BAT file that will automatically open a subdirectory on a hard disk that contains the word processing software program and then automatically start the program.

ADDITIONAL EXTERNAL DOS COMMANDS

Entire texts have been written to describe DOS commands and how the user can employ them effectively. So far, in this module, we have described only the most commonly used commands. However, in this section, we'll describe additional commands that, although not used as often, are still very important.

THE MODE COMMAND

The **MODE command,** an external command, tells the computer to switch from one setting to another. It can initialize the computer's mode of operation in regard to whether a color or a monochrome monitor is being used; whether information is routed to the printer through the parallel printer port or the serial communications port (a *port* is where the printer is plugged in to the computer); and which port you plug your modem in. The command is used only when the default configuration needs to be changed to work with the software you are using. For example, the default mode of operation for monitors is monochrome. If you want your monitor display to be in color, you would need to use the MODE command.

THE BACKUP COMMAND

The **BACKUP command** allows you to make backup copies of the files on your data disk—regardless of whether it's a hard disk or a floppy disk—onto another disk. The command allows you to specify the name of the file (or files) you want to copy, the disk drive where the file (or files) is located, whether you want the target disk to be erased before the backup copies are placed on it, and whether you want to copy only files that have been updated since a certain date or time. The syntax for the BACKUP command is shown in Figure A.27. Once you've keyed this command in and pressed RETURN, DOS will prompt you to make sure the correct disk is in the drive and to insert additional disks if the disk in your target drive becomes full.

THE SORT AND FIND COMMANDS

DOS gives the user the capability to sort the contents of files. What if you want a directory list in alphabetical or chronological order of all files you have stored on your data disk? You could issue the DIR command and send the output to a file instead of to the screen (as you did in the batch file with the TREE command). Then you could use the **SORT command** to sort the contents of the file. The SORT command allows you to specify how to sort a file and whether you want the file in ascending or descending order.

FIGURE A.26
Batch file. This is a listing of the batch file called **TREEPRNT.BAT**, which will send the output of the TREE command to the printer.

```
ECHO OFF
CLS
ECHO   THIS BATCH COMMAND FILE WILL LIST ON THE PRINTER
ECHO   ALL OF THE SUBDIRECTORIES AND FILES LOCATED ON
ECHO   YOUR DATA DISKETTE.  MAKE SURE YOUR PRINTER IS ON
ECHO   BEFORE YOU CONTINUE.
PAUSE
TREE B:\F >B:\DISKSTAT
ECHO   WHEN YOU ARE PROMPTED TO GIVE THE NAME OF YOUR LIST DEVICE,
ECHO   PRESS THE RETURN KEY.
PRINT B:DISKSTAT
```

FIGURE A.27
Syntax of the **BACKUP** command.

BACKUP command syntax

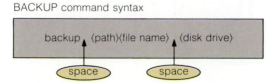

DOS's FIND command allows the user to locate a string of characters in a file. For example, what if you have a file that contains 200 names and addresses, but you can't remember whether you keyed in Lindsay Upham's name? You can use the **FIND command** to search for the occurrence of the name; the output of the command will tell you whether or not the string was found. The syntax for the SORT and the FIND commands is shown in Figure A.28.

THE DISKCOPY COMMAND

DOS's **DISKCOPY command** allows the user to copy entire floppy disks at once, while formatting the target disk—the disk being copied to—as it copies. You simply tell the command where your source disk is and where your target disk is, and then you press the RETURN key. This command doesn't recognize files, only tracks and sectors, so the target disk becomes a mirror-image copy of the source disk.

One disadvantage to using the DISKCOPY command—and why many users prefer to use the COPY command to copy all the files from one disk to another—is that often a file becomes fragmented on a disk, which means that it is stored on different portions of a disk. This is not apparent to the user in any other way but that it slows retrieval time. Using the DISKCOPY command will make the target file fragmented just like the source file. However, when files are copied using the COPY command, each target file is copied in one contiguous piece (that is, not fragmented).

SUMMARY

To be effective and efficient at work, business users need to understand some basic fundamentals about a microcomputer's operating system. To execute operating system commands, the user must be familiar with the operating system's disk-drive

---

FIGURE A.28
Syntax of the SORT command and the FIND command.

SORT command syntax

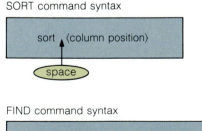

FIND command syntax

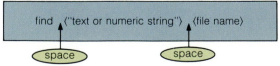

naming conventions, command hierarchy, command syntax, and file-naming conventions. Understanding the disk-drive naming conventions allows users to correctly specify different disk drives when issuing commands. Knowing about the command hierarchy, or the order in which the operating system executes different types of commands, helps the user to understand why or why not a command has been executed as intended. If the command you try to execute doesn't fall into any category in the command hierarchy, or if you use incorrect syntax, you will get an error message on the screen. Knowing the rules for naming files will allow you to quickly proceed with your work. In the DOS operating system, a file name can't be longer than eight characters, and an extension can't be longer than three characters.

As shown in Figure A.29 (page 506), operating system software gives the user many different types of commands with which to manage disk storage. These commands fall into the following categories: (1) standard user commands, (2) directory commands, and (3) batch commands. Standard user commands allow you to perform common activities, such as copying files or formatting disks. Directory commands allow you to create, use, and maintain directory structures that keep files that relate to one another in their own subdirectory—or sub-subdirectory—on a disk. Batch commands allow you to create batch command files to automate frequently performed procedures. In DOS, all batch files end with the extension BAT.

DOS is the most widely used operating system in the business environment today. To use it effectively, you must follow its rules and conventions carefully. Most business professionals require some training in the use of DOS before they reach that level of effectiveness.

KEY TERMS

AUTOEXEC.BAT file
BACKUP command
batch command
batch command file
boot
CHDIR command
CHKDSK command
CLS command
command syntax
COPY command
COPY CON command
default disk drive
DIR command
directory structure
DISKCOPY command

ECHO
ECHO OFF
ERASE command
extension
external command
file name length
file-naming conventions
FIND command
FORMAT command
initialize
internal command
MKDIR command
MODE command
operating system
    commands

RENAME command
RMDIR (RD)
    command
root directory
SORT command
subdirectory (file
    drawer)
sub-subdirectory (file
    folder)
system prompt (A>)
TREE command
TYPE command

FIGURE A.29
DOS command summary.

Command Name	Purpose	Syntax
1. FORMAT	To prepare disks for storage	format <drive name>
2. DIRECTORY	To let you view the names of the files stored on a disk	dir <drive name> /w/p optional
3. COPY	To make copies of files	copy <drive name><file name> <drive name><file name> where you're / what you're where you're / new name copying from / copying copying / optional
4. RENAME	To change the name of a file	rename <drive name><file name> <new file name>
5. TYPE	To see the contents of a file	type <drive name><file name>
6. ERASE	To erase one or more files from a disk	erase <drive name><file name(s)>
7. CHECK DISK	To analyze the directories on a disk and the amount of internal memory available for use.	chkdsk <drive name>
8. MAKE DIRECTORY	To make a subdirectory on a disk	mkdir
9. CHANGE DIRECTORY	To move into a subdirectory on a disk	chdir } <drive name><path>
10. REMOVE DIRECTORY	To remove a subdirectory on a disk	rmdir
11. TREE	To allow you to see the subdirectories on a disk	tree <drive name>
12. BACKUP	To allow you to make backup copies of files on an entire disk	backup <path><file name> <disk drive>
13. SORT	To put the contents of a file into a specified order	sort <column position>
14. FIND	To see if a file contains a certain text or numeric string	find <"text or numeric string"> <file name>

EXERCISES

SHORT ANSWER

1. How do you know if your computer has booted or not?

2. How would you find out how much internal memory you have in your computer and what the total capacity is of your data disk?

3. Why do many users prefer to use the COPY command instead of the DISK-COPY command when copying all the files from one disk to another?

4. If your computer has a hard disk, when might it be potentially disastrous to format it?

5. When might you find it necessary to rename files?

6. Why is it significant to know whether the command you want to use is an internal or an external command?

7. Why is it important to know the disk-drive and file-naming conventions of the operating system you are using? What are DOS's disk-drive and file-naming conventions?

8. Give an example of when it would be valuable to create a directory structure on your storage device.

9. Why is it important to know about batch files? Why do you think it would be especially important to know about batch files in a business environment where only a few people know how to use the operating system?

10. What might the reason(s) be for a computer not to boot when it is turned on?

HANDS-ON EXERCISES

1. Boot your computer.

2. Check the status of your data disk and internal memory.

3. Format your data disk.

4. Erase all files from your data disk. (*Note:* Remember how the global character (*) can help you do this quickly.)

5. Perform the steps to create some of the text files in the "Getting Ready to Practice More DOS Commands" section so that we can work with them in some of the next few exercises.

6. List the files present on your data disk. What information do you see on your screen as output from the command?

7. List the files present on your DOS disk. Now list them using (a) the wide-display option, and (b) the page-display option. What information does the page-display option give you that the wide-display option doesn't?

8. Copy all of the files from your DOS disk that have an extension of COM onto your data disk. How much space do you have left on your data disk, if any?

9. On your data disk, make a copy of the file called TEXT3.DOC under your name (such as NANCY or TOM).

10. Rename the file TEXT2.DOC on your data disk NEWNAME.DOC. Erase the file called TEXT1.DOC from your data disk.

MODULE B

B
WORD PROCESSING:
WORD PERFECT

This module will familiarize you with word processing and demonstrate how useful word processing software can be for you—both personally and professionally. We provide you with a list of the most useful features available in word processing software and describe the hardware requirements necessary for effective word processing. We recommend you read the section on "Operating System Software Fundamentals" in Module A before you proceed with this module.

■

When you have completed this module, you will be able to:

- Define the term *word processing* and describe the document cycle
- Describe the features of word processing that are important to know when:
  —entering and editing text
  —spell-checking
  —using a thesaurus
  —saving and retrieving
  —printing
  —merging
- Use WordPerfect to create, edit, and save a document

WORD PROCESSING SOFTWARE OVERVIEW

For those of us who are not trained typists, the thought of typing a letter can quickly turn a good mood into a bad one—that is, if we are using a typewriter instead of a computer and word processing software. The process of using a typewriter is familiar to most of us. You begin typing your letter, paying close attention to pressing the correct keys. You finish typing the letter. You reread it, hoping you won't come across any misspelled words—but you do. Or you omitted a critical sentence right in the middle of your letter. So you have to start all over again.

With the help of word processing software programs, computers give us the ability to avoid such trying situations. Word processing software programs are used on all types of computers. Some computers (called *dedicated word processors*) are designed to perform *only* word processing activities. This module focuses on the capabilities of word processing software used on microcomputers.

WHAT IS WORD PROCESSING?

Word processing is nothing new; people have been processing words for hundreds of years. For our purposes, **word processing** refers to the preparation of text (words, sentences, paragraphs) for creating, editing, or printing documents (for example, memos, letters, or manuscripts). **Word processing software** allows us to create, edit, store and retrieve, and print documents.

When a user presses a key on a typewriter, a character is immediately printed out on paper in hardcopy form. However, when a user of a computer loaded with word processing software presses a key, the character is stored electronically in internal memory, "printed" only on the screen. This innovation gives the computer user one major advantage over the traditional typewriter user: Characters stored electronically can be manipulated easily by the tools made available through the word processing program. The user can change text again and again without having to start over, correcting mistakes without disturbing the rest of the document. Only after the document is "perfect" is it printed in hardcopy form.

As more and more microcomputers are used in the business workplace, more and more word processing software programs are being written for use with micro-computers. Bookstore and computer store shelves are full of books on different microcomputer word processing software packages. If you're smart, you'll ask around to see what people think is the best word processing software in terms of ease of use and available features or used the most in your particular industry. You should also check software reviews in magazines on microcomputer software.

HARDWARE CONSIDERATIONS

Before you purchase a word processing package, you need to consider the hardware you'll be using with the software because different word processing packages require different hardware. Word processing hardware requirements fall into the follow-ing categories: (1) internal memory, (2) disk storage, (3) keyboard configuration, and (4) printed output.

The first and most important hardware consideration is internal memory. Inter-nal memory requirements vary from one word processing software package to an-other. Early software was designed to "fit" easily into 64 K of random access memory (RAM). However, as the sophistication of software has increased, so has the require-ment for internal memory. Some newer software packages require a minimum of 256 K RAM. If the computer doesn't satisfy the internal memory requirements of your word processing software, you won't be able to use the software.

Another important hardware consideration relates to disk storage. The capacity of your disk storage device(s) affects the size of the largest document you can work with. Although some 5 1/4-inch floppy disks and 3 1/2-inch diskettes are capable of storing between 1 and 2 MB, many 5 1/4-inch floppies in use today store only a maximum of 362 K, which can present a problem to the user. On average, one page of text takes up approximately 2 K of disk storage space. On a 362 K diskette, this translates into a theoretical capacity of 181 pages of text per disk; however, this capacity is not practically achievable because many word processing programs auto-matically create backup copies of files being updated; some even create a temporary "in-progress copy," taking up storage space. This reduces the actual capacity of the 362 K disk to approximately 70 pages.

Keyboard configuration is another important hardware consideration. Because such a large part of word processing involves typing, you should make sure you feel comfortable with the layout of your keyboard. Word processing software uses certain keys on the keyboard frequently; these keys may vary from program to program. Among these keys are the function keys, the INSERT key, the DELETE key, the CONTROL key, the ALTERNATE key, and the SHIFT key (see Figure 3.5 for a description of the keyboard and key functions). Before you buy word processing software, make sure your keyboard has all the necessary keys to use it effectively.

The final hardware consideration is the printer. You must have a printer that is compatible with your software program; otherwise, you'll never be able to output your documents in hardcopy form. The documentation manual that accompanies your word processing software lists compatible printer models. You should, of course, review this list before you purchase either a printer or a word processing program, depending on which you purchase first. With hundreds of printer manufacturers in the marketplace today, and even more models of printers to choose from, a program can't be compatible with all of them. Most software is compatible with the more popular models.

THE DOCUMENT CYCLE

The **document cycle** involves using word processing software to perform the following activities: (1) entering, (2) editing, (3) spell-checking, (4) saving and retrieving, and (5) printing a document. A sixth feature—merging text from separate documents into a single document—may also be part of the cycle. Each step in the document cycle involves using a number of different features of your word processing software. To execute these features, most word processing software uses menus, commands (which are invoked by typing two or three keys at the same time or in succession), or special function keys. In the "In the Lab" section of this module, you will primarily use special function keys along with a succession of other specific keystrokes to execute WordPerfect commands. The next section describes the features that relate to each step in the document cycle.

WORD PROCESSING FEATURES

Some people find the concept of writing with a computer difficult to grasp. They are used to using the traditional tools for word processing—pen or pencil and paper, or a typewriter. It's natural to think that a new way of doing things is going to be difficult, because one is suddenly confronted with unfamiliar procedures. If you are one of these people, you will probably put pen and paper aside after working through this module, because you'll find that computer-based word processing makes writing much easier. The following sections will familiarize you with the features included in most word processing packages.

ENTERING TEXT

After you have loaded your word processing software into internal memory (see Module A for instructions on booting your computer), the next step is to enter, or key in, your text. When entering text, you will be dealing with (1) cursor movement, (2) word wrap and the RETURN key, (3) scrolling, and (4) formatting.

In most word processing programs, the **cursor** is a blinking or highlighted line (or block) about as wide as a character, which marks either where the next character will be entered or the starting point of the next command operation. As you type in a character, the cursor moves to the right. You can control where the cursor is positioned in a document when you perform editing operations (such as inserting or deleting a sentence in the middle of a paragraph); in other words, the cursor can be moved in ways other than one character at a time. This feature is especially useful when working with large documents. In the "In the Lab" section of this module, you will learn how to move the cursor around a document using the WordPerfect software program.

Another important feature of computer-based word processing is **word wrap.** To begin typing a new line on a typewriter, you press the **RETURN key** when the print mechanism hits the right-hand margin so that it will return to the left-hand margin. When using a computer and word processing software, you don't have to press the RETURN key at the end of every line. When the cursor reaches the right-hand margin, it automatically returns to the left-hand margin of the line below. In other words, the cursor *wraps around* to start a new line when it reaches the right margin. If a word is being typed that is too big to fit on the current line, the cursor will automatically take the whole word down to the next line.

What if you want to start a new line because you've reached the end of a paragraph, or you want some blank lines in your document? If you press the RETURN key, a new line will be created. However, the RETURN key should be used only when you need to end a paragraph or include some blank lines in your document. As you will learn later, using the RETURN key instead of allowing the word wrap feature to operate makes it very tedious to format text—that is, to set up how you want your pages to look when they are printed out.

Entering text almost always involves **scrolling**—the automatic movement of text up or down the screen. Many, if not most, of the documents you create will be too large to see all at once on the screen. Your monitor can hold at the most 24 to 25 lines of text. What happens when you're entering a document that is longer than 25 lines? Your document will move up, or *scroll,* off the top of your screen. As shown in Figure B.1, your screen acts like a **window** through which you see portions of the text you have entered. To see portions of text that have scrolled off the screen, you need to move the cursor to the portions of text you want to see (you will learn how to do this shortly). To see an entire document longer than 25 lines, you must print it out.

What if you want to underline a sentence or phrase in your document? What if you want certain parts of your text to appear darker, or bolder, when printed out? What if you want to change the margins of your document to be either larger or smaller, or to center text in your document? These are all **formatting** tasks that are easy to accomplish using word processing software. You may choose to wait to format your document until the editing stage of the document cycle, after you've entered the basic text.

EDITING TEXT

Let's say you've used word processing software to create a resume to send out to a potential employer. You now want to send the same resume out to another potential employer, but you want to **edit** it (make changes to it) to focus on the different job description. A number of features can be used to edit a document. Two of the most important editing features involve inserting and deleting text. When using a typewriter, you usually have to retype an entire sentence (if not an entire page) if you want to insert a word in the middle of a sentence. However, with word processing software, to insert text in or delete text from a document all you have to do is to move the cursor to the location where you want to start the operation and then press the appropriate keys. Once you've performed the desired operation, most software programs will automatically format your revised text to fit within the margins you have set. In the tutorial section of this module ("In the Lab"), you will have a chance to practice inserting and deleting text.

Another convenient editing feature of word processing programs is the ability to perform **block operations.** For example, what if you decide to move the first paragraph of your document to the end of your document? By using block operations, you can move, delete, and copy sentences, paragraphs, and even pages by telling the software where the beginning and end points are of the text block you want to move. Once you have defined the block of text, you issue the appropriate command to move, delete, or copy it. Most word processing software also offers the capability of creating a separate file out of a block of text. This feature allows you to save parts of documents you will be using again and to incorporate them into new documents.

Most word processing software also features the ability to search for and replace text in a document. For instance, perhaps you used the name John instead of Jack in many places throughout your document. If your document is 20 pages long, to find each occurrence of "John," erase it, and type in "Jack" would take a long time. With the **search and replace** capability, you tell the software what word or phrase

FIGURE B.1
The window. Most screens allow you to see only 24 to 25 lines of text at one time—through a "window." The text moves (scrolls) up and down the screen to get to different areas of the text.

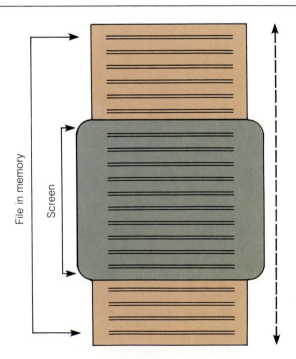

File in memory

Screen

you want to search for and what word or phrase you want to replace it with. Then—presto!—say good-bye to John and hello to Jack.

SPELL-CHECKING AND USING A THESAURUS

Many word processing software packages can check for spelling errors in your document. (With some packages this capability is considered a utility that you must buy separately.) It's amazing how many errors the spelling checker finds even after you've looked for spelling errors yourself. When you choose the menu option to check the spelling of your document, a spelling dictionary (which accompanies your word processing program) is loaded into memory. The words in your document are then compared to the words in the dictionary. The spelling checker flags each word in your document that it can't match in the dictionary and asks you to correct the word. Sometimes, if the dictionary doesn't contain a word like it, the checker will flag a word that is spelled correctly; spelling checkers allow you to skip correcting words that are flagged even though they're spelled correctly. Spelling checkers also let you add words to the dictionary, which is very useful if your profession uses special terminology or if you must often use proper names in your documents. If you don't add these words to the dictionary, it will flag them as misspelled every time you **spell-check** your document.

Many word processing packages also include the capability to identify words with similar meanings through use of a computerized thesaurus. The user simply uses the thesaurus menu to choose a word to be compared with words of similar meaning in the thesaurus dictionary, and the program will list on the screen all the appropriate words. This feature is useful when you know what you want to say but just can't find the right words.

SAVING AND RETRIEVING

After you've created a document (and before you turn your computer off), you must issue a command to save your document—that is, to place a permanent copy of your document on your disk storage device. Otherwise, you will lose all the text you keyed in since you turned the computer on. When you are working with a large document, you should **save** your document periodically (*while* you're working on it) so that you don't lose it if the power fails. When you first save your document, you have to give it a name (as you learned in Module A, the name should be no more than eight characters long). If you save the document again after making changes and/or additions to it, you will be replacing the original document. If you want to keep several versions of a document, you will have to save each one with a different name. We'll go through the procedure to save documents in the "In the Lab" section of this module.

At the beginning of a word processing session, after you have loaded your word processing software into internal memory, you might want to edit a document that you stored previously. You will need to choose the menu option that will allow you to **retrieve** a copy of the document from your storage device and place it into internal memory.

PRINTING

Once you've created a document and you're pleased with it, you'll probably want to print the document out on a printer. Printing a document involves connecting your printer to your computer, turning the printer on, and then issuing the command to print your document. However, before you actually print your document, you may want to enhance the final appearance of the printed page—that is, to change the formatting.

For example, you may want to change the justification of your document; in other words, you may want all text to be evenly aligned along the left margin and ragged on the right margin (no "broken" words), evenly aligned along both the left and the right margins ("justified"), or centered (ragged on both sides) (Figure B.2). Or you may want to change the size of the **margins** that will appear on the printed page (Figure B.3); when a document is printed, the software tells the printer to skip a few lines at the top of the page for the top (or head) margin, at the bottom of the page for the bottom margin, and at the left and right sides of the page. You may also want to change the line spacing of your document from single- to double- or triple-spaced.

FIGURE B.2
Unjustified (ragged right);
justified; and centered text.
Changing the justification
of your document affects
how text is aligned along
the margins of the page.

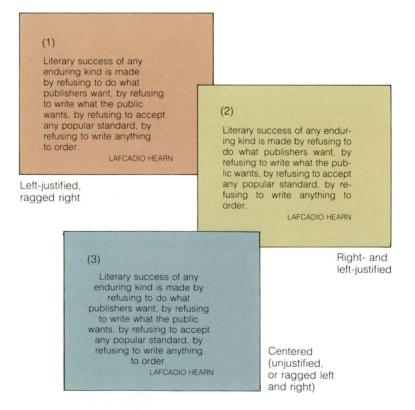

(1)

Literary success of any
enduring kind is made
by refusing to do what
publishers want, by refusing
to write what the public
wants, by refusing to accept
any popular standard, by
refusing to write anything
to order.
                    LAFCADIO HEARN

Left-justified,
ragged right

(2)

Literary success of any enduring kind is made by refusing to
do what publishers want, by
refusing to write what the public wants, by refusing to accept
any popular standard, by refusing to write anything to
order.
                    LAFCADIO HEARN

Right- and
left-justified

(3)

Literary success of any
enduring kind is made by
refusing to do what
publishers want, by refusing
to write what the public
wants, by refusing to accept
any popular standard, by
refusing to write anything
to order.
                    LAFCADIO HEARN

Centered
(unjustified,
or ragged left
and right)

You may want certain parts of your document to be underlined or in bold for emphasis, such as your name and address in a resume. Most word processing software can send codes to the printer to tell it to print underlines or print a string of text twice to make it darker. Word processing software can also put headers or footers on a page (Figure B.3). **Headers** and **footers** are descriptive information that appears at the top or bottom of every page. Headers and footers generally contain such information as page number, date, and document title. Although defined from within the program, headers and footers in most word processing packages appear only on your printed output.

MERGING

Think of how much time you would save if you could send out 50 personalized resumes to potential employers in less than an hour! Word processing software can help you do so by allowing you to bring information from two files together, a process that is called **merging** (Figure B.4).

FIGURE B.3
Margins. Word processing software allows you to change the size of the margins that will appear on the printed page and to insert a header or a footer. Here, the footer is "B.3."

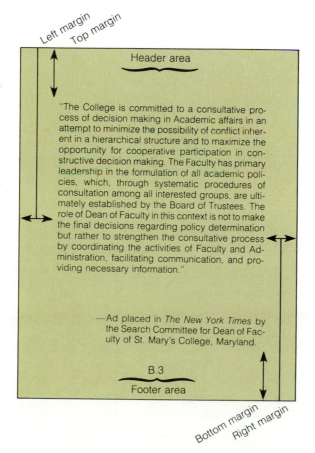

Left margin Top margin

Header area

"The College is committed to a consultative process of decision making in Academic affairs in an attempt to minimize the possibility of conflict inherent in a hierarchical structure and to maximize the opportunity for cooperative participation in constructive decision making. The Faculty has primary leadership in the formulation of all academic policies, which, through systematic procedures of consultation among all interested groups, are ultimately established by the Board of Trustees. The role of Dean of Faculty in this context is not to make the final decisions regarding policy determination but rather to strengthen the consultative process by coordinating the activities of Faculty and Administration, facilitating communication, and providing necessary information."

—Ad placed in *The New York Times* by the Search Committee for Dean of Faculty of St. Mary's College, Maryland.

B.3

Footer area

Bottom margin Right margin

In this case, the first file used in the merging process is the stored resume—the document. The second file is often referred to as the *data file*, which, in this example, contains the names and addresses of the potential employers. Data files must be set up according to a specific format, depending on the word processing program you use. In the tutorial section, we'll show you how a WordPerfect data file should look. To prepare for a merge, you must put specific codes in your document so that your software will know what information from your data file should appear in which locations in your document.

IN THE LAB:

WORD PROCESSING USING WORDPERFECT

In this tutorial, you will have the opportunity to create a document using the educational version of WordPerfect, a very popular word processing software pack-

FIGURE B.4
Merging. This editing feature of word processing software allows the user to bring together information from two separate files.

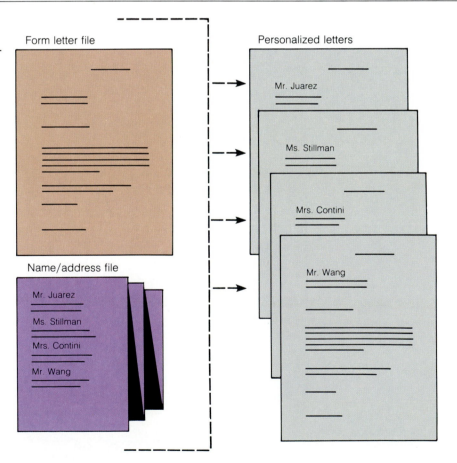

age. You will learn how to use most of the word processing features discussed in this module thus far. Because WordPerfect's features are similar to those of most word processing programs today, gaining experience with WordPerfect will help you if you ever have to learn how to use another word processing software package. Concepts and procedures are similar from one word processing package to another.

The educational version of WordPerfect (used in this tutorial) is limited in two ways. First, the maximum file size you can create is 5 K, which translates into a little more than two pages of text. If you want to create and print a document that is longer than two pages, you will have to link smaller documents together. We describe the procedure for doing this in the Saving and Retrieving section of this tutorial. Second, the characters "*WPC" will appear throughout your document in unpredictable locations—unacceptable characters if your intention is to use this educational version in the future to generate reports. To print out your document without these characters, you must print the document file using the *complete* version of WordPerfect, which you can purchase for $125.00 with our special rebate offer.

In this tutorial, we assume you are using an IBM PC or compatible microcomputer that has two floppy disk drives (drives A and B), that your copy of the WordPerfect program will be retrieved from drive A, and that the document you will be creating will be saved onto a data disk in drive B. Throughout this module we will be referring to drives A and B. If you are using a computer with a hard disk, you will probably need to change these references to include drive C, depending on from where you will retrieve a copy of WordPerfect and to where you will save your documents (consult your instructor or computer lab assistant for guidance).

THE BUSINESS SITUATION

Sporting Life is a sporting goods store that carries a wide variety of sporting goods—from baseball bats and volleyballs to scuba diving equipment and aerobic workout gear. You, the store's manager, have recently purchased a computer and have just finished a course on how to use the computer's operating system. You learned how to name files, refer to disk drives, and use some common operating system commands. Now you are eager to learn how to use the word processing software package called WordPerfect; you bought this package because you knew you were going to send out personalized letters to regular clients telling them of special upcoming sales. You are currently planning a sale on ski equipment and would like to announce it in the next couple of days.

The first activity of this tutorial will lead you through the document cycle and help you create some document files. If at any time during this tutorial you have questions about a term, refer to the previous section on Word Processing Features.

LOADING WORDPERFECT AND USING FUNCTION KEYS

We assume that you have booted your computer with an operating system disk in drive A. To load the WordPerfect program instructions into internal memory and to use its set of commands, replace the operating system disk in drive A with the WordPerfect program disk. Now key in the following after the "A" prompt to load WordPerfect:

```
A>WP
```

Press the RETURN key. (*Note*: If you are using an IBM AT, press the ENTER key instead of the RETURN key.) Once the instructions have been loaded, a copyright page should appear. Press any key, and an empty page with status information at the bottom should appear.

> **QUICK REFERENCE:**
> **LOADING WORDPERFECT**
> 1. After the A prompt, type WP.
> 2. Press the RETURN key.
> 3. Press any key to display an empty page with status information on the bottom of the screen.

Note: If you are using a monochrome monitor, the letters at the bottom of your screen might be "breaking up"—that is, they may not look solid. WordPerfect can be used with either a monochrome monitor or a color monitor. If the letters are breaking up on your monochrome screen, do the following: (1) Copy the Word-Perfect master disk onto a disk formatted with DOS. (2) Go through the step described above to load this new copy of WordPerfect into memory. (3) Press CTRL F3. (4) Press the 4 key to select colors. (5) Press the 2 key to select monochrome characteristics (single-color monitor). (6) Press the 1 key or the 2 key to select how underlining will be shown. (7) Press the F7 key to exit.

What do you see on the screen? In the upper left-hand corner of the page, the cursor is blinking and waiting for you to enter text. In the bottom right-hand corner of the page, you should see status information that tells you what position ("Pos") the cursor is in. Note that your cursor is in position 10, not position 1. This default position automatically creates a left margin of nine characters when you print the document. Nine characters comprise the default left margin; you can change it with a command if you want it to be smaller or larger. Before we actually exercise your typing skills, we'd like to teach you how to access WordPerfect's commands.

WordPerfect's commands are accessed by pressing a **function key** (function keys have the letter *F* and a number and are usually located on the far left of most keyboards) and either the **ALTERNATE (ALT), SHIFT, or CONTROL (CTRL) keys.** Figure B.5 shows the WordPerfect template that indicates what each function key will do. (The template is placed around the function keys on the IBM keyboard. Don't worry if yours doesn't fit; you can still refer to it.) Note that four different commands are listed for each function key, each in a different color. To perform commands printed in *black*, you simply tap the function key corresponding to your choice. To perform commands printed in *blue*, hold the ALT key down and tap the appropriate function key. To perform commands printed in *green*, hold the SHIFT key down and tap the appropriate function key. Finally, to perform commands printed in *red*, hold the CTRL key down and tap the appropriate function key.

QUICK REFERENCE:
USING THE FUNCTION KEYS
To use the commands shown in:
1. BLACK, press the function key alone.
2. BLUE, press the ALT key and the function key.
3. GREEN, press the SHIFT key and the function key.
4. RED, press the CTRL key and the function key.

What keys would you press to **center** a title on a page? The word *center* is your hint. As you have probably figured out, you need to hold the SHIFT key down and tap the F6 key. Now it's time to exercise your typing skills. *Note:* In this tutorial, don't press any keys unless we instruct you to do so.

FIGURE B.5
WordPerfect template. This command identifier fits around the function keys on most keyboards. It is color coded to help the user remember which special key to hold down while tapping a function key—the ALT key (blue), the CTRL key (red), the SHIFT key (green), or no second key (black).

Beginning a Document: Cursor Movement and Moving Text

Your cursor should still be blinking in the upper left-hand corner of your screen, marking where the first character you type will appear. At this point, you can't move your cursor anywhere because you don't yet have any text for the cursor to move around in. Your document is empty. To put characters into this empty space, press any of the following keys: (1) keys labeled with letters, numbers, and special characters; (2) the **TAB key,** which puts five "blank" characters into your document; (3) the **SPACE bar,** which puts one "blank" character into your document; or (4) the RETURN key. The spaces (called *hard spaces*) created by using the TAB, SPACE bar, or RETURN keys are considered by the word processing program to be characters, even though the spaces don't appear as characters in the normal sense. (You can think of hard spaces as invisible characters.) To move your cursor around in your document, you will use the **arrow keys** and the PgUp and PgDn ("page up" and "page down") keys.

In the next few sections, you are going to create a business letter (Figure B.6) to one of Sporting Life's clients, and at the same time learn about many of Word-Perfect's word processing features. To show how many blank lines should be in the letter, "[Rtn]," which stands for pressing the RETURN (or ENTER) key, appears in the left margin to mark each blank line. Don't type [Rtn]; it's just a marker.

Your cursor should still be in the upper left-hand corner of your screen. Type in the date. (*Note:* When typing in numbers on an IBM PC keyboard, or a keyboard that has a number pad that is used both for entering arithmetic and for moving the cursor, use the numbers listed across the *top* of the keyboard, not the ones on the number pad to the right; you'll be using the number-pad arrow keys to move around in your document.)

You now have some text in your document, so you can move the cursor with the arrow keys. To try this, tap the left-arrow key four times. Your cursor should be positioned on the "1" of 1989.

Next we want to type in Mr. Henderson's name four lines down. To create four blank lines, press the RETURN key four times. What happened when you pressed the RETURN key with the cursor in its current position? The number 1989 was brought down *with* the cursor. You should always check the cursor position before you press the RETURN key. You can get 1989 back up to its original position by deleting the blank lines: Move the cursor with your up arrow and then your right arrow to the position where you want the "1" of 1989 to be positioned (Figure B.7). Tap your **DELETE (DEL)** key until 1989 is back in its original position. Move the cursor one character to the right of 1989. Press the RETURN key four times. You should now be in the correct position to key in Mr. Henderson's name and address.

Key in the following:

Text:	Followed by:
Mr. Robert Henderson	Press RETURN
111 Fallenbranch Lane	Press RETURN
Hillsbrook, CA 94010	Press RETURN four times
Dear Mr. Henderson:	Press RETURN twice

What if we want to insert a line above the street address that states what company Mr. Henderson works for? Move the cursor to the first "1" of 111. Press the RETURN key. Now press the up-arrow key once to move the cursor to the blank line that was just created. Key in the following: Henderson Securities, Inc. As you can see, with word processing software, it's not difficult to insert text into a document because you can move text with the RETURN key. You can also move text

FIGURE B.6
Sporting Life letter

```
October 3, 1989
[Rtn]
[Rtn]
[Rtn]
[Rtn]
Mr. Robert Henderson
111 Fallenbranch Lane
Hillsbrook, CA 94010
[Rtn]
[Rtn]
[Rtn]
[Rtn]
Dear Mr. Henderson:
[Rtn]
    We at Sporting Life would like to introduce you to our
new product line of ski clothing and equipment. Our
clothing line includes a wide variety of items from a
number of different high-quality manufacturers. Ski
jackets, ski pants, and ski sweaters, all in the latest
fashion, are here for you to see. For two weeks, October
7-21, we are giving valued past customers like yourself a
20% discount on all ski clothing items!
    Our ski equipment inventory also comprises high-
quality items. If you buy a complete package of skis,
boots, and poles, you can take advantage of a 20% discount
on the entire package.
    Mr. Henderson, we offer you this challenge: Check
around town. If you can find a store that offers a better
selection of ski clothing and ski equipment at a better
price, we'll match that price. But don't waste too much
time with this challenge, because with these savings,
you'll be able to find more of our inventory on the slopes
than in the store!
    Hope to see you soon.
[Rtn]
[Rtn]
        [your name]
        Manager,
        Sporting Life
```

with the SPACE bar and the TAB key. Tap your left-arrow key four times so that you're positioned on the "I" of "Inc." Press the SPACE bar five times. Note that the text moved over to the right five times. Now press your TAB key twice; the text should move over ten spaces.

You should now be in print position 45. To put "Inc." back in the correct position, use the left-arrow key to move the cursor back to print position 32. Tap your DELETE key until "Inc." is back in the appropriate location.

QUICK REFERENCE:
DELETING AND INSERTING

Delete text, spaces, or blank lines by using the arrow keys to position the cursor on the text, space, or blank line that you want to delete and then tapping the DELETE (DEL) key until the item you're deleting is gone.

Insert text, spaces, or blank lines by using the arrow keys to position the cursor where you want the new items to appear and then either typing in the text (for inserted text), pressing the SPACE bar or TAB key (for inserted spaces), or pressing the RETURN key (for blank lines).

Tap your down-arrow key until you are at the bottom of your document. You should be on line 14 in print position 10. This is the bottom of the document's first page. What if your document is a total of three pages in length and you are asked to move to the end of it? WordPerfect's default page length is 54 lines. Would you have to tap your down-arrow key 162 times to reach the bottom of your document? No. WordPerfect provides easier ways to move around in documents, depending on where you want to go (Figure B.8). If your document is three pages long, for

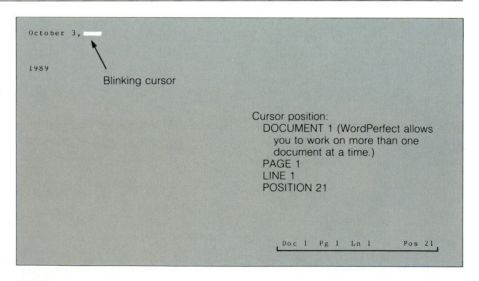

FIGURE B.7
Getting "1989" back to its original position. Position the cursor where you want the "1" of "1989" to be positioned and tap the DEL key. The status line at the bottom of the screen tells you what document, what page, what line, and what character position from the left your cursor is in.

October 3,

1989

Blinking cursor

Cursor position:
DOCUMENT 1 (WordPerfect allows you to work on more than one document at a time.)
PAGE 1
LINE 1
POSITION 21

Doc 1   Pg 1   Ln 1   Pos 21

example, you could simply tap the PgDn key twice to go to the top of the third page. Or you could press the following three keys in sequence:

HOME, HOME, and down-arrow

(The **HOME key** is number 7 on your numeric keypad.) In the rest of this tutorial, you will be using many of the cursor-moving methods listed in Figure B.8.

COMPLETING A DOCUMENT: WORD WRAP

You should now be ready to key in the rest of the letter to Mr. Henderson. Press the TAB key once. Your cursor should have moved five spaces to the right. Begin typing

FIGURE B.8
WordPerfect's cursor-movement methods. WordPerfect offers many ways to move the cursor around a document.

Horizontal Movement	Keys
Character left and right	Left- and Right-Arrow keys
Word right	Ctrl, Right-Arrow
Word left	Ctrl, Left-Arrow
Right edge of screen	Home, Right-Arrow
Left edge of screen	Home, Left-Arrow
Far right of the line	Home, Home, Right-Arrow
Far left of the line	Arrow
Vertical Movement	**Keys**
Line up and down	Up- and Down-Arrow keys
Top of screen	Home, Up-Arrow, or Minus $(-)$ key
Bottom of screen	Home, Down-Arrow, or Plus $(+)$ key
Top of current page	Ctrl, Home, Up-Arrow
End of current page	Ctrl, Home, Down-Arrow
Top of previous page	PgUp
Top of next page	PgDn
Beginning of document	Home, Home, Up-Arrow
End of document	Home, Home, Down-Arrow
Go To page #	Ctrl, Home, #
# Lines up	Esc, #, Up-Arrow
# Lines down	Esc, #, Down-Arrow

the rest of the letter. Don't press the RETURN key at the end of each line; press it only at the end of each paragraph. Otherwise the word-wrapping feature won't work. When you have finished typing in the last line of the document, which contains the text "Sporting Life," press the RETURN key. The cursor should now be on line 35 in print position 10.

QUICK REFERENCE:
USING WORD WRAP
When typing in paragraphs, don't press the RETURN key at the end of each line. Press the RETURN key only at the end of each paragraph.

SAVING AND RETRIEVING A DOCUMENT

Now you are going to issue your first WordPerfect command. You are going to save your document to disk—before someone comes by and accidentally trips over the cord to your computer, pulling the plug out of the socket. Right now your document resides only in internal memory; a loss of power to the computer would mean a total loss of all the work you've done so far. As we pointed out earlier, it's especially important to periodically save large documents.

You can save a WordPerfect document in three ways. You can save your document without leaving it (F10); save your document and then clear memory, which means an empty page will appear on the screen (F7 + N response to a query on the screen); or you can save your document and then exit WordPerfect (F7 + Y response). Because we are going to lead you through some editing and formatting exercises, we don't want you to clear memory or exit WordPerfect yet. Press F10 to initiate the SAVE command. You will be prompted to key in the name of the document to be saved. To tell WordPerfect you want your document to be saved onto the data disk in drive B under the name of DOC1, key in

B:DOC1

and then press RETURN. Your document will be saved onto your data disk in drive B.

QUICK REFERENCE:
SAVING A DOCUMENT
Use one of three methods:

—*Save without leaving your document:* (1) Press F10; (2) key in the document name; (3) press RETURN.

—*Save and exit your document:* (1) Press F7; (2) press Y; (3) key in the document name; (4) press RETURN; (5) press N.

—*Save and exit WordPerfect:* (1) press F7; (2) press Y; (3) key in the document name; (4) press RETURN; (5) press Y.

Now we want to make sure that the document DOC1 exists on your data disk.

The F5 key is the **LIST-FILES key.** Tap your F5 key. Key in B: to tell WordPerfect you want to see the files present on the data disk in drive B. Then press the RETURN key. You should see the name of the file DOC1, how much space it takes up on the disk, and the date and time it was created. To get back to your document, tap the F1 key—the CANCEL key. This will cancel the current command and return you to your document.

QUICK REFERENCE:
LISTING FILES ON A DISK
1. Press F5.
2. Key in B:.
3. Press RETURN.
4. Press F1 to return to your document work area.

To see what happens when you save a document more than once, pretend you've made some changes to the document and save DOC1 again. Press the F10 key. You will be asked "REPLACE B:\DOC1? (Y/N)." Key in Y. The "altered" document you have in internal memory has just replaced the document you had on your data disk. In this way you can update files.

QUICK REFERENCE:
SAVING THE SAME DOCUMENT MORE THAN ONCE
1. Follow one of the procedures listed above in the Quick Reference for Saving a Document until you have keyed in the document name and pressed RETURN.
2. Press Y to replace.

Although we aren't going to do it now, you should know how to retrieve a file. Hold the SHIFT key down and tap the F10 key. You will then be prompted for the name of the file to retrieve. Key in the name and then hit the RETURN key. If you have forgotten the name of the file that you want to retrieve, you can use the F5 key to list the data disk's files on the screen. You can then retrieve a file from within the LIST-FILES (F5) command (Figure B.9).

QUICK REFERENCE:
RETRIEVING A DOCUMENT
Method One:
1. Press SHIFT F10.
2. Key in the name of the file to retrieve.
3. Press RETURN.

Method Two:
1. Press F5.
2. Use the arrow keys to highlight the file you want to retrieve.
3. Press 1 to retrieve.

EDITING A DOCUMENT

You are going to execute a number of different editing commands, including inserting and deleting text and performing block operations, to make your document look like the one in Figure B.10. In this section, the following tasks will be performed on the letter you keyed in earlier (DOC1):

1. The name and address have to be changed. The fastest way to perform this activity is to first mark the name and address as a block of text and then, with one command, to erase the block. Key in the new name and address.

2. In the salutation and the body of the letter, the name "Mr. Henderson" must be changed to "Miss Dennis."

3. A new paragraph with a list of discounted items needs to be inserted in the document.

4. The first three lines of the last paragraph need to be indented and made into a separate paragraph.

5. The last few lines in the first paragraph must be moved to a position below the list of discounted items.

6. The closing line must be edited.

TASK 1—Position your cursor on the "M" of "Mr. Henderson" at the very top of your document.

1. ALT F4
   Hold the ALT key down and tap the F4 key to activate Block Mode.

FIGURE B.9
List files. This is an example of a LIST-FILES (F5) screen display. To execute one of the commands listed at the bottom of the screen, such as retrieving or deleting a file, you must first use an arrow key to move the cursor to highlight the file on which you want to perform an operation; then tap the key with the number that corresponds to the command you want to execute.

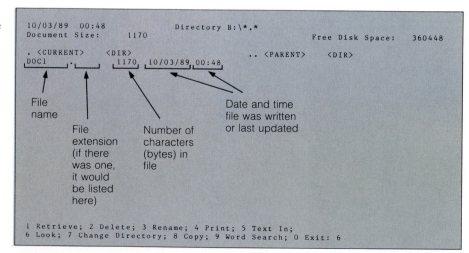

2. Tap the down-arrow key three times to highlight Mr. Henderson's name and address.

3. Now that the block is highlighted, press the DELETE key (DEL). Word-Perfect will then ask "Delete Block (Y/N)?" Respond by tapping Y. The block should have disappeared.

FIGURE B.10
The new DOC1. This is what your letter will look like after you have worked through the editing exercises in this section.

```
October 3, 1989


Miss Michele Dennis
1841 Kelton Ave.
San Mateo, Ca. 94010


Dear Miss Dennis:

     We at Sporting Life would like to introduce you to our new
product line of ski clothing and equipment.  Our clothing line
includes a wide variety of items from a number of different
high-quality manufacturers.  Our ski equipment inventory also
comprises high-quality items.  If you buy a complete package of
skis, boots, and poles, you can take advantage of a 20% discount
on the entire package.

     We are also offering special discounts on children's
clothing and equipment.  The following items are on sale:

                              Discount
     1.   Ski Pants          20%
     2.   Ski Sweaters       15%
     3.   Ski Goggles        40%
     4.   Skis, Boots, and Poles   25%

Ski jackets, ski pants, and ski sweaters, all in the latest
fashion, are here for you to see.  For two weeks, October 7-21,
we are giving our valued past customers like yourself a 20%
discount on all ski clothing items!

          Miss Dennis, we offer you this challenge:
          Check around town.  If you can find a store
          that offers a better selection of ski
          clothing and ski equipment at a better price,
          we'll match that price.

But don't waste too much time with this challenge, because with
these savings, you'll be able to find more of our inventory on
the slopes than in the store!

     Hope to see you soon.

     [your name]
     Manager,
     Sporting Life
```

QUICK REFERENCE:
DELETING A BLOCK
1. Use arrow keys to position cursor at beginning of block you want to delete.
2. Press ALT F4.
3. Use arrow keys to move cursor to end of block.
4. Press the DELETE (DEL) key.
5. Press Y to delete.

TASK 2—Key in the new name and address for Miss Dennis (see Figure B.10).

TASK 3—Move the cursor down to the "M" of "Mr. Henderson" in the salutation. Delete "Mr. Henderson" by tapping the DELETE key and then key in Miss Dennis's name. Move your cursor down to the second paragraph in the document and delete Mr. Henderson's name, replacing it with Miss Dennis's name.

TASK 4—Position your cursor on the first line of the second paragraph of the document and press the RETURN key twice to insert two blank lines. Then tap the up arrow twice to position the cursor at the beginning of the area where you want to place the new paragraph (the one with the discount listings in Figure B.10). Key in the new paragraph; remember not to press the RETURN key until you've finished the paragraph. You can line up the item descriptions and discount amounts by using the TAB key. We'll lead you through keying in the first item:

1. Press the TAB key seven times. Type Discount. Press RETURN.
2. Press the TAB key once. Type 1. Press the TAB key.
3. Type Ski Pants.
4. Press the TAB key four times. Type 20%. Press RETURN.

Repeat Steps 2 through 4 until you've finished the list. When repeating Step 4, use your judgment about how many times to press the TAB key to line up the discount amounts. If you press the TAB key too many times, just tap the left-arrow key to get back to the correct position.

TASK 5—Position your cursor in position 10 on the first line of the last paragraph. Tap the DEL key once to delete the tab. Press the RETURN key once. Your objective now is to indent the first three sentences of the last paragraph. Let's first indent the whole paragraph and then we'll insert two blank lines by pressing the RETURN key twice to move the last line down out of the indented area. *Note:* The **INDENT** command will affect a paragraph only up to the first place the RETURN key was pressed.

To indent the text from both margins ten spaces, hold the SHIFT key down and tap the F4 key twice. Then tap your down-arrow key a few times until all the text is indented. To move the last line of this paragraph out of the indented area, position the cursor on the "B" of "But." Press the RETURN key twice.

QUICK REFERENCE:
INDENTING TEXT
—*On the left margin only:*
Press F4 once for each group of five spaces you want to indent.

—On both margins:
Press SHIFT F4 once for each group of five spaces you want to indent.

TASK 6—The last activity is to move the paragraph that is below the list of discounted items up into the first paragraph. Then the lines in the first paragraph beginning with "Ski jackets, ski pants . . ." need to be moved down to below the list of discounted items. Quite a few steps are involved in moving text when using WordPerfect, but it won't seem so tedious after you have done it a few times. Here are the steps to accomplish this move:

1. Position the cursor in position 10 of the paragraph that is right below the list of discounted items. Hold the ALT key down and tap the F4 key to invoke Block mode.

2. Press the RETURN key to highlight the entire paragraph; this is a shortcut to highlighting the paragraph (as opposed to tapping the down arrow four times).

3. To move this block to the first paragraph:
   a. Hold the CTRL key down and tap the F4 key. This invokes the Move set of commands.
   b. Choose option 1 (Cut Block).
   c. Move the cursor to where you want the block to be placed in the first paragraph, which is on the "S" of "Ski jackets."
   d. Hold the CTRL key down and tap the F4 key, which again invokes the Move set of commands.
   e. Choose option 5 (Text). Your text should now be positioned in the correct location. Tap the DEL key once to delete the tab. The rest of the first paragraph should have been pushed downward one line because you moved a RETURN up with this block of text.

QUICK REFERENCE:
MOVING A BLOCK
1. Use arrow keys to position cursor at beginning of block.
2. Press ALT F4.
3. Use arrow keys to move cursor to end of block.
4. Press CTRL F4.
5. Press 1.
6. Position cursor where you want block moved.
7. Press CTRL F4.
8. Press 5.

To move the remainder of this paragraph to the location below the discounted items:

1. Position the cursor on the "S" of "Ski jackets" and invoke Block mode by holding the ALT key down and tapping the F4 key.

2. Press the RETURN key to highlight the rest of the paragraph.

3. To move this block down below the discounted items:
   a. Hold the CTRL key down and tap the F4 key. This invokes the Move set of commands.
   b. Choose option 1 (Cut Block).
   c. Move the cursor to where you want the block to be placed, which is two lines below the list of discounted items in position 10.
   d. Hold the CTRL key down and tap the F4 key, which again invokes the Move set of commands.
   e. Choose option 5 (Text). Your text should now be positioned in the correct location.

Your document should now look like the one in Figure B.10. If it doesn't, review the steps we've performed so far. The purpose of this editing exercise has been to demonstrate that you can easily make changes to your documents.

Right now you have an edited version of DOC1 in internal memory. Save this edited document onto your data disk in drive B under the name DOC2.

SPELL-CHECKING A DOCUMENT AND USING THE THESAURUS

Included on your WordPerfect diskette is a file called README.DOC that contains a demonstration of how to use WordPerfect's spelling checker and Thesaurus programs. Because it's only a demonstration, it's of little use to you when you are working with your documents. Nonetheless, this demonstration will introduce you to the useful capabilities of the spelling checker and the thesaurus. If you are interested in seeing how to use these capabilities, retrieve the file called README.DOC (follow the instructions in the Saving and Retrieving section) and follow the instructions on the screen.

PRINTING A DOCUMENT

Now it's time to print your document out on the printer. However, first we're going to add a footer to your document by using one of WordPerfect's many print features. Figure B.11 shows the **Print Format menu** that can be accessed by holding the CTRL key down and tapping the F8 key. Figure B.12 shows the **Line Format menu** that can be accessed by holding the SHIFT key down and tapping the F8 key, and Figure B.13 shows the **Page Format menu** that can be accessed by holding the ALT key down and tapping the F8 key. From this last menu we are going to create a footer that includes the current page number. Perform the following steps:

1. Access the Page Format menu by holding down the ALT key and tapping the F8 key.
2. Tap 6 to access the Headers or Footers menu.
3. Tap 3 for Footer A.
4. Tap 1 for "Every Page."
5. To center your footer on each page, hold the SHIFT key down and tap the F6 key.

6. Key in THIS IS A FOOTER. To enter the code so that consecutive page numbers will appear in the footer, tap the SPACE bar a few times and then hold the CTRL key down and tap the letter N (what you will see on the screen is ^N).

7. Tap the F7 key to EXIT to the Page Format menu.

8. Tap the F7 key again to return to your document.

FIGURE B.11
WordPerfect's Print Format menu. This menu shows the options you have to change the format of your document when you print it.

```
Print Format Menu:  All of the settings you see in this menu
(such as "10" for Pitch) are the current settings.  If you want
to change any of them, you must select the number corresponding
to the option you want to change.  Each of the options is
described briefly below:

Pitch:  If you want to change the number of characters that will
print in an inch, choose option 1.

Font:  If you want to change the type style that will be used
when printing, choose option 1.

Lines:  If you want to change the number of lines that will print
in a vertical inch, choose option 2.

Right Justification:  You have the option of printing your
document with a jagged right margin (option 3) or an even right
margin (option 4).

Underline Style:  Options 5-8 allow you to control how
underlines will display when they are printed.

Sheet Feeder Bin Number:  Some printers allow you to feed paper
into the printer automatically using one or more special feeder
bins.  If your printer has more than one feeder connected to it,
option 9 allows you to specify which feeder you want to use.

Insert Printer Command:  You can use option "A" if you want to
instruct the printer to, for example, print in a larger type
size, or print characters darker.
```

```
Print Format

     1 - Pitch                        10
         Font                          1

     2 - Lines per Inch                6

  Right Justification                 On
     3 - Turn off
     4 - Turn on

  Underline Style                      5
     5 - Non-continuous Single
     6 - Non-continuous Double
     7 - Continuous Single
     8 - Continuous Double

     9 - Sheet Feeder Bin Number       1

     A - Insert Printer Command

     B - Line Numbering               Off

Selection: 0
```

QUICK REFERENCE:
CREATING A FOOTER ON EVERY PAGE
1. Press ALT F8.
2. Press 6.
3. Press 3.
4. Press 1.
5. Key in the footer text (key in ^N if you want a page number to appear).
6. Press F7 twice.

A footer should be set up to print at the bottom of each document page. You'll know if this has happened after you perform the necessary commands to print your document. To send your document page to the printer, hold the SHIFT key down and tap the F7 key (Print). Tap number 1 for Full Text. In a few seconds, your document should be printing out on the printer!

QUICK REFERENCE:
PRINTING A DOCUMENT
1. Press SHIFT F7.
2. Press 1 (or another number corresponding to how much of your document you want to print).

Note: As mentioned earlier, the educational version of WordPerfect will insert *WPC in unpredictable locations throughout your document. Also, to print a document that is longer than the maximum file size supported by this educational version (approximately 2 pages), you can create smaller documents under different file names and then link them together before you print. See the Quick Reference below for the procedure to follow to link files.

FIGURE B.12
WordPerfect's Line Format menu.

```
  1 2 Tabs; 3 Margins; 4 Spacing; 5 Hyphenation; 6 Align Char: 0



        Tabs:  Options 1 and 2 allow you to change the tab settings --
        currently there is a tab set every five spaces.  When you tap the
        TAB key your cursor should jump five spaces.

        Margins:  The left margin is currently set in position 10 and the
        right margin is currently set in position 74.  Choose option 3 if
        you want to change these settings.

        Spacing:  If you want to change the line spacing to double-or
        triple-spaced (the current spacing is single), choose option 4.

        Hyphenation:  Choose option 5 if you want WordPerfect to
        automatically hyphenate a word that is too long to fit on the
        current line when the cursor reaches the right margin.


        Align Char:  If you want to key in a column of numbers that are
        aligned vertically by the decimals or commas in the numbers, you
        would choose option 6 to specify this.
```

FIGURE B.13
WordPerfect's Page Format menu.

Page Number Position: Choose option 1 if you want to change
where the page number appears at the bottom of the pages in your
document.

New Page Number: If you want the first page of your document to
begin with a page number other than "1" then choose option 2.

Center Page Top to Bottom: Choose option 3 if you want the text
you've typed in to be centered on the page when it is printed
from top to bottom. This option is convenient if you need to
create a title page.

Page Length: If you want to change the number of lines that will
print on a page from 54 (the current setting) to something else,
choose option 4.

Top Margin: Choose option 5 if you want to change the number of
lines that are automatically left blank for a margin at the top
of your document.

Headers and Footers: Choose option 6 if you want to include a
header and/or a footer in your document.

Page Number Column Positions: This option (option 7) differs
from option 1 because it allows you to place page numbers in
positions past position 158.

Suppress for Current Page only: Choose option 8 if you don't
want headers, footers, or page numbers to appear on the current
page when it is printed.

Conditional End of Page: Choose option 9 if you want a certain
number of lines to be kept together on the same page. This
command is frequently used to keep tables from printing on two
pages. The entire table will be printed on the same page.

Widow/Orphan: Choosing option "A" will protect you from widows
(a term used to describe the first line of a paragraph printed on
the bottom of a page) and orphans (a term used to describe the
last line of a paragraph printed on the top of a page).

```
Page Format

        1 - Page Number Position

        2 - New Page Number

        3 - Center Page to Bottom

        4 - Page Length

        5 - Top Margin

        6 - Headers or Footers

        7 - Page Number Column Positions

        8 - Suppress for Current page only

        9 - Conditional End of Page

        A - Widow/Orphan


Selection: 0
```

QUICK REFERENCE:
LINKING DOCUMENTS TOGETHER BEFORE PRINTING
1. Retrieve your first document.
2. Move your cursor to the end of this document.
3. Retrieve your second document. This second document will be "tagged" onto the end of the first document. Continue in this fashion until you have retrieved all the text you want to print out.

SUMMARY

The term *word processing* refers to the processing of text for (1) creating, (2) editing, and/or (3) printing documents. Word processing software allows us to create, edit, store and retrieve, merge, and print documents. Figure B.14 shows a summary of the commands used to perform most of these activities using WordPerfect, a popular word processing package used in business today. It is difficult to find a microcomputer user today who doesn't use word processing software.

In word processing, the document cycle involves using software to (1) enter, (2) edit, (3) spell-check, (4) save, and (5) print a document. Each step uses a number of features that your word processing program offers to you. When entering text, you should know how to move the cursor and what effect pressing the RETURN key has when the cursor is positioned in the middle of a sentence. When working with a document that is longer than 25 lines, you should know how to scroll through your document on the screen to see all the text.

To edit text you need to know how to insert and delete text. Block operations, which can save you a lot of time, allow you to move, copy, or delete large sections of text. You should also know how to spell-check your documents (if your program has the capability), save and retrieve your documents, and print your documents. When printing, you may want to change the appearance of your document on the printed page by changing margins, justification, line spacing, or by adding a header or a footer.

Word processing programs also offer us the ability to create personalized form letters. The process involves creating a document file and a data file and merging them. These files must be created according to the specifications of your particular word processing program.

FIGURE B.14
WordPerfect Command Summary. (Keys separated by commas should be pressed in sequence, one after the other. A key followed by a slash [/] should be held down while following key or keys are pressed.)

Commands	Key(s)
Block	ALT/F4
Bold	F6
Center	SHIFT/F6
Cancel	F1
Delete (ch to left)	BACKSPACE
Delete (ch cursor is on)	DEL
Delete (wd cursor is on)	CTRL/BACKSPACE
Delete EOL	CTRL/END
Exit	F7
Format Line	SHIFT/F8
Page	ALT/F8
Print	CTRL/F8
Help	F3
Indent	F4
Justification	CTRL/F8,3, or 4
List-Files	F5
Margin	SHIFT/F8,3
Margin Release	CTRL/TAB
Move cursor	arrow keys
a word at a time	CTRL/RIGHT or LEFT-ARROW
to beg of doc	HOME,HOME,UP-ARROW
to end of doc	HOME,HOME,DOWN-ARROW
Move text	CTRL/F4
Print	SHIFT/F7
Retrieve doc from disk	SHIFT/F10
also use	F5, highlight, 1
Retrieve deleted text	F1
Reveal Codes	ALT/F3
Save	F10
also use	F7
Screen	CTRL/F3
Spacing	SHIFT/F8,4
Spell	CTRL/F2
Switch	SHIFT/F3
Tab (set/rel)	SHIFT/F8,1
Tab Ruler Line	CTRL/F3,1,UP-ARROW
Thesaurus	ALT/F1
Typeover (toggle)	INS
Underline	F8

KEY TERMS

ALT key
arrow keys
block operation
center
CTRL key
cursor
data file
DEL key
document cycle
document file
edit
footer
formatting
function keys

header
HOME key
INDENT
left-justification
Line Format menu
LIST-FILES key
margin
merge
Page Format menu
Print Format menu
retrieve
RETURN key
right-justification
save

scrolling
search and replace
SHIFT key
SPACE bar
spell-check
TAB key
unjustified
window
word processing
   software
word wrap
word processing

EXERCISES

SHORT ANSWER

1. Why does a spelling-checker program sometimes think correctly spelled words are wrong?
2. Describe the process involved with merging two files together to create a form letter.
3. Why is the ability to perform block operations so valuable?
4. What are the typical steps of the document cycle?
5. Describe the hardware considerations of using word processing software and a microcomputer.
6. What are some useful features to know when you print documents?
7. What are some features to know when you enter text?
8. What is meant by the term *word processing?*
9. What are some text-editing features you should know?
10. Describe a time when you could have really used a word processing program.

HANDS ON

Complete the following exercises in order:

1. Create the document pictured in Figure B.15. Save this document on your data disk under the name B:CARRERO1.

2. Determine the number of bytes the file called CARRERO1 contains.

3. Insert the following paragraph between the current second and third paragraphs in the document to Luis Carrero. This paragraph should be indented ten spaces from both sides. Save this updated document under the name B:CARRERO1. (*Hint*: You will need to replace the old file.)

> You may be interested in a special offer that will be available for the next two months. For customers who have registered for two or more seminars, we are offering a third seminar—on a word processing package of your choice—for half the usual fee.

4. Print CARRERO1 out on the printer using all of the default settings.

5. Print CARRERO1 out again. Make sure the document is left-justified and that there's a footer at the bottom of the page that contains your name (for example, Sean's Document).

FIGURE B.15
B:CARRERO1

```
January 7, 1989


Mr. Luis Carrero
32100 Pacific Avenue
San Francisco, CA 94100


Dear Mr. Carrero:

     Thank you so much for meeting with me regarding
microcomputer training seminars.  I'm sure you will be satisfied
with the training session we will be conducting for you and your
staff next month.

     The training will provide each participant with practical
experience using the keyboard and typical storage devices.  As a
result, working with the computer will be a comfortable
experience for your staff, not a frustrating one.  And as we
discussed, each of you will be provided with a student manual and
a reference text.

     If you have any questions, please don't hesitate to call.
We look forward to the training session.

     With best regards,


     Natasha Erochina
     Training Coordinator
```

MODULE C

ELECTRONIC SPREADSHEETS: LOTUS 1-2-3 AND SUPERCALC4

The electronic spreadsheet has become one of the most significant information processing tools in history. Learning to use this tool is so easy that in a short time the user can master the basics well enough to produce a simple spreadsheet. To help you gain a practical understanding of this software, this module provides an overview of the features of electronic spreadsheet processing, followed by a tutorial ("In the Lab") using Lotus 1-2-3, a popular spreadsheet software package. (*Note:* Those of you using SuperCalc4 will find the keystrokes for this package in the margins of the tutorial.)

■

When you have completed this module, you will be able to:

- Identify the advantages of using an electronic spreadsheet as opposed to a manual spreadsheet
- Describe the procedures for creating reliable spreadsheets
- Describe what you see when electronic spreadsheet software has been loaded into internal memory, and name the three modes of spreadsheet operation
- Create an electronic spreadsheet using Lotus 1-2-3 or SuperCalc4

ELECTRONIC SPREADSHEET OVERVIEW

A spreadsheet is essentially a grid of rows and columns with headings determined by the situation. Headings used by an accountant who is figuring out a company's projected taxes over the next five years would differ from the heads used by an inventory manager of an automobile factory who is trying to calculate the need for certain parts over the next two years. But in both cases, the users would put numbers into rows and columns and then perform calculations on them. Until fairly recently, spreadsheets (or worksheets) were done by hand. It might have taken days or weeks to complete a spreadsheet; if one number had to be changed, the whole spreadsheet would have to be recalculated and corrected by hand!

Electronic spreadsheet software, which eliminates this tedious and time-consuming activity, is now being used on approximately one out of every two microcomputers in the business community. Spreadsheet software is indispensable to the business professional who does tax planning or prepares financial statements, such as cash projections or budgets. Engineers, scientists, teachers, accountants, architects, graphic designers, and many other professionals also find useful applications for spreadsheet software. The following pages will explain what the business user needs to know about this tool.

MANUAL VERSUS ELECTRONIC SPREADSHEETS

As we mentioned, a manual spreadsheet (Figure C.1) is composed of rows and columns. The intersection of a row and column is called a **cell**. The spreadsheet is used to accumulate financial data that is later used in calculations to derive totals or percentages. Spreadsheet organization helps the user produce nicely aligned and organized reports. However, to do this manually requires pencils, erasers, a calculator, and lots of time. Everything in manual spreadsheets, except the lines that form the rows and columns, must be done by hand.

For many people, making the text and numbers legible is more painstaking than deriving the spreadsheet's data! However, real frustration is experienced when a number that affects other numbers in a spreadsheet must be changed. All affected numbers must be erased and re-entered.

Electronic spreadsheet software and the microcomputer have made it much easier to produce accurate spreadsheets quickly.

1. *Electronic spreadsheets can be larger than manual ones.* A manual spreadsheet is usually no larger than the sheet of paper that fits on top of the desk. An electronic spreadsheet ranges in size from 128 to 256 columns and 2048 to 10,000 rows. The Lotus 1-2-3 (Version 2.01) spreadsheet contains 8192 rows and 256 columns. The SuperCalc4 spreadsheet contains 9999 rows and 255 columns. Measured in feet, the Lotus spreadsheet would be approximately 118 feet tall and 128 feet wide. The large size of the electronic spreadsheet allows the user to develop larger reports than is possible using a manual spreadsheet. Of course, it's impossible to see an entire electronic spreadsheet on the screen at once. Your screen acts as a window through which you see only a small portion of the spreadsheet (Figure C.2). You must print the spreadsheet to see it in its entirety.

2. *Electronic spreadsheets can perform mathematical calculations, including adding, subtracting, multiplying, and dividing.* The user puts the specifications for a calculation in a cell in the form of a formula, and the spreadsheet performs the calculation and displays the answer in the cell. In a manual spreadsheet, to perform calculations the user must have a calculator, a pencil, and a piece of paper. And the user must manually record the result of the calculation in the appropriate cell in the spreadsheet. When using an electronic spreadsheet, if you want to divide 362 by 24,000, you need only enter the following into the appropriate cell (if using either Lotus 1-2-3 or SuperCalc4): 362/24000. The answer will automatically be displayed in the cell.

3. *Cells in electronic spreadsheets can contain formulas.* In an electronic spreadsheet, cells hold not only text and numbers but also formulas that allow the user to refer to certain cells. For example, instead of putting 362/24000 in a cell, you could put a formula into it that will divide 362 by a number in a certain cell location in the spreadsheet. Instead of displaying

FIGURE C.1
Manual spreadsheet. This manual spreadsheet is used to keep track of expenses. If a mistake is made entering any expense amounts, three other cells in the spreadsheet are affected.

EXPENSE TYPE	JAN	FEB	MAR	TOTAL	
Telephone	85	79	82	246	
Rent	600	600	600	1 800	
Utilities	35	42	70	147	
Auto	50	45	196	291	
Other	121	135	140	396	
Total	891	901	1 088	2 880	

the formula in a cell, the spreadsheet displays the calculation designated by the formula.

4. *In electronic spreadsheets, calculations are immediate.* In the manual spreadsheet in Figure C.1, data has been entered into columns B through D (Jan., Feb., and Mar.), and the results of calculations have been placed into the bottom row of the spreadsheet and in column E (Total). In this spreadsheet, if you need to change March's telephone expense from 82 to 92, you'll need to change three additional cells in the spreadsheet, all of which involve calculations. Figure C.3 shows this same spreadsheet as it would appear on the screen in electronic form if you were using Lotus 1-2-3. The electronic spreadsheet contains hidden formulas in column E and in row 10. These formulas, described later in this section, refer to other cells in the spreadsheet. To change the amount for March's telephone expense in the electronic spreadsheet, you rekey it, and the formulas that refer to that cell location automatically recalculate changes.

FIGURE C.2
Spreadsheet window. Your screen acts as a window through which you see only a portion of a large electronic spreadsheet. Spreadsheet software packages give you a variety of ways to move around the spreadsheet.

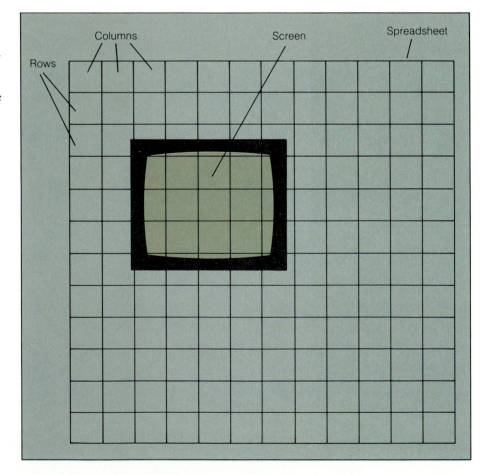

5. *Electronic spreadsheets can be stored and retrieved.* Business professionals often produce the same report over and over again, updating each report with the current date and data. If you want to change the electronic spreadsheet in Figure C.3 to reflect expenses for April through June, you need only retrieve from disk storage a copy of the old spreadsheet (saved under the name of QTR1), change the text for the month headings, and then change the data. The TOTAL formulas will automatically recalculate the locations affected by the changes. You don't need to rekey any other text. You can then save this spreadsheet under a new name (QTR2). In this way, reports can be updated easily.

HARDWARE CONSIDERATIONS

To use spreadsheet software efficiently, you must know how it uses computer hardware. Spreadsheets are stored on disk. During processing, internal memory holds a copy of the main module of the operating system and a copy of the electronic spreadsheet program. The rest of internal memory is used like a scratch pad where you build your spreadsheet. The size and sophistication of your spreadsheet application is limited by the amount of internal memory left on the "scratch pad." The maximum amount of user internal memory in PC-compatible computers is 2 MB; however, most microcomputers currently used in business are limited to 640 K. In the latter case, after the operating system software and the spreadsheet program are loaded, the user is left with less than 400 K of internal memory to build an application. This limitation has proved annoying for the more sophisticated user who cannot obtain a microcomputer with more than 640 K of internal memory. As a result, special hardware, called *expanded memory*, has been developed to allow the

FIGURE C.3
Immediate calculations. In this electronic spreadsheet, column E and row 10 contain formulas that automatically recalculate amounts when the monthly expense data is changed.

```
A1: [W13] ^EXPENSE                                                                    READY

          A              B              C              D              E
1    EXPENSE
2    TYPE            JAN            FEB            MAR            TOTAL
3    ------------------------------------------------------------------------
4    TELEPHONE         85             79             82             246
5    RENT             600            600            600            1800
6    UTILITIES         35             42             70             147
7    AUTO              50             45            196             291
8    OTHER            121            135            140             396
9    ------------------------------------------------------------------------
10   TOTAL            891            901           1088            2880
11   ================================================================
12
13
14
15
16
17
18
19
20
01-Jan-80   12:18 AM
```

user to build larger applications. This product allows the user to add from 2000 K to 8000 K of additional memory.

As a spreadsheet application becomes larger and more sophisticated, the mathematical processing required begins to take more and more time. To help solve this problem, the newest electronic spreadsheet products incorporate the software necessary to use a math coprocessor chip (if the user has installed one on the computer's motherboard), which increases the speed of computation by about 100 times.

ELECTRONIC SPREADSHEET DEVELOPMENT PROCEDURES

If you're planning to build a house yourself, you should have a good idea of why and how you're going to build it. To build the house properly, you'll follow procedures that have been used many times by other people. So it is if you are planning to develop an electronic spreadsheet.

Specific guidelines have evolved for developing electronic spreadsheets on the basis of the collective experience of the many people who have built them. If you take shortcuts instead of following these procedures, you will develop spreadsheets that aren't reliable. Recent studies done by several major universities found that 90% of all spreadsheets developed by nonprogramming professionals contained at least one error. And business decisions are being made on the basis of spreadsheets like these!

The steps for consistently developing a reliable spreadsheet are as follows:

1. *Establish your objectives*—It's easy to build a spreadsheet that doesn't save you any time at all. However, if you clearly formulate objectives for the spreadsheet before you start building it, you will know whether or not your particular needs will be met by an electronic spreadsheet, as well as what direction to take if you decide to proceed.

2. *Define your requirements*—Once you've decided to build a spreadsheet, you're ready to define your requirements—in other words, redefine your objectives much more precisely. For instance, you must determine where data will be entered into the spreadsheet, the type of processing that will take place, and the kind of output you want.

3. *Build the spreadsheet*—If Steps 1 and 2 were completed in sufficient detail, Step 3 should be relatively simple—that is, keying the necessary text and formulas into the cells.

4. *Test the spreadsheet*—The biggest mistake you can make when using electronic spreadsheets is to assume that they automatically produce correct information and that they will inform you of any serious problems. After you have finished building your spreadsheet, you must test it carefully to ensure that it works exactly as you intended. One way to perform the test is by entering sample data into the spreadsheet and having it perform a few calculations; then perform the same calculations manually to see if you get the same results as the electronic spreadsheet. If you do get the same results, you can rely on the accuracy of the information produced by the electronic spreadsheet.

5. *Use the spreadsheet*—After you have tested it, you should write down a list of procedures for using the spreadsheet, so that someone who hasn't seen your spreadsheet before will understand how to use it, if necessary. It's also a good idea to make a backup copy of your spreadsheet, in case someone accidentally erases it from your disk storage device.

ELECTRONIC SPREADSHEET FEATURES

This section focuses on the features of electronic spreadsheet processing that you should know to use the software effectively.

LOADING THE SPREADSHEET SOFTWARE

Once you have told the operating system software to load a copy of the electronic spreadsheet program instructions into the internal memory of your computer, you are ready to begin communicating with the program. You should see the upper left corner of the huge electronic spreadsheet on your screen. To see more of the spreadsheet, you can use your arrow keys to cause the screen to scroll.

The **spreadsheet area** of the screen display comprises rows and columns that are labeled with letters and numbers that allow you to identify cells in the spreadsheet. A cell is the intersection of a row and a column. In Figure C.4, cell A1 contains the text EXPENSE, and cell B4 contains the number 85.

At the top or bottom of your screen, depending on the particular spreadsheet program you are using, you see the **Command/Data Entry area**. Most electronic spreadsheet programs display the following types of information in this area: status

FIGURE C.4
Electronic spreadsheet. A cell in an electronic spreadsheet area is identified by row number and column letter—for example, cell A1 contains **EXPENSE**. The Command/Data Entry area indicates what cell you're in and what's in the cell; it also gives you command options and descriptions. The Indicator area displays any error messages or messages about certain keys that have been pressed (such as the **NUM LOCK** key).

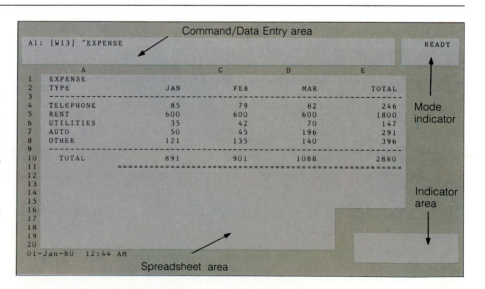

information telling you what cell the cursor is in, what the format of the cell is (we'll discuss formatting options later), and what the actual contents of the cell are. In Figure C.4 for example, the Command/Data Entry area indicates that the cursor is currently positioned on cell A1 (A1:), that the column has been widened to 13 characters ([W13]), and that the text EXPENSE is in the cell ('EXPENSE). In addition, when you instruct the spreadsheet program to issue a command, the list of available commands appears in the Command/Data Entry area along with a description of what a specific command will do for you. Also, characters that you're entering into specific cells in the spreadsheet are displayed here until you press the RETURN key. To the right of the Command/Data Entry area is a message that tells you what mode of operation you're currently working in (modes of operation will be described in the next section).

Most electronic spreadsheet programs also have an **Indicator area,** which is positioned either on the top or the bottom of the screen. This area indicates, for example, whether the CAPITAL LOCK or NUMBER LOCK keys have been pressed, or whether an ERROR MESSAGE exists. For instance, if you are using SuperCalc4 and you attempt to save your work but give an invalid file name (such as one that contains more than eight characters), the message "Filename Error" will appear in the bottom right-hand corner of the screen (in the Indicator area).

THE THREE MODES OF OPERATION

Electronic spreadsheets operate in one of three modes: Ready Mode, Entry Mode (sometimes broken down into LABEL and VALUE modes), or Menu Mode. (The exact mode names will vary depending on the spreadsheet program you are using.)

If you are in **Ready Mode,** you can move the cursor around in the spreadsheet. You need to be able to move the cursor for two reasons. First, to put data into a specific cell, such as cell D8, you need to move the cursor to that cell before you key in the data. When you build a spreadsheet, you will be entering data in many cells. Second, to view a spreadsheet that is larger than the screen, you need to move the cursor. Businesspeople make spreadsheets that average in size from 15 to 65 columns, and from 20 to 60 rows. How do you access the part of your spreadsheet that you can't see on the screen? For example, in Lotus 1-2-3, if your cursor is positioned in cell A1 and you press the right-arrow key about ten times, the screen contents will scroll to the left when the cursor reaches the far right of the screen. Likewise, if you press the down-arrow key past the bottom of the screen, the screen scrolls upward. Scrolling the screen by using the arrow keys is the means by which you can see and use the rest of the spreadsheet area available to you.

The second mode is called **Entry Mode.** You are in this mode *after* you have positioned the cursor in the cell into which you want to enter text, numbers, or a formula and have typed one key. Once you type that key, the mode indicator will tell you that you're in Entry Mode. If you are using SuperCalc4, no matter whether you're typing text or a formula, the mode indicator will say ENTRY. If you are using Lotus 1-2-3 and have entered text, the mode indicator will say LABEL. If you have entered a number or formula, the mode indicator will say VALUE. Once you have pressed the RETURN key to complete the entry of data into the cell, you will be back in Ready Mode and can move the cursor around the spreadsheet again.

The third, and probably most powerful, mode of operation is **Menu Mode.** The commands in most electronic spreadsheets are organized hierarchically—meaning that subselections exist under main command headings. Figure C.5a shows the command hierarchy for Lotus 1-2-3's Range group of commands. In both Lotus 1-2-3 and SuperCalc4, Menu Mode is invoked by pressing the slash key (/). A list of the main command options appears in the Command/Data Entry area. Once you prepare to choose a command option by moving the cursor to it (and thus highlighting it), the choices available under that option are then displayed in this area (Figure C.5b). To choose a command option, tap the ENTER or RETURN key when it is highlighted. By proceeding in this fashion, you go deeper and deeper into the hierarchical command structure of the electronic spreadsheet. When you have reached the "bottom" of a command (the lowest level of the command hierarchy), the electronic spreadsheet usually returns you to Ready Mode. If for some reason you don't want to complete a command, an option is usually available that will allow you to go back up the command structure to Ready Mode. In both Lotus 1-2-3 and SuperCalc4, you can back out of a structure by tapping the ESCAPE (ESC) key or the BACKSPACE key.

ENTERING TEXT, NUMBERS, AND FORMULAS

No matter whether you want to enter text, numbers, or formulas into a cell, you must remember to first move the cursor to the appropriate cell and then key in the data. Keying in text and numbers is simple—until the text or number becomes wider than the column. The default column width for most electronic spreadsheet programs is nine characters. (The term *default* refers to the assumptions the electronic spreadsheet program makes about a spreadsheet until the user tells it otherwise.) If you want to change the default column width, you must invoke Menu Mode and choose the command that allows you to change column width. For instance, look at Figure C.6; cell A3 contains the text INCOME AND EXPENSE BUDGET SPREADSHEET (you can tell by looking in the Command/Data Entry area), and cell B3 contains the text 1987-1988. Because the columns haven't been widened—that is, the default column width values are in effect—you can't see all of the text in cell A3. Cell A1 contains DENNIS & GRASSO TEXTILE COMPANY; even though cell B1 appears to contain GRASSO, it actually contains nothing. The contents of cell A1 overlay cell B1 because cell B1 is empty.

Entering formulas into cells is also simple. A **formula** is a mathematical expression that defines the relationships among various cells in an electronic spreadsheet. Figure C.7 shows the arithmetic and logical operators that can be used in Lotus 1-2-3 formulas. These operators are similar to those found in most electronic spreadsheet programs.

USING FUNCTIONS

An electronic spreadsheet program provides many powerful functions to use in formulas, as well as mathematical shortcuts. A **function** is a subset of a formula. Sometimes a formula consists of nothing but a function. Other times you will use a function *in* a formula to make the formula shorter.

FIGURE C.5
Command hierarchy structure. (a) The command hierarchy for Lotus 1-2-3's RANGE group of commands. As you can see, a number of different formatting and other options exist under this command; (b) what the screen looks like after the / key has been pressed, displaying the options available under the RANGE command.

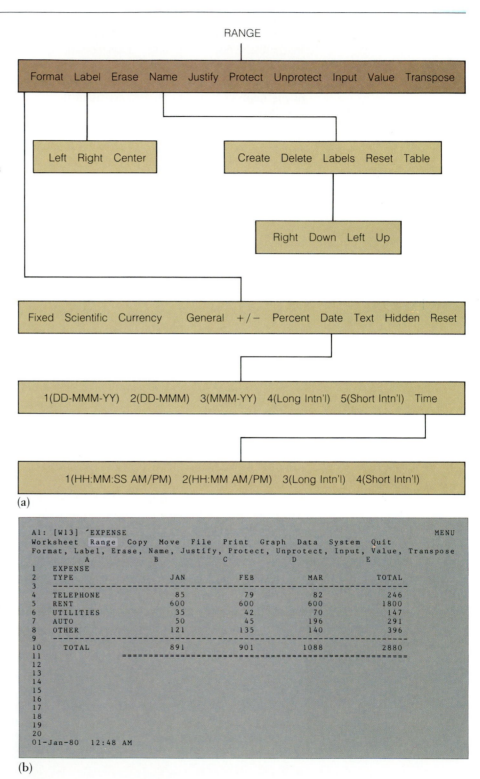

(a)

(b)

FIGURE C.6

Hidden cell contents. If the text in a cell is wider than the default column width allows (cell A3), only a portion of the text is displayed in the cell. However, as indicated by the Command/ Data Entry area display, the entire text is indeed present in the cell.

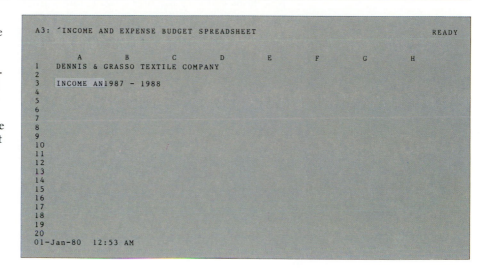

```
A3: ´INCOME AND EXPENSE BUDGET SPREADSHEET                                    READY

           A       B       C       D       E       F       G       H
   1   DENNIS & GRASSO TEXTILE COMPANY
   2
   3    INCOME AN1987 - 1988
   4
   5
   6
   7
   8
   9
  10
  11
  12
  13
  14
  15
  16
  17
  18
  19
  20
  01-Jan-80   12:53 AM
```

FIGURE C.7

Formula operators. The arithmetic and logical operators used in Lotus 1-2-3 formulas.

Mathematical Operators		Logical Operators	
=	Equal	#NOT#	Not
<	Less than	#AND#	And
<=	Less than or equal to	#OR#	Or
>	Greater than		
>=	Greater than or equal to		
<>	Not equal		

Functions can save the user a tremendous amount of time. For example, in Figure C.8, there is a column of numbers in column B. In cell B19, we want a formula that will add the contents of all cells from B5 to B17. Without the use of a function, the formula in cell B19 could be written as follows:

```
(B5 + B6 + B7 + B8 + B9 + B10 + B11 + B12 + B13 etc.)
```

Think about the amount of time it would take to add a column of 100 numbers! To save time when adding ranges of numbers—a **range** is one or more cells that form a rectangle (Figure C.9)— electronic spreadsheet programs use a function (often referred to as the **SUM function**) to simplify the process. In Lotus 1-2-3 and SuperCalc4, the SUM Function in cell B19 would be:

```
Lotus 1-2-3:     @SUM(B5..B17)

SuperCalc4:      SUM(B5:B17)
```

With this function, the user simply specifies the beginning and end of the range of cells to be added, encloses the range in parentheses, and keys in the text @SUM (all of Lotus 1-2-3's functions are preceded by @) or SUM in front of the first parenthesis.

Different types of functions can be used as mathematical shortcuts in formulas. Some functions allow the user to determine the minimum, maximum, and average of a range of cells. In Lotus 1-2-3, these functions would be expressed using the @MIN, @MAX, and @AVG functions. And in SuperCalc4, these functions would be expressed using the MIN, MAX, and AVERAGE functions. Another function, the **DATE function,** allows mathematical calculations to be performed on the date. For example, the DATE function can determine the number of days that have passed since January 1, 1900. You will use the DATE function later on in the tutorial.

FIGURE C.8
Functions. The user can save time by using the SUM function in cell B19 to calculate the total amount of the checks. Spreadsheet programs provide a number of different functions.

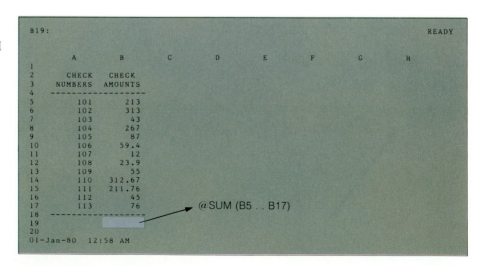

Spreadsheet programs also provide the user with a powerful function that can perform an "if . . . then" analysis. For example, what if you want to know if one cell (C5) has a greater value in it than another cell (D5) and to perform a certain calculation depending on the answer? You would perform an **if . . . then** analysis—in Lotus 1-2-3, you would use the IF (@IF) function. Depending on whether the "test" is true or false (whether C5 is greater than D5), a certain action is performed. In conversational terms, the syntax of the command—using cells C5 and D5 as examples—is as follows: IF the amount in cell C5 is greater than the amount in cell D5, THEN perform a certain action (for instance, add the two amounts); otherwise, perform a different action (for example, subtract the two amounts).

Use of the IF function can get quite sophisticated when you start including multiple tests in the statement. For instance, instead of having just one test (for example, IF C5 is greater than D5, THEN . . .), you might have two tests (IF C5 is greater than D5 and C5 is greater than E5, THEN . . .). This illustration is just a sample of what the IF . . . THEN function can do; to demonstrate any more is

FIGURE C.9
Spreadsheet ranges.

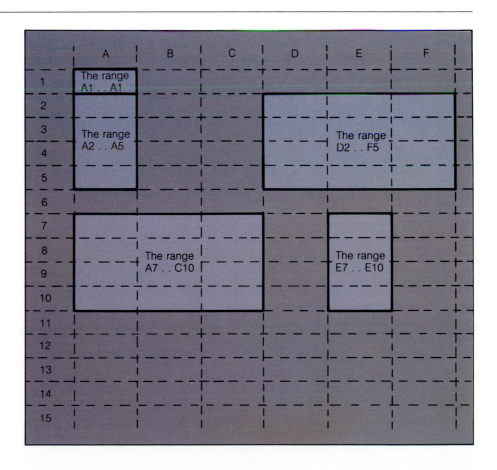

beyond the scope of this module. You will get a chance to try out the IF function in the tutorial. Figure C.10 shows some of the commonly used Lotus 1-2-3 functions.

COPYING

The text and formulas in cells can be quite long. What happens if you want to place a text string that is 30 characters long in 25 places in the spreadsheet? Do you have to key in 750 characters? No. The process of getting text and formulas into a large number of cells is really quite simple. It involves using a spreadsheet command that allows you to **copy.** Generally speaking, the steps for copying text from one cell into many other cells are as follows:

1. Initiate the COPY command.
2. Tell the software where the text is that you want to copy—the column letter and row number.
3. Tell the software what cell or cells you want the text copied into.

The COPY command is used the same way to copy formulas; however, formulas sometimes need to be "prepared" before they can be copied. When a formula is copied into one or more cells, the spreadsheet program analyzes the cell from which the formula is being copied and the cell(s) the formula is being copied to. It determines the net displacement (or change in column and row position) of the two locations and changes the cell references in the copied formula(s) to reflect their new locations in the spreadsheet.

What if you don't want your copied formulas to change? Depending on the spreadsheet program you are using, you can use different ways of "freezing"—or keeping constant—a cell reference in a formula so that when it is copied the cell

FIGURE C.10
Common Lotus 1-2-3 functions.

Function	Purpose
@SUM(range)	Adds together a range of cells.
@MAX(range)	Determines the maximum value in a range of cells.
@MIN(range)	Determines the minimum value in a range of cells.
@AVG(range)	Determines the average value in a range of cells.
@COUNT(range)	Determines the number of entries in a range of cells.
@DATE	Allows you to perform calculations using dates.
@IF	Allows you to perform a test. If the test is true, a certain action is taken; if the test is false, a different action is taken.

reference doesn't change. In Lotus 1-2-3 and SuperCalc4, we freeze cell coordinates (that is, the column letter and the row number) in formulas by using a dollar sign ($). Figure C.11 shows the different ways you can freeze a cell reference in a formula. As you'll see in the "In The Lab" section of this module, it's important to know how to keep cell references constant in order to prepare a formula to be copied. If you don't know how to prepare formulas to be copied, you may end up keying in all of your formulas individually, which will take up a lot of time unnecessarily.

FORMATTING

Figure C.12 shows a spreadsheet before and after it has been formatted. As you might have guessed, **formatting** commands allow the user to improve the appearance of a spreadsheet. You can choose from a number of formatting commands.

The first command used in Figure C.12(b) formatted the numbers in columns B through E in the **currency format**. Numbers that are formatted this way are displayed with a dollar sign and a specified number of decimal places. In this figure, the numbers were formatted to two decimal places. The numbers in column F were formatted in the **percent format**; it's much easier to understand the percent numbers after formatting has taken place.

As you can see, the column headings are left-aligned in Figure C.12(a). To give the columns a neater appearance, a command was used to right-align the headings within their cells (Figure C.12(b)). In electronic spreadsheet programs, labels (text) can be left-aligned, centered, or right-aligned in a cell, but numeric values can't. Depending on the default assumptions of the software, numbers are usually right-aligned in a cell. The columns were widened in Figure C.12(b) to provide more space between the numbers in the columns.

SAVING

While you are working with a spreadsheet program, the spreadsheet specifications reside in internal memory. If you want a permanent copy of the specifications that

---

FIGURE C.11
Spreadsheet programs give the end-user a number of different ways to freeze cell references in formulas. These are the different ways a Lotus 1-2-3 cell reference can be frozen.

Reference	Description
C7	Both column and row references are frozen.
C$7	Only row reference is frozen.
$C7	Only column reference is frozen.
C7	Neither column nor row reference is frozen.

you can retrieve later, you must issue a spreadsheet command that will save your specifications onto disk. The spreadsheet specifications you have saved, which are referred to as a **template,** consist of all the text, numbers, and formulas you have entered into the spreadsheet. If you want to update the template later, you simply retrieve a copy of it from disk, add new data, and then save the updated template.

PRINTING

You have the option of printing a spreadsheet in one of two forms: as a report or as a list of specifications. Figure C.12 shows examples of printed spreadsheet reports.

FIGURE C.12
Before and after. To improve the appearance of the spreadsheet (a), a number of different formatting commands were used (b).

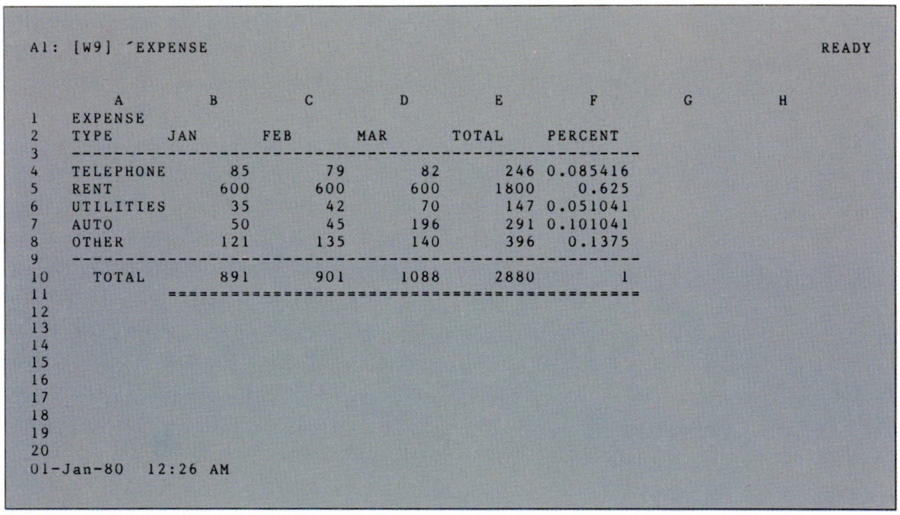

```
A1: [W9] 'EXPENSE                                                             READY

         A         B          C          D          E          F          G          H
1   EXPENSE
2   TYPE      JAN       FEB        MAR        TOTAL      PERCENT
3   ----------------------------------------------------------
4   TELEPHONE       85         79         82        246 0.085416
5   RENT           600        600        600       1800    0.625
6   UTILITIES       35         42         70        147 0.051041
7   AUTO            50         45        196        291 0.101041
8   OTHER          121        135        140        396   0.1375
9   ----------------------------------------------------------
10    TOTAL        891        901       1088       2880        1
11            ==============================================
12
13
14
15
16
17
18
19
20
01-Jan-80   12:26 AM
```

(a)

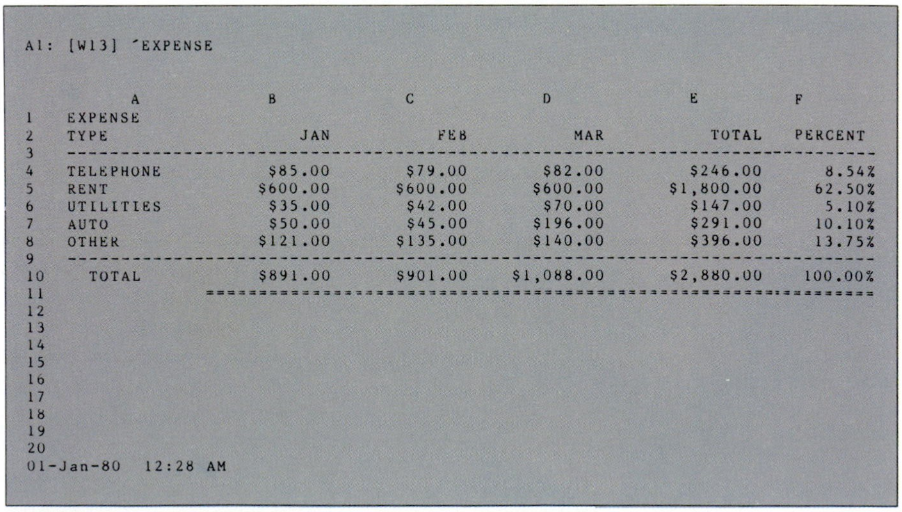

```
A1: [W13] 'EXPENSE

           A              B              C              D              E            F
1   EXPENSE
2   TYPE                  JAN            FEB            MAR            TOTAL    PERCENT
3   ---------------------------------------------------------------------------------
4   TELEPHONE          $85.00         $79.00         $82.00          $246.00      8.54%
5   RENT              $600.00        $600.00        $600.00        $1,800.00     62.50%
6   UTILITIES          $35.00         $42.00         $70.00          $147.00      5.10%
7   AUTO               $50.00         $45.00        $196.00          $291.00     10.10%
8   OTHER             $121.00        $135.00        $140.00          $396.00     13.75%
9   ---------------------------------------------------------------------------------
10    TOTAL           $891.00        $901.00      $1,088.00        $2,880.00    100.00%
11               ==================================================================
12
13
14
15
16
17
18
19
20
01-Jan-80   12:28 AM
```

(b)

In Lotus 1-2-3, this form is called the **As-Displayed format,** which is what you see on the screen (SuperCalc4 refers to this as the *Formatted format*). To see what formulas you have in each cell of the spreadsheet and how each cell is formatted, you need to print out the report specifications. In Lotus 1-2-3, this form is called the **Cell-Contents format** (SuperCalc4 refers to this as the *Contents format*). It's a good idea to print out a Cell-Contents format for every spreadsheet you create, so that you can recreate the spreadsheet's specifications if the spreadsheet is accidentally erased. Figure C.13 shows the application specifications for the report in Figure C.12b.

FIGURE C.13
List of specifications. This printout shows the characteristics of every cell that contains data in the spreadsheet in Figure C.12(b).

```
A1:  [W13]  ^EXPENSE
A2:  [W13]  ^TYPE
B2:  [W13]  "JAN
C2:  [W13]  "FEB
D2:  [W13]  "MAR
E2:  [W15]  "TOTAL
F2:  [W14]  "PERCENT
A3:  [W13]  \-
B3:  [W13]  \-
C3:  [W13]  \-
D3:  [W13]  \-
E3:  [W15]  \-
F3:  [W14]  \-
A4:  [W13]  ^TELEPHONE
B4:  (C2)  [W13]  85
C4:  (C2)  [W13]  79
D4:  (C2)  [W13]  82
E4:  (C2)  [W15]  @SUM(B4..D4)
F4:  (P2)  [W14]  (E4/E$10)
A5:  [W13]  ^RENT
B5:  (C2)  [W13]  600
C5:  (C2)  [W13]  600
D5:  (C2)  [W13]  600
E5:  (C2)  [W15]  @SUM(B5..D5)
F5:  (P2)  [W14]  (E5/E$10)
A6:  [W13]  ^UTILITIES
B6:  (C2)  [W13]  35
C6:  (C2)  [W13]  42
D6:  (C2)  [W13]  70
E6:  (C2)  [W15]  @SUM(B6..D6)
F6:  (P2)  [W14]  (E6/E$10)
A7:  [W13]  ^AUTO
B7:  (C2)  [W13]  50
C7:  (C2)  [W13]  45
D7:  (C2)  [W13]  196
E7:  (C2)  [W15]  @SUM(B7..D7)
F7:  (P2)  [W14]  (E7/E$10)
A8:  [W13]  ^OTHER
B8:  (C2)  [W13]  121
C8:  (C2)  [W13]  135
D8:  (C2)  [W13]  140
E8:  (C2)  [W15]  @SUM(B8..D8)
F8:  (P2)  [W14]  (E8/E$10)
A9:  [W13]  \-
B9:  (C2)  [W13]  \-
C9:  (C2)  [W13]  \-
D9:  (C2)  [W13]  \-
E9:  (C2)  [W15]  \-
F9:  (P2)  [W14]  \-
A10: [W13]  ^   TOTAL
B10: (C2)  [W13]  @SUM(B4..B8)
C10: (C2)  [W13]  @SUM(C4..C8)
D10: (C2)  [W13]  @SUM(D4..D8)
E10: (C2)  [W15]  @SUM(E4..E8)
F10: (P2)  [W14]  @SUM(F4..F8)
B11: [W13]  \=
C11: [W13]  \=
D11: [W13]  \=
E11: [W15]  \=
F11: [W14]  \=
```

A number of other printing options are also available. For example, what if you want to print your spreadsheet in report form, but it is too wide or too long to fit on the paper in the printer? If you tell the spreadsheet program you have a narrow piece of paper in the printer and then proceed to print the wide spreadsheet, the program will start on one piece of paper and then automatically print the excess on the next page. All it takes is a bit of cutting and pasting to restore the spreadsheet to its full width. Figure C.14 shows Lotus 1-2-3's print menu.

PROTECTING

To prepare a spreadsheet for use by other people, you should protect the cell contents so that they aren't accidentally erased by the other users when they enter data. After you have tested your spreadsheet to make sure all the formulas are correct, you first use one command to **protect** all the cells in the spreadsheet and then use a second command to "**unprotect**" only those cells into which data will be entered. You will learn more about this in the tutorial.

FIGURE C.14
Lotus 1-2-3's print menu. These are some of the options you have to control the appearance of your printed spreadsheet.

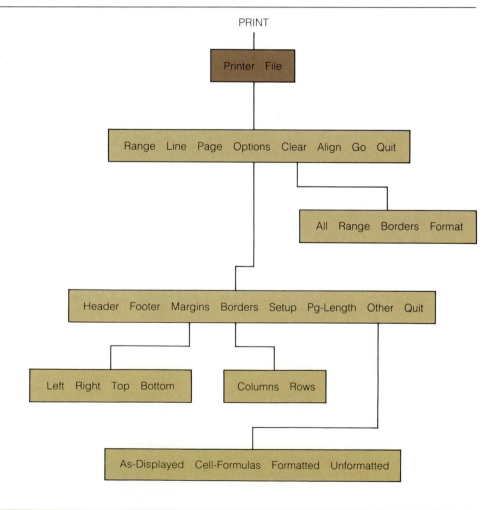

IN THE LAB:

USING LOTUS 1-2-3/SUPERCALC4

In this tutorial you will have the opportunity to create a spreadsheet using the Lotus 1-2-3 and/or SuperCalc4 spreadsheet packages. (SuperCalc4 is an electronic spreadsheet that works very much like Lotus 1-2-3.) The keystrokes for SuperCalc4 will be displayed in the margin. In this section, you will practice using most of the electronic spreadsheet features discussed in the module thus far. These features are common to almost all electronic spreadsheet programs available today. Having experience with one of these packages will help you learn other electronic spreadsheet programs, because they are all similar in concept and organization. (The main difference between Lotus 1-2-3 and SuperCalc4 is that SuperCalc4's Command/ Data Entry area is on the bottom of the screen.)

We assume that you are using a microcomputer with two floppy disk drives (drives A and B), that your copy of Lotus 1-2-3 or SuperCalc4 will be retrieved from drive A, and that the spreadsheet template you will be creating will be saved onto a data disk in drive B. If you are using a computer that has a hard disk, you will probably need to substitute drive C for either drive A or drive B, depending on where you will retrieve a copy of Lotus 1-2-3/SuperCalc4 and where you will save your spreadsheet template. (*Note:* If you are using SuperCalc3, the command sequences may differ slightly from those given in the margin of this tutorial. Consult the documentation manual that accompanies your version of SuperCalc for the correct command sequences.)

THE BUSINESS SITUATION

You are the manager of Sporting Life, a sporting goods store that carries a full line of sports equipment and clothing. Over the last few years, sales have increased to more than $900,000. Recently you acquired a computer and had a lesson in how to use operating system software. You also acquired electronic spreadsheet software because you were told that many activities performed manually at Sporting Life can be performed more quickly and easily using this type of software. One activity that your staff finds time consuming is keeping track of unpaid invoices.

At Sporting Life, when an invoice is sent to a client, the client is told to return a copy of it along with a check for the total amount due within 30 days. However, up to now you have had no efficient way of tracking unpaid invoices (or accounts receivable)—that is, the invoices that are over 30 days old. At any given point, you probably have invoices totaling about $10,000 that are overdue. You want to set up a way of keeping track of how old the invoices are so that, when an invoice is over 30 days old, the customer will be penalized.

In the following pages, you will build an electronic spreadsheet that will keep track of Sporting Life's unpaid invoices. This spreadsheet will make use of three functions that were discussed earlier in the module ("Using Functions"). First, because the calculations in your spreadsheet will be based on a comparison of the current date and the invoice date, you will enter the dates into the spreadsheet using the @DATE function; in this way, you can determine the number of days that have passed since an invoice was issued by subtracting the invoice date from the current date. A penalty will be calculated depending on whether more than 30 days have passed.

Second, the @IF function will be used to calculate the penalty. Third, you will use the @SUM function to calculate the total amount of all penalties and total amounts due. The total amounts due will be calculated by adding the invoice amounts and the penalty amounts.

LOADING LOTUS 1-2-3 AND SUPERCALC4

Before you can do anything, you must load the operating system and the electronic spreadsheet software into internal memory. (Refer to Module A for instructions on how to load the operating system.) You should now have the operating system prompt on the screen. To load a copy of Lotus 1-2-3's program instructions into internal memory, first place your Lotus 1-2-3 disk in drive A and close the disk drive gate. Now key in 123 and then press the RETURN key (this key is labeled ENTER on some keyboards). You should now see a screen of blank cells.

For SuperCalc4 Users:

Put the SuperCalc4 #1 program disk in drive A as specified. After the system prompt, key in SC4 and then press RETURN. An initial screen containing text will appear. At this point take out your #1 SuperCalc4 diskette from drive A and put in your #2 SuperCalc4 diskette. Press the SPACE bar to continue to a screen of blank cells.

MOVING THE CURSOR

Your cursor should now be positioned in cell A1. To move the cursor, you need to use the arrow keys on your keyboard. Tap your right-arrow key four times. The cursor should now be positioned in cell E1. Tap your down-arrow key five times. The cursor should be in cell E6. Tap your left-arrow key two times. Your cursor should now be positioned in cell C6. If at any time you want to return the cursor to cell A1, press the HOME key on your number pad. Figure C.15 shows you some additional methods for efficiently moving around in the Lotus 1-2-3 spreadsheet. As spreadsheet applications grow in size, efficient methods for moving around in a spreadsheet become increasingly important.

ENTERING DESCRIPTIVE TEXT

You are now ready to begin building the spreadsheet template. Start by entering the text for the spreadsheet into the correct cells. This text will serve as the frame of reference for the rest of the spreadsheet. Don't worry if you make a spelling error or put text in the wrong cell; we will show you how to edit cells in the next step.

To enter text into a cell, do the following:

1. Use the arrow keys to position the cursor in the cell in which you want to enter text.

2. Type in the text (you will see the text that you type displayed in the Command/Data Entry area). When you are finished, press the RETURN (ENTER) key to enter the text into the cell.

3. Position the cursor in the next cell into which you want to enter text. Follow the procedure given in Step 2 above.

Now key the following text in the designated cells (*Note:* you can use either upper or lowercase letters):

CELL LOCATION	YOUR KEYSTROKES (TEXT)
1. A1	OPEN INVOICE REGISTER
2. A3	CURRENT DATE:
3. A5	INVOICE
4. A6	NUMBER
5. B5	INVOICE
6. B6	DATE
7. C5	INVOICE
8. C6	AMOUNT
9. D5	DAYS
10. D6	PASSED
11. E6	PENALTY
12. F5	TOTAL
13. F6	DUE
14. D18	TOTAL:

FIGURE C.15
Moving the cursor. These methods of moving the cursor are common to most spreadsheet packages.

Keys	Purpose
HOME	Moves cursor to cell A1 from anywhere in the spreadsheet.
END	When used prior to any of the arrow keys, it will move you to the last cell in an empty or filled space.
LEFT ← RIGHT →	Used to position the cursor either left or right one column.
UP ↑ DOWN ↓	Used to position the cursor either up or down one row.
PGUP	Used to move the cursor up an entire screen.
PGDN	Used to move the cursor down an entire screen.

Your spreadsheet template should now look like the one in Figure C.16.

EDITING CELL CONTENTS

To edit a cell using Lotus 1-2-3 or SuperCalc4, you can proceed in one of two ways: (1) Position the cursor on the cell you want to edit and then retype the contents. When you press the RETURN key, the retyped material will replace the old contents; or (2) position the cursor on the cell you want to edit and press the F2 key (Function 2). The contents of the cell will appear in the Command/Data Entry area so that you can edit it there, one character at a time. Once you're done editing characters, press the RETURN key to place the edited contents back in the cell. With the latter approach, you don't have to rekey the entire entry if you simply want to make a small change to the contents of the cell.

ENTERING FORMULAS

So far, you've entered only descriptive text into this spreadsheet. To add processing "power" to the spreadsheet, we need to add some formulas. You will enter four formulas and, later, you'll copy them. The following is a description of the formulas you will enter:

1. In cell D8, you will enter a formula that subtracts the invoice date (B8) from the current date (C3). (You will be entering the current date into cell C3 later. For now, this formula will refer to an empty cell.) As described earlier, copying formulas isn't always as simple as copying text, because electronic spreadsheets automatically adjust cell references in formulas when they are copied. Sometimes, as in this case, you won't want a cell reference to adjust

FIGURE C.16
Open invoice (accounts due) register template. At this point, only text has been entered in the spreadsheet template.

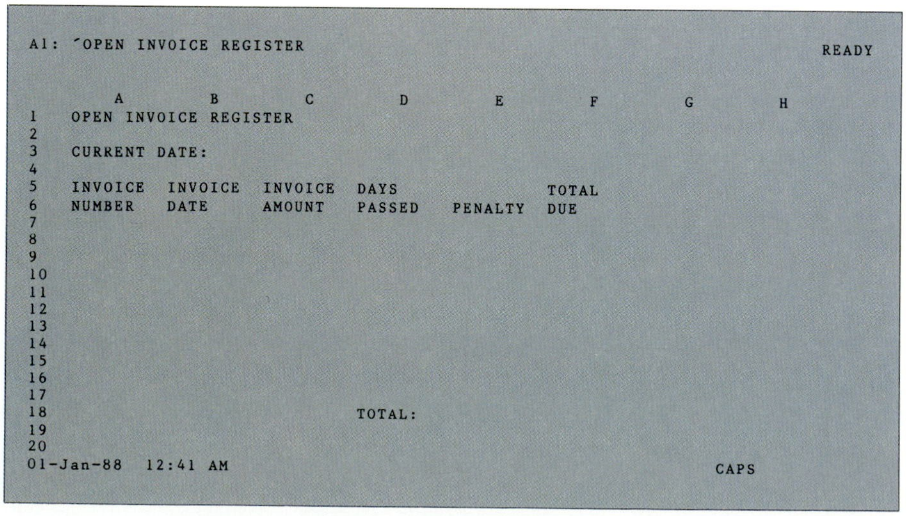

```
A1:  ^OPEN INVOICE REGISTER                                                    READY

           A          B          C          D          E          F          G          H
     1   OPEN INVOICE REGISTER
     2
     3   CURRENT DATE:
     4
     5   INVOICE    INVOICE    INVOICE    DAYS                  TOTAL
     6   NUMBER     DATE       AMOUNT     PASSED     PENALTY    DUE
     7
     8
     9
    10
    11
    12
    13
    14
    15
    16
    17
    18                                    TOTAL:
    19
    20
    01-Jan-88   12:41 AM                                                       CAPS
```

in a formula: We don't want the reference to the current date (C3) to adjust, because every formula in column D will need to refer to that specific cell. We need to "freeze" the reference to cell C3 in our formula by using the dollar sign ($).

2. In cell E8, you will enter a formula that tests to see if the number of days that have passed since the original invoice date (D8) is greater than 30. If it is greater, a 5% penalty will be calculated (C8*.05). If it isn't greater, no penalty will be calculated.

3. In cell F8, you will enter a formula that adds the invoice amount and the penalty amount.

4. In cell E18, you will enter a formula that adds the range of cells between cells E8 and E16 to calculate the total of all penalty amounts.

Key the following formulas into the designated cells:

CELL LOCATION	YOUR KEYSTROKES
1. D8	(C3-B8)
2. E8	@IF(D8>30,C8*.05,0)
3. F8	(C8+E8)
4. E18	@SUM(E8..E16)

For SuperCalc4 Users:
Key the following formulas into the designated cells (uppercase or lowercase):

CELL LOCATION	YOUR KEYSTROKES
1. D8	(C3-B8)
2. E8	IF(D8>30,C8*.05,0)
3. F8	(C8+E8)
4. E18	SUM(E8:E16)

Your spreadsheet should now look similar to the one in Figure C.17. If it doesn't, review the steps we have discussed so far. Zeros appear in all cells that contain formulas because no numerical data has been entered yet.

USING THE MENUS

Because in the next step we're going to show you how to save the work you've done on your spreadsheet thus far—which involves using a menu—we need to show you first how to use Menu Mode. To enter Menu Mode, tap the slash (/) key. At the top of your screen you should see a number of different menu options. Your cursor should be highlighting the Worksheet group of commands, and the WORKSHEET command options should be displayed on the second line.

For SuperCalc4 Users:
Your cursor should be highlighting the Arrange option, and the description for that option—"Sort spreadsheet (entire or partial) by a column or row"—should be displayed on the very bottom of your screen.

To choose a menu option, you can either (1) position the cursor on the menu option you want to choose (by using the right- and left-arrow keys) and then press the RETURN key, or (2) tap the first character of the option you want to choose. In most spreadsheet programs, each option begins with a unique first character.

SAVING THE SPREADSHEET TEMPLATE

Even though your spreadsheet isn't complete, you should save it now, as a precaution against accidentally losing your work. Right now your spreadsheet template resides in internal memory. If you turn your computer off, your spreadsheet will be lost! To retain a permanent copy of your template, you must name it and save it onto your disk in drive B. The name you will give your template is INVOICE. Press the following keys:

For SuperCalc4 Users:
/,S,B:INVOICE,[Rtn]

1. Press the HOME key. The cursor will jump to cell A1. When you retrieve this template later, the cursor will be in cell A1, because spreadsheet programs remember where the cursor was at the time the template was saved.
2. /,F,S,B:INVOICE,[Rtn]

The procedure for saving a template a second (or third or fourth . . .) time is the same as the procedure for saving it the first time—except that at the end of the save procedure, you will be asked if you want to replace the original file called INVOICE (stored on your data disk) with the template in internal memory. If you do, respond by tapping R for Replace. Otherwise, save the updated template under a different name (then you will have a copy of the original template *and* a copy of the edited template).

For SuperCalc4 Users:
If you save your template a second time, you will be asked if you want to overwrite your file on disk. If you do, tap O and then A, for all. Otherwise, save your template under a different name.

RETRIEVING THE SPREADSHEET TEMPLATE

To practice retrieving your spreadsheet template, save a copy of your spreadsheet template using the procedures described in the last section and then turn your computer off. To continue work on the spreadsheet called INVOICE, you will need to retrieve a copy of it from your data diskette. After you reboot your computer, key in the following:

/,F,R,B:INVOICE,[Rtn]

You now have on the screen a copy of your INVOICE template.

For SuperCalc4 Users:
/,L,B:INVOICE,[Rtn],A
INVOICE has been retrieved. *Note:* SuperCalc4 puts the extension .CAL onto your template files.

COPYING FORMULAS

When you are using a spreadsheet package, copying first involves choosing the option to copy from the menu and then specifying what cell you want to copy from (the cell that contains the formula to be copied) and what range of cells you want the formula to be copied into. In the next few steps, we'll lead you through copying a few formulas in the spreadsheet. The keys or groups of keys we want you to press will be separated by commas. (*Note:* Don't key in the commas.) When you see [Rtn], press the RETURN key. As you press the following keys (uppercase or lowercase), remember why you're pressing them and note how your menu changes. (*Note:* If you are in Menu Mode at this point, you won't need to press the first slash [/] key in Step 1.)

CELL LOCATION	YOUR KEYSTROKES
1. D8	/,C,[Rtn],D9..D16,[Rtn],
2. E8	/,C,[Rtn],E9..E16,[Rtn],
3. F8	/,C,[Rtn],F9..F16,[Rtn],
4. E18	/,C,[Rtn],F18,[Rtn],

For SuperCalc4 Users:

CELL LOCATION	YOUR KEYSTROKES
1. D8	/,C,[Rtn],D9:D16,[Rtn]
2. E8	/,C,[Rtn],E9:E16,[Rtn]
3. F8	/,C,[Rtn],F9:F16,[Rtn]
4. E18	/,C,[Rtn],F18,[Rtn]

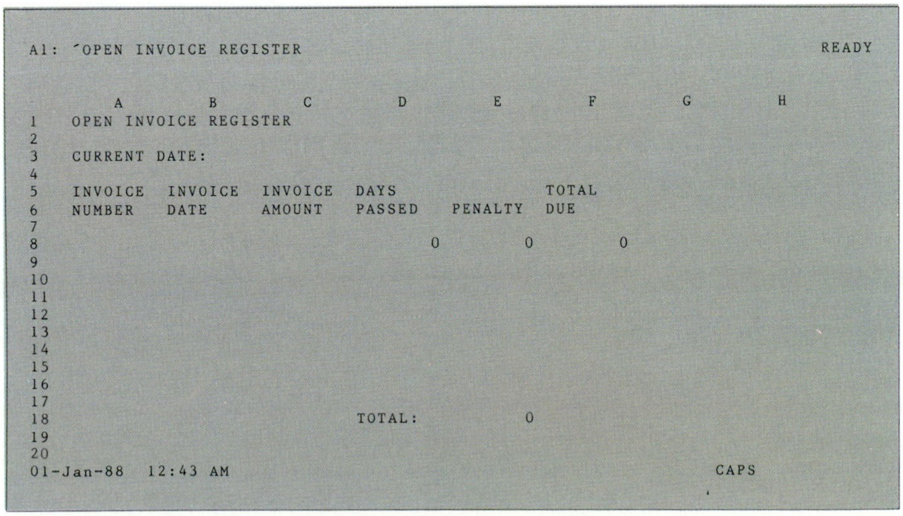

FIGURE C.17
Template with formulas. Four different formulas have been entered; they soon will be copied to other cells. Zeros appear in the cells now because no numerical data has yet been entered.

```
A1:  ^OPEN INVOICE REGISTER                                                    READY

           A         B         C         D         E         F         G         H
    1  OPEN INVOICE REGISTER
    2
    3  CURRENT DATE:
    4
    5  INVOICE   INVOICE   INVOICE   DAYS                TOTAL
    6  NUMBER    DATE      AMOUNT    PASSED    PENALTY   DUE
    7
    8                                          0         0         0
    9
   10
   11
   12
   13
   14
   15
   16
   17
   18                                TOTAL:              0
   19
   20
   01-Jan-88   12:43 AM                                            CAPS
```

Note that you moved to the cell that you wanted to copy from each time. This enabled you to simply press the RETURN key when Lotus 1-2-3/SuperCalc4 prompted you to enter the range to copy from.

ENTERING UNDERLINES

In this step you are going to enter underlines into your spreadsheet to make it appear more organized. To enter an underline using Lotus 1-2-3, you must fill a cell with dashes to mark the beginning of where you want the underline to be. Then copy the dashes into the other cells in which you want the underline to appear. To fill a cell with dashes, Lotus 1-2-3 uses the "backslash-fill" command. Key in the following:

CELL LOCATION	YOUR KEYSTROKES
1. A7	\,-
2. A17	\,-

You should now have dashes in cells A7 and A17. The next step is to copy these dashes into the appropriate cells. Perform the following copy commands:

CELL LOCATION	YOUR KEYSTROKES
1. A7	/,C,[Rtn],B7..F7,[Rtn]
2. A17	/,C,[Rtn],B17..F17,[Rtn]

Your spreadsheet template should now look like the one in Figure C.18.

For SuperCalc4 Users:

To enter an underline using SuperCalc4, key in a single quote (') followed by a dash (-) into the first cell you want to contain an underline. Doing this will put an underline across the entire row of your spreadsheet. If you want the underline to cover only a few columns, position the cursor in the first column where you *don't* want an underline to appear, key in another single quote ('), and then tap the RETURN key. Key in the following (remember that commas separate the keystrokes—don't key the commas in):

CELL LOCATION	YOUR KEYSTROKES
1. A7	',-,[Rtn]
2. G7	',[Rtn]
3. A17	',-,[Rtn]
4. G17	',[Rtn]

When you are using the method described above for Lotus 1-2-3/SuperCalc4, the underline will automatically widen when you widen a column. Your screen should look similar to the one pictured in Figure C.18.

ENTERING THE CURRENT DATE

You are now going to enter the current date to exemplify the need to format your spreadsheet, which we'll do in the next step. The format for this function is as follows:

@DATE(YY,MM,DD)

YY refers to "year," MM refers to "month," and DD refers to "day." To enter the date March 16, 1988, into cell C3 using the DATE function, key in the following:

@DATE(88,03,16)

You should see the number 32218 in the cell. This is the number of days that have passed since January 1, 1900. By itself, this number isn't very meaningful; you need to format it to be displayed in Lotus 1-2-3's date format. *Note:* The number 32218 will remain in the cells in column D until a corresponding Invoice Date has been entered. Examine the formula you entered into column D to understand why.

For SuperCalc4 Users
Key in the following:
DATE (03,16,88)
The date should appear as 3/16/88 in the cell.

FORMATTING NUMBERS AND TEXT

In this step, you are going to format the appearance of the numbers in the spreadsheet—that is, how they will be displayed. The Current Date cell (C3) will be formatted in the date format. Because you will later be entering invoice date data

FIGURE C.18
Spreadsheet template with copied formulas and underlines. Note that zeros still appear because numerical data has not yet been entered.

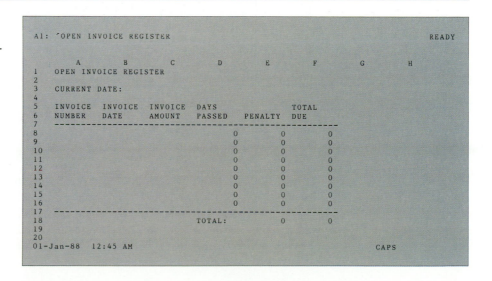

using the Date function into the Invoice Date column, you will also format that column in the date format. You will then format the Invoice Amount, Penalty, and Total Due columns in the currency format. If a series of asterisks (*) appears in some cells after they are formatted, don't be alarmed. This is Lotus 1-2-3's way of telling you that the column isn't wide enough to display the number. In the next step, you will widen columns. (*Note:* In the following few steps, it doesn't matter if you move to the specified cell locations before issuing the format commands, because in each case, the range to be formatted is referred to directly in the command sequence.)

CELL LOCATION	YOUR KEYSTROKES
1. C3	/,R,F,D,[Rtn],C3,[Rtn]
2. B8	/,R,F,D,[Rtn],B8..B16,[Rtn]
3. C8	/,R,F,C,[Rtn],C8..C16,[Rtn]
4. E8	/,R,F,C,[Rtn],E8..E18,[Rtn]
5. F8	/,R,F,C,[Rtn],F8..F18,[Rtn]

Note that in Steps 4 and 5, you were able to format through an underline. Also, you could have combined Steps 4 and 5 if, in Step 4, you had referred to the range E8..F18, which would have immediately formatted columns E and F in the currency format.

We will format the column headings so that they are lined up above the numbers displayed in this spreadsheet.

CELL LOCATION	YOUR KEYSTROKES
A5	/,R,L,R,A5..F6,[Rtn]

Your spreadsheet template should now look similar to the one pictured in Figure C.19. If it doesn't, review the steps done so far.

For SuperCalc4 Users:

CELL LOCATION	YOUR KEYSTROKES
1. C8	/,F,E,C8:C16,[Rtn],$,[Rtn]
2. E8	/,F,E,E8:E16,[Rtn],$,[Rtn]
3. F8	/,F,E,F8:F16,[Rtn],$,[Rtn]
4. A5	/,F,E,A5:F6,[Rtn],T,R,[Rtn]

WIDENING COLUMNS

Unless you tell Lotus 1-2-3/SuperCalc4 otherwise, all columns will be the default width—nine characters wide. Often, however, nine characters isn't wide enough to see all of the text or numbers you place into cells. To be able to see all the numbers in the cells in your spreadsheet, you are going to widen columns B, C, and F. To widen a column, position the cursor anywhere in the column you want to widen *before* you issue the command keystrokes. The steps are as follows:

COLUMN LOCATION	YOUR KEYSTROKES
1. B	/,W,C,S,10,[Rtn]

These keystrokes widened column B to 10 characters.

2. C	/,W,C,S,10,[Rtn]

These keystrokes widened column C to 10 characters.

3. F	/,W,C,S,13,[Rtn]

These keystrokes widened column F to 13 characters.

For SuperCalc4 Users:

COLUMN LOCATION	YOUR KEYSTROKES
1. C	/,F,C,C,[Rtn],W,10,[Rtn]
2. F	/,F,C,F,[Rtn],W,13,[Rtn]

ENTERING DATA

Now that you've entered all of the text and formulas into your spreadsheet, it's time to enter some spreadsheet data. (Remember, after you have entered the data, test the formulas by performing the calculations manually and checking the results against the results in the spreadsheet.) (*Note:* Enter data into the first three columns only. Everything else in the spreadsheet is a calculation based on a formula.)

Each Invoice Date will have to be entered using the DATE function. The rest of the information will be entered directly without using a function.

FIGURE C.19
Formatted spreadsheet template with the current date.

```
A1:  ^OPEN INVOICE REGISTER                                                        READY

        A         B          C          D          E          F          G
1    OPEN INVOICE REGISTER
2
3    CURRENT DATE:        ********
4
5    INVOICE   INVOICE   INVOICE      DAYS                  TOTAL
6     NUMBER     DATE     AMOUNT     PASSED   PENALTY         DUE
7    ---------------------------------------------------------------------
8                                    32218    $0.00        $0.00
9                                    32218    $0.00        $0.00
10                                   32218    $0.00        $0.00
11                                   32218    $0.00        $0.00
12                                   32218    $0.00        $0.00
13                                   32218    $0.00        $0.00
14                                   32218    $0.00        $0.00
15                                   32218    $0.00        $0.00
16                                   32218    $0.00        $0.00
17   ---------------------------------------------------------------------
18                                  TOTAL:    $0.00        $0.00
19
20
01-Jan-88   12:48 AM                                                         CAPS
```

We'll lead you (both Lotus 1-2-3 and SuperCalc4 users) through entering the data for the first two invoices. As you enter this data, note how your formulas calculate immediately. Refer to Figure C.20 to enter the rest of the invoice data. Key the following data into the designated cells (press the RETURN key after each keystroke):

CELL LOCATION	YOUR KEYSTROKES
1. A8	38105
2. B8	@DATE(88,01,14)
3. C8	1200
4. A9	38106
5. B9	@DATE(88,01,20)
6. C9	750

For SuperCalc4 Users:

CELL LOCATION	YOUR KEYSTROKES
1. A8	38105
2. B8	DATE(01,14,88)
3. C8	1200
4. A9	38106
5. B9	DATE(01,20,88)
6. C9	750

FIGURE C.20
Completed open invoice
spreadsheet.

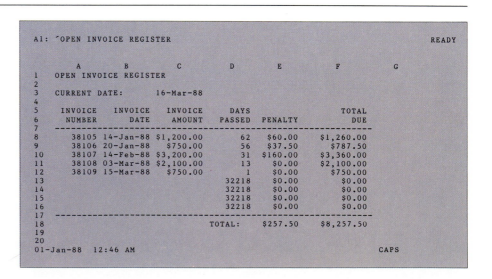

ADDING, CHANGING, AND DELETING DATA

Pretend a week went by between the time you saved your spreadsheet template and the time you retrieved it to input some new data. How do you add it to the spreadsheet? How do you change some existing data or delete some existing data? To add data, position the cursor in the cell where you want to enter data and then key in the data. Enter a new Invoice Number into A13 (key in any data). Then position your cursor in cell B13 and key in a new Invoice Date (key in any data). To change existing data, follow the instructions given in "Editing Cell Contents." To erase data from your template, press the following keys (in the following, [range] should be replaced with the appropriate range of cells you want to delete, such as A8..C8):

For SuperCalc4 Users:
/,B,[range],[Rtn]

/,R,E,[range],[Rtn]

Remember that none of your changes will be retained if you don't resave your spreadsheet template.

PROTECTING THE SPREADSHEET TEMPLATE

In the business environment, other people will certainly be using the spreadsheet you created. As described earlier, many electronic spreadsheet programs provide you with the capability of protecting certain cells in your spreadsheet so that nobody can accidentally erase them.

The recommended procedures for protecting your spreadsheet are as follows:

1. Issue the command to protect the entire spreadsheet.
2. Now issue the command to unprotect the range(s) of cells in your spreadsheet template into which you or others will be entering data.

In Lotus 1-2-3, use these keystrokes to protect the formulas in your spreadsheet:

1. /,W,G,P,E,
   These command keystrokes protect the entire spreadsheet.
2. /,R,U,C3,[Rtn]
   These command keystrokes unprotect the Current Date cell so that you can update the spreadsheet with the current date.
3. /,R,U,A8..C16,[Rtn]
   These command keystrokes unprotect the Current Date cell so that you can add, change, or delete data from the Invoice Number, Invoice Date, and Invoice Amount columns.

For SuperCalc4 Users:
The specific keystrokes to protect the formulas in your spreadsheet are as follows:
1. /,P,A1:F18,[Rtn]
2. /,U,C3,[Rtn]
3. /,U,A8:C16,[Rtn]

The unprotected portions of your spreadsheet template should now be highlighted.

Printing the Spreadsheet Template

To print your Lotus 1-2-3 spreadsheet in both the As-Displayed and Cell-Contents formats, press the following keys:

1. /,P,P,R,A1..F18,[Rtn],A,G,
   These keystrokes will print your spreadsheet's As-Displayed format. The A stands for "align" and helps to make sure your spreadsheet prints beginning at the top of the page. When your printer stops printing, continue with Step 2.

2. /,P,P,R,A1..F18,[Rtn],O,O,C,Q,A,G,
   These keystrokes will print your spreadsheet's Cell-Contents.

For SuperCalc4 Users:

To print your spreadsheet in both the Formatted and the Contents formats, press the following keys:

1. /,O,P,R,A1:F18,[Rtn],A,G,[press any key]
   These keystrokes will print your spreadsheet's Formatted format. The A stands for "align" and helps to make sure your spreadsheet prints beginning at the top of the page. When your printer stops printing, continue with Step 2. [Tap the Escape (ESC) key a few times to return to Ready Mode.]

2. /,O,P,R,A1:F18,[Rtn],O,R,C,Y,Q,Q,A,G,[press any key]
   These keystrokes will print your spreadsheet's Contents format. SuperCalc4 may prompt you to "press any key" again to print a second page.

The procedure for keeping track of unpaid invoices at Sporting Life has been greatly simplified. Your staff is probably eager to learn more about spreadsheet software and how to use it to automate more of their accounting activities.

Summary

Electronic spreadsheets provide the business professional with an extremely valuable way to produce information and update reports easily. Electronic spreadsheets are composed of rows and columns; the intersection of a row and column is called a *cell*. If a formula is placed in it, each cell can act like a miniature calculator. The capabilities of spreadsheet cell formulas combined with those of a spreadsheet command menu enable the user to create very powerful applications.

When creating a spreadsheet template, users must pay attention to the recommended spreadsheet development procedures. These procedures involve: (1) establishing objectives, (2) defining requirements, (3) building the spreadsheet, (4) testing the spreadsheet, and (5) using the spreadsheet. If these procedures are not followed, the likelihood is great that the spreadsheet will contain errors.

Most spreadsheets operate in one of the three modes: (1) Ready Mode, (2) Entry Mode, and (3) Menu Mode. Knowing which mode you're in is important so that you can answer questions such as "Why can't I move the cursor around the spreadsheet?" or "Why is the function appearing as text in the cell, instead of the answer the function should be deriving?"

A variety of features are common to almost all electronic spreadsheet programs, including the ability to enter text, numbers, and formulas into cells. A number of different functions can be used to speed up the process of keying in a complex formula, such as the DATE and the SUM functions. Electronic spreadsheet programs also allow the user to execute many powerful commands that will perform such tasks as copying, formatting, saving, printing, and protecting. The best way to learn about the power available within an electronic spreadsheet program is to use one. (Figures C.21 and C.22 on pages 574–576 provide command summaries of Lotus 1-2-3 and SuperCalc4.) In this tutorial, you have practiced using Lotus 1-2-3 and/or SuperCalc4. As a result, you should be prepared to tackle any other spreadsheet program; once you've used one spreadsheet program, you will find it relatively easy to use another type.

KEY TERMS

As-Displayed format	Entry Mode	protect
cell	formatting	range
Cell-Contents format	formula	Ready Mode
Command/Data Entry area	function	spreadsheet area
	IF . . . THEN function	SUM function
COPY command	Indicator area	template
currency format	Menu Mode	unprotect
DATE function	percent format	
electronic spreadsheet		

FIGURE C.21   Summary of Commands for Lotus 1-2-3

Command	Comments
/File Retrieve	Retrieves a file from disk and displays it on screen.
/Worksheet Column Set-width (number)	Adjusts the column width in which the cell pointer is currently located.
/Worksheet Global Column-width (number)	Adjusts all column widths.
/Worksheet Insert Column [RETURN]	Inserts a new column to the left of the column in which the cell pointer is currently located.
/Worksheet Insert Row [RETURN]	Inserts a new row above the row in which the cell pointer is currently located.
/Copy (range to copy from) (range to copy to) [RETURN]	Copies one cell, or a group of cells, to a different location.
@SUM (beginning cell..ending cell)	Sums a group of cell.
/Range Erase (beginning cell..ending cell) [RETURN]	Erases a range of cells from the current worksheet on screen.
/File Save (filename) [RETURN]	Saves the current worksheet, under the file name you designate, to disk. This version will replace an older version if an older version exists.
/Print Printer Range (beginning cell..ending cell) [RETURN] Align Go	Sends the current worksheet, defined by the range, to the printer.
/Move (from) [RETURN] (to) [RETURN]	Moves cell entries from one location to another.
/Worksheet Status	Displays the current status of your worksheet.
/Worksheet Column Hide (cell address)	Hides a column of information designated by the cell address.
/Worksheet Column Display (cell address)	Displays a previously hidden column.
/Range Name Create [RETURN] (indicate range of cells) [RETURN]	Allows you to label a range by a name (like SALES) rather than by cell addresses (like B7..F7).
@MIN(range)	Displays the minimum value of a range.
@MAX(range)	Displays the maximum value of a range.
@AVG(range)	Displays the average value of a range.
/Range Format Percent (number of decimal places) (range) [RETURN]	Edits numbers in specified range to percent format.
/Worksheet Global Format Currency (number of decimal places) [RETURN]	Formats all numbers on the worksheet to display currency format with designated number of decimal places.
/Worksheet Global Column-width (number of characters) [RETURN]	Adjusts all columns to designated width except those adjusted using the /Range Format command.
/Worksheet Titles Vertical	Freezes that portion of the worksheet to the left of the cell pointer.
/Worksheet Titles Clear	Clears titles frozen horizontally and vertically.

Command	Comments
/Worksheet Titles Horizontal	Freezes that portion of the worksheet above the cell pointer.
/Worksheet Titles Both	Freezes that portion of the worksheet above and to the left of the cell pointer.
[F6]	Switches between windows.
/Worksheet Window Unsync	Allows the worksheets in two separate windows to scroll unsynchronized.
/Worksheet Window Clear	Removes the window partition from the worksheet.
/File Xtract [RETURN] filename.ext [RETURN] (cell range) [RETURN]	Extracts and saves a portion of the current worksheet in a separate worksheet file. Saves formulas in the extract file.
/File Xtract Values filename.ext [RETURN] (cell range) [RETURN]	Extracts and saves a portion of the current worksheet in a separate worksheet file. Does not save formulas.
/File Combine Copy Entire-File filename.ext [RETURN]	Incorporates all or part of a worksheet file into the current worksheet at the location of the cell pointer.
/Range Justify (cell range) [RETURN]	Treats a continuous column of text as a paragraph, rearranging the words so that none of the lines is longer than a specified width.
/Print Printer Range (cell range) [RETURN] Options Setup \015	Turns on compressed print.
/Worksheet Column Set-Width (number)	Sets the current column to the desired width.
/Range Label Center (cell range) [RETURN]	Centers the labels in designated range.
/Worksheet Insert Column [RETURN]	Inserts a column to the left of the cell pointer.
/Worksheet Delete Row [RETURN]	Deletes row designated by cell pointer.
/Range Format Currency 2 [RETURN] (cell range) [RETURN]	Changes the cell range to currency format with two decimal places.
/Data Sort Data-Range [RETURN] Primary-Key (field name) [RETURN] Ascending [RETURN] Secondary-Key (field name) [RETURN] Ascending [RETURN] Go	Sorts the database by the Primary-Key field name in ascending order and then by the Secondary-Key field name in ascending order.
/Data Query Input (cell range) [RETURN] Criterion (cell range) [RETURN] Find	Searches the database for the criterion specified by the Criterion cell range. Use up arrow or down arrow to search through database.
/Range Erase (cell range) [RETURN]	Erases the contents of cell range.
[F7]	Repeats the most recent data query.
/Print Printer Range (cell range) [RETURN] Options Setup Margins 132	Sets the printed page to 132 columns rather than the standard 80.
/File Save filename.ext [SPACE] P [RETURN] (type password) [RETURN] (type password again) [RETURN]	Establishes a password for a file.
/Worksheet Erase Yes	Clears the current worksheet from the screen and memory but not from the disk.

FIGURE C.22   Summary of Commands for SuperCalc4

Use the F1 function key or ? after typing / to get a description of these commands.

/A	The **Arrange** command—sorts cells in ascending or descending order.
/B	The **Blank** command—removes or empties contents of cells or graphs. Specify range.
/C	The **Copy** command—duplicates graphs or contents and displays format of cells.
/D	The **Delete** command—erases entire rows or columns.
/E	The **Edit** command—allows editing of cell contents.
/F	The **Format** command—sets display format at Entry, Row, Column, or Global levels.
/G	The **Global** command—changes global display or calculation options.
/I	The **Insert** command—adds empty rows or columns.
/L	The **Load** command—reads spreadsheet or portion from disk into the workspace.
/M	The **Move** command—inserts existing rows or columns at new positions.
/N	The **Name** command—defines named ranges.
/O	The **Output** command—sends display or cell contents to printer, screen, or disk.
/P	The **Protect** command—prevents future alteration of cells.
/Q	The **Quit** command—ends use of the SuperCalc program.
/S	The **Save** command—stores the current spreadsheet on disk.
/T	The **Title** command—locks upper rows or left-hand columns from scrolling.
/U	The **Unprotect** command—allows alteration of protected cells.
/V	The **View** command—displays data as pie, bar, line, area, X-Y, or Hi-Lo graphics.
/W	The **Window** command—splits the screen display.
/Z	The **Zap** command—erases spreadsheet and format settings from workspace.
//	Additional commands //D accesses Data Management options.

EXERCISES

SHORT ANSWER

1. Describe specifically what you see when you first load your spreadsheet program into internal memory and the empty spreadsheet appears on the screen.

2. Why does your computer need to have a large amount of internal memory to use an electronic spreadsheet program effectively?

3. If you develop a spreadsheet that others are going to be using, why should you protect certain portions of it? What portions of it wouldn't you protect?

4. Describe the procedures for developing an electronic spreadsheet.

5. What are some advantages of using an electronic spreadsheet compared with using a manual spreadsheet?

6. What are the two different forms in which an electronic spreadsheet can be printed?

7. Why is it important to have efficient ways of moving the cursor around an electronic spreadsheet?

8. Describe the procedure for copying text and what you need to consider when copying formulas. Why is it important to review the formulas you have copied to make sure they are correct?

9. What is the purpose of formatting a spreadsheet?

10. Describe what is meant by the term *menu hierarchy*.

HANDS ON

1. Retrieve a copy of the INVOICE spreadsheet you created in the tutorial. Do the following:
   a. Change the Current Date to July 21, 1988.
   b. Add the following data:

Invoice Number	Invoice Date	Invoice Amount
38110	16-Mar-88	1200
38111	23-Mar-88	800
38113	09-Apr-88	1400

   c. Save the updated template onto your data disk under the same name you retrieved it under (INVOICE).

2. Add a column heading entitled PERCENT in cell G6. Enter a formula into cell G8 that divides F8 by F18. (Make sure the formula has a frozen reference to cell F18.) Copy the formula in the range F9..F16. Once the formula has been copied, format it to be displayed in the percent format, with two decimal places. Save this updated template under the name of INVOICE1 onto your data disk.

3. Clear internal memory. You should now have a blank electronic spreadsheet on the screen. Create the spreadsheet shown in Figure C.12b. Save it onto your data disk under the name of QTR1.

Challenge: There is one problem with the spreadsheet you created in the tutorial entitled INVOICE. It has to do with the Days Passed column. We don't want any date to appear in this column unless some invoice data has been entered. Use the IF . . . THEN function to annotate, or improve, the formula currently in cell D8 that says the following: If an invoice amount has been entered, then determine the number of days that have passed since the invoice date; otherwise, put a zero in the cell. Once you've accomplished this, copy this formula into the range D9..D16.

MODULE D

MICROCOMPUTER DATABASE MANAGEMENT SYSTEMS: dBASE III PLUS

Modern database management systems for microcomputers provide the business user with the means of managing and manipulating large amounts of data. They were introduced to the business community for use on microcomputers at about the same time as electronic spreadsheets; received with great enthusiasm, both types of software packages are powerful, easy to use, and often used together. This module will introduce you to database management systems (DBMS) software and demonstrate how important it can be to you as a business user.

PREVIEW

When you have completed this module, you will be able to:

- Describe what a database management system is and what the hardware considerations are for its use
- Describe the features of using a DBMS that are important to know about when you are:
  —creating and adding data
  —searching a database
  —sorting and indexing a database
  —changing the database structure
  —combining data from two database files
  —creating and printing reports
- Use dBase III Plus to create and manage a database
- Use dBase III Plus to create and print a report

DATABASE MANAGEMENT SYSTEM (DBMS) OVERVIEW

Picture an office with a row of file cabinets that extends as far as you can see—and you're responsible for them! You use your filing system mainly to track customer-related information, and everything is perfectly organized in alphabetical order. Not even one customer name is out of place! You know exactly where to look to find information on each customer. Great. But what if you need to pull out all folders that contain information on customers who live in a particular area? Your alphabetical organization scheme would no longer be useful. Your manual filing system has become a problem. You need a microcomputer database management system!

As described in Chapter 12, a **database management system (DBMS)** is a software tool designed to facilitate the creation and maintenance of an information database in order to produce reports. The term **database** describes a collection of data stored for a variety of business purposes. This module will explain the features of the **microcomputer-based DBMS.**

HARDWARE CONSIDERATIONS

Three major hardware considerations affect the use of a DBMS. First, and most important, because databases in the business environment tend to grow quite large, the user needs a *high-capacity* disk storage device (preferably a hard disk) with rapid access time so that data can be moved quickly to and from internal memory. (Because the database you will be working with in the "In the Lab" section is relatively small, you won't need a hard disk.) Many of your business files will become very large over time (assuming you continue to add data to them), so you need a large storage area. Also, some commands you will be using, such as the SORT command, require that all or part of your existing file be copied into a new file—another reason for having a high-capacity disk storage device.

Second, the user must be able to easily back up, or make duplicate copies of, disk contents—the best way to back up large database files is to use a streaming tape storage device (see Chapter 4). With one COPY command, you can copy the entire file (or entire disk contents) onto the tape.

Third, internal memory must also be considered. A DBMS stores only a small amount of data in internal memory at any time during processing. However, if your file is small enough (less than 300 K) to be loaded into a RAM disk (see Chapter 4), then performance can be improved substantially. Loading your DBMS file into RAM reduces to zero the mechanical delay inherent in disk drives.

DBMS FEATURES

As with any software package, you must be familiar with the concepts and features of a DBMS before you start to use it. This section will introduce you to these concepts and features so that when you come to the tutorial section, you will understand the whys and whats of DBMS processing.

CREATING A DATABASE

After you have loaded your DBMS software into internal memory, you can begin using its commands to create or manage a database. Creating a database is often referred to as creating the **database structure**—defining exactly what you want each field in a database record to look like. (*Note:* If you don't understand the meaning of terms like *field*, *record*, and *file*, refer to the "Data Hierarchy" section of Chapter 4.) Think of this activity as defining how many folders you want in a file drawer and what kind of information each folder should contain. Figure D.1 shows a database file structure that was defined using dBase III Plus, a popular DBMS used on microcomputers in the business environment today. This file structure was saved onto a data disk under the name of EMPLOYEE. To create a structure, the following items must be defined:

1. *Field Name*—You must give a unique name to each field of data you want to store. With dBase III Plus, which you'll learn how to use in the tutorial section of this module, a **field name** can be no longer than ten characters. To manipulate the database, you will often be required to refer to one or more elements of data by their field names.

2. *Field Type*—DBMS programs require you to define what type of information will be stored in the field. With most DBMS programs, data can be one of five types: (1) **character**—data that is **nonnumeric,** such as name and address information; (2) **numeric**— data that will be used in calculations, such as dollar amounts; (3) **date**—data that must be entered in a specific date format so that calculations can be performed on it; (4) **logical**—data that indicates whether a field is true or false (such as data regarding a person's marital status, where true = married and false = single); and (5) **memo**— data in the form of a long paragraph of text.

3. *Field Width*—You must determine what the maximum size of the field will be. For example, if you are defining the structure for a field that is to contain an employee's last name, what is the longest name you will probably have? Will it be ten, twenty, or thirty characters long? You must be sure that enough space is available for all the data you want to enter.

4. *Decimal Places*—For each numeric field, you must determine the number of **decimal places** you want. Most users store numbers to two decimal places (such as $10.00) instead of no decimal places (such as $10).

You must think carefully at the start so you won't have to change your database structure later, after you've entered a number of different records. (To change a database structure, you must go through a specific procedure that can take a lot of time, depending on the DBMS program you use.) Before the employee database file structure was created, for example, thought was given to having a separate field for SIRNAME, FIRSTNAME, and LASTNAME because (1) the database can now be sorted into alphabetical order by last name and (2) the individual name fields can be referenced in a report. For example, you might want to include only SIRNAME (to store Mr., Ms., Miss, or Mrs.) and LASTNAME fields in a specific report.

ADDING DATA TO A DATABASE

Once you have defined your database structure, you can add data to it. However, first you must tell the DBMS software to which file you want to add data or which file you want to use. DBMS programs make this requirement because more than one database file (or storage drawer) may be stored on the same disk. The procedure for adding new records to a database file (such as data about a new employee) is straightforward and involves issuing a command. In the "In the Lab" section of this module we lead you through adding records to a database.

FIGURE D.1
Database structure. What you would see on the screen if you used dBase III Plus to create a database structure to store employee data. The following items were defined: (1) field name, (2) field type, (3) field width, and (4) number of decimal places.

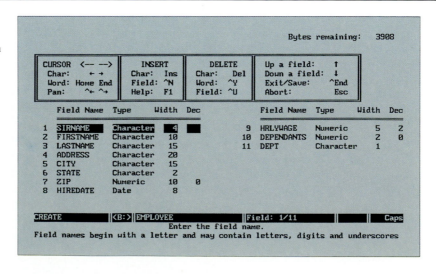

Figure D.2 pictures a listing of the database file called EMPLOYEE (whose structure was pictured in Figure D.1) after twelve records have been entered.

SEARCHING A DATABASE

What if you want to see a list—either on your screen or printed out—of only those elements of your database that meet certain criteria? In a manual file system, depending on how the folders are organized, you might need a long time to perform special searches for information such as the following: "Pull out the folders in the employee filing cabinet for every employee who makes more than $15.00 per hour." If the folders are organized in alphabetical order by name, performing this task will involve pulling each folder out of the cabinet and looking at all the hourly wage (HRLYWAGE) figures. This could take hours! In contrast, performing **searches** with DBMS software and database files stored in computer-usable form is fast and, once you get comfortable with the procedure, easy. As long as you know the field names defined in your database structure (such as SIRNAME and FIRSTNAME) and are familiar with the types of operations you can perform, you can ask the DBMS for the answer to any number of questions about your database.

There are four categories of database management operations: (1) arithmetic operations, (2) relational operations, (3) logical operations, and (4) string operations.

ARITHMETIC OPERATIONS   You can perform **arithmetic operations** on the numeric fields in your database. The arithmetic operators are:

+	Addition
−	Subtraction
*	Multiplication
/	Division
()	Parentheses are used for grouping operations

FIGURE D.2
EMPLOYEE database file.
These records were keyed into the EMPLOYEE database structure that was shown in Figure D.1.

SIRNAME	FIRSTNAME	LASTNAME	ADDRESS	CITY	STATE	ZIP	HIREDATE	HRLYWAGE	DEPENDENTS	DEPT
Mr.	Alan	Sampson	122 Westwood Street	San Mateo	CA	94001	05/06/89	17.00	0	A
Ms.	Victoria	Costigan	155 Washington Lane	San Bruno	CA	95609	02/14/89	18.00	0	B
Miss	Ahmad	Arguello	2100 Morrell Place	San Mateo	CA	94001	01/04/89	19.00	0	A
Mr.	Mark	Termeunde	41 Pacific Avenue	San Francisco	CA	94104	01/05/89	11.00	0	B
Ms.	Nancy	Busterud	310 Filbert Street	San Francisco	CA	94109	03/16/89	21.00	0	B
Mr.	Rolando	Rodriguez	1440 Occidental St	San Mateo	CA	94001	05/11/89	19.50	0	A
Mr.	Donald	Hutchinson	3100 Woodside Way	San Mateo	CA	94001	02/06/88	21.00	0	A
Miss	Donna	Bowman	3118 Pine Street	San Francisco	CA	94104	11/13/88	16.50	0	B
Ms.	Sandra	Smolley	4313 Wilhaggin Drive	San Mateo	CA	94001	11/04/88	23.00	0	A
Mr.	Clayton	Fong	3200 Anderson Street	San Bruno	CA	95609	11/04/88	10.50	0	B
Miss	Betsy	Dunne	58 Leavenworth	San Francisco	CA	94109	01/03/88	17.00	0	A
Mr.	Britt	McConnell	1200 3rd Street	San Francisco	CA	94001	09/01/89	17.00	0	A

RELATIONAL OPERATIONS   **Relational operations** are used to analyze the contents of fields. For example, you would need to use a relational operator if you want to list the records in your EMPLOYEE database file that have an hourly wage field that contains an amount greater than 15. The following relational operators are used to perform relational operations:

>	Greater than
<	Less than
=	Equal to
>=	Greater than or equal to
<=	Less than or equal to
<>	Not equal to

The result of a relational operation is always a true (T) or false (F) answer. Another operation is usually performed on the basis of the answer, such as listing the record on the screen.

LOGICAL OPERATIONS   **Logical operations** allow you to search your database for special information. For example, you might want to list on the screen all the records that have an hourly wage (HRLYWAGE) amount that is greater than 15 *and* a department (DEPT) field that equals San Diego. There are three logical operators:

1. AND   Allows you to specify two conditions that must exist for a specific action to be taken.

2. OR   Allows you to specify one of two conditions that must exist for a specific action to be taken. For example, test to determine if CITY = San Francisco OR CITY = San Mateo. This command would allow you to screen out all records except those containing data on residents in San Francisco or San Mateo.

3. NOT   Allows you to specify that a condition not be true for a specific action to be taken. For example, test to determine if CITY is NOT equal to San Francisco. This command would allow you to screen out all records for people living in the city of San Francisco.

STRING OPERATIONS   **String operations** allow you to search for the occurrence of a specific group of text characters in your database. The text ARG is a **string** (group) of three characters. For example, if you are working with an enormous database, you might want to list on the screen only those files whose last name (LASTNAME) begins with the letters ARG.

SORTING VERSUS INDEXING

When you ask a DBMS to list, or search for, specific records based on certain criteria, the list displays the record data in the order you input it to the database file. How, then, can you list records in chronological order (by date), for example? By using the SORT command or the INDEX command. Note that these two commands offer you very different ways to access the data in a file in a particular sequence. As described below, **indexing** files into a particular order is generally preferable to **sorting** files into order.

When the SORT command is used, a copy of the original file is produced in sorted order (the DBMS will prompt you to give the newly sorted file a new name). Therefore, if you don't have at least twice as much space left on your disk as the size of your database file, the SORT command won't work.

In contrast, the INDEX command does not produce a complete new copy of the file. As a result, the INDEX command takes less time than the SORT command to put a database file into order. The INDEX command creates a small index file containing the key field (the field you are using to determine the order) in the order (as you have defined it) that you want the database to be put into. You can have a file indexed into any number of orders (for example, last-name order, chronological order, order of increasing pay rates). When you want to display database files in a certain order, you tell the DBMS which index file to use. These index files don't take up much space on your data disk, so you don't have to worry about indexing your files too often or in too many different ways.

CHANGING A DATABASE'S STRUCTURE

What happens if, after you've entered hundreds of records, you realize you need to change the structure of your database? Perhaps you want to add a field to each record in the EMPLOYEE database—for example, employee number (EMPNUM). In the early days of DBMS software, this procedure would have been difficult. Recent versions of DBMS software make the problem easier to deal with; however, certain database structure changes are more difficult to accomplish than others.

One of the most common structure changes that users make affects **field width**—sufficient space was not allotted initially. As you will see in the tutorial section, changing the field width is easy. However, changing the **type** of a **field**—for example, from character to numeric—is a little more difficult.

COMBINING DATA FROM TWO FILES

Occasions will arise when you will want to combine data from two files to form a third file. For instance, let's assume you have a Customer database file containing the following fields in each record: (1) customer name, (2) customer address, and (3) invoice number. You've entered data for these fields into 150 records. And let's say you also have an Invoice database file that contains the following fields in each record: (1) invoice number, (2) invoice amount, and (3) amount paid. Now you want a Customer-Invoice database file. The process for creating this new file is as follows:

1. Create a new database structure that includes the same name and data type characteristics for each field in the existing database structures. (Of course, you will have only one field for Invoice Number in the new database file.)

2. Use the command that matches records according to a key field and copies data into fields with matching names. (You would tell the DBMS to copy customer name, customer address, and invoice number from the Customer file into the new database file.)

3. Copy the invoice amount and amount paid field data from the Invoice file into the new database file. You will need to match invoice numbers to copy the data into the appropriate locations in the new database file.

CREATING AND PRINTING REPORTS

You've learned that you can manipulate a database by sorting, indexing, and/or listing records that meet your specifications or criteria. Frequently you will want the results of these manipulations to be output in a more polished form that can be circulated throughout your company for review.

In our discussion of database management system software in Chapter 12, we briefly described the report module. We told you that it is usually menu-driven and that it asks you for the details (contents) of the report. When you manipulate a database through sorting, indexing, or extracting, you can output the results to the report module, which allows you to include totals and subtotals, perform arithmetic on the numeric fields in your database, and add stylized headings and subheadings, thus improving the overall appearance of the report.

For instance, you may want to include in a report for your company's executives (using data from the Employee database) a listing containing Lastname, Firstname, Hiredate, and Hrlywage fields for all the employees who work in Department A. Without using the report module—using only a simple LIST command—the listing would look something like Figure D.3. But if you used the report module, the listing might look like Figure D.4.

IN THE LAB:

USING dBASE III PLUS DBMS SOFTWARE

In this tutorial, you will have the opportunity to create and manage a database using dBase III Plus, a popular DBMS package. You will learn to use most of the features discussed thus far. These features are common to most DBMS programs, so your experience using dBase III Plus will help you learn to use other DBMS packages.

We assume you are using a microcomputer with two floppy disk drives (drive A and drive B), that your copy of dBase III Plus will be retrieved from drive A, and that the database you create will be saved onto a data disk in drive B. If you are using a computer with a hard disk, you will probably need to substitute drive C for drive A or B, depending on from where you will retrieve a copy of dBase III Plus and to where you will save your documents.

THE BUSINESS SITUATION

You manage the sporting goods store called Sporting Life. Over the last few years the store has grown substantially, doubling the number of employees. You serve nearly 500 regular customers, plus other new customers. You are interested in tracking customer information in the form of a computer-usable database file so that you can easily retrieve information about customers and send mailers out to special customers. This tutorial will teach you to create and manage Sporting Life's customer database and generate information for mailers. (*Note:* Read the section on "Saving the Database" in this tutorial before you end your working session—if you don't end your working session properly, your database file might be damaged.)

LOADING dBASE III PLUS AND USING THE MENUS

We assume that you have booted your computer with an operating system disk in drive A of your computer. To load the dBase instructions into internal memory and to use its set of commands, replace your operating system disk in drive A with your dBase System 1 disk. To load the instructions on this disk into internal memory, key in the following after the A prompt:

    A>DBASE

Press the RETURN key. After a brief copyright message appears on the screen, a message appears telling you to replace your System 1 disk with your System 2 disk. Follow this instruction and then press the RETURN (Enter) key.

FIGURE D.3
Using the LIST command to list database records.

```
Record#   LASTNAME       FIRSTNAME   HIREDATE    HRLYWAGE
      1   Sampson        Alan        05/06/89       17.00
      3   Arguello       Ahmad       01/04/89       19.00
      6   Rodriguez      Rolando     05/11/89       19.50
      7   Hutchinson     Donald      02/06/88       21.00
      9   Smolley        Sandra      11/04/88       23.00
     11   Dunne          Betsy       01/03/88       17.00
     12   McConnell      Britt       09/01/89       17.00
```

FIGURE D.4
Using the report module to list database records.

```
                    DEPARTMENT "A"
                LISTING OF EMPLOYEES
                        for
                     FALL 1989


        LAST          FIRST       DATE        HOURLY
        NAME          NAME        of          WAGE
                                  HIRE


        Sampson       Alan        05/06/89    17.00
        Arguello      Ahmad       01/04/89    19.00
        Rodriguez     Rolando     05/11/89    19.50
        Hutchinson    Donald      02/06/88    21.00
        Smolley       Sandra      11/04/88    23.00
        Dunne         Betsy       01/03/88    17.00
        McConnell     Britt       09/01/89    17.00
```

QUICK REFERENCE:
LOADING dBase III Plus
1. Place your System 1 disk in drive A.
2. After the A prompt, type DBASE.
3. Press RETURN.
4. Replace your System 1 disk with your System 2 disk.
5. Press RETURN.

You should now see the initial dBase menu display. The cursor is highlighting the Setup group of commands, which are listed below the highlighted word *Setup*. The format of this list of commands is often referred to as a **pull-down menu.** Moving the cursor with the right- or left-arrow key (located on the keyboard number pad) will cause another group of commands to be listed, or pulled down. Tap your right-arrow key once. The commands that allow you to create a database have been pulled down. Tap your right-arrow key seven more times until you are back at the Setup group of commands. Note that some options that are pulled down in the different menus are brightly lit and some are dimly lit. The dimly lit options can be used only when certain conditions exist; the brightly lit options can be used now. You will understand what we mean by "conditions" as you progress through this tutorial.

You can also highlight a group of commands by typing the first letter of the option. For example, to highlight the Retrieve group of commands, tap the letter R. To again highlight the Setup group of commands, tap the letter S. To highlight a command in the list that has been pulled down, use your up- and down-arrow keys. Tap your down-arrow key six times until you are highlighting the Database file option again. To select an option (which we don't want you to do now), you need to highlight the option and then press the RETURN key.

QUICK REFERENCE:
USING THE MENUS
1. Use your right- and left-arrow keys to "pull down" the commands corresponding to each group name, or tap the first letter of the group name.
2. To choose options within a group of commands, use your up- and down-arrows to highlight the option you want, and then press the RETURN key to begin execution of the command.

What else do you see on the screen? You should see the status bar on the bottom, which tells you about the current status of activities (Figure D.5).

CREATING THE DATABASE STRUCTURE

To create a database you must highlight the Create group of commands using the right-arrow key. Then choose the Database File group of commands by first highlighting the option (your cursor should be highlighting it already) and then tapping the RETURN key. A new menu should appear that lists a number of disk drives; dBase III Plus is asking you "Where do you want to store your database file(s)?" Because your data disk is in drive B, highlight B: and press the RETURN key. You will then be prompted to enter the name you want to give your database file. Because you are going to be creating a customer database file for Sporting Life, let's name the file CUSTOMER. Key in CUSTOMER and press the RETURN key.

QUICK REFERENCE:
CREATING A DATABASE STRUCTURE
1. Highlight the Create group of commands.
2. Choose the Database File group of commands.
3. Choose option B:.
4. Key in a name for your database; press the RETURN key.

Your screen should now look very much like the screen display in Figure D.6.

FIGURE D.5
dBase III Plus main menu. What you see (after the copyright message) when dBase III Plus is first loaded into internal memory.

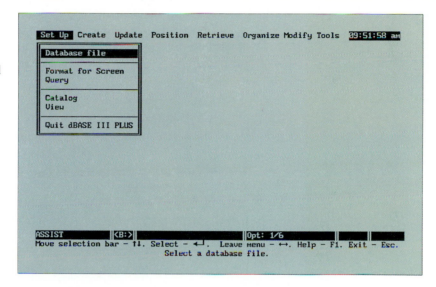

FIGURE D.6
Create database screen. dBase is waiting for you to define the structure of your database.

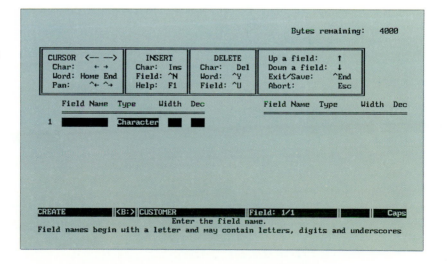

Information about moving the cursor appears at the top of your screen, followed by a blank area that will be used to define the structure for your database. To define the structure, key in the following (if you are using an IBM AT, press the ENTER key instead of the RETURN key; pressing the RETURN key will be symbolized by [Rtn]):

FIELD NAME		DATA TYPE	FIELD WIDTH			
1. SIRNAME	[Rtn]	C	4 [Rtn]			
2. FIRSTNAME	[Rtn]	C	10 [Rtn]			
3. LASTNAME	[Rtn]	C	15 [Rtn]			
4. ADDRESS	[Rtn]	C	30 [Rtn]			
5. CITY	[Rtn]	C	15 [Rtn]			
6. STATE	[Rtn]	C	2 [Rtn]			
7. ZIP	[Rtn]	C	10 [Rtn]			
8. INVNUM	[Rtn]	N	4 [Rtn]	[Rtn]		
9. INVAMT	[Rtn]	N	7 [Rtn]	2	[Rtn]	
10. AMTPAID	[Rtn]	N	7 [Rtn]	2	[Rtn]	
11. INVDATE	[Rtn]	D				

Your screen display should now look like the one in Figure D.7. Note that dBase automatically put the number 8 into Invdate's field-width column. Press RETURN to tell dBase III Plus you don't want to put any more fields in the records in this database. Then press RETURN once more to confirm your decision. You will be asked if you want to input records now. Press N for No. (You could have added data at this point, but we want you to practice using a database first.)

You should now be back where you left off at the main menu. *Note:* On your disk in drive B, you now have a file called CUSTOMER.DBF. dBase III Plus automatically gives all of your database files the extension of .DBF.

FIGURE D.7
Defining your database structure. What your screen should look like after defining the last field for the Customer database.

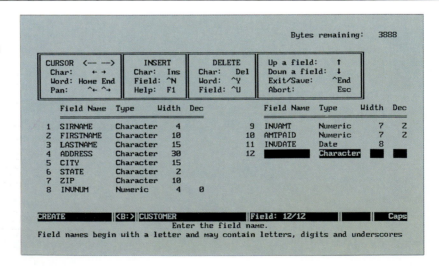

USING A DATABASE AND ADDING RECORDS

To add records to a file, you first need to specify to which file you want to add records (even though you only have one database file on your disk, CUSTOMER.DBF). Move the cursor to the Setup group of commands. Because you want to access the Database File group of commands and your cursor is already highlighting it, press the RETURN key. Highlight B: to tell dBase which disk drive the database file is in, and then press RETURN. The cursor should now be highlighting the file called CUSTOMER.DBF. If other files were on your disk, they would be listed here also. Press RETURN to use the CUSTOMER.DBF file. dBase will then ask you if the file is indexed or not (we describe indexing files later in this tutorial). Key in N. The status area at the bottom of your screen should indicate that you are using the CUSTOMER file located on a disk in drive B. The procedure you've just practiced is similar to pulling a file drawer open so that you can put documents into it.

QUICK REFERENCE:
USING A DATABASE YOU'VE CREATED
1. Highlight the Setup group of commands.
2. Choose the Database File group of commands.
3. Choose option B:.
4. Highlight the file you want to use; press the RETURN key.
5. Depending on whether your file is indexed or not, tap Y or N.

To add data to your open file, highlight the Update group of commands. Press RETURN to choose the Append option. A blank form that looks like the one in Figure D.8 should appear on the screen. To put data into this first record, key in the following:

1. Mr.   [Rtn]
2. Sean   [Rtn]

FIGURE D.8
Adding data to the Customer database. After you issue the command to add data to the customer database, this screen should appear.

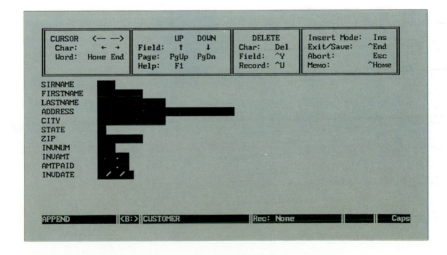

3. Wheeler   [Rtn]

4. 132 Walnut Lane   [Rtn]

5. San Francisco   [Rtn]

6. CA

7. 94122   [Rtn]

8. 2131

9. 132.11

10. 0   [Rtn]

11. 071488

dBase should now be waiting for you to enter information into the second record. What if you made a mistake when entering data into the first record? Can you go back to it? Fortunately, as shown at the top of your screen, dBase gives you a number of methods for moving to records and within records. To move to the previous record, press the PGUP key on your number pad. Your cursor should now be positioned on the M of "Mr." You can use the up- and down-arrow keys to move the cursor from field to field and the left- and right-arrow keys to move the cursor from character to character within fields. If you want to delete a character, position the cursor on the character and tap the DEL key. If you want to insert a character, or characters, tap the INS key (insert). (Note that when you tap the INS key, your status line indicates that insert mode is "on.") Tap your PGDN key to move to the next record to enter data.

Figure D.9 shows a listing of the database after you have entered nine more records. Refer to this figure and key in the rest of the data to the file. When you have entered the last data, press the RETURN key, and wait for a second. Because you left an entire record blank, dBase will assume that you don't want to add any more data to the database and will take you back to the main menu. Even though you are at the main menu, your CUSTOMER.DBF file is still open. dBase will assume that any command you issue pertains to this file.

QUICK REFERENCE:
ADDING DATA TO A DATABASE FILE
1. Once you've gone through the steps described in the Quick Reference on "Using A Database You've Created," highlight the Update group of commands.

FIGURE D.9
Customer database listing.

Record#	SIRNAME	FIRSTNAME	LASTNAME	ADDRESS	CITY	STATE	ZIP	INVNUM	INVAMT	AMTPAID	INVDATE
1	Mr.	Sean	Wheeler	132 Walnut Lane	San Francisco	CA	94122	2131	132.11	0.00	07/14/89
2	Mr.	Arnold	Schwartz	1330 Silver Street	San Mateo	CA	94019	2132	245.00	0.00	02/14/89
3	Mr.	Roy	Anchorman	13 Wayside Drive	San Francisco	CA	94102	2132	500.00	200.00	02/27/89
4	Miss	Judith	Kater	4311 Pacific Avenue	San Francisco	CA	94102	2140	1400.00	800.00	04/08/89
5	Mr.	Walter	Tindell	100 Eastman Drive	San Mateo	CA	94019	2138	350.00	0.00	03/15/89
6	Ms.	Anne	Henning	1440 Diego Way	San Francisco	CA	94102	2136	1400.00	700.00	06/12/89
7	Mr.	Tom	Hendrickson	1200 5th Avenue	San Mateo	CA	94019	2134	150.00	0.00	06/01/89
8	Mr.	Jack	Coyle	900 Golden Gate Way	San Francisco	CA	94102	2142	125.00	0.00	08/03/89
9	Ms.	Michele	Grasso	1300 Edgewood Drive	San Mateo	CA	94102	2145	1000.45	0.00	01/04/89
10	Ms.	Joan	Vieau	55 Francisco Street	San Francisco	CA	94102	2147	1150.75	150.00	06/15/89

2. Choose the Append option.
3. Key in the data. When you're at the bottom of a record and have pressed the RETURN key, dBase will automatically move you to the next record so you can enter more data.
4. Refer to the menu at the top of the screen to move around in the current record and between records in order to make editing changes.
5. When you've finished entering data and the cursor is on a blank record, press RETURN.

SAVING THE DATABASE

Although this might sound obvious, one of the most important things to learn about using a DBMS program is how to save your work. With dBase III Plus, the procedure doesn't involve issuing a SAVE command; instead, it involves going through the correct procedure to exit the program. When you exit the program, all your database management activities (such as adding or deleting activities) will be saved in the database.

To exit dBase III Plus, choose the Setup group of commands. Then choose the Quit dBase III Plus option. By choosing this option, you are saving your work, after which you will return to the DOS prompt (A>). At the end of each working session, you should go through the exit procedure.

QUICK REFERENCE:
SAVING YOUR WORK
1. Highlight the Setup group of commands.
2. Choose the Quit dBase III Plus option.

SEARCHING THE DATABASE

You now have a database on your data disk called CUSTOMER.DBF that contains ten records of customer data. How do you retrieve data from the database? How do you even know for sure the records exist? First, make sure you have gone through the necessary steps to open the CUSTOMER.DBF file for use. Then choose the Retrieve group of commands. Now select the List option by pressing the RETURN key. Press RETURN again to execute the command. You will be asked if you want to send the output to the printer. Type N so that the information is displayed on the screen. Because there are so many fields of data in each record, they can't all fit on one line, so they wrap around to the next line. Note that part of the city field and all of the state, zip, invoice number, invoice amount, and invoice date fields wrap around to the next line.

QUICK REFERENCE:
LISTING A DATABASE—ALL RECORDS, ALL FIELDS
1. Make sure you have a database in "use."
2. Highlight the Retrieve group of commands.
3. Choose the List option.
4. Choose the Execute the Command option.
5. Type Y or N, depending on whether you want the database to be listed on the screen or printed out.

Let's be a little more selective about what fields are displayed on the screen so that the display looks neater. This time, you will display only the last name (LAST-NAME), invoice number (INVNUM), invoice amount (INVAMT), amount paid (AMTPAID), and invoice date (INVDATE) fields. You must first highlight the Retrieve group of commands. Then choose the List option by highlighting it and pressing the RETURN key. Then highlight the Construct a Field List option and press the RETURN key. To select a field to be displayed, highlight the field and then press the RETURN key. Highlight each field listed above that you want to display and press the RETURN key after each is highlighted. In the status area at the bottom of your screen you should see a list of the fields you selected for display.

To tell dBase you have finished selecting fields for display, tap the right-arrow key. Then highlight the Execute the Command option and press the RETURN key to list the designated fields on the screen. Type N when asked if you want to send the output to the printer. Your display should look like the one in Figure D.10.

QUICK REFERENCE:
LISTING YOUR DATABASE—
ALL RECORDS, SELECTIVE FIELDS
1. Highlight the Retrieve group of commands.
2. Choose the List option.
3. Choose the Construct a Field List option.
4. Highlight each field you want listed and press RETURN for each.
5. Tap the right-arrow key when you've finished selecting fields.
6. Choose the Execute the Command option.
7. Type Y or N, depending on whether you want the database to be listed on the screen or printed out.

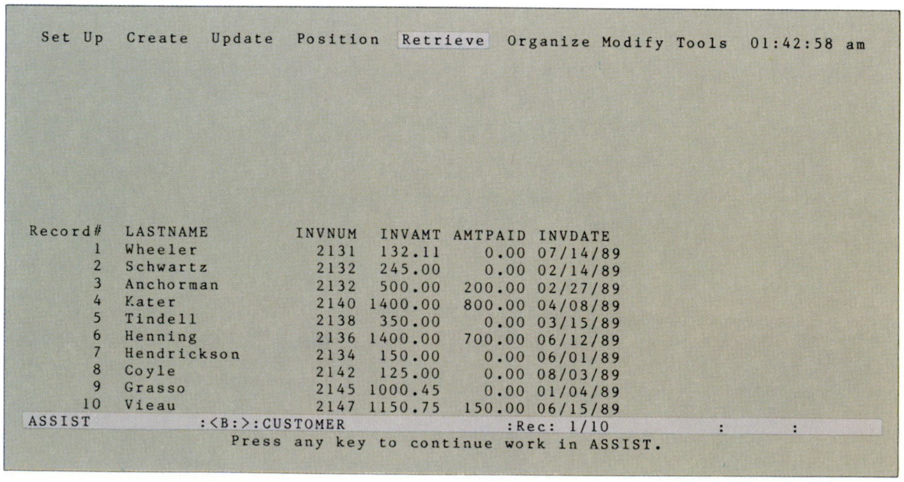

FIGURE D.10
Listing of specific fields. It's easy to be selective about which fields are listed when you perform a search operation. In this search operation, the following fields were listed: (1) LAST-NAME, (2) INVNUM, (3) INVAMT, (4) AMTPAID, and (5) INVDATE.

```
Set Up  Create  Update  Position  Retrieve  Organize Modify Tools  01:42:58 am




Record#   LASTNAME       INVNUM   INVAMT  AMTPAID  INVDATE
     1    Wheeler         2131    132.11     0.00  07/14/89
     2    Schwartz        2132    245.00     0.00  02/14/89
     3    Anchorman       2132    500.00   200.00  02/27/89
     4    Kater           2140   1400.00   800.00  04/08/89
     5    Tindell         2138    350.00     0.00  03/15/89
     6    Henning         2136   1400.00   700.00  06/12/89
     7    Hendrickson     2134    150.00     0.00  06/01/89
     8    Coyle           2142    125.00     0.00  08/03/89
     9    Grasso          2145   1000.45     0.00  01/04/89
    10    Vieau           2147   1150.75   150.00  06/15/89
ASSIST              :<B:>:CUSTOMER              :Rec: 1/10        :        :
              Press any key to continue work in ASSIST.
```

In the following steps, we are going to perform a number of data searches using the CUSTOMER.DBF file so that you can see how easily data can be retrieved.

Step 1—*List the records in which the CITY field is equal to San Francisco.* Choose the Retrieve group of commands and choose the List option. Then choose the Build a Search Condition option. Because our search is based on the CITY field, highlight that field and then press the RETURN key. Now highlight the operator you want. In this case, you want to see the records in which CITY is equal to San Francisco, so press RETURN because you are already highlighting the "equal to" option. Now enter the character string you are searching for—that is, San Francisco. This character string must be keyed in exactly as you keyed it into the database initially; if you capitalized the S of "San" and the F of "Francisco," you must do so here, too. But as the screen message reminds you, don't enter quotation marks. Make sure you've spelled the text correctly. Press the RETURN key. Press RETURN again if you're highlighting "No more conditions." Then highlight the Execute the Command option and press the RETURN key. Don't send your output to the printer. On the screen, you should now see the list of every record in which CITY is equal to San Francisco. Because there are too many fields in a record to be displayed on one line, each record takes two lines. As a result, in the next step, you will be selective about which fields are displayed on the screen.

QUICK REFERENCE:
LISTING YOUR DATABASE—
SELECTIVE RECORDS, ALL FIELDS
1. Highlight the Retrieve group of commands.
2. Choose the List option.
3. Choose the Build a Search Condition option.
4. Highlight the field(s) you want to use in your search and press the RETURN key.
5. Choose the operator you want.
6. Key in the character string or number that you're searching for. Press RETURN.
7. Choose the No More Conditions option.
8. Choose the Execute the Command option.
9. Type Y or N, depending on whether you want the database to be listed on the screen or printed out.

Step 2—*List the fields in which CITY is equal to San Francisco.* As in Step 1, choose the Retrieve group of commands and then the List option. Then choose the Construct a Field List option and highlight the following to specify that you want to display only these fields: (1) LASTNAME, (2) INVAMT, (3) AMTPAID, and (4) INVDATE. (Press the RETURN key after each field is highlighted.) Tap your right-arrow key to tell dBase you've finished selecting fields.

To tell dBase you want to display only those records that have a CITY field equal to San Francisco, follow exactly the steps described in Step 1, starting with where it says to choose the Build a Search Condition option. Your screen listing should look like the one in Figure D.11.

Step 3—*List the records in which CITY is not equal to San Francisco.* Repeat Step 1, except that when you choose operators, choose the "Not equal to" operator (<>).

Step 4—*List the records in which the ZIP field is equal to 94011.* Repeat Step 1, except instead of specifying the CITY field as the one on which you want to build a search condition, specify the ZIP field.

Quiz: List the records in which Invoice amount is greater than or equal to 200.00.

In the following searches, you will be using multiple conditions to retrieve specific data:

Step 5—*List the records in which the CITY field is equal to San Francisco and the AMTPAID field is equal to 0.00.* Choose the Retrieve group of commands and the List option. Then choose the Build a Search Condition option. As you did in Step 1, highlight the CITY field, the "equal to" option, and then key in San Francisco. Highlight the Combine With .AND. option to tell dBase you want to perform a multiple search. Highlight the AMTPAID field, the "equal to" option, and then key in 0. Then specify No More Conditions and choose the option to Execute the Command.

Step 6—*List the name and address fields of people who live in San Mateo and have an INVAMT field greater than 200.00.* Choose the Retrieve group of commands and the List option. Then choose the Construct a Field List option and highlight the following to specify you want to display only these fields: (1) SIRNAME, (2) LASTNAME, (3) ADDRESS, (4) CITY, (5) STATE, (6) ZIP. (Press

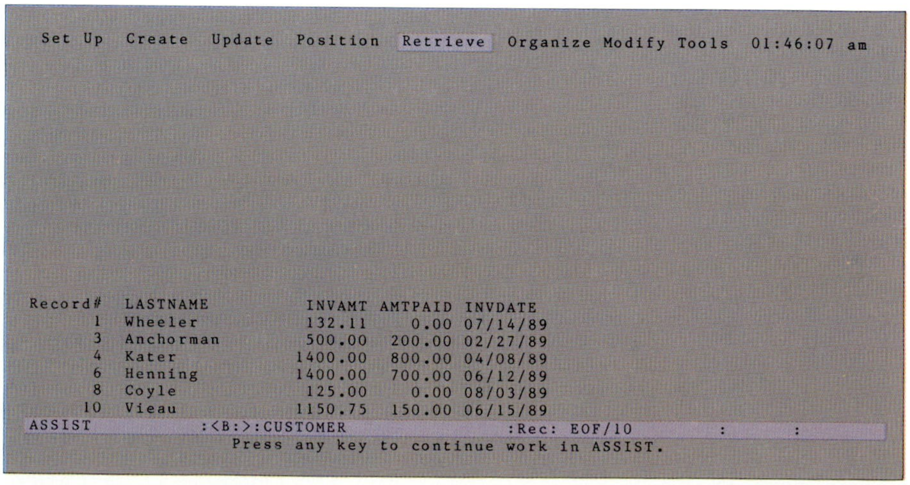

FIGURE D.11
Customer database CITY field listing. In this search operation, four fields were listed in the Customer database for records in which the CITY field was equal to San Francisco.

```
Set Up  Create  Update  Position  Retrieve  Organize Modify Tools  01:46:07 am
```

```
Record#  LASTNAME        INVAMT AMTPAID INVDATE
      1  Wheeler         132.11    0.00 07/14/89
      3  Anchorman       500.00  200.00 02/27/89
      4  Kater          1400.00  800.00 04/08/89
      6  Henning        1400.00  700.00 06/12/89
      8  Coyle           125.00    0.00 08/03/89
     10  Vieau          1150.75  150.00 06/15/89
ASSIST             :<B:>:CUSTOMER              :Rec: EOF/10        :        :
              Press any key to continue work in ASSIST.
```

the RETURN key after each field is highlighted.) Tap your right-arrow key to tell dBase you've finished selecting fields. Then choose the Build a Search Condition option. Highlight the CITY field, the "equal to" option, and then key in San Mateo. Highlight the Combine With .AND. option to tell dBase you want to perform a multiple search. Highlight the INVAMT field, the "equal to" option, and then key in 200. At this point specify No More Conditions and then choose the option to Execute the Command.

Step 7—*List the names and addresses in all records in which CITY is equal to San Francisco or Burlingame.* Choose the Retrieve group of commands and the List option. Then choose the Construct a Field List option and highlight the following fields to specify you want to display only these fields: (1) SIRNAME, (2) LAST-NAME, (3) ADDRESS, (4) CITY, (5) STATE, (6) ZIP. (Press the RETURN key after each field is highlighted.) Tap your right-arrow key to tell dBase you have finished selecting fields. Then choose the Build a Search Condition option. Highlight the CITY field, the "equal to" option, and then key in San Francisco. Highlight the Combine With .OR. option. Highlight the CITY field again, the "equal to" option, and then key in Burlingame. At this point specify No More Conditions and then choose the option to Execute the Command.

As you can see, DBMS software provides almost limitless ways to perform searches on your database files.

SORTING THE DATABASE

You have decided that you want your Customer database to be listed in order of invoice. You can accomplish this either by sorting or by indexing the database. In this section, you will use dBase's SORT command. As you learned earlier, sorting a database creates a new file that contains all the sorted records, which can be a problem if you are short of disk space. Make sure the CUSTOMER.DBF file is in use and then list the LASTNAME and INVNUM fields on your display screen to familiarize yourself with the current order of the CUSTOMER.DBF file. To sort this database file, do the following:

1. Choose the Organize group of commands.
2. Next choose the Sort option.
3. Choose the field you want to sort on, namely the INVNUM field.
4. Tap your right-arrow key to leave this menu.
5. Select the disk drive you want to store the sorted file on. You should specify B:.
6. Name the new file SORT1.

To see if the sort worked, select the Retrieve group of commands and the List option. Then choose the Execute the Command option. List the records on your display screen. What do you see? The records aren't in INVNUM order? They had better not be. You're still looking at your original CUSTOMER.DBF file. To look at the sorted file, you need to go through the steps to use the file SORT1.DBF. List the LASTNAME and INVNUM fields of the SORT1.DBF file on your display screen. The listing should look like the one in Figure D.12.

QUICK REFERENCE:
SORTING A DATABASE
1. Highlight the Organize group of commands.
2. Choose the Sort option.
3. Choose the field you want to sort on.
4. Tap the right-arrow key to leave the menu.
5. Select the disk drive to store the sorted file.
6. Give the sorted file a name. Press RETURN.

If you don't want both the CUSTOMER.DBF file and the SORT1.DBF files to remain on your data disk, taking up space, you can simply copy the contents of the sorted file into the CUSTOMER.DBF file by going through the following steps:

1. Choose the Organize group of commands.

2. Choose the Copy option.

3. Specify the disk drive.

4. Type the name CUSTOMER, because that's the file name you want to copy into (dBase will add the .DBF part of the file name, so you don't have to type it in).

5. When dBase asks you if you want to replace the existing file named CUS-TOMER on your disk, type Y.

If you now go through the steps to use the CUSTOMER.DBF file and then list the contents of the file on the screen, you will see that the file is in INVNUM order.

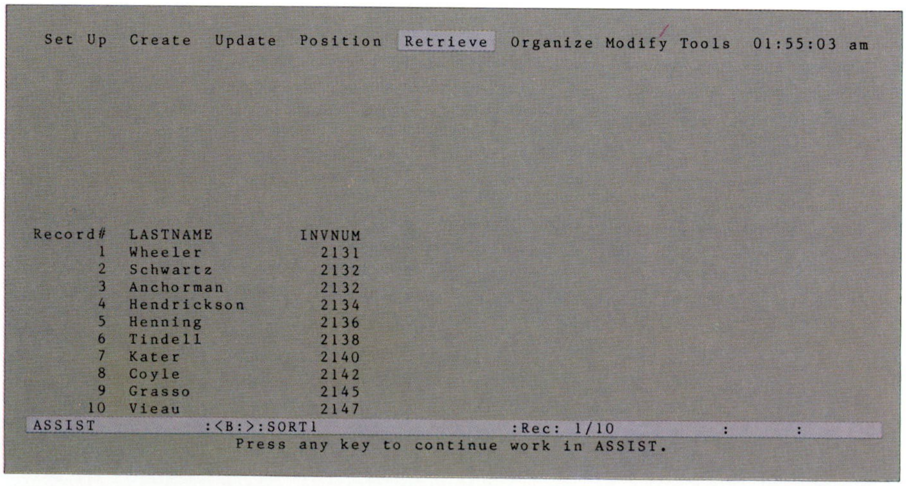

FIGURE D.12
SORT1.DBF file. This shows the LASTNAME and the INVNUM fields in the new sorted file.

```
 Set Up  Create  Update  Position  Retrieve  Organize Modify Tools  01:55:03 am




   Record#  LASTNAME       INVNUM
        1  Wheeler          2131
        2  Schwartz         2132
        3  Anchorman        2132
        4  Hendrickson      2134
        5  Henning          2136
        6  Tindell          2138
        7  Kater            2140
        8  Coyle            2142
        9  Grasso           2145
       10  Vieau            2147
 ASSIST            :<B:>:SORT1                    :Rec: 1/10       :        :
                   Press any key to continue work in ASSIST.
```

Because the objective of the last few steps was to conserve disk space, you should now perform the necessary steps to erase the file called SORT1.DBF. Choose the Tools group of commands. Then choose the Erase option. Highlight the SORT1.DBF file and press the RETURN key. The SORT1.DBF file has been deleted.

Indexing the Database

As described earlier, there are advantages to putting a database in order using the INDEX command instead of the SORT command. With the INDEX command, you don't have to create a new file that contains all the sorted records as you do when you use the SORT command; instead, you create small index files that take up very little space in storage. The next few steps will show you how to put the CUS-TOMER.DBF file into INVAMT order using the INDEX command.

1. Choose the Organize group of commands.
2. Choose the Index option.
3. Key in the name of the field you want to sort on. (Key in INVAMT.)
4. Specify the disk drive where you want the index file to be stored (B:).
5. Key in INVAMT as the name of the index file.

If you go through the steps to list the records in the CUSTOMER.DBF file right now, you'll see that they are in INVAMT order. In addition, on your data disk, you have a file called INVAMT.NDX, because dBase puts the extension of .NDX on all index files.

Let's go through the steps to create another index file that will put the CUS-TOMER.DBF database into CITY order.

1. Choose the Organize group of commands.
2. Choose the Index option.
3. Key in the name of the field you want to sort on. (Key in CITY.)
4. Specify the disk drive where you want the index file to be stored (B:).
5. Key in CITY as the name of the index file.

If you go through the steps to list the records in the CUSTOMER.DBF file right now, you'll see that they are in CITY order.

Remember that when you first go through the steps to use a database, you are asked whether the file is indexed. dBase is simply asking you what order you want the database file in. To illustrate, pretend the CUSTOMER.DBF file isn't in use. Go through the steps to use this file by first choosing the Setup group of commands and the Database File option. Choose the B: option and the CUSTOMER.DBF file. When you are asked if the file is indexed, key in Y. You should see your two index files listed on the screen. At this point, dBase wants to know in what order you want your database to be in. Press the RETURN key if you're currently highlighting the INVAMT.NDX file. The INVAMT.NDX file is now the active index. For a reason we'll explain in the next paragraph, now highlight the CITY.NDX file and press the RETURN key. Then tap your right-arrow key to return to the main menu.

At this point, if you list the CUSTOMER.DBF file now it will be in INVAMT order.

Why did we have you also choose the CITY.NDX file if it doesn't affect the current order of the database? Because when you add or delete records from your database, each index file you choose when you set up your database file for use will be automatically updated. dBase allows no more than seven index files for each database.

<u>QUICK REFERENCE:</u>
INDEXING A DATABASE
1. Choose the Organize group of commands.
2. Choose the Index option.
3. Key in the name of the field you want to index on.
4. Select the disk drive to store the index file.
5. Give the index file a name. Press RETURN.

EDITING THE CONTENTS OF A DATABASE

As manager of Sporting Life, you foresee the need to change records in the Customer database often because the invoice number and amount information will change as checks are received and additional items are ordered. You also realize that you will need to add a field to each record in the database—a field that stores each customer's telephone number. In this section we will lead you through the following: (1) editing records using the **EDIT command**, (2) editing records using the **BROWSE command**, (3) deleting records using the BROWSE command, and (4) modifying the structure of the database using the Modify group of commands.

To change the contents of a database record, you must first make sure the database file you want to edit (CUSTOMER.DBF) is in use—along with the index files you created, because you want them to be updated automatically when you make changes to the database.

Step 1—*Editing records using the EDIT command.* It's easy to edit a record if you know the record number. But when you have a database file that contains 100 records, it's almost impossible to remember what the number is for a particular record. Therefore, before you use the EDIT command to edit a record, you often have to search for the record you want (in order to make that record current). Pretend your CUSTOMER.DBF file contains over 100 records. You know you have to change Sean Wheeler's address from "132 Walnut Lane" to "142 Walnut Street." To make this record current, you need to search for it. Perform the following steps:

1. Choose the Position group of commands from the main menu.
2. Choose the Locate option.
3. Choose the Build a Search Condition option.
4. Choose the FIRSTNAME field, because you're going to specify that it must be equal to Sean.
5. Choose the "equal to" option.

6. Key in Sean.

7. Choose the Combine With .AND. option, because in the next step you're going to specify that the LASTNAME field must be equal to Wheeler.

8. Choose the LASTNAME field.

9. Choose the "equal to" option.

10. Key in Wheeler.

11. Choose the No More Conditions option.

12. Choose the Execute the Command option.

You should see a message at the bottom of the screen that says Sean Wheeler's record is Number 1. To edit this record, perform the following steps:

13. Choose the Update group of commands from the main menu.

14. Choose the Edit option.

15. You should now see Sean Wheeler's record on the screen waiting for you to edit it. Tap your down-arrow key to the ADDRESS field and key in the correct street address.

16. To save your changes, as it tells you in the menu at the top of the screen, you must hold the CTRL key down and tap the END key on your number pad. You should be back at the main menu.

The process of using the EDIT command may seem cumbersome, but you will find it easy after a while.

Step 2—*Editing records using the BROWSE command.* When you use the BROWSE command to edit the contents of a database, the contents of your database file are listed on the screen from the current record downward. To make the first record the current record so that the entire database will be listed on the screen, and then to enter Browse mode, perform the following steps:

1. Choose the Position group of commands.

2. Choose the Goto record option.

3. Choose the Top option.

4. Choose the Update group of commands.

5. Choose the Browse option.

6. You should now see the first four fields (columns) of data listed on the screen. You can now move the cursor around and edit the fields the cursor is in.

The screen isn't wide enough to display each record in its entirety at once, so you need to know how to move the cursor around the fields in your database. The menu at the top of the screen will guide you around your database. Practice moving your cursor. Figure D.13 lists the ways to move around the database fields. After editing using the BROWSE command, to save your changes and return to the main menu, hold the CTRL key down and tap the END key on your number pad.

Step 3—*Deleting records using the BROWSE command.* Follow Step 2. To delete the first record in your database, do the following:

1. Position the cursor anywhere in the record.

2. As the menu at the top of the screen instructs, hold the CTRL key down and tap the U key. At the bottom right of the screen, the indicator says "Del." Note that the record is still shown on the screen because it has only been "marked" for deletion. We need to use another group of commands to delete the record. dBase forces you to perform two steps to delete records so that you don't delete records unintentionally.

3. Exit Browse mode by holding the CTRL key down and tapping the END key on your number pad.

4. To permanently delete the first record from your database, choose the Update group of commands.

5. Choose the Pack option.

The message that tells you how many records were copied also tells you how many records are in your database file at this point.

Step 4—*Modifying the structure of the database using the Modify group of commands.* To add a field for PHONE to each record in your database, do the following:

1. Choose the Modify group of commands.

2. Choose the Database File option.

FIGURE D.13   Cursor Movement in Browse Mode

Command	Key
One character to the right	→
One character to the left	←
One field to the right	END
One field to the left	HOME
Move the screen one field to the right	CTRL + →
Move the screen one field to the left	CTRL + ←
Up one record	↑
Down one record	↓
Up one screen	PGUP
Down one screen	PGDN

3. Tap your down-arrow key until you are positioned on the blank field number 12.

4. Define this field as follows:
Field name: PHONE
Field type: C
Field width: 13

When you've finished keying in the preceding specifications, press the RETURN key to move the cursor down to the next record and then press the RETURN key twice more to tell dBase you've finished editing the database structure and you want to save the updated structure.

The easiest way to add phone numbers to the CUSTOMER.DBF file is to enter Browse mode by following Step 2 and then moving the cursor over to the PHONE field and entering the phone numbers. Go ahead and enter any phone numbers into the CUSTOMER.DBF file.

CREATING A REPORT

In this section you are going to create a report that looks like the one in Figure D.14. You will save the specifications for the report in a report file; dBase will add the extension .FRM to the file name. Perform the following steps to create this report:

1. Make sure the CUSTOMER.DBF file is in use (if it is, its name will be listed at the bottom of the screen).

2. Choose the Create group of commands.

3. Choose the Report option.

4. Specify B:. This is where your report file will be stored.

5. Give this file the following name: REPORT1.

You should see on the screen all the characteristics dBase assumes your report will have. To give your report a title, press RETURN (because you're highlighting the Page title option) and key in the following: CUSTOMER NAME AND ADDRESS LISTING. Press the RETURN key four times to return to the menu.

FIGURE D.14
Report. This report was generated using the REPORT1 file.

```
                      CUSTOMER NAME AND ADDRESS LISTING

        LAST NAME     FIRST NAME ADDRESS                    CITY           ZIP


        Wheeler       Sean       132 Walnut Lane            San Francisco  94122
        Schwartz      Arnold     1330 Silver Street         San Mateo      94019
        Anchorman     Roy        13 Wayside Drive           San Francisco  94102
        Kater         Judith     4311 Pacific Avenue        San Francisco  94102
        Tindell       Walter     100 Eastman Drive          San Mateo      94019
        Henning       Anne       1440 Diego Way             San Francisco  94102
        Hendrickson   Tom        1200 5th Avenue            San Mateo      94019
        Coyle         Jack       900 Golden Gate Way        San Francisco  94102
        Grasso        Michele    1300 Edgewood Drive        San Mateo      94102
        Vieau         Joan       55 Francisco Street         San Francisco  94102
```

To increase the amount of information that can fit on the printed page, change the left margin to zero (0) by highlighting the Left margin option, pressing the RETURN key, typing in 0, and then pressing the RETURN key again. To leave this menu, tap the right-arrow key.

To create the first column of this report (LASTNAME data), perform the following steps:

1. Tap the right-arrow key once to highlight the Columns group of commands.
2. Choose the Contents option.
3. Key in the following: LASTNAME. You should see the format for the report starting to build itself at the bottom of the screen.
4. Choose the Heading option.
5. Key in the following: LAST NAME (because this is the heading, use two words).
6. Press the RETURN key four times to go back to the menu.
7. Press the PGDN key to define the next column.

To create the second column of your report (FIRSTNAME data), perform the following steps:

1. Choose the Contents option.
2. Key in the following: FIRSTNAME.
3. Choose the Heading option.
4. Key in the following: FIRST NAME.
5. Press the RETURN key four times to go back to the menu.
6. Press the PGDN key to define the next column.

To create the third column of your report (ADDRESS data), perform the following steps:

1. Choose the Contents option.
2. Key in the following: ADDRESS.
3. Choose the Heading option.
4. Key in the following: ADDRESS.
5. Press the RETURN key four times to go back to the menu.
6. Press the PGDN key to define the next column.

To create the fourth column of your report (CITY), perform the following steps:

1. Choose the Contents option.
2. Key in the following: CITY.
3. Choose the Heading option.
4. Key in the following: CITY.
5. Press the RETURN key four times to go back to the menu.
6. Press the PGDN key to define the next column.

To create the fifth and final column of your report (ZIP), perform the following steps:

1. Choose the Contents option.
2. Key in the following: ZIP.
3. Choose the Heading option.
4. Key in the following: ZIP.
5. Press the RETURN key four times to go back to the menu.
6. Press the PGDN key.

Now that you've defined all the columns you want to see in your report, you must save the report format. To do this, tap your right-arrow key twice to highlight the Exit group of commands. Choose the Save option.

VIEWING A REPORT

To view your report, perform the following steps:

1. Choose the Retrieve group of commands.
2. Choose the Report option.
3. Specify B:.
4. Press the RETURN key to choose the REPORT1.FRM format.
5. Choose the Execute the Command option, and tap N when asked if you also want to print this report out on the printer.

You should see all the records in your database displayed on the screen according to the format you defined in REPORT1.FRM. What if you want to see only those records in which the INVAMT field is greater than 200.00? To accomplish this, you need to build a search condition. Perform the following steps:

1. Choose the Retrieve group of commands.
2. Choose the Report option.
3. Select B:.
4. Choose the REPORT1.FRM format.
5. Choose the Build a Search Condition option.
6. Choose the INVAMT field.
7. Choose the "greater than" option.
8. Key in 200.
9. Choose the No More Conditions option.
10. Choose the Execute the Command option to see the report on the screen (tap N when you are asked about sending the output to the printer). Only those records that have an INVAMT field greater than 200.00 should be listed in the report.

PERFORMING CALCULATIONS

What if you want to know the total amount of all the INVAMT fields or the AMTPAID fields in the CUSTOMER.DBF database file? Most DBMS programs make this request relatively easy to accomplish. To determine the total of all the INVAMT fields, perform the following steps:

1. Choose the Retrieve group of commands.
2. Choose the Sum option.
3. Choose the Construct a Field List option.
4. Choose the INVAMT field.
5. Tap your right-arrow key to return to the previous menu.
6. Choose the Execute the Command option.

The answer should appear at the bottom left of the screen. With what you now know about building search conditions, you should be able to combine a search condition and a calculation. For example, you could specify that you want to find the sum of all invoices for people who live in San Francisco. The possibilities are almost limitless.

SUMMARY

Database management systems software is being widely used in the business environment today for a number of very good reasons. This tool has made it easy for the non-computer professional to create and manage business information in the form of computer-usable database files and to generate custom-tailored reports from this information.

When you create a database file, you must first define exactly what kind of data you want to store. This activity is often referred to as "creating the structure" for the database. In creating the structure, the following items need to be defined: (1) field name, (2) field type, (3) field width, and (4) number of decimal places. You should give careful thought to your structure so that potentially difficult revisions don't need to be made to the structure after a large number of records have been entered. Once the structure for a database has been defined, the user can then begin adding data.

One of the main advantages of using a DBMS program to manage a database is the ease with which information can be extracted or searched for. To perform searches, the following types of operations can be used: (1) arithmetic operations, (2) relational operations, (3) logical operations, and (4) string operations. DBMS programs also make it easy to order database files differently through the use of sorting and indexing. Ordering files using indexing is much faster than using sorting, and the use of disk storage space is more efficient.

The uses for DBMS software in the business environment are virtually limitless because of the numerous capabilities the software provides and the ease with which non-computer-specialists can learn to use it.

FIGURE D.15   dBase III Plus Summary of Commands in ASSIST

Command	Comments
Set Up	
Database File	Opens a database file that exists on disk and optionally sets one or more index files active.
Format for Screen	Not covered.
Query	Not covered.
Catalog	Not covered.
View	Not covered.
Quit dBASE III Plus	Ends the session of dBASE III Plus.
Create	
Database File	Creates a database file, defines its structure, and allows entry of records.
Format	Not covered.
View	Not covered.
Query	Not covered.
Report	Creates a report form that contains the information on report layout.
Label	Creates a label form that contains information on the label layout and fields.
Update	
Append	Adds records to the database file.
Edit	Allows editing (modifying) of database records, viewed one record at a time.
Display	Lists specified records and fields to the monitor or printer, pausing when the screen is filled.
Browse	Displays the database in a multiple-record format, one row per record.
Replace	Not covered.
Delete	Marks specified records for deletion from the database file.
Recall	Unmarks specified records.
Pack	Copies all unmarked records, creating a new version of the same database file, but without any marked records.
Position	
Seek	Quickly locates an expression in the field for which the database is indexed in the master index file.
Locate	Not covered.
Continue	Not covered.
Skip	Not covered.
Goto Record	Positions the record pointer at the beginning or end of the open database file, or at any specified record.

(continued)

FIGURE D.15   continued

Command	Comments
Retrieve	
List	Displays specified fields and records to the monitor or printer, without any pauses.
Display	Displays specified fields and records to the monitor, with pauses when the screen is filled.
Report	Uses a report form to prepare a report containing selected records.
Label	Uses a label form to prepare labels from selected records.
Sum	Sums a numeric field for specified records in a database.
Average	Averages a numeric field for specified records in a database.
Count	Counts the number of records in a database that meet specified conditions.
Organize	
Index	Creates an index file (.NDX) that keeps the database file organized on an expression (usually a single field), even when changes are made to the database file.
Sort	Creates a copy of the database file that is sorted on one or more fields, in ascending or descending order.
Copy	Not covered.
Modify	
Database file	Not covered. Makes changes to the structure of the database.
Format	Not covered.
View	Not covered.
Query	Not covered.
Report	Not covered. Makes changes to an existing report form (.FRM).
Label	Not covered. Makes changes to an existing label form (.LBL).
Tools	
Set drive	Sets the default drive for the data disk.
Copy file	Not covered. Copies files, such as for backup purposes.
Directory	Displays the names of files on the data disk.
Rename	Not covered. Renames a disk file.
Erase	Not covered. Deletes a disk file.
List structure	Displays to monitor or printer the structure of the active database file.
Import	Not covered.
Export	Not covered.

KEY TERMS

arithmetic operations
BROWSE command
character (nonnumieric)
    data
computer-based database
    management system
database
database management
    system (DBMS)
database structure

date data
decimal places
EDIT command
field name
field type
field width
indexing
logical data
logical operations

memo data
numeric data
pull-down menu
relational operations
search
sorting
string
string operations

EXERCISES

SHORT ANSWER

1. What is involved in defining a structure for a database?
2. Explain the difference between sorting and indexing.
3. What hardware considerations are involved in using DBMS software?
4. Describe the different kinds of mathematical operations that can be performed to derive information from a database.
5. Why is it important to give careful thought to how the structure for a database is defined?
6. What is meant when someone says "I need to change the structure of this database"? Why would this need to be done?
7. Why would you need to combine two database files to make a third file?
8. What is the advantage of listing your database using a special report file rather than just executing a command to retrieve or search for certain information?
9. Describe a business situation in which it would be advantageous to use DBMS software to manage a database file.
10. What is a microcomputer-based DBMS?

HANDS ON

The following exercises should be completed in order:

1. Load your DBMS software into internal memory.
2. Create on your data disk a database to collect student registration information. Give this database the name of STUDENT. The database should have the following structure:

FIELD NAME	TYPE	WIDTH
FIRSTNAME	C	4
LASTNAME	C	15
ADDRESS	C	25
CITY	C	15
STATE	C	2
ZIP	C	13
COURSE1	C	5
COURSE2	C	5
COURSE3	C	5
PHONE	N	13
AGE	N	2

3. Add the following records to the STUDENT database file:

    Sanderson, Sally, 141 Sansome St, San Francisco, CA, 94108, IS100, IS10, IS5, (415)555-4156, 19

    Androtti, Ronald, 2131 Washington, Berkeley, CA, 94709, IS100, IS10, IS5, (415)555-1900, 20

    Ng, Henry, 4100 Haight St, Berkeley, CA, 94709, IS101, IS100, IS10, (415)555-2001, 21

    Solkowitz, Renee, 101 Bush St, San Francisco, CA, 94108, IS10, IS5, (415)555-3121, 20

    Yoshida, Yukiko, 1411 Stanford Way, Berkeley, CA, 94109, IS100, IS10, (415)555-4110, 22

4. Save the STUDENT database data by exiting your DBMS program.

5. Load your DBMS program into internal memory and issue the command to use the STUDENT database file. Do the following:
    a. List all the records in the database, but don't send the output to the printer.
    b. List the records (only) for students who live in San Francisco.

6. If your STUDENT database is currently in use, perform the following searches:
    a. List those records in which COURSE1 is equal to IS100 and COURSE2 is equal to IS10.
    b. List those records in which AGE is greater than 20 and CITY is equal to San Francisco.

7. Use the SORT command to put the STUDENT database into order of AGE. Give the newly sorted file the name of SORTED1. List the contents of SORTED1 on the screen.

8. Create an index called LASTNAME to put the STUDENT database file into LASTNAME order.

9. Add three more records to the STUDENT database. Make sure the STUDENT database is in use and the index called LASTNAME is active.

10. Create a report file named CLASSRPT (to be used with the STUDENT database) that has the following specifications:
   a. TITLE = UNDERGRADUATE
          STUDENT REGISTRATION
          LISTING
   b. COLUMN 1 FIELD NAME = LASTNAME
      COLUMN 1 FIELD HEADING = LAST NAME
   c. COLUMN 2 FIELD NAME = FIRSTNAME
      COLUMN 2 FIELD HEADING = FIRST NAME
   d. COLUMN 3 FIELD NAME = COURSE1
      COLUMN 3 FIELD HEADING = 1ST COURSE
   e. COLUMN 4 FIELD NAME = COURSE2
      COLUMN 4 FIELD HEADING = 2ND COURSE
   f. COLUMN 5 FIELD NAME = COURSE3
      COLUMN 5 FIELD HEADING = 3RD COURSE

MICROCOMPUTER-BASED GRAPHICS: LOTUS 1-2-3 AND SUPERCALC4

All types of business users recognize that the use of graphics can improve the effectiveness of any informational presentation. The introduction of microcomputer-based graphics software into the business community has made it possible for users to produce professional-looking graphs at very low cost. This module will demonstrate how to use an electronic spreadsheet package to create a variety of business charts.

Before you read this module, we recommend you read the section on loading DOS in Module A and all of Module C.

PREVIEW

When you have completed this module, you will be able to:

- Explain why the user should know how to use graphics in the business environment and describe the difference between dedicated graphics and spreadsheet-based graphics
- Describe what pie, line, bar, and area charts are and what they are used for
- Use Lotus 1-2-3 and SuperCalc4 to create a pie chart, a line chart, and a bar chart

OVERVIEW OF GRAPHIC REPRESENTATION

Graphic representation of data is more effective than simple text for the same reason that road maps are easier to follow than written or dictated directions. By nature, people remember what they see in the form of images and symbols better than they remember detailed text or speeches. **Graphics,** which are the pictorial representation of words and data, provide us with a superior method of presentation. **Computer graphics** are images that have been generated by a computer; **microcomputer-based business graphics**—the topic of this module—are images that have been generated by a microcomputer to present business-related information. Graphics can be produced in a variety of forms to suit the specific needs of the business professional: Microcomputer images can be displayed on the screen, photographed, plotted on paper in color, or made into a transparency that can be used with an overhead projector.

Studies have shown that the use of graphics can greatly increase the effectiveness of communication; however, some business professionals still refuse to use graphics to present information. One reason for their refusal is that they have gotten along without using graphics in the past and are reluctant to learn something new. But, as you have just seen, graphics can make their job much easier and would certainly make their presentations more effective.

SPREADSHEET-BASED VERSUS DEDICATED GRAPHICS PACKAGES

The type of software used on microcomputers to generate graphics falls into two categories: (1) spreadsheet-based software packages and (2) dedicated graphics packages. The sole purpose of a **dedicated graphics package** is to provide the user with the capability to produce graphics, whereas a **spreadsheet-based package** (described in Module C) provides the user with a number of different processing capabilities in addition to the capability to produce graphics.

Compared with spreadsheet-based graphics packages, dedicated graphics packages provide the user with a greater amount of flexibility in presenting data and information in different formats, types, colors, and sizes. When a dedicated graphics package is used, the data to be included in a graph must usually be input directly to the program as the graphic image is created. (Some new dedicated packages are able to "import" data from other software packages—such as Lotus 1-2-3—to be included in the graph.)

Spreadsheet-based graphics are used by the person who has entered data into a spreadsheet and who wants to see the data in graphic form. In this case, the kinds of style choices offered by dedicated graphics packages are not needed; simple graphs will do. Often, if something fancier is needed, the user will use the spreadsheet-based graph to get a general picture of what the data looks like in graphic form and then recreate the graph using a dedicated graphics package. In the tutorial section of this module, you will create a few different business charts using two spreadsheet-based packages—Lotus 1-2-3 and SuperCalc4 (the keystrokes for SuperCalc4 will be in the margin).

HARDWARE CONSIDERATIONS

The type of hardware you need to turn your microcomputer into a graphics work-station depends mostly on what you will be using the graphics for. If you are presenting information to a small group, you could use your monitor to display graphics. However, the screen image can often appear distorted; for instance, a pie chart, which should appear round, might appear jagged and oval. When presenting information to large groups, unless you have a projection device to enlarge the screen image, you are better off using slides, transparencies, and/or giving the audience copies of each graph. To do so, one must transfer the specifications for the screen image via a cable to an output device, such as a printer or a plotter, which then draws the image on transparency film or paper. A slide image is created by taking a picture of the screen directly using a 35-mm camera loaded with slide film. The best quality of graphic output is usually produced by printers and plotters. If you plan to use your video display screen as the presentation medium, make sure you have a graphics card in your computer. And if you want to display colors, make sure your monitor is a color monitor and that you have a *color* graphics card in your computer.

Choosing the right printer for your graphics output is only slightly less confusing than choosing a computer. You must consider so many factors: Will you need to use different typefaces (styles of type)? Is color really important to you, or will black and white be adequate? Will your software package support the printer you intend to use? Certain types of printers are capable of creating graphics; others are not. (See Chapter 6 for information on printers.) No matter what output method you choose, make sure your software package is compatible with your output device.

FORMS OF BUSINESS GRAPHICS PRESENTATION

The most common forms used for presenting business information graphically are (1) pie charts, (2) line charts, (3) bar charts, and (4) area charts. In the following sections, we refer to the spreadsheet data shown in Figure E.1.

PIE CHARTS

A **pie chart,** which is a circle with wedges that look like slices of pie, is the best chart to use when illustrating parts of a whole. For example, if your purpose is to show in graphic form what percent each type of expense in Figure E.1 is of the whole, you should use a pie chart (Figure E.2a). To avoid confusion, you should never create a pie chart with more than twelve slices—preferably not more than eight; otherwise, the chart becomes cluttered and loses meaning.

Sometimes the technique of **exploding** is used in pie charts. This technique "blows up," or enlarges, a particular part of the chart for emphasis. For example, if you want to emphasize the fact that the OTHER expense category represents a large percentage of TOTAL expenses, you could enlarge that wedge of the pie chart, or "explode" it (Figure E.2b). Most spreadsheet-based graphics programs give the user the capability of exploding one or more pieces of a pie chart.

You can label the slices of a pie chart in two ways. You can either place the descriptive text on or near the appropriate slice or you can use a legend, a descriptive label set off to the side, top, or bottom of the chart that describes a specific data element—such as "Rent" or "Telephone." Both charts in Figure E.2 use legends set off to the right side of the chart to label each element.

LINE CHARTS

When you need to show trends over time, the **line chart** is the appropriate chart form to use (Figure E.3). The angles of the line reflect variations in a trend, and the distance of the line from the horizontal axis represents quantity. For example, if you want to show Hotaling Stationers' expense trends over the first three months of the year in the form of a line chart, the chart would look like the one in Figure E.3. Note that it's easy to see that AUTO expenses took a big jump in March and that UTILITIES also increased substantially.

FIGURE E.1
Expense data for Hotaling Stationers. This spreadsheet is used by Hotaling Stationers to calculate their Actual Expenses.

	A	B	C	D	E	F
1			ACTUAL EXPENSES			
2			HOTALING STATIONERS			
3	EXPENSE					
4	TYPE		JAN	FEB	MAR	TOTAL
5	-------					
6	TELEPHONE	$85.00	$79.00	$82.00	$246.00	
7	RENT	$600.00	$600.00	$600.00	$1,800.00	
8	UTILITIES	$35.00	$42.00	$70.00	$147.00	
9	AUTO	$50.00	$45.00	$196.00	$291.00	
10	OTHER	$121.00	$135.00	$140.00	$396.00	
11	-------					
12	TOTAL	$891.00	$901.00	$1,088.00	$2,880.00	
13						
14						
15						
16						
17						
18						
19						
20						

01-Jan-80   04:02 AM

FIGURE E.2
Pie chart. These charts
show what percentage each
of Hotaling Stationers' expenses is of total expenses.
(Percentages have been
rounded up.)

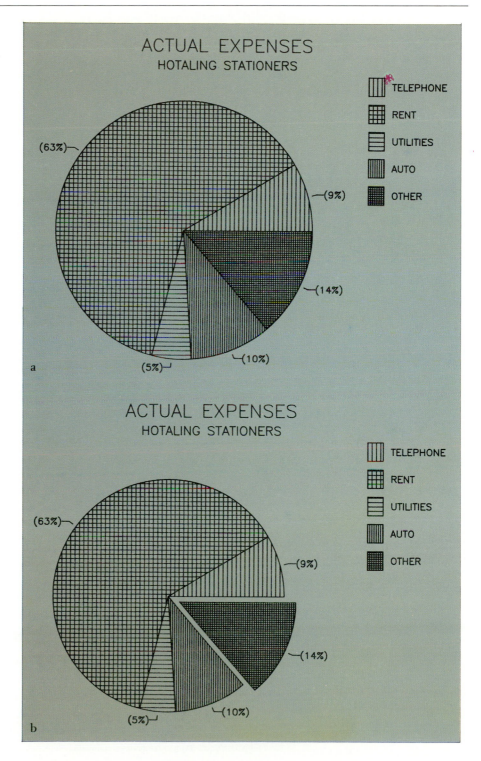

When you create a line chart, you must define the scale for the vertical axis of the chart by specifying the lowest (zero in Figure E.3) and the highest numbers (200) on the scale, as well as the number of intervals between the two points (3). You must also define the points of comparison on the horizontal axis—that is, the text and the number of intervals. For example, do you want to compare the expense amounts for January, February, and March? Or do you want to compare the expense amounts for 1986, 1987, and 1988?

BAR CHARTS

When the purpose is to compare one data element with another data element, a **bar chart** is the appropriate form to use. Figure E.4 compares the total monthly expense amounts for Hotaling Stationers. In this bar chart, it's easy to see that March's expenses were the highest and that January's expenses were the lowest. The chart in Figure E.4 is a simple bar chart. It provides no information about what types of expenses were incurred. Grouped bar charts and stacked bar charts are variations of the simple bar chart. A **grouped bar chart** (Figure E.5a) is used to show how data elements compare over time. A **stacked bar chart** (Figure E.5b) is used to show how the components of a data element compare over time.

As with line charts, when you create a bar chart you must define the scale for the vertical axis and the points of comparison on the horizontal axis.

AREA CHARTS

Area charts share some characteristics with line charts and stacked bar charts. An area chart with a single line is almost identical to a line chart with a single line except

FIGURE E.3
Line chart. This chart shows Hotaling Stationers' expense trends over the first three months of the year.

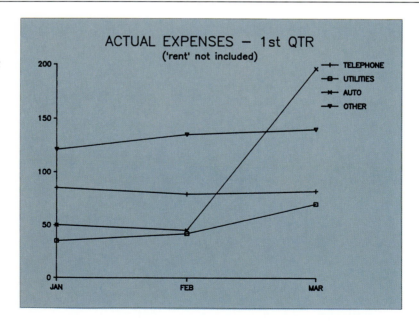

that the area below the line is shaded. The shading helps to emphasize the trend of the line. An area chart that has more than one line is similar to a continuous stacked bar chart.

PRINCIPLES OF BUSINESS GRAPHICS PRESENTATION

No matter how sophisticated your graphics software may be, you would probably be better off using no graphics at all if you don't follow certain basic principles for creating charts: simplicity, unity, emphasis, and balance.

SIMPLICITY

Many things can cause your chart to look confusing: for example, using too much color, using too much descriptive text, including too many variables (such as too many pie slices in a pie chart). It's natural to try to tell the whole story in one chart, but doing so may defeat the whole purpose of using graphics. You use a chart to symbolize numbers or words because most people tend to find graphics easier to understand than straight text and tables. If you include too much text or detail in a chart, the visual aspects become muddied and the symbols difficult to understand. Always try to keep your charts simple.

FIGURE E.4
Bar chart. This chart compares the total monthly expense amounts for Hotaling Stationers.

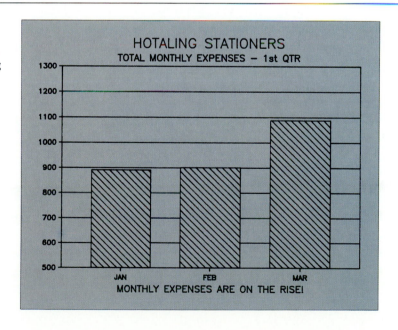

UNITY

To be understandable, your graph must clearly relate all the elements of data it contains—that is, it must appear as a unit. For instance, if you use too much space between the variables (such as between bars in a bar chart), you will probably destroy the unity of your chart. Framing, or boxing, a graph can help to unify it.

FIGURE E.5
Bar chart variations. (a) A grouped bar chart, which compares groups of items over time; (b) a stacked bar chart, which breaks out the components of each data item for comparison.

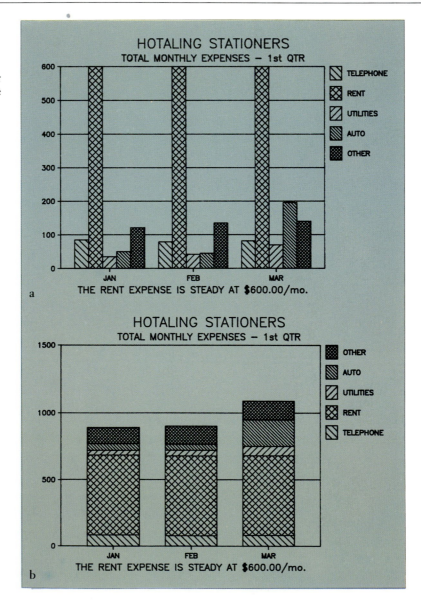

Emphasis

Emphasis is used to make certain data elements stand out. For example, exploding the OTHER pie slice emphasizes it in part (b) of Figure E.2. No matter what type of chart you create, you can emphasize different parts by using colors and shading.

Balance

Your graph should look balanced—both as a unit and in the context of the rest of the page. One factor that affects balance is the position of descriptive text, including titles and legends. Changing the position of such text affects the balance of the graph. Changing the shading, color, and thickness of the lines used in a graph will also affect balance. For instance, if you create a bar chart made up of eight bars, don't specify a dark color for the four larger bars on the right of the chart and a light color for the smaller bars on the left side. Because dark colors appear heavy, they will make the bar chart look out of balance by "weighing down" the right side.

In the Lab:

Business Graphics Using Lotus 1-2-3/SuperCalc4

In this tutorial, you will create a few charts using Lotus 1-2-3 and/or SuperCalc4, two popular electronic spreadsheet packages. The general use of these two packages was covered in Module C. Work through Module C before starting the tutorial in this module.

We assume you are using a microcomputer with two floppy disk drives (drive A and drive B), that your copy of the Lotus 1-2-3 or SuperCalc4 program will be retrieved from drive A, and that the files you create will be saved onto a data disk in drive B. If your computer has a hard disk, you will probably need to substitute a reference to drive C for A or B, depending on from which drive you are retrieving a copy of the software program and to which drive you will be saving your charts.

The Business Situation

As the manager of Sporting Life, for a number of months you've been using a spreadsheet-based program to track sales of sporting goods. Because in your presentations you prefer to use graphics to present sales trends, you have decided to learn how to use your spreadsheet program to create graphs of the data you enter.

The sales data for your ski line is presented in Figure E.6. You will use Lotus 1-2-3 to present this data in graphic form. (Throughout the tutorial we will put corresponding SuperCalc4 keystrokes in the margin.)

GETTING STARTED

Before you proceed with this tutorial, read or work through Module C, which describes the features of electronic spreadsheets and shows you how to use Lotus 1-2-3 and SuperCalc4. Because many terms we use in this module were defined in Module C, we won't define them again here. Before you start learning the graphics commands available with these spreadsheet packages, you need to create the specifications for the spreadsheet template pictured in Figure E.6. If you've worked through Module C, you should be able to do this. Here are a few hints about the spreadsheet:

1. The spreadsheet keeps track of sales by quarter for both ski equipment and ski clothing. A subtotal is calculated for each item; this involves using the @SUM function.

2. A total is calculated in column F by using the @SUM function to add the quarterly amounts for each type of ski item. For example, the formula in cell F7 should say the following: @SUM(B7..E7). To complete this spreadsheet, you will copy this formula into the two cells below, and copy others into the appropriate cells. *Note:* This spreadsheet doesn't require that you use any absolute references. (Refer to the tutorial section in Module C to review the procedure for copying formulas.)

For SuperCalc4 Users:
SUM(B7:E7)

3. Subtotal amounts are calculated in rows 10 and 16 by using the @SUM function. For example, the formula in cell B10 should say the following:

    @SUM(B7..B9)

For SuperCalc4 Users:
SUM(B7:B9)

4. A total is calculated in row 18 that adds the two subtotal amounts. For example, the formula in cell B18 should say the following:

    (B10 + B16)

5. None of the rest of the data in this template involves a calculation.

FIGURE E.6
Sporting Life ski sales.

```
              A            B          C          D          E          F          G
  1   SPORTING LIFE:   SKI ITEMS
  2   NUMBER OF ITEMS SOLD IN 1987
  3
  4   TYPE            QTR1        QTR2       QTR3       QTR4      TOTAL
  5
  6   EQUIPMENT
  7   POLES             50          53         17         53        173
  8   BOOTS             71          62         22         69        224
  9   SKIS              78          59         30         81        248
 10   **  SUBTOTAL     199         174         69        203        645
 11
 12   CLOTHING
 13   GLOVES            92          85         47         95        319
 14   PANTS            151         137         63        161        512
 15   SWEATERS         160         129         98        152        539
 16   **  SUBTOTAL     403         351        208        408       1370
 17
 18   **  TOTAL        602         525        277        611       2015
 19
 20
                                                                             CAPS
```

Create the spreadsheet template pictured in Figure E.6. Save it onto your data disk under the name SALES. In the next section we lead you through presenting this data in different business graphs. When creating a graph using a spreadsheet package, you must supply the following types of information:

1. What type of graph do you want to create?
2. Where is the data, or variables, that you want to graph?
3. What are the labels for the X axis?
4. Do you want to include a legend in this graph?
5. What is the title of your graph going to be?
6. When you output this graph on a hardcopy output device, what size do you want the graph to be?

CREATING A BAR CHART

In this section, you will create a bar chart that compares the subtotals for ski equipment sales (Variable A) and the subtotals for ski clothing sales (Variable B) for each of the four quarters. When you are done, the bar chart should look like the one in Figure E.7.

You should now be looking at the SALES spreadsheet template on the screen. In the following steps, we will use commas to separate the keys, or groups of keys, we want you to press. When you see [Rtn], press the RETURN key (ENTER on some keyboards). Throughout this tutorial, as you press keys per our instructions, note the reason why you're pressing them and note how your menu changes.

FIGURE E.7
Sporting Life bar chart.
(Graphics shown in this section are output from Lotus 1-2-3.)

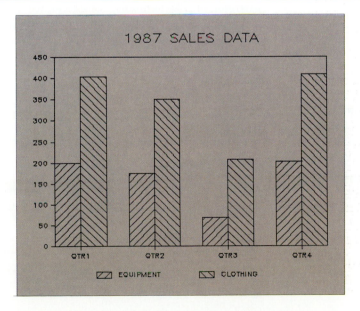

1. To specify the type of graph you want to create and the variables you want to include in it, key in the following:

/,G,T,B,A,B10..E10,[Rtn],B,B16..E16,[Rtn],V

For SuperCalc4 Users:
/,V,G,1,B,D,B10:E10,[Rtn],D,[press the SPACE bar],B16:E16,[Rtn],S

You should now see your graph on the screen without any labels. Press any key to continue. Your graphing menu should still be on the screen.

2. To specify the labels for the X axis, key in the following:

For SuperCalc4 Users:
/,V,T,B4:E4,[Rtn],S

X,B4..E4,[Rtn],V

You should now see labels along the X axis that identify the four quarters. Press any key to continue. Your graphing menu should still be on the screen.

3. To specify a legend and a title, key in the following:

O,L,A,EQUIPMENT,[Rtn],L,B,CLOTHING,[Rtn],T,F,1987
   SALESDATA,[Rtn],Q,V

For SuperCalc4 Users:
/,V,V,A6,[Rtn],V,[press the SPACE bar],A12,[Rtn],H,M,A2,[Rtn],Q,S
The heading will be slightly different from the one created with Lotus 1-2-3.

You should see your completed graph on the screen. Press any key to continue. Your menu should still be on the screen.

4. In this step, you will save the graph specifications for this bar chart onto your disk under the name BAR1. Lotus 1-2-3 will automatically supply the extension of .PIC to this file, which you will use later to output your graph. This .PIC file can be used only for outputting your graphs. To save your graph specifications so that you can use them later for output, key in the following:

S,BAR1,[Rtn]

For SuperCalc4 Users:
You don't have to save your graph specifications in a special file. Just make sure you save your spreadsheet template after you have specified your graph settings so that you can recall them at a later time.

5. The last step is to give the graph's specifications a name within the spreadsheet file and to then save the sales template with the name in it; in this way, when you retrieve the file called SALES at a later date, you can view your graph again by referring to the name you gave your graph specifications and change them if you want to. To name your graph specifications and then save your spreadsheet (your menu should still be on the screen), press:

N,C,BAR1,[Rtn],Q, /,F,S,SALES,[Rtn],R

CREATING A PIE CHART

This section's objective is to create a pie chart that shows what percentage each quarterly total is of the year's sales. When you are done, the pie chart should look like the one in Figure E.8.

1. Right now the specifications for the last graph you created, the bar chart, are in internal memory. Because you are going to create a new graph, clear internal memory of the previous specifications by keying in the following:

   /,G,R,G

For SuperCalc4 Users:
SuperCalc4 doesn't have any corresponding keystrokes.

2. To specify the type of graph you want to create and the variables you want to include, key in the following (the graphing menu should still be on the screen):

   T,P,A,B18..E18,[Rtn],V

For SuperCalc4 Users:
/,V,2,G,P,D,B18:E18,[Rtn],S

You should see your pie chart with the percentages allocated automatically for each piece of the pie. No descriptive text has been entered yet. Press any key to continue.

FIGURE E.8
Sporting Life pie chart.

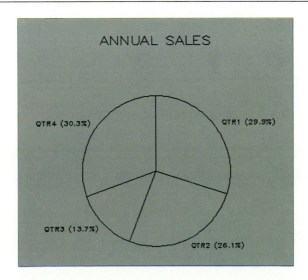

3. To enter labels and a title:

X,B4..E4,[Rtn],O,T,F,ANNUAL SALES,[Rtn],Q,V

For SuperCalc4 Users:
/,V,2,T,B4:E4,[Rtn],H,M,A2,Q,S

You should now see the completed pie chart on the screen. Press any key to continue. The graphing menu should still be on the screen.

4. To save your graph specifications so that you can output this graph later, key in the following:

S,PIE1,[Rtn]

5. To name your graph specifications and then save your spreadsheet (your graphing menu should still be on the screen):

N,C,PIE1,[Rtn],Q,/,F,S,SALES,[Rtn]

The SALES spreadsheet now has the graph specifications for two different graphs stored in it—BAR1 and PIE1. If necessary, these specifications can be recalled at a later date for editing.

CREATING A LINE CHART

In this section, you will create a line chart that compares equipment sales by type across the four quarters. When you are done, the line chart should look like the one in Figure E.9.

1. Right now the specifications for the last graph you created (the pie chart) are in internal memory. Because you are going to create a new graph, clear internal memory of the previous specifications by keying in the following:

/,G,R,G

2. To specify the type of graph you want to create and the variables you want to include in it, key in the following (the graphing menu should still be pictured on the screen):

T,L,A,B7..E7,[Rtn],B,B8..E8,[Rtn],B9..E9,[Rtn],V

For SuperCalc4 Users:
/,V,3,G,L,D,B7:E7,[Rtn],D,[press the SPACE bar],B8:E8,[Rtn],D,[press the SPACE bar],[press the SPACE bar],B9:E9,[Rtn],S

You should see your line chart with the lines mapped out, but without any labels. Press any key to continue.

3. To specify the X axis labels and titles:

X,B4..E4,[Rtn],O,T,F,EQUIPMENT SALES,[Rtn],T,S,1987,[Rtn], Q,V

For SuperCalc4 Users:
/,V,3,G,T,B4:E4,[Rtn],H,M,A2,[Rtn],S,A1,[Rtn],Q,S

You should now see the completed line chart on the screen. Press any key to continue. The graphing menu should still be on the screen.

4. To save your graph specifications so that you can output the graph later, key in the following:

S,LINE1,[Rtn]

5. To name your graph specifications and then save your spreadsheet (your graphing menu should still be on the screen):

N,C,LINE1,[Rtn],Q, /,F,S,SALES,[Rtn],R

The SALES spreadsheet now has the graph specifications for three different graphs stored in it—BAR1, PIE1, and LINE1. You can recall any of these graph specifications and view and/or edit them at any time.

Printing Your Charts

Right now on your data disk you have three graph files that you've saved onto your disk; each has the extension PIC. These are the files that you will use to print your charts according to the following steps.

FIGURE E.9
Sporting Life line chart.

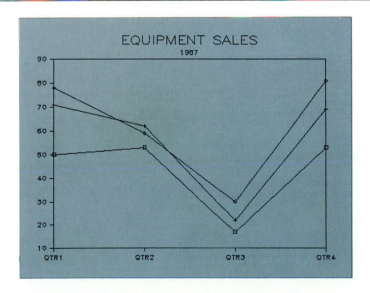

1. To load the instructions that are stored on the Lotus PrintGraph disk into memory press:

   /,Q,Y,[highlight the PrintGraph option],[Rtn],[replace 1-2-3 diskette with one labeled "PrintGraph"],[Rtn]

2. To select an image to print:
   —Highlight the Image-Select option and press RETURN. You should see a list of your graph files on the screen.
   —Use the arrow keys to choose the graph you want to print and press the SPACE bar.
   —If you want to view the graph at this point, press F10.

3. To print the image (make sure your printer is turned on):
   —Tap the ESC key to return to the previous menu.
   —Choose the Align option.
   —Choose the Go option.

4. To exit PrintGraph and return to Lotus 1-2-3:
   —Choose the Exit option.
   —Replace your PrintGraph disk with the Lotus 1-2-3 disk. Follow the screen prompts.

For SuperCalc4 Users:

1. To choose an output device:
   /,G,G,D,[highlight the model of printer or plotter you want to use],[Rtn],[tap the ESC to return you to Ready mode]

2. To print a graph:
   /,V,[press the number corresponding to the "view" of your data you want to print—bar chart (1), pie chart (2), line chart (3)], [press the F9 key to print]

SUMMARY

The use of graphics in the business environment has increased substantially over the past few years as users have become aware of the effectiveness of using graphics in informational presentations. This effectiveness is the result of the development of microcomputer-based graphics packages and the concurrent decrease in the cost of producing graphics. Studies have shown that using graphics to present trends and comparisons instead of straight text and tables is effective and convincing.

Microcomputer graphics software falls into one of two categories: dedicated graphics and spreadsheet-based graphics. Dedicated graphics packages, which are more flexible graphically than spreadsheet-based packages, are used only to produce graphics. They allow the user to choose from a variety of formats, type styles, colors, and sizes. Spreadsheet-based graphics programs are generally used by the person who has entered data into a spreadsheet and wants to see quickly how the data looks in graphic form. Figure E.10 summarizes the commands used to produce graphs with Lotus 1-2-3. (See the summary in Module C for a SuperCalc4 command summary.)

FIGURE E.10 Lotus 1-2-3 Command Summary for Graphics

Command	Comments
/Graph Type Line	Selects line graph format.
/Graph X	Defines X-axis labels.
/Graph A, B, C, D, E, F	Defines Y-axis data ranges.
/Graph View	Displays graph on screen.
To Clear Graph	Press any key.
/Graph Options Titles First	Enter first title line of graph.
/Graph Options Titles Second	Enter second title line of graph.
/Graph Options Titles X-axis	Enter X-axis title.
/Graph Options Titles Y-axis	Enter Y-axis title.
/Graph Options Titles Second /C2	Accesses the cell contents of C2 as second title.
/Graph Options Legend A	Enter the legend for the A range.
/Graph Options Data-labels	Enter data labels for each data point.
/Graph Options Grid Horizontal	Allows horizontal lines to form a grid within the graph.
/Graph Reset B	Resets B defined data range.
/Graph Options Grid Clear	Clears grid from graph.
[F10]	Displays the graph currently specified.
/Graph Name Create	Saves the current graph settings under a graph name. Used for what-if analysis.
/Graph Reset Graph	Clears or cancels graph or range settings.
/Graph Name Use NAME	Makes a named set of graph settings current and draws the graph.
/Graph Type Bar	Designates a bar graph.
/Graph Options Color	Displays your graph in color rather than black and white.
/Graph Options B&W	Displays your graph in black and white. This is the default setting.
/Graph Save NAME	Stores the current graph in a graph file called NAME.PIC for later printing using PrintGraph.
/File Save	Saves the worksheet with the current graph settings.
/Graph Type Stacked-bar	Designates a stacked bar graph.
/Graph Type XY	Designates an X-Y graph.

PrintGraph Commands

Command	Comments
A>Pgraph 123	Loads (add 123 to file name to load custom device driver).
Image-select	Select the graph file (filename.PIC) you wish to print.
Align	Aligns the printhead with the beginning of the paper.
Go	Begins the graph printing process.

Four forms of charts are most commonly used in business. The pie chart is the best form to use to present the parts of a whole. If your objective is to show the trends over time, the line chart is the best form. If you want to compare one data element to another, you should use a bar chart. And if you want a particularly dramatic representation of a trend, use an area chart.

No matter which chart form you choose, however, you must remember to keep it simple, unified, and balanced, and you should emphasize appropriate parts of the chart. If your purpose is to emphasize a certain part of the chart, use color, a special type style or type size, or another feature (such as exploding a pie slice) to make the element stand out.

KEY TERMS

area chart	graphics	pie chart
bar chart	grouped bar chart	spreadsheet-based
computer graphics	line chart	graphics package
dedicated graphics	microcomputer-based	stacked bar chart
package	business graphics	
exploding		

EXERCISES

SHORT ANSWER

1. What are the four principles of presentation?

2. Describe a business situation in which straight text might be more effective than a chart in making an informational presentation.

3. What is the difference between a dedicated graphics package and a spreadsheet-based graphics package?

4. What hardware considerations should you keep in mind if you are planning to use your microcomputer as a graphics workstation?

5. How is an area chart similar to both a line chart and a stacked bar chart?

6. Why are business graphics important to the user?

7. If your objective is to show the trend of sales for two different products over a period of four years, which type of chart would be the best to use? Why?

8. If your objective is to show that the sales for a particular item represent a large percentage of total sales, which type of chart would be the best to use? Why?

9. When would you use a spreadsheet-based graphics package instead of a dedicated graphics package, and vice versa?

HANDS ON

On the basis of the following information, create the charts described below.

1ST QUARTER EXPENSES
DIVISION A

	JAN	FEB	MAR	TOTAL
Telephone	85	79	82	246
Rent	600	600	600	1800
Utilities	35	42	70	147
Auto	50	45	196	291
Other	121	135	140	396
***TOTAL	891	901	1088	2880

1ST QUARTER EXPENSES
DIVISION B

	JAN	FEB	MAR	TOTAL
Telephone	73	82	65	220
Rent	610	610	610	1830
Utilities	40	62	45	147
Auto	50	45	75	170
Other	150	95	137	382
***TOTAL	923	894	932	2749

1. Create a pie chart that graphs Division A's first quarter totals for each item.

2. Create a grouped bar chart (or side-by-side chart) that would best compare the totals for January, February, and March for Divisions A and B.

3. Create a simple line chart to show the trend of the monthly totals for Division B.

4. Create a simple bar chart that graphs the totals for each type of expense for Division A.

5. Create a pie chart to show what percentage each type of Division A's expenses is of the whole for January.

6. Choose the best type of chart to show Division B's first quarter totals as a percentage of the whole. Emphasize the "Other" slice.

7. Choose the best type of chart to compare the totals for each type of expense in Divisions A and B.

8. Choose the best type of chart to compare the trends of the monthly totals for Divisions A and B.

9. Choose the best type of chart to graph the totals for each type of expense for Division B.

10. The title of your chart is "EXPENSES ARE LOWER IN DIVISION B". Create a chart that would most effectively illustrate this title.

Appendix
BASIC Programming
for the User

Introduction to BASIC

It's important for users like yourself to have some exposure to a traditional programming language like those described in Chapter 8. First, in the business environment it is likely that you will have to communicate to a professional programmer what you'd like a software program to do to meet your needs. By knowing some of what's involved in creating a program, you can be much more effective at communicating your needs. Second, it is also likely that you will at some point be using one of the newer software development tools for microcomputers described in Chapter 8, such as an electronic spreadsheet package or a database management system. Having some experience with a traditional programming language, no matter how limited, will help you appreciate the power of these newer software development tools.

We have chosen BASIC to demonstrate the use of a traditional programming language, because it is considered the easiest of the traditional programming languages to learn to use. Again, our objective isn't for you to learn everything there is to know about the BASIC programming language, but to give you some "basic" experience using a traditional programming language for the reasons described above.

A Brief History

BASIC was developed at Dartmouth College in an attempt to improve a system used by scientists doing numeric calculations. Originally the users had to submit cards to a centrally located card reader, which would then instruct the computer to run a program; the output was printed a few hours (or even days) later.

A timesharing system that improved efficiency and ease of use demanded an interactive language—BASIC—that would allow each user to type programs into a terminal (similar to a personal computer) on whose screen the output would be displayed immediately.

Since its invention, BASIC has been adopted by almost all computer and microcomputer manufacturers. However, because the manufacturers found the language to be limited, they would change it slightly to make use of enhancements particular to various machines. Thus, different versions (called *dialects*) of BASIC emerged, as illustrated in Table 1. Note which computer you will be using, and, as each BASIC instruction is presented, refer to the table to see how your machine BASIC differs from generic BASIC; your instructor will mention any other differences as you work through this appendix.

An Interpreter and a Compiler

BASIC can be used either as an *interpreter* or as a *compiler*. As you recall from the text, most computer languages take the code that the programmer writes and instantly convert it to the machine's own language. Because the machine can run the program only after it has been converted, you must write the entire program before trying it out. With interpretive languages like BASIC, each line is converted to machine language, one at a time, greatly simplifying the testing process; the only disadvantage is that an interpreted program must be converted to machine language each time it is run. This constant conversion slows processing.

Writing a program using a compiler is a three-step process:

1. Create the program (called *source code*) in a form readable by people.
2. Run the compiler (which inputs the source code and outputs a machine language readable by the computer).
3. Execute the machine language program.

Compiling a program takes time, but a compiled program will run much faster than an interpreted program. Programmers will often create and revise a program using the interpreter and then compile the program after it has been tested and all corrections made.

PRINT: Displaying Numbers

This section will show you how to use BASIC as a calculator and how to display the results.

Typing Mistakes

The best way to learn is to do, and you will learn much quicker if you dare to make mistakes. Don't worry about breaking the computer by mistyping something. The computer can take care of itself. If you have access to a computer, try out the examples shown. If you have questions about how BASIC will respond to a particular instruction, try it and see.

TABLE 1   Features of Most Common BASIC Dialects

	Minimal BASIC	Microsoft IBM	AWS/ TRUE BASIC	VAX II PDP II	Apple	TAS 80	Comments
Arrays—beginning subscript	0	0	1	0	0	0	
OPTION BASE	N	Y	Y	N	N	N	
END	Y	Y[1]	Y	Y[2]	Y[1]	Y[1]	[1]not required
FOR…NEXT	Y	Y	Y	Y	Y[3]	Y	[2]must be last physical line
GOSUB… RETURN	Y	Y	Y	Y	Y	Y	[3]tests at end of loop
IF…THEN	Y[4]	Y	Y	Y	Y	Y	[4]restricted to IF…THEN line #
IF…THEN… ELSE	N	Y	Y	Y	N	Y	
nested IF… THEN…ELSE	N	Y	N	Y	N	Y	
INPUT	Y	Y	Y	Y	Y	Y	
With prompt format	N	Y INPUT "msg";[5] INPUT "msg",	Y INPUT PROMPT[6] "msg";	Y INPUT "msg";[7]	Y INPUT "msg";[6]	Y INPUT "msg";[7]	[5]semicolon gives ? comma suppresses ? [6]? not displayed [7]? displayed
LET	Y	Y	Y	Y	Y	Y	
Multiple statements per line	N	Y[8]	N	Y[9]	Y[8]	Y[8]	[8]separate with colon : [9]separate with backslash \
ON…GOSUB… RETURN	N	Y	Y	Y	Y	Y	
PRINT	Y	Y	Y	Y	Y	Y	print zones vary
READ…DATA	Y	Y	Y	Y	Y	Y	
REM	Y	Y[10]	Y	Y[11]	Y	Y[10]	[10]can substitute apostrophe ' [11]can substitute exclamation point !
To save a file	SAVE FILE-NAME	SAVE "FILE-NAME"	SAVE FILE-NAME	SAVE or SAVE FILE-NAME	SAVE FILE-NAME	SAVE "FILE-NAME"	
To load a file	LOAD FILE-NAME	LOAD "FILE-NAME"	OLD FILE-NAME	OLD FILE-NAME	LOAD FILE-NAME	LOAD "FILE-NAME"	
WHILE… WEND	N	WHILE… WEND	DO WHILE… LOOP	WHILE… NEXT	N	N	

Y = Yes, available in this dialect   N = No, not available in this dialect   [1-11] = See note in comment column

Each instruction has a particular format, or syntax. If you do not follow the correct syntax, BASIC will usually display an error message. You can then reenter the instruction correctly.

PRESSING RETURN

After you type a line, the computer will wait for you to type a signal that you are finished with the line. You give this signal by tapping the RETURN (or ENTER or CR) key. This key is usually a large one located to the right of the alphabetic keyboard. It is similar in purpose and in placement to the carriage return key on a typewriter. (See Figure 3.5 for a description of the keyboard.)

THE CURSOR

As you type, you'll notice a blinking light on the screen that indicates where the next character will appear. This is the *cursor*. When you press RETURN, the cursor moves to the beginning of the next line. The cursor always lets you know where you are on the screen.

A SIMPLE CALCULATOR

Let's try using BASIC as a calculator. We will do this by using the PRINT statement. (In this and following examples, we will underline everything that you type in and not underline what BASIC displays in reply.)

```
PRINT 3 RETURN
3
```

We typed PRINT followed by a space, the digit 3, and pressed RETURN. BASIC responded by displaying the digit 3.

```
PRINT 2 + 2 RETURN
4
```

We typed PRINT followed by a space and the numeric expression 2 + 2. BASIC evaluated the expression and displayed the result.

Here is another example:

```
PRINT 3, 2 + 2 RETURN
3               4
```

COMMAS AND SEMICOLONS

Note that we can make BASIC type two values on one line by placing a comma between calculations. Let's try some more examples:

```
PRINT 1,2,3,4,5 RETURN
1        2        3        4        5

PRINT 1,   2,   3,   4,   5 RETURN
1        2        3        4        5
```

Notice what happened: BASIC divided the display line into *print zones*. These print zones are commonly spaced 14 columns apart, creating five print zones on an 80-column screen. (The exact number will depend on the dialect.) The comma between the values causes BASIC to skip to the next print zone for each value. By using commas, we can print output in neat columns. The extra spaces between values on the PRINT line, as in the second example, do not affect the spacing of the output.

Numeric values are displayed with a minus sign in front if the value is negative and a space in front if the value is positive. In most dialects they are also followed by a space.

If you want to print values next to one another, you use the semicolon, which suppresses movement to the next print zone. Here is an example:

```
PRINT 1;-2;3 + 3  RETURN
   1  -2   6
```

Using the semicolon, results are printed next to one another, with the space for the sign in front and a space after.

The comma and the semicolon are used as *delimiters* to separate values. Because of this, no commas are placed in values over 999. To print 12,345 we must type `PRINT 12345`. If we write `PRINT 12,345`, BASIC will interpret it as the two numbers 12 and 345.

USING THE PRINTER

In our discussion we will be printing to the screen; however, the same information can be printed on the printer if your system has one. In most systems this is done with the LPRINT statement. LPRINT uses the same syntax as PRINT. However, LPRINT directs output to the printer instead of the screen. On some systems, simultaneously pressing the CTRL and PrtSc keys or the CTRL and P keys will cause all output that is sent to the screen to be sent to the printer as well. Because each dialect varies on how to send data to the printer, we will not give examples using the printer. Check with your instructor if you are to use a printer.

BLANK LINES

A blank line often improves readability in reports or screen displays. The PRINT statement used alone (PRINT) will cause a blank line.

TEST YOUR LEARNING

1. What are BASIC dialects?
2. How do commas and semicolons affect PRINT?
3. How can BASIC be used as a calculator?

4. What will be printed by each of these statements? Try to predict what will happen, then try it on your computer.

   a. `PRINT 1, 2, 3, 1 + 2 + 3`
   b. `PRINT 1,500; 2,567`
   c. `PRINT 1,234,500`
   d. `PRINT 1 2 3`

5. Write a line to print the following:
   a. the sum of 400 plus 35
   b. the number 5321

6. Write a statement that will print the values 3,567,16.2, and -3 in separate print zones. Then write a statement to print the values next to each other.

CONSTANTS

In the preceding PRINT examples, we used numbers and numbers added to one another. Because the values of numbers do not change, they are called *constants*. All *numeric constants*, such as those displayed in the examples above, consist entirely of numbers. Other examples of numeric constants are as follows:

```
5     3.1416     -739.2     276387
```

Constants consisting of characters (such as letters, punctuation, and other special characters) may be printed by placing quotes around the constant. Consider the following example:

```
PRINT "Hi, I am a string constant!" RETURN
Hi, I am a string constant!

PRINT "The interest rate is 5%" RETURN
The interest rate is 5%
```

Constants of alphanumeric characters (letters or numbers) are called *string constants* or just *strings*. They are often used to prepare report headings and titles. In contrast to numeric constants, string constants print without leading or trailing spaces. All characters within the quotes, including spaces, print exactly as they appear. The quotes themselves do not print; they just define the beginning and ending of the string for BASIC.

As with numeric constants, more than one string constant may be printed on the same line. The constants may be separated by commas to cause printing in the next print zone or by semicolons to cause printing in the next available position. In fact, both numeric and string constants may be printed on the same line.

```
PRINT "The sum of 4 and 7 is"; 4 + 7 RETURN
The sum of 4 and 7 is 11
```

TEST YOUR LEARNING

1. What are constants?
2. What is a string constant?
3. What is a numeric constant?
4. Write a statement that will print your last name, age, and birth date on one line with each item in separate print zones.
5. Write a statement to print the name of your city, your state, and your zip code. Use a separate constant for each. Separate the constants with semi-colons.

PROGRAMS AND LINE NUMBERS

So far we have been writing instructions in the *immediate* (or *direct*) *mode*. As soon as we typed the line and pressed RETURN, BASIC executed the statement. If BASIC performed only one statement at a time, as in the examples shown so far, its use would be limited. Fortunately, BASIC does much more. We can tell it to follow a series of instructions. Just as a cook can follow a recipe step by step, BASIC can follow the instructions of a program step by step. But, what exactly is a *program?*

WORKSPACE AND NOTECARDS

Imagine that inside your computer's primary storage or memory is a workspace consisting of a set of notecards (see Figure 1). On each notecard is a BASIC statement that tells the computer what to do. Each notecard also has a number; the cards are kept in numeric order.

To write a program, we type a series of BASIC program lines. The program lines are like the numbered notecards in the preceding analogy; the computer's memory is the workspace. A program line is composed of a line number (such as 10 or 100 or 1000), a space, and a BASIC statement. The following is a program with the instructions shown in Figure 1.

```
100 PRINT "Student Name", "Score" RETURN
110 PRINT RETURN
120 PRINT "Adams, M.", 85 RETURN
130 PRINT "Jones, K.", 92 RETURN
140 PRINT "Mitchell, L.", 75 RETURN
```

This time when you press RETURN the statement is not executed immediately. The line number indicates to BASIC that the instruction is to be stored in the workspace as a line in a program. This is called the *indirect mode.*

You will note that we have numbered the lines in increments of ten. Although you don't need to follow this practice, you'll find it helpful because it will allow you to insert other lines as you develop your program.

END

At the end of the program, we type the BASIC statement END. END tells BASIC to stop executing the program and return control to the user. Some dialects of BASIC require this statement as the last physical line of the program. For others, END may occur anywhere in the listing but should be the last statement executed by the program. For still other dialects, END is optional. We will add an END statement to our program.

```
999 END  RETURN
```

LIST

We now have a program stored in the workspace of the computer. In the remainder of this section we will present the commands that allow you to view, modify, and make permanent copies of a program. Because all of these commands instruct BASIC to do something with the program, they are not part of the program itself and are not preceded by a line number.

LIST instructs BASIC to show us the program that is currently in the workspace. This is what happens when we type LIST and press RETURN:

```
LIST  RETURN
100  PRINT  "Student Name", "Score"
110  PRINT
120  PRINT  "Adams, M.", 85
130  PRINT  "Jones, K.", 92
140  PRINT  "Mitchell, L.", 75
999  END
```

To see selected lines we use a form of LIST. The following statement will list just Lines 120 through 140.

FIGURE 1
A program is like a set of notecards

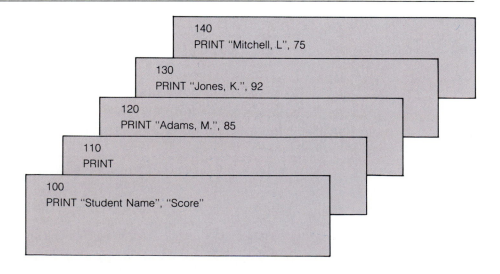

```
LIST 120-140 RETURN
120 PRINT "Adams, M.", 85
130 PRINT "Jones, K.", 92
140 PRINT "Mitchell, L.", 75
```

If you want a printed copy of your program, you can list your program on the printer. Again, each system varies on how to do this. One common way is to use the command LLIST in place of LIST. Check with your instructor regarding the system you are using.

RUN

Typing in all of these BASIC lines is like writing a recipe. Let's see how our recipe (program) "tastes."

Type RUN to instruct BASIC to execute all the lines of the program in its workspace.

```
RUN RETURN
Student Name   Score

Adams, M.      85
Jones, K.      92
Mitchell, L.   75
```

After RUN was entered and RETURN pressed, BASIC began with the first line of the program and executed each one until the END statement was reached.

SAVE

When you end your session or turn the computer off, the workspace is cleared, erasing the program (see Figure 2). This sample program is only a few lines long and so would not take too long to retype. However, soon our programs will be much longer and we would not want to retype them each time to use them.

FIGURE 2
The workspace gets erased

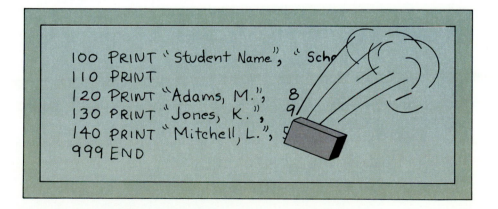

Luckily BASIC provides us with a way to save our program onto permanent storage. To do so, we must first assign a name to the program. The rules for program names vary with each dialect. In our examples we will use file names of eight or fewer characters. Let's call our program SCORES and make a copy with the following command:

```
SAVE "SCORES" RETURN
```

(Some dialects require quotes around the name of the file, others do not, as shown in Table 1.) If you turn your computer off now, the program will disappear from memory. But the copy we saved will remain on the disk (or tape). Note that there is no line number used with SAVE. It is a command that we want BASIC to execute immediately, not part of a program.

LOAD

When we wish to copy our program back into our workspace, we can type the following:

```
LOAD "SCORES" RETURN
```

A copy of the program that we saved with the name SCORES is now in the workspace. Again, some dialects require the quotes, others do not. Also, some dialects use the word OLD instead of LOAD:

```
OLD SCORES RETURN
```

Some computers may need you to specify the disk drive on which the program is to be saved. One common way to identify disk drives is to give them names such as A, B, or C. On such a system you may be required to place your personal diskette in the drive named B. To save your file to drive B you will need to prefix the file name with B:. Here is an example that saves the file SCORES on drive B.

```
SAVE B:"SCORES" RETURN
```

When you wish to retrieve the program, use the following command:

```
LOAD B:"SCORES" RETURN
```

If you were to forget to include the B:, the system may look on the wrong drive and report:

```
File not found,
```

NEW

Let's try typing and running a new program.

```
10 PRINT "This is a new program." RETURN
20 PRINT RETURN
999 END RETURN
RUN RETURN
```

```
This is a new program.

Student Name  Score

Adams, M.       85
Jones, K.       92
Mitchell, L.    75
```

What happened? Why did the messages from the previous program appear? Type LIST to find out what program is currently in memory.

```
LIST RETURN
10 PRINT "This is a new program."
20 PRINT
100 PRINT "Student Name", "Score"
110 PRINT
120 PRINT "Adams, M.", 85
130 PRINT "Jones, K.", 92
140 PRINT "Mitchell, L.", 75
999 END
```

Because our old program is still in the workspace, the new line we typed was inserted into the existing program. To get a new, clean workspace we must type the BASIC command NEW (without line number).

```
NEW RETURN
LIST RETURN
```

Nothing is listed, showing that now we have a new, clean workspace with all old program lines removed. We can now begin to enter a new program.

CORRECTING LINES

So far, we have typed in all the lines without error. Being human, we won't be able to keep this up for long; luckily BASIC provides ways for us to correct mistakes.

If we discover an error before we press RETURN, we can backspace, deleting the error, and retype the remainder of the line. However, if we discover the error only after we have pressed RETURN, this method won't work. For example, suppose that the score for Jones should be 95 not 92, and we don't realize it until later. To correct the error, we must first load the program back into the workspace.

```
LOAD "SCORES" RETURN
```

To correct the line we retype it:

```
130 PRINT "Jones, K.", 95 RETURN
```

When we now list the program we see that the retyped line replaces the former line with that same number:

```
LIST RETURN
100 PRINT "Student Name", "Score"
110 PRINT
```

```
120 PRINT "Adams, M.", 85
130 PRINT "Jones, K.", 95
140 PRINT "Mitchell, L.", 75
999 END
```

At this point the correction has been made only to the copy of the program that is in the workspace. Because we wish to correct the permanent copy also, we must save the corrected version.

SAVE "SCORES" RETURN

The program currently in the workspace replaces the former program that we stored with the name SCORES.

ADDING LINES

At this point we wish to add more students to our program. We can add lines by simply typing more PRINT statements and assigning line numbers that will place them in the proper sequence.

```
123 PRINT "Bradly, J", 72 RETURN
126 PRINT "Duncan, A.", 86 RETURN
135 PRINT "Lopez, M.", 88 RETURN
150 PRINT "Thompson, F.", 70 RETURN
128 PRINT "Franklin, B.", 73 RETURN
```

Let's LIST the program again. Notice that BASIC inserted the new lines in the proper sequence.

```
LIST RETURN
100 PRINT "Student Name", "Score"
110 PRINT
120 PRINT "Adams, M.", 85
123 PRINT "Bradly, J", 72
126 PRINT "Duncan, A.", 86
128 PRINT "Franklin, B.", 73
130 PRINT "Jones, K.", 95
135 PRINT "Lopez, M.", 88
140 PRINT "Mitchell, L.", 75
150 PRINT "Thompson, F.", 70
999 END
```

REMOVING LINES

BASIC's DELETE command will delete one or more lines.

DELETE 10   will delete just Line 10.

DELETE 10 - 100   will delete all lines from Line 10 to and including Line 100.

DELETE 10 -   will delete all lines from Line 10 to the end of the file.

DELETE - 10   will delete all lines from the start of the file up to and including Line 10.

To delete Line 140 that we have added to our demonstration program type, we key:

```
DELETE 140  RETURN
```

When we LIST the program we will see that Line 140 is erased.

```
LIST  RETURN
100 PRINT "Student Name", "Score"
110 PRINT
120 PRINT "Adams, M.", 85
123 PRINT "Bradly, J", 72
126 PRINT "Duncan, A.", 86
128 PRINT "Franklin, B.", 73
130 PRINT "Jones, K.", 95
135 PRINT "Lopez, M.", 88
150 PRINT "Thompson, F.", 70
999 END
```

In some dialects DELETE typed by itself will delete all the program lines from the workspace!

An alternate way to delete one line is to type just the line number. Typing 140 RETURN has the same result as DELETE 140 RETURN.

RENUM

Because we have been adding and deleting lines, the line numbers are no longer in increments of ten. BASIC provides the RENUM command to renumber the lines. There is no common syntax for this command, so you will have to check with your instructor about the options available on your computer.

Typing just RENUM will usually renumber the first line number to 10 and the remaining lines in increments of 10. Let's renumber our demonstration program.

```
RENUM  RETURN
LIST  RETURN
10 PRINT "Student Name", "Score"
20 PRINT
30 PRINT "Adams, M.", 85
40 PRINT "Bradly, J.", 72
50 PRINT "Duncan, A.", 86
60 PRINT "Franklin, B.", 73
70 PRINT "Jones, K.", 95
80 PRINT "Lopez, M.", 88
90 PRINT "Thompson, F.", 70
100 END
SAVE "SCORES"  RETURN
```

COMMANDS VERSUS STATEMENTS

At one time many restrictions used to affect which instructions could be executed in direct and indirect mode. For these historical reasons, those instructions that are usually used in the immediate mode (such as RUN and LIST) are called *commands*, whereas others that are usually placed in programs (such as PRINT) are called *statements*.

For most systems the difference is transparent to the user; that is, the user won't perceive a difference. Although the PRINT statement is usually executed as part of a program (indirect mode), you have already seen that it can be executed immediately (direct mode), when no line number is given. Likewise, although RUN and LIST are usually executed in direct mode, in most dialects they can be placed as part of a program.

What's important is that when a line number precedes an instruction, the instruction becomes part of a program and will not be executed until the program is run. When no line number precedes the instruction, it is executed as soon as RETURN is pressed.

TEST YOUR LEARNING

1. What is a workspace?
2. What happens if you forget to SAVE your file?
3. What happens if you forget to type NEW?
4. How do you correct a BASIC line?
5. How do you delete a BASIC line?
6. What does RENUM do?
7. Write a program to print a list of the following monthly household expenses.

```
Rent        450
Car         175.85
Food        359
Other       75
```

a. Save the program using the name EXPENSE. (You will use this program in future exercises.)
b. Load the program and run it again.

8. Make the following changes to the program EXPENSE that you wrote in the previous exercise: Change the car payment to 155.35. Add a new expense category: Pets, 35 and print it after Food. Run the program to test the changes. Renumber the lines and list the program. Save this updated version, keeping the same name.

ARITHMETIC EXPRESSIONS

So far we have used only addition in arithmetic expressions. As in arithmetic, BASIC uses the plus sign (+) to represent addition and the minus sign (−) to represent subtraction. However, multiplication is represented by the asterisk (*) and division by the forward slash (/). Be sure not to use the letter "x" when you want to multiply two numbers. BASIC will interpret "x" as a letter and not the multiply operator. To show exponentiation, some versions of BASIC use the up caret ($\hat{}$) while others use the up arrow ($\uparrow$). These symbols represent the *arithmetic operators*. Here are some examples of printing *arithmetic expressions*:

```
Statement            Meaning                          Result
PRINT 5 + 2 - 3      5 plus 2 minus 3                 4
PRINT 12.2 * 6       12.2 times 6                     73.2
PRINT 150 / 12       150 divided by 12                12.5
PRINT 25^3           25 raised to the third power     15625
```

ORDER OF PRECEDENCE

What is the value of the numeric expression 1 + 2 / 3 * 4? Depending on whether we add, divide, or multiply first, we can arrive at different answers. BASIC examines each expression to see what operators are used in it. The order that BASIC uses in solving numeric expressions is called the *order of precedence*. As shown in Table 2, it first performs exponentiation. Next it performs all the multiplication and division. Finally it performs addition and subtraction. At each level BASIC performs the operations moving from the left to the right.

PARENTHESES

The order of precedence may not reflect how we want the expression to be evaluated. As in algebra, we can insert parentheses to tell BASIC to solve the enclosed expression first. When solving for the value of an expression that contains parentheses, BASIC looks first at the expression within parentheses and evaluates it as any other numeric expression, following the order of precedence for operators. Then it evaluates the remainder of the expression outside the parentheses. As in algebra, sets

---

TABLE 2   Order of Precedence for Arithmetic Operators

Operator	Meaning	Example
^	Exponentiation	3 ^ 2 = 9
*, /	Multiplication and division	3 * 2 = 6 6 / 2 = 3
+, −	Addition and subtraction	3 + 2 = 5 3 − 2 = 1

Expressions in parentheses are evaluated first.
When ties in precedence occur, expressions are evaluated from left to right.

of parentheses may be placed within other sets. (Be sure you type the ordinary parentheses symbols. The other special bracket symbols—[ ]{ }—are not valid here.)

Parentheses may also be used to make an expression clear and understandable to users even though BASIC does not require them.

Here are some examples of printing expressions with and without parentheses:

```
Statement                         Order of Evaluation      Result
PRINT 1 + 2 * 3                        1 + 6                  7
PRINT 2 * 3 + 4 * 5                    6 + 20                 26
PRINT 2 * (3 + 4) * 5                  2 * 7 * 5              70
PRINT 4 + 7 * (6 - 4) / (2 + 5)       4 + 7 * 2 / 7 = 4 + 2   6
```

TEST YOUR LEARNING

1. How does BASIC decide which arithmetic operations to perform first?
2. How can you force BASIC to change this order?
3. What value will be printed by each of these statements? Type each in your system to check your answer.

   a. PRINT 10 + 4 / 2 - 3
   b. PRINT 1 + 2 + 3 + 4 * 5
   c. PRINT 5 + 6 * 8 / 4
   d. PRINT 4 * 4 - 9 / 3

4. Write a line in BASIC to perform the following calculation and print the result.

   a. 3(4) + 2(12 + 3(5))
   b. 5(7 - 10)/5

5. A painter needs to estimate how much paint will be needed to cover an area of 3600 square feet. One gallon of paint covers 300 square feet.
   a. Write a program to calculate and display the number of gallons needed.
   b. Paint costs $12 per gallon. Add a line to the program that will print the cost.
   c. Save this program using the name PAINT. (You will use this program in future exercises.)

LET AND VARIABLES

We have learned how to do simple computations; however, sometimes we need to store or save values. BASIC allows us to store values in *variables* by using the LET statement. First we must give the variable a name and then specify the value to be stored in it. The variable name is placed to the left of an equal sign and the value assigned to it is placed to the right of it. The following is an example of using the *numeric variable* B4:

```
LET B4 = 45 RETURN
PRINT B4 RETURN
45
```

After BASIC executes the above LET statement, B4 will have the value of 45. The PRINT statement displays this value.

BASIC knows that B4 is a variable name and not a constant because it begins with a letter (so it can't be a numeric constant), and it doesn't have quotes around it (so it can't be a string constant).

VARIABLE NAME VERSUS VARIABLE VALUE

A variable is like a mailbox—it displays a name, such as A or C7, and has mail (values) inside, such as 12 or −200.3. As with a mailbox, the contents of a variable can change. If we type LET B4 = 57, the value of B4 will be changed from 45 to 57 (see Figure 3). We can also place the results of an arithmetic expression in a variable.

```
LET B4 = (10 + 5) / 3 RETURN
PRINT B4 RETURN
5
```

FIGURE 3
Variable name and contents

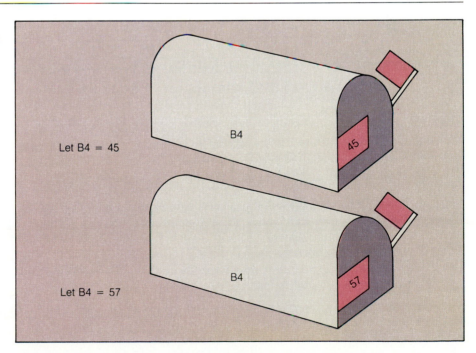

Let B4 = 45

B4

45

Let B4 = 57

B4

57

GOOD VARIABLE NAMES

The rules for naming variables vary from dialect to dialect; however, all dialects of BASIC require that variable names begin with a letter. Some dialects are limited to two-character names, a letter and (optionally) one digit. Upper and lower case letters are considered the same for variables.

With two-letter variable names, it is difficult to make variable names that reflect the use of the variable. Other dialects of BASIC allow for long names that can better describe the variable. Examples of a long name are COST and DISCOUNT. Some dialects allow up to eight characters, some have a maximum of 40, and others allow over 200. Special characters such as periods or dashes may be used in some dialects as separators, as in the name YEAR.TO.DATE.TOTAL.

Warning: Although some dialects, such as Apple BASIC and early Radio Shack, allow the user to enter long variable names, they will recognize only the first two characters of the variable name. In these versions the names CUSTACT and CUSTBAL will be interpreted as the same variable because they both begin with CU.

When possible, avoid short variable names or abbreviations. Although they are clear to BASIC, short names confuse the people who work with the program. We will use descriptive names in all of our examples.

MISSPELLING VARIABLE NAMES

Misspelling is a problem with long variable names. Whenever BASIC encounters a numeric variable for the first time, it initializes the variable to zero. If you type the following, BASIC would print 0:

```
LET COST = 10 RETURN
PRINT CSOT RETURN
```

To BASIC, CSOT is a new variable to which it assigns an initial value of zero. You must always verify that you have correctly spelled each variable name. BASIC won't say that you have made an error; it will just give you an erroneous result.

STRING VARIABLES AND DOLLAR SIGNS

BASIC also allows us to store names and other character data in variables. To differentiate these from numeric variables, BASIC requires that we name the variables that store strings of characters (*string variables*) with a dollar sign at the end of the name.

For example, to define CUSTNAME$ as a string variable, we can type the following:

```
LET CUSTNAME$ = "Margaret Johansen" RETURN
PRINT CUSTNAME$ RETURN
Margaret Johansen
```

RESERVED WORDS

Variables can't have the same names as *reserved words*, such as the statements PRINT and LIST, which have special meaning to BASIC. The list of reserved words varies from system to system; the quick reference at the end of this appendix lists those that we discuss. Check with your instructor for a complete list for your dialect.

USING VARIABLES IN A PROGRAM

In the program SCORES we want to calculate and print the average score. We will do this by using two variables. The one named TOT.SCORE will store the total of all the scores, and AVG.SCORE will store the average. Here is the program with this code added:

```
10  PRINT "Student Name", "Score"
20  PRINT
30  PRINT "Adams, M.", 85
40  PRINT "Bradly, J", 72
50  PRINT "Duncan, A.", 86
60  PRINT "Franklin, B.", 73
70  PRINT "Jones, K.", 95
80  PRINT "Lopez, M.", 88
90  PRINT "Thompson, F.", 70
100 LET TOT.SCORE = 85 + 72 + 86 + 73 + 95 + 88 + 70
110 LET AVG.SCORE = TOT.SCORE / 7
120 PRINT
130 PRINT "Average Score", AVG.SCORE
999 END
RUN RETURN
Student Name   Score

Adams, M.        85
Bradly, J.       72
Duncan, A.       86
Franklin, B.     73
Jones, K.        92
Lopez, M.        88
Thompson, F.     70

Average Score  81.28571
```

FORMATTED OUTPUT

Notice how the result printed. In most cases we would want the number rounded to one or two decimal places. BASIC provides formatting statements to round, to place dollar signs in currency amounts, and to align numeric values on the decimal point. Because these statements vary widely from dialect to dialect, we will not cover them in this generic discussion of BASIC.

A related issue involves how some dialects of BASIC store the fractional parts of numbers. On some versions of BASIC you may get unexpected results from arithmetic operations. Consider the following:

```
PRINT 10 * .0715 RETURN
.7150001                    ← this should be .715
```

This problem occurs because (on some machines) BASIC uses binary arithmetic (which provides no exact representation for .01). Formatted printing will usually help to solve this problem.

Test Your Learning

1. What is a variable?

2. How does BASIC know whether a variable should store numeric or string data?

3. What are the restrictions for naming variables? (Check the rules for your dialect.)

4. Write statements to assign the following values to the variables listed below. If your system allows only two-character names, use just the first two names shown below.

Value	Variable Name
45	COUNTER
34.57	P2
Gross Pay	MESSAGE$
Sacramento	CITY$

5. A house measures 75 feet by 50 feet and costs $45 per square foot to build. Write a program that calculates and prints the total number of square feet and then calculates and prints the total cost.

6. a. Load the program PAINT that you wrote as an exercise in the previous section. Modify the program so that the number of gallons is stored in the variable GALLONS and the cost of the paint is stored in the variable PAINT.COST.

   b. The painter charges 15¢ a square foot in addition to the cost of the paint. Have the program calculate and print the total amount the painter will charge. Store this amount in the variable JOB.COST. Save the program, keeping the same name.

7. Your gross pay is $300.00, from which the following is withheld:

   Social Security tax, which is .0715 of the gross
   Federal withholding tax, which is $45.00
   Disability insurance, which is .009 of the gross

   The resulting net pay is $230.85. Write a program that will calculate and print the amount of each tax, then calculate and print net pay.

PROGRAM DOCUMENTATION AND REM

Programs are written by and for people. Well-written programs are easy to under-stand. They contain notes to the reader, called *documentation* (see Chapter 9), that tell what the programs do and provide other important information. Business programs tend to be used for ten years or more. During this time many programmers will be called upon to change the program to meet current business needs. Documentation helps these programmers modify existing programs quickly and correctly. Let's look at some types of documentation.

PROGRAM IDENTIFICATION BLOCK

Every program should contain information that identifies it by giving its name, who wrote it, and a short statement about what the program does. The BASIC statement that allows for making remarks in a program is REM. The REM statement is not executed by BASIC, therefore we can put any characters or message after REM that we wish. These comments will appear when the program is listed and serve as an explanation to the reader. Let's load the program SCORES and add documentation.

<u>LOAD "SCORES"</u> RETURN

The following new lines will identify the program. We will use asterisks to make the lines stand out.

```
1 REM ***************************************** RETURN
2 REM      Program Name:  SCORES RETURN
3 REM         Written by EB Cohen RETURN
4 REM         December 25, 1988 RETURN
5 REM RETURN
6 REM     This program prints student scores RETURN
7 REM         and the average score RETURN
8 REM ***************************************** RETURN
```

DATA DICTIONARY

To make our program usable by others, we also need to tell the reader what the variable names stand for. Variable names like TOT.SCORE and AVG.SCORE are self-evident; but if we use a dialect of BASIC that allows only two-character variable names (like TS and AS), then we must create REM statements that tell what TS and AS mean. The list of variable names and their meanings is called a *data dictionary*.

We have used up most of the available line numbers at the start of the program, so we will need to RENUMber the program before we add the data dictionary. Here is a listing of the renumbered program with the data dictionary:

<u>RENUM</u> RETURN
<u>LIST</u> RETURN

```
10 REM ****************************************
20 REM      Program Name:   SCORES
30 REM           Written by EB Cohen
40 REM           December 25, 1988
50 REM
60 REM     This program prints student scores
70 REM         and the average score
80 REM ****************************************
90 REM *          DATA DICTIONARY            *
100 REM
110 REM TOT.SCORE = total score
120 REM AVG.SCORE = average score
130 REM ****************************************
140 REM
150 PRINT "Student Name", "Score"
160 PRINT
170 PRINT "Adams, M.", 85
180 PRINT "Bradly, J.", 72
190 PRINT "Duncan, A.", 86
200 PRINT "Franklin, B.", 73
210 PRINT "Jones, K.", 95
220 PRINT "Lopez, M.", 88
230 PRINT "Thompson, F.", 70
240 LET TOT.SCORE = 85 + 72 + 86 + 73 + 95 + 88 + 70
250 LET AVG.SCORE = TOT.SCORE / 7
260 PRINT
270 PRINT "Average Score", AVG.SCORE
280 END
SAVE "SCORES" RETURN
```

Multi-Statement Line

Sometimes we will want a remark on the same line as another statement. We can do this by placing a colon (or backslash, depending on the dialect) between the statements.

```
190 LET AVG.SCORE = TOT.SCORE / 7   :REM Calculate average score
```

Although BASIC allows other statements to be placed on the same line, for ease of reading and understanding we recommend doing so only with a REM statement. Because BASIC ignores all characters after REM, you can't add another statement after it.

Some dialects allow REM to be replaced by an apostrophe (') or exclamation point (!)

Wrap-Around

As you write programs you may find that a line of code is greater than 80 characters. For example, we could have written the line to print the average score as follows:

```
240 PRINT AVG.SCORE = (85 + 72 + 86 + 73 + 95 + 88 + 70) / 7 REM:
print average score
```

As we type the 80th character of this line we reach the end of the screen. No problem. As we continue typing, the 81st character appears in the first column of the next row on the screen. This feature is called *wrap-around*. To BASIC the program line is not ended until the RETURN key is pressed. Some dialects have a maximum line length, others do not. A common maximum line length is 254 characters, just over 3 lines on an 80-column terminal. To improve readability, spaces should be inserted between words in the statement.

Test Your Learning

1. What is documentation?
2. Why is documentation important?
3. How do you get a line to hold more than a single statement?
4. What happens when a line is greater than 80 characters? What is the maximum line length for your dialect of BASIC?
5. a. Load the program EXPENSE you wrote as an exercise for the previous section on programs. Add documentation to this program and save the updated program.
   b. Do the same for the program PAINT that you modified as an exercise in the previous section.

INPUT

Let's enter a new program that calculates the mark-up rate for a given product.

```
NEW RETURN
10 LET PRICE = 130 RETURN
20 LET COST = 100 RETURN
30 PRINT "Mark-up rate "; (PRICE - COST) / COST RETURN
40 END RETURN
RUN RETURN
Mark-up rate .3
```

This program calculates the mark-up rate for only one value of PRICE and COST. We would like to use this program to compute mark-up for all sorts of products; do we need to revise our program for each item? No. The INPUT statement allows us to get the values of PRICE and COST from the user. Here's how INPUT works.

Without Prompt

When BASIC executes the INPUT statement, it displays a question mark on the screen and waits for the user to enter something and press RETURN. We could change Line 10 in the program to read:

```
10 INPUT PRICE RETURN
```

Now RUN the program.

```
RUN RETURN
?
```

BASIC is executing Line 10 and waiting for us to enter a value and press RETURN. It will then store the value in variable PRICE and proceed to the next line.

Type the amount 150 and press RETURN; the program will continue as before.

```
? 150 RETURN
Mark-up rate  .5
```

Now we have the ability to enter any amount as the price. Try running the program and entering different values.

WITH PROMPT

The question mark is pretty cryptic: How does the user know what the program is asking for? We could PRINT a message or *prompt* just before executing the INPUT statement.

```
5 PRINT "What is the value for PRICE"; RETURN
10 INPUT PRICE RETURN
```

When we run the program, the prompt "What is the value for PRICE?" will appear. The semicolon (;) at the end of the PRINT statement keeps the cursor from advancing to the next line.

```
RUN RETURN
What is the value for PRICE? 130 RETURN
Mark-up rate  .3
```

Note that because the need for a prompt with INPUT is so common, almost all BASIC dialects allow the prompt message to be placed directly in the INPUT statement; therefore, we can replace Lines 5 and 10 with one line:

```
DELETE 5 RETURN
10 INPUT "What is the value for PRICE"; PRICE RETURN
```

The prompt is placed within quotes and followed by a semicolon. Because the syntax for this statement varies, check Table 1 for the correct format for your system. Some dialects use a colon instead of the semicolon; some automatically place the question mark after the prompt, others don't. Our examples will show a dialect that uses a semicolon and automatically generates a question mark.

INPUTTING MORE THAN A SINGLE VARIABLE

We can input more than one value with a single INPUT statement.

```
DELETE 10 RETURN
20 INPUT "What are the values for COST and PRICE"; COST, PRICE RETURN
```

In this example of INPUT, we are asked to enter two numbers. We must type one number, a comma, and the other number. The comma separates the numbers. When the line is executed, the first value entered is placed in the variable COST, and the second is placed in the variable PRICE.

```
RUN RETURN
What are the values for COST and PRICE? 100, 130 RETURN
Mark-up rate .3
```

You must enter the same number of values as variables in the INPUT statement. If you don't, BASIC will display an error message. Here is the message one dialect displays:

```
What are the values for COST and PRICE? 100 RETURN
?Redo from start
What are the values for COST and PRICE?
```

At this point you simply type the correct number of values and press RETURN. The program will then continue.

INPUTTING STRING VALUES

You may also input string values with the INPUT statement. For example, to have the user enter the customer's last name, we use the following:

```
200 INPUT "Customer last name"; CUST.LAST.NAME$ RETURN
```

The important thing to remember is that string data must be entered into a string variable. If we used the variable name CUST.LAST.NAME (instead of CUST.LAST.NAME$), BASIC would display an error message telling us we used the wrong variable type.

TEST YOUR LEARNING

1. What does INPUT do?
2. a. Why would you use a prompt?
   b. Does your system allow a prompt? If so, what punctuation mark is used after the prompt?
   c. If your system does not allow a prompt in the INPUT statement, how can you display a prompt?
3. Write a program that asks the user to input his or her name and a number. Use a prompt to tell the user what to do. Then print the number preceded by the message "The number you entered is".
4. Write a program that uses a single INPUT statement to allow the user to enter two numbers. Print the sum and the product of these numbers.
5. Load the program EXPENSE from the previous exercises. Change the program so that the user is asked to enter the amounts for each expense item. Save this updated version.

6. The formula for calculating the area of a circle is pi (pi = 3.1416) times the radius squared. Write a program that asks the user to input the radius of the circle and prints the area for that radius.

7. Modify the program PAINT from previous exercises so that the following data is input by the user: length of the area to be painted, width of the area, number of square feet that one gallon will cover, cost of one gallon of paint, and the painter's fee per square foot. As before, have the program calculate and print the number of gallons needed, the cost of the paint, and the total cost of the job. Make sure the program is well documented and clear prompts are given to the user.

8. You wish to determine your gas mileage and cost for gas on a trip. Write a program that accepts as input the beginning mileage, the ending mileage, the total number of gallons of gas, and the cost per gallon. The program displays as output the average miles per gallon and cost of gas per mile.

READ AND DATA

Many programs have data that seldom change. A good example of such data is the tax rates, which usually remain constant for at least a year. We can place the social security and state disability rates in a program in several ways. We could ask the user to enter them each time the program is run, as in the following:

```
1000 INPUT "Please enter social security tax rate: ", SS.RATE
1010 INPUT "Please enter state disability tax rate: ", SDI.RATE
1020 LET SS.AMOUNT = GROSS * SS.RATE
1030 LET SDI.AMOUNT = GROSS * SDI.RATE
```

or we could code them into the program:

```
1000 LET SS.AMOUNT = GROSS * .0715
1010 LET SDI.AMOUNT = GROSS * .009
```

The disadvantage with the first method is that the program relies on the user to remember and enter the tax rates correctly each time the program is run. The second method eliminates this possibility for error, but when rates change, the programmer must search for each LET statement and change the values. If the rates are also used in other lines, the programmer must be sure to find all places where they are used.

STORING VALUES

The DATA statement offers us a way to store values that rarely need to be changed. We can store the values with this statement:

```
NEW RETURN
100 DATA .0715, .009 RETURN
```

The values given in the DATA statement are placed in a data list when the RUN command is given and before any program statements are executed. The values are stored sequentially in the same order as they appear in the program listing.

RETRIEVING VALUES

To retrieve the values we use the READ statement:

```
100 DATA .0715, .009 RETURN
110 READ SS.RATE RETURN
120 READ SDI.RATE RETURN
130 LET SS.AMOUNT = GROSS * SS.RATE RETURN
140 LET SDI.AMOUNT = GROSS * SDI.RATE RETURN
```

When the READ statement is executed, BASIC assigns the next unread value in the data list to the variable named in the READ statement. Thus, the first value of .0715 is assigned to SS.RATE and the second value of .009 is assigned to SDI.RATE.

Line 100 shows that more than one value may be stored with a single DATA statement. The values are separated by commas. Also, more than one value may be read with a single READ statement. Lines 110 and 120 could be replaced by this single line:

```
110 READ SS.RATE, SDI.RATE
```

Strings as well as numbers can be placed in DATA statements. However, a string DATA value must be read into a string variable. For example, we can store a heading in a DATA statement and print it using the following statements:

```
500 DATA Gross
510 READ HDG1$
520 PRINT HDG1$
```

Note that although quotes are not always needed around string constants in DATA statements, they may be used. The following short program uses DATA statements to store headings, tax rates, and gross amounts, which are retrieved for use in the program using READ statements. Note that in this example the DATA statements appear at the end of the program. Remember, the values in DATA statements are placed in the data list *before the program is executed*. Therefore, it doesn't matter where the DATA statements are placed in the program as long as the values appear in the sequence in which they are to be read. Table 3 shows the DATA list for this program and the variables to which the values are assigned by the READ statements.

```
NEW RETURN
100 REM Program to demonstrate use of READ and DATA RETURN
110 REM Calculate and print taxes for several gross amounts RETURN
120 REM RETURN
130 READ HDG1$, HDG2$, HDG3$ RETURN
140 PRINT HDG1$, HDG2$, HDG3$ RETURN
150 PRINT RETURN
```

```
160 READ SS.RATE, SDI.RATE  RETURN
170 READ GROSS1  RETURN
180 PRINT GROSS1, GROSS1 * SS.RATE, GROSS1 * SDI.RATE  RETURN
190 READ GROSS2  RETURN
200 PRINT GROSS2, GROSS2 * SS.RATE, GROSS2 * SDI.RATE  RETURN
210 READ GROSS3  RETURN
220 PRINT GROSS3, GROSS3 * SS.RATE, GROSS3 * SDI.RATE  RETURN
1000 REM  RETURN
1010 REM   *** DATA statements ***  RETURN
1020 DATA Gross, SS Amount, SDI Amount  RETURN
1030 DATA .0715, .009  RETURN
1040 DATA 100, 500, 1000  RETURN
1050 END  RETURN
RUN  RETURN
Gross          SS Amount        SDI Amount

   100          7.150001          .9
   500         35.75            4.5
  1000         71.5             9
```

In this example we used DATA statements to store the gross salaries. Normally we would use the INPUT statement to enter these values because they change for each employee. However, when learning programming or when testing programs, DATA statements are frequently used in place of INPUT.

RESTORE

We can re-read the same DATA values in the program using the RESTORE statement. RESTORE causes the next READ statement to begin with the first DATA value in the list.

If we try to read more items than the list holds without using RESTORE, BASIC will display an error message such as: `Out of DATA in 170`, in which 170 is the number of the line where the error occurred.

TABLE 3   Data List for Demonstration Program

Value	Assigned to This Variable
GROSS	HDG1
SS AMOUNT	HDG2
SDI AMOUNT	HDG3
.0715	SS.RATE
.009	SDI.RATE
100	GROSS1
500	GROSS2
1000	GROSS3

TEST YOUR LEARNING

1. What does the DATA statement do?

2. How are the values stored by DATA statements retrieved?

3. What value will be assigned to each variable and what will be printed by the following sets of program lines? One set has an error; what's wrong with it? Try each on your computer.

```
10 DATA 20, 450, Range 1
20 DATA 50, 900, Range 2
30 READ R1.MIN, R1.MAX, R1.DISC$
40 READ R2.MIN, R2.MAX, R2.DISC$
50 PRINT R1.MIN, R1.MAX, R1.DISC$
60 PRINT R2.MIN, R2.MAX, R2.DISC$
70 END
```

```
10 DATA 20, 450
20 DATA 50, 900
30 DATA Range 1, Range 2
40 READ R1.MIN, R1.MAX
50 READ R2.MIN, R2.MAX
60 READ R1.DISC$, R2.DISC$
70 PRINT R1.MIN, R1.MAX, R1.DISC$
80 PRINT R2.MIN, R2.MAX, R2.DISC$
90 END
```

```
10 DATA Range 1, Range 2
20 DATA 20, 450
30 DATA 50, 900
40 READ R1.MIN, R1.MAX
50 READ R2.MIN, R2.MAX
60 READ R1.DISC$, R2.DISC$
70 PRINT R1.MIN, R1.MAX, R1.DISC$
80 PRINT R2.MIN, R2.MAX, R2.DISC$
90 END
```

4. Write a program to read the names of the days in the week from DATA statements and to display them on the screen.

5. Modify the program PAINT so that the square feet that one gallon of paint covers and the painter's fee per square foot are stored in DATA statements instead of input by the user.

PROGRAM PLANNING

Up to now we have written very simple programs. Before moving on to more realistic programming, let's study how to plan a program using *structured programming* concepts (see Chapter 9). To illustrate these planning techniques, we'll develop a program that calculates the withholding taxes and net pay for employees. At the end of this appendix we'll write the full program for this application.

PROBLEM DEFINITION

The first and most important step in programming is to define the problem. You may have a perfectly written program, but it is useless if it doesn't solve the correct problem. As part of the problem definition, write down exactly what you want the program to do, including a description of the input to the program and the desired output. Until you can do this, you can't begin to write the program.

Here is the problem definition for the payroll problem we want to solve: By federal and state laws, employers are required to withhold several taxes from an employee's gross pay and to remit these funds to the government—that is, to calculate and provide for withholding federal income tax, social security tax (known as FICA), and state disability tax. States vary on the amounts to be withheld.

The program uses 1986 tax rates for a biweekly payroll, taking as its input each employee's name, gross salary, number of allowances (or exemptions), and marital status. It computes and displays the amount to be withheld and the net pay (gross less amount to be withheld) for each employee. It accumulates the total gross pay, total amount withheld, and total net pay, and displays these totals after all employee information has been entered.

MODULES

After defining the problem, the next step is to break the program that is supposed to solve it into logical sections, or *modules*. The payroll program has three major modules. The first, usually called *initialization*, is used to set variables (such as the tax rates) to their initial values and to perform other housekeeping functions. The second module processes the data for each employee. The third prints the totals.

We can represent these modules graphically using a *structure chart*, as shown in Figure 4. An organization chart has many similarities to a structure chart: The top boxes in each represent the modules or people that control the program flow or activity in the boxes under them, and the bottom boxes represent the level at which most of the detail work is done.

The upper modules or "manager modules" of a structure chart direct processing to the proper place at the proper time. The worker modules each perform one simple task.

TOP-DOWN PROGRAMMING

A program is much easier to write, test, and modify if we break each of the top modules into smaller and smaller modules, much as we would write an outline. The process is called *top-down programming*. For example, if we must calculate pay, we might create submodules to compute regular pay, compute overtime pay, and compute deductions.

PSEUDOCODE

As we break the problem into submodules, we will get to a point where the module can no longer be decomposed. At this stage we will code the module using *pseudo-code*, an English-like programmer's shorthand that can outline the steps that the module must perform. Pseudocode is BASIC without commas or exact syntax; indeed, the actual translation to BASIC code is quite simple. The pseudocode for processing the employee pay data might read as follows:

```
Enter employee name, allowance, gross pay, marital status
Compute amount subject to withholding
Compute amount to withhold
    Compute federal tax
    Compute social security tax
    Compute state disability tax
    Compute amt withheld = federal + soc sec + state disability
Compute net pay = gross - amt withheld
Print detail line
Add to totals
```

At this point, we need to learn some more BASIC before we can learn how to translate the pseudocode of our plan into actual code. We also need to learn the three structures of programming: sequence, repetition, and selection.

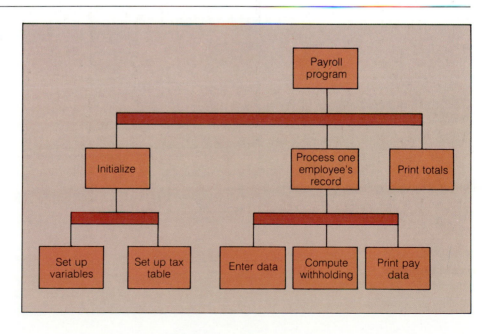

FIGURE 4
Preliminary structure chart of payroll program

FLOW CHARTS

Pseudocode is useful both for program design and for program documentation. As you recall from Chapter 9 of this text, another aid to program documentation is the *flowchart*. The most common flowchart symbols are repeated in Figure 5. We will use flowcharts to help explain concepts.

Note: Because you are now familiar with when to press RETURN, we will no longer explicitly show "RETURN" or underline the lines in the programs.

TEST YOUR LEARNING

1. Define
   a. module
   b. pseudocode
   c. structure chart
   d. top-down programming

SEQUENCE

Before the invention of structured programming, programs were written and revised in an unorganized fashion. Structured programming was founded in Israel in 1964

FIGURE 5
Basic flowchart symbols

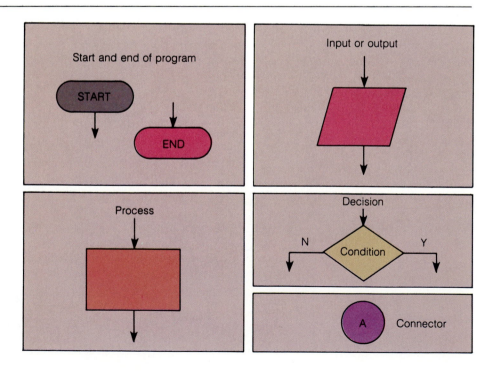

when mathematicians Corrado Bohm and Guiseppe Jacopini proved that all programs can be written using just three structures. Figure 6 shows flowcharts for each of these structures.

In all the programming we have done so far, program execution falls straight down from the top of the program to the bottom. This simple structure (going down the list of instructions one at a time, executing each in its turn) is in fact one of the three fundamental structures of structured programming, called *sequence*.

REPETITION (OR ITERATION)

We will find that much of the power of programming comes from our ability to direct program execution to parts of the program other than the next line. For

FIGURE 6
Three programming structures

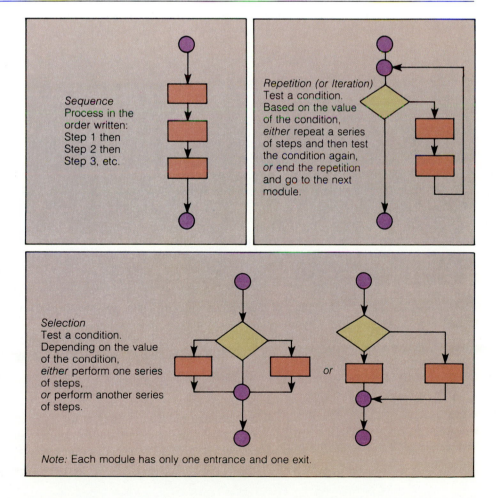

Sequence
Process in the order written:
Step 1 then
Step 2 then
Step 3, etc.

Repetition (or Iteration)
Test a condition.
Based on the value of the condition,
either repeat a series of steps and then test the condition again,
or end the repetition and go to the next module.

Selection
Test a condition.
Depending on the value of the condition,
either perform one series of steps,
or perform another series of steps.

or

Note: Each module has only one entrance and one exit.

example, in the payroll program we will want to repeat the steps that calculate withholding and net pay without writing these instructions separately for each employee.

THE LOOP

You are already familiar with the concept of *repetition*, or looping. When following the recipe for baking a cake, we are told to mix the batter until it is smooth. The cookbook author does not write 100 or 1000 lines that say "beat batter one time," because sometimes the batter would be underbeaten and other times overbeaten. In effect, the author tells us to loop. We are told (1) if the batter is smooth, move on to the next instruction; otherwise, (2) beat the batter once and go back to (1). In this way, we beat the batter the exact number of times needed. Another term used for looping is iteration.

FOR . . . NEXT

BASIC provides two sets of special instructions to support looping. The first set, FOR and NEXT, executes a set of instructions an exact number of times. Consider the following demonstration program:

```
NEW
10 REM Demonstration program for FOR . . . NEXT
20 FOR COUNT = 1 TO 5
30    PRINT "The current count is ";COUNT
40 NEXT COUNT
50 END
RUN
The current count is 1
The current count is 2
The current count is 3
The current count is 4
The current count is 5
```

The FOR statement in Line 20 begins the loop. The variable COUNT is used to keep track of the number of times the loop has been executed (see Figure 7). It is called the *counter*, *control variable*, or *loop index*. Following COUNT are the initial and maximum values for the counter.

Line 30 is the *loop body*. Any number of instructions can be included here as part of the loop body. (In this case, only one line forms the loop body.) The loop body will be executed each time the loop is repeated.

The NEXT statement in Line 40 defines the end of the loop. Although not all dialects require it, the counter used in the FOR statement is again listed following the word NEXT.

When this loop is entered, COUNT is initialized to the first value specified in the FOR statement. At Line 20, COUNT is initialized to 1. The value of COUNT is then tested against the ending value specified in the FOR statement (which is 5 in this example). Because it is not greater than the ending value, the loop body (line 30) is executed. When the NEXT statement in Line 40 is reached, control passes back to the FOR statement in Line 20. The value of COUNT is incremented by one. This repetition continues until the value of COUNT is greater than 5. Then control passes to the line after the NEXT, Line 50. In this manner the loop is repeated a total of five times.

Note that we add spaces before the statements in the body of the loop to indent it. This indentation, which makes the loop body more readable, helps us to make the program easily maintainable and understandable.

FOR . . . NEXT WITH STEP

We will want the counter for most applications to be incremented by one; however, using the STEP clause we can increment the counter by a value other than one.

```
20 FOR COUNT = 1 TO 5 STEP 2
```

FIGURE 7
Flowchart of
FOR . . . NEXT loop

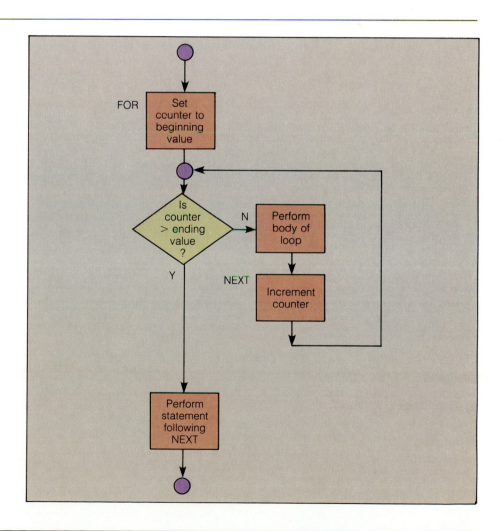

Changing Line 20 to include STEP 2 causes the counter to be incremented by two each time the loop is executed. The loop will now be executed three times and COUNT will have the values of 1, 3, and 5.

```
RUN
The current count is 1
The current count is 3
The current count is 5
```

Both the starting and ending values in the FOR statement may be variables. The following program asks the user to input the number of students and uses this value for determining how many times the loop will be repeated. The program also accumulates the total score by adding the current score to the total on each pass through the loop. In Line 20 this total is initialized to zero. Although most dialects of BASIC will initialize it to zero for us, it is good programming practice to explicitly initialize all variables.

```
10   REM    -----     Initialize Accumulators    ----
20   LET TOTAL.SCORE = 0
30   REM    -----     Enter Number of Students    ----
40   INPUT "Number of Students"; NUM.STUDENTS
50   REM    -----     Enter Each Student and Score    ----
60   FOR STUDENTS = 1 TO NUM.STUDENTS
70       INPUT "Student Name"; STUDENT.NAME$
80       INPUT "Student Score"; SCORE
90       LET TOTAL.SCORE = TOTAL.SCORE + SCORE
100  NEXT NUM.STUDENTS
110  REM    -----     Print Average Score    -----
120  PRINT
130  PRINT "Average Score", TOTAL.SCORE / NUM.STUDENTS
140  END
```

The FOR . . . NEXT loop allows us to write one set of instructions for processing, which will be repeated for each employee. The following code will calculate the social security and state disability taxes for each of four employees and print the total gross pay and net pay for each.

```
NEW
10 REM ******   Initialize Variables   ******
20 LET TOT.GROSS = 0
30 LET TOT.WITHHOLDING = 0
40 READ SS.RATE
50 READ SDI.RATE
60 DATA .0715, .009
70 REM    ******  Process Each Employee  ******
80 FOR NUM.EMP = 1 TO 4
90    REM        **  Input Data              **
100     INPUT "Employee's name: "; EMPNAME$
110     INPUT "Gross pay: "; GROSS
120   REM        **  Perform Calculations   **
130     LET SS.AMOUNT = GROSS * SS.RATE
140     LET SDI.AMOUNT = GROSS * SDI.RATE
```

```
150     LET WITHHOLDING = SS.AMOUNT + SDI.AMOUNT
160     LET TOT.GROSS = TOT.GROSS + GROSS
170     LET TOT.WITHHOLDING = TOT.WITHHOLDING + WITHHOLDING
180  REM        **   Print Pay Data           **
190     PRINT EMPNAME$, GROSS, WITHHOLDING, GROSS - WITHHOLDING
200 NEXT NUM.EMP
210 REM ******   Print Final Totals    ******
220 PRINT "Totals", TOT.GROSS, TOT.WITHHOLDING, TOT.GROSS - TOT.WITHHOLDING
230 END
```

Nested FOR . . . NEXT Loops

One FOR . . . NEXT loop may be placed inside another FOR . . . NEXT loop to form *nested loops*, as the following program demonstrates. When the outer loop is entered for the first time, the counter OUTER has the value of 1. The inner loop is then entered. This loop is repeated twice with INNER having the values of 1 and 2. OUTER is then incremented by the NEXT statement in line 130 and the outer loop is executed again. The outer loop is performed a total of three times. The inner loop is performed a total of six times, twice each time the outer loop is performed. Note again that the statements inside each loop are indented.

```
10   REM   --   Initialize Accumulators   --
20   LET OUT.COUNT = 0
30   LET IN.COUNT = 0
40   REM   --   Begin Outer Loop   --
50   FOR OUTER = 1 TO 3
60      PRINT "Outer Loop Number"; OUTER
70      LET OUT.COUNT = OUT.COUNT + 1      :REM Count Outer Loop
80      REM    --   Begin Inner Loop   --
90      FOR INNER = 1 TO 2
100         PRINT "   Inner Loop Number"; INNER
110         LET IN.COUNT = IN.COUNT + 1    :REM  Count Inner Loop
120      NEXT INNER
130 NEXT OUTER
140 PRINT "Number of times Outer Loop was executed"; OUT.COUNT
150 PRINT "Number of times Inner Loop was executed"; IN.COUNT
160 END
RUN
Outer Loop Number 1
   Inner Loop Number 1
   Inner Loop Number 2
Outer Loop Number 2
   Inner Loop Number 1
   Inner Loop Number 2
Outer Loop Number 3
   Inner Loop Number 1
   Inner Loop Number 2
Number of times Outer Loop was executed 3
Number of times Inner Loop was executed 6
```

Have you ever wondered just how many gifts were given in the song "The Twelve Days of Christmas"? Here's a program that uses nested loops to solve that query. Figure 8 is the flowchart for this program.

```
10   REM    ***  Initialize Total Gifts    ***
20   LET TOTAL.GIFTS = 0
30   REM    ***  Count Gifts for Each Day ***
40   FOR DAY = 1 TO 12
50       LET DAY.GIFTS = 0
60       FOR GIFT = 1 TO DAY
70           LET DAY.GIFTS = DAY.GIFTS + GIFT
80       NEXT GIFT
90       PRINT "On Day"; DAY; "the number of gifts is"; DAY.GIFTS
100      REM    ***  Add to Total Gifts    ***
110      LET TOTAL.GIFTS = TOTAL.GIFTS + DAY.GIFTS
120  NEXT DAY
130  REM    ***  Print Total Gifts   ***
140  PRINT "Total number of gifts is:"; TOTAL.GIFTS
150  END
RUN
On Day 1 the number of gifts is 1
On Day 2 the number of gifts is 3
On Day 3 the number of gifts is 6
On Day 4 the number of gifts is 10
On Day 5 the number of gifts is 15
On Day 6 the number of gifts is 21
On Day 7 the number of gifts is 28
On Day 8 the number of gifts is 36
On Day 9 the number of gifts is 45
On Day 10 the number of gifts is 55
On Day 11 the number of gifts is 66
On Day 12 the number of gifts is 78
Total number of gifts is: 364
```

WHILE . . . WEND

WHILE and WEND are the other set of statements that create loops in BASIC. (WEND is a contraction of W for WHILE and END for end of the WHILE loop.) Although most dialects of BASIC have this set of statements, they may vary slightly; we will discuss the most common version. (*Note:* The WHILE and WEND statements are not available in most Tandy or Apple BASIC. We'll present a way to simulate the WHILE loop when we discuss the GOTO statement. You may wish to read that section at this time. Consult your instructor if you need to simulate the WHILE . . . WEND loop.)

The WHILE statement consists of the word WHILE followed by some condition. If the condition is true, all the statements between the WHILE and WEND statements are executed. Control then returns to the WHILE statement. If the condition is false, processing is directed to the statement following the WEND.

FIGURE 8
Flowchart of nested
FOR . . . NEXT loop

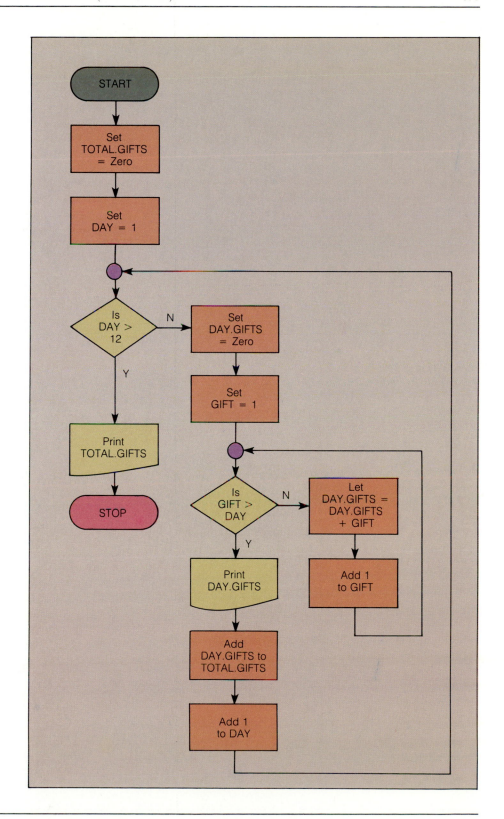

Here is an example of a WHILE . . . WEND loop.

```
NEW
10 REM Demo program for WHILE...WEND
20 INPUT "What is your check balance"; BALANCE
30 WHILE BALANCE > 0
40    INPUT "How much is this check"; CHECK
50    LET BALANCE = BALANCE - CHECK
60    PRINT "Current Balance: "; BALANCE
70 WEND
80 PRINT "Oops, you are overdrawn"
90 END
```

This program asks the users for their checkbook balance and repeatedly asks for checks until the account is overdrawn. At that point, it prints the message "Oops, you are overdrawn" (see Figure 9).

The loop consists of Lines 30 through 70. It begins with the WHILE statement in Line 30 and ends with the WEND in Line 70. When program execution reaches

FIGURE 9
Flowchart of
WHILE . . . WEND

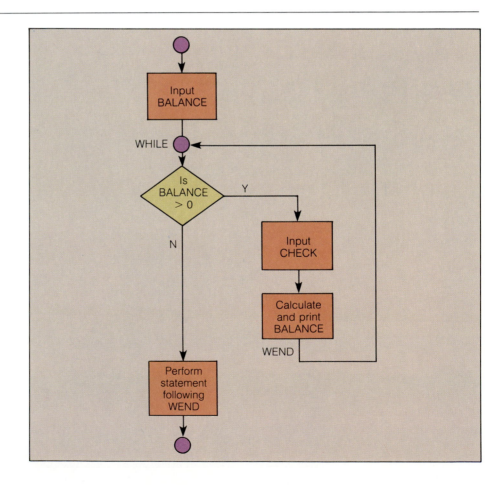

Line 30, it tests the condition after the word WHILE. In this case, the condition is BALANCE > 0. If the condition is true, control passes to the line after the WHILE. Control then passes sequentially from Line 40 to 50 to 60 to 70, the WEND statement. The WEND statement returns control to its matching WHILE at Line 30 where the condition is checked again. If the condition is false, control passes to the line after the WEND.

Here is the demonstration program in action:

```
RUN
What is your check balance? 100 RETURN
How much is this check? 50 RETURN
Current Balance: 50
How much is this check? 51 RETURN
Current Balance: -1
Oops, you are overdrawn
```

More on Conditions

In the earlier example, we used the symbol > to represent "greater than." There are six such symbols, called *relational operators*.

>	greater than
<	less than
=	equal
=> (or >=)	equal or greater than
=< (or <=)	equal or less than
<> (or ><)	not equal

These relational operators can be used to construct *conditions* that can be evaluated as either true or false. Here are some more conditions:

```
AMOUNT <> 99999
HOURS <= 40
ANS$ = "YES"
```

In addition to the relational operators, the *logical operators* AND, OR, and NOT can be used to create more complex conditions.

Suppose we want to perform a module for all males under age 25. We could use the following WHILE selection:

```
WHILE SEX$ = "M" AND AGE < 25
```

In this case both conditions (SEX$ = "M" and AGE < 25) must be true for the loop to be executed. If either condition is false, the entire condition will be evaluated as false. In that case, processing will continue on the line following the WEND.

When two conditions are joined with OR, if at least one of them is true, the entire condition is evaluated as true. To select all customers living in the states of California or Arizona we would write:

```
WHILE STATE$ = "CA" OR STATE$ = "AZ"
```

The third logical operator, NOT, reverses true and false. For example, NOT BALANCE > 0 is true when BALANCE is less than or equal to zero and is false when BALANCE is greater than zero.

PROCESSING WITHIN A WHILE . . . WEND LOOP

In all of the sample programs so far, each time we wanted to use a different set of values we had to rerun the program. WHILE . . . WEND loops are commonly used to overcome this problem. The user signals the desire to enter another set of values or to end the program. If the user signals "another set," the loop is repeated. If the signal is "quit," the program is ended. Let's see how to do this with WHILE . . . WEND by using it to rewrite the employee processing loop of the payroll program.

```
70  REM     ******  Process Each Employee  ******
75  INPUT "Do you wish to enter another employee (YES/NO)"; ANS$
80  WHILE ANS$ = "YES"
90      INPUT "Employee's name: "; EMPNAME$
100     INPUT "Gross pay: "; GROSS
110     LET SS.AMOUNT = GROSS * SS.RATE
120     LET SDI.AMOUNT = GROSS * SDI.RATE
130     LET WITHHOLDING = SS.AMOUNT + SDI.AMOUNT
140     PRINT EMPNAME$, GROSS, WITHHOLDING, GROSS - WITHHOLDING
150     LET TOT.GROSS = TOT.GROSS + GROSS
160     LET TOT.WITHHOLDING = TOT.WITHHOLDING + WITHHOLDING
165     INPUT "Do you wish to enter another employee (YES/NO)"; ANS$
170 WEND
```

The question is asked once before the loop is entered to "prime the loop" and again at the end of the loop.

There is a second way to write the loop. Instead of having a separate question ("Do you want to enter another employee (YES/NO)"), we can signal completion by entering a predetermined value for one variable, such as employee name. We need to be sure that this signal value is not one that would be a valid value for the application. In this example DONE will be entered as the employee name to signal the end of entry.

```
70  REM     ******  Process Each Employee  ******
75  INPUT "What is the Employee's name (enter DONE to quit) "; EMPNAME$
80  WHILE EMPNAME$ <> "DONE"
100     INPUT "Gross pay: "; GROSS
110     LET SS.AMOUNT = GROSS * SS.RATE
120     LET SDI.AMOUNT = GROSS * SDI.RATE
130     LET WITHHOLDING = SS.AMOUNT + SDI.AMOUNT
140     PRINT EMPNAME$, GROSS, WITHHOLDING, GROSS - WITHHOLDING
150     LET TOT.GROSS = TOT.GROSS + GROSS
160     LET TOT.WITHHOLDING = TOT.WITHHOLDING + WITHHOLDING
165     INPUT "What is the Employee's name (enter DONE to quit) "; EMPNAME$
170 WEND
```

Notice again how we prime the loop. The first time, the user is asked to enter EMPNAME$ before the loop is entered. A second INPUT statement appears at the end of the loop. The first statement primes the loop using the first employee. The placement of the second INPUT statement ends the loop immediately after DONE is entered.

Data Validation

WHILE . . . WEND is commonly used immediately after INPUT to ensure that the value of the data that the user has entered is within the correct range. This is called *data validation* or *input validation*. In the first example in the preceding section, we asked the user to enter YES if processing is to continue. What if the user had answered NO, or XVCBR, or even yes? In all of these cases, processing would have ended. (Uppercase characters are not equal to lowercase, therefore YES does not equal yes.) We want the user to enter either YES or NO. We also want to check that the value of GROSS is greater than zero and less than 5000. To have the program check for this, we can add the following:

```
75 INPUT "Do you wish to enter another employee (YES/NO)"; ANS$
76     WHILE ANS$ <> "YES" AND ANS$ <> "NO"
77         INPUT "Please enter YES or NO", ANS$
78     WEND
100    INPUT "Gross pay: "; GROSS
101        WHILE GROSS < 0 OR GROSS > 5000
102            INPUT "Please enter an amount between 0 and 5000"; GROSS
103        WEND
165    INPUT "Do you wish to enter another employee (YES/NO)"; ANS$
166    WHILE ANS$ <> "YES" AND ANS$ <> "NO"

167        INPUT "Please enter YES or NO"; ANS$
168    WEND
```

As you can see, adding validation increases the length of the program. Most programs are like this. Because users are human, they make mistakes. If a program is to prevent these mistakes from being accepted, as all programs should, a considerable portion of the program will be devoted to data validation.

Test Your Learning

1. What is a loop?

2. How can you create loops in BASIC?

3. Name the three parts of the FOR . . . NEXT loop and describe the function of each part.

4. How does the WHILE . . . WEND loop differ from the FOR . . . NEXT loop?

5. What is the difference between AND, OR, and NOT?

6. How can you validate input in BASIC?

7. Write a program that asks the user to input the name, hours, and hourly rate for each of five employees. Calculate and print the gross wages (hours times rate) for each employee. After all five have been entered, print a blank line followed by the total gross wages.

   a. If your dialect has WHILE . . . WEND or a similar construct, have the program validate that the hours are within the range 0 to 40.

   b. If your dialect has WHILE . . . WEND, change the program to allow any number of employees to be entered. Instruct the user to enter DONE as the name when entry is complete.

8. a. Modify the program PAINT (from earlier exercises) to use a FOR . . . NEXT loop to input the measurements of three rooms. Calculate and display the total area as well as the cost of the paint and the total job.

   b. Now change the program so that the user inputs the number of rooms to be painted. (This number is used as the ending value in the FOR statement.)

9. Write a program that asks the user for an employee's name, gross monthly pay, and the percentage of the pay he or she wants withheld and deposited in a credit union. Using a FOR . . . NEXT loop, calculate and print the monthly balance for 12 months, assuming an interest rate of 1 percent per month. The output should appear as follows:

```
Employee? Sarah Gentry
Monthly Gross? 500
Percent to credit union (enter 10% as 10)? 10
Month              Balance
 1                  50
 2                  105
 3                  165.5
 4                  232.05
 5                  305.255
 6                  385.7805
 7                  474.3585
 8                  571.7944
 9                  678.9738
10                  796.8712
11                  926.5584
12                  1069.214
```

SELECTION

The last of the three structures of structured programming is *selection* (refer to Figure 6). Recall the recipe example in the previous section. It has an ingredients section that uses selection, which states,

```
IF cake is to feed 5 - 7 people, THEN use 3 cups flour
IF cake is to feed 8 - 10 people, THEN use 4 cups flour
IF cake is to feed 11 - 12 people, THEN use 5 cups flour
```

Note that the syntax of this selection process is the word IF, a condition, the word THEN, and a statement to be executed if the condition is true.

IF . . . THEN

BASIC uses IF and THEN just like the example above. The syntax consists of the reserved word IF followed by a logical condition, the reserved word THEN, and a BASIC statement. If the condition is true, the action following THEN is executed. If the action is false, the action is not taken. Therefore, we could replace Line 80 in the checkbook program with this line:

```
80 IF BALANCE < 0 THEN PRINT "Oops, you are overdrawn!"
```

When the new Line 80 is executed, *if* the value of BALANCE is less than 0, *then* the PRINT statement is executed; otherwise, the PRINT statement is not executed. Processing continues with the next line. The flowchart for the IF . . . THEN statement is shown in Figure 10.

In this next example we want to determine the number of overtime hours. If the value of the variable HOURS is greater than 40, then OT.HOURS is set to the HOURS less 40. If HOURS is 40 or less, OT.HOURS remains zero. To assure that any prior

FIGURE 10
Flowchart of IF . . . THEN

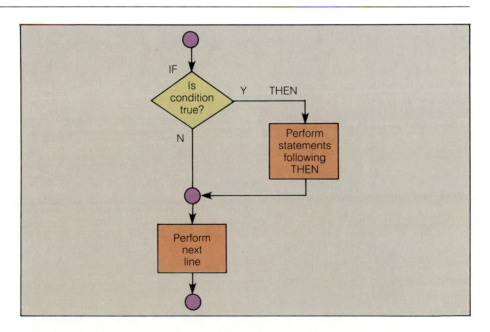

value of OT.HOURS is not retained, we initialize it to zero before the IF . . . THEN statement.

```
2000   LET OT.HOURS = 0
2010   IF HOURS > 40 THEN LET OT.HOURS = HOURS - 40
```

IF . . . THEN . . . ELSE

We frequently want to perform one action if a condition is true and another if the condition is false. Most dialects of BASIC provide the IF . . . THEN . . . ELSE statement, an extension of the IF . . . THEN statement that allows selection of one action or another. (See Table 1 to determine if it is available on your system.)

The syntax of this statement is the reserved word IF followed by a logical condition, the reserved word THEN, a BASIC statement, the reserved word ELSE, and another BASIC statement. If the condition is true, the statement following THEN is executed. If the condition is false, the statement following ELSE is executed. One and only one of the THEN and ELSE clauses is executed. A flow-chart of this statement is shown in Figure 11.

We can replace the two lines that determine overtime with this one line:

```
2010   IF HOURS > 40 THEN LET OT.HOURS = HOURS - 40 ELSE LET OT.HOURS = 0
```

In this case the ELSE clause sets OT.HOURS to zero, eliminating the need for a separate statement to initialize it.

FIGURE 11
Flowchart of
IF . . . THEN . . . ELSE

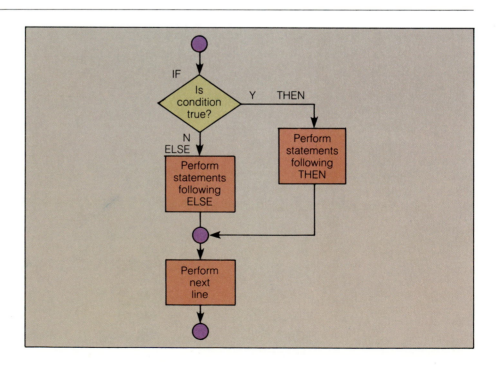

Here's another series of statements that give a 10 percent discount to customers 65 and over.

```
1200 LET TAX = .06
1210 IF AGE < 65 THEN LET PRICE = PRICE + TAX * PRICE ELSE LET PRICE = .9 *
(PRICE + TAX * PRICE)
```

Note that it took more than one screen width (80 columns) to write the last statement. Rather than accept the spacing that the screen gives us, we'll rebreak the line to improve readability. This clearly separates the actions to be taken on the true and false conditions:

```
1210 IF AGE < 65 THEN LET PRICE = PRICE + TAX * PRICE
                 ELSE LET PRICE = .9 (PRICE + TAX * PRICE)
```

NESTED IF . . . THEN . . . ELSE

Many dialects support a more complex version of the IF statement that allows you to nest one IF statement within another (see Table 1).

To demonstrate, we'll write a statement to select a salesperson's commission factor. Two items determine the commission: the employee's gross sales and the bonus rate assigned to that employee. If the gross sales figure is greater than 20,000, and the bonus rate is 2, the commission factor is to be 4. If gross sales is greater than 20,000, but the bonus rate is not 2, then the commission factor is to be 3. If gross sales is 20,000 or less but greater than 10,000, the commission factor is to be 2. If gross sales is 10,000 or less the commission factor is to be 1.

Before writing the code, let's write this proposal as pseudocode.

```
IF Gross > 20000
   THEN IF bonus = 2
           THEN LET commission factor = 4
           ELSE LET commission factor = 3
   ELSE IF Gross > 10,000
           THEN LET commission factor = 2
           ELSE LET commission factor = 1
```

Now we'll rewrite the pseudocode in BASIC as one nested IF . . . THEN . . . ELSE statement. (See Figure 12 for the flowchart of this statement.)

```
50 IF GROSS > 20000 THEN IF BONUS.RATE = 2 THEN LET COMMISSION.FACTOR = 4
     ELSE LET COMMISSION.FACTOR = 3 ELSE IF GROSS > 10000
     THEN LET COMMISSION.FACTOR = 2 ELSE LET COMMISSION.FACTOR = 1
```

If you're using APPLE BASIC or another dialect that doesn't support nested IF's, you can write the following statements to replace the one above:

```
50 IF GROSS > 20000 AND BONUS.RATE = 2 THEN LET COMMISSION.FACTOR = 4
60 IF GROSS > 20000 AND BONUS.RATE <> 2 THEN LET COMMISSION.FACTOR = 3
70 IF GROSS =< 20000 AND GROSS > 10000 THEN LET COMMISSION.FACTOR = 2
80 IF GROSS =< 10000 THEN LET COMMISSION.FACTOR = 1
```

TEST YOUR LEARNING

1. What is selection?

2. Where is processing directed if the condition following the IF is false?

3. a. Under what conditions will the following lines print the message "Paid In Full" and under what conditions will it print "Balance Due"?

```
10 LET MESSAGE$ = "Paid In Full"
20 PRINT "Balance";
30 INPUT BALANCE
40 IF BALANCE > 0 THEN LET MESSAGE$ = "Balance Due"
50 PRINT MESSAGE$
```

   b. Under what conditions will each of these three messages print?

```
10 PRINT "Balance";
20 INPUT BALANCE
30 IF BALANCE > 5000 THEN LET MESSAGE$ = "Over Limit"
   ELSE IF BALANCE > 0 THEN LET MESSAGE$ = "Balance Due"
   ELSE LET MESSAGE$ = "Paid In Full"
40 PRINT MESSAGE$
```

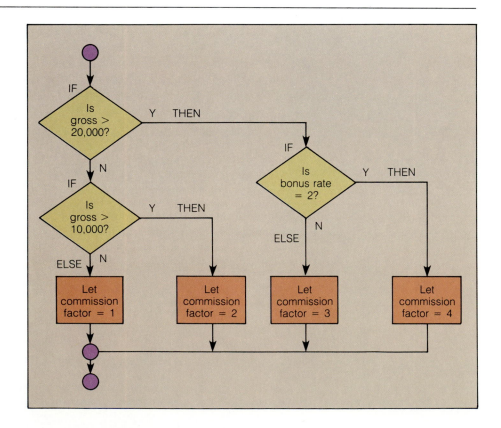

FIGURE 12
Flowchart of nested
IF . . . THEN . . . ELSE

4. Write a program that asks the user to enter two numbers. If the first number is greater or equal to the second, print the sum of the numbers. If the first number is less than the second, print their product.

5. Depending on its weight and size a package will be sent by different mail services. If the package weighs less than one pound, it will be sent first class no matter what the size. If it weighs less than 25 pounds, and the height times the width times the length (in inches) is not greater than 1728, then it will be sent third class. Otherwise, it will be sent parcel post. Write a program that asks the user to enter the weight, height, length, and width and prints a message indicating which way the package is to be sent.

6. Using IF . . . THEN, write a program to do the following:
   a. Ask the user to input the salesperson's name and gross sales. If the gross sales is greater than 5000, set the bonus sales to the gross minus 5000.
   b. Using FOR . . . NEXT, modify the program to input five salespeople. After entry is completed print the total bonus sales.
   c. Because the cutoff for the bonus may not always be 5000, place this value in a DATA statement.
   d. If WHILE . . . WEND is available on your system, change the loop to allow for any number of salespeople to be entered. Ask the user to enter QUIT as the name when entry is completed.

MODULARITY

In our earlier discussion of program planning we discussed the techniques of dividing programs first into major modules and then into successively smaller ones. The next two statements, GOSUB and RETURN, allow us to make each module of structured programming into a separate BASIC module.

GOSUB . . . RETURN

The GOSUB statement and its companion statement, RETURN, allow us to branch to another location in the program, perform any number of processing steps, and then continue processing where we left off.

To illustrate the use of these stastements let's write a short program that does the following:

```
Ask user to enter hours worked
 IF the hours are greater than 40
    THEN Calculate the number of hours over 40
         Multiply the overtime hours times the overtime rate = overtime pay
         Add the overtime pay to the total overtime pay
         Increment the count of employees with overtime
    Calculate gross pay
    Increment the count of employees
    Add gross pay to total pay
```

Now we write the above in BASIC, using GOSUB to direct us to the module that processes overtime pay.

```
10 REM    ***    Calculate Overtime and Regular Pay    ***
500 REM      --      Initialize      --
510 LET NUM.EMPL = 0
520 LET NUM.OT.EMPL = 0
530 LET TOT.PAY = 0
540 LET TOT.OT.PAY = 0
550 LET RATE = 9
560 LET OT.RATE = 13.5
1000 REM     --      Enter Employee Pay Data     --
1010 INPUT "Enter Employee Number (9999 to quit) ";EMPL.ID
1020 WHILE EMPL.ID <> 9999
1030    LET OT.PAY = 0
1040    INPUT "Enter Total Hours Worked "; HOURS
1050    IF HOURS > 40 THEN GOSUB 2000      :REM     process overtime
1060    LET PAY = HOURS * RATE + OT.PAY
1070    LET TOT.PAY = TOT.PAY + PAY
1080    LET NUM.EMPL = NUM.EMPL + 1
1090    INPUT "Enter Employee Number (9999 to quit) ";EMPL.ID
1100 WEND
1110 REM     --      Print Totals     --
1120 PRINT "Num of Empl", "Total Pay", "Num with OT", "Total OT Pay"
1130 PRINT NUM.EMPL, TOT.PAY, NUM.OT.EMPL, TOT.OT.PAY
1140 END
2000 REM      --      Process Overtime  --
2010 LET OT.HOURS = HOURS - 40
2020 LET OT.PAY = OT.HOURS * OT.RATE
2030 LET TOT.OT.PAY = TOT.OT.PAY + OT.PAY
2040 LET NUM.OT.EMPL = NUM.OT.EMPL + 1
2050 LET HOURS = 40         :REM Set Regular Hours to 40
2060 RETURN
```

In Line 1050 we placed GOSUB in an IF statement. If the condition (HOURS > 40) is true, then GOSUB will direct processing to Line 2000. At Line 2000 we begin the processing for overtime pay. We end this module with the RETURN statement. RETURN returns processing to the line following GOSUB (Line 1060).

With GOSUB we can write the major module (calculating total pay) separately from the lesser module (calculating overtime pay). The instructions that make up the overtime module become a kind of program within a program, called a *subroutine*.

STOP

Note the placement of the END statement in the example we have just shown. Line 1140 is the last line that the program is to *execute*; therefore, we placed the END statement here to signal that processing is completed and control is to be returned to the user. Some dialects require that END be the last *physical* line in the program. What do we do when we actually want processing to stop at Line 1140? One solution uses the STOP statement. STOP is similar to END in that it halts processing and returns control to the user; differences between the two statements vary from dialect to dialect. STOP usually displays a message indicating the line at which processing was halted, whereas END does not. The other differences are not significant to our discussion at this point.

To satisfy the requirement of some dialects that END be the last physical statement, we could modify the program changing Line 1140 to read `1140 STOP` and add the line `9000 END`.

We'll cover another alternative in the discussion of the GOTO statement.

PROGRAMMING WITH SUBROUTINES

To achieve even greater modularity we can write all the processing instructions in subroutines. As is common in business applications, the following program consists of three major modules: (1) initialize the variables; (2) process each transaction; (3) do final processing. Using GOSUB we can easily change this program to make each module a separate subroutine.

```
10 REM   ***    Calculate Overtime and Regular Pay  ***
20 GOSUB 500          :REM initialize
30 WHILE EMPL.ID <> 9999
40     GOSUB 1000   :REM process employee
50 WEND
60 GOSUB 2000         :REM print totals
70 END
80 REM
500 REM     --       Initialize    --
510 LET NUM.EMPL = 0
520 LET NUM.OT.EMPL = 0
530 LET TOT.PAY = 0
540 LET TOT.OT.PAY = 0
550 LET RATE = 9
560 LET OT.RATE = 13.5
570 INPUT "Enter Employee Number (9999 to quit) ";EMPL.ID
580 RETURN
590 REM
1000 REM     --       Enter Employee Pay Data    --
1010    LET OT.PAY = 0
1020    INPUT "Enter Total Hours Worked "; HOURS
1030    IF HOURS > 40 THEN GOSUB 1090      :REM     process overtime
1040    LET PAY = HOURS * RATE + OT.PAY
1050    LET TOT.PAY = TOT.PAY + PAY
1060    LET NUM.EMPL = NUM.EMPL + 1
1070    INPUT "Enter Employee Number (9999 to quit) ";EMPL.ID
1080 RETURN
1090 REM        --       Process Overtime   --
1100 LET OT.HOURS = HOURS - 40
1110 LET OT.PAY = OT.HOURS * OT.RATE
1120 LET TOT.OT.PAY = TOT.OT.PAY + OT.PAY
1130 LET NUM.OT.EMPL = NUM.OT.EMPL + 1
```

```
1140 LET HOURS = 40          :REM Set Regular Hours to 40
1150 RETURN
1160 REM
2000 REM       --      Print Totals      --
2010 PRINT "Num of Empl", "Total Pay", "Num with OT", "Total OT Pay"
2020 PRINT NUM.EMPL, TOT.PAY, NUM.OT.EMPL, TOT.OT.PAY
2030 RETURN
```

Note that the INPUT for the first employee number is a part of the initialization subroutine. This INPUT primes the WHILE . . . WEND loop.

WHY USE MODULES

Modular programming may seem a bit cumbersome to you. Why use a subroutine when you can just write those few instructions "in line"? The reasons become clear when the programs become lengthy and when each subroutine consists of many lines of code. The modular approach allows the programmer to write in a logical fashion, coding the general outline first and then coding each section separately. In the past, programmers would be almost finished writing a program only to discover a major flaw in their logic, which often required rewriting nearly the entire program. With modular programming the basic logic is written and checked first. Because each set of steps is written as a separate module, changes and corrections made to that section don't require changes to other modules.

THE "ONE" RULE

Three guidelines for writing modules are contained in what is known as the *"One" rule*, which has three parts:

- A *module does but one task*. If we have two tasks to do, we write two modules.

- A *module has only one entrance*. A module should be entered only through its first line—the line number indicated by the GOSUB that directed processing to this module. Although a number of different GOSUB's may direct control to the same module, none should branch to a line in the middle of the module.

- A *module has only one exit*. This is the line with RETURN at the end of the module. There should be only one RETURN within the module.

Unfortunately, BASIC allows us to break this rule without warning us of the consequences. If we do break the "One" rule, our program will not be truly structured; in addition, it will be prone to error and difficult to follow or modify.

MENUS

We will frequently write a program that asks the user to select from a number of processing options, which are usually displayed as a numbered list on the screen (such as shown in Figure 13). This list is called a *menu*. The user is asked to enter one of the numbers to indicate the selected option. With GOSUB we can direct processing to the desired section of the program and return to the menu when that section has been completed.

USING GOSUB FOR MENUS

Here is a program that displays the menu in Figure 13. At this point only a message is displayed when an option is selected. The detailed instructions have not yet been written.

```
100 REM    ***  Ask User to Select Option   ***
110 REM
120 LET FINISH = 0
130 WHILE FINISH = 0
140    PRINT "1 = Add new client"
150    PRINT "2 = Display current client"
160    PRINT "3 = Modify existing client"
170    PRINT "4 = Print report"
180    PRINT "5 = End processing"
190    PRINT
200    INPUT "Please enter your selection (1-5): "; CHOICE
210    WHILE CHOICE < 1 OR CHOICE > 5
220       INPUT "Please enter a selection between 1 and 5: ";CHOICE
230    WEND
240    IF CHOICE = 1 THEN GOSUB 1000
250    IF CHOICE = 2 THEN GOSUB 2000
260    IF CHOICE = 3 THEN GOSUB 3000
270    IF CHOICE = 4 THEN GOSUB 4000
280    IF CHOICE = 5 THEN GOSUB 5000
290 WEND
300 END
```

FIGURE 13
Menu presents options to user

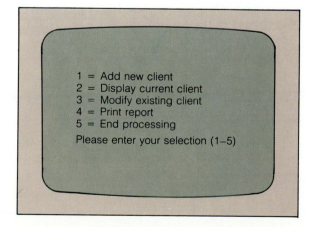

1 = Add new client
2 = Display current client
3 = Modify existing client
4 = Print report
5 = End processing

Please enter your selection (1–5)

```
1000 REM   *** Add a new client  ***
1100 PRINT "Module to add new client"
1120 RETURN
2000 REM   *** Display current client   ***
2010 PRINT "Module to display current client"
2020 RETURN
3000 REM   *** Modify existing client   ***
3010 PRINT "Module to modify existing client"
3020 RETURN
4000 REM   *** Print report ***
4010 PRINT "Module to print report"
4020 RETURN
5000 REM   *** End processing   ***
5010 LET FINISH = 9
5020 PRINT "Module to end processing"
5030 RETURN
```

ON . . . GOSUB . . . RETURN

ON . . . GOSUB is a powerful extension of GOSUB. It directs processing to any selection of modules, depending on the value of a variable. With this extension we can replace the series of IF statements in the menu program (Lines 240–280) with the following single ON . . . GOSUB statement:

```
240    ON CHOICE GOSUB 1000, 2000, 3000, 4000, 5000
```

The ON . . . GOSUB statement evaluates the variable named, in this case CHOICE. If CHOICE has the value of 1, processing branches to the first line number following the GOSUB (Line 1000 in our example). If the value of CHOICE is 2, processing continues at the second line number, and so on.

TEST YOUR LEARNING

1. What does GOSUB do? What other statement is associated with it and what does it do?

2. How is a menu used in a program?

3. On your system, what are the differences between END and STOP?

4. What rule should all modules follow? What are the three parts to this rule?

5. What is the difference between GOSUB and ON . . . GOSUB?

6. Using GOSUB, write a program that contains these three modules: (a) Initialization in which accumulators are set to zero. (b) Processing loop in which each student's last name and score are entered. (Use WHILE . . . WEND if available; otherwise, use FOR . . . NEXT and ask the user to enter the number of students.) Count the students and total the scores. (c) Final processing in which the number of students and average score is printed.

7. Write a program that displays the following menu for a payroll program. If the user enters an invalid choice, display a message asking the user to reenter

a number within the valid range. Have each module display a message, then return to the menu.

```
Payroll Menu

1 = Enter New Employee
2 = Terminate Employee
3 = Enter Pay Data
4 = Print Pay Checks
5 = Print Payroll Reports
9 = End Processing


Your Selection?
```

8. The XYZ Company carries four products, numbered 1 through 4. Each has a different price and discount schedule for high-volume customers as shown in the following table:

```
Product #1        Price $100.00
Qty:  0-100 = 0%    101-300 = 10%    301-1000 = 15%    over 1000 = 20%
Product #2        Price $495.00
Qty:  0-10  = 0%    11- 20 = 5%      21 - 50 = 10%     over 50 = 15%
Product #3        Price $5.95
Qty: 0-1000 = 5%    1000-5000 = 10%  over 5001 = 12%
Product #4        Price $10,000
Qty: no discounts
```

Write a program that asks the user for the product number and quantity ordered, then computes the total list price and the discounted price. Use a separate subroutine for each product type. Allow the user to enter as many orders as desired. At the end of the program print for each product the total number ordered, the total list price, and the total discounted price. Also print the above totals for all orders.

GOTO

GOTO is perhaps the most controversial statement in BASIC. Like GOSUB, GOTO directs processing to another line in the program; however, GOTO does not have a statement that returns processing to the point from which it branched. Controversy has arisen because the misuse of GOTO can cause programs that jump from here to there. Indiscriminate use of GOTO creates programs that are very difficult to test or modify. Structured programming developed as a way of controlling this misuse; indeed, at one time it was called "GOTO-less programming." Programmers don't agree on the use of GOTO: Some believe it should never be used; others believe GOTO should be used only in certain restricted situations. Still others feel that GOTO has many valid uses.

VALID USES

Programmers agree that GOTO can be used if it does not cause branching that violates the "One" rule. Thus it can be used for *forward branching*—a process that transfers control to a line that follows the GOTO statement. It does not jump processing into or out of a loop, or into or out of a subroutine. The following is an example of forward branching.

```
10 LET PRICE = 75
20 LET DISCOUNT = 0
30 INPUT "Quantity"; QTY
40 IF QTY < 100 THEN GOTO 60
50 LET DISCOUNT = .1        :REM apply discount
60 LET SELL.PRICE = QTY * (PRICE - PRICE * DISCOUNT)
70 PRINT "The selling price is"; SELL.PRICE
80 END
```

The GOTO statement in line 40 caused branching to line 60 when the value of QTY is less than 100. This example could also be written using GOSUB.

```
10 LET PRICE = 75
20 LET DISCOUNT = 0
30 INPUT "Quantity"; QTY
40 IF QTY => 100 THEN GOSUB 80      :REM apply discount
50 LET SELL.PRICE = QTY * (PRICE - PRICE * DISCOUNT)
60 PRINT "The selling price is"; SELL.PRICE
70 END
80  REM  **   Apply Discount    **
90  LET DISCOUNT = .1
100 PRINT "discount taken"
110 RETURN
```

Because of the advantages of modularity, we recommend the use of GOSUB in place of GOTO wherever possible.

GOTO IN PLACE OF STOP

Some dialects require END to be the last physical line of a program. We have discussed the use of STOP to halt processing at a line other than the last line. However, STOP usually displays the message "Break in line nnn," which can be disconcerting to the user. To avoid this problem, we can replace STOP with a GOTO statement that directs processing to the END statement:

```
10 LET PRICE = 75
20 LET DISCOUNT = 0
30 INPUT "Quantity"; QTY
40 IF QTY => 100 THEN GOSUB 80      :REM apply discount
50 LET SELL.PRICE = QTY * (PRICE - PRICE * DISCOUNT)
60 PRINT "The selling price is"; SELL.PRICE
70 GOTO 120           :REM   Go To End
80  REM  **   Apply Discount**
90  LET DISCOUNT = .1
```

```
100 PRINT "discount taken"
110 RETURN
120 END
```

Using GOTO and IF to Simulate WHILE . . . WEND

Another valid use of GOTO is to simulate the WHILE . . . WEND construct in those dialects that don't have it. Using GOTO, we could write the checkbook balance example that we wrote during the discussion of WHILE . . . WEND like this:

```
10 'Demonstration segment to simulate WHILE...WEND using GOTO
20 INPUT "What is your check balance"; BALANCE
30 IF BALANCE <= 0 THEN GOTO 80
40     INPUT "How much is this check"; CHECK
50     LET BALANCE = BALANCE - CHECK
60     PRINT "Current Balance: "; BALANCE
70 GOTO 30
80 PRINT "Oops, you are overdrawn"
90 END
```

BASIC allows us to omit the word GOTO in the IF . . . THEN statement. Line 30 could be written as:

```
30 IF BALANCE <= 0 THEN 80
```

As a second example, let's rewrite Lines 30 through 50 of the overtime program (from the section on GOSUB) using GOTO in place of WHILE . . . WEND:

```
20 GOSUB 500        :REM initialize
30 IF EMPL.ID = 9999 THEN GOTO 60
40     GOSUB 1000   :REM process employee
50 GOTO 30
60 GOSUB 2000       :REM print totals
70 END
```

Test Your Learning

1. Why should you avoid using GOTO?

2. What is a legitimate use of GOTO?

3. What BASIC statement is best for directing processing elsewhere in the program?

4. How can you correct the problem with the following program?

```
10   LET C3 = 0
20   IF C3 > 20 THEN GOTO 50
30   LET C3 = C3 + 6
40   PRINT C3
50   GOTO 20
60   END
```

5. Write a program that uses GOTO to simulate a FOR . . . NEXT loop. Execute the loop a total of four times. On each pass through the loop, print the value of the counter. (Remember to add one to the counter on each pass.)

6. Rewrite the following WHILE . . . WEND loop using GOTO.

```
100   INPUT "Customer Name (or EXIT to end)"; CUST.NAME$
110   WHILE CUST.NAME$ <> "EXIT"
120       PRINT CUST.NAME$
130       INPUT "Customer Name (or EXIT to end)"; CUST.NAME$
140   WEND
```

7. What happens in this program? (*Note:* This "spaghetti code" led to the development of structured programming.)

```
10    INPUT "Enter First Number (9999 to end)"; N1
20    IF N1 > 10 THEN GOTO 90
30    IF N1 > 50 THEN GOTO 110
40    PRINT "First Number is "; N1
50    INPUT "Enter Second Number"; N2
60    PRINT "First times Second is "; N1 * N2
70    IF N1 = 9999 THEN GOTO 130
80    GOTO 10
90    LET N2 = 25
100   GOTO 60
110   LET N1 = 30
120   GOTO 50
130   END
```

DEBUGGING BASIC

A program can have various types of errors. A *syntax error* occurs when BASIC executes a line that it doesn't understand. For example, consider the following:

```
1230 PRIMT "This line has PRINT misspelled"
RUN
Syntax error
```

BASIC has not the foggiest idea what PRIMT means. BASIC will find syntax errors for us, but only when the line is actually executed. When the line is encountered, BASIC will tell us that it has found a syntax error by displaying a message on the screen.

Another type of error is the *logic error*. Here the program makes perfect sense to BASIC, yet it does not solve our problem. This can occur, for example, when we type GOSUB 2000 when we meant to type GOSUB 3000. Or we meant to pay overtime as time and a half, but our program mistakenly gives double time. The program runs, but the output is wrong.

As you are probably aware, errors in programs are called *bugs*. Therefore, the process of finding and correcting errors in programs is called *debugging*. Because it is inevitable that any program you write will have some bugs, several techniques have been developed to decrease the number of bugs and to quickly correct those that do occur.

INCREMENTAL DEBUGGING

Because BASIC gives error messages when syntax errors occur, one of the easiest ways to find this type of error is to use BASIC. In other words, run your program as you type it in. Then debug any syntax errors. Repeat this process by typing in some more modules, running, and debugging. BASIC will point out any syntax errors.

For example, as part of a payroll program we have a module in which the employee data is entered. We can write just those lines and test them before writing any code that processes the data.

```
3100 REM   ***          enter pay data          ***
3110 REM
3120 INPUT "What is the gross pay"; GROSS
3130 WHILE GROSS < 0 OR GROSS > 5000
3140   INPUT "Please enter an amount for gross between 0 and 5000 ", GROSS
3150 WEND
3160 INPUT "Please enter the number of allowances ", NUMALLOWANCES
3170 PRINT "Please enter filing status:"
3180 PRINT "  1 = single"
3190 PRINT "  2 = married"
3200 INPUT "  Employee's status"; STATUS
3210 WHILE STATUS < 1 OR STATUS > 2
3220     INPUT "Status must be 1 or 2, please reenter"; STATUS
3230 WEND
9999 END
```

Even though this is just a section of the program, we can RUN these lines to make sure they contain no syntax errors. By stopping to check for errors as we code, we can easily catch and correct most syntax errors as we make them.

TEST DATA

To test logic errors we need to create some *test data* for which we know the correct output. The test lines we have just written contain no output, but we can check that the variables GROSS, NUMALLOWANCES, and STATUS contain the correct values by displaying their values on the screen in two ways. We could run the lines and then type PRINT in the immediate mode.

```
PRINT GROSS, NUMALLOWANCES, STATUS
```

Or we can insert temporary lines into the program to display these values. To our sample we can add:

```
3221 PRINT "The values of GROSS, NUMALLOWANCES and STATUS are: ";
     GROSS, NUMALLOWANCES, STATUS
```

We will remove this temporary line only when we are satisfied that the variables are being calculated and stored correctly.

Top-Down Debugging

A more formalized type of incremental debugging is *top-down debugging*, a companion to top-down programming. Like incremental debugging, top-down debugging calls for you to test your program as you code it; but it also calls for you to test the modules in a certain order, from top to bottom.

The essence of top-down debugging is to test each module as you write it, starting with the uppermost modules. In this way you can detect and correct the errors at each level as you go along. An error in an upper module that is not detected until after the minor modules have been written can result in hours or days of rewriting. For this reason the upper modules are tested first and most often. Taking the time to test at each step will actually reduce the total time it takes to produce the final, bug-free product. In this case, taking time saves time.

How can we test a module that uses other modules that have not yet been written? We write dummy or *stub modules* for the lesser modules. We made use of stub modules in the earlier program segment that displayed the menu. The stub may contain as little as a simple PRINT statement to inform us control has reached that module.

In the section on program planning, we discussed a program to calculate withholding taxes. To begin writing this program we would first code the three top modules shown in Figure 4.

```
NEW
1000 REM ***************************
1010 REM        Main Module
1020 REM ***************************
1030 GOSUB 2000          :REM Initialize
1040 WHILE EMPNAME$ <> "DONE"
1050    GOSUB 3000       :REM Process one employee's record
1060 WEND
1070 GOSUB 4000          :REM Print Totals
1080 END
2000 REM ***********************
2010 PRINT "Insert lines to initialize here"
2020 INPUT "What is the Employee's name (enter DONE to quit)"; EMPNAME$
2030 RETURN
3000 REM ***********************
3010 PRINT "Insert lines to process employee here"
3020 INPUT "What is the Employee's name (enter DONE to quit)"; EMPNAME$
3030 RETURN
4000 REM ***********************
4010 PRINT "Insert lines to print totals here"
4020 RETURN
```

We can now run the program to ensure this part works correctly. If all is well, we proceed to write and test each submodule.

Using STOP and CONT

We have discussed the use of STOP to halt processing at some location other than the physical end of the program. We also noted that STOP displays a message that indicates at which line processing was halted. This function becomes very useful while debugging. We can insert temporary STOP statements to halt processing at a particular spot in the program. When the program encounters the STOP instruction, it passes control back to the user. The program is put in a suspended state with all variables keeping their values. This allows us, using PRINT in the immediate mode, to find out what values different variables have. We can even change the value of variables using LET in immediate mode.

To continue the program at this point, type CONT. When you press RETURN, the program will resume where it left off. This ability to halt processing temporarily, modify the value of variables, and then continue is a major difference between STOP and END.

Test Your Learning

1. Compare incremental debugging with top-down debugging.
2. How can STOP and CONT be used for debugging?

Arrays

Up to this point, when we have wanted to hold data in a program, we've assigned a separate variable name to each data element. We have used numeric data variables that hold only numeric values and string data variables that hold non-numeric or character values, such as names and addresses.

data element	variable name
3	COUNT
14.56	PRICE
"BETTY BOYD"	EMPNAME$

Single Dimension Arrays

Frequently we need to store a list within a program. Think of a "To-Do" list in which you note various tasks. If there are seven items on your list you could number them and refer to the first as "To-Do #1," the second as "To-Do #2," and so on.

```
To-Do List
1.   Do Laundry
2.   Pay Bills
3.   Cut Lawn
4.   Finish Math Assignment
5.   Go to Store
6.   Call Jane and Jack
7.   Clean Kitchen
```

Instead of assigning a different variable name to each item, we can place the list in BASIC using an *array*. We assign a name to the array (or list) using the same rules as for ordinary variables. Following the name, in parentheses, is a number or a numeric value. This number is called the *subscript*. The subscript tells BASIC to which item in the list we are referring. For example, if we want to put the above "To-Do" list into a BASIC program as an array we could assign it the name `TODO$`. Because this list contains string data, we gave it a string name. To refer to the fifth item, "Go to Store" we would use `TODO$(5)`. The value of `TODO$(5)` is "Go to Store." The value of `TODO$(3)` is "Cut Lawn."

The elements of the array `TODO$` and their values are as follows:

```
Array Name:          TODO$
Element Name         Value of Element
TODO$(1)             Do Laundry
TODO$(2)             Pay Bills
TODO$(3)             Cut Lawn
TODO$(4)             Finish Math Assignment
TODO$(5)             Go to Store
TODO$(6)             Call Jane and Jack
TODO$(7)             Clean Kitchen
```

Before we can use this array, we must instruct BASIC that `TODO$` refers to an array and that the maximum number of entries or *elements* in the array is seven. The DIM (DIMension) statement does this. We use the DIM statement `DIM TODO$(7)` to instruct BASIC to establish the string array `TODO$`, reserving room in its workspace for elements with subscripts up to seven.

Now we can write a short program to enter and print this list.

```
100 DIM TODO$(7)
200 PRINT "Enter up to seven things for your To-Do List"
210 FOR ITEM = 1 TO 7
220     INPUT "Enter next item: ", TODO$(ITEM)
230 NEXT ITEM
240 REM
300 PRINT "Current To-Do List"
310 FOR ITEM = 1 TO 7
320     PRINT ITEM, TODO$(ITEM)
330 NEXT ITEM
340 END
```

Note that we use the variable `ITEM` as a subscript in Lines 220 and 320. Much of the power of arrays comes from this use of subscripts.

As a final note, even though we dimensioned the array `TODO$` to seven, in many dialects it will actually have eight elements, with subscripts 0 through 7. In this program we have ignored the element with the subscript of zero. BASIC does not require a DIM statement for single dimension arrays with 10 or fewer elements; however, good programming practice dictates always dimensioning arrays.

Parallel Arrays

To represent some data, we need more than one list. Consider the following tax table that is used for calculating the amount of federal income tax to withhold.

If you earn over	but not over	your tax is	plus this percent	of the amount over
$0	$57	$0	.00	
$57	$173	$0	.12	$57
$173	$385	$13.92	.15	$173
$385	$605	$45.72	.19	$385
$605	$913	$87.52	.25	$605
$913	$1154	$164.52	.30	$913
$1154	$1373	$236.82	.34	$1154
$1373		$311.28	.37	$1373

The table contains five columns of data. For any given earned amount we can use one line of the table to compute our tax. For example, if we earn $500, we use the fourth line. Our tax is $45.72 plus 19% of ($500 − $385). These five sets of lists are parallel. Collectively they form a table.

We could program this table by using five arrays, but notice the redundancy in the arrays. All the information in the "but not over" and "amount over" columns is found in the "If you earn" column. We can store all this information in BASIC using just three parallel arrays: one for the lower limit of the range, one for the minimum tax, and one for the rate.

Lower	Amount	Rate
0	0	.00
57	0	.12
173	13.92	.15
385	45.72	.19
605	87.52	.25
913	164.52	.30
1154	236.82	.34
1373	311.28	.37

The following program segment will READ the values from DATA statements and store them into three parallel arrays. Note that subscripts allow us to use a FOR . . . NEXT loop to read the values from the DATA statements into the arrays.

```
2170 REM   *****************************************
2180 REM      read in withholding table
2190 REM
2200 DIM LOWER(8), AMOUNT(8), RATE(8)
2210 FOR ITEM = 1 TO 8
2230    READ LOWER(ITEM), AMOUNT(ITEM), RATE(ITEM)
2250 NEXT ITEM
```

```
2270 REM   *******************************************
2280 REM              Data Statements
2290 REM   *******************************************
2380 REM   ****    1986 tax table for single, biweekly     ****
2390 REM lower, amount, rate
2400 DATA    0,    0.00,  .00
2410 DATA   57,    0.00,  .12
2420 DATA  173,   13.92,  .15
2430 DATA  385,   45.72,  .19
2440 DATA  605,   87.52,  .25
2450 DATA  913,  164.52,  .30
2460 DATA 1154,  236.82,  .34
2470 DATA 1373,  312.76,  .37
2480 REM
```

Now that the values are stored in the arrays we can write the code to calculate the tax (amount to withhold for given earnings). To find the proper range, we'll test the earnings against the lower limit. If it is greater than this amount but less than or equal to the next limit, then the amount to withhold is the minimum amount plus the rate times the difference between the limit and the earnings. This method works for all except the last range (because there is no "next limit" for that one). We'll test for that range separately.

In the following code, the FOR . . . NEXT loop checks the amount subject to withholding against the limits for each step except the last. If the amount falls within any of these ranges, the amount to withhold is calculated according to the following formula: Subtract the lower limit from the amount subject to withholding. Multiply the difference times the rate for this range. Add the product to the base amount for this range. For the last range there is no upper limit. Therefore, if the amount subject to withholding is greater than the last limit, we perform the calculation using the data for the last range.

```
3500 REM   ****     Compute Amount to Withhold     ****
3510 LET WITHHOLDING = 0
3520 REM   **            search tax array            **
3530 FOR I = 1 TO NUM.IN.TABLE-1
3540    IF SUBJECT > LOWER(I) AND SUBJECT <= LOWER(I+1)
             THEN LET WITHHOLDING = AMOUNT(I) + RATE(I) *
             (SUBJECT - LOWER(I))
3550 NEXT I
3560 REM   **           check for last range          **
3570 IF SUBJECT > LOWER(NUM.IN.TABLE) THEN LET WITHHOLDING =
        AMOUNT(NUM.IN.TABLE) + RATE(NUM.IN.TABLE) *
        (SUBJECT - AMOUNT(NUM.IN.TABLE))
3580 REM   **       calculate social security and SDI **
3590 LET SS.AMOUNT = GROSS * SS.RATE
3600 LET SDI.AMOUNT = GROSS * SDI.RATE
3610 REM   **        calculate total withholding      **
3620 LET WITHHOLDING = WITHHOLDING + SS.AMOUNT + SDI.AMOUNT
3630 RETURN
3640 REM
```

MULTIDIMENSION ARRAYS

In the previous discussion we learned how to load the tax rates for a single person on a biweekly payroll into three arrays. However, not all employees are single; we also need the tax rates for married employees. We could create a separate set of parallel arrays with separate names for the married rates. Fortunately BASIC provides a simple way of expanding an array to more than one dimension by the use of multiple subscripts. Let's look first at the array LOWER that contains the lower limit for each income bracket. Instead of representing the lower limits as a list, we need to represent them as a table as shown below:

```
                        TABLE
                SINGLE              MARRIED
Range 1         0                   0
Range 2         57                  100
Range 3         173                 398
Range 4         385                 795
Range 5         605                 980
Range 6         913                 1199
Range 7         1154                1419
Range 8         1373                1859
```

To identify an element in a list we need only give the row in which it appears. For a table, we need to give both the row and the column. In the single dimension array, to retrieve the third range for a single person we referenced it as LOWER(3). To reference it from a similarly named table, we use LOWER(3,1) (row 3, column 1); to reference the third range for a married person we use LOWER(3,2) (row 3, column 2). The first subscript indicates the range; the second subscript indicates the marital status (1 equals single, 2 equals married).

We can now change our subroutine to build two-dimensional arrays for the tax rate tables. Note that the DIM statement in Line 2200 has been changed to reflect the creation of arrays with eight rows and two columns.

```
2170 REM    ************************************************
2180 REM       read in withholding table
2190 REM
2200 DIM LOWER(8,2), AMOUNT(8,2), RATE(8,2)
2210 FOR J = 1 TO 2
2220     FOR I = 1 TO 8
2230         READ LOWER(I,J), AMOUNT(I,J), RATE(I,J)
2240     NEXT I
2250 NEXT J
2260 RETURN
2270 REM    ******************************************
2280 REM              Data Statements
2290 REM    ******************************************
2370 REM
2380 REM        **** 1986 tax table for single, biweekly   ****
2390 REM lower, amount, rate
2400 DATA    0,   0.00, .00
2410 DATA   57,   0.00, .12
```

```
2420 DATA    173,    13.92,  .15
2430 DATA    385,    45.72,  .19
2440 DATA    605,    87.52,  .25
2450 DATA    913,   164.52,  .30
2460 DATA   1154,   236.82,  .34
2470 DATA   1373,   312.76,  .37
2480 REM
2490 REM         **** 1986 tax table for married, biweekly    ****
2500 REM lower, amount, rate
2510 DATA      0,     0.00,  .00
2520 DATA    100,     0.00,  .12
2530 DATA    398,    35.76,  .17
2540 DATA    795,   103.25,  .22
2550 DATA    980,   143.95,  .25
2560 DATA   1199,   198.70,  .28
2570 DATA   1419,   260.30,  .33
2580 DATA   1859,   405.50,  .37
2590 REM
```

TEST YOUR LEARNING

1. What is an array? What is an element of an array? What is a subscript?

2. What does DIM do?

3. a. Write a statement to dimension an array with up to 12 elements.
   b. Write a statement to dimension an array that represents the sales in five locations for each of 12 months.

4. Write a program to read the names of each month and the number of days in that month from DATA statements and load them into two arrays: one, a string array containing the names of the months; the other, a numeric array containing the number of days in the month.

5. a. Write a program that prompts the user to enter the description and cost for nine products. Place this data in two single-dimension arrays.
   b. Add a second part of the program that displays the name of each product and asks the user the quantity ordered. Store the response in a third array. When entry is completed, print a report listing the name, price, quantity ordered, and total cost for the items ordered. If zero is ordered for a particular product, do not print it. At the end of the list print the total cost for all items.

6. There are five manufacturing areas in the company. Management wants an analysis of the output of each area over a six-month period. Write a program to do the following:

   Ask the user to enter for each department its name and total output for each of six months. Place the names in a single-dimension array and the output in a two-dimension array (one subscript will be department number and the other, month).

   Total the output for each department and compute the average total output.

At the end of the program, display a report that shows the department name, the total output, and the amount that the output is over or under the average.

A Sample Program

In prior sections, we have discussed and coded portions of a payroll withholding program. At this point we will put them all together into a complete program.

Specifications

We have already given the general specifications for this program. These are the steps for calculating the various taxes:

Federal Income Tax

1. Calculate the amount subject to withholding by multiplying the number of allowances times the allowance rate for a biweekly payroll and subtracting the result from the gross.
2. Select the table appropriate for the employee's marital status.
3. For this table, select the range appropriate for the employee's amount subject to withholding that was calculated in Step 1.
4. Use the tabled values to calculate the amount to withhold.

Social Security (FICA) Tax

1. Multiply the gross pay times the social security tax rate.

State Disability Insurance (SDI) Tax

1. Multiply the gross pay by the current SDI rate.
   (Both social security and SDI have a maximum amount to be withheld during the calendar year. This sample program does not check for the limits; to do so would require that the program have access to year-to-date data.)

Design

The complete structure chart for this program is shown in Figure 14. The program line numbers for each module are noted on each of the boxes.

Annotated Program Listing

```
100 REM  ***      Sample Payroll Program: PAYROLL   ***
110 REM  Written by EB Cohen
120 REM  11/11/87
130 REM  This is a sample program for calculating net pay.
```

FIGURE 14
Structure chart for payroll
program

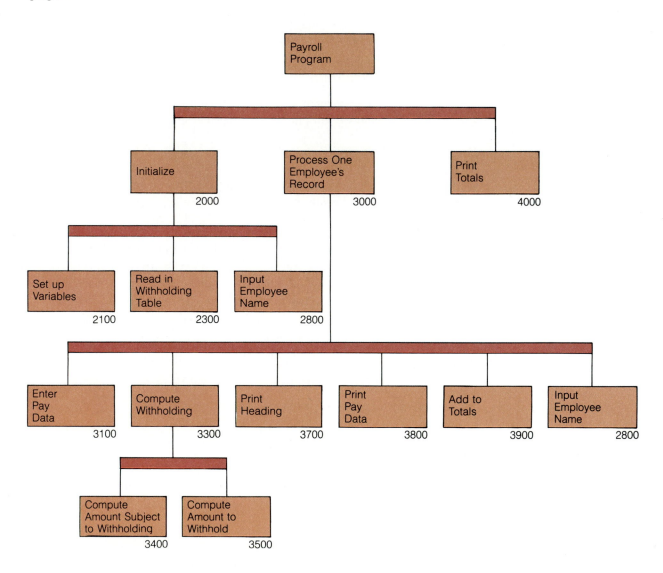

```
140 REM   It uses Arrays and READ...DATA
200 REM   *********************************
210 REM   ****    Data Dictionary         ****
220 REM   ALLOWANCE          ALLOWANCE.RATE times NUMALLOWANCES
230 REM   ALLOWANCE.RATE     Rate per allowance for biweekly payroll
240 REM   AMOUNT             Base amount of tax on table (array)
250 REM   EMPNAME$           Employee's name
260 REM   GROSS              Gross Pay
270 REM   I                  Counter for loop
280 REM   J                  Counter for loop
290 REM   LOWER              Lower limit on tax table (array)
300 REM   NUMALLOWANCES      Number of allowances for employee
310 REM   NUM.IN.TABLE       Number of tax rates in table
320 REM   NUM.STATUS         Number of marital status categories
330 REM   RATE               Percentage rate in tax table (array)
340 REM   SDI.AMOUNT         Amount to be withheld for SDI
350 REM   SDI.RATE           Tax rate for State Disability Insurance
360 REM   SS.AMOUNT          Amount to be withheld for Social Security
370 REM   SS.RATE            Tax rate for Social Security
380 REM   STATUS             Marital status for employee
390 REM   SUBJECT            Calculated amount subject to withholding
400 REM   TOT.GROSS          Total gross wages
410 REM   TOT.WITHHOLDING    Total amount withheld
420 REM   WITHHOLDING        Amount to be withheld for this employee
1000 REM   *************************************************
1010 REM   *************************************************
1020 REM
1030 GOSUB 2000          :REM   Initialize
1040 WHILE EMPNAME$ <> "DONE"
1050    GOSUB 3000       :REM   Process one employee's record
1060 WEND
1070 GOSUB 4000          :REM   PRINT TOTALS
1080 END
1090 REM   *************************************************
1100 REM   *************************************************
```

After initializing the tax rate tables and other variables, the program will process one employee at a time. The user will enter DONE as the employee's name to signal that entry is complete. At that point the program will print the final totals and end.

```
2000 REM   ****             Initialize      ****
2010 GOSUB 2100          :REM   set up variables
2020 GOSUB 2300          :REM   read in withholding table
2030 GOSUB 2800          :REM   input employee name (initial input)
2040 RETURN
2050 REM   *********************************************
2100 REM   ***         set up variables               ***
2110 REM              set totals to zero
2120 LET TOT.GROSS = 0            :REM total gross
2130 LET TOT.WITHHOLDING = 0      :REM total withholding
2140 REM   *******      read data constants      **********
```

```
2150 READ NUM.STATUS              :REM number of filing categories
2160 READ NUM.IN.TABLE            :REM number of tax brackets in table
2170 READ ALLOWANCE.RATE          :REM allowance per deduction
2180 READ SS.RATE                 :REM social security rate
2190 READ SDI.RATE                :REM state disability insurance rate
2200 RETURN
2210 REM  **********************************************
```

To allow for ease of modification when the tax rates change, all of the tax data is placed in DATA statements. When any rates change, only the corresponding DATA statements need to be changed.

```
2300 REM ****           read in withholding table          ****
2310 REM         define arrays for withholding table
2320 DIM LOWER(NUM.IN.TABLE, NUM.STATUS), AMOUNT(NUM.IN.TABLE, NUM.STATUS),
        RATE(NUM.IN.TABLE, NUM.STATUS)
2330 FOR J = 1 TO NUM.STATUS
2340     FOR I = 1 TO NUM.IN.TABLE
2350         READ LOWER(I,J), AMOUNT(I,J), RATE(I,J)
2360     NEXT I
2370 NEXT J
2380 RETURN
```

Note that this code is the same as was presented earlier in the chapter, except the variables NUM.STATUS and NUM.IN.TABLE are used in the DIM and FOR statements in place of actual numbers. This practice allows changes in these criteria to be implemented without rewriting these instructions.

```
2390 REM  *********************************************
2400 REM         Data Statements - 1986 Tax Rules
2410 REM  *********************************************
2420 REM  Number of filling status categories and entries in tables
2430 DATA 2, 8
2440 REM  Dependent allowance for biweekly payroll
2450 DATA 41.54
2460 REM  Social Security and Disability tax rates
2470 DATA .0715
2480 DATA .009
2490 REM
2500 REM        ****   single biweekly tax table   ****
2510 REM lower, amount, rate
2520 DATA    0,    0.00, .00
2530 DATA   57,    0.00, .12
2540 DATA  173,   13.92, .15
2550 DATA  385,   45.72, .19
2560 DATA  605,   87.52, .25
2570 DATA  913,  164.52, .30
2580 DATA 1154,  236.82, .34
2590 DATA 1373,  312.76, .37
2600 REM
```

```
2610 REM         ****    married biweekly tax table   ****
2620 REM lower, amount, rate
2630 DATA     0,    0.00,  .00
2640 DATA   100,    0.00,  .12
2650 DATA   398,   35.76,  .17
2660 DATA   795,  103.25,  .22
2670 DATA   980,  143.95,  .25
2680 DATA  1199,  198.70,  .28
2690 DATA  1419,  260.30,  .33
2700 DATA  1859,  405.50,  .37
2710 REM
2800 REM     ********* Input employee name *************
2810 PRINT
2820 INPUT "What is the Employee's name (enter DONE to quit)"; EMPNAME$
2830 RETURN
2840 REM
```

The first employee name is entered as part of the initialization before executing the main WHILE . . . WEND loop. All remaining names will be entered at the end of the loop.

```
3000 REM     ********     Process one employee record    *******
3010 REM     ***************************************************
3020 GOSUB 3100            :REM enter pay data
3030 GOSUB 3300            :REM compute withholding
3040 GOSUB 3700            :REM print heading
3050 GOSUB 3800            :REM print pay data
3060 GOSUB 3900            :REM add to totals
3070 GOSUB 2800            :REM input employee name
3080 RETURN
3090 REM
3100 REM     ***             enter pay data              ***
3110 REM
3120 INPUT "What is the gross pay"; GROSS
3130 WHILE GROSS < 0 OR GROSS > 5000
3140    INPUT "Please enter an amount for gross between 0 and 5000"; GROSS
3150 WEND
3160 INPUT "Please enter the number of allowances"; NUMALLOWANCES
3170 PRINT "Please enter filing status:"
3180 PRINT " 1 = single"
3190 PRINT " 2 = married"
3200 INPUT " Employee's status"; STATUS
3210 WHILE STATUS < 1 OR STATUS > 2
3220     INPUT "Status must be 1 or 2, please reenter"; STATUS
3230 WEND
3240 RETURN
3250 REM
3300 REM     ***          Compute Withholding          ***
3310 REM
3320 GOSUB 3400            :REM Compute Amount Subject to Withholding
3330 GOSUB 3500            :REM Compute Amount to Withhold
3340 RETURN
```

```
3350 REM
3400 REM  ****   Compute Amount Subject to Withholding   ****
3410 LET ALLOWANCE = ALLOWANCE.RATE * NUMALLOWANCES
3420 IF GROSS - ALLOWANCE > 0 THEN LET SUBJECT = GROSS - ALLOWANCE
        ELSE LET SUBJECT = 0
3430 RETURN
3440 REM
```

The amount subject to withholding is the gross less the number of allowances times the rate per allowance. We must handle the possibility that this result could be less than zero.

```
3500 REM   ****     Compute Amount to Withhold   ****
3510 LET WITHHOLDING = 0
3520 REM   **            search tax array          **
3530 FOR I = 1 TO NUM.IN.TABLE-1
3540    IF SUBJECT > LOWER(I,STATUS) AND SUBJECT <= LOWER(I+1,STATUS)
           THEN LET WITHHOLDING = AMOUNT(I,STATUS) + RATE(I,STATUS) *
                (SUBJECT - LOWER(I,STATUS))
3550 NEXT I
3560 REM   **        check for last range          **
3570 IF SUBJECT > LOWER(NUM.IN.TABLE,STATUS) THEN LET WITHHOLDING =
        AMOUNT(NUM.IN.TABLE,STATUS) + RATE(NUM.IN.TABLE,STATUS) *
        (SUBJECT - AMOUNT(NUM.IN.TABLE,STATUS))
3580 REM   **      calculate social security and SDI **
3590 LET SS.AMOUNT = GROSS * SS.RATE
3600 LET SDI.AMOUNT = GROSS * SDI.RATE
3610 REM   **        calculate total withholding      **
3620 LET WITHHOLDING = WITHHOLDING + SS.AMOUNT + SDI.AMOUNT
3630 RETURN
3640 REM
```

To find the proper range, we must find the one in which the amount subject to withholding is greater than the lower limit but less than or equal to the next limit. The FOR . . . NEXT loop checks the amount subject to withholding against the limits for each step except the last. If the amount falls within any of these ranges, the amount to withhold is calculated according to the following formula: (a) Subtract the lower limit from the amount subject to withholding. (2) Multiply the difference times the rate for this range. (3) Add the product to the base amount for this range. For the last range there is no upper limit; therefore, if the amount subject to withholding is greater than the last limit, we perform the calculation using the data for the last range.

Social security and SDI are calculated by multiplying the gross times the rate for each of these taxes.

The three taxes are added together to give the total amount to be withheld.

```
3700 REM      Print Heading
3710 PRINT
3720 PRINT "Emp Name","Gross","Deductions", "Withholding","Pay"
3730 PRINT
3740 RETURN
3800 REM      Print Withholding
```

```
3810 REM
3820 PRINT EMPNAME$, GROSS, NUMALLOWANCES, WITHHOLDING, GROSS - WITHHOLDING
3830 RETURN
3900 REM      Add to Totals
3910 REM
3920 LET TOT.GROSS = TOT.GROSS + GROSS
3930 LET TOT.WITHHOLDING = TOT.WITHHOLDING + WITHHOLDING
3940 RETURN
4000 REM  *********************************************
4010 REM  **********      Print Totals      *************
4020 REM
4030 REM
4040 PRINT "TOTALS",TOT.GROSS, , TOT.WITHHOLDING, TOT.GROSS-TOT.WITHHOLDING
4050 RETURN
4060 REM      *** End of Listing ***
```

Sample Output

```
What is the Employee's name (enter DONE to quit)? JOE DOE
What is the gross pay? 1300
Please enter the number of allowances? 4
Please enter filing status:
   1 = single
   2 = married
   Employee's status? 2
Emp Name        Gross           Deductions   Withholding    Pay

JOE DOE         1300            4            287.06         1012.94


What is the Employee's name (enter DONE to quit)? BETTY BOYD
What is the gross pay? 1900
Please enter the number of allowances? 1
Please enter filing status:
   1 = single
   2 = married
   Employee's status? 1
Emp Name        Gross           Deductions   Withholding    Pay

BETTY BOYD      1900            1            1037.619       862.381

What is the Employee's name (enter DONE to quit)? DONE
TOTALS          3200                         1324.679       1875.321
```

Test Your Learning

1. The ABC company needs a program to keep track of its inventory. It has twelve products in its inventory. These products are assigned product numbers 1 through 12.

   a. Write a program that builds a table that holds the current quantity on hand for each product. Use either READ and DATA or INPUT to establish the initial quantities.

b. Write a program that displays a menu and asks the user to select one of the following options:

```
1 = Add to existing inventory
2 = Take from existing inventory
3 = Display current quantity for selected product
4 = Print report of current quantity for all products
5 = End processing
```

c. Write separate modules to perform each of these tasks.

Use top-down programming and testing. Validate that the product number entered is 1 through 12 and the quantity is 999 or less.

When Option 2 is selected, test the quantity remaining after the order is placed. If the quantity is less than 10, display a message directing the user to reorder this product. If the order would result in a quantity less than zero, change the order to the quantity on hand and display a message that says the order has been changed to the number on hand and directs the user to reorder the product.

2. The ABC company has expanded to two more locations. Modify the program described in Exercise 1 to keep track of the inventory at each of the three locations. (Use two-dimension arrays.) The program should allow the user to add, delete, or inquire about any product at any of the locations. The report produced in Option 4 will show the quantity of each product at each location as well as the total quantity at all locations.

SUMMARY

You have learned some fundamentals of BASIC. Although we have not covered more advanced topics (such as report design, sequential and random files, or graphics), you should now have an understanding of the concepts of program design and enough knowledge of BASIC to write simple programs.

QUICK REFERENCE OF SELECTED RESERVED WORDS

DATA	Statement	places value in data list
DELETE	Command	removes one or more lines from BASIC's workspace
DIM	Statement	allocates space for array
END	Statement	terminates execution
FOR . . . NEXT	Statements	loop for a given number of times
GOSUB . . . RETURN	Statements	temporarily transfer control to a module
GOTO	Statement	permanently transfers control
IF . . . THEN . . . ELSE	Statements	select which statements to execute
INPUT	Statement	gets values for variables from the user
LET	Statement	assigns a value to a variable
LIST	Command	displays the program in the workspace
LOAD	Command	copies a program from storage into the workspace
NEW	Command	clears the workspace
ON . . . GOSUB	Statement	transfers control based on value
PRINT	Statement	displays values
READ	Statement	retrieves values from DATA list
REM	Statement	used for documentation
RENUM	Command	renumbers the lines of a program
RESTORE	Statement	restarts at beginning of DATA list
RUN	Command	causes a program to execute
SAVE	Command	copies a program from the workspace to storage
STOP	Statement	pauses execution, CONT resumes
WHILE . . . WEND	Statements	create a loop

GLOSSARY

access time Average time to locate instructions or data from secondary storage device and transfer to computer's internal memory.

accumulator Register in internal memory to hold accumulated data.

acoustic coupler A modem consisting of cradle of two rubber cups to hold telephone receiver and transmit data via sound signals (converted from digital to analog form) over the telephone line. *Compare* **direct-connect modem.**

Ada High-level programming language developed by Department of Defense for military systems; supports real-time procedures, automatic error recovery, and flexible input and output operations.

Add-on memory board Circuit board plugged into expansion slot on motherboard to increase capacity of microcomputer's internal memory.

address bus Part of CPU used to access internal memory storage locations containing data needed by instructions.

addressing scheme Computer design feature that determines amount of internal memory CPU can control at any one time.

algorithms Well-defined rules for solving a problem; may include diagrams.

alphanumeric data Data that can include letters, digits, and special symbols such as punctuation marks; it cannot be mathematically manipulated. *Compare with* **numeric data.**

American National Standards Institute (ANSI) Organization that develops standards for all high-level programming languages.

American Standard Code for Information Interchange (ASCII, pronounced *"as-*key") A standard 8-bit code used in data communications, microcomputers, and many minicomputers; 128 valid characters can be formulated with ASCII.

Amplitude Size of voltage or magnitude of wave form in data or voice transmission.

Analog signal Signal that is continuously varying and represents range of frequencies; the telephone system is based on analog signals. *See* **digital signal.**

ANSI *See* **American National Standards Institute.**

Apple DOS Disk operating system introduced by Apple Computer Corp. in late 1970s.

applications controls Controls to ensure input and processing of data is accurate, complete, and authorized; (1) input controls, (2) processing controls, (3) output controls, and (4) authorization controls.

applications generator Software system that generates computer programs in response to user's needs. The system consists of precoded modules performing various functions. The user selects the functions he or she needs and the applications generator determines how to perform the tasks and produces the necessary instructions for the software program.

applications software Program or programs designed for specific task—for example, a payroll or billing.

arithmetic/logic unit (ALU) Part of the CPU that performs all arithmetic and logical (comparison) functions.

arithmetic operations The operations of addition, subtraction, multiplication, division, and exponentiation.

array   Data organized in rows and columns. When stored in internal memory, it allows data to be read quickly by a search of a table. Also called **matrix.**

artificial intelligence (AI)   Field of study concerned with using computers to simulate human thought processes such as imagination and intuition.

ASCII *See* **American Standard Code for Information Interchange.**

assembly language   Language using low-level symbolic abbreviations to represent machine-language instructions. Assembly language is specific to different makes and models of computers. Assembly languages are also known as **second-generation languages** and **low-level programming languages.**

asynchronous transmission   Sending one character or bit at a time, each bit preceded by a "start" bit and followed by one or two "stop" bits and an error check bit (or parity bit). An inexpensive and widely used but relatively slow form of data communication. Also called **start-stop transmission.**

automated teller machine (ATM)   *See* **financial transaction terminal.**

auxiliary storage   *See* **secondary storage.**

backup file   Copy of file to ensure data and programs are preserved if original file is damaged or destroyed.

band printer   *See* **line printer.**

bandwidth   Speed at which data can be transmitted on a communications frequency.

bar-code reader   Input scanning device for reading the light and dark bar codes (stripes) on products that represent their inventory stock numbers or product numbers. The scanner analyzes the bars for width and spacing and translates this data into electrical signals for the computer. Two types of scanners are the hand-held wand and the counter top scanner.

BASIC (Beginner's All-Purpose Symbolic Instruction Code)   High-level interactive programming language designed to teach how to program; now the primary language used on microcomputers.

batch   Group of documents or transactions intended for input to the computer in a controlled fashion.

batch commands   Commands used to create **batch command files,** which automate frequently used command sequences and make procedures easier for users unfamiliar with the computer's operating system. Batch command files are considered external command files because their instructions are not loaded into internal memory at the time the computer is booted.

batch processing   Technique whereby data is collected over a period of time and then is processed at one time for output.

belt printer   *See* **line printer.**

binary code   Scheme for encoding data using binary digits.

binary digit (bit)   In binary notation, either 1 or 0. The digit 1 represents an "on" electrical (or magnetic) state; the digit 0 represents an "off" state. A group of adjacent bits (usually eight) constitutes a byte or single character.

bit   *See* **binary digit.**

bit-mapped display   CRT screen display system in which each possible dot is controlled by a single character in memory. Also known as dot-addressable or all-points-addressable display.

block   Group of contiguous records on magnetic tape. Each block is separated on the tape by a gap (interblock gap) to compensate for the tape's acceleration and deceleration as it moves past the read/write head.

block operations   By using block operations, it it possible to move, delete, and copy entire sentences, paragraphs, and pages by issuing commands to the software.

boot   To start up the computer.

bpi   *See* **recording density.**

bus   An "electronic highway" or communication path linking several devices. The CPU may have a data bus, an address bus, and a control bus.

bus network   Communication network in which all messages are transmitted to the entire network, traveling from the sender in both directions along the cable until a message reaches the computer for which it was intended. A central computer is not required to control activity.

byte   A group of contiguous bits, usually eight, that form a character.

C   High-level programming language introduced by Bell Laboratories for use in writing systems software. Though complex to learn, C can be used on a variety of machines.

camera output microfilm/microfiche (COM) system   Equipment that captures computer output on microfilm or microfiche.

card reader   Device that translates the holes in punched cards into electrical signals, which are input to the computer.

cartridge-tape drive   Device that reads magnetic tape in form of a large cassette; often used as alternative type of secondary storage to hard disk. The most popular tape cartridges use 1/4-inch tape in reels up to 1000 feet long. *See also* **streaming tape method.**

cathode-ray tube (CRT)   Electronic screen used with computer terminals to display data entered into a computer and information available from it. Its principal components are an electron gun, a yoke, a shadow mask, and a phosphor-coated screen. Also called **video display screen.**

centralized computer facility A single computer department in a company established to provide sole data processing support to all other departments.

central processing unit (CPU) The part of the computer composed of electrical circuitry directing most of the computer system's activities. The CPU consists of the control unit, the arithmetic/logic unit (ALU), and the processing registers.

character *See* **byte.**

character box Fixed location on a video display screen where a standard character can be placed. Most screens can display 80 characters of data horizontally and 25 lines vertically, or 2000 character boxes (called *character-mapped display*)—the number the electron gun can target. The more pixels that fit into a character box, the higher the resolution of the resulting image. Each character box is "drawn" according to a prerecorded template stored in ROM.

character-mapped display *See* **character box.**

character printer *See* **letter-quality printer.**

characters per second (CPS) Measure of speed of printers and other output devices.

child record In hierarchical database, record subordinate to parent record. *Compare with* **parent record.**

chip Integrated circuit made of silicon and containing electronic components; can be as little as 1/4-inch square.

clock Device in CPU that synchronizes all operations in a machine cycle.

coaxial cable Type of thickly insulated copper wire for carrying large volumes of data—about 1800–3600 voice calls at once. Often used in local networks connecting computers in a limited geographic area.

COBOL (COmmon Business Oriented Language) High-level programming language for business. Its commands and syntax are English-like and thus appropriate for business applications.

color monitor *See* **RGB monitor.**

command syntax *See* **syntax.**

common carrier *See* **public network.**

compiler Computer program that translates a high-level language program (source program) into machine-language instructions (object program) all at once. *Compare with* **interpreter.**

computer Data processing device made up of electronic and electromechanical components that can perform computations, including arithmetic and logical operations. Also known as **hardware.**

computer-based information system Computer system for collecting data, processing it into information, and storing the information for future reference and output. The system consists of five components: people, computer hardware, manual and computerized processing procedures (software), data, and information. It has four major phases of activity: input, processing, output, and storage.

computer literacy Basic understanding of what a computer is and how it can be used as a resource.

computer professional Person with formal education in technical aspects of computers—e.g., a programmer, systems analyst, or computer operator.

computer system System of hardware, software, and people for converting data into information.

concentrator Communications device that multiplexes low-speed communications lines onto one high-speed line; it is more "intelligent" than a multiplexer because it can store and forward transmissions.

control bus One of three buses in CPU; it carries the control signals generated by the control unit to the appropriate computer system components.

controller Device that allows multiple terminals and printers to share a communications link.

control program *See* **supervisor.**

control structure Used in structured programming to solve problems in programming logic. There are three control structures: sequence, selection (if-then-else), and iteration (or looping—do-while).

control unit Part of the CPU that reads, interprets, and sees to the execution of software instructions.

coprocessor chip Special integrated circuit designed to speed up numeric processing. It allows the microcomputer to do parallel addition.

counter Area in internal memory that records number of times a condition is encountered during processing.

CP/M (Control Program/Microcomputers) Disk operating system designed to operate on 8-bit microcomputer systems using the Intel 8080 or Zilog Z80 microprocessor families.

CPS *See* **characters per second.**

CPU *See* **central processing unit.**

CRT *See* **cathode-ray tube.**

cursor Indicator on video display screen that shows where next character input will appear.

daisy wheel printer Printer with plastic or metal disk with typeface impressions of characters on outside tips of spokes; the print character is forced against ribbon and paper.

data   Raw, unevaluated facts, concepts, or instructions; after processing, data becomes information.

data access area   Exposed part of a disk.

database   Large group of stored, integrated (cross-referenced) data that can be retrieved and manipulated to produce information.

database administrator (DBA)   Person who coordinates all related activities and needs for a corporation's database. A DBA has six major responsibilities: (1) database implementation, (2) coordination with user, (3) backup, (4) recovery, (5) performance monitoring, and (6) system security.

database management system (DBMS)   Comprehensive software tool that allows users to create, maintain, and manipulate an integrated base of business data to produce relevant management information. A DBMS represents the interface between the user and the computer's operating system and database.

database management system (DBMS) software   Program that allows storage of large amounts of data that can be easily retrieved and manipulated to produce management reports.

data bus   Communication link that carries data between components of the computer system.

data dictionary   A reference tool that specifies all elements in a database and the relationships among them.

data file   *See* file.

data flow diagram   Graphic representation of flow of data through a system.

data independence   Data that is independent of applications programs being used, so that it is easy to access and change.

data integrity   An attribute of data that describes its accuracy, reliability, and timeliness.

data processing   Operations for refining, summarizing, categorizing, and otherwise manipulating data into a useful form for decision making.

data redundancy   The situation where the same data appears in different files, often in different formats, which makes updating files difficult.

data storage hierarchy   The levels of data stored in a computer file: (1) files, (2) records, (3) fields, (4) bytes, (5) bits.

data transfer rate   Time required to transfer data from disk into a computer's internal memory.

DBMS   *See* database management system.

decentralized computer facility   Separate computer facility established to service the needs of each major department or unit in an organization.

decision support system (DSS)   A computer-based information system for assisting managers in planning and decision making. A DSS may use database management systems, query languages, financial modeling or spreadsheet programs, statistical analysis programs, report generators, or graphics programs to provide information. A DSS may be general or institutional.

dedicated data entry system   Terminals connected to a minicomputer that do nothing but input and store data.

dedicated line   Communication line leased by a company for its own transmission purposes.

default disk drive   The disk drive that is automatically affected by commands unless the user specifies another drive.

demodulation   Process of converting analog signals sent over a telephone line into digital form so that they can be processed by a receiving computer.

desktop publishing software   Programs that enable user to use a microcomputer and a desktop-size laser printer to produce high-quality publications.

desktop terminal   A keyboard and video display screen connected to a central computer but fitting on top of the user's desk.

detail reports   Computer-produced reports for operating (lower-level) managers that contain specific information about routine activities; such reports are highly structured—their form is predetermined.

digital signal   Signal that is discontinuous and discrete; it consists of bursts that form a transmission pattern. Computers communicate with each other in streams of bits transmitted in digital signals—a series of on and off electrical pulses. *See* analog signal.

digitizer   Device that can be moved over a drawing or photograph that converts the picture to data that can be stored, printed out, or shown on a video display screen.

direct access   Situation in which records are stored and retrieved in any order. Also called **random access.**

direct-connect modem   Modem that directly connects computer to telephone line, resulting in less interference and higher data transmission speeds (300–2400 bps or higher). An internal direct-connect modem is placed inside the computer; an external direct-connect modem is outside the computer. *Compare* acoustic coupler.

direct implementation   One of three approaches to system implementation; the change is made all at once, with the old system being halted at the same time the new system is activated. *Compare* parallel implementation, phased implementation.

directory commands   Internal commands used in microcomputers to create directory structures on a storage device.

directory structure   Method of organizing a database, using a hierarchical directory.

disk A revolving platter on which data and programs are stored.

disk cartridge Form of secondary storage (5–10 MB) consisting of a 5 1/4- or 3 1/2-inch cartridge containing one or two platters and enclosed in a hard plastic case; the cartridge is inserted into the disk drive much like a music tape cassette.

disk drive Device into which a floppy disk or disk pack is placed for storing and retrieving data.

disk drive gate Door of disk drive, which must be closed for the read/write operation to be performed.

diskette *See* **floppy disk.**

disk operating system (DOS) Internal command instructions for microcomputers. DOS was developed in 1978 by Intel Corporation. IBM added program enhancements and released IBM PC-DOS in 1981; by 1985, DOS had become the industry standard for microcomputers.

disk pack Removable direct-access storage medium holding 6–12 magnetic platters usually 14 inches in diameter; capacity is 150–250 MB.

distributed computer facility Centralized and decentralized computer facilities combined; users have own computer equipment, but some computer terminals are connected to a bigger computer in a remote location.

document cycle Use of word processing software for entering, editing, spell-checking, saving and retrieving, and printing a document. The cycle may also include merging text from separate documents into a single document.

DOS *See* **disk operating system.**

dot-matrix printer Impact printer using pin-like hammers to strike a ribbon against paper in computer-determined patterns of dots, making possible a variety of type styles and graphics.

dot pitch In a CRT screen, distance between any two adjacent holes in the shadow mask. The smaller the dot pitch, the more precise the image.

double-density *See* **recording density.**

double-sided disk Disk storing data on both sides.

double-sided disk drive Disk drive with read/write heads for both top and bottom surfaces of a disk.

drive capstan In a tape drive, a small cylindrical pulley used to regulate speed of tape. *See also* **stop capstan.**

drive gate *See* **disk drive gate.**

drum plotter Special-purpose output device for reproducing computer-generated drawings. Paper is placed on a drum and stationary pens move across the paper as the drum revolves.

DSS *See* **decision support system.**

dynamic memory access (DMA) chip Integrated circuit responsible for managing the internal memory, keeping track of which memory locations are available for use.

EBCDIC *See* **Extended Binary Coded Decimal Interchange Code.**

E-cycle *See* **execution cycle.**

editing Process of changing text—e.g., inserting and deleting.

electrically erasable programmable read-only memory (EEPROM) Type of memory much the same as erasable programmable read-only memory except that changes can be made to an integrated circuit electrically byte by byte under software control.

electroluminescent (EL) display Type of video display screen with light-emitting layer of phosphor and two sets of electrodes surrounding the phosphor layer—one side forming vertical columns (usually 512), the other side forming horizontal rows (usually 256). To form a pixel on the screen, current is sent to row-column intersection, and the combined voltages cause the phospor to glow at that point.

electron gun A component of a CRT; it creates an image on the screen by firing a beam of electrons at the inside of the screen, which causes the phosphors to glow. The electron beam is directed across the screen horizontally and vertically by the magnetic field produced by the yoke under the control of the computer software.

electronic banking Service enabling customers to access banking activities from home via a terminal or personal computer connected to their telephones.

electronic bulleting boards Information services that can be reached via computers connected to telephone lines that allow users to place or read messages from other users.

electronic communications *See* **telecommunications.**

electronic mail Transmission and storing of messages by computers and telecommunications.

electronic shopping Service through which users can order merchandise by using microcomputers and telecommunications to browse through products listed on remote databases.

electronic spreadsheet software *See* **spreadsheet software.**

electrostatic plotter Special-purpose output device for reproducing computer-produced drawings. The plotter produces images on specially treated paper with small dots of electrostatic charges, and the paper is then run through a developer to make the image appear.

erasable programmable read-only memory (EPROM) Type of memory in which with the help of a special device using ultraviolet light, the data or instructions on an integrated circuit can be erased and new data can be recorded in its place.

E-time   Time required to complete the execution cycle in a CPU.

event-initiated reports   Reports generated for middle managers only when certain conditions exist, such as changes requiring immediate attention—e.g., equipment breakdown.

exception reports   Reports generated for middle managers that show out-of-the-ordinary data—e.g., inventory reports listing only items numbering fewer than ten in stock.

execution cycle (E-cycle)   Activity in CPU that includes execution of instruction and subsequent storing of result in a register. *See also* **instruction cycle, machine cycle.**

executive workstations   Terminals used by managers to assist them in their daily activities. These workstations can be operated by themselves or in connection with a mainframe computer; they usually have voice and data communications capabilities and built-in software.

expanded memory   In a microcomputer, internal memory that has been added over and above the 640 K maximum (up to 8 MB); it consists of an add-on memory board and special driver software.

expert system   Kind of software consisting of knowledge and rules for using it gathered from human experts in a particular occupation. One of the first practical applications of artificial intelligence, it consists of (1) a natural language interface with the user, (2) a knowledge base, (3) an inference machine to solve problems and make logical inferences, and (4) an explanation module to explain the conclusions to the user.

Extended Binary Coded Decimal Interchange Code (EBCDIC, pronounced "*eb*-see-dick")   The most popular code used for IBM and IBM-compatible mainframe computers. Unlike ASCII, it uses all 8 bits to represent data, making 256 characters or bit combinations available.

external command instructions   General-purpose instructions kept in secondary storage for "housekeeping tasks" on microcomputers such as the sorting of files and formatting of disks. Also called **utility programs.**

external commands   Commands not often used by typical microcomputer user and therefore stored on the operating system disk.

external label   Identifying paper label placed on magnetic tape reel.

external modem   Direct-connect modem that is outside the microcomputer and uses its own power supply; it is connected to the computer by a cable.

fiber optics   Form of computer communications in which signals are converted to light form and fired by laser in bursts through thin (2000ths of an inch) insulated glass or plastic fibers. Nearly 1 billion bits per second can be communicated through a fiber optic cable.

field   Group of related characters (bytes) of data.

fifth-generation language   *See* **natural language.**

file   Group of related records. A file may contain data (data file) or software instructions (program file).

file management system   System of organizing business data and information in sequential order in a single file on magnetic tape. The approach does not allow easy grouping of records within a file or establishing relationships among records in different files.

file-name length   A convention specified by different operating systems—e.g., DOS specifies 1–8 characters in file names.

file protection ring   Plastic ring inserted into back of magnetic tape reel to protect tape from accidentally being written on; a tape can be written on only when the ring is in place.

financial transaction terminal   Terminal used in banking activities to access a central computer. It may be an automated teller machine (ATM) or specialized terminal used by bank tellers.

first-generation language   *See* **machine language.**

fixed disks   Magnetic disks for secondary storage that cannot be removed from the disk drive.

flatbed plotter   Special-purpose output device for reproducing computer-generated drawings. Paper is placed flat and pens move horizontally and vertically across it.

flat screen technologies   Describes three kinds of technologies developed for video display screens for laptop computers: *See* **electroluminescent display, gas plasma display, liquid crystal display.**

floating point   Scientific form of notation used to handle large numbers; the decimal point is allowed to move around, or "float."

floppy disk   Thin plastic (Mylar) disk enclosed in paper or plastic covering that can be magnetically encoded with data. Originally 8 inches in diameter, standard floppy disks are now 5 1/4 and 3 1/2 inches.

footer   Descriptive information (such as page number and date) that appears at the bottom of each page of a document.

formatting   (1) Putting magnetic track and sector pattern on a disk to enable the disk to store data or information. (2) In word processing, the alteration of text by addition of underlining or boldface, change of margins, centering of headings, etc.

FORTRAN (FORmula TRANslator)   One of the first high-level languages; used for technical and scientific applications, primarily on minicomputers and mainframes.

fourth-generation languages (4GLs) High-level languages, primarily of three kinds, that allow noncomputer professionals to develop software. *See* **applications generator, query language, report generator.**

frequency Number of times signal repeats the same cycle in a second.

front-end processor A computer used in a computer center to handle data transmission and communications from outside terminals and devices to allow the main computer to concentrate solely on processing applications as quickly as possible.

full-duplex transmission mode Communications transmission that sends data in both directions simultaneously.

function keys Specialized keys on a microcomputer keyboard for performing specific tasks with applications software.

gas plasma display Used as video display screen in some laptop microcomputers. Gas plasma display uses three pieces of glass sandwiched together. The inner layer has numerous small holes drilled in it. The outer two layers are placed on both sides of the middle one, and the holes are filled with a gas mixture, usually a mixture of argon and neon. Both outer layers of glass have a thin grid of vertical and horizontal wires. A pixel appears at a particular intersection when the appropriate horizontal and vertical wires are electrified.

GB *See* **gigabyte.**

general controls Organizational controls that apply to overall processing activities of all computer-based systems. They apply to five areas: (1) the organization, (2) system and program documentation, (3) software, (4) physical security, and (5) management practices.

general-purpose register A register in the CPU that provides work space for data during processing; such registers are used for a variety of purposes, including arithmetic operations.

gigabyte (GB) One billion bytes.

half-duplex transmission mode Two-way data communications in which data travels in only one direction at a time.

hard card Type of storage device consisting of a circuit board that is plugged into a microcomputer expansion slot. A hard card can store about 20 MB of data.

hardcopy Printed or filmed output, such as paper, which can be read by people. *Compare with* **softcopy.**

hard disk A secondary storage device consisting of a rigid metal platter connected to a central spindle, and with the entire unit, including read/write heads, enclosed in a permanently sealed container. Hard disks store much more information than do floppy disks.

hard-sectored disk A hard or floppy disk that always has the same number and size of sectors, as determined by the manufacturer. *Compare with* **soft-sectored disk.**

hardware *See* **computer.**

hashing Mathematical calculation performed by computers on key field values in order to retrieve specific records. Hashing uses a mathematical formula that almost always produces a unique number by dividing the key field number by the prime number closest to, but not greater than, the number of records to be stored. The resulting number is then translated into a disk surface number, sector number, and track number.

header Descriptive information (such as page number and date) that appears at the top of each page of a document.

header label *See* **internal label.**

hierarchical database model Type of database organization in which data is arranged into related groups resembling a family tree, with child records subordinate to parent records. A parent record can have many child records, but each child record can have only one parent record. The record at the highest level, or top of the "tree," is called the root record.

hierarchical network Star networks configured into a single multilevel system, with a single large computer controlling all network activity. However, a computer connected into the main computer can have a star network of devices connected to it in turn. Also known as **tree network.**

hierarchy chart *See* **structure chart.**

hierarchy-input-processing-output (HIPO) design Systems design method using two types of diagrams: (1) the hierarchy diagram or visual table of contents (VTOC), which resembles an organizational chart and presents a view of the new system broken down into its major functions and subfunctions (modules), and (2) the input-processing-output (IPO) diagram, which provides an overview of a module's input, processing, and output activities.

high-level language Programming language designed to run on different computers with few changes—e.g., COBOL, FORTRAN, and BASIC. Most high-level languages are considered to be "procedure-oriented" because the program instructions comprise lists of steps, or procedures, that tell the computer not only what to do but how to do it. Also known as **procedural language.**

history file Data file created to collect data for long-term reporting purposes.

hub   Round opening in the center of a floppy disk, which enables the disk to fit over a spindle in the disk drive.

I-cycle   *See* **instruction cycle.**

impact printer   Output device that makes direct contact with paper, forming the print image by pressing an inked ribbon against the paper with a hammer-like mechanism. Impact printers are of two types. *See* **letter-quality printer, dot-matrix printer.**

indexed sequential access method (ISAM)   Method of secondary storage whereby records are stored sequentially but with an index that allows both sequential and direct, random access. Used almost exclusively with random access microcomputer storage devices to provide maximum flexibility for processing.

index hole   Hole in protective jacket enclosing floppy disk that enables the disk to be positioned over a photoelectric sensing mechanism. When a hole in the disk passes under the index hole in the jacket each time the disk revolves, it activates a timing mechanism that determines which portion of the disk is over or under the read/write heads.

information   Data processed into usable form by the computer. It is the basis for decision making.

information centers   In many large organizations, an area staffed by experts on the hardware, software, and procedures used in the company who can help users with these matters. In companies without a mainframe, it is often called a personal computer support center.

information reporting system   *See* **management information system.**

information service   *See* **public databank.**

information system   An organization's framework of standards and procedures for processing data into usable information; it can be manual or computer-based.

ink-jet printer   Nonimpact printer that resembles dot-matrix printers in that it forms images or characters with dots. The dots are formed not by hammer-like pins but by droplets of ink fired through holes in a plate.

input controls   Manual and computerized procedures to safeguard the integrity of input data, ensuring that all such data has been accurately put into computer-usable form.

input/output (I/O) operations   Instructions provided by a program for inputting data into internal memory and outputting information.

input screen   On a video display screen, a kind of format that is a combination of displayed text and pictorial data that identifies the elements of data to be entered and in which order they are to be entered. Input screens allow

data entry operators to verify visually all data being entered.

instruction   A set of characters directing a data processing system to perform a certain operation.

instructions   *See* **software.**

instruction cycle (I-cycle)   In the CPU, the operation whereby an instruction is retrieved from internal memory and is decoded, alerting the circuits in the CPU to perform the specified operation.

integrated software package   Software combining several applications into a single package with a common set of commands. Word processing, electronic spreadsheets, database management systems, graphics, and data communications have been combined in some such packages.

integrated workstation   *See* **executive workstation.**

interblock gap (IBG)   Blank sections between groups or blocks of records on magnetic tape, to allow for the acceleration and deceleration of tape through a tape drive.

internal command instructions   Instructions loaded into internal memory when microcomputer is booted where they direct and control software and hardware.

internal commands   Commands used the most by typical microcomputer users and that reside in internal memory; includes standard user commands. *See* **directory commands, batch commands.**

internal label   Label recorded on tape magnetically, which is examined by a program before processing begins to ensure that it is the correct tape. Also known as **header label.**

internal memory   *See* **primary storage.**

internal modem   Direct-connect modem that is inside a microcomputer; it is located on a circuit board plugged into an expansion slot and draws power directly from the computer's power supply. No special cable is required.

international network   Network providing intercontinental voice and data communications, often using undersea cable or satellites.

International Standards Organization (ISO)   Organization working to develop standards for high-level programming languages, communications, and compatibility among computers.

interpreter   Language processor that converts high-level program instructions into machine language one instruction statement at a time. *Compare with* **compiler.**

interrecord gap (IRG)   Space left between records when data is written on magnetic tape.

iteration (do-while) control structure   In structured programming, the structure that allows an activity to be repeated (iterated) as long as a certain condition remains true. Also known as a **loop.**

I-time   Time required for CPU to execute instruction cycle.

justification   In word processing, the activity of evenly aligning words on a margin.

K   *See* **kilobyte.**

key   *See* **key field.**

keyboard   Device resembling typewriter keyboard for entering data and computer-related codes. Besides standard typewriter keys, it often has special function keys, cursor movement keys, and numeric keys.

key field   Unique element of data contained in each record; used to identify the record and to determine where on the disk the record should be stored or retrieved using direct access storage and retrieval method.

keypunch machine   Device to transcribe data from a source document by punching holes into cards via a keyboard using a special code.

key-to-disk data entry   System used for high-volume data entry; it consists of several terminals connected to a dedicated computer, usually a minicomputer, that stores data on magnetic disks.

key-to-diskette data entry   System of data entry in which data is stored on floppy diskettes. Later data may be automatically transferred from diskettes to magnetic tape for a main computer system.

key-to-tape data entry   System of data entry in which data is represented by magnetized spots on magnetic tape.

kilobyte (K)   1024 bytes.

language processors   Programs that translate high-level languages and assembly languages into machine language. Also known as **translators.**

laser printer   Output device in which a laser beam is directed across the surface of a light-sensitive drum to record an image as a pattern of tiny dots. As with a photocopying machine, the image is then transferred to the paper a page at a time.

latency period   *See* **rotational delay.**

left justification   Words at the left margin are evenly aligned.

letter-quality printer   Impact printer in which, like a typewriter, a hammer presses images of fully formed characters against a ribbon. *See* **daisy wheel printer, thimble printer.**

light pen   Input device consisting of a light-sensitive photoelectric cell that, when touched to a video display screen, is used to signal the screen position to the computer.

line printer   Output device in which a whole line of characters is printed practically at once. Includes band printers, belt printers, and print-chain printers, in which a printable character is located on a band, belt, or print chain, with a separate print hammer for each print position across the width of the paper guide. As the band, belt, or print chain revolves around the print line, the hammers are activated as the appropriate characters pass in front of them.

liquid crystal display (LCD)   Used as video display screen in some laptop microcomputers. LCD uses a clear liquid chemical trapped in tiny pockets between two pieces of glass. Each pocket of liquid is covered both front and back by thin wires. When current is applied to the wires, a chemical reaction turns the chemical a dark color, thereby blocking light. The point of blocked light is the pixel.

local area network (LAN)   Communications network connected by wire, cable, or fiber optics link that serves parts of a company located close to each other, generally in the same building or within two miles of one another. LANs allow workers to share hardware, software, and data.

logical database design   Detailed description of database model from business rather than technical perspective; it involves defining user information needs, analyzing data element requirements and logical groupings, finalizing the design, and creating the data dictionary. Every element of data necessary to produce required management information system reports is identified and the relationship among records is specified. *See also* **schema, subschema.**

logical operations   Operations consisting of three common comparisons: equal to, less than, and greater than. Three words used in basic logical operations are AND, OR, and NOT.

logical record   Record defined by user according to logic of the program being used; it is independent of the physical records.

logic error   In programming, an error caused by incorrect use of control structures, incorrect calculation, or omission of a procedure.

loop   *See* **iteration (do-while) control structure.**

low-level programming language   *See* **assembly language.**

machine cycle   In the CPU during processing, the instruction cycle and the execution cycle together, as they apply to one instruction.

machine language The language the CPU understands; data and instructions are represented as binary digits. Each type of computer responds to a unique version of machine language. Also known as **first-generation language.**

magnetic-ink character recognition (MICR) Data entry technology used in processing checks; it involves the reading of numeric characters and special symbols printed on checks with magnetic ink.

mainframe computer The most powerful type of computer, usually housed in a controlled environment, that can support many powerful peripheral devices and the processing requirements of hundreds of users.

main memory *See* **primary storage.**

management Individuals responsible for providing leadership and direction in an organization's areas of planning, organizing, staffing, supervising, and controlling of business activities. Management may be low-level (operating or supervisory), middle-level, and upper-level.

management information system (MIS) Computer-based processing and/or manual procedures within a company to provide useful and timely information to support decision making on all three levels of management. Also called *information reporting system.*

margins Space between the right, left, top, and bottom edges of printed text and the edge of the paper.

mass storage system System for storing enormous amounts of data; it may consist of as many as 2000 data cartridges. Each cartridge may be retrieved individually and positioned under a special read/write head for data transfer.

master file File used to store data permanently for access and updating. *Compare with* **transaction file.**

matrix *See* **array.**

MB *See* **megabyte.**

media Type of material on which data is recorded—e.g., paper, magnetic tape, or magnetic disk. Singular form: medium.

megabyte (MB) 1000 K—approximately 1 million characters.

megaHertz (MHz) One million hertz; a measure of speed at which computers perform operations.

memory *See* **primary storage.**

merging Bringing together information from two different files.

microcomputer Small general-purpose computer system that uses a microprocessor chip as its CPU. It can usually be used by only one person at one time. Also known as personal computer, desktop computer.

microprocessor Integrated circuit containing the CPU circuitry for a microcomputer.

microwave system Communications technology using the atmosphere above the earth for transmitting signals point to point from tower to tower. Such systems are extensively used for high-volume as well as long-distance communication of both data and voice in the form of electromagnetic waves similar to radio waves but in a higher frequency range. Microwave signals are said to be "line-of-sight" because they cannot bend around the curvature of the earth.

middle management Level of management dealing with decisions covering broader range of time than decisions made by operating managers.

millions of instructions per second (MIPS) Unit of measure for speed at which a computer processes software.

minicomputer Computer that is similar to but less powerful than a mainframe computer; it can support 2–50 users and computer professionals.

MIPS *See* **millions of instructions per second.**

MIS *See* **management information system.**

modem Device for translating digital signals from a microcomputer into analog signals for transmission over telephone lines and then back into digital signals again for processing. Modem stands for MOdulate/DEModulate. *See also* **acoustic coupler, direct-connect modem.**

Modula-2 High-level programming language as an improvement of Pascal; it is better suited for business use than Pascal and can be used as an applications software development tool.

modulation Process of converting digital signals from a microcomputer into analog form so that data can be sent over a telephone line.

module In programming, a small, easy-to-work-with unit in a program that has only a single function, a single entry, and a single exit point. Also known as **subroutine.**

monitor Device for viewing computer output. Also known as **cathode-ray tube (CRT), screen, video display screen.**

monochrome monitor Device for viewing text and in some cases graphics in a single color, commonly green or amber. It has only one electron gun. *Compare with* **RGB monitor.**

motherboard Main circuit board in a microcomputer system. It normally includes the microprocessor chip (or CPU), internal memory chips, all related support circuitry, and the expansion slots for plugging in additional components.

mouse Hand-held input device connected to a microcomputer by a cable; when the mouse is rolled across the desktop, the cursor moves across the screen. A button on the mouse allows users to make a menu selection or issue a command.

MS-DOS *See* **disk operating system.**

multiplexer Device that allows several terminals to share a single communications line.

multiprocessing Activity in which operating system manages simultaneous execution of programs with two or more CPUs. This can entail processing instructions from different programs or different instructions from the same program. *Compare with* **multitasking.**

multiprogramming *See* **multitasking.**

multitasking Activity in which more than one task or program is executed at a time. A small amount of each program is processed, and then the CPU moves to the remaining programs, one at a time, processing small parts of each. Also known as **multiprogramming.**

natural language High-level programming language supposed to resemble human speech. Similar to query language, eliminates the need for user to learn specific vocabulary, grammar, or syntax. Examples of natural languages are Clout for microcomputers and Intellect for mainframes. Also known as **fifth-generation language.**

network Collection of data communications hardware, computers, communications software, and communications media connected so that users can share information. *See also* **international network, private network, public network.**

network database model Type of database organization similar to hierarchical model but allowing multiple one-to-many relationships; each child record can have more than one parent record. Access to the database can be from a number of points, not just the top.

nonimpact printer Output device that does not print by making direct contact with paper. *See* **ink-jet printers, laser printers, thermal printers.**

nonvolatile storage Type of storage that is relatively permanent; that is, computer instructions and data are not lost when the power is turned off.

numeric data Element of data that can be mathematically manipulated. *Compare with* **alphanumeric data.**

object program Program consisting entirely of machine-language instructions. *Compare with* **source program.**

off-line processing Delayed, heavy-duty processing of transactions after regular processing has been completed. *Compare with* **on-line processing.**

off-the-shelf software Applications software that can be purchased in a computer store, as opposed to software that is custom-written by a programmer.

on-demand reports Reports requested by middle management on a case-by-case basis.

one-to-many relationship In hierarchical database model, the parent-child relationship between two record types; one parent record has many child records.

on-line processing Processing in which data is input immediately; it is not data that is stored temporarily in a transaction file for later processing. *Compare with* **off-line processing.**

on-line real-time processing Processing in which each transaction is fully processed when input, there is immediate feedback, and action can be taken right away. All related computer files affected by the transaction are updated immediately, and printed output can be produced on the spot.

open wire Earliest type of telephone line, composed of unsheathed, uninsulated copper wires strung on telephone poles.

operating environments Systems software products designed to improve procedures for using systems software and applications software. They reside in internal memory, along with the supervisor, after the computer has been turned on.

operating management The lowest level of management in an organization; such managers deal mostly with decisions covering a relatively narrow time frame, actualizing the plans of middle management and controlling daily operations. Also known as **supervisory management.**

operating system (OS) Set of internal command instructions or programs to allow computer to direct own resources and operations. In microcomputers, called a **disk operating system.**

operating system/2 (OS/2) Operating system intended to take advantage of 80286 and 80386 microprocessors and support multitasking and software applications requiring up to 16 MB of internal memory.

operating system command Internal or external command that allows users to manage disks and disk files.

operating systems software Program that starts up the computer and functions as the principal coordinator of all hardware components and applications software programs.

operational decision makers Low-level managers who typically make structured decisions regarding daily business operations.

optical character recognition (OCR) Input device that reads hardcopy data from source documents into computer-usable form; such devices use light-sensitive equipment to read bar codes, optical marks, typewritten characters, and handwriting.

optical-mark reader (OMR) Device that reads data recorded on preprinted sheets with special pencil and converts it into computer-usable form.

optical storage Secondary storage technology using a high-power laser beam to burn microscopic spots in a disk's surface coating. Data is represented by the presence and the absence of holes in the storage locations. A much lower-power laser beam is used to retrieve the data. Much more data can be stored in this way than with traditional storage media and it is faster and cheaper; data cannot be erased or changed.

OS/2 *See* **operating system/2.**

output Computer-produced output may be text, graphics, voice, or computer-usable.

output file File created to produce data as output that will be used as input by another program or application.

page printer *See* **laser printer.**

parallel addition Describes activity in which each calculation is processed simultaneously in a single operation in the ALU. *Compare with* **serial addition.**

parallel implementation One of three approaches to system implementation; the old system and new system are run at the same time for a specified period, then the old system is discontinued when the new system is judged satisfactory. *Compare* **direct implementation, phased implementation.**

parent record In hierarchical database model, the record higher in the structure than child records. Each child can have only one "parent"—that is, each record may have many records below it but only one record above it, a one-to-many relationship. Deletion of a parent record automatically deletes all child records.

parity bit Check bit; used in error detection.

Pascal High-level programming language for large and small computer systems; developed to teach programming as a systematic and structured activity. It has strong mathematical and scientific processing capabilities.

PC-DOS *See* **disk operating system.**

periodic reports Reports for middle management produced at predetermined times—e.g., payroll reports, inventory status reports.

phased implementation One of three approaches to system implementation: a system is so large it is implemented one phase at a time. *Compare* **direct implementation, parallel implementation.**

physical database design In design of a database, the stage following the logical design. Physical design involves specifying how best to store data on the direct-access storage devices so that it can be updated and retrieved quickly and efficiently.

physical records *See* **block.**

pixel Picture element, a glowing phosphor on a CRT screen. Small pixels provide greatest image clarity (resolution).

PL/1 (Programming Language 1) High-level, general-purpose programming language for computation and heavy-duty file handling. Primarily used on minicomputers and mainframes.

plotter Output device used to create hardcopy drawings on paper in a variety of colors. *See also* **drum plotter, electrostatic plotter, flatbed plotter.**

point-of-sale (POS) terminal Input/output device used like a cash register to print sales transaction receipt and to send sales and inventory data to a central computer for processing.

port Electrical interconnection—e.g., on microcomputer the point where the printer is plugged into the computer.

portable terminal Input/output device users can carry with them to remote locations and connect via telecommunications lines to a central computer. Dumb terminals can send and receive data to and from the main computer; smart terminals permit some data to be entered and edited before the connection to the main computer.

post-implementation evaluation In systems design, a formal evaluation of a new system after operation for several months and after systems maintenance has been done to determine if the system is meeting its objectives.

power supply Source of electrical power to components housed in the system unit of a microcomputer.

primary storage The internal memory of a computer, where data and instructions are held for immediate access by the CPU. Also known as **internal memory, main memory.** *Compare with* **secondary storage.**

print-chain printer *See* **line printer.**

printer Output device that prints characters, symbols, and sometimes graphics on paper. *See also* **impact printer, nonimpact printer.**

private network Network supporting voice and data communications needs of a particular organization.

procedural language *See* **high-level language.**

procedure In an information system, specific sequence of steps performed to complete one or more information processing activities.

processing registers   In the CPU, the registers holding data or instructions being acted on. Their size determines the amount of data that can be processed in a single cycle.

program   Group of related instructions that perform specific processing tasks.

program files   Programs stored on magnetic disk or tape.

program flowchart   Diagram using standard ANSI symbols to show step-by-step processing activities and decision logic needed to solve a programming problem.

program independence   Attribute of programs with information in similar arrangements. Programs that are not independent—e.g., some with the date first and expense items second, others vice versa—require programmers to write programs using these specific file formats.

programmable read-only memory (PROM)   Type of memory chip in which data or program instructions are not prerecorded when it is manufactured; thus, users can record their own data or instructions, but once it is done, it cannot be changed.

protocol   In telecommunications, formal rules for communicating, including those for timing of message exchanges, the type of electrical connections used by the communications devices, error detection techniques, methods required to gain access to communications channels, and so on.

protocol converter   Specialized intelligent multiplexer that facilitates effective communications between microcomputers and the main computer system.

prototyping   In systems analysis and design, the process of building a small, simple model of a new system in order to get feedback from users as quickly as possible. Report generators, applications generators, and DBMS software packages may be used.

pseudocode   "Fake code"; programming code not actually entered into the computer but using English-like statements (instead of flowchart symbols) to represent program logic. It is more precise in representing logic than regular, idiomatic English but does not follow a specific syntax. It uses four statement keywords to portray logic: IF, THEN, ELSE, and DO.

public databank   An information service providing users with access, for a fee, to large databases. Also known as **information service.**

public network   Network providing subscribers with voice and data communications over a large geographical area. Also known as **common carrier, specialized common carrier.**

quad-density   *See* **recording density.**

query language   A type of language that allows users to ask questions about, or retrieve information from, database files by forming requests in normal English statements. Learning the specific grammar, vocabulary, and syntax is usually a simple task. The definitions for query language and for database management systems software are so similar that they are usually considered to be the same.

RAM   *See* **random access memory.**

RAM-resident software   In a microcomputer, software always available to the user because it resides in internal memory at all times.

random access   *See* **direct access.**

random access memory (RAM)   Volatile temporary storage for data and program instructions; data can be stored and retrieved at random, no matter where it is. RAM is used for storing operating systems software and for temporary storage of applications program instructions, input data, and output data.

raster scan rate   Measure of number of times per second the image on a video display screen can be refreshed—that is, "lit up" again. Because the phosphors hit by the electron beam do not glow very long, the beam must continuously sweep the screen. With a low raster scan rate, the screen will seem to flicker.

read-only memory (ROM)   Type of memory in which instructions to perform operations critical to a computer are stored on integrated circuits in permanent, nonvolatile form.

read/write head   Recording mechanism in magnetic storage devices that "reads" (accepts) the magnetic spots of data and converts them to electrical impulses and that "writes" (enters) the spots on the magnetic tape or disk. Most disk drives have two read/write heads to access the top and bottom surfaces of a disk simultaneously.

record   Collection of related fields.

recording density   Number of bits per inch (bpi) that can be written onto the surface of a magnetic disk. Disks and drives have three kinds of recording densities: (1) single-density, (2) double-density, or (3) quad-density.

register   Temporary storage location within the CPU to quickly accept, store, and transfer data and instructions being used immediately. An instruction that needs to be executed must be retrieved from internal memory and placed in a register for access by the ALU. The larger the register (the more bits it can carry at once), the greater the processing power.

relational database model   Type of database organization in which many tables (called relations) store related data elements in rows (called tuples) and columns (called attributes). The structure allows complex logical relationships between records to be expressed in a simple fashion. Relational databases can cross-reference data and retrieve data automatically, and data can be easily added, deleted, or modified. Data can be accessed by content, instead of address, as occurs with hierarchical and network models.

relational operation   Operation comparing two elements of data to determine if one element is greater than, less than, or equal to the other.

report file   Data file in a small computer system storing information for reports for transfer to a special computer system for printing.

report generator   High-level language similar to a query language, which allows users to ask questions of a database and retrieve information from it for a report. The user cannot alter the contents of the database file but has great control over the appearance of the output.

resolution   Clarity of the image on video display screen. Three factors measuring resolution are lines of resolution (vertical and horizontal), raster scan rate, and band width.

retrieving   In word processing, obtaining previously created documents from a storage device and placing them in internal memory.

RGB monitor   Device for viewing text and graphics in various colors. It has three electron guns and the screen is coated with three types of phosphors: red, green, and blue. Each pixel is made up of three dots of phosphors, one of each color, and is capable of producing a wide range of colors. *Compare with* **monochrome monitor.**

right justification   Words at the right margin are evenly aligned.

ring network   Telecommunications in which messages flow in one direction from a source on the loop to a destination on the loop. Computers in between act as relay stations, but if a computer fails, it can be bypassed.

ROM   *See* **read-only memory.**

root directory   In the hierarchy of the directory structure, when a microcomputer program is booted, the first directory displayed is the root directory. This contains subdirectories, which can in turn contain sub-subdirectories. The root directory is similar in concept to the filing cabinet.

root record   In hierarchical database model, the record at the highest level or top of the "tree." Root records, which are the key to the structure, connect the various branches.

rotational delay   In a disk drive, the time required for the disk to revolve until the correct sector is under or over the read/write heads.

RPG (Report Program Generator)   High-level programming language designed to help small businesses generate reports and update files easily. It can be used to solve clearcut and relatively simple problems.

satellite system   In telecommunications, a system that uses solar-powered satellites in stationary orbit above the earth to receive, amplify, and retransmit signals. The satellite acts as a relay station from microwave stations on the ground (called earth stations).

saving   Activity of permanently storing data from a microcomputer's internal memory on a disk.

schema   Describes organization of relational database in its entirety, including names of all data elements and ways records are linked. A subschema is part of the schema.

screen   *See* **monitor.**

scrolling   Activity of moving text up or down on the video display screen.

search and replace   In word processing, the activity of searching for and replacing text in a document.

secondary storage   Any storage device designed to retain data and instructions in permanent form. Secondary storage is nonvolatile: data and instructions remain intact when the computer is turned off. Also called **auxiliary storage.** *Compare with* **primary storage.**

second-generation language   *See* **assembly language.**

sector   One of several pie-shaped "wedges" on a hard or floppy disk used for storage reference purposes. The point at which a sector intersects a track is used to reference the data location. *See* **hard-sectored disk, soft-sectored disk.**

seek time   In a disk drive, the time required for the drive to position the read/write heads over the proper track.

selection (if-then-else) control structure   In structured programming, the control structure that allows a condition to be tested to determine which instruction(s) will be performed next.

semiconductor   Material that conducts electricity poorly but that, when "impurities" are added to it, can be used to form electrical circuits. The integrated circuits in the internal memory of almost all computers today are based on this technology.

semistructured decision   Decision typically made at the middle management level that, unlike structured decisions, must be made without a base of clearly defined informational procedures. *Compare with* **structured decision.**

sequence control structure   In structured programming, the control structure that specifies that all events take place in sequence, one after the other.

sequential storage and retrieval   Method of file storage in which data is retrieved one record at a time in the sequence in which it was recorded on the storage medium.

serial addition   Describes activity in which each calculation is processed one digit at a time in the ALU. *Compare with* **parallel addition.**

setting time   In a disk drive, the time required to place the read/write heads in contact with the disks.

shadow mask   In a CRT, a shield with holes to prevent dispersion of the beam from the electron gun so that only a small, precise portion of the beam is allowed to reach the screen. The distance between any two adjacent holes in the shadow mask is referred to as **dot pitch.**

simplex transmission mode   Communications transmission in which data travels only in one direction at all times.

single-density disk   *See* **recording density.**

single-sided disk   Floppy disk storing data on one side only.

smart cards   Credit-card sized personal transaction computers that can be inserted into special card-reading point-of-sale terminals. The cards have memory chips containing permanent records that are easily updated each time the card is used. The transaction data stored on the card can later be read into the computer to update the user's bank records.

softcopy   Output produced in a seemingly intangible form such as on a video display screen or provided in voice form. *Compare with* **hardcopy.**

soft-sectored disk   A disk that is marked magnetically by the user's computer system during formatting, which determines the size and number of sectors on the disk. *Compare with* **hard-sectored disk.**

software   Instructions given to the computer to tell it what to do and when and how to do it. Frequently made up of a group of related programs. There are three general categories. *See* **applications software, software development tool, systems software.**

software development tool   Programming language such as BASIC, COBOL, or FORTRAN used to write programs and other supplemental tools.

software package   Software and documentation usually created by professional software writers to perform general business functions.

source document   Document such as an order form on which information is recorded for later entry in computer-usable form.

source program   Program written in high-level programming language. *Compare with* **object program.**

specialized common carrier   *See* **public network.**

speech coding   Form of coding relying on human speech as providing reservoir of sounds for building the words and phrases to be output. Sounds are codified and stored on disk to be retrieved and translated back as sounds such as these heard in some cars, toys, and games.

speech synthesis   Use of basic speech sounds that are created electronically, without the use of a human voice.

spelling checker   In word processing, programs that check a document for spelling errors.

spreadsheet software   Software program enabling user to create, manipulate, and analyze data and develop personalized reports involving the use of extensive mathematical, financial, statistical, and logical processing.

star network   Telecommunications network with a central computer system linked to a number of smaller computers and/or terminals (called nodes). The central computer acts as traffic controller between all nodes and terminals and controls communications to locations outside the network.

start-stop transmission   *See* **asynchronous transmission.**

stop capstan   In a tape drive, a cylindrical pulley used to hold the tape still long enough for data to be written or read. *See also* **drive capstan.**

storage hardware   Devices that accept and hold computer instructions and data in a form that is relatively permanent, commonly on magnetic disk or tape.

strategic decision maker   Manager in upper-level management who makes unstructured decisions—unpredictable and long-range, not just about past and/or current activities. Such decisions tend to be directed toward strategic planning, allocation of resources, and policy formulation. *See also* **upper management.**

streaming tape method   Storage method in which data is written onto a tape in one continuous stream, with no starting or stopping, no IBGs or IRGs. Tape cartridges have 10–60 MB capacities.

structure chart   In systems analysis, a chart for diagramming an organization and breakdown of modules. Also known as **hierarchy chart.**

structured decision   Predictable decision that can be made about daily business activities by following a well-defined set of routine procedures; typically made by operating managers.

structured design   A top-down system to ensure that agreement is reached as early as possible on major design decisions. Its goals are simplicity, refinement by level, and modularity. Two diagrams are used to document the overall design of a new system: **structure charts and data flow diagrams.**

structured programming Method of programming using top-down design and three control structures to break down main functions into smaller modules for coding purposes.

structured walkthrough In programming, a method whereby a group of programmers meet to review a program designed by another programmer in order to identify what is not clear or workable.

stub testing Process by which several high-level modules in a program are tested before the program is designed for the rest of the lower-level modules; the objective is to eliminate as many errors as possible without having to write the whole program first. A stub is an unprogrammed module.

subdirectory File on a storage device that contains other files and other subdirectories; it is part of the hierarchical directory structure. A subdirectory resembles a file drawer containing file folders.

subroutine *See* **module.**

subschema Part of the schema of a relational database; it refers to the way certain records are linked to be useful to the user.

sub-subdirectory Low in the hierarchy of the directory structure, it is contained within a subdirectory of the root directory. A sub-subdirectory resembles a file folder.

summary report Report for middle managers that reviews, summarizes, and analyzes historical data to help plan and control operations and implement policy formulated by upper management. Summary reports show totals and trends.

supervisor The "captain" of the operating system, it remains in a microcomputer's internal memory and calls in other parts of the operating system as needed from secondary storage and controls all other programs in the computer. In a multitasking environment, a supervisor coordinates the execution of each program. Also known as **control program.**

supervisory management *See* **operating management.**

synchronous transmission Form of transmitting groups of characters as blocks with no start and stop bits between characters. Characters are sent as blocks with header and trailer bytes (called flags) inserted as identifiers at the beginnings and ends of blocks. Synchronous transmission is used by large computers to transmit huge volumes of data at high speeds. *Compare with* **asynchronous transmission.**

syntax Rules and patterns required for forming programming language sentences or statements that tell the computer what to do and how to do it.

syntax error In programming, an error resulting from incorrect use of the rules of the language the program is being written in.

systems development life cycle (SDLC) Formal process by which organizations build computer-based information systems. Participants are users, data processing staff, management of all departments, and computer specialists. The SDLC is used as a guide in establishing a business system's requirements, developing the system, acquiring hardware and software, and controlling development costs. It is generally divided into six phases: (1) analyze current system; (2) define new system requirements; (3) design new system; (4) develop new system; (5) implement new system; and (6) evaluate performance of new system.

systems flowchart Tool of systems design to diagram and document design of a new system and present an overview of the entire system, including data flow (points of input, output, and storage) and processing activities.

systems maintenance The phase after a new system has been implemented when adjustments must be made— e.g., correction of minor processing errors.

systems requirement report Report concluding the second phase of systems development life cycle; it enables managers to determine the completeness and accuracy of the new system requirements, as well as the economic and practical feasibility of the new system.

systems software Programs that are the principal interface between all hardware, the user, and a software package.

systems test Phase of testing all programs and related procedures for operating a new system.

system unit Main computer system cabinet in a microcomputer, which usually houses the power supply, the motherboard, and the storage devices.

tactical decision maker Middle-level manager who generally deals with semistructured decisions.

TB *See* **terabyte.**

telecommunications Movement of voice and data over long distances, such as by telephone lines, through the use of computers. Also known as **electronic communications.**

teleconferencing Electronic linkage of several people who participate in a conversation at the same time.

terabyte (TB) One trillion bytes.

terminal Input/output device; it typically consists of a video display screen, a keyboard, and a connecting cable. A *dumb* terminal is entirely dependent for all its capabilities on the computer system to which it is connected; it cannot do any processing of its own. A *smart* terminal is able to do some editing and storage of data without interacting with the central computer system, but it cannot be used for programming. An *intelligent* terminal can input and receive data, as well as allow users to edit and program.

thermal printer A nonimpact printer that uses heat to produce an image. The print mechanism heats the surface of chemically treated paper, producing dots as characters. No ribbon or ink are used.

thermal transfer printer Nonimpact thermal printer with a print head that is heated and applied to an inked ribbon coated with wax. The heat melts the wax, which in turn sticks to the surface of regular paper.

thimble printer Letter-quality impact printer similar to daisy wheel printer, except that the spokes curve upward instead of lying flat.

third-generation language *See* **high-level language.**

timesharing computer system System that supports many user stations or terminals simultaneously. A front-end processor may be used to schedule and control all user requests entering the system from the terminals, enabling the main computer to concentrate solely on processing.

token ring network Telecommunications network in which each computer obtains exclusive access to the communications channel by "grabbing" a "token" and altering it before attaching a message. This altered token acts as a message indicator for the receiving computer, which in turn generates a new token, freeing up the channel for another computer. Computers in between the sender and the receiver examine the token and regenerate the message if the token is not theirs. Thus, only one computer can transmit a message at one time.

top-down design In structured programming and systems design, the act of identifying the main functions of a program and then breaking them into smaller units (modules).

touch screen Video display screen sensitized to receive input from touch of a finger.

track On magnetic tape a row or channel running the length of the tape. On disks, a track is one of the circular bands.

track density Number of tracks on magnetic medium. Common track densities are 48 tracks per inch (tpi) and 96 tpi. Track density affects disk capacity.

transaction file Temporary storage file in which information is stored in computer-usable form until needed for processing. *Compare with* **master file.**

transaction information system Information system supporting day-to-day business operating activities or transactions; usually the first and most important objective of an information system. A computer-based transaction information system is focused at the operating (lowest) level of a business. Also called an operations information system (OIS) or an electronic data processing (EDP) system.

transaction log Complete record of activity affecting contents of a database during transaction period. This log aids in rebuilding database files if damaged.

translator *See* **language processors.**

tree network *See* **hierarchical network.**

TRS-DOS Disk operating system for Tandy/Radio Shack microcomputers.

turnaround document Computer-produced output document forwarded to a recipient, who records any additional data on it and returns it to the sender.

twisted-pair cable Insulated pairs of wires twisted around each other; they are often packed into bundles of a thousand or more pairs, as in telephone lines.

UNIX Operating system initially created for minicomputers; it provides a wide range of capabilities, including virtual storage, multiprogramming, and timesharing.

unjustified text Text with an unaligned (ragged) margin.

unstructured decision Decision rarely based on predetermined routine procedures; involves the subjective judgment of the decision maker and is mainly the kind of decision made by upper management. Unstructured decisions are supported by management information systems in the form of highly summarized reports covering information over long time periods and surveying activities outside as well as inside the company.

upper management The level of management dealing with decisions that are broadest in scope and cover the longest time frame. Top managers include only a few powerful people who are in charge of the four basic functions of a business: (1) marketing, (2) accounting and finance, (3) production, and (4) research and development. A manager at this level is also known as a **strategic decision maker.**

user Person receiving the computer's services; generally someone without much technical knowledge who makes decisions based on reports and other results that computers produce.

utility programs *See* **external command instructions.**

vertical recording Form of recording on disks in which magnetic spots are placed on end, with the "north pole" on top. This technology is designed to save space on the recording surface.

video display screen Device for viewing computer output. Two main types are cathode-ray tube (CRT) and flat panel. *See also* **monitor.**

virtual memory   An operating system element that enables the computer to process as if it contained almost an unlimited supply of internal memory. It enables a program to be broken into modules, or small sections, that can be loaded into internal memory when needed. Modules not currently in use are stored on high-speed disk and retrieved one at a time when the operating system determines that the current module has completed executing. Also known as **virtual storage.**

virtual storage   *See* **virtual memory.**

voice input device   Input device that converts spoken words into electrical signals by comparing the electrical patterns produced by the speaker's voice to a set of prerecorded patterns. If a matching pattern is found, the computer accepts it as a part of its standard "vocabulary" and then activates and manipulates displays by spoken command.

voice output   Synthesized sound; computer output used in situations where other softcopy output is inappropriate, as in automotive systems.

volatile storage   Form of memory storage in which data and instructions are lost when the computer is turned off.

wand   *See* **bar-code reader.**

window   Most video display screens allow 24–25 lines of text to be viewed at one time, and this portion is called a "window." By moving (scrolling) text up and down the screen, other windows of text become available.

word processing   Preparation of text for creating, editing, or printing documents.

word processing software   Program enabling user to create and edit documents: inserting, deleting, and moving text. Some programs also offer formatting features such as variable margins and different type sizes and styles.

word wrap   In word processing, when the cursor reaches the right-hand margin of a line it automatically returns ("wraps around") to the left-hand margin of the line below and continues the text.

write/protect notch   On a floppy disk, a notch in the protective cover that can be covered to prevent the read/write head from touching the disk surface so that no data can be recorded or erased.

yoke   In a CRT, the cylinder placed in front of the electron gun that can generate a controlled magnetic field (like a directional magnet). The yoke directs the electron beam of the electron gun across the screen horizontally and vertically.

INDEX

WordPerfect
CORPORATION
School Software Direct Order Form

Qualifying teachers, as well as college, university, and other post-secondary students, can now purchase Word-Perfect Corporation (WPCORP) software directly from WPCORP at a reduced price. To qualify, a participant must be teaching or currently enrolled as a full-time student, and must agree in writing not to resell or transfer any package purchased under this program.

If you satisfy these qualifying conditions and would like to purchase software directly from WPCORP under the School Software Program, complete the following six steps and sign at the bottom of the form.

Step 1. From the list below, select the appropriate software for your computer (please note that each student is limited to *one* package of WordPerfect) and mark an "x" in the corresponding blank(s).

	Product	Disk Size	Computer	Price*
___	WordPerfect 4.2	5¼"	(IBM PC/XT/AT/Compatibles)	$125.00
___	WordPerfect 4.2	3½"	(IBM PC/XT/AT/Compatibles)	125.00
___	WordPerfect 1.1	5¼"	(Apple IIe/IIc)	59.00
___	WordPerfect 1.1	3½"	(Apple IIe/IIc)	59.00
___	WordPerfect 1.1	3½"	(Apple IIGS)	59.00
___	PlanPerfect 3.0	5¼"	(IBM PC/XT/AT/Compatibles)	99.00
___	PlanPerfect 3.0	3½"	(IBM PC/XT/AT/Compatibles)	99.00
___	WordPerfect Library	5¼"	(IBM PC/XT/AT/Compatibles)	59.00
___	WordPerfect Library	3½"	(IBM PC/XT/AT/Compatibles)	59.00
___	WordPerfect Executive	5¼"	(IBM PC/XT/AT/Compatibles)	79.00
___	WordPerfect Executive	3½"	(IBM PC/XT/AT/Compatibles)	79.00

Step 2. Make a photocopy of your current Student ID or Faculty card *and* a photocopy of some well-known form of identification displaying your social security number, such as your Driver License or Social Security Card. (WPCORP will hold this information strictly confidential and use it only to guard against duplicate purchases.) Your school ID must show current enrollment. If it does not show a date, you must send verification of current enrollment. If you have serious reservations about providing a social security number, call Educational Development at (801) 227-7131 to establish clearance to purchase any of the above software products at these special prices.

Step 3. Enter your social security number: __ __ __ — __ __ — __ __ __ __

Step 4. Enclose payment for the total cost of the package(s) ordered with personal check, money order, Visa, or MasterCard.

Account #_____

Expiration Date _____ ☐ VISA ☐ MasterCard

(Make check or money order payable to WordPerfect Corporation.)

Step 5. List your shipping address: ⧅ Times Mirror/Mosby

Ship To _____

_____

_____

Phone _____

Step 6. Enclose this signed and completed form, the photocopies of your identification cards, and your signed check or money order (or Visa or MasterCard account number and expiration date) in an envelope and mail to School Software Program, WordPerfect Corporation, 288 West Center Street, Orem, UT 84057.

The information provided herein is correct and accurate, and I will abide by the restricting conditions outlined by WPCORP in this document. I understand that at its sole discretion, WPCORP may refuse any order for any reason.

Signature _____ Date _____

*Utah residents add 6.25% sales tax.